Jeanne N. Knutson

General Editor

HANDBOOK
OF
POLITICAL
PSYCHOLOGY

Jossey-Bass Publishers

San Francisco • Washington • London • 1973

HANDBOOK OF POLITICAL PSYCHOLOGY
Jeanne N. Knutson, General Editor

Copyright © 1973 by: Jossey-Bass, Inc., Publishers
615 Montgomery Street
San Francisco, California 94111
and
Jossey-Bass Limited
3 Henrietta Street
London WC2E 8LU

Library of Congress Catalogue Card Number LC 72-5893

International Standard Book Number ISBN 0-87589-174-8

Manufactured in the United States of America

JACKET DESIGN BY WILLI BAUM

FIRST EDITION

Code 7317

The
Jossey-Bass
Behavioral Science Series

General Editors

WILLIAM E. HENRY, *University of Chicago*

NEVITT SANFORD, *Wright Institute, Berkeley*

PREFACE

$\mathbb{B}$ehavioral science today is heavily influenced by widespread demands for its increased relevance to the problems of society. The rapidly growing interest in political psychology can be seen as an attempt, by behavioral scientists in a number of disciplines, to accept that challenge. We have, on the one hand, a rich and incrementally developed literature covering the social and intrapsychic determinants of human behavior. On the other hand, political life presses our awareness with demands for solutions to intricate problems of violence, alienation, racism, and despair—problems that crucially affect the quality and the quantity of human life today. Political psychology, then, is an interdisciplinary effort: knowledge gained by behavioral scientists is focused on critical human needs, so that the good life—which is the ancient promise of the polity—can be better realized.

In the past three decades, political psychology has become the professional interest of scholars in virtually all behavioral disciplines. This growing interest is reflected in research reports and theoretical essays covering all aspects of political life as seen through the lens of individual-level determinants. The student of politics wishing to grasp the major dimensions and accomplishments of this research has had available no article, chapter, or separate book that conceptualizes the field of political psychology as a whole and takes a close look at its major subdivisions in a rigorous and thorough fashion. He has had no intellectual guide to help him assess what is generally understood about the determinants of political behavior and what large gaps exist in our present knowledge.

Increasingly, a pressing need has developed among scholars and students to examine political psychology in terms of its intellectual roots, alternative strategies of inquiry, available models, past research findings, and unmet research needs. From a number of directions, it has been urged that those engaged in socially relevant research step back and examine the priorities, assumptions, and limitations both of analytic frameworks and of "objective" methods of assessment. Such an inquiry requires a major intellectual commitment, and bringing a disparate group of noted scholars to make such a commitment is in itself a considerable political and psychological feat. The obvious competence of the contributors is well reflected in the quality of the following chapters, in spite of the enormity of their task of summarizing and criticizing a subarea in which each has made original contributions and the lack of available guidelines to assist in this assignment.

As work on the *Handbook of Political Psychology* proceeded, the conceptual and methodological inadequacies of much past work in political psychology became obvious, as did the need to gain new perspectives about the ongoing work in various subfields. In response to their dissatisfaction with much of what they reviewed, the contributors to this volume have jointly made a greatly needed intellectual contribution by creatively analyzing and critically assessing the issues, the models, and the methods of inquiry employed in the sector of political psychology they discuss. While each chapter is necessarily written from the author's own vantage point, the reader will find the analysis comprehensive and the tenor—as Fred Greenstein's concluding chapter notes—pluralistic.

This volume thus provides intellectually sophisticated, original—frequently iconoclastic—analyses of pressing theoretical and empirical concerns. It should therefore prove invaluable to the professional scholar who is making his own contribution to the development of political psychology. The forcefully stated arguments—those with which he disagrees as well as those he finds congenial—will certainly stimulate his own intellectual process. The following chapters also make it possible for upper-division and graduate students to acquire a meaningful awareness of particular areas of substantive and methodological interest, and provide a detailed, comprehensive bibliography to guide their further research. For those of us who have been busily cultivating our own small gardens, the *Handbook of Political Psychology* presents an enlightening opportunity to become acquainted with other subdivisions of political psychology. It further offers us the chance to examine the methods of inquiry to which we have become wedded and makes a concerted effort to move research in various substantive areas away from complacent reliance on a single mode by examining the special advantages and limitations of different methodologies in the study of political behavior.

The discussion in this book begins with a stimulating integration of the intellectual traditions which have flowed into political psychology and have provided the basis for its distinctive interdisciplinary approach. The *Handbook* then turns to an examination of the three basic psychological constructs by which political behavior is most frequently analyzed: personality, attitudes, and beliefs. Each of the contributors to this part not only delimits in an original statement the special conceptual approach of the construct which is discussed in terms of available models, but additionally attempts the difficult task of distinguishing the theoretical and empirical usage of his construct from that of the other two constructs.

From this analysis of basic psychological constructs, the book moves on to consider the manner in which stable orientations toward political belief and activity are formed and maintained. In this part, three major orienting approaches—socialization, authoritarianism, and anomie-alienation—are assessed. These approaches, which together are responsible for hundreds of research efforts, are summarized and their contributions are criticized by three contributors whose seminal work in these areas well exemplifies the social relevance of political psychology.

The *Handbook* then turns to a discussion of the critical areas in which the nexus of individual and polity has been assessed in theory and in the field. The three areas—leadership; aggression, violence, revolution, and war; and international politics—further reflect the social importance of work in political psychology, as well as its broadly interdisciplinary subject matter. Analysis here indicates additionally the dynamic, evolving nature of theory in political psychology and thus well illustrates the value of the integrative task on which our efforts here are predicated.

The analysis of methods of inquiry in the following part of the book is of particular value to the student of political behavior because three of the methods discussed (experimentation, simulation, and projective techniques) have been seldom utilized in past research, and the remaining two (survey research and psychobiography) have been generally employed with less than optimal rigor. Each of the contributions in this part of the *Handbook* emphasizes the growing importance of methodological sophistication in political research, the value of research which includes multimethod analysis, and the exciting opportunities for future research which a careful understanding of the potential of each method makes visible.

Finally, the *Handbook* concludes with an incisive overview which well emphasizes the interdisciplinary, broadly conceived approach to the study of political behavior which is stressed by each of the collaborators in this volume. The final chapter emphasizes the contributors' consistent awareness of the dangers of psychological reductionism and intrapsychic overdeterminism and their continuing understanding of the value of multivariate models and complementary methods of inquiry. In our definition, political psychology weds intrapsychic determinants to political processes as these processes are intellectually experienced by the various disciplines. While each of the chapters addresses issues of particular interest to educators, political scientists, sociologists, psychologists, and historians, the integrating focus remains a concern with individual-level determinants of political behavior.

Today, the students of political psychology are legion, and the field is becoming increasingly international. A different group of these scholars, addressing themselves to the same topics, would doubtless have had a number of other points to make. The thoughtful and authoritative statements offered in the following chapters should stimulate this necessary further theoretical and empirical work. The success of this *Handbook* will be seen in the furtherance of a sense of community, of intellectual purpose, and of methods of inquiry by those with a concern for the relevance of the individual in the study of political behavior. The attainment of these goals has been already fostered: the interaction of the contributors to this book with one another and with a much wider group of peers who served to clarify and criticize judgments by sharing knowledge and viewpoints has begun a process that both refines and elucidates. The collaborators in this first edition of the *Handbook of Political Psychology* hope that it is but a beginning.

Los Angeles
June 1973   JEANNE N. KNUTSON

CONTENTS

CONTRIBUTORS

ALFRED H. BLOOM has assisted Herbert C. Kelman on a book on the social psychology of international relations. Bloom is a graduate student in social psychology at Harvard University, working in Hong Kong on his Ph.D. dissertation in the area of individual conceptions of political authority. He graduated summa cum laude in romance languages from Princeton University in 1967, spent a year studying international politics in France on a Fulbright-Hays grant, and received his masters' in social psychology from Harvard University in 1971.

RUFUS P. BROWNING is a political scientist at the University of California, Davis. He received his doctorate from Yale University and has taught at the University of Wisconsin, the University of California, Berkeley, and Michigan State University. His current research includes a computer simulation of political bargaining and a study of decision-making in experimental schools.

JAMES CHOWNING DAVIES is professor of political science at the University of Oregon and has taught at the California Institute of Technology and the University of California, Berkeley and Los Angeles. He has held fellowships from the Rockefeller Foundation, the Social Science Research Council, and the Carnegie Foundation. His interests in political psychology range widely, with major emphasis on socialization and revolution. His current interest is in constructing a political theory concerning the initiation, growth, stabilization, decay, and overthrow of governments.

BETTY GLAD is associate professor and head of the Department of Political Science at the University of Illinois at Urbana. She is on the council of the Midwest Political Science Association and is vice-president of the International Studies Association, Midwest. She has served on the editorial board of *PS* and chaired the Committee on the Status of Women of the Midwest Political Science Association. Her primary research interest has been the impact of modal psychological and ideological structures on American foreign policy-making.

FRED I. GREENSTEIN is Henry Luce Professor of Politics, Law and Society at Princeton University; he was previously professor and chairman of the Department of Government at Wesleyan University. He is on the editorial board of the *British Journal of Political Science* and the *Journal of Youth and Adolescence* and was previously on the editorial board of the *American Political Science Review*. He is a former member of the Political Science Advisory Panel of the National Science Foundation and a member of the Committee on Pre-Collegiate Education of the American Political Science Association. His primary interests within political psychology have been socialization and personality research.

HERBERT H. HYMAN is professor of sociology at Wesleyan University; previously, he was on the faculty of Columbia University for many years. His long and varied experience in survey methods includes the position of associate director of the Columbia Bureau of Applied Social Research, membership in the National Opinion Research Center at the University of Chicago, and the position of program director of surveys for the United Nations Research Institute. He is on the editorial board of the *Public Opinion Quarterly* and is associate editor of *Sociological Methodology*. He is past president of the American Association for Public Opinion Research.

DANIEL KATZ is professor of psychology and program director of the Survey Research Center at the University of Michigan. He is on the editorial board of the *Journal of Cross-Cultural Psychology* and has served on the editorial boards of numerous other journals, including *Human Relations,* the *Journal of Social Issues,* and the *Journal of Conflict Resolution,* as well as being editor of the *Journal of Abnormal and Social Psychology* and of the *Journal of Personality and Social Psychology.* He is a past president of the Society for the Psychological Study of Social Issues and of Divisions One and Eight of the American Psychological Association. Among his numerous honors is the 1965 Kurt Lewin Memorial Award for outstanding contributions to the integration of social research and social action. He has made major contributions in the areas of social psychology, personality, and attitudes.

HERBERT C. KELMAN is Richard Clarke Cabot Professor of Social Ethics at Harvard University and was previously professor of psychology and research psychologist at the Center for Research on Conflict Resolution at the University of Michigan. He is past president of the Society for the Psychological

Study of Social Issues and of Division Eight of the American Psychological Association, is vice-president of the International Studies Association, and has served on numerous editorial boards, including those of the *Journal of Personality and Social Psychology,* the *International Studies Quarterly, Psychiatry,* and *Human Relations.* He was the recipient of the Kurt Lewin Memorial Award for 1973. His research interests include social influence and attitude change, nationalism and political ideology, international relations, and ethics in social science.

JEANNE N. KNUTSON is senior research associate in psychology and political science at The Wright Institute in Berkeley and member, Psychiatry Department, Ross-Loos Medical Group, Los Angeles. She has a Ph.D in political science and is completing a Ph.D. in psychology (social psychology and psychopathology). She has had internships in clinical psychology at Cedars-Sinai Medical Center, Los Angeles, and at the Los Angeles Psychiatric Service. She has held pre- and post-doctoral research fellowships from the National Institute of Mental Health and is presently studying black and white patterns of political socialization under a research grant from the Society for the Psychological Study of Social Issues. Her current work includes an analysis of the long-term effects of personality on political belief and activity, the use of projective techniques in the study of political socialization, psychological models of political recruitment, and a case study of visualization in the treatment of hysteria.

ROBERT E. LANE is professor of political science at Yale University and past president of the American Political Science Association. He has received fellowships from the Fund for Advancement of Education, the Social Science Research Council, and the Center for Advanced Study in the Behavioral Sciences, and has been given awards by the Ford Foundation, the Carnegie Foundation, the Social Science Research Council, and the Woodrow Wilson International Center for Scholars. He was a senior Fulbright-Hays scholar in 1972–1973. He has published numerous works in political psychology, with special emphasis on ideology, beliefs, and opinions.

JOHN B. MCCONAHAY is director of the Psychology and Politics Program in the graduate school and assistant professor of political science and psychology at Yale University. He has been a National Institute of Mental Health research fellow and was a research assistant on the Los Angeles Riot Study carried out by the University of California, Los Angeles. He has published articles and a book on urban violence, and he is on the editorial board of the *Journal of Conflict Resolution.* His current research and writing are in the areas of political ideology and the effects of human crowding upon aggression and political socialization.

RICHARD G. NIEMI is associate professor of political science at the University of Rochester. He has received fellowships and research grants from the National Science Foundation, the National Institute of Mental Health, and the Ford Foundation. His major research interests are probability models of collective decision-making and political socialization. In the latter area he is currently working on a panel study of political change and development over the eight-year period after high school.

NEVITT SANFORD is scientific director of The Wright Institute in Berkeley and was previously professor of psychology and director of the Institute for the Study of Human Problems at Stanford University. Before that, he was professor of psychology at the University of California, Berkeley. He is past president of the Society for the Psychological Study of Social Issues and of Division Eight of the American Psychological Association. He received the 1970 Kurt Lewin Memorial Award for outstanding contributions to the integration of social research and social action and has been on the editorial boards of numerous journals, including the *Journal of Social Issues* and the *Journal of Abnormal and Social Psychology*. His major interests include socialization and personality development during the college years, authoritarianism, and social action research.

M. BREWSTER SMITH is professor of psychology and vice-chancellor of the Division of Social Sciences at the University of California, Santa Cruz. He was formerly the chairman of the Psychology Department at the University of Chicago and was director of the Institute of Human Development and professor of psychology at the University of California, Berkeley. He is past president of the Society for the Psychological Study of Social Issues and was editor of the *Journal of Abnormal and Social Psychology* and the *Journal of Social Issues*. His major research interests currently lie at the boundary of personality and social psychology, concerning the self in experience and action.

J. MILTON YINGER is professor and chairman of the Department of Sociology and Anthropology at Oberlin College. He has been on the editorial boards of *Social Problems*, the *American Sociological Review,* and the *Journal of Conflict Resolution*. He is the secretary of the American Sociological Association. From 1965–1970, he held a research grant from the Office of Education to study the effects of educational intervention on the culturally disprivileged. He has been a Guggenheim Fellow and, in 1958, received (with G. E. Simpson) the Anisfield-Wolf Award in Race Relations for the best work of nonfiction in race relations. He has made major contributions to the sociology of religion, to the study of race and minority group relations, and to developing a field view of personality, areas of interest in which he continues to work.

HANDBOOK
OF
POLITICAL
PSYCHOLOGY

1

WHERE FROM AND
WHERE TO?

James Chowning Davies

Political science in America started in the late nineteenth century. It began as the study of institutions, with such influential works as Woodrow Wilson's *Congressional Government*, published in 1885. In its early decades the new discipline largely ignored two basic phenomena: the effect of people on political institutions (and vice versa) and the political effect, on both people and institutions, of rapid social change and instability.

After World War I, however, while most American political scientists reflected the public mood of turning away from the unsettling and the unpleasant, some young professionals began to seek understanding of the forces inside people's heads that help to establish, maintain, or disestablish political institutions. In the 1920s, these young political scientists ventured into what their respectable peers and elders looked down on as the ill-reputed house of psychology. Companionships developed. A few progeny appeared. Then, after World War II, in the 1950s, the liaisons and their issue became accepted, institutionalized, and even sanctified. There was a baby boom: hundreds of studies in the behavior of the public—in stable democracies.

Studies of political behavior were typically legitimated only when they analyzed voters and lobbyists and legislators and administrators who behaved as rational bargainers in the familiar political marketplaces. Unions between political science and psychology that produced analyses of political misbehavior—when people "vote" with their feet, their lungs, and even with sit-ins and guns—remained illegitimate. Even in the 1960s and 1970s, after decades of wars, revolutions, rebellions, and riots, the predominant trend remained the study of stable, safely observable, and easily quantifiable phenomena. Political behaviorists still largely ignored the causes and effects of deep changes that alter the behavior of people in turbulent times.

The long-range prospect of continuing this neglect is that citizens and leaders will continue to face new problems with the same shock of ignorance that numbed their reactions to World War I and to revolution in Russia, Latin America, and Asia after both world wars. The short-range prospect is that political science will lose both its readers and its followers. One of the major purposes of this volume and this chapter is to demonstrate the enormous potential fruitfulness of more frequent and deeply involved and meaningful relationships between psychology and political science.

Natural scientists have learned to control floods and epidemics by understanding their causes. When social scientists pay less exclusive attention to healthy bodies politic, they too will be able to diminish the suffering and destruction that accompany profound and rapid social change. The contributors to this book seek to call attention to more fundamental causes, to more generally significant political phenomena, than just those that occur in calm times in calm countries. It is the minds of men that—either with calmness or agitation—resist change or welcome it. We can fruitfully look for the fundamental causes in the minds of men.

$B = f \, (OE)$

The discussion in this and many later chapters is organized around a basic behavioral equation: all observable behavior, including political behavior, is a function (or product) of the interaction between the organism and the environment. $B = f \, (OE)$. The equation is by no means novel and would indeed be a banality if it had not been neglected or garbled. The present form of the equation differs from earlier ones (like that of Lasswell and Kaplan, 1950, pp. 4–6) in that it explicitly locates nonenvironmental determinants in the human organism. For a consideration of the basic equation and its political implications, see Davies, 1963, ch. 1; in the present chapter the term *situation* is replaced with the more inclusive *environment*.

In some writings, the organic part of the equation is left unnecessarily vague, by such terms as *unconditioned response, predisposition to respond,* or *nonenvironmental determinants.* These terms avoid saying what these responses, predispositions, and nonenvironmental determinants are and where they come from. Some writers altogether ignore the organic part in their preoccupation with environmental influences under such terms as *stimulus, training, conditioning, socialization, politicization,* and *personality formation.* In many analyses, even such self-evident organic needs as food, rest, sex, and stimulation become undifferentiated parts of the activity of human beings, who thereby become indistinguishable from other animals. In this chapter, however, the basic premise is that every one of the enormously important environmental forces depends, for its effect on behavior, on the existence of a *selectively* responsive organism. Because of its enormously intricate nervous and endocrine systems, the human organism interacts in very precise ways with specific aspects of the environment. If it did not, it would behave in a randomized, entropic nonpattern comparable to that of marbles being shaken in a box or to the nonpattern of molecules of gas bouncing against each other inside a closed container.

The work of the many investigators who have contributed to the development of politically relevant psychology is divided into three main categories in this chapter: (1) theory and research emphasizing the organism as the major determinant; (2) theory and research emphasizing the close social environment in its *direct,* proximal influences on the behavior of individuals and groups; and (3) theory and research emphasizing the broad social environment in its *indirect, mediated,* distal influences on such behavior. In addition, there is a summary of some of the work on the central control systems (the nerves and the endocrines) that has been done by physiologists, in Chapter 9. This latter work will some day be directly relevant to an explanation of all major aspects of political behavior, but at present it is only directly relevant to explaining violence.

The basic distinction between kinds of environmental influences is significant and calls for clarification before we go farther. *Proximal* influences, including group influences, are those in which the influencing person is directly in contact with the selectively responding human organism, the human individual. The actions—verbal and otherwise—of parents, spouses, friends, teachers, preachers, and speakers at political rallies are proximal influences. Each of the persons with whom the individual is in direct contact is a proximal influencer. *Distal* influences are those which are carried to the individual by a proximal influencer. Churches, trade unions, social classes, economic and political institutions provide distal influences, and they are always mediated by a person who is in direct, proximal contact with the individual. A workingman, for example, may identify with the working class generally, but in every case the identification is mediated by people in circumstances with whom he (more exactly, his highly selective and—by the time of early adulthood—highly conditioned sensory, memory, and response system) is in direct contact. Nonpersonal influences fall similarly into the proximal and distal categories. An individual who sees a beautiful view while hiking in the mountains is being proximally influenced. An individual who reads a book about mountains is being distally influenced. The major preoccupation in this chapter is with those proximal and distal—those direct and mediated—influences that are between people.

Human Organism as a Determinant of Behavior

General interest in the social significance of the human organism developed somewhat earlier than did political science as a discipline. The major starting point was the publication in 1859 of Charles Darwin's *Origin of Species,* which sought to demonstrate the organic continuity between men and other species. This argument, like the prior argument that the earth is not the center of the universe, was a shock to human egocentricity. Only a generation after this shock to men's egocentricity came another, to their rationality. This was the assertion that men's behavior is almost totally controlled by forces of which they are unaware. That is, most of the conscious reasons men give to explain their behavior are rationalizations of unconscious forces.

Sigmund Freud (1856–1939) remains the great pioneer in this effort to place men mentally in their natural organic context, as Darwin has placed them physically in that context. The work of most of the psychologists discussed in this section—including those who stressed the environment—derives from the genetic psychology that Freud based in the human organism, notably in the glands and the brain.

Freud conceptualized mental processes as a threefold complex: the id, the ego, and the superego. The id (the libido or Eros) is the force that impels an individual to create and procreate, the instinct that seeks life and is the energy for life's development and perpetuation (Freud, 1933). These libidinal, erotic forces emerge whether or not the individual tries to deny them or is even conscious of them. The ego is the force that enables him to become aware of the libidinal forces and exercise some control over them.

This potential for control, however small, is crucial. Because it exists, men can live in some kind of harmony with themselves and with their fellow men. Indeed, the libido is the basis for not only the sexual ties between people but also—when the sexual goal is inhibited and controlled—for social and political ties. Although civilization produces deep anxieties when it frustrates the natural desire for sex, civilization also performs the necessary function of so inhibiting that desire by deflecting it from sex to other activities as to make society and culture possible (Freud, 1930). Civilization is a necessary external source of control.

This external control gradually is internalized by the individual on whom his parents, as his ideal figures, exert their influence and that of civilization, whose agents the parents are—in our terms, the proximal influencers who mediate social influences. The mother and the father give affection when the growing child acts in accordance with parental (and also, invariably, social) restrictions and demands; they withdraw affection when the child does not. This internalization, which Freud called the superego and equated with conscience, is a necessary part of the establishment, maintenance, and advancement of civilization. In a continuous interpersonal, intergenerational process of interaction both individuals and civilization develop and perpetuate themselves.

One of Freud's original disciples, Alfred Adler (1870–1937), broke with Freud because of what Adler regarded as Freud's total emphasis on sex and his rather tardy concern for the social influences on behavior. In *Understanding Human Nature* (1927), Adler insisted that sex is only one of many manifestations of men's desire for superiority, which includes a "striving for recognition." When this desire is frustrated, individuals develop a neurosis, an "inferiority complex." They can rid themselves of this inferiority feeling by developing their "social feeling," their sense of community with their fellow men. This social feeling and the empathic identification with others are innate tendencies not necessarily related, in Adler's emphatic view, to sexual impulses. Empathy makes it possible for people to be influenced by others, sometimes excessively so, particularly during childhood by parents. This "authoritative influence" can instill in individuals a habit of unreasoned obedience, even to public authority figures. Empathy, authority, and thus unreasoned obedience can give rise to race hatred (ethnocentrism), capital punishment, and war. Therefore, if social harmony is to prevail, a careful balance must be maintained between overspecifying and overgeneralizing the sense of empathy.

The most striking difference between Freud and Adler is their opposing view of internal conflict. Freud described the conflict as being fundamentally between internal forces within the individual—the life instinct (Eros) and the death instinct, which we will consider in Chapter Nine as it relates to Freud's analysis of war. Adler argued that internal conflict results from the failure of the environment to properly nurture the individual's social feeling. *Properly* nourished, this feeling can cause everyone to "feel himself bound to his fellow man" and so to internalize as part of himself "the welfare of humanity."

On the genetic, psychoanalytic grounds established by Freud, Erich Fromm (b. 1900) developed and expanded the analysis of broad social and political phenomena that Freud (1922, 1930) had undertaken only in his sixties (long after he had established his major theories) and that Adler (1927) had only begun to systematize. However, Fromm sidestepped a consideration of innate determinants. He said that "although there are certain needs . . . common to man, . . . man's nature, his passions, and anxieties are a cultural product" (1941, pp. 12–13). Influenced possibly as much by Marx as by Freud, Fromm focused on the social and cultural matrix that produces mental crises in entire peoples, entire civilizations.

In Fromm's view (1941), the central crisis facing Western civilization results from the interaction of two tendencies within a developing individual: "growth of self-strength" and "growing aloneness," which together produce the dilemma of independence and interdependence. This dilemma within the minds of individuals is improperly managed in the modern world with its intense frustrations, and tends to produce what Fromm called the authoritarian personality. Such a personality type, which he said became very prevalent, for historic and contemporary reasons, in the German lower middle class, exhibits strong feelings of "powerlessness, anxiety, and isolation" and as a result develops a sado-masochistic "love for the powerful" and "hatred for the powerless." Fromm also included within this personality type some less central characteristics: pettiness, hostility, and asceticism ("thriftiness with feelings as well as money") (pp. 211–212).

William McDougall (1871–1938) was a British contemporary of Freud, but was influenced by the earlier American psychologist William James (1842–1910), particularly by his *Principles of Psychology,* which appeared in 1890. Like Freud and James, McDougall began his professional career on a base of rigorous laboratory training in physiology. But his major contribution, again like that of Freud and James, was no direct product of the laboratory and also bore no evident relationship to any influence of the Vienna psychoanalytic school. McDougall's *Introduction to Social Psychology* (1908), a mainly theoretical work, became enormously influential in both England and America.

McDougall listed seven major instincts, to each of which he conjoined an emotion. The combinations are these: flight and fear, repulsion and disgust, curiosity and wonder, pugnacity and anger, self-abasement (or self-assertion) and negative (or positive) self-feeling, and finally the parental instinct and the tender emotion. In what seems more like an afterthought, he added other instincts to the seven major ones: reproduction (sex), eating, gregariousness, acquisition, and construction.

The innovative aspect of McDougall's list is its considerable length. He avoided, as had James, reducing innate predispositions either to the self-preservation instinct, which is the solitary instinct lying at the base of Social Darwinism as it derives from Darwinian biology, or to the sexual instinct, which Freud said was the one basic life urge—although Freud broadened its definition to make sex mean the same thing as all the meanings of love. One can reduce innate drives to Eros (and the death instinct) as Freud did, or leave the question vague, as Fromm did. But either reducing or evading the issue of innate drives makes it more difficult to explain such profound, earth-shaking phenomena as revolution and such seemingly self-evident phenomena as political stability.

An even more extended listing of basic needs was developed by Henry Alexander Murray (b. 1893) in his *Explorations in Personality* (1938). Borrowing and integrating ideas from Freud, Jung, Adler, James, McDougall, and others, the book marks some kind of ultimate in specification of innate behavioral tendencies. Murray defined need as "an organic potentiality or readiness to respond in a certain way under given conditions. [It is] a latent attribute of an organism" (p. 61). He states that all needs are complex electrochemical processes taking place within the central nervous and endocrine systems. But he separates needs into two main classes: primary or "viscerogenic" and secondary or "psychogenic," the latter having "no localizable bodily origins." In regard to this latter category he implicitly acknowledges the non-existence of physiological research that can help establish the organic loci of perhaps, for our purposes, the most important of the organic tendencies to respond.

The viscerogenic needs are inspiration (of air), water, food, sex, lactation, expiration (of air), urination, defecation, harmavoidance, heatavoidance, coldavoidance, noxavoidance, and sentience (for sensuous stimuli). The psychogenic needs are acquisition, conservance, order, retention, construction, superiority, achievement, recognition, exhibition, inviolacy, infavoidance (need to avoid failure, ridicule), defendance, counteraction, dominance, deference, similance (need to identify with others), autonomy, contrarience (need to be unique), aggression, abasement, blamavoidance, affiliation, rejection, nurturance, succorance (need to receive aid), play, cognizance (need to explore, to satisfy curiosity), and exposition (need to explain, interpret) (pp. 77–83).

Murray considers all these needs to be specific "pushes" from within that are directed in an orderly way toward something whose achievement is pleasant or away from something that is unpleasant. Correlative to the organic need is the environmental "press," which is "a threat of harm or promise of benefit to the organism" (pp. 40–41).

If Freud may be accused of reductionism—of oversimplifying the distinguishable basic driving forces—Murray may be charged with elaborationism. The scheme is really to elaborate to be readily usable as a coherent set of drives, at least to explain political behavior. Its boldness lies in denying oversimplification, in diminishing the tendency to reduce everything to a simple, general (but, neverthless, directional) energy state, as in Freud's concept of the libido.

Starting with research on one of the needs on Murray's list, David McClelland (b. 1917) produced the first psychologically empirical attack (1961) on a problem that had hitherto been analyzed sociologically and for the most part only theoretically by Max Weber (1904) and R. H. Tawney (1926). This problem is to explain what Weber called the Protestant Ethic. According to McClelland, the Protestant ethic—

the hard work, the frugality, the confident future orientation toward production of material wealth, the social exclusiveness of the elect—occurs not just in Protestant but also in Catholic, Communist, Occidental, and Oriental nations. The basic common phenomenon is the need for achievement, and McClelland relates this need to the process of modernization. His behavioral research shows the inadequacy of institutional analysis. It is not capitalism or socialism or even protestantism that spontaneously activates the need for achievement. This organically based need, latent in a premodern society, becomes active whenever a favorable environment develops, whatever ideology or institutional structure may accompany its development.

Abraham Maslow (1908–1970) generated a list of basic drives (1943b) that is some kind of midpoint between reductionism and elaborationism. It is more applicable to political analysis than Freud's very brief or Murray's very long list. Maslow specified five categories of needs; physical, security, social-affectional, self-esteem, and self-actualization needs. More important, however, for social and political analysis is his assertion that the basic needs are hierarchically ordered. When an individual is deprived of a need in the first category (of physical needs), this condition will activate the central control systems so that he will pursue its satisfaction before returning to any other (nonphysical) activity. If an individual is playing a game, reading, or working at a job that is either physically or mentally tiring, and *gets* tired, he will stop the play or the work and rest. Furthermore, not until the physical, security, and social-affectional needs are at least minimally satisfied will the individual seek satisfaction of his self-esteem needs. A person will suffer a variety of degradations rather than go without food, clothing, and shelter or without the company of those close to him. And only when there is a relatively steady satisfaction of at least some of his self-esteem needs will he be able easily to pursue his self-actualization needs.

The idea of priority, of hierarchy, makes it possible to explain patterns of political behavior that otherwise seem irrational. To give a rudimentary example, an individual who is very hungry is *un*able to turn his attention to political concerns at the very time when his political action may get him some food. An individual who feels unaccepted and unloved will be too preoccupied with his social-affectional needs to be able to develop a concern for politics. If he does turn to politics, he quite likely will become excessively demanding of affection, either from his followers (on Hitler, see Langer, 1972) or from his beloved leader. Empirical support for the hierarchy will be touched on in discussing the research of Harlow, Spitz, and Bowlby on emotionally deprived monkeys and children. The political implications of the hierarchy, both theoretically and empirically, have been explored by Davies (1963, ch. 1–2; 1972), Aronoff (1967), Inglehart (1971b), and Knutson (1972a).

There does appear to be an incongruity in the appearance of security as one of the need categories along with the physical, love, esteem, and actualization needs. Security seems to be related to the other needs in an instrumental way: one seeks to gain a sense of security *in the pursuit of* his physical, love, esteem, and actualization needs; one does not normally pursue security for its own sake (Davies, 1963, ch. 1; 1970, pp. 617–618; 1972; Kagan, 1972, p. 55). Furthermore, the need system becomes more coherent if two other instrumental needs—knowledge and power—are listed with security. So conceived, the instrumental needs for security, knowledge, and power are akin to these in Murray's list: superiority, defendance, counteraction, dominance, aggression, cognizance, and exposition. While the instrumental needs do not as such appear in Maslow's need hierarchy, not only security but also knowledge and power are convenient and probably necessary units of analysis for both theory and research in political behavior (Davies, 1972).

From Freud to Murray and Maslow, the primary emphasis among motivational psychologists as here described has been on the organism. But Adler and Fromm, as we have noted, strongly emphasized the environment. Another psychiatrist, Harry Stack Sullivan (1892–1949), stressed the environment even more, at times arguing that the individual must adjust to society instead of expecting society to adjust to him. In Sullivan's view, the neurotic is fundamentally someone who has failed to achieve satisfactory interpersonal relations. The mentally healthy person, according to Sullivan (1940), is the one who has adjusted his behavior to the norms of the society he lives in. The "radical," in contrast, has adjusted only to his ingroup; he and his group are paranoid with respect to the outside world, and the ingroup norms serve to justify and organize the destructive impulses of the radical.

This ends our discussion of psychologists—from Freud to Sullivan—who heavily emphasized the central nervous system as the entity that, in various ways and amounts influences—or must adapt to—the environment. In the next section we move to a discussion of work that most heavily emphasizes the environment and its ability to control the organism.

Environment as Determinant: Direct, Proximal Influence

Among the studies of direct, proximal influences we here include the work of stimulus-response psychologists, situationalists, and developmentalists.

Stimulus-Response Psychology. The grandsire of all environmental determinists in psychology is Ivan Petrovitch Pavlov (1849–1936). He was an exact contemporary of Freud, the grandsire of all genetic, organic determinists. Freud emphasized the role of organic (mainly sexual) determinants but by no means neglected the role of the environment (in the form of socially derived repressions and suppressions). Pavlov heavily emphasized the environment but did not neglect the organism. For him, behavioral events proceed from stimulus to (organic) neural processes to response.

In Pavlov's view, instincts are simply reflexes, reactions to internal and external stimuli. In addition to the more basic instinctual reflex, the hunger drive, however, he also observed the "freedom" and "investigatory" reflexes in his dogs—their dislike of the harness that kept them in the experimental apparatus and their alertness to a variety of stimuli that had nothing to do with the hunger drive. In this respect, Pavlov evidently anticipated two of the needs in Murray's list—the need for autonomy and the need for cognizance.

Pavlov's great contribution, summarized in his *Conditioned Reflexes* (1927), lies in his demonstration that higher vertebrates (and by implication men) can learn —be trained, conditioned—to associate a symbolic stimulus (a conditioned stimulus) with a nonsymbolic stimulus (an unconditioned stimulus). He trained dogs first to expect a food reward (the unconditioned, natural, real stimulus) whenever they were placed in the laboratory apparatus. He then trained them to anticipate the reward by activating, in advance of the reward, a bell, buzzer, metronome, or mild shock (the conditioned stimulus). When fully trained, the dogs would make an anticipatory response to food, by salivating, when *only* the conditioned stimulus was presented.

Pavlov's research—which was well endorsed by the postrevolutionary Soviet regime, with whose environmental determinism Pavlov's views were compatible—laid the groundwork for much modern learning theory and for a broad "objective" line of research that has argued the great manipulability—and the eventual emancipation—of all mankind. His presuppositions about manipulability were consistent with the optimistic view associated with environmental determinists—from John Locke (for whom the human mind was a blank sheet, on which society wrote what it chose to write) to Karl Marx (who argued that the human products of the immiserating capitalist system could be emancipated quite simply if that system were changed).

John B. Watson (1878–1958), an American successor to Pavlov, virtually eliminated central nervous activity from Pavlov's sequence of stimulus, neural processes, and response. Watson became almost totally preoccupied with the observable. In his view, hunger is a set of stomach contractions and thought is a series of muscle movements. He said at one point, "Give me a dozen healthy infants . . . and I'll guarantee to take any one at random and train him to become any type of specialist I might select—doctor, lawyer, artist, merchant-chief, and yes, even beggarman and thief, regardless of his talents, penchants, tendencies, abilities, vocations, and race of his ancestors" (Watson [1924], 1961, p. 104). Although he did recognize some "unlearned original responses," including fear, rage, and love, he preferred those that require no abstract classification because they are readily observable—responses such as sneezing, hiccoughing, crying, penis erection, urinating, defecating, eye movements, limb and torso movements, smiling, feeding, crawling, walking. Edward Chace Tolman, the distinguished motivational-behavioral psychologist, called this approach "muscle-twitch psychology."

The irony is that Watson was as much at home within American capitalism as Pavlov was within Soviet socialism. Without some criteria—whether derived from a structured view of human nature or a set of political ethics—it is manifestly possible to condition stimulus-response psychology to any ideology, any social and political system.

The most recent theorist among stimulus-response psychologists is somewhat less like Watson in his dogmatism and more like Pavlov in his distinction as a scientist. And he is perhaps more polemically inclined than either. B. F. Skinner (b. 1904) designed what has become known as the Skinner box, the container in which an experimental subject (a pigeon or a rat) becomes an active participant in gaining its reward. Instead of learning (as Pavlov's dogs did) that he will be fed when a bell rings, a subject learns that if he does what he is expected to do (like pushing a bar) he will be rewarded. The technique is called *operant conditioning* and tends to integrate positive action on the part of a subject with positive reward, thereby producing the response which both experimenter and subject desire.

Skinner frankly faced the social and political implications of his stimulus-response psychology. In *Walden Two* (1948), he argues that people generally do not want to make their own decisions and prefer to be governed by those who understand them. These governors, in turn, must be skilled enough to be able successfully to condition people to accept the social harmony and good life that they really want but do not know how to get. In *Beyond Freedom and Dignity* (1971), Skinner backs off, at least in emphasis, from the extreme elitism of *Walden Two*. He nevertheless insists that people think they are free when in fact they are only unbuttoned—which is quite different from saying they think they are free when they are conditioned to social control. They would do well, in his view, to rid themselves of the notion that freedom and dignity, *as they have been written about,* really have much to do with the good life.

Skinner (1971) depreciates any psychology that uses such concepts as goals, intentions, or purposes. "We find the purpose of the skilled movement of the hand in the consequences that follow it." And "we do, indeed, feel things inside our own skin, but we do not feel the things [like purpose] we have invented to explain behavior. . . . We do feel certain states of our bodies associated with behavior, but . . . they are by-products and not to be mistaken for causes" (pp. 12–14). But after vociferously kicking intent and purpose out the back door, Skinner welcomes them quietly at the front door. "The intentional design of a culture and the control of human behavior it implies are essential if the human species is to continue to develop" (p. 167). Two pages later he uses the word again, but in quotation marks. "What is needed is more 'intentional' control, not less, and this is an important engineering problem" (p. 169).

However, changing from his *Walden Two* position, Skinner in his second polemic does not consistently advocate control by an elite group but rather by the individual himself. His criteria for control are what is "natural" for developing human beings, but he does not explain how anything can be natural to a being with no definable nature. We do not know very much about the organism, he says, but eventually physiology will tell us more about what goes on under the skin. In any event, it is evident from his manner of writing that Skinner likes people and dislikes frustrating environments—aversively conditioning environments, as he calls them.

This is sophisticated and benign behaviorism, having as its purpose the eventual removal of external controls, as the individual moves toward autonomy (Hall, 1972). Such behaviorism is far removed from Watson's incredible belief in the near-total manipulability of humans. Supposedly Skinner looks forward to the withering away of the state. At least Marxism does. The problem is what controls to establish and who are to establish them in the interim. In *Walden Two,* psychologists are in control, but later Skinner backs away from according power to them or any other elite group. Lenin did not back away from the issue: the vanguard of the proletariat are the custodians of liberation.

Behaviorists, as well as Leninists, express honestly their compassion and responsible concern for humanity. What behaviorists and Leninists alike lack is any very specific set of standards by which they will appraise the appropriateness of control. At the same time they both presume to have remarkable confidence in their own ability to lead the way. They lack knowledge but want power to act on the basis of the vaguest criteria, the most prescientific premises of their scientism.

Situationalism. A substantial category of proximally oriented psychological work does not neatly fall into the behaviorist classification. This residual category is composed of situationalists (mainly the Gestaltists), who analyze behavior in terms of the present (rather than the historical) environmental antecedents of actions. Freud and his descendants concentrate on the patient's history of interpersonal relationships. Behaviorists focus on the effects of uncomplicated signaling stimuli that can condition behavior when the subject learns to associate a reward with the signal. Situationalists consider the complex and powerful influences of those small chunks of society that we call face-to-face or proximal groups, in contacts that are of relatively brief duration (Smith, 1971).

One of the most innovative pieces of research in this category was done on the basis of the autokinetic effect, the innate tendency of the brain to perceive a stationary point of light as moving, in a totally dark room, when there is no other stimulus to serve as a reference to the point of light. Sherif (1936, 1947) added a social dimension. He placed an innocent subject in a darkened room, together with a stooge of the experimenter, the stooge being told to say that the point of light had moved a certain number of inches. The amount of movement that innocent subjects then reported seeing tended to approximate the amount mentioned by the stooge. Sherif thereby demonstrated that social reference groups can influence perceptions.

The enormous power of a group to distort perceptions was explicated in experiments undertaken by Asch (1952). College students, who were presumably rather mature and surely above average in autonomy, were placed, usually alone, with a group of students who were the experimenter's stooges. The stimulus in this case was not a point of light but a set of lines whose length the innocent subjects were asked to compare with a standard, criterion line. When quite alone, subjects were able to judge almost perfectly which of a set of comparison lines was the same length as the criterion line. When they were in the group of stooges, however, and the stooges unanimously agreed that a line which in fact was *not* the same length as the criterion line *was* the same length, innocent subjects made errors in about a third of all their judgments—errors in the direction of their conniving fellow group members. (See Chapter Three in this volume.)

Extensive studies by some Yale psychologists (Hovland, Janis, and Kelley, 1953) spell out a variety of relationships involving the interaction between communicators and communications on the one hand and opinion change in communicatees on the other. One of these studies examines the effect of the communicator on the change in opinions held by the communicatee. When the communicator was a person with whom the communicatee could positively identify, he tended to change his opinion in the direction argued by the communicator; the communicatee was less likely to change his opinion when he disliked or mistrusted the communicator. This finding is less of a surprise than the finding that, after a lapse of time, opinions tended to change in the direction of the argument of the disliked communicator— and then to reverse again when the communicatee was reminded of who said that which he was now coming to accept. The implications are potentially enormous and relate to the success of prophets and polemicists (and housewives) in changing the views of people who despise or depreciate them. Radical change, violent and nonviolent, has typically been advocated by social rejects, from Socrates to Christ, from Mahomet to Marx. The continuing difficulty is that, consistent with the Yale findings, these prophets finally get accepted and their teachings established—and then finally ignored.

A significant integration of a variety of seemingly discontinuous but related research has been made by Leon Festinger in *A Theory of Cognitive Dissonance* (1957). Without establishing the loci in the brain, he argues that man has an irrepressible need to establish consistency in his opinions—to order and rationalize them. In quite different language, Festinger is talking about what Freud called the reality principle. He emphasizes the need to eliminate dissonance not only between one belief and another but also between belief and act. He elaborates on the social circumstances in which dissonance is diminished and intensified.

Two major statements within the situationalist category (Dollard and others, 1939; Berkowitz, 1962) deal with a very basic problem: the causes and circumstances of frustration and aggression. Discussion of these statements is contained in Chapter Nine in this volume.

Developmentalism. In the theory and research thus far considered under the environmental determinant category (from Pavlov to Hovland and others), little attention has been paid to the organic part of the equation $B = f$ (OE). In contrast, developmentalists symmetrically emphasize the necessity of *inter*action between organism and environment for normal development of the individual.

In the 1950s Harry Harlow and his associates began to publish reports of their research with monkeys that had been taken from their mothers at birth and "raised" by artificial mothers—wire-cloth and terry-cloth mothers with monkey-like faces and one rubber nipple, from which milk could be drawn. The effects were dramatic. When afforded contact with the artificial mother, the infant monkeys clung to it, even when blasts of air frightened or suddenly emerging spikes actually hurt the little monkeys. As soon as they could, they returned to their offensive fake mothers. Other monkeys, raised in isolation from any contact, became generally withdrawn in their posture, varying apathy with rage at environment and at themselves. Sometimes they would bite at their hands or arms till they reached bone. As they grew, they developed little ability to play with their normally raised agemates and when they were physically mature had no interest in sex.

When mother-deprived female monkeys were involuntarily impregnated, they became frightfully cruel mothers, sometimes killing their unwanted offspring by biting their skulls. But the severely mistreated infant monkeys nevertheless clung to their emotionally deprived mothers—and in time, in some kind of elemental group therapy, changed their mothers into rather normally affectionate creatures (Harlow, 1953; Harlow and Zimmerman, 1958; Harlow and Harlow, 1962; Harlow and Suomi, 1970).

Similar phenomena were observed by René Spitz (b. 1887), a child psychiatrist trained by Freud. Spitz studied what happened to infants raised in a foundling home. These children had had normal contact with their own or surrogate mothers during the first three months of life and then were deprived of contact with them for at least three months. The infants were given adequate physical attention by nurses, who fed, bathed, and changed them. But the nurses averaged eight infants each to care for and so could spend only a fraction of the time of a normal mother with a single child. The effects were similar to those in Harlow's monkeys. Of the ninety-one children raised in this well-run foundling home, thirty-four died before their second birthday. Those who survived were "human wrecks who behaved either in the manner of agitated or apathetic idiots" (Spitz, 1949, 1959). For a careful specification of the step-by-step sequence of development when there is normal interaction between child and mother, see Bowlby (1969, ch. 14–16).

A study of the physical effects of deprivation on brain tissue (undertaken by David Krech, Mark Rosenzweig, and others at the University of California, Berkeley) has demonstrated the inextricable relationship between the developing organism and the environment. In this study, genetically identical laboratory rats were divided into two groups. In one, the rats were raised in what the experimenters called an enriched environment: their cages were placed in brightly lighted rooms, and they had abundant handling by experimenters and many toys and other rats to play with. In the other group, the rats were well fed and housed, but in darkened rooms with minimal handing by experimenters and neither toys nor other rats to play with. After about two months of these different environments, the enriched rats were alert and sociable; the deprived rats were apathetic and dull. Then the two groups of rats were killed and their brains compared. The enriched group had larger brain weights than the deprived ones and statistically significant differences in amounts of two chemicals (acetylcholinesterase and cholinesterase) that are involved in the passing of electrical signals across nerve synapses (Krech, 1968; Quay and others, 1969).

Working with normal children in normal environments, the Swiss psychologist Jean Piaget (b. 1896) observed the process by which children began, at the age of six or seven, to develop rules and judgments of right and wrong. This period is of course much later than the critical postnatal period (the period studied by Harlow, Spitz, and Krech and Rosenzweig). By age six or seven the children whom Piaget (1932) studied had already passed through the "egocentric" stage of confusing self and non-self and had entered the "cooperative" stage, when they began to change from accepting rules as parentally or divinely established and became able to deliberate and decide on their own rules for play. Again, as in the earlier stages studied by Harlow and others, there is apparently a crucial interaction between developing organism and environment that makes possible the establishment of cooperation, of rule making rather than rule obeying.

Some theorists have attempted integrations of what is known about successive stages of development. Erik Erikson (b. 1902) conceptualized "eight ages of man," starting in infancy and culminating in maturity: basic trust, autonomy, initiative, industry, identity, intimacy, generativity, and ego integrity. Each stage develops on its predecessor—in a process that Erikson, using a term from embryology, calls "epigenesis." If failure in development should occur at any stage, the individual probably will be unable to develop normally through the stages that follow (Erikson, 1950, ch. 7; 1963, ch. 7 and p. 273).

A further refinement of the stages in the interaction process in a developing human being has been made by Kohlberg (1964, esp. p. 400; 1968). He describes six stages in moral development. A growing child successively changes the bases for conformity to rules: (1) to avoid punishment, (2) to obtain rewards, (3) to avoid disapproval, (4) "to avoid censure by legitimate authorities and resultant guilt," (5) to maintain the respect of the impartial spectator judging in terms of community welfare, and (6) "to avoid self-condemnation."

These writers and the experimenters discussed before them are working on the basic building blocks whereby the initial interactions between infants and their maternal environment gradually form the structure of society. This interplay between individuals and this interdependence of organism and environment are what lead to the development of social and political institutions whose growth, establishment, and disestablishment are inextricably related to the growth of individual human beings, from infancy to maturity.

It is not yet possible to generate a broad theory of political development on the empirical psychological basis of the work done by such as Erikson, Spitz, and Kohlberg. But some of the foundations for such work are already in existence. Normal organic growth processes have, as Spitz put it (1959, p. 43), "a life of their own." But this life will not develop unless the environment is supportive of the stage of development for which the organism is ready. Spitz refers to this interaction of organism and environment as "dependent development" (meaning the same thing that Erikson means by "epigenesis"). An infant cannot reach Erikson's "ego integrity" or Kohlberg's "internalized conscience" without having gone through a continuous process of building and interacting as his organism make its demands and as an environment responds in the epigenetic process.

One implication of developmental analysis, of the finding of the necessity for effective continuous interaction between organism and environment, is not mentioned by any of these investigators. Maslow's hierarchy reminds us that the physical needs precede all others. An organism that lacks food and good health is ill prepared to undertake any developmental interactions if the environment fails to feed it. Unfed people die. Unfortunately there are perhaps billions of people on earth so malnourished that bodily needs absorb almost their entire attention.

The political involvement of emotionally deprived people may be one of basic indifference (unconcern for anything beyond rudimentary social interaction) interrupted by an occasional outburst of rage against society, against humanity, against self. But for those people whose deprivation is physical and therefore even more fundamental, political involvement is perhaps even nearer to absolute zero. When it does appear, it is likely to take the form of totally asocial concern of each individual for his own survival.

Environment as Determinant: Mediated, Distal Influences

Studies of mediated, distal influences emphasize the role of the great society, the vast groupings in which the individual appears to have an undifferentiated and relatively passive role and in which the emotional considerations are supposedly minimal. They deal, that is, with such processes as modernization, industrialization, and immigration—and with such influences as regional, religious, and political party affiliation as these affect the individual's political behavior.

These processes generally take place in intensely personal contexts, with an often strongly emotional reaction on the part of the person influenced by such seemingly impersonal forces. That is, they generally are mediated by direct, affect-laden contacts with specific events and specific individuals that serve as carriers of the impersonal influence. A person who is compelled to increase his output in order to increase the enterprise's profit, in order to provide private or public capital for economic expansion, is made to do this not by a book or a concept but by a boss. A person who lives through the numerous traumata of leaving an old and defined community for a new, exciting, and unpredictable society does so in no impersonal way. He cries when he leaves his parents at the bus station, the pier, or the airport. He swallows his pride in the new society when the boss calls him a peasant, a Wop, a Bohunk, or a Nigger. After achieving some job security, he gets together with real-life compatriots or fellow landsmen to begin to act, in a real movement of people who passionately oppose their common degradation.

However, it is sometimes inconvenient to reduce analysis to the immediate interpersonal level; furthermore, some influences may affect large bodies of people in much the same way. Socioeconomic status plays an enormous role, in both developing and developed industrial societies, in establishing patterns of political behavior. So do such phenomena as social mobility and religious affiliation. Some writers using such units of analysis have reduced men to undifferentiated particles in a homogeneous mass. To avoid the opposite error of supposing that every environmental influence is uniquely personal, we need to consider forces that are of broad and indirect origin.

Karl Marx (1818–1883) was a developmentalist before that genre developed among psychologists. But Marx conceived the great determinants of development to be not within the individual or in the interaction processes that Harlow and Spitz examined. The grand determinants for Marx were the interactions of vast classes within vast systems: between the feudal lords and system against which the bourgeoisie revolted and between the bourgeoisie and the capitalist system against which the proletariat was beginning to revolt. This last revolt was to be the product of the aggregation of vast "masses" in wretched urban slums, often worked quite literally to death by the machines and system which they did not control. What this system did, however, was to unite the wage-enslaved "masses" in some consciousness of their common class interest (Marx and Engels, 1848).

On a common-sense level, the analysis makes much psychological sense. People who are oppressed do tend to form a unified group. But there are at least two problems with the analysis. One is that people who are so poor that their entire preoccupation is with staying alive and striving for some minimal nuclear family solidarity are not going to revolt: they will get food and shelter for themselves, their spouses, and children by whatever means necessary. Their "morality" is individual and primitive social survival rather than class survival. Only when their basic material needs are met (so that they no longer need to struggle each against all others or at least all other families) can they afford to become conscious of their common class interest. The other problem is that, once they have achieved a modicum of control over the productive forces by such means as collective bargaining and the strike, they are apt for a time to become conservative, opposed to further change and hostile to those who advocate it. McCarthyism—the era of communist baiting in America in the 1950s—was more a populist protest than a capitalist inquisition (see Stouffer, 1955).

The need hierarchy helps us explain these events. The process of development —seeking satisfaction of the physical, social, dignity, and finally self-actualization needs—takes place a step at a time, in the epigenetic manner that both Spitz and Erikson described. The interest of working people in free speech, in the creative arts, indeed in individuation and individual autonomy, requires the prior secure satisfaction of the social-affectional and dignity needs. In their vision of the good society, writers who objectively were in the bourgeois class like Marx, Engels, and Lenin ignored the need of poor people to go through the stages of development that their own parents (even their ancestors) had already passed through. Their sympathy with the poor (that is, with factory workers and most peasants) began after these pioneers among the intellectuals of their time had emerged out of a bourgeois class identification to a classless, human identification. They envisioned the good society that was appropriate to themselves as pioneers who had subjectively rejected class identification, but they were not yet able to rid themselves of a doubtless unconscious identity as members of the intelligentsia.

Such a good, classless society was not yet then, in the mid-nineteenth century —if it is even in the late twentieth century—within the realm of real possibility for unemancipated factory workers and poor peasants whose major and almost constant day-to-day concern was with sheer survival and who could not share the human, personal basis (or even universally apply the ideological basis) of the identifications of humanitarian intellectuals. The work—not just in words but also in deeds—of Marx, Engels, and Lenin was enormously influential in developing a sense of common interest among poor people; I am arguing, because of their moral identification with poor people and not because of the intellectual validity of their argument or their evidence. Visions of the good life, as poor people saw or see it, are inescapably based more solidly on material abundance than on the possibility of identifying with other people not as poor people who also need material goods more than anything else but as human beings whose differences are in their stages of development rather than in their nature.

If Marx was psychologically rather innocent, the French sociologist Durkheim (1858–1917) was not. His intimate analysis of the effects of industrialization on individuals, spelled out in *The Division of Labor* (1893), remains a sophisticated original source of explanation, nearly a century after he wrote it. Rural people commence their involvement in the industrializing modern world by entering the factory system, which severs their original social ties, binds them to the machines they tend, and dissects their coherent skills into tiny identical, repetitive pieces. Urban and factory influences produce in them what Durkheim called anomie, the sense of rootlessness and normlessness that alienates industrial workers from past and present associations and from themselves as individuals. (See also Chapter Seven in this volume.) At the same time, Durkheim emphasized, the division of labor becomes the principal source of social solidarity. An individual in primitive rural society is not so much free as he is stunted. Cities, factories, the specialization of job function do alienate, routinize, and even regiment the lives of people; but they also make possible a more total emancipation of man, who is otherwise stunted by his poverty and thus limited to concerning himself with only survival, with satisfying his material needs.

W. I. Thomas (1863–1947), nominally a sociologist like Durkheim, developed over several decades a rather systematic psychological system in which he concentrated on analysis of the great adjustment problems of poor people who emigrated from rural Poland to urban Chicago. He concluded that the individual and the situation *define each other* and that the individual modifies the environment by defining and solving problems according to his "wishes" and tendencies. By way of John B. Watson's "unconditioned responses" of fear, rage, and love, Thomas (1923) developed a list of "wishes," "the forces which impel action." These are the desires for new experience, security, response, and recognition. Curiously, he gave but slight mention to a couple of rather basic forces that impel action—hunger and sex; but he did note that the wish for response is related to the love instinct (including sex). And he described the wish for recognition in words that make it sound much like Maslow's needs for self-esteem and self-actualization. Altogether it is a remarkable list, and it became the basis, as noted in Chapter Nine in this volume, for a major theoretical work by Lyford Edwards on revolution.

Two other sociologists, Robert and Helen Lynd, made a major advance when they interviewed a sample of a city population and produced a massive study of the citizens' manner of living and their social (including political) interactions—more specifically, their pattern of work, family life, education, leisure, church activities, and government. The study demonstrated the wide range of phenomena that can be examined when systematic and direct contact is established with ordinary people. Using some of the techniques of cultural anthropologists plus quantitative analysis of questionnaire data, the Lynds (1929, 1937) established trends that were broadened and deepened in future decades of basic social and political research. They did factually what in various ways had been done fictionally by Charles Dickens in England, Émile Zola in France, and Upton Sinclair in America: they showed what life is like in an industrialized community.

In 1950 appeared a book that grew out of Erich Fromm's (1941) description of the (Nazi) authoritarian character. *The Authoritarian Personality,* in which four psychologists (Theodore Adorno, Else Frenkel-Brunswik, Daniel Levinson, and Nevitt Sanford) collaborated, is a broadly based quantitative study undertaken at the University of California, Berkeley. It examines where socially the authoritarian personality type appears and what its relationships are to such political phenomena as fascism and democracy. The book is crude in its methodology and naïve in its political concepts. Yet it is one of the most profoundly influential studies to appear since World War II and one of the first explicit efforts to link psychological and political concepts. One of the original collaborators in the study, Sanford, has written a new appraisal for this volume (see Chapter Six). Analysis at this point would be redundant.

Backtracking a bit, we turn to the development of research in political attitudes as these relate to voting behavior. The pioneer in this research, Paul Lazarsfeld (b. 1901), studied patterns of persistent and changing social characteristics (notably socioeconomic status, religion, and residence), the factors that he said determine political preference. His ground-breaking study (Lazarsfeld, Berelson, and Gaudet, 1944) was of the 1940 election and was done in a single city, as the Lynds' work was. The trend of political analysis of voting based on a sampling of the entire nation was developed to some kind of methodological ultimate in the work done under the direction of Angus Campbell (b. 1910) at the University of Michigan Survey Research Center. The Survey Research Center provided probably the most intensive (or at least extensive) analysis of the process of public opinion formation that has ever been undertaken in a stable polity. The center seems less prepared and inclined to get at the roots of change or of intense political instability. It has ventured into analysis of public *attitudes* toward political disturbances that produce violence (Blumenthal and others, 1972) but not the *tendencies* within individuals and societies that produce political violence.

Two authors have concerned themselves not with public opinion in stable democracies but with various social-psychological aspects of political development.

Daniel Lerner (b. 1917) used data gathered in several Middle Eastern nations by the Bureau of Applied Social Research at Columbia University and produced some concepts and findings that are applicable to developing nations all over the world. He emphasized, in different language, the need for what Adler called the community sense, and he asserted that empathy—in this context the feeling of a citizen toward his fellow nationals—is a crucial antecedent of modernization (1958). Walt Whitman Rostow (b. 1916) is a broad-gauged economic historian who looked into contemporary developmental processes and thus into the future (1952). His novel phrase, "the revolution of rising expectations," became a cliché that has concealed the significance of his findings about the "propensities" that, in certain favorable circumstances, impel people toward material development. Without adequate elaboration, he emphasized the psychological foundations of his theory.

This summary of some notable contributions to political psychology has been too brief, but it does suggest the very varied origins of relevant ideas and research. In the range of intellectual disciplines it has included psychoanalysts and social psychologists. It has also included sociologists and economists, who might turn in their graves at having psychology imputed to them. But the wide range of contributions only demonstrates the impossibility of classification on any other basis than what each has added to our understanding of the roots of political action. Broadly construed, that is what this book is about. It is not about psychology or political science but about political behavior, and there are no a priori disciplinary barriers to its understanding. Now we can turn to have a look at some more explicitly political writings, having by now some foreknowledge of the ancestry of these later works.

Some Progeny of the Union of Psychology and Political Science

The first notable liaisons between psychology and political science developed at the University of Chicago under the encouragement of the political scientist Charles Merriam. He saw the exciting possibilities of psychological (and even physiological) attachments (Merriam, 1934, pp. 20, 43–44) but was never himself able to exploit them.

The Work of Lasswell. One of Merriam's numerous intellectual progeny, Harold Dwight Lasswell (b. 1902) was the first to enter boldly into the psychological house of political ill repute, establish a liaison, and sire a set of ideas and influences of great vitality. And, like Merriam, he not only produced progeny but encouraged others to do likewise. He thus became not only the intellectual father but also a kind of grandfather of many of the political psychologists who developed after him.

Perhaps the most cited of Lasswell's succinct formulas appears in his *Psychopathology and Politics* (1930, pp. 75–76): Political man is the product of private motives, displaced on a public object, and rationalized in terms of public interest. In *Power and Society* (1950), which he coauthored with Abraham Kaplan, there is a more fundamental and symmetrical statement on the "fundamental units" of political behavior. They are specified as "response, environment, and predisposition" (p. 3). This becomes the fundamental equation: response is "a function of E[nvironment] and P[redisposition]" (p. 6). This is substantially the same as the equation with which this chapter started.

Lasswell formally recognized the basic part that predispositions play in determining behavior but avoided a direct consideration of these "nonenvironmental" determinants of response. He wrote at a time when the stimulus-response Watsonian behaviorist psychology was still a dominant influence, and so it is understandable that he shied away from these nonenvironmental (that is, organic) forces. Instead, he chose to list as a related set of basics a system of "pyramids," as he first called them (Lasswell, 1935), or "values," as he came to call them (Lasswell and Kaplan, 1950). The "pyramids" are safety, income, and deference; the "values" are divided into two broad categories, welfare and deference. Since values are objects sought in the environment, they correspond more to what Murray called "presses" than to organically based needs.

The values that Lasswell considers are the more or less visible objects that all people pursue, in ways that vary with individuals and cultures. The welfare values include well-being (health), wealth (income in goods and services), various kinds of skills, and enlightenment. The deference values include power, respect, rectitude, and affection. The kinship of these valued objects to basic needs is evident, but Lasswell avoided establishing the relationship. He does not say what nonenvironmental characteristics predispose people to want these things, because "no generalizations can be made a priori concerning the scale of values of all groups and individuals" (Lasswell and Kaplan, 1950, p. 56). By saying that it is the values—and, by inference, the predispositions—that make objects valuable, Lasswell avoids the organic half of his basic equation, which neither Freud, McDougall, Murray, Maslow, nor even the sociologist W. I. Thomas avoided. This avoidance has made it more difficult to make political inferences from Lasswell's writings that are of cross-cultural validity.

One of Lasswell's early main interests was analysis of symbols and their use by political elites to elicit "blood, work, taxes, applause from the masses" (Lasswell, 1951, p. 311). Propaganda—that is, symbol manipulation by the elite that is in power —succeeds when it handles "aggressiveness, guilt, weakness, affection" (Lasswell, 1951, p. 317). Propaganda generated by the counterelite, including a revolutionary elite, "selects symbols which are calculated to detach the affections of the masses from the existing symbols of authority, to attach these affections to challenging symbols, and to direct hostilities toward existing symbols of authority" (p. 322).

Lasswell's preoccupation with analysis of the elite, those who get the most of what there is to get, at times seems to spill over into the assumption that the elite are more important than the "mass," that it is important to learn the skills of symbol manipulation in order to keep the "masses" compliant: "The consensus on which order is based is necessarily nonrational; the world myth must be taken for granted by most of the population. The capacity for the generality of mankind to disembarrass themselves of the dominant legends of their early years is negligible" (Lasswell, 1935, p. 181). In sum: "The study of politics is the study of influence and the influential" (Lasswell, 1951, p. 295). Even in his study of revolutions, the major preoccupation is with the elites who lead their publics and with their use of symbols to incite them (Lasswell and Lerner, 1965). This preoccupation continued at least to 1956, when he suggested as an alternative to the murderous destruction of nuclear weapons a minimization of coercion by the gentler device of the "paralysis" bomb or a "paralyzing" beam of sound or some other high-energy source which could immobilize a city (Lasswell, 1956, p. 968).

Another preoccupation is his concern with equalizing the amount of values that each person should get. In *Democratic Character* (1951), he emphasized the necessity for sharing power, respect, and other values if a democratic society is to come into being—and he presumed that such a society *should* come into being. In 1956 he reiterated his growingly explicit and equalitarian values and argued for the universalization of what had been deemed only the white man's heritage: "the dignity of freedom."

There nevertheless remained a kind of stewardly willingness to manipulate people, not in the brutal manner of punishment but by techniques which Skinner called positive reinforcement. "Since the basic postulate of behavior is the maximization of indulgences over deprivations, our task is to consolidate democratic conduct by directing the indulgences toward those who act democratically, and the deprivations toward those who do not" (Lasswell, 1951, p. 513). The democratic task, ironically, is one that must be shouldered by the elite.

The dilemma that has faced elitists from Plato to Marx and Lenin, with eighteenth-century libertarians (including Rousseau) in between, is also expressed by Lasswell. None of these individuals successfully resolved the dilemma involved in the asymmetrical possession and exercise of influence in every real society in every actual era on this earth. The task of increasingly equalizing power and dignity, as a task of those who have more of both, is manifestly as hard to specify on paper as it is to accomplish in reality. Lasswell avoided the extravagant rhetoric of those so attached to an ideal that they lose contact with the realities and the responsibilities of power in any society, however democratic.

The theoretical contributions of Lasswell have been truly large. His professional contribution has been truly enormous: he was the first to insist successfully on the need to bring psychology into political analysis. He more than any other person insisted that unconscious forces which so significantly determine how people behave politically must be subjected to analysis. His ideas were not always consistent, but he stated his concepts and his orientation so forcefully that they were at last listened to. The large body of theory and research mentioned in the previous parts of this chapter had for the most part been around before Lasswell wrote. And political science had continued to ignore psychology.

Unfortunately, the very broad range of Lasswell's interests was ignored or narrowly viewed by most of the political scientists—many of them his disciples—who subsequently studied political behavior. Lasswell was at last listened to, but with ears that were sensitive to only a narrow range of his ideas, which resonated so broadly with political reality under conditions of stability *and* instability. For decades after Lasswell wrote his *World Politics and Personal Insecurity* in 1935, political scientists continued to study political behavior under stable circumstances, when social and political developments proceed slowly and institutions operate effectively. Writing sometimes as a technologist on symbol manipulation, he nevertheless saw the ineffectiveness of symbol manipulation when people are not symbolically but really deprived and when symbols do not relate to their real problems, their changing value expectations (their basic needs as they emerge) (Lasswell, 1951, p. 435). Many of Lasswell's heirs-evident, in their concentration on the low volatility of political behavior in stable democracies, have failed to appreciate that they themselves are not meeting the knowledge expectations of students and publics and elites. There is an increasingly evident need, expectation, and valuation of explanations of more universal applicability, in stable and unstable circumstances, in democracies and nondemocracies.

Some Research Developments Since Lasswell. Research in political behavior since the end of World War II has taken four somewhat different directions along lines that are not quite parallel and extend to differing lengths. The first of these is the study of voting behavior in stable democracies. The second is cross-national comparative research, in polities that are relatively stable and democratic (that is, the nations studied are at least not dictatorships and not undergoing revolution or widespread violence). The third line of research is in the genesis, the origins, of behavioral patterns that become established in childhood, the starting point generally being set at the age of about six, when children begin their schooling. The first of the trends has been the dominant one. The second and third have provided relief from the rather static study of behavior under stable circumstances, a study that has become increasingly dull, repetitious, and a precious picking of nits. The fourth is systematically psychological political biography.

The principal systemic frame of reference of each of these major trends has continued to be political stability—behavior shaped by stable environmental conditions among relatively contented people. This limitation, particularly in the first two lines, has amounted to settling for half a loaf of what was fresh in the 1940s but already stale in the 1960s. The limitation was not established by the wide range of Lasswell's concerns or by the vast breadth and depth of widely known psychological theory and research, only some of which has been recounted in the earlier part of this chapter. But this limited research has nevertheless produced some work of enduring utility, and the limitation is gradually being removed, most notably in the third line of research, in what has come to be called political socialization (see Chapter Five in this volume) and finally in research in political instability, a trend that now promises to become established (see Chapter Nine).

The first line of research is exemplified by the opinion and attitude studies that have emerged from the University of Michigan Survey Research Center (A. Campbell and others, 1960, 1966). This work is lineally descended from the studies of such pioneers as the Lynds and Lazarsfeld, but with refinements and innovations. Voting behavior has been analyzed as a function of the relationship between such social characteristics as rural-urban immigration, urban-rural residence and socioeconomic status on the one hand and orientations toward party, candidates, and issues on the other. Most innovative has been the study of the correlates of the sense of political efficacy, the sense that taking part in politics makes a difference for the single individual among scores of millions. And the research has ventured beyond national boundaries, to study voting behavior in such nations as Norway, England, and France—which, of course, are relatively stable democracies.

Various traditions and other irrational (but psychologically explicable) forces have inhibited the use of the great instrument of survey research to achieve the comprehensiveness and depth that other techniques and writers outside the University of Michigan have attempted. Two examples of stepping beyond secure methodologies and frames of reference may be mentioned. Both remain within the framework of analyzing stable polities, but both range broadly. Lester Milbrath (b. 1925) produced a remarkable synthesis in a study of political participation (1965). It is so nicely ordered and develops such a logical sequence of statements and propositions as to "how and why" people get involved in politics that it reads a bit like a geometry text. But it is far richer in data: it is a summation of the state of a well-matured subdiscipline. And it notes, without elaboration, that there is a lack of research on relationships between individual needs (both physical and mental) and political behavior.

The other study lacks the elegantly ordered development of Milbrath's synthesis but probes more deeply. Robert Lane (b. 1917) in *Political Life* (1959b) considers as wide a range of behavioral relationships as Milbrath does, but he boldly introduces a listing of human needs (economic, affectional, understanding, relief of tension, power, and self-esteem). It is even more significant that Lane spends at least a fourth of the book in considering the political consequences of such needs. To be sure, he remains within the framework of research data in the United States, but the data he uses had been largely ignored by behaviorally oriented political scientists. The synthesis that Lane was striving for in *Political Life* remained psychologically unstructured, but the volume was a pioneering effort—less extremely confident than Lasswell and more sedulously aware of the necessity of gathering evidence to evaluate theoretical propositions.

In *Political Ideology* (1962), Lane achieved unprecedented depth and a much more psychologically concerted analysis of the origins of political beliefs and values of fifteen people, all of them in what may loosely be called the upper-working class or lower-middle class. His observations of the fifteen are applicable to perhaps a majority of citizens in a stable society undergoing rapid internal change, but survey research has not yet undertaken to use the concepts around which Lane built his research. *Political Ideology* is less a study of ideology than of the roots of political belief systems, of political attitudes. Lane's fifteen people have a sincere but shallow belief in the values of democracy, of hard work and reward for it only among the rich and powerful when they have indeed worked hard. They also share a sense of futility at trying to control any major aspect of political life; at the same time, they have a fear of change. They both respect and resent those who have wealth and power; but they resent and do not respect those who radically criticize the existing (American) political system, perhaps as poor people within the Russian imperial and Soviet systems have resented internal radical criticisms of their government. Lane presents a rather frightening picture of the ambivalence toward authority and toward stable systems themselves. Such beliefs are perhaps prevalent in any greatly diversified society among individuals who are less than successful by that society's standards. They feel unconnected and powerless within a colossal system that they fear—and fear to change.

Some of the roots of assent to stability have been analyzed in a study of five nations. Again, the broad matrix is of basic stability, but there is an impressive new use of survey techniques to ascertain the incidence of political dispositions among major segments of the population of the United States, Great Britain, Germany, Italy, and Mexico. Gabriel Almond (b. 1911) and Sidney Verba (b. 1932) in *The Civic Culture* (1963) found varying and generally diminishing degrees of both political participation and sense of the efficacy of participation in these five nations. The diminutions generally were in the order of the nations listed, from the United States as the highest to Mexico as the lowest. Among numerous other relationships, they found something consistent with Lane's study of fifteen lower-status Americans:

a higher degree of participation and political self-confidence among people of higher socioeconomic status—possibly because the parents in such families encourage participation in the making of family decisions. Almond and Verba note that in those countries where there is a greater participation by all family members in family decision making (the United States and Britain), there is also a greater amount of participation in intermediary groups of a religious, political, or other social sort. In these countries, they found, people feel politically more efficacious (1963, ch. 11, 7).

In the late 1950s a new development started in political psychology, on research beginnings of the 1940s and theoretical foundations that are as new or old as Erikson, Freud, Rousseau, and even Plato in his concern for the training of the youth. The new development retains the continuing emphasis on behavior in stable polities, but it has undertaken to examine the most fundamental dynamic process of all: the origins and growth of political tendencies in the individual as he moves from birth and familial nurturance as a child to political maturity as a citizen. (See Chapter Five in this volume.)

Herbert Hyman, in his pioneering *Political Socialization* (1959), ordered and summarized a substantial body of theory and research on how political tendencies first get established. A notable work cited is that of Theodore Newcomb (1943, 1947), studying the changes in political outlook of girls of generally conservative upper-middle-class background, as they lived through the liberal atmosphere of four college years. But Hyman went back earlier than the influences of late adolescence. He compared the socialization process in working-class and middle-class families and covered the age range from grade school up to middle age and the kind of group influence from the family to age-peer groups in school.

In a related effort, Sidney Verba did not emphasize the developmental sequence but nevertheless considered proximal social influences on the establishment of basic political predispositions. And in his *Small Groups and Political Behavior: A Study of Leadership* (1961) he synthesized the extant research. Much of the research focus of *The Civic Culture* (which, as we have noted, Verba coauthored with Almond) was established in Verba's early work, where he noted the need for undertaking comparative analysis in different societies.

The two major initial research studies of the early stages of political (as distinct from total) socialization appeared more or less simultaneously and quite independently. In 1957 Fred I. Greenstein completed the planning and began the interviewing of grade school and high school students who provided the data first for his doctoral dissertation at Yale University (1959) and then an article on "The Benevolent Leader: Children's Images of Political Authority" (1960) and a book, *Children and Politics* (1965). That same year two others, David Easton and Robert Hess at the University of Chicago, began to publish the results of their studies of grade and high school students (Hess and Easton, 1960; Easton and Hess, 1962).

The findings of these more or less simultaneous and quite separated sources are not the same but generally confirm each other. Consistently with Hyman (and Lane's *Political Ideology*), Greenstein compared differences in the basic interactions between parents and children in working-class and middle-class families, noting the more frequent tendency of children in the former class to show feelings of inadequacy, limited imagination, and deference. He noted that working-class boys are relatively more interested in politics than working-class girls are, and that working-class women are less interested in politics than middle-class women are. But in general working-class boys and girls showed less interest than middle-class boys and girls. In short, studying the same epiphenomena as Almond and Verba (1963, ch. 7, 12) but with a deeper probe, Greenstein found a more pronounced tendency among middle-class than among working-class families to socialize children in the direction of equal deference and involvement in decision making. It adds up to evidence of the increasingly obvious irony that people of middle-class origin are more equalitarian and on that dimension more democratic than people of working-class origin. For a more direct comparison of what they call "elites and masses" in democracies, see Dye and Zeigler (1970, esp. ch. 5).

Hess and Easton (1960) emphasize the relationship between attitudes toward father and attitudes toward the president. For children in the early years of grade school, the image of the father and the image of the president tend to be much alike. By the time children finish grade school, however, they have developed more distinctly separate images of father and president, in the direction of seeing the latter as working harder and knowing more than father does.

Two more recent books, by Dawson and Prewitt (1969) and by Langton (1969), both entitled *Political Socialization,* show the considerable strides that have been made in research, in the decade since Hyman delimited the field. But with rare exceptions (see Davies, 1965), no direct effort has been made to consider the *pre*school influences of parents on political socialization. If Freud—and such major institutions as the Catholic Church and totalitarian parties of left and right—are correct in saying that the first six years are the most crucial ones, then the largely unexplored *political* consequences of the training during those years are most crucial. The political implications of the research of Harlow and Spitz and Krech and associates, as described above, remain unexamined. Langton (1969, ch. 2) found marked differences in political attitudes among children raised in families where both mother and father were present and those raised in father-absent families. This research describes the political product of interactions that do commence at or near birth but does not, perhaps could not, examine the process that produces the product.

Another line of research is the political biography on a psychological base. Again, as in political socialization, this volume has a separate chapter on psychobiography (see Chapter Eleven). It is enough here for me to mention works that seem particularly promising or successful. One of the most brilliantly intuitive psychobiographies appeared well before there was such a word. It is Lord Charnwood's *Abraham Lincoln,* first published in 1916. Edgar Snow did a similar and classic study of Mao Tse-tung in 1938. Intuition of the same special sort that Charnwood and Snow possessed became happily joined with thorough and systematic knowledge in Erik Erikson. On the foundation of his *Childhood and Society* (1950—second edition, 1963), he wrote his landmark studies of Martin Luther (1958) and of Gandhi (1969). The work of Erikson (and before him Henry Murray and Sigmund Freud) has inspired not only later psychobiographies but also theory and research in the background of political elites and nations undergoing development (Pye, 1962).

The problems in psychobiography are quite special. It seeks to explain the personalities of leaders who seem to share little in common other than being leaders. Knowledge about the early childhood influences in the lives of political leaders is invariably fragmentary. Even less is known or knowable about the reasons that leaders became such while their brothers, sisters, parents, and children usually are individuals of no great distinction. We can trace back from the broad, fast-running river of the leader's public career to the headwaters of his childhood, but we cannot yet explain why most such headwaters do not become such big rivers. More abstractly, how much of the behavior of leaders is a function of the development of their complex organisms, over decades, and how much is the product of their complex environments, over decades, is perhaps impossible to know.

We are likely to be able to predict fairly well where the broad class of political elitists comes from but to predict quite badly which of the few individual members of this elite will become chiefs of state. Members of the elite, including modern revolutionary leaders, below the very topmost level, are more likely to emerge from the middle class or from some other above-average status than from the working class or from rural backgrounds (Brinton, 1965, pp. 95–100; Strauss, 1973)—although occasionally the sons of carpenters, poor farmers, and factory workers do become even immortal agitators and chiefs of state. Such findings remind us to be less surprised at the clergy background of Woodrow Wilson, Malcolm X, and Martin Luther King; the lawyer background of Karl Marx; or the high government official background of Nikolai Lenin and Mohandas Gandhi—and more surprised at the poor farmer background of Abraham Lincoln. They remind us to be most surprised at any present scheme for predicting who among those now living will be chiefs of state in any land in the year 2001.

The conceptual tools and measuring devices with which we can ascertain adequately *why* some men become political leaders indeed remain rather rudimentary. But some analysis explaining the *style* of men who become leaders has become increasingly sensitive and psychologically sophisticated. The study of Wilson by the Georges (1956) and of the first American Secretary of Defense, James Forrestal, by Rogow (1963) indeed show the limitations imposed by scant knowledge of childhood influences that Freud and Erikson have psychoanalytically emphasized (and Harlow and Krech behaviorally emphasized). Yet the work of the Georges and of Rogow succeeds. The Georges, however, do not discuss the relevance of the fact that Wilson, a wartime president whom the war tore apart, was eight and living in Georgia during the Civil War when the violent march of Sherman's army laid much of Georgia waste.

A very bold and successful systematization has been made by James David Barber (1972a), the boldest step yet in establishing a typology applicable to all the American presidents from Taft to Nixon. The study establishes personality types and makes a successful case for the predictability of style of presidential rule, partly on the basis of tendencies that began in childhood. Although the book does not say who will become president, it cogently argues how presidents will act. And Barber does take note of the fact that Wilson experienced war, firsthand, at a very tender age.

Toward General Political Theory on a Psychological Base

In the previous sections of this chapter I have skimmed selectively—necessarily too selectively to be encyclopedic—the surface of a vast and rapidly growing body of writing that bears on the manifestations and causes of political action. Those writings that have been discussed are by no means a cross section of those that have been written. I have sought to compensate for what I regard as a hypertrophy of research in epiphenomena, phenotypes, and other evidences of the sometimes self-evident or long since demonstrated, by ordering the discussion in accordance with a theoretical rather than epiphenomenal basis—$B = f \ (OE)$—and by discussing first the organic emphases. There is not a dystrophy but a kind of atrophy of theory and research that can help us link observable acts with their deeply and generally antecedent causes in the human organism, notably the nervous and endocrine systems. Aristotle sought such relationships. So did Hobbes, whose *Leviathan* (1651) founded its analysis of political institutions on a theory of human nature. And likewise Lasswell has sought to relate fundamental determinants to observable effects—and vice versa.

The concern in American studies of political behavior for precisely validating the self-evident, in each of its infinite nuances, seems almost an industrial phenomenon, consistent with the ability to turn out identical and shiny automobiles that speedily move nowhere and everywhere. The ability to produce printouts on the computer has displaced the ability to think and postulate more fundamental causal relationships. While Mendelian genetics has been transformed into microbiology and traditional somatic physiology has been transformed into neurology and endocrinology, the study of political behavior for the most part has continued to pursue that which is no longer novel. In turbulent times it has studied stability. In a time when systems are under intense pressure, political science as a total discipline has studied not the pressure so much as the container—the behavior not of people but of institutions.

There are three exceptions to the heavy emphasis on the epiphenomenal, on the study of manifest effects—three efforts to establish the fundamental linkages between people and institutions, in stable and in turbulent times, that Hobbes attempted. None of them is a finished product, an ultimate statement, but each has reflected an effort to link things more fundamentally and each has reflected the scientific commitment to seek empirical validations for assertions that of necessity remain untested hypotheses. And a fourth effort has involved the empirical testing of phenomena about which there has been some light laughter or solemn scholarly headshaking, about supposedly vague notions that were deemed really untestable.

The earliest of these broad-gauged efforts was undertaken by Christian Bay in his *Structure of Freedom* (1958). Frankly avowing a reality which affects everyone but which most social scientists are either prudish or schizophrenic about—a set of values—Bay has attempted to examine such empirical foundations as exist for distinguishing the human purposes that government should serve and those it should stay away from.

The second of these efforts, growing out of a doctoral dissertation (Davies, 1952), was undertaken by me, in a book (Davies, 1963) whose title was filched from Graham Wallas (1858–1932) on *Human Nature in Politics* (1908). In my study of the relationships, I attempted to order the presentation of ideas and research that bear—less explicitly in a normative context than in Bay's writing—on some of the basic psychological questions.

The third of these efforts is Robert Lane's *Political Thinking and Consciousness* (1969). In this work, Lane examines the ways in which people become not just knowledgeable about politics but aware of themselves as self-conscious participants in the political process.

The fourth book, Jeanne Knutson's *Human Basis of the Polity* (1972a), is not the first effort to test Maslow's concept of a hierarchy of basic needs but the first effort empirically to apply it in its political context.

The concept of basic needs, mentioned by all four of these writers, has become increasingly central to the thinking of each of them. The statement of what needs are indeed basic—in varying degrees and at different times common to the entire human species—is different in each of the four writers, but each emphasizes them: whatever behavioral characteristics human beings do have in common, these writers assert, they surely include some needs. In my *Human Nature in Politics* they are the subject matter of the first two chapters. Lane mentions them somewhat unsystematically in his *Political Life* and then very centrally in his *Political Thinking and Consciousness*.

Another characteristic of all four of the books is that each shows a sense of awareness of the evolution of political theory. In an era of political behaviorists who, as Arthur Koestler might have put it, are a generation without an umbilical cord, these four writers have not sat and mystically contemplated their navels. They are research oriented. But they show an awareness of their intellectual heritage in political theory.

All of these works and any works in political psychology are only beginnings, but in an age when publics and individual citizens are asking fundamental questions and when political "apathetics" and other rebels have threatened to tear down governments unresponsive to their demands, these works and some others have not been limited to ascertaining whether the shift in political loyalties means that the new majority is Democratic, Republican, Undecided, or Not Ascertained. They have sought to assemble ideas and research that can have more enduring value.

In such directions political psychology can go. In such directions, toward more fundamental explanations, political science cannot go without psychology. Systematic knowledge of it is as basic to political science as organic chemistry is to biology and as physics is to chemistry. There is no other way to find answers to the fundamental questions of why governments, as Jefferson put it, are instituted among men and why men assert the right to alter or abolish government that does not serve their needs. If indeed that is fundamentally why Americans and other people have revolted, the study of what men want is a rather appropriate place to begin to study the stability and instability of their political institutions.

2

PERSONALITY IN THE STUDY OF POLITICS

Jeanne N. Knutson

In discussions of political behavior, scholars and laymen alike make widespread use of personality concepts, because intuitively and impressionistically we all sense that the type of person who occupies a certain role has a good deal to do with the way the role is performed. Furthermore, although again it is more observational than evidential, certain types of people do seem to occupy certain roles. Hence, we tend to stereotype the personality aspects of role performance: the businessman's Babbitry, the pedantic nature of a professor or preacher, the hoarding tenacity of the peasant—plus myriad racial and cultural stereotypes which have also dogmatically and at times existentially circumscribed the lives of those the labels seem to fit.

For their thoughtful critiques of a draft version and for a good deal of the clarity of the present chapter, I would like to express appreciation to Alexander L. George, Daniel Katz, and M. Brewster Smith.

However, a second—and still impressionistic—examination of personal evidence forces us to conclude that personality stereotypes are a blend of veracity and mendacity and therefore do not accurately represent any given group. In fact or fiction, we all are acquainted with informal and humanitarian teachers, spendthrift peasants, bourgeois revolutionaries, and other common "aberrations." Thus, we are initially forced to acknowledge that *the relationship between personality and social-political behavior is one of contingency:* what is true is so only in a certain degree, in some cases, and on certain occasions. At this point the professional student of political behavior, when faced with a research problem in which personality is clearly a relevant dimension, turns to a standard volume on personality theory. Unfortunately, he quickly discovers that there is no one personality theory, but rather a veritable smorgasbord of theoretical systems. Thus, the scholar who is interested in studying the effect of personality on political behavior is forced to become familiar with the major theoretical systems in order to acquire an understanding of useful models and constructs. Also (as the following section attempts to make clear), the scholar who wishes to employ intrapsychic determinants in his research design must do more than simply pick a congenial theoretical framework within which to work.

Additionally, since each personality theory is stated in general terms without clear behavioral referents, the problem of operationalizing the selected personality theory becomes paramount and leads the political psychologist into the thorny pathways of methodological acrimony and ambiguous research findings. The thoughtful researcher, therefore, must be wary lest the availability of a particular personality theory or frequently employed personality scale overdetermine and deleteriously shape his research strategies and goals.

Conceptualizing Personality

Both historically and currently, personality as a concept has lacked behavioral referents and objective specificity and therefore has eluded rigorous analysis and assessment. Historically, the existence of religious, moral, and legal norms seemed to obviate the need for scientific examination. Currently, the concept of personality remains difficult to objectify largely because of its theoretical development in the clinical tradition (Hall and Lindzey, 1957)—a tradition in which intuition has been valued as highly as empiricism. Additionally, the increasingly popular social learning theories have retarded the analysis of personality as a trans-situational construct (see Alker, 1972). As the following discussion will suggest, equally deleterious to the scientific usage of personality have been the antiempiricist assumptions upon which the concept has usually been based. It is thus initially necessary to examine those assumptions and to delimit personality in terms which allow its scientific study.

To begin with, in its scientific usage today, the concept *personality* has no common currency. Indeed, its meaning is very much determined by the theoretical persuasion of the scholar who is using the term. Although at least ten such viewpoints exist (Misiak and Sexton, 1966, pp. 169–170), two main assumptions are general to most of these viewpoints. In the first place, personality is generally conceded to refer to the "internal dispositions" or "stable attributes" which an individual brings to a situation. As part of this assumption, most personality theories posit some organization by which intrapsychic attributes are grouped. This organization constrains the effects of intrapsychic attributes and outer (extrapsychic) stimuli. Second, as Lazarus (1963, p. 37) notes: "One hallmark of personality is consistency, or stability. If we had no consistent personal qualities, we could not conceive of personality, since we would all be continually changing so much that we would scarcely be recognizable."

Thus, common definitions of personality assume two meanings: (a) organized internal dispositions and (b) stability or consistency over time. To Allport (1937, p. 48), who recorded over fifty then current definitions: "Personality is the dynamic organization within the individual of those psychophysical systems that determine his unique adjustments to his environment." Murray's (1968, p. 6) statement is more definitive: "A personality at any designated moment of its history (in middle life, for example) is the then-existing brain-located, imperceptible and problematical hierarchical constitution of an individual's entire complex stock of interrelated substance-dependent and structure-dependent psychological properties (elementary, association, and organizational)."

As the above definitions imply, personality in some unspecified way is seen to refer to *organized, stable internal predispositions* which each individual brings to a situation. These dispositions orient his behavior, and they vary among individuals. A major confounding factor, however, is recognized by all personality theorists (though acknowledged in idiosyncratic terms). That factor is the situational specificity of the relationship between any one behavior and the personality construct to which it refers.

> Even when there is little or no consistency at the level of behavioral acts, there may be great stability or consistency in the hypothetical structures and processes that determine these surface acts. To borrow an attractive expression from [Allport, 1937, p. 351], "the same heat that melts the butter hardens the egg." The same structure, when reflected in different circumstances, may have superficially different, even opposite effects. This kind of consistency of determining structures and processes is of the utmost importance in personality theory [Lazarus, 1963, p. 39].

An empirically useful (that is, rigorously scientific) personality theory, then, must specify behavioral referents for its constructs; it must also delimit the situational specificity of these behaviors and/or the interaction pattern beween personality constructs and situational determinants. Thus, a third assumption underlying definitions of personality is that behavior is related to a system of intrapsychic determinants in knowable ways and that these ways vary with the parameters of the external situation. For example, in the Berkeley study of authoritarianism (see Chapter Six in this volume), a person could be viewed as possessing the trait of "aggressiveness," even though he acted aggressively only toward physically weaker persons and was compliant when challenged by a physical or psychological superior.

At least two major obstacles, however, confound attempts to measure personality according to the assumptions discussed. First, personality is unmeasurable because it is global or general; that is, it is inclusive of the organization of all internal traits. Second, personality is a *mediating construct;* that is, it cannot be measured directly but can only be *inferred* from instances of behavior (which themselves are nonspecific). Like other concepts, it exists only as a theoretical construct (Kelly, 1955) and thus requires specification in terms of entities which can be directly observed.

But in spite of these obstacles, a basis can be provided for the empirical use of personality in the study of behavior. This basis necessitates (a) conceptualizing personality in terms less encompassing than the overarching concept itself and (b) specifying behavioral referents, thus providing "decision rules" by which the presence or absence of a particular aspect of personality may be objectively judged. Hence, though personality exists as a global (and as such unmeasured) concept, by convention different personality theorists have specified their meanings of personality in terms of subconcepts with more or less clear objective referents (although these may be specified to vary with the situation). These subconcepts, which the global concept *personality* encompasses, are such entities as traits, values, needs, drives, and habits—subconcepts stemming from the general psychological theory that is intellectually compatible to the theorist developing his view of personality (Sanford, 1968b, p. 589). However (as Sanford points out), methods of "dividing" personality often involve "arbitrary cuts" in the interest of some practical aim or "abstracting" features which appear of topical concern, proclivities which have provided the basis for most trait measurement efforts.

Perhaps the best-known and certainly the largest (as well as perhaps the most instructive) attempt at an *inclusive* definition of personality traits was begun by Allport and Odbert (1936) and carried out by Cattell (1957), whose search in a standard English dictionary netted some 18,000 trait terms; from this initial list, Cattell compiled a list of 4504 terms and then further reduced this list to 171 "synonym groups," which presumably spanned the "personality sphere." Ratings of these elements were submitted to cluster and then factor analysis, from which appeared five distinct, independent (and statistically orthogonal) factors. (These factors are Extroversion, Agreeableness, Conscientiousness, Emotional Stability, and Culture. See Norman, 1963, p. 577). Yet, after all this effort to objectify traits, the best evidence to date suggests that these five independent factors are commonly used English-language constructs that exist in the minds of the raters employing them—leaving unanswered the more pressing question of whether these concepts also have intrapsychic meaning for the subjects so rated. This conclusion was forced by the ingenious work of Passini and Norman (1966), who illustrated through a study in which the same five factors emerged from judges' ratings of the personalities of complete strangers that the existence of these traits was located in the minds of the raters. (For another attempt to build a trait system, see Guilford, 1959.) Similar to the work of trait theorists in substance, if not in terminology, are efforts to develop inclusive lists of needs which serve to motivate behavior (see Cronbach, 1963; Fromm, 1955; Linton, 1945; Murray, 1938).

Personality theorists who employ a trait model adhere to certain assumptions about intrapsychic functioning. The trait model, as Mischel (1968, p. 6) notes, is cumulative, in that indicators are related additively to the inferred underlying disposition. (Through summing the frequency of behavioral indications of a trait, one arrives at the intensity or quality of the trait the person possesses.) Trait theorists not only measure individual traits in an additive manner; they also summate groups of traits possessed by a person on the assumption that including more traits in their model of personality allows a more complete understanding of the personality of the subject. Thus, for example, if a subject's behavior is scored on the needs for creativity, endurance, intraception/extraception, and change (Murray, 1938), it is assumed that one will know more about the subject's personality than if his behavior is scored for only one of these needs.

As should be clear from the above, a trait thus refers to a theoretically limited and empirically isolable aspect of a person's total personality. A trait focuses on individual (behaviorally relevant) differences on a single dimension. Trait statements are inherently unconcerned with the question of intrapsychic organization (relations between traits) and do not generally speak predictively regarding the existence and intensity of other hypothesized traits.

Other personality theorists attempt to make a global or holistic estimate which is suggestive of a person's *total* psychic functioning. This group emphasizes the necessity of *first understanding the organizing principle of intrapsychic functioning* in order to assess, for example, whether passivity implies a dependent character or is a reaction formation (as in a passive-aggressive) against the expression of aggressive impulses. Maslow (1943c, 1954), for example, has conceptualized human behavior in terms of a hierarchy of five basic need areas: physiological, safety or security, affection and belongingness, esteem (both self and social), and self-actualization. Because of the contingent influence of personality on behavior and the theoretical complexity of these need areas, however, such holistic personality constructs can only with difficulty be defined in ways that allow their empirical validation and the assessment of their effect on political behavior. (For works that attempt such linkage, see Knutson, 1972a; Simpson, 1971; Davies, 1963.)

Holistic theorists assume that the personality concepts which they have abstracted address themselves to the total manner of a person's functioning—to the structure, dynamic organization, and operation of any one personality. In this tradition, Maslow (1943b, pp. 528–529) speaks of discrete "syndromes" of personality:

> In our definition of the syndrome, the main quality which characterizes the whole ("meaning," "flavor," or aim) can be seen in any of its parts if these parts are understood not reductively, but holistically. Of course this is a theoretical statement and we may expect to find operational difficulties with it. Most of the time we shall be able to discover the flavor or aim of the specific behavior only by understanding the whole of which it is a part. And yet there are enough exceptions to this rule to convince us that the aim or "flavor" inheres in the part as well as in the whole.

This holistic viewpoint is thus grounded in understanding the organizing principle (for example, the dominant need area) of each personality and in the belief that an adequate measure of a single personality's functioning is predictive of all aspects of the personality.

While holistic theorists agree that constructs such as traits, narrowly defined needs, and drives have a large degree of commonality (thus allowing nomothetic statements), they stress that any one personality can be completely understood (and thus completely predicted) only in relationship to itself. Nomothetic analysis, then, can bring some general understanding of the operation of personality in behavior;

however, "the issue concerning uniqueness is settled in terms of predictive power, which is greater when idiographic knowledge is employed" (Allport, in Smith, 1971). Such a holistic viewpoint of course characterizes the psychoanalytic theories (Hall and Lindzey, 1957; Sarnoff, 1962) in which the understanding and predictibility gained by such holistic labels as "obsessive compulsive" and "hysterical, conversion type" need to be optimally supplemented by in-depth study of the person to whom the label is being applied.

While most nomothetic analyses of personality to date have been based on trait approaches and holistic models have generally been reserved for clinically oriented case studies, such a distinction has been based more on convenience than necessity. As was exemplified in a recent study (Knutson, 1972a), it is feasible to employ a holistic model on a nomothetic level. For discussions of the interrelated (rather than dichotomous) nature of nomothetic and idiographic levels of personality analysis, see Falk (1956) and Beck (1953).

Explicitly, holistic theorists consider each personality as an open system, with its own logical imperatives and organizing principle. Theorists with this perspective emphasize the necessity of knowing the function (D. Katz, 1960) that a particular behavior serves for a person in order to understand what the behavior implies about his personality. This functional principle is seen as the key to unlocking the manner in which outer stimuli and intrapsychic constraints are organized. From this viewpoint, it is meaningless to state that a man who works for many political causes possesses the trait of "active orientation." A relevant statement (which necessarily implies a phenomenological stance) would rather label his personality as self-actualizing, other-directed, hysterical, and so forth. Such a label would not only subsume the meaning of the observed behavior but would also be predictive of the individual's functioning along dimensions yet unstudied.

Holism in personality theory is not only grounded in a consideration of the individual psyche, but—adding to the difficulty of employing such concepts in rigorous empirical research—holism is inclusive of every isolable subconcept in the personality area. For example, Murray (1968, pp. 6–7) declares (in a statement which classically summarizes the indistinct and qualitative nature of much holistic theory):

> In this PS [personological system], "personality," the most comprehensive term we have in psychology, is given a functional meaning embracing everything from basic temperamental variables—for example, energy level, hedonic level, affective state of being—to such higher mental processes as may be devoted to superpersonal (cultural) endeavors—for example, artistic, historical, scientific, philosophical. Consequently, even by restricting one's attention (as one inevitably must do and should do) to the most important properties, a personality cannot yet be adequately represented as a functional and temporal whole in less than 5000 words, let us say; certainly not by a short list of traits.

From the above distinctions, it is apparent that a holistic personality construct would be much more difficult to employ in political research than would a trait theory, in which specified, disparate traits (with presumably clearer behavioral referents) are used to *stand for* the concept of personality. Yet ease of measurement is perhaps deceptive, for (at least from a holistic perspective) when an individual's functioning is assessed in terms of several discrete areas, most of his predispositions may be left unmeasured—and an understanding of the interactions among his predispositions in the various, discrete dimensions may be obviated as well. For example, a trait theorist who sets out to measure aggressiveness and conformity does not necessarily make any assumptions about the traits of intellectuality and creativity as well (nor about the relationships between these traits—although he may hypothesize the existence of certain patterns of covariance), but a holistic theorist who makes a global personality-relevant statement clearly does make such assumptions.

While Murray, Freud, Erikson, and others who employ a holistic approach to personality discuss this viewpoint in different terms from those used by Maslow, the basic belief is remarkably similar: Each behavior in which a person is psychically engaged provides an expression of some aspects of his total personality structure; that is, his basic needs, drives, motivations, as well as his idiosyncratic manner of coping, his response patterns, his habits. The obverse of this belief is extremely important in understanding the holistic viewpoint. Organization is more basic than analytic elements. A person's total personality forms a gestalt, the parts of which can be separated only theoretically and then with peril to the meaning of the part in the person's psychic economy (Katz, 1960). Thus, the employment of the holistic view stems from dissatisfaction with the usefulness of knowing *only* that a person has a certain intelligence quotient or dogmatism score, or uses a certain number of cognitive categories of certain width through which to process the information about his world, or tends to register a certain degree of anxiety (masculinity, introspection, and so forth) in relation to a sample or standardized population.

Both trait and holistic definitions of personality remain hypothetical constructions, with an explicit existence limited to the eye of the beholder. Between these constructs and measurable phenomena lie levels of inference which greatly compound the difficulty of measuring personality. Yet *personality can be understood only as an inference from behavior.* As Murray (in Smith, 1971, p. 356) has noted, it is imperative to "distinguish between the facts and manifestations of personality, on the one hand, and the formulation or conception of personality on the other. . . . The distinction is the same as that between symptoms and signs versus diagnosis. Personality is a diagnosis." Further compounding the problem of measurement, we have seen that a discrete, observable behavior (that is, a somatic or verbal response) cannot be tied to a specific functional or dynamic meaning: behavioral correlates of personality are dependent upon situational parameters.

For many research problems, personality may not be a useful variable to include—in spite of the Siren's call to employ easily available and easily administered scales. In a number of politically important areas, situational, role, and demographic factors offer the most parsimonious avenue to predicting political behavior. Thus, the first job of the political psychologist interested in employing personality variables in his research design is to make sure that he has explicated an adequate theoretical basis for the inclusion of the dimension of personality.

In order to operationalize a research design in which personality is hypothesized to have an integral part, the political psychologist must first conceptualize clearly what he means by the concept *personality*. The next step is to delineate attributes of personality which can be subjected to scientific study (that is, quantified or in other ways objectively assessed) as well as to specify how these attributes, which stand for the concept *personality,* relate to the concept as a whole. (To these concerns we turn in the pages that follow.) MacIver's (1937, p. 26) pointed statement about the measurement of attitudes aptly summarizes these issues: "In their zeal for measurement [psychologists] fail to ask, what *in* the attitude is it that we are undertaking to measure? We do not measure *things,* but only certain quantitative aspects of things. We do not measure a table, but its length and breadth and height and weight. We do not measure the sun, but its radiation, the composition of its light, its size, its weight, its apparent motion among the stars, and so forth. What *aspects* then of an attitude do we set out to measure?" And how, we must add, do these aspects relate to the personality and behavioral dimensions which we have defined as our areas of concern?

Defining and Assessing Personality

The area of personality measurement has proved to be a difficult domain for those concerned with objective assessment. After the great flush of success accompanying the Woodworth Personal Data Sheet in World War I (Holtzman, 1968), there followed the sobering realization that a good deal of the early promise was due to artifacts of the measurement situation and that "much of what is called behavior rating in fact involves higher-order behavioral interpretation, and research on the correlations between diverse behavior ratings actually correlates diverse behavioral interpretations or constructions" (Mischel, 1968, pp. 68–69).

Basically, the difficulties in measuring personality center around the inevitable levels of inference involved. One level of inference is added as objective and measurable phenomena must—in every personality system—stand for the personality concept. Personality is understandable only in behavioral terms: "Personality *measurements,* if they discriminate at all, always express, in a pure or impure form, explicitly or implicitly, a personality concept in terms of which the differential behavior may be understood. Personality *concepts,* if they are not hopelessly vague or inconsistent, always imply specifiable behavioral differences in people" (Block, 1968, p. 30). Yet— to add additional layers of inference—we have seen that a discrete item of observable behavior cannot be tied to a specific meaning: behavioral correlates of personality are dependent upon situational parameters. Conversely, the same behavior may be expressive of different intrapsychic meanings for different individuals, as well as having different meanings for the same individual at different times. An inadequate appreciation of these factors has been responsible for much unfounded criticism of progress in personality research. (See Alker, 1972.)

Thus, the first requirement of a system of personality measurement is to specify, in terms of a trait or holistic theoretical perspective, the behavioral correlates by which personality is defined *and* to make these definitions situation specific. Otherwise, as Mischel (1968) rightly notes, so-called "objective" tests lose their objectivity because intuitive interpretation is needed to assess the meaning of standard scores. Such specification of the meaning of behavior includes a definition of the role of "moderator variables" (Wallach, 1962; Kogan and Wallach, 1964)—that is, interactions among several variables which shape the influence between any one variable and the rest of the data. (For example, as we noted in the case of authoritarianism, the presence of psychological or physical authority mediates or moderates the expression of aggression.)

Let us consider this requirement in the light of Lane's (1962) excellent in-depth study of the roots of the political ideology of fifteen working-class citizens. Much of Lane's discussion focuses on the personality traits that distinguish a democrat from an undemocrat. His conclusions in this regard are based on a wide-ranging analysis of democratic theory and his largely impressionistic evidence from these fifteen men. On the basis of Lane's data and additional items derived from democratic theory, it would be possible to conceptualize a cluster of personality correlates of democratic behavior (see Knutson, 1972a, ch. 5), such as open-minded-ness, tolerance of others and of ambiguity, and low anxiety level, and then to define these variables in terms of measurable, situation-specific behavior (including, but not limited to, performance on questionnaire items). For example, "tolerance of am-biguity" could be defined, as it was in a study by Block and Block (1951), as the lack of development of a frame of reference in an experiment employing the auto-kinetic effect of apparent light movement.

Next, the political variables need also to be made behaviorally specific. System-supportive "democratic behavior" could perhaps minimally be defined as referring to such variables as voting in the last four presidential elections, paying taxes regularly, possessing a certain degree of political information, and obeying laws protecting the person and property of others. (Democratic behavior could of course be defined in a number of other ways—for instance, by specific outcomes of interpersonal relations as defined in a laboratory experiment or by the prevalence of certain story themes on TAT cards, as discussed in Chapter Fifteen in this volume. In this case, however, the use of such methods would run the very real risk of measuring personality traits a second time, under the guise of political outcomes.)

At this point, it is possible to offer a series of testable hypotheses: "Personality variables x, y, and z will be predictive of (positively correlate with) a cluster of un-democratic behaviors, defined as a, b, and c." We could then replicate Lane's inten-sive analysis of fifteen working-class citizens and supplement our data gathering with an analysis of fifteen convicts at the state prison who have identical demographic profiles but have never engaged in any of the activities which we have defined as supportive of democratic systems. Objective scoring methods, plus a blind analysis of our open-ended interviews by two coders unfamiliar with our assumptions, would then allow us to test whether it is possible to separate, *on the basis of personality traits,* subjects whose behavior conforms to our minimal requirements of a democrat from those whose behavior does not conform.

Unless political psychologists proceed through such steps as outlined above, continual impressionistic work with personality variables becomes intellectually limit-ing on several counts. First, we run into the very real danger that our model of the personality correlates of democratic behavior has developed along with our data analysis and has been subjectively tailored to fit our data, thus offering no testable analysis of any point which we may set out to study. Second, we obviate the addi-tional opportunities which more systematic research provides to extend and revise our theories. Such opportunities come not only when our hypotheses are supported but, perhaps even more when they are not—and, continually, when we take the rewarding time to engage in deviant case analysis (Peak, 1953).

A second step to the measurement of personality involves a choice of methodology. For example, if one wishes to measure anxiety, Block (1968, p. 31) notes that there are at least four basic ways of proceeding:

(1) A subject may be observed in his everyday life and actions (presumably without his actions' being affected by these observations) and from his behaviors a judgment is made as to whether he is anxious; (2) a subject may be asked, by means of a questionnaire, to state directly (or in ways he may not completely understand) whether he is anxious; (3) a subject may be placed in a controlled or test situation designed to elicit special behaviors or projects relevant to anxiety; (4) a subject's physiological reactions may be assessed by various instruments, to determine whether he shows certain responses or changes presumed to be indicants of anxiety.

As will be discussed (also see Knutson, 1972c), political psychologists have unnecessarily limited the methods they have employed to study personality. Since each method imposes inherent limitations on the types of data that may be acquired, some methods are more appropriate for certain purposes than are others. (The special value of certain major approaches is discussed in the methodology section of this book.)

In addition, the measurement of personality makes a third requirement—that of cross-situational measurement, an area which Mischel (1968, pp. 86, 78) has summarized as being fraught with peril for the quantifier: "The correlations between measures by themselves cannot be interpreted as evidence for the associations between the labeled traits because diverse trait names often cover highly similar operations that require subjects to do similar things . . . [and] the correlations obtained among personality measures to some extent may simply reflect their common associations with intelligence and education." As Campbell and Fiske (1959) note, it is necessary to ascertain construct validity through the employment of a multitrait-multimethod matrix, in which the designated trait is more highly correlated with itself across methods than it is correlated with other traits within any one method. It is also necessary to show what is *not* being measured, as well as what is being measured—and thus to achieve what Campbell and Fiske (1959; Campbell, 1960) have labeled "discriminant validation."

When one ascertains that a subject's score is *indicatively similar across methods and over time,* he may feel some assurance that he is tapping a dimension with some stability and consistency and (if the scientific requirements of the above methods are observed) some validity for the construct being measured. One may not, however, assume that the subject's "personality" is being measured—except in the limited sense of one dimension, which has been isolated for the purpose of a specified research design.

However, when—in terms of Maslow's (1954) need hierarchy, for example—one aligns subjects on a dimension of self-actualization, one makes a different set of assumptions—assumptions that need to be specified in advance. In terms of holistic theory, one is measuring an intrapsychic organizing principle, which, by a predetermined theoretical stance, specifies the position of the subject on a host of other dimensions, allowing for the process that Cronbach and Meehl (1955) have carefully defined as "construct validity." Thus, a person categorized as "self-actualizing" is assumed in holistic terms also to be categorized as (relative to other subjects) creative, flexible, empathic, open-minded, and so forth (Knutson, 1972a) and as *not* dogmatic, rigid, extrapunitive, and so forth. (For a classic discussion of the demands made by a hierarchical model employing stages or "milestones," see Loevinger, 1966.) Hence, while holistic personality theory allows the concurrent measurement of a number of dimensions, it makes much heavier demands upon the accuracy of the measuring instrument.

Part of the difficulty in personality research to date appears to stem from lack of rigor in areas of conceptualization, definition, and assessment. In addition, inadequate attention has been paid to the criterion problem of validating the meaning of the measures employed (as was done in the classic study of authoritarianism; see Chapter Six). Only by attending to the criterion problem can newly developed measures become the basis for cumulative knowledge; others who employ them then have some confidence in their meaning. Another difficulty rests on a fundamental conceptual difference between those personality researchers who see promise in their work and those who feel that the utility of personality constructs has been disproved. Hunt (1965, p. 81) clearly states this issue: "If one takes the square of the coefficient of correlation as a rough, 'rule-of-thumb' index of the proportion of the variance attributable to persons, it would appear to be limited to somewhere between 4 and 25 percent of the total. This is incredibly small for any source which is considered to be *the* basis of behavioral variation, but we personologists have blamed our instruments rather than our belief in the importance of static dimensional traits."

Personality—in what could be labeled "the fallacy of reductionism"—frequently and mistakenly has been considered synonymous with behavior. Consequently (as suggested by the quotation above), personality measures which in standardized situations *at best* account for 25 to 30 percent of the variance are rejected as but tangentially related to the end goal of predicting and understanding BEHAVIOR. The alternative view—that intrapsychic factors *do* account for only about one third of the variance in most overt behavior (realizing of course that some behaviors are totally determined by inner or outer constraints)—is given little currency. As discussed in more detail below, I would suggest that social and cultural predispositions are responsible for another 25 to 30 percent of the variance, leaving approximately half of the variance to be accounted for, under usual conditions, by the actual field situation(as manipulated, for example, by the laboratory experiment).

Most writers today (as this volume attests) agree that a multivariate approach which encompasses all the above factors is necessary for the analysis of political behavior. In employing personality constructs as part of such an approach, certain critical issues involving the linkages between personality and political behavior need to be delimited. It is to this task that we now turn.

Influence of Personality on Behavior

In political psychology, it has become a truism that personality—in some unspecified way—affects political beliefs and political activity. This assumption can be traced back to Plato, who expressed a concern with the promotion of personality growth supportive of the polity. It received general professional acceptance through the seminal work of Harold Lasswell, whose books (1930, 1948) advanced the thesis that political behavior results from intrapsychic predispositions being displaced on public objects. Yet, in all the years since Lasswell's early work, the assumption that personality at least partially determines political beliefs and political behavior has received inadequate critical analysis.

This statement should not be taken to imply that a relationship between the intrapsychic and the political is totally unsupported. On the contrary, a wide variety of correlational studies have successfully predicted politically relevant attitudes, beliefs, and behaviors from personality variables. Both theoretically and empirically, however, such correlational studies have failed to support Lasswell's contention. Theoretically, the studies have generally avoided the difficult task of clearly explicating the specific linkages by which personality influences political behavior and, in turn, is influenced by political behavior. Empirically, these studies have generally failed to illustrate the *stability or coherence* (or both) of personality over time as well as its constant (or predictably variable) relationship to matters political. (The best evidence for the consistency of personality over time appears in Block and Haan, 1971; Jones, Bayley, MacFarlane, and Honzik, 1971; Kagan and Moss, 1962.)

The theoretical view that personality is a stable and/or consistent attribute that shapes an individual's political beliefs and activity retains a powerful intellectual appeal, an appeal grounded in psychiatric experience and in clinical data fed into the literature of politics (Greenstein, 1969; Greenstein and Lerner, 1971; Knutson, 1972a). Perhaps this view is most clearly expressed in the frequently made distinction between indirect and direct political learning (Dawson and Prewitt, 1969); according to this view, certain hypothetical levels and processes of learning account for both intrapsychic stability and the constraints of experience, societal values, and situation (Smith, 1968c; Greenstein, 1969).

In a seminal analysis, Almond (1960b, p. 28) has discussed the difference between "manifest" and "latent" socialization. Manifest socialization "takes the form of an explicit transmission of information, values, or feelings vis-à-vis the roles, inputs, and outputs of the political system." It is the most obvious and frequently studied means of transmitting cultural values and approved norms of behavior and includes the variables of adult reference-group constraints, formal learning in school and church, and other structured life experiences. Yet, in Almond's view, the individual has much earlier begun a process of "latent" socialization, which "takes the form of a transmission of information, values, or feelings vis-à-vis the roles, inputs, and outputs of social systems such as the family which affects attitudes toward analogous roles, inputs, and outputs of the political system." Such factors as personal values, self-concept, unfulfilled needs, and sense of competence (or ego strength) tap the personality dimension of such a latent, personally consistent manner of responding.

Theoretically, such a model can be expressed as shown in Figure 1. In this model, basic personality needs (such as the need for security, in Maslow's theory; the need for trust, in Erikson's model; or a thwarted need for aggression, in Freud's analysis) are seen as developing at an early stage in the child's life cycle, so that the school-age child's personality can be characterized holistically in terms of certain ascendant needs, which are organized in a dynamic pattern. (See, for example, the excellent analysis of esteem needs in elementary children by Coopersmith, 1967.) The above model—moving one step back from Rokeach's (1960) assertion that an

FIGURE 1.   LINKAGES BETWEEN PERSONALITY AND POLITICS

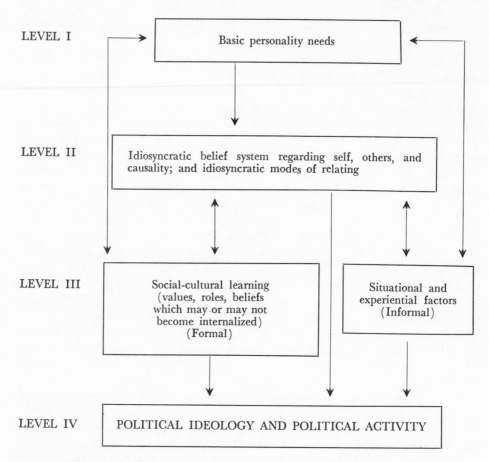

individual's belief system is built on (radiates out from) certain basic, "central," or "primitive" (that is, unquestioned) beliefs—suggests that a person's unquestioned views of himself, of human nature in general, and of the nature of causality are determined by his basic personality needs. Supportive of this viewpoint, as I have illustrated and reviewed elsewhere (Knutson, 1971; 1972a), is the fact that certain need-related attitudes almost invariably cohere. If, for example, other people are seen as trustworthy, control tends to be internal (see Rotter, 1966), and the viewpoint is optimistic, tolerant, and efficacious.

Our earlier discussion of the ways in which personality is conceptualized is directly related to Levels I and II. When a political psychologist speaks in holistic terms, he is of course referring to Level I. When he speaks, on the other hand, of such traits as dogmatism, machiavellianism, low self-concept, intrapunitiveness, and aggressiveness, he is making dynamic statements about Level II as it relates to political behavior—rather than dynamic and genetic statements about the nomothetic or idiographic origin and organization of the stuff of which politics is made. (This does not imply a value judgment about the advisability of employing either level of analysis. For some purposes, a knowledge of psychogenesis and total personality configuration may be essential; for others, it will be superfluous.)

A study by Browning and Jacob (1964) of the frequently held view in political psychology (see below) that power motivation is a major determinant of political activity provides an excellent example of an adequate Level II analysis. Drawing a representative sample ($N = 50$) of the elected officials in two parishes in Louisiana and, in an eastern city, a random sample ($N = 23$) of businessmen-politicians, these investigators used a projective technique to measure the needs for power, achievement, and for affiliation. The study produced two important findings: (1) None of the individual motivations discriminated between politicians and nonpoliticans of similar occupation and status; but (2) "politicians in high-potential positions scored much higher in both achievement and power motivation than their matched sample." Thus, the authors concluded that the effect of these personality traits is mediated by situational constraints. Avoiding the knotty, costly, and clouded search for total personality configurations and developmental understanding, Browning and Jacob present a Level II analysis which inventively delimits one area where individual predispositions interact with environmental constraints; and they adequately address the question of why certain types of roles may be peopled by certain types of actors.

By contrast, a recent analysis of presidential character (Barber, 1972a) suggests some of the limitations of an examination that remains at Level II. Barber amply and in fascinating detail documents the contention that personality does indeed shape presidential actions and presents (pp. 445–454) a valuable analysis of likely relationships between presidential character and the situational and psychic needs of the constituency. Turning to the weightier question of the linkages by which personality influences political behavior, Barber offers two dimensions (active-passive; positive-negative), from which he develops a fourfold categorization of the presidents whose character he analyzes. Unfortunately, his model of personality styles is too general to be predictive of the behavior of the men whom he studies, and the reader is left with the impression that a person's psychic energy level and affective orientation are an inadequate basis by which to judge his future performance in specified situations. For example, in Barber's "active-negative" category Wilson, Hoover, Johnson, and Nixon become uneasy bedfellows. When the idealistic, humanitarian, socially sensitive Hoover is linked with the pragmatic, power-oriented, and often consciously ruthless Johnson, one becomes aware that intrapsychic needs, goal states, and internalized values are as important as coping strategies in "predicting performance."

Because one looks in vain for clear decision rules by which a future president's specific behavior could be predicted or which place him in this rough categorization, one is unfortunately forced to conclude that while Barber's argument is a useful coarse division of presidential character, it needs to be supplemented by Level I analysis, which specifies the needs the individual seeks to gratify as well as the organizing principle of those needs. (For example, Barber's evidence suggests that three of his "active-negative" subjects—Wilson, Johnson, and Nixon—were motivated by the often interwoven needs to express aggression and enhance self-esteem, while Hoover lacked libidinal gratification and was motivated by needs for affection and belongingness.) Finally, since the influence of personality is contingent, it would be necessary (after assessing basic needs) to understand the multidetermined ways in which these basic personality needs influence political behavior, given specific personal values and political constraints.

Let us look again at our model of intrapsychic linkages. Once established, basic personality needs (usually mediated by the person's belief system and standardized modes of relating) interact with direct political learning and situational and experiental factors (Level III)—which, in turn, interact with (and thus may modify) basic personality needs. For example, a person who is self-actualizing and who thus has a personalized belief system characterized by empathy, flexibility, and tolerance may nevertheless—through direct learning of social values in an intolerant society (Maslow, 1957; Pettigrew, 1958)—accept intolerance as a major belief. Yet, through personal experiences (such as interpersonal relationships or a university education) his values and attitudes may be modified so that they more closely fit his idiosyncratic belief system (which includes the belief that human beings are intrinsically valuable); and this changed orientation may be sustained in later years. Thus, it is important to note, social changes in values and beliefs come about because direct socialization, until verified by experience and consonant with inner needs, is tentative —as studies of major shifts in college years have shown (Newcomb, 1943; Sanford, 1962b). Finally, "growth" experiences may fulfill psychic needs and allow the person to function on a more competent intrapsychic level; or, on the darker side, psychic trauma—as exemplified in the life of Kurt Schumacher (Edinger, 1965)—may cause a basically healthy person to become, in Maslow's terms, psychically deprived. Such changes in basic personality needs would then initiate correlative changes on Level II and the formal belief area of Level III.

An instructive example of the importance of distinguishing among Levels I, II, and III is found in a study of political socialization among black children (Liebschutz and Niemi, 1972). Using as baseline data a 1969 survey of 886 children in grades 2 through 8, the authors examined the effects on the children's politically relevant attitudes of a curriculum designed to improve the self-concept of disadvantaged black children. (These attitudes included a sense of political efficacy and evaluations of various political authority figures and of the fairness of laws). In results that are both psychologically and politically important, the authors found (a) that there were some changes during the experimental intervention toward increased realism in political evaluations and a greater sense of political efficacy—although the changes are generally small and may not be statistically significant; and (b) that this concerted intervention apparently had no long-term effects on political attitudes. Unfortunately, the concept of the self (the independent variable) is not clearly specified, nor do we learn whether a regression effect occurred in this area also. What does seem apparent, however, is the difficulty of changing personality predispositions on Level II and the formal side of Level III once they are established—especially when the target attitudes must represent a departure from the reality experienced by the child (the informal side of Level III) and the unmet basic needs which can be hypothesized to motivate ghetto children (Knutson, 1972a).

The careful reader will note, at this point, some differences between the above model and Brewster Smith's well-known "map for analysis of personality and politics" (1968c; also see Chapter Three in this volume). Most obvious is Smith's inclusion of factors that shape Level III elements; because of our focus on personality, such factors are omitted here. A more important, substantive difference is that our model makes divisions in Smith's "Personality Processes and Dispositions" level. With our concern here for the importance of intrapsychic dynamics, our model stresses the tentative nature of social learning and the necessity (in order to successfully predict behavior over time) that there be a close fit between Levels I and II, on the one hand, and Level III, on the other. Much of the socialization research (see Chapter Five in this volume), for example, has focused on the means by which social agents instill social values and attitudes and on counting what these values and attitudes (and, presumably, behaviors) are. The above model emphasizes the necessity of determining the consistency and stability of Levels III and IV in terms of their relevance for the psychic needs and perspectives of the individual (Levels I and II).

Finally, turning to Level IV, our model illustrates that personality predispositions, social and cultural values, and situational and experiential constraints (as well as the interaction between these three factors) lead to a political ideology and to a level of political activity. Under this model, even though peripheral attitudes (that is, attitudes in which the person has no psychic investment) may be incongruent, on a deeper and more meaningful level the person holds a consistent political ideology. When a survey analyst declares that on a set of basic political issues a respondent's attitudes are inconsistent, the personality theorist must point out the need to find a deeper level, on which consistency may rest securely and meaningfully (Sears, 1969), and this can be done only by attending to the psychological meaning of the attitudes for the person in question. Thus, only when basic personality needs are uncovered is it possible to make "psychological sense" of an activist who advocates both extending human rights of ethnic groups and sterilization of "welfare mothers" in order to control population, or a citizen who abhorred the organized inhumanity in Vietnam but supported his president's perseverative hostility in that part of the world. (See Zellman and Sears, 1971, in this connection.)

The above model offers a further caveat, which has been a constant theme of this chapter: that is, the multidetermined nature of the behavior and beliefs in which political psychologists are interested. As Maslow stated in an early article (1943c, p. 384): "Motivation theory is not synonymous with behavior theory. The motivations are only one class of determinants of behavior. While behavior is almost always motivated, it is also almost always biologically, culturally, and situationally determined as well." Indeed, Kagan (1972) posits the view that there is no necessary relation between motive and either action or affect.

As others have also noted, behavior is a result of the interaction of personality predispositions, social and cultural precipitants, and the field situation. I would suggest that a major reason for the lack of generality of political *and* of personality research is that too many researchers explore one of these dimensions as if it operated in a vacuum. Yinger (1965, p. 587) caustically sketches the relevance of such work:

If one lives in an environment that never falls below 0° C. or goes above 100° C. he can afford to predict, solely on the basis of the "traits" of H_2O, that it is a liquid. This is an adequate way of saying that H_2O, a compound with certain potentialities, is liquid under certain conditions which, being constant, can be disregarded. That does not mean, however, that the conditions are not always involved in producing the results.

Research on Political Relevance of Personality

One can employ a number of conceptual schemes by which to categorize the personality-relevant research in political psychology. In the two major, summative works in this area (Greenstein, 1969; Greenstein and Lerner, 1971), Greenstein has utilized a tripartite division of the literature into studies of individual political actors, types of political actors, and aggregates of political actors. Sigel (1970, pp. 232–236), on the other hand, classified the literature on personality and politics into analyses of populations and biographies of individuals—with the latter subdivided into the "hero" school and the motivational or "antihero" school. Lane (1968) discussed the relevance of personality to ideology, as well as to legislative, judicial, and electoral behavior; Levinson (1968) covered "ideology-personality constellations," using such categories as conservatism, liberalism, authoritarianism, and alienation. (For other major discussions, see Milbrath, 1965; Lane, 1959b.)

In this chapter, I shall follow a somewhat different approach—one dictated by what I see as the relevance of personality for the study of political behavior and belief (Knutson, 1972a). In considering broadly popular behaviors, such as joining a major political party or voting in presidential elections, we now recognize that personality variables are unlikely to account for a significant amount of the variance, because of the well-studied importance of social and cultural factors in determining a person's basic political orientation (Campbell and others, 1960; Flacks, 1967) and his conformance with modal political activity. Milbrath and Klein (1962, p. 54) have noted another constraint on the impact of personality on political behavior: "Political participation seems to be a special case of a general social participation pattern. Personality factors requisite for general social participation are also requisite for political participation, but their presence does not necessarily produce political activity. We are not aware of any study which has isolated a personality trait which drives people specifically into politics; even the much discussed "drive for power" finds many alternative modes of expression."

The literature of political psychology, however, suggests that personality variables are selectively felt at a number of points in the political process. One point, for example, involves the selection process for leadership roles; another is the inner predispositions which lead individuals to engage in deviant forms of political activity or to adhere to deviant political beliefs (although it must be underscored that no intrapsychic commonality accounts for all forms of deviancy). Personality factors are also selectively felt in the process of political learning because values and patterns of behavior are inculcated which may or may not find the psychic resonance necessary for their behavioral actualization. Again, personality is clearly important in understanding the manner in which a person carries out the roles to which (often because of cultural and societal constraints) he has been assigned. In this regard, personality serves to define the use of coping or defensive mechanisms (Kroeber, 1966)—that vital distinction which precludes or advances the overall attainment of political goals. In a similar way, personality variables allow the political psychologist to gauge psychic energy level—which is predictive of the person's ability to engage in all forms of social behavior, including that categorized as political.

Thus, it is useful to assess the personality and politics literature from the relationship between personality and two dimensions of political involvement: activity and ideology. Under the first category belong questions as to the amount (apathetic, conforming, activist), type (leader, follower, isolate, joiner, decision-maker or implementer) and quality (flexible, rigid, creative) of activity. In the second category fall questions as to the direction and ideological intensity which political activity is likely to take. (It is important to note that little research has been done on the critical relational area between the activity and ideology dimensions.)

Throughout the accumulating research, a basic principle which appears is that *the influence of personality is directly related to the specificity of the politically relevant behavior*. For broadly popular acts, in other words, social and cultural norms often "carry the action" so that behavior does not engage deep levels of intrapsychic functioning. Hence, to become a legislator appears to require. either considerably more or less esteem (Barber, 1965) than to be a member of the citizenry who elect the legislators. Similarly, it seems to require more psychic competence to adopt a deviant political stance than to work for a major political party (Knutson, 1971). A second major principle (discussed above but worth keeping in mind as we review a sample of the literature) is that the effect of personality is mediated by and mediates social, cultural and experiential factors.

Level of Activity. A number of personality traits relating to individual political activity have been isolated. One of the most frequently studied is the trait of efficacy or competence (Douvan and Walker, 1956). Interest in this concept became widespread with the development by the University of Michigan's Survey Research Center of a scale measuring "political efficacy" (Berelson, Lazarsfeld, and McPhee, 1954; Campbell, Gurin, and Miller, 1954). As a recent analytic discussion of this dimension makes clear (Renshon, 1972), both the unidimensionality of this scale and its theoretical basis have been accepted without a thoughtful critique, which legitimization required. Nevertheless, a multitude of studies, in addition to the voting studies carried out by the SRC itself, have demonstrated that there is a relationship between an inner feeling of potency and the degree of political activity in which one engages (Eulau and Schneider, 1956; Janowitz and Marvick, 1953; Milbrath, 1965; Agger, Goldstein, and Pearl, 1961; Almond and Verba, 1963; Rosenberg, 1954; Barber, 1972a). In personality theory, a sense of efficacy has been related to the degree of psychic competence a person possesses (Smith, 1968b).

A second dimension of personality which has been related to political activity is authoritarianism (see also Chapter Six in this volume). As I have summarized elsewhere (Knutson, 1972a), research to date has presented a conflicting view of the contribution of authoritarianism to the level of political activity. This lack of clarity is, in no small measure, due to the fact that authoritarianism is clearly compounded of intrapsychic as well as social (demographic) factors (Greenstein, 1969). In terms of the model of personality linkages presented earlier in this chapter, it seems likely that authoritarianism (in general use, a Level II variable) influences political activity in ways dependent upon the personality needs (Level I) of the individual who scores high on this trait and the values (Level III) into which he has been socialized. Thus, authoritarians with affiliative needs will be likely to join social and political groups, a relationship which Lane (1955) found to occur in one set of data. But, as a study by Janowitz and Marvick (1953) suggests, security needs may account for the correlations found between authoritarianism and age, lack of education, and lower socioeconomic status, as well as for the relationship between authoritarianism and isolationist attitudes, lack of political efficacy, and nonvoting in the 1948 election. That there are different predispositions to authoritarianism is clear from past research on the F scale (see the interesting work by Pettigrew, 1958), but how such differences relate to the effect of authoritarianism on political activity level has never been adequately studied. In terms of the model discussed in this chapter, authoritarianism appears to present an example of the need for an holistic approach to the study of personality and politics.

Another area in which a personality trait has proved useful in the under-standing and prediction of political activity is that of anomie and alienation (see Chapten Seven in this volume for a more detailed discussion; see also Knutson, 1972a, ch. 3). This dimension has been conceptualized and measured in rather different ways, including a sense of powerlessness or internal-external control (Rotter, 1966; De Charms, 1968), a generalized sense of despair or meaninglessness defined as "the breakdown of the individual's sense of attachment to society" (Srole, 1956; see also McClosky and Schaar, 1965) or more focused types of alienation (Seeman, 1966, 1967a, 1967b, 1971, 1972). A sense of powerlessness, as Seeman has shown, is related to a lack of political knowledge and knowledge in other specified areas in which control-relevant information is not of value to the subject; equally important, a sense of powerlessness is clearly separable from a sense (in Marxian terms) of alienation from work. The sense of powerlessness (as opposed to other types of alienation) is rather clearly related to a lack of engagement in social and political activity, but because this dimension has been repeatedly correlated with lower socio-economic status and has been conceptually indistinct in terms of psychic and societal roots (Knutson, 1972a), its meaning in personality terms calls for careful assessment.

Another personality trait in which a good deal of theoretical work has been invested is that of power motivation. Since Lasswell's (1930) early statements about the importance of political activity as a compensation for unfulfilled needs for esteem, it has been a largely unexamined truism that power motivation, as a psychologically distinct and unitary dimension, is exceedingly important in explaining political activity levels. This is true even though Lasswell (1954) later qualified his earlier dictum in major ways, and even though the differential importance of power motiva-tion in political behavior has been carefully delimited in a number of places (George, 1968; Knutson, 1972a; Lane, 1959b).

The limited empirical work here to date (for instance, Browning and Jacob, 1964) has generally failed to substantiate this motivation as a simplistic indicator of political involvement. Thus, the intuitively important variable effect of power striving remains a major area for future research and presents two major caveats. First, as Horney (1937) pointed out a number of decades ago, any need—including the need for power—can be neuroticized or healthy and adaptive and, within these strictures, may serve various functions. The possibility of healthy, creative needs for power has been given relatively little attention to date in theory and even less in research. (For a discussion of the varying needs which power seeking and attainment may serve, see George, 1968; Knutson, 1972a, p. 69.) Second, it is quite simplistic to view political leaders (or anybody else) as driven by one narrowly defined need. For example, Maslow (1954) has analyzed the need for self-esteem as composed of a number of separate subneeds; the gratification of each presumably can bring a sense of fulfillment to the esteem need area. I would suggest that research here should focus on the idiosyncratic ordering of politically relevant needs for which any one political leader strives—an ordering which, as George (1968) notes, is sensitive to the person's perception of the situational opportunities for their gratification. For example, the person who strives for power but also places a high value on human life (as Robert Kennedy appeared to do), is quite different from the leader (such as Hitler) who was motivated by unfulfilled power needs but devalued human life.[1] (For work in the area of value ordering, see Rokeach, 1968.)

Each of the above personality traits, as the reader might imagine, has been studied—not only to determine its relation to political participation but also to assess the quality and quantity of role performance by individuals who have successfully passed through the political selection (or self-selection) process. For example, a number of studies (for instance, Nie, Powell, and Prewitt, 1969a, 1969b) have suggested that individuals lacking such traits as efficacy, if they are members of organizations that value political participation, may nevertheless be politically active, though lacking in political knowledge or concern. Fragmentary evidence suggests, however, that participation without a sense of psychic competence shapes political activity in a negative stance (Thompson and Horton, 1960) and that to the extent to which participation is correlated with lack of competence, a democratic system is inherently weak (Cnudde and Neubauer, 1969).

Another psychological trait shown to affect the quality of a person's political activity is the attribute of dogmatism (Rokeach, 1960), a trait referring theoretically to the structure (as opposed to the content) of a person's belief system. In a lengthy series of laboratory experiments, Rokeach showed that subjects can be placed along a continuum going from closed-mindedness to open-mindedness and that individuals at the closed-minded end of the continuum differ in a number of politically important ways from those at the open-minded end of the continuum. First of all, closed-minded individuals are typified by anxiety and have difficulty assimilating new information. Consequently, they may reject information outright if it conflicts with their beliefs; or they may perceptually distort the information so that they can accept it (for instance, a voter who approves of Eugene McCarthy can also support George Wallace because "both are for the individual and opposed to the system which denies individuality"); or they may accept—but *not* integrate—the new information if it comes from a valued authority ("I am totally opposed to the war in Vietnam, but President Nixon feels that we should continue to fight until the Vietnamization policy works and he must be right, because he's president"); or—if the change in beliefs required by information from a positive authority is too great—they may devalue the authority.

Further, closed-minded subjects are likely, without analysis, to accept and act on new information which appeals to them. Consequently, as Rokeach (1960, p. 240)

---

[1] The reader should note that a construct such as power can be considered either an intrapsychic need or the goal objective of such a need, depending on its function in the individual's psychic economy.

showed experimentally, open-minded individuals take considerably *longer* to solve problems when presented with a new, conflicting piece of evidence, because of their need to analyze before assimilating or rejecting the information. On the other hand, "problem solving proceeds more smoothly in closed persons when new beliefs are presented all at once than when presented gradually because of their proclivity to easily accept without assimilation 'packaged' information" (pp. 287–288). While there have been few applications of this personality trait to the study of political role performance and activity level, its relevance in such study is obvious. Suggestive in this respect is the frequent finding of voting studies that "the most partisan people protect themselves from the disturbing experience presented by opposition arguments by paying little attention to them" (Lazarsfeld, Berelson, and Gaudet, 1944, pp. 89–90), offering the testable hypothesis that undeviating partisanship may be associated with an intrapsychic trait which closes off new information. The above evidence also suggests that the individual who changes his beliefs and joins a mass movement—accepting wholly, as a matter of faith, dogma stemming from positively valued authorities—may also be typified by this personality trait. (The reader should note that thus far in this literature review, we have been able to discuss psychodynamics without needing to take up the more difficult problem of psychogenesis.)

In the area of leadership, dogmatism offers a useful concept for studying people who close off new information in a manner dysfunctional to their announced political goals. This phenomenon has been illustrated in the detailed study by Edinger (1965) of the German Social Democratic leader Kurt Schumacher. It can also be seen to operate in the recurring, self-made crises of Woodrow Wilson (George and George, 1956). Indeed, as the Georges illustrate by the supportive function served by Colonel House and others, dogmatic individuals frequently arrange their life space so that conflicting information is filtered out before it reaches their input channels. For example, at one point in his career, Wilson's problems clearly stemmed from "his deliberate refusal to make use of the channels of information that were available to him. [In another instance] . . . Wilson did not care to listen to opinions he did not welcome" (Janis, 1959, p. 13). This phenomenon can also be observed in the tacit understanding among Hitler's staff: "For God's sake, don't excite the Fuehrer—which means do not tell him bad news—do not mention things which are not as he conceives them to be" (Von Wiegand, in Langer, 1972, p. 76). A similar, less extreme, example of information control has been observed to operate in Nixon's milieu (Barber, 1972a, p. 439).

An interesting discussion of the dysfunctional nature of closed-mindedness in political leaders is found in an article by Janis (1959), which thoughtfully traces a number of sources of decisional conflicts. Janis concludes that a leader's decisions may improve in quality (and his "decisional conflicts" may be reduced) if he is given more accurate information and learns, in advance, the possible consequences of his acts. In view of Rokeach's work, this appears an overoptimistic conclusion, since the dysfunctional nature of at least part of the decision making which Janis uses as evidence can be attributed to something other than inadequate or inaccurate information; namely, to the inability of closed-minded persons to avail themselves of, to assess, and to integrate information because of the "unconscious affective charge" (to employ Janis's phrase) which conflicting, nonsupportive information entails.

The trait of dogmatism was also employed in a study (DiRenzo, 1967) of leadership roles in Italy. Using a sample drawn from the Chamber of Deputies of the Third Republican Parliament of Italy and a nonrandom control group, DiRenzo found a significant difference between the mean dogmatism scores of the two groups, with the political leaders being more closed-minded. Because of his inadequate control group, more convincing is the relation that he found between dogmatism and political ideology: the two groups lowest in dogmatism were on the left extreme, and the two highest were on the right extreme (p. 123). The author (pp. 152–153) comments: "The more open-minded parties in our political sample are those that have gained progressively in strength; the more closed-minded parties are those that have lost strength, even to the point of passing out of existence. . . . These data support the explanation of dogmatism correlating with threatened existence." (For a critical review of DiRenzo's book, see Greenstein, 1970b.)

The answers provided by personality variables to the question of who is available for leadership roles have been, as Sigel (1970) points out, varied indeed. Generally, two schools of thought have arisen which speak to this phenomenon (also see Chapter Eight in this volume). First, Lasswell (1930, 1948)—in an analysis of political leaders, a number of whom had been hospitalized for psychiatric reasons—persuasively argued that a political leader projects his neurotic needs into the public sphere and enters political life in search of their fulfillment. (DiRenzo's study can be seen as supportive of this view.) Lasswell (1951) later modified this thesis to account for his observation that in a democracy the successful political leader is not likely to be driven by compensatory personality needs; his initial argument, however, has continued to have widespread appeal. A second theoretical stance (Lane, 1959b; Knutson, 1972a, forthcoming) is summarized by Rutherford (1966, p. 390) in these terms:

> If an individual suffers from intrapsychic conflict, so much energy will be consumed by the struggle within the person that no surplus will remain to cope with conflict in the political arena. Interpersonal relations and ego strivings will thus suffer to a great extent. Those experiencing intrapsychic conflict, then, would be expected to withdraw from political participation rather than project upon political objects. We would have this proposition: the higher the level of political participation, the greater the psychic energy need, the less the intrapsychic conflict, and, hence, the more rational the participant.

Rutherford, in the same article, then attempts to refute this position by presenting evidence from a patient-governed ward of a psychiatric hospital. He reports that these patients before they were hospitalized, had reported participating in politics as much as the average citizen in upper socioeconomic groups and more than would be expected for lower socioeconomic groups. Furthermore, he found only a small (.294) correlation between clinical judgment of mental health and participation on the patient council; in fact, manic-depressive and paranoid schizophrenic types were overrepresented among the patient council leaders, compared with their number in the ward population.

The Rutherford article, by overstating the position he is attempting to refute, gives us an opportunity to look closely at the theoretical stances involved. One school (which we will label here the Lasswell-Rutherford position) advances the view that unfulfilled personality needs, far from being a barrier to participation, *may* actually motivate psychically deprived citizens to seek fulfillment by engaging in political activity because of the special need gratifications available through political activity. Thus psychically deprived individuals will tend to be overrepresented among the population of political leaders. The other school of thought (which we will call the Lane-Knutson viewpoint) holds (1) that psychically deprived individuals are less likely to seek active political roles than are more psychically fulfilled persons— particularly when the role requirements are stressful; and (2) that unfulfilled psychic needs are eventually dysfunctional to role performance in terms of the individual's own political goals.[2]

Supporting our everyday observations, a number of studies have pointed out that persons who lack psychic competence do serve important functions in political systems (as Tucker, 1965, argues in the case of the dictator) and that political activity also serves to meet the particular needs of these individuals. See, for example, the psychobiographic studies of Civil War political leader Thaddeus Stevens (Brodie, 1966); of Abraham Lincoln, a president with severely unmet basic needs (Clark, 1933); of Secretary of State James Forrestal (Rogow, 1963); of Chicago mayor Anton Cermak (Gottfried, 1962); of Secretary of State Charles Evans Hughes (Glad, 1966); of Reformation leader Martin Luther (Erikson, 1958); and the previously mentioned studies of Kurt Schumacher (Edinger, 1965) and Woodrow Wilson (George and George, 1956). Moreover—as studies of Hitler (Langer, 1972) and Stalin (H. Salisbury, 1969; Deutscher, 1949) and Lasswell's (1930) early analyses of political leaders indicate—severely pathological responses may occasionally be instrumental in achieving and solidifying a position of political importance.

In aggregate terms, however, the Lane-Knutson position begins by noting that a person will be likely to engage in social and political activity to the extent that his basic psychic needs have been met. As I have illustrated in terms of Maslow's need hierarchy with a nonrandom sample of 495 ordinary citizens, there is a significant correlation between political participation and fulfillment of psychic needs (Knutson, 1972a). The correlation, while significant, certainly is not large enough to disallow the view that unmet psychic needs may produce political activity ($r = .14$), although an examination of the relationships (see Table 1) indicates that the most fulfilled citizens are twice as likely to engage in active political roles as are those with unfulfilled psychic needs. (It is also possible that gratification of psychic needs is related to the concomitants of participation, such as social status and education.)

The second part of the Lane-Knutson position interprets the low correlation and the evidence that unmet needs are not an absolute barrier to participation. According to this position, persons who engage in political activity as a means of compensating for unresolved needs will eventually face critical situations; at such times, the necessary (intrapsychically compulsive) fulfillment of unmet psychic needs will disallow the attainment of valued political goals. In such a psychically rigidified situation (discussed above as episodic in the careers of Wilson and others), the individual's behavior is shaped by unconscious or preconscious psychic needs rather

---

[2] As Alexander George notes (in a personal communication), compensatory need gratification and dysfunctional role performance do not necessarily go together.

Table 1.

CONTINUUM OF MENTAL HEALTH VERSUS POLITICAL PARTICIPATION

	Low	Middle	High	Percent
Psychically deprived	36.6	37.4	26.1	100
Low self-actualizers	33.3	40.8	25.8	100
High self-actualizers	23.5	32.3	44.1	100

Source: Knutson, 1972a, p. 236.

Note: Psychically deprived refers to those subjects categorized as primarily motivated by physiological, safety, affiliative or esteem needs, with the balance of the subjects categorized as either low (less fulfilled) or high (more fulfilled) self-actualizers, depending on their scores on the indices of psychic deprivation. Low, middle, and high participation were ascertained by a modification of the Woodward-Roper (1950) Political Participation Index, which sums reported political activities, such as voting and attending political meetings.

than by objective, consciously articulated, political parameters. This process is concisely discussed by Langer (1972, pp. 74–75) as follows:

> This is a very fundamental trait in Hitler's character structure. He does not think things out in a logical and consistent fashion, gathering all available information pertinent to the problem, mapping out alternative courses of action, and then weighing the evidence pro and con for each of them before reaching a decision. His mental processes operate in reverse. Instead of studying the problem, as an intellectual would do, he avoids it and occupies himself with other things until unconscious processes furnish him with a solution. Having the solution he then begins to look for facts that will prove that he is correct. In this procedure he is very clever, and by the time he presents it to his associates, it has the appearance of a rational judgment. Nevertheless, his thought processes proceed from the emotional to the factual instead of starting with the facts as an intellectual normally does. It is this characteristic of his thinking process that makes it difficult for ordinary people to understand Hitler or to predict his future actions. . . . [This method] is not without its shortcomings. He becomes dependent on his inner guide, which makes for unpredictability on the one hand and rigidity on the other. The result is that he cannot modify his course in the face of unexpected developments or firm opposition.

The frequency of episodes in which intrapsychic considerations operate virtually unchallenged depends on the individual's ego strength and on the degree to which it functions in a coping rather than a defensive manner (Kroeber, 1966). Thus, level of ego functioning (which, in turn, is related to severity of psychic deprivation) determines a person's ability to find an adaptive situation which meets both inner and outer constraints. Hence, the Lane-Knutson position also addresses the degree of successful role performance and, given the severity of the leader's unmet needs, the likelihood that he will be able to choose his time and manner of exit from public life.

Any attempt to compose a fourfold table of health and political activity is doomed to failure, because personality is too complex and various to be neatly categorized; if one attempts such abstracting, he risks losing the essential heuristic and predictive powers which legitimate a model. In assessing the relation between psychic competence and political activity level or role-performance ability, we need to look at *what* the unmet need is and the *manner* in which the person characteristically deals with this need (sublimation, in the case of Abraham Lincoln's need for affection, produced very different results politically than repression and denial of the same need did in the case of Thaddeus Stevens). This point has been beautifully illustrated by Erik Erikson (1958, 1969), whose works have analyzed how Martin Luther and Mahatma Gandhi were able to integrate inner and outer reality in ways that fulfilled both their own unmet needs and the requirements of the history into which they were born and which they helped to make.

Direction of Ideology. The previous section has provided a number of clues to the ways in which personality variables may assist in our understanding of the direction (for example, conformist or deviant, left or right) and intensity which political activity may take. To begin with, DiRenzo (1967) found dogmatism associated with a right-wing political stance, although Rokeach (1960) had presented evidence (derived from very small samples) that his measure is unrelated to direction of political ideology. Studies such as that by DiRenzo have, however, failed to substantiate the lack of ideological relevance of the dogmatism scale and have generally found a conservative bias in this measure of cognitive functioning (Parrott and Brown, 1972). Barker (1963), for example also found dogmatism associated with rightist activity, although the correlation was not as strong as that between authoritarianism and rightist activity. On the other hand, in a study of political activists ranging from left-wing radicals to members of the American National Socialist White People's party (Knutson, 1971), a significant correlation occurred between authoritarianism and left-wing political activity and ideology and *also* between dogmatism and left-wing political activity and ideology. (Correlations between dogmatism and left direction ranged from .46 to .69; those between authoritarianism and left direction ranged from .67 to .80.) As this sample was distinguished from the others in this area (being composed of political leaders, instead of college students, and of subjects whose political beliefs reflected a much wider range of ideology than student samples offer), its results are worth replicating.

The original Berkeley study (Adorno and others, 1950) found a relationship between authoritarianism and a rightist political orientation. This finding was replicated by Leventhal, Jacobs, and Kudirka (1964), but the relationship held only when the hypothetical choice offered the subjects placed the conservative candidate in the Republican party. These various studies suggest that authoritarianism (and its variant, dogmatism) may be related to the preference for closed-minded candidates or dogmatic ideologies—which are at times, but not always, found on the right.

A recent study (Putnam, 1971) identifies a dimension of cognitive style which enriches our understanding of the dimension of dogmatism, and of personality factors related to intensity of political activity. In a study based on in-depth interviews with ninety-three members of the British House of Commons and eighty-three members of the Italian Chamber of Deputies, a factor called "ideological style" was derived from the data. Subjects rated high in ideological style tended to be "generalizers." Generalizers are those who deduce their analysis from a general, abstract theory instead of dwelling on particular, technical questions. Those high in ideological style also tend to refer to a specific ideology or doctrine to buttress their arguments, and they employ utopias as the basis for judging policy. They "also tend more frequently to be motivated by ideological satisfactions, to interpret political phenomena such as parties in terms of more abstract schema, and to reject a merely 'possibilist' approach to politics" (Putnam, 1971, p. 665). In both leadership samples, such "ideological style" was related to extreme (left and right) positions on the political spectrum. Ideological style was also correlated (in both samples) with alienation from existing political and social institutions. Most important for our discussion, however, these ideologues are *not* distinguished by a dogmatic unwillingness to compromise, by valuing ends more than means, *or* by their scores on moral absolutism, authoritarianism, political distrust, or social distrust.

Putnam (1971) did find, however, that his index of partisan hostility, while not significantly positively correlated with his index of ideological style, was also correlated with political extremism. He concludes: "Some extremists are 'ideological' and some extremists are 'hostile,' but they are rarely the same extremists" (p. 672). Finally, he notes that partisan hostility is, in both samples, inversely correlated with age, which he sees as a reflection of shifts in societal values as well as (age) cohort-specific experiences.

Putnam's analysis underlines the impossibility of our finding any simple relationship between political behavior and personality variables. Here, the same behavior—political extremism—is clearly correlated with at least two different (and largely unrelated) intrapsychic traits, both of which appear to be Level II variables. Some extremists were characterized by an abstract, goal-oriented, and somewhat messianic and idealistic cognitive style. Other extremists were identified by their hostility toward political outgroups, their unwillingness to compromise, their authoritarianism, and their moral absolutism. Uncovering such contingent relationships is intellectually demanding, but such relationships are more psychically accurate—and hence more meaningful—than earlier, more simplified models of political behavior.

This distinction between complex and contingent theses versus less satisfying but simpler theses is well illustrated by two studies of political conservatism. McClosky (1958), in a well-known study, looked at a large number of personality variables in relation to what he defined as conservatism and found, on all counts, a clear relationship between traditional conservatism and various measures of psychic deprivation. From the items of his conservatism scale made available, it appears that McClosky was correlating personality variables with a punitive, negativistic view of human nature, rather than with the view of conservatism as dedicated to the conservation and gradual change of things established. A later study (Schoenberger, 1968) illustrated that if conservatives are defined by dedication to furthering social and economic viewpoints rather than by agreement with a negative view of human nature, conservative party affiliation is inversely related to authoritarianism and positively related to support of civil liberties. As in the study by Putnam (1971), these two studies of conservatism taken together suggest again that there may be at least two types of extremists: ego-defensive and ideological (in Putnam's sense). A number of other studies (Anderson and others, 1965; Simmons, 1965; Nettler and Huffman, 1957) have shown that there is no general conservatism or liberalism factor.

On the basis of research to date, we can conclude only that personality variables undoubtedly are related to the direction of political ideology. In order to understand what linkages exist, a good deal of prior work is required to conceptualize an ideological stance as consistent and to empirically demonstrate that it differentiates those who are active in various political groups so-labeled *before* one can take up the weightier question of what personality characteristics relate to what ideological stance.

As with activity level, the direction of political activity appears to be multi-determined. DiPalma and McClosky (1970) found psychic fulfillment consistently correlated with a conformist, majoritarian political view, although this relationship was much weaker in higher educational than in noncollege levels. On the other hand, Block and her associates (Block, Haan, and Smith, 1969; Block, 1972) have illustrated —with careful studies of student radicals—that there are meaningful, statistically significant personality differences between student deviants whose political activity is an affirmation of parental values and those for whom it represents generational discontinuity. Thus, work in this area seems particularly suitable for the employment of a holistic personality model, enabling the researcher to understand the function of the ideological stance adopted from the phenomenological view of his subject's personality.

One further, impressive development in the study of personality and ideology needs to be mentioned; namely, the exciting work of Inglehart (1971a, 1971b) on intergenerational value changes in Western Europe. Using Maslow's need hierarchy, Inglehart examined political preferences specific to different generations or age cohorts. He found, in line with the differential growth of affluence in the West European countries, major differential shifts in political preferences. The older generations tend to select acquisitive values (characteristic of unfulfilled physiological and safety needs). But the younger generations of West Europeans express preferences for what Inglehart calls "postacquisitive" or "postbourgeois" values—values which, he persuasively argues, have grown in political importance as lower psychic needs have been gratified through decades of continued economic prosperity.

Inglehart's work offers a substantive base for the generally polemical assertions of Reich (1970) about a sweeping value change in America today. It also provides additional understanding of the differences in the "liberalism" of working-class and middle-class citizens (Lipset, 1960) and elucidates the psychic basis of the increasingly clearly explicated causal chain in democratic development (Lerner, 1958; Knutson, 1972a, pp. 276–281; Cnudde and Neubauer, 1969; Aronoff, 1967, 1970). If one assumes (as this chapter clearly does) that psychic health, like physical health, is universally based on the satisfaction of certain needs, personality-related differences in ideology across cultures become a matter of investigating the ratio and social distribution of personality types in a specific polity, as well as the cultural values and situational constraints which interact with personality to produce ideological stances in that nation.

A Case of Relative Deprivation

As the above literature review illustrates, the uses of personality in the study of political behavior have been manifold. Indeed, applications of personality to political concerns can probably be found in all the chapters of this book. Like the man on the street, the professional student also sees great utility in employing personality as a means of conceptualizing the political phenomena with which he deals. As the above discussion also suggests, however, much of the work in the area of personality remains tentative; carefully constructed, replicated designs are few indeed.

Further, we scholars have sometimes repeated the sins of our forefathers, who used personality as a conveniently simplistic way of categorizing political activity. When we try to understand those political beings whom our research interests necessitate examining, we are able to see with the wisdom of distance that Machiavelli's view of personality as action-oriented and manipulative did not adequately describe human nature, that Hobbes's opinion of human nature as overdetermined by the need for security did not fully describe reality, and even that Marx's belief that human nature had *one* major determinant (Fromm's and Freud's viewpoints as well) is not too helpful. We are less able to see, I think, that theoretical viewpoints which categorize political behavior of the right or left in terms of one set of intrapsychic determinants; that see leadership behavior either as stemming from the achievement of mental health or as a reaction to unfulfilled needs; or that divide all political actors in terms of ad hoc fourfold tables are also likely to be of little use in the study of political behavior.

The analysis of personality and political behavior in cumulative terms requires first of all a delimitation of research areas in which personality is likely to be a meaningful dimension (see Knutson, 1972a, ch. 5 for a longer discussion of what these major areas of political behavior appear to be). When such a research focus has been selected, it is then essential to adequately conceptualize personality and further define it as measurable behavior. Next, as specific behaviors (for example, voting, making successful decisions, becoming a student activist) are repeatedly shown to correlate with separable personality traits, these traits need to be related to each other in terms of a conceptual framework which sees an individual in holistic terms (but allows for nomothetic statements). Finally, it is necessary to consistently engage in deviant case analysis—so that, for example, we can understand why undogmatic individuals adopt a right-wing viewpoint or why individuals with severely unmet personality needs become successful leaders.

Given these priorities, it is necessary to move back and forth from methods which focus in depth on a single actor and methods which are suitable for aggregate analysis. (See Beck, 1953.) The psychobiography, for example, has added a good deal to our knowledge of the deviant political leader, whose personality departs markedly from our expectations of the requirements for political success. In-depth interviews and projective techniques also increase our understanding of deviant types and enable us to define new personality constraints which require laboratory experimentation and the scaling abilities of a psychometrician to delineate. In addition, survey research is available to allow us—once our understanding is refined—to ascertain the patterns of variance and the range of attributes with which we deal.

By working back and forth between the individual and the aggregate level, between attempts to uncover and analyze separate traits and efforts to amalgamate them into a holistic view, we will arrive at an understanding of the relevance of personality for the study of political behavior which is richer, more complex, and more satisfying than present knowledge makes possible. Such a process is far from novel. As Freud's theoretical and clinical work brilliantly illustrates, the study of personality continues to require that its practitioners be open-minded, creative, intellectually tentative, and theoretically well grounded as they seek, through observation and introspection, to understand the complex interaction between personality and behavior.

3

POLITICAL
ATTITUDES

M. Brewster Smith

In the initial, classical review of the topic of attitudes, written at a time that from present perspectives seems almost antediluvian, Gordon W. Allport (1935) began by saying, "The concept of attitude is probably the most distinctive and indispensable concept in contemporary American social psychology." Through many vicissitudes during the intervening years, attitudes have remained a central topic in the psychologist's social psychology; they have also figured prominently in the sociologist's variant of this interdisciplinary field. Although the social psychologists of whatever persuasion who have used the term seem to have known what they were talking about, the vast literature concerning attitudes includes a substantial controversial literature about their definition. In this case as in so many others, definitional controversy is a tedious, but not wholly sterile, enterprise. As we shall see, fundamental issues of conceptual strategy are involved.

Conception of Attitudes

For present purposes, a working definition that is as unpretentious as I can make it seems desirable: "The concept of attitude, although variously defined, is most commonly employed to designate inferred *dispositions,* attributed to an individual, according to which his thoughts, feelings, and perhaps action tendencies are organized with respect to a psychological object" (Smith, 1968a, p. 458). Even such an informal definition embraces a controversial theoretical commitment to a strategy that accounts for observed social behavior by extracting analytically two classes of inferred, reconstructed determinants: features of the *situation* of action, and inferred *dispositions* or properties of the behaving *person* (see Lewin, 1951). This strategy, which is one that I feel at home with and prefer, is by no means necessary for social psychology and behavioral science. It has never been attractive to behaviorists and other positivists, who like to stay as close as possible to observables. In fact, the truly radical behaviorist (Skinner, 1957; Bem, 1967) has no use at all for the concept of attitude, which he dissolves into particular behaviors, verbal and otherwise, viewed as under the control of particular discriminative stimuli and contingencies of reinforcement. Various compromise positions—for instance, merging attitudes with habits (Doob, 1947) or treating attitudes not as dispositions but as a special class of behaviors—have been taken by theorists influenced by positivism. (See D. T. Campbell, 1963, for a view that holds cognitive and behavioral concepts of attitudinal dispositions to be essentially equivalent.)

The choice between a dispositional or a positivistic-behavioral commitment can hardly be based on established fact. It is not a matter of right or wrong. Certainly, the Skinnerians have shown that they are able to push their approach surprisingly far into the precincts of human action—though I think only by letting a good deal of common-sense "dispositional" psychology in through the back door (Smith, 1973). My own commitment to a dispositional orientation rests on two grounds.

One has to do with a broad view of the "image of man" (Chein, 1972) that is compatible with human freedom and dignity, and therefore with politics, and also with empirical, self-corrective, and thus on the whole cumulative science. The reductive, positivistic view of Skinner (1971) has no meaningful place for politics, which concerns the allocation of power among human *actors* in a polity. The values of liberty and justice, traditional to normative political theory, require a concept of human agency. And a view of man as an actor, politically and otherwise, needs concepts to formulate man's more enduring dispositions. Such an analysis of variable social behavior into more or less stable personal attributes and variable properties of the situation of action corresponds with Heider's (1958) analysis of "common-sense psychology," and I take that as an advantage if our aim is to give a systematic account of human action in the world of living human concerns.

The second is pragmatic. Because human beings as we know them grow up in language communities in which, however imperfectly and mysteriously, communication takes place, we do have approximate access to one another's thoughts and feelings, from which we can make approximate inferences about each other's more enduring orientations. Neither as naïve human actors nor as social scientists are we restricted to the Skinnerian world of fragmented behaviors. We can listen to one another; we can even conduct systematic interviews and administer verbal scales. Although inferences from the data of communication can mislead as well as inform, we have good warrant to depend on them in social science as in everyday life. A conceptual framework that excludes inferred psychological dispositions from any legitimate place is so severely restrictive that in practice even the committed behaviorist does not stay consistently within it. Henceforth, therefore, I will take for granted a dispositional view of attitudes.

To return to my working definition, a few additional comments are in order. Definitions of attitudes often specify that attitudes are relatively enduring learned dispositions. But it seems unnecessary to build duration or, for that matter, learned acquisition into the definition. The crux of the definition, and also the point on which virtually all proposed definitions agree, is that attitudes are "organized with respect to a psychological object." Attitudes are *toward* something: a thing, a concept, a policy, a person, a political party—or even the *self*. They also involve organization—a structured set of beliefs held in readiness; a readiness to feel and to act toward the object in different but coherently specifiable ways depending upon features of the immediate situation in which the object is encountered. One of the founders of social psychology, William McDougall (1921), a great and presently underrated theorist, adapted this concept from Shand (1914) as the basis upon which mental life is organized, though he and Shand used the term *sentiment* instead of attitude.

The dispositions with which we are concerned govern both thoughts (beliefs) and feelings (affect), which are hardly separable. As Osgood, Suci, and Tannenbaum (1957) have shown with the Semantic Differential, the primary, preemptive dimension for any concept tends to be *evaluative*, pro or con. The main tradition of psychological research in attitude measurement has overwhelmingly stressed this pro-con dimension (see Scott, 1968). If one were to attend only to this tradition, a working definition of attitude might restrict it to dispositions of favorableness or unfavorableness toward objects. But survey research and qualitative studies, including studies of particular relevance to politics, are equally concerned with the cognitive content of beliefs.

My working definition fudges in its reference to "action tendencies," because I do not want to take the route of definition to decide empirical-theoretical issues that are very much alive. In political psychology, we are of course ultimately interested in behavior—what the person does (which includes what he says on a given occasion). The complexities involved in the relation between attitudes and behavior will be touched upon below. It is still not clear, however, whether behavioral consequences are more profitably viewed as *following from* a given set of beliefs and feelings, given the person's appraisal of his immediate situation, or whether a "behavioral component" needs to be built into the conception of attitude itself (Katz and Stotland, 1959).

In this chapter I will not take seriously the specification of *political* attitudes. This term could obviously be given either a narrow reading (of attitudes toward political objects such as issues, parties, candidates, or leaders) or a broader one (to include whatever attitudes of political actors are thought to be relevant to their political actions). I. will generally have the broader meaning in mind, with no concern about boundaries. I will be concerned rather with interpreting the social-psychological literature on attitudes for its relevance to political psychology—focusing mainly on the nature of attitudes and the processes involved in their development and change. (See also Chapters Four and Five in this volume.)

My review will perforce be selective and personal. There are forty-three pages of references in McGuire's (1968) definitive chapter on attitudes and attitude change in the *Handbook of Social Psychology*. Two excellent books (Insko, 1967; Kiesler,

Collins, and Miller, 1969) have been devoted to a critical examination of theories of attitude change, the main focus of recent psychological attention; and a very fat one (Abelson and others, 1968) treats the single topic of consistency theories. Sears' (1969) chapter on political behavior for the *Handbook of Social Psychology* is in fact mainly a substantive treatment of political attitudes as they bear on voting in national American politics; it has sixteen pages of references. Clearly, then, I must aim more at perspective than at summary. The serious student will need to refer to the sources just mentioned.

Some History

The scholarly history of the concept of attitudes is shorter than Allport's (1935) review suggests. In his day, Allport felt the need for legitimizing the concept by tracing ambiguous linkages to the history of experimental psychology. Given the solid social-psychological use of the concept since his chapter was written, we can forgo such legitimizing pseudohistory. I have already mentioned a more germane theoretical antecedent in McDougall's (1921) concept of sentiment. The term *attitude* was launched in social psychology (sociological version), however, by Thomas and Znaniecki (1918) in the methodological preface to their classic monographic study *The Polish Peasant*. For Thomas and Znaniecki, *attitude* and *value* are complementary terms. Attitude refers to any disposition of a person toward an object, while any object becomes a value by virtue of being target of a person's attitude. Thus launched conceptually, attitudes became fully established in social psychology when Thurstone (1928) directed his sophistication in psychophysics to the problem of their measurement. What could be more legitimizing? In fact, a sophisticated theory of attitude measurement has developed from the beginnings launched by Thurstone (see Scott, 1968), a line of development that has thus far mainly served the legitimizing function. For better or worse, the theoretically interesting experimental studies of attitude of the last two decades have mostly used very simple, even naïve indices of attitude: single items presented for agreement or disagreement, or ad hoc and a priori "scales" assembled without regard for psychometric nicety. The methodological inventiveness of the experimenters has been invested almost wholly in the manipulations of experimentation, not in the mapping and measurement of attitudinal variables. As for descriptive analyses of public attitudes, particularly relevant to political psychology, these have mainly drawn upon the techniques of survey design and analysis, not of attitude scaling (see Hyman, 1955; and Chapter Twelve in this volume).

The research of the early period—reviewed by Allport (1935) and by Murphy, Murphy, and Newcomb (1937), who each declared attitudes to be a central topic of social psychology—was in fact not very interesting or substantial. The characteristic approach was descriptive and correlational (mainly on college sophomores, at that), with little sustained attention to the conditions under which attitudes are formed and modified and little effort to connect the psychology of attitudes with more general explanatory principles.

One of the more substantial studies of this period (Murphy and Likert, 1938) came up with little that was more solid or reliable than the finding that among college students radicalism was somehow associated with dissatisfaction. (Strictly speaking, radicalism-conservatism is a personality trait rather than an attitude, since it lacks a psychological object. As a trait, however, it is defined by consistencies among attitudes toward a variety of social objects.) It was popular to correlate radicalism-conservatism with personality traits like introversion-extraversion—also being newly and crudely measured. There was little by way of theory to guide the venture, and little by way of theory resulted from it. More recently, Eysenck (1954a) has pursued a similar strategy with explicit theory and more sophisticated methods, but his study is badly faulted and its conclusions cannot be accepted (see Christie, 1956).

About the time of World War II, then, the psychology of attitudes was at low ebb. Maybe it was still the central topic of social psychology, but it did not attract the bright young investigators, some of whom were finding exciting new directions in the experimental group dynamics of Kurt Lewin. Several developments in the late 1930s and the 1940s radically changed the complexion of the field. As a result, during the 1950s and 1960s attitudes at last really earned a central place at the heart of a burgeoning, primarily experimental social psychology.

One development, which began in the late 1930s with the invention of public opinion polls (later rechristened for scientific purposes as sample surveys), carried the study of attitudes off the campus into the territory of real political life. The major thrust was under sociological auspices. Paul Lazarsfeld in particular introduced analytic methods for treating successive interviews with "panels" of respondents, and employed this approach in studying the determinants of voting decisions in presidential campaigns (see, for example, Lazarsfeld, Berelson, and Gaudet, 1944). The emphasis was on demographic predictors of the voting decision, such as rural-urban residence, socioeconomic status, and religious affiliation. Survey methodology in the study of attitudes (though not directly political ones) was substantially advanced in the wartime studies, directed by the sociologist Stouffer, that resulted in the volumes of *The American Soldier* (Stouffer and others, 1949).

But psychologists too were employing the new survey technology—initially, under the leadership of Rensis Likert and Angus Campbell, in the Bureau of Program Surveys of the United States Department of Agriculture and later at the Survey Research Center of the University of Michigan. When these psychologists turned their attention to the study of voting decisions, they placed focal emphasis on attitudes—such as toward candidate, toward party, and toward campaign issues. (For a classic later example in this tradition, see A. Campbell and others, 1960; see also the review by Sears, 1969.) They typically paid much more attention than sociologists to the beliefs—cognitive structures—embedded in these attitudes. Whether under psychological or sociological auspices, survey research has provided the major descriptive substantive content of the psychology of political attitudes. More than any other research tradition, it has brought their study into contact with the realities of political life.

A second development (reviewed in detail by Sanford in Chapter Six) followed from the surge of academic interest in psychoanalytic theory that, in the immediate postwar years, accompanied the launching of a self-conscious clinical psychology. The studies brought together in *The Authoritarian Personality* (Adorno and others, 1950) drew upon a liberalized psychoanalytic theory (in keeping with the emerging dominance of "ego psychology" in psychoanalytic circles) to give a motivational interpretation of anti-Semitic and more generalized ethnocentric attitudes in terms of defensive personality processes. En route, the authors extended their interpretation to antidemocratic or "fascist" orientations generally. The F scale, devised to measure these orientations, staked a claim for itself in an ambiguous common ground overlapping attitudes, ideology, and personality. Over the ensuing decade, its availability led to a large amount of research, much of which was unfortunately consumed in exploring the scale's technical defects. The tide of research interest in the topic unfortunately waned at about the point when more adequate measures were becoming available (Kirscht and Dillehay, 1967). In the present context, *The Authoritarian Personality* is important because it reintroduced interest in the psychodynamic basis of political attitudes, emphasizing more systematic methods and more explicitly delimited and elaborated theory than was characteristic of Lasswell's (1930) initial ground-breaking foray.

The third major development began with wartime experimental studies of the impact of army films for internal propaganda, and emerged full blown shortly after the war as a new laboratory-based experimental social psychology, in which attitude change was the focal topic of experiment and theory. Carl Hovland, a brilliant experimental psychologist who was drawn in as a consultant to direct a program of research on army-orientation films (Hovland, Lumsdaine, and Sheffield, 1949), carried forward the research at Yale after the war in a vigorous collaborative program on persuasive communication. Unlike the earlier studies of propaganda and attitude change (Murphy, Murphy, and Newcomb, 1937), the Yale studies were guided by theories drawn from general psychology. The predilection of Hovland and his closest collaborators was for the kind of learning theory identified with Yale and the names of Clark Hull and Kenneth Spence, but the program was actually guided by a theoretically neutral empirical scheme that mapped the effects of persuasive communication into those attributable to the source of the communication, to the content of the communication, to the predispositions of the audience, and to responses induced to the communication. (This scheme can be traced to Lasswell.) Different theoretical models could be drawn upon, and were, for hypotheses. A programmatic statement that presented an impressive initial series of experiments (Hovland, Janis, and Kelley, 1953) was followed by a series of monographs that filled in much of the picture sketched in the initial volume. (See Hovland and Janis, 1959; Rosenberg and Abelson, 1960; M. Sherif and Hovland, 1961.)

Added to this manifestly fruitful research program, which seemed to be yielding a new "experimental rhetoric," was a simple, new, imperialistic theory pushed with proselytizing enthusiasm by an incomparably ingenious experimentalist. The proselytizing experimentalist was Leon Festinger, the theory concerned "cognitive dissonance" (Festinger, 1957), and the heyday of experimental social psychology (the late 1950s and the 1960s) followed. In other respects the timing was right: through the National Institute of Mental Health and the National Science Foundation, the federal government released unprecedented resources to train researchers in the behavioral sciences and to support their basic research. That the new laboratory studies of attitude change came to concern themselves with abstruse theoretical and methodological issues was for the time being an advantage, not a handicap. Under the system of research grants by peer review, the new field expanded under its own directives, with few external brakes applied.

The study of attitude change, then, suddenly became integrally linked with the competitive extension and elaboration (not just the application) of general theories in psychology. But these process-oriented developments proceeded in virtual isolation from the content-oriented tradition of field research using survey methods.

(In Chapter Twelve, Hyman comments on the negligible contribution of experimental methods to political psychology. For a more broadly based and positive view of the role of the experiment in political psychology, see McConahay's discussion in Chapter Thirteen.)

Toward the end of the decade, disillusionment began to set in (Ring, 1967). There were a variety of grounds for discontent. It became apparent to those who did not already know it that experimentation is no royal road to truth: ambiguities abound in the experimental realization of theoretical concepts. Although the heavy social investment in experimental social psychology produced gains in the sophistication of experimental design and in alertness to alternative possibilities of interpretation, experimentation (which came to involve increasingly intricate stage management) did not seem to be paying off as much as hoped in replicable results. And the issues to which the experiments were being addressed were getting increasingly detached from the real world of social—and political—behavior.

The preciousness of much work in experimental social psychology also ran afoul the tide of social concern and discontent that was sweeping the campuses with its call for "relevance." Newly aroused ethical sensitivities were disturbed by the manipulative cast of social-psychological experimentation, especially by its heavy reliance upon deception to bring social reality into the laboratory. And questions were raised, too, as to whether the experimenters themselves were being deceived (Rosenthal and Rosnow, 1969). Meanwhile, cold winds from Washington added their force to these intrinsic trends. "Basic" research no longer could enjoy a growth economy, and the carrot of funds began to point in the direction of problem-focused studies.

Concomitantly with these developments, social psychologists who had sequestered themselves in the laboratory were becoming interested in field studies. Ingenuity was being directed to stage-managing field experiments that tested social-psychological hypotheses in real-life settings with unwitting participants. (Ethical problems here, too!) An influential early example, which displayed the value and the great appeal of such an approach, was the exploration of the "unresponsive bystander" problem—why he so often remains uninvolved when help is urgently needed (Latané and Darley, 1970). D. T. Campbell (1969a) was providing a rationale for social psychologists to regard "reforms as experiments" and contributing to the development of techniques for doing so. Field experimentation was thus added to survey research as an alternative—or a complement—to the laboratory.

As I write this chapter, it is too early to predict the extent to which the pendulum will swing. I hope that a better balance in research strategies will result, not just a change of fashion (Smith, 1972). It is already clear, however, that the substantial recent reviews of theoretically oriented experimental studies of attitudes (Abelson and others, 1968; Insko, 1967; Kiesler, Collins, and Miller, 1969; McGuire, 1968) adopted a more sanguine view of past and future achievements than comes easily to us today.

The Yield of Attitude Research

My own appraisal, as the reader surely understands, will be cast in the emerging, more skeptical mode. There have been gains from two decades of eager experimentation, but their contribution to political psychology is surely far less than that of the steady, relatively untheoretical progress toward describing and in part understanding the attitudinal determinants of political behavior, especially voting, by means of sampling surveys (see the review by Sears, 1969). I will discuss the yield of experimental attitude research for political psychology under two headings: empirical generalizations and the relevance of theory.

Empirical Generalizations. Experimental studies of persuasive communication have yielded a number of generalizations that can be fitted into an untheoretical map, like the one with which Hovland, Janis, and Kelley (1953) began. For a readable summary of this "scientific rhetoric" I quote at length from Zimbardo and Ebbeson's (1969, pp. 20–23) introduction to the psychology of attitude change. (Zimbardo and Ebbeson draw, in turn, from Karlins and Abelson, 1970.) The backup for these dogmatically phrased statements is most fully available in McGuire's (1968) compendious chapter in the *Handbook of Social Psychology.*

A. The Persuader
1. There will be more opinion change in the desired direction if the communicator has high credibility.
Credibility is:
    a. Expertise (ability to know correct stand on issue).
    b. Trustworthiness (motivation to communicate knowledge without bias).
2. The credibility of the persuader is less of a factor in opinion change later on than it is immediately after exposure.
3. A communicator's effectiveness is increased if he initially expresses some views that are also held by his audience.
4. What [the members of] an audience [think] of a persuader may be directly influenced by what they think of his message.
5. The more extreme the opinion change that the communicator asks for, the more actual change he is likely to get.
    a. The greater the discrepancy (between communication and recipient's initial position), the greater the attitude change, up to extremely discrepant points.
    b. With extreme discrepancy, and with low-credibility sources, there is a falling off in attitude change.
6. Communicator characteristics irrelevant to the topic of his message can influence acceptance of its conclusion.
B. How to Present the Issues
1. Present one side of the argument when the audience is generally friendly, or when your position is the only one that will be presented, or when you want immediate, though temporary, opinion change.
2. Present both sides of the argument when the audience starts out disagreeing with you, or when it is probable that the audience will hear the other side from someone else.
3. When opposite views are presented one after another, the one presented last will probably be more effective. . . .
4. There will probably be more opinion change in the direction you want if you explicitly state your conclusions than if you let the audience draw their own, except when they are rather intelligent. Then implicit conclusion drawing is better.

5. Sometimes emotional appeals are more influential, sometimes factual ones. It all depends on the kind of audience.

6. Fear appeals: The findings generally show a positive relationship between intensity of fear arousal and amount of attitude change, if recommendations for action are explicit and possible, but a negative reaction otherwise.

7. The fewer the extrinsic justifications provided in the communication for engaging in counternorm behavior, the greater the attitude change after actual compliance [*if* it occurs—MBS].

8. No final conclusion can be drawn about whether the opening or closing parts of the communication should contain the more important material.

9. Cues which forewarn the audience of the manipulative intent of the communication increase resistance to it, while the presence of distractors simultaneously presented with the message decreases resistance.

C. The Audience as Individuals

1. The people you want most in your audience are often least likely to be there. There is evidence for selective seeking and exposure to information consonant with one's position, but not for selective avoidance of information dissonant with one's position.

2. The level of intelligence of an audience determines the effectiveness of some kinds of appeals.

3. Successful persuasion takes into account the reasons underlying attitudes as well as the attitudes themselves. That is, the techniques used must be tailored to the basis for developing the attitude.

4. The individual's personality traits affect his susceptability to persuasion; he is more easily influenced when his self-esteem is low.

5. There are individuals who are highly persuasible and who will be easily changed by any influence attempt, but who are then equally influenceable when faced with countercommunications.

6. Ego involvement with the content of the communication (its relation to ideological values of the audience) decreases the acceptance of its conclusions. Involvement with the consequences of one's response increases the probability of change and does so more when source-audience discrepancy is greater.

7. Actively role-playing a previously unacceptable position increases its acceptability.

D. The Influence of Groups

1. A person's opinions and attitudes are strongly influenced by groups to which he belongs and wants to belong.

2. A person is rewarded for conforming to the standards of the group and punished for deviating from them.

3. People who are most attached to the group are probably least influenced by communications which conflict with group norms.

4. Opinions which people make known to others are harder to change than opinions which people hold privately.

5. Audience participation (group discussion and decision making) helps to overcome resistance.

6. Resistance to a counternorm communication increases with the salience of one's group identification.

7. The support of even one other person weakens the powerful effect of a majority opinion on an individual.

8. A minority of two people can influence the majority if they are consistent in their deviant responses. [The last two propositions pertain to small face-to-face groups—MBS.]

E. The Persistence of Opinion Change

1. In time, the effects of a persuasive communication tend to wear off.

  a. A communication from a positive source leads to more rapid decay of attitude change over time than one from a negative source.

  b. A complex or subtle message produces slower decay of attitude change.

  c. Attitude change is more persistent over time if the receiver actively participates in, rather than passively receives, the communication.

2. Repeating a communication tends to prolong its influence.

3. More of the desired opinion change may be found some time after exposure to the communication than right after exposure (sleeper effect) [which is greater for communications from less trustworthy or negatively evaluated comunicators—MBS].

How the reader reacts to such a list must be a virtual Rorschach test of his orientation to social research. Most of the points seem obvious, yet the contraries of many of them could reasonably be maintained. The passage quoted is a fair rendition of the *empirical* outcome of an enormous amount of research—some of it directed primarily to more esoteric theoretical issues. As a rhetoric of political communication, it surely contributes to political psychology. Yet qualifications must be introduced about the evidential status of these assertions and about the adequacy of this account of persuasive communication for political psychology.

Some of the propositions quoted (for instance, A-2, B-1, E-1, 2, 3) concern the longer-run consequences of exposure to a communication. But most of the research on which this summary is based tests the immediate effects of very brief and therefore, in the long run, inconsequential communications. A confident scientific rhetoric would have to be based upon research that followed the effects of more extensive exposure to persuasive communication through longer time.

As Proposition C-1 recognizes implicitly, research on attitude change pertains mostly to what can be done to captive audiences. Except under totalitarian circumstances, political communication in the real world faces conditions quite other than those studied in the laboratory. (See Hovland, 1959, for a discussion that attempts to reconcile the contrasting results of experimental studies of attitude change in response to attempts at persuasive influence, which typically find change to spare, and sample survey studies in the field, which typically do not.) Only McGuire (1964) has made a concerted attempt to study the conditions under which communication can induce resistance to counterpersuasion, and he limited his research to the special case of cultural truisms (like the precepts of good hygiene) that are not normally exposed to attack in the ordinary arena of communication.

A more important empirical reservation is that the propositions listed do not give sufficient prominence to the underlying fact of psychological inertia—resistance to change—which, after all, is the sensible response to any isolated new fact that challenges a person's existing attitudes (Janis and Smith, 1965). Particularly when the issue is important and therefore engages with well-established systems of belief and attitude, or with the norms of groups with which the person is identified, resistance makes sense from the perspective of adaptation, unless or until compelling evidence or social pressure is introduced. The fact of resistance, in persuasive communication as well as in psychotherapy, makes the claims of would-be persuaders less menacing than they would otherwise be if taken at face value.

More seriously, this experimental rhetoric is incomplete. It utterly ignores the impact of rational argument as such: cogent versus irrelevant considerations, weighty versus trivial arguments, logical versus illogical reasoning. If the set of propositions gives the global impression of manipulativeness and disrespect for the political actor, the impression is fair. Although, to be sure, most political actors do operate at a discouragingly low level of rationality (Sears, 1969), the fact is that researchers have not brought the intrinsic features of rational argument under experimental scrutiny. The manipulative flavor of the conclusions drawn has to be understood in this context.

Relevance of Theory. Since attitudes are learned in the first place, and enduring change in attitudes is a matter of further learning, *theories of learning* are one major approach to the conceptualization of attitude change. Attitudes can also be seen as embodying the results of information processing and in turn affect the way that a person conceives and judges aspects of his world. *Theories of the cognitive processes* are therefore a second source of hypotheses about attitude change. And as organized dispositions toward psychological objects, attitudes are important components of personality. A third group of theoretical orientations to attitude change thus have their roots in *personality theory.* These differing theoretical orientations highlight different research questions that involve different variables, so they are perhaps best regarded as complementary rather than competitive.

Let us first look briefly at learning theories. We have already noted that Skinner's radically behavioristic treatment of learning bypasses attitudes, along with all other dispositional concepts, and focuses on the stimulus control of discrete responses as it is established and maintained by specified contingencies of "reinforcement" (Skinner, 1957). This is a program that can be argued in principle, and illustrated, but hardly carried out in adequate detail to meet the needs of students of political behavior. The analyst of political behavior can nevertheless learn from the Skinnerians to attend closely to the payoff contingencies of reward and punishment ("reinforcement") under which particular politically relevant behaviors are "acquired" and to the current contingencies under which they are maintained. Such attention to significant detail can be a healthy corrective to the sloppy habits that a global functionalism may seem to countenance. (The functionalist perspective is presented at some length below.) As a critical perspective, moreover, Skinnerian behaviorism usefully questions the assumption that attitudes are intrinsically structured. (The degree to which public beliefs and attitudes *are* structured in the sense of patterns of correlations across persons is readily exaggerated; see Converse, 1964.) To the extent that the coherence of beliefs, attitudes, and behavior can be accounted for by external contingencies, the concept of intrinsic structure can be misleading. What people *say* and what they *do* are surely governed in part by different contingencies, different positive and negative sanctions. The Skinnerians usefully remind us of this, though I do not believe that their theoretical strategy can be extended to deal adequately with the domain of political psychology.

Psychologists have drawn on the broader framework of stimulus-response

(S-R) learning theory for a conceptual language to apply in the study of attitude change, which they analyze in terms of the familiar categories of stimulus and response, incentives, reinforcement, generalization, discrimination, and conflict. As illustrated in the work of the Yale group (Hovland, Janis, and Kelley, 1953), the categories of learning theory serve heuristically to set the terms of empirical problems and to suggest lines of interpretation that give direction to subsequent investigation—rather than to generate specific hypotheses. Campbell (1963) suggests that in this kind of use, the S-R and cognitive languages may well be intertranslatable and equivalent for most purposes. The student of political psychology need feel under no obligation to learn the S-R language, I think, unless he wishes to pursue some of the technical psychological literature. The recent stream of interest in the experimental psychology of verbal learning has yet to influence attitude research and theory, to which it might be thought to be especially relevant.

As mentioned, *cognitive theories* are another source of hypotheses about attitude change. There has always been a strong cognitive emphasis in the psychology of attitudes. As the philosophical basis for dogmatic positivism lost its legitimacy and psychologists ceased to be cowed by its dictates (see Koch, 1959), cognitively oriented theories of attitudes came into greater prominence.

In the traditional alignment of controversy in systematic psychology, learning theories were linked with behaviorism and cognitive theories with Gestalt psychology. During the period of behavioristic predominance, the Gestalt psychologist Asch attacked the stimulus-response account of "prestige suggestion" (a traditional topic in the earlier literature on attitude change) in a series of studies that are described in his excellent textbook (Asch, 1952). The controversy centered on how to interpret the empirical fact that people tend to evaluate a slogan or literary passage more highly when it is attributed to a prestigious source than when it is attributed to a source toward whom they feel less favorable. The S-R account asserted an essentially mechanical process of associative learning, in which the positive or negative affect aroused by the source adheres to the message (on the model of classical conditioning). Asch's Gestalt-oriented view held, to the contrary, that attribution serves rather to provide a new context of meaning; this new context induces changes in the cognitive object, so that changed evaluuative judgments and accompanying affect are then appropriate. At least two issues apparently are involved. One has to do with the *priority* of cognitive as compared with affective factors in attitude change. Do people change their feelings about an object because they have come to see it differently, or do they change their beliefs about it to fit prior alterations in their feelings? The evidence now seems clear that both processes occur; what may be primary is a tendency to bring beliefs and feelings into congruence (Rosenberg, 1960). From present perspectives, the second issue also seems less clearly drawn than it did in 1950: Are the processes of influence to be interpreted in associative or in meaningful terms? Recent elaborations of associative theory, which emphasize central mediational processes intervening between stimulus and response, tend to converge with the older cognitive theories. Heat has dissipated from controversy as theorists socialized to feel at home with stimulus-response or with cognitive terminologies came to see their differences as more a matter of linguisic preference and conceptual strategy and less a question of truth versus falsity.[1]

[1] The discussion of Asch is adapted from Smith (1968a), p. 461.

During the heyday of experimental research on attitude change, the main focus of attention concerned theories of cognitive consistency (Abelson and others, 1968). The topic became elaborated to such an extreme that it defies responsible summary in my allotted space. I will therefore restrict myself to identifying a few of the main contenders in the barest terms, preparatory to venturing some judgments about the contribution of consistency theories to political psychology.

One kind of consistency that seems firmly established but because of its obviousness (once established) has not attracted a great deal of research is that between beliefs and feelings (Rosenberg, 1960); that is, there is a strong tendency for people to bring their beliefs and feelings into line. The tendency of voters to support the issue stands of their preferred party has been interpreted by Sears (1969) as reflecting such a rationalizing trend toward consistency. Along somewhat similar lines, Rosenberg and Abelson (1960) developed a formal model for assessing the degree of "balance" in attitudinal structures, conceived as networks in which affectively evaluated cognitive elements are linked by positive, negative, or null relations. Thus, to draw on one of their examples, a state of imbalance is illustrated by a student who favors coeds at Yale, wants good grades, yet believes that having coeds at Yale would interfere with getting good grades. The imbalance motivates a search for a balance-producing resolution, which might be attained by changing the affective sign (+ or −) of "coeds at Yale" or of "good grades" or of the imputed relation between the terms, or by introducing further cognitive differentiation in one or the other term. Attitude change is accounted for by pressures to restore balance when new information has upset it. The formal model, which develops widely influential ideas suggested by Heider (1958), has not been extensively tested.

The ability of cognitive-affective consistency theory, taken rather loosely, to suggest political strategies is illustrated by Rosenberg (1967) in regard to peace-oriented politics of the Cold War era (Rosenberg also draws on the broader gamut of empirical generalizations and theories about attitude change) and by Rosenberg, Verba, and Converse (1970) in regard to peace advocacy during the Vietnam war. In a handbook for "doves," the latter authors urge that "the great persuasion task is to show Americans that some of the doubts they already feel are indeed very legitimate ones, and that the ['hawkish'] Southeast Asian policy which they still endorse and mildly favor does, in fact, violate their positive values and advance negative ones" (p. 97). The relative lack of firmly crystallized, consistent structure in "dovish" or "hawkish" attitudes (Converse and Schumann, 1970) suggested to the authors that the appropriate cultivation of inconsistencies could change public attitudes in the direction they favored.

By far the greatest experimental attention has been devoted to Festinger's (1957) theory of cognitive dissonance. The theory itself is simple (too simple, its critics maintain). Any two cognitive elements—beliefs or bits of knowledge—may be either *consonant, dissonant,* or *irrelevant* to one another. Dissonance occurs when one element follows psychologically from the contrary of the other. Thus, my knowledge that I have irretrievably purchased a new house is dissonant with my awareness of each of the disadvantages entailed in my purchase. The total amount of dissonance that a person experiences is a function of the *importance* of the elements in a dissonant relationship and of the *proportion* of relevant relations that are dissonant. People tend to attempt to reduce dissonance when it arises: states of dissonance have motivational properties. Dissonance may be reduced in three major ways: by changing one or more of the elements involved in dissonant relations, by adding new cognitive elements that are consonant with already existing cognitions, and by decreasing the importance of the dissonant elements. A general tendency for cognitions to be brought into correspondence with impinging reality is assumed.[2]

In many respects this capsule summary is misleading, though accurate. One could never guess from it the main preoccupations of dissonance research or the nature of its contribution. In the first place, dissonance theory has been applied by Festinger and others to a much narrower range of phenomena than was implied by Festinger's initial general statement: mainly to the case in which a person's knowledge of what he has just done is dissonant with his awareness of grounds for *not* having done it—a special case indeed. Thus, the *smaller* the bribe or threat used to induce a person to take a public stand contrary to his private attitude, the *more* likely he is subsequently to change his private attitude in the direction of his public action. Knowledge that one has sold out for a small price is more dissonant with knowledge of one's discrepant private attitude than is knowledge that the "price is right," and it therefore results in greater pressure to attitude change (when other routes for the reduction of dissonance are excluded experimentally). Such "nonobvious" predictions have been the stock in trade of dissonance theorists.

Nowhere in research on dissonance theory is the amount of dissonance independently assessed, and the impression that "cognitive elements" can be isolated, weighed, and counted is wrong. Festinger and his followers compensate for the weakness of the theory in this respect (the lack of coordinating definitions to link it with social reality) by great ingenuity in the creation of special experimental situations where the presumed balance of elements is such that predictions can be generated. The theory is thus ill adapted to application in the interpretation of social behavior outside the laboratory.

Much of the ingenuity of Festingerian experimentation goes into "conning" the experimental subject into taking a stand or engaging in a specified behavior while under the impression that he has a free choice. The predictions of the theory mostly concern what happens *after* this behavior because of the cognitive discrepancies that it gives rise to. The elaborate manipulations employed to set up situations in which the theory can be tested are themselves more a matter of artistry than of theory. This whole line of research has tended to substitute experimental ingenuity for theoretical explicitness.

Several years ago I was taken to task by some of my colleagues for the following appraisal of dissonance theory:

> The conjecture may be ventured that, in the long run, dissonance theory will turn out to have made sense of certain paradoxical feedback effects of a person's behavior upon his attitudes but to have said little that is important about the main themes governing the formation of attitudes and the direction of behavior. Or it may become incorporated in a more comprehensive theory that deals with these themes. The lure of the paradoxical "nonobvious prediction" can deflect attention from the main story,

---

[2] The foregoing paragraph is adapted from Smith (1968a), p. 463.

which may be "obvious" but needs to be formulated and specified [Smith, 1968a, p. 464].

I now feel comfortable in standing by this assessment. There is some solid residue from the flood of research oriented to dissonance theory, but it is clearly no longer at the "cutting edge" of apparent advance in social psychology. Attention has turned elsewhere.

Paradoxically, the consistency theories, dissonance theory among them, are poles apart from the cognitive theory of Asch (1952), which, Gestalt-wise, exaggerated the rationality of human judgments. (Asch claimed that even if people have to decide and act on inadequate or distorted information, they still can be counted on to behave rationally in the world as they see it. The kind of irrationality brought to light by Freud embarrassed him, and he could only treat it residually.) Consistency theory has turned out to be mainly a theory of rationalization, not of rationality. In its alternative versions, it gives a good account of the strain toward a simple complacent view of oneself and the world, which, we can agree, is all too characteristic of political attitudes. It has much less to say about the circumstances in which some people, some of the time, come to attend to uncomfortably insistent facts and even to seek them out—though both Rosenberg and Abelson (1960) and Heider (1958) before them had the promising thought that we move toward views that are more complex cognitively because simpler ones make trouble for us, either in our commerce with reality or in keeping our own inner peace.

An additional cognitively oriented approach to attitude change remains to be considered. This approach—the application of psychological theories of judgment (Sherif and Hovland, 1961; Sherif, Sherif, and Nebergall, 1965)—has, I think, more direct applicability to political attitudes and behavior than the consistency theories, though it is less fully developed and tested in research. According to this approach, a person's attitude on a controversial issue corresponds to the range of discriminable opinion positions that he finds acceptable. The person's *latitude of acceptance* is typically narrower than the accompanying *latitude of rejection* when he is highly ego-involved with the issue or when his position is extreme. In responding to a persuasive communication that advocates a particular position on the issue, he first locates it on a subjective pro-con scale of favorability with respect to the issue. The persuasive effect of the communication on the recipient will depend heavily on the distance between the recipient's own stand and where he locates the position advocated by the communication on his scale of judgment. Maximal persuasive effects are to be expected when the position advocated in the communication falls within the recipient's latitude of acceptance but near its boundary. (If the position advocated falls centrally in the person's latitude of acceptance, he agrees with it, but there is no occasion for persuasion.) Under these conditions, the recipient is likely to minimize its judged distance from his own position (*assimilation effect*) and to be open to its influence. When the position of the communication falls within his latitude of rejection, he is likely to exaggerate its judged distance from his own stand (*contrast effect*) and to resist influence. On issues that do not "ego-involve" the recipient, relatively broad latitudes of acceptance may be expected. Under these circumstances the more the position of the communication differs from that of the recipient, the greater the persuasive effect, within broad limits. High ego involvement, however, is accompanied by narrow latitudes of acceptance. With high ego involvement, therefore, contrast effects are likely to magnify the perceived discrepancy between the positions of the communication and the recipient. A more discrepant communication would thus be expected to be less effective.[3]

An additional concept drawn by Sherif from the psychology of judgment concerns the *anchoring* of judgments to particularly strong or salient reference points. If I know that a particular weight is "heavy," I am likely to judge any lesser weight as "light." So with opinions: depending on which ones define a "radical" position on my subjective scale, my judgments of what is "liberal" will vary. The extreme or end stimuli in any continuum of judgment are especially likely to serve as anchors when a person has had little experience with an ordered stimulus series on the particular dimension, when the potential range of stimulus values is unknown, or when no explicit standards for judgment are provided (Kiesler, Collins, and Miller, 1969, pp. 241–242).

There are problems with the theory, and data from the fairly substantial body of research that it has stimulated are not entirely consistent with it. On the whole, however, principles of social judgment are directly suggestive about important phenomena of political life. In observing the radical protest politics of the late 1960s, for example, I often thought that a constructive political consequence of dramatizing an uncompromisingly pure and extreme position—say, on the Vietnam war—is to establish a new extreme "end anchor" in people's scales of political judgment. The extreme position will not initially attract many supporters, and when it is promoted without benefit of invitation to reasonable compromise, it is hardly designed to do so. But to the extent that it catches the public eye sufficiently to anchor a new end point on people's subjective scales, it may lead people to redefine what they regard as a "moderate" position and thus contribute to shifting the grounds of political debate.

Another group of theories, personality-oriented theories of attitudes, were low in prestige during the boom years of laboratory experimentalism, if only because individual differences in personality cannot themselves be manipulated as independent variables. (But the empirically oriented Yale program nonetheless paid attention to personality variables as facilitating, limiting, or interacting with the independent variables of persuasive communication; see Hovland and Janis, 1959.) Before surveying the theories that guided such research as did go on, we need to clear up a confusion that I think prevails in references to personality factors in political psychology.

For most writers outside of psychology, "personality" has come to connote the realm of deep motivational dynamics typified by Freudian psychoanalysis. When researchers announce, with disappointment or with satisfaction, that they have tried and failed to show the relevance of "personality factors" to some class of outcomes in political and social life, attempts to show the effects of variables in this realm are usually at issue. A less restrictive conception of personality is also possible, and I think has much to recommend it.

According to this view, personality is the overall organization of a person's dispositions—a view congruent with that elaborated by Knutson in Chapter Two.

---

[3] This paragraph is adapted from Smith (1968a), p. 462.

From this perspective, attitudes themselves are important *components* of personality and also may be regarded as influenced by the encompassing personality system in which they are embedded. Social psychologists have focused mostly on relatively superficial attitudes, leaving the more central ones to clinicians (like attitudes toward the self and complementary attitudes toward the world, such as hopefulness and trust or suspiciousness and despair). But there is nothing inherent to the concept of attitude that pushes it outside the realm of personality or even toward its periphery.

Researchers of many persuasions have drawn upon psychoanalytic theory for hypotheses about the motivational sources of attitude formation and change. Although Sarnoff (1960) has attempted the most direct and explicit application to the theory of social attitudes, the most substantial impact has undoubtedly come via the theory of the authoritarian personality (Adorno and others, 1950; see Chapter Six in this volume). The prejudiced person, and by implication the proto-fascist, uses his attitudes to maintain a rigid and defensive posture; bolsters his vulnerable self-esteem by identifying with the strong and rejecting the weak; and resolves his own uncertainties and keeps his unacceptable impulses in check (while giving them covert expression) by cleaving moralistically to a world of clear-cut alternatives, one in which the safe areas of conventional respectability seem bounded by unknown dangers and conspiracies. This is a special theory of a particular type of political-social orientation that I would myself place in a broader framework of functional theory (see below). The theory is better than much of the research that has been adduced to support or to refute it. It is still very much alive and relevant.

Christie's concept of Machiavellianism (Christie and Geis, 1970) occupies a similar position—intermediate between attitudes, ideology, and personality—though its sources are not psychoanalytic. Scores on the "Mach scale," drawn in part from Machiavelli's writings, tap an orientation of manipulativeness and cynicism about human nature that turns out to have behavioral consequences in accord with expectations in contrived experimental situations. The dimension has obvious relevance to political behavior.

A theoretical approach to attitudes and attitude change that has yet to be elaborated would draw upon conceptions of the *self*. The data upon which such a theory could build come not from the laboratory with its pallid "ego involvements" (Sherif and Cantril, 1947) but from the engagements of self in life crises—including the crises artificially provoked by the Chinese communists in "brainwashing" and "thought reform" (Lifton, 1961; Schein, Schneier, and Barker, 1961) and in psychotherapy. Laboratory studies of attitude change have perforce been confined to attitudes that do not make too much difference to people, and the theories to which they have given rise may well be correspondingly limited.

In successful cases of "brainwashing," a person's deep-seated convictions are attacked and their social supports withdrawn to achieve a profound reorientation of attitudes. The metaphor of "death and rebirth" comes naturally here, as in the case of religious conversion. If attitudes that have become central constituents of the self are to be changed, the person's very sense of identity must be challenged; guilt is evoked, confessed, and expiated. The person is then given practice in performing the roles of his prescribed new identity and is supported in this identity by a new set of social relationships. Erikson (1958) has given a strikingly similar account of Martin Luther's transformation from a young layman into a monk. The parallels between attitude change in self-involving life situations and in psychotherapy (in faith healing and brainwashing as well) have been noted in a provocative and readable book (Frank, 1961) that has in no way been superseded.

The most systematic recent attempt to formulate the common ingredients of these "self-reconstitution" processes is by Sarbin and Adler (1970–1971), whose conception of the self is embedded in the more general perspective of social role theory. They note the following common themes: the enactment of symbolic death and rebirth, the importance of the group or the "other" as a source of role demands and a model for identification, the use of ritual behavior, reliance on proprioceptive stimuli to manipulate "core anchorages" of the self, and the prominence of "trigger" events that enhance the process of conversion. In the cases they examined, they observe that "three central processes appear to be at work: (1) a physical and/or psychological assault (symbolic death); a developing confusion about self and other beliefs (the bridge between death and rebirth); (2) surrender and despair (becoming a nonperson); and (3) a working through, active mastery, reeducation or adaptation process (the rebirth experience)" pp. 614–615. Unfortunately, largely because of the emphasis on laboratory studies of attitudes, these important processes have not been treated in most formal presentations of attitude theory. Among the academically based contributions that can be drawn upon to extend this view of fundamental, self-involving attitude change is Rokeach's (1960, 1968) structural treatment of personal belief and value systems, in which (among other distinctions) he contrasts a central region of primitive beliefs about the self and world with a peripheral region comprising beliefs received on authority.

A final set of personality-oriented theories to be considered has come to be known as the *functional* approach, because their angle of access is concerned with the functions that opinions and attitudes serve in the ongoing economy of personality. During the era dominated by laboratory experiments, functional theory did not enjoy much prestige among experimental social psychologists, although the variant proposed by Katz and Stotland (1959) generated its share of research. We have already noted that personality-oriented theories did not fit the experimentalist mold of focusing on independent variables that could be manipulated. The laboratory era was also a time of formalization, of miniature theories that seemed to lend themselves to definitive test. In contrast, functional theory attempted to create a coherently eclectic framework in which, for example, the defensive processes highlighted by psychoanalysis have an appropriate place—but only *a* place, not an exclusive billing.

From the standpoint of aspirants to hard science, another drawback inheres in any functional approach: it is admittedly only a way station en route to a more detailed causal analysis. Only from a dubious teleological standpoint can functions be regarded as explanations. In his focus on the adaptive transactions of the human organism, the functional theorist rests his pragmatic case on the de facto teleology of the adaptive process. He insists that although functions are not causes, an analysis of how a person's opinions and atitudes are useful to him is bound to be relevant to a causal understanding of their acquisition, maintenance, and change. In the social psychology of attitudes, he would argue, we may need to go through the naturalistic functionalism of Darwin before it makes sense for us to aspire to the causal models of Watson and Crick. Psychology has a bad habit of aping the most advanced models of the hard sciences, whether it is ready for them or not.

If we are concerned with understanding the personal basis of political attitudes and their contribution to political behavior, some of the features of the functional approach that put off the experimentalists may even be appealing. This may explain why the schema advanced in *Opinions and Personality* (Smith, Bruner, and White, 1956) may have had more currency among political scientists than it has had in psychology. Greenstein's *Personality and Politics* (1969), which featured it saliently, surely has much to do with its currency in his discipline.

Functional Approach

The functionalist conceptual map presented in Figure 1 is an outgrowth of my attempts to apply the approach developed in *Opinions and Personality* to the analysis of various problems involving social attitudes and behavior—in particular, McCarthyism, civil liberties, and anti-Semitism. I have also found it useful in teaching.[4] It is *not* a theory that can be confirmed or falsified, but rather a declaration of intellectual strategy to be judged as profitable or sterile rather than as true or false. As a framework, it provides a roost for verifiable assertions. My main claim for it is that it may help to counterbalance the normal human tendency to stress the exclusive importance of the variables or theories that one is momentarily captured by. A second claim is that such an armchair "path analysis" of relationships between types of variables can undercut prevalent disputes between partial accounts regarded by their proponents as mutually exclusive but perhaps better regarded as complementary.

For the moment, disregard the tangle of arrows in the fine structure of the map, and look only at the five major panels identified by Roman numerals. In keeping with the psychological focus of the map, Personality Processes and Dispositions (Panel III) occupy the center of the stage. Because we are used to reading them from left to right, I have put the payoff in Political Behavior (Panel V) at the extreme right. Imagine that panel to include any politically relevant actions that we may be interested in: voting, information seeking, influence attempts, administrative decision making, or even question answering. Our observational data come from this panel and the other peripheral ones; only by reconstruction and inference do we arrive at the contents of Panel III.

Starting with Political Behavior (Panel V), the arrows (marked A and B) that link it with Personality Processes and Dispositions (Panel III) and with The Situation as Immediate Antecedent of Action (Panel IV) represent Lewin's methodological premise: All social behavior is to be analyzed as a joint resultant of characteristics of the person, on the one hand, and of his psychological situation, on the other. To specify the contribution of either requires taking the other into account. To take this feature of the map seriously is to regard the old quarrel between psychologists and sociologists about the relative importance of personal dispositions versus situations as silly and outmoded: the two classes of determinants are jointly indispensable. Depending on the behavioral outcome in question and historical contingencies, one or the other may control more of the variance; one or the other may also be strategically more accessible if we are interested in influencing the behavior. Thus, changing the law (Panel IV) may be a better way of reducing racist

---

[4] This section is adpated from Smith (1968d).

FIGURE 1. A FUNCTIONAL MAP: POLITICAL ATTITUDES IN THEIR PERSONAL AND SOCIAL CONTEXT. ADAPTED FROM SMITH (1968d)

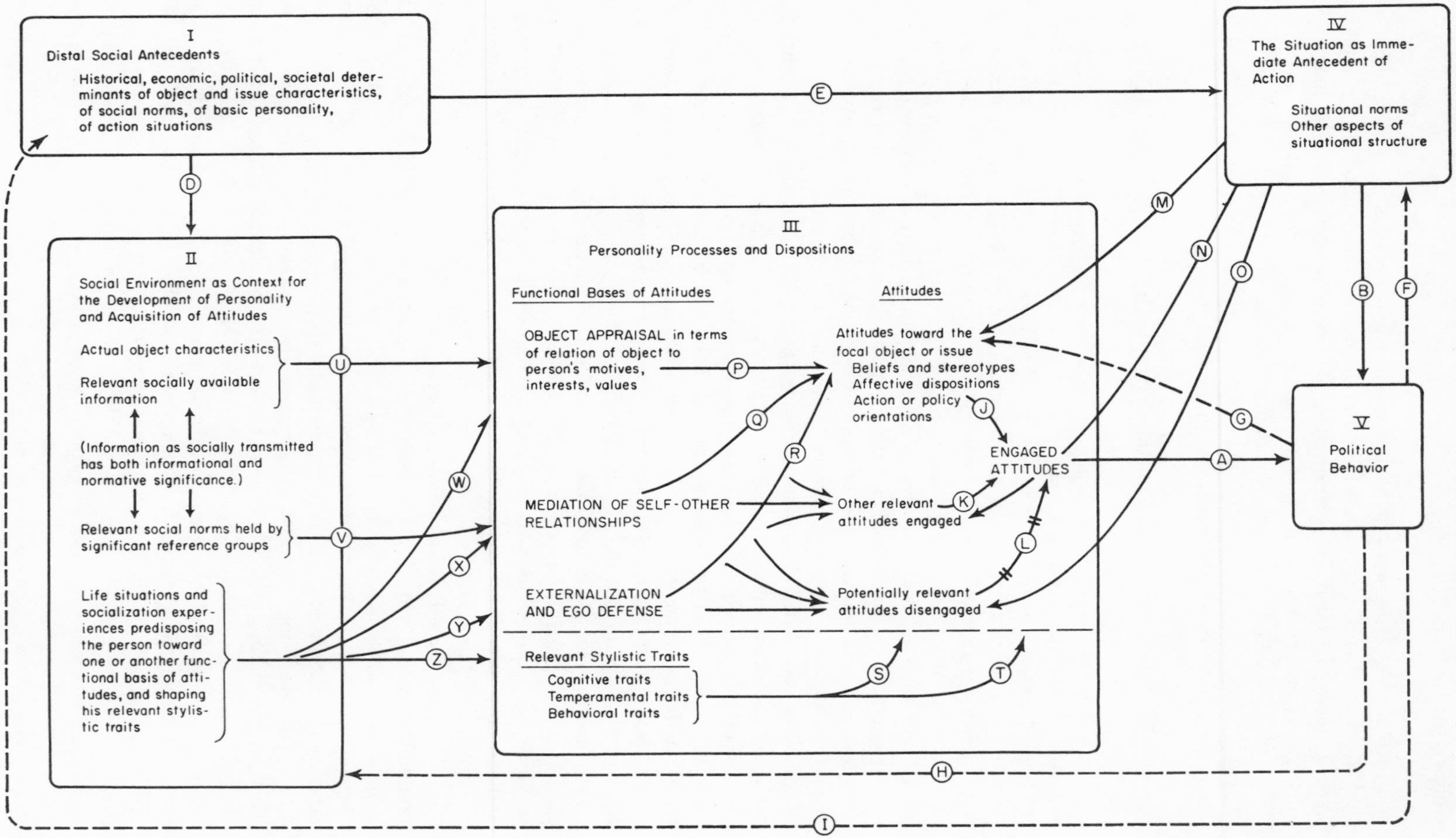

I
Distal Social Antecedents

Historical, economic, political, societal determinants of object and issue characteristics, of social norms, of basic personality, of action situations

II
Social Environment as Context for the Development of Personality and Acquisition of Attitudes

Actual object characteristics

Relevant socially available information

(Information as socially transmitted has both informational and normative significance.)

Relevant social norms held by significant reference groups

Life situations and socialization experiences predisposing the person toward one or another functional basis of attitudes, and shaping his relevant stylistic traits

III
Personality Processes and Dispositions

Attitudes

Attitudes toward the focal object or issue
Beliefs and stereotypes
Affective dispositions
Action or policy orientations

ENGAGED ATTITUDES

Other relevant attitudes engaged

Potentially relevant attitudes disengaged

Functional Bases of Attitudes

OBJECT APPRAISAL in terms of relation of object to person's motives, interests, values

MEDIATION OF SELF-OTHER RELATIONSHIPS

EXTERNALIZATION AND EGO DEFENSE

Relevant Stylistic Traits
Cognitive traits
Temperamental traits
Behavioral traits

IV
The Situation as Immediate Antecedent of Action

Situational norms
Other aspects of situational structure

V
Political Behavior

behavior than attempting to change personality—even if one grants the correctness of the theory of authoritarianism.

Causal antecedents can be traced back from each of the two panels that show immediate determinants of action. From Personality (Panel III) a cluster of arrows leads us to Panel II, Social Environment as Context for the Development of Personality and Acquisition of Attitudes. Both the environment of socialization (Panel II) and the immediate situation of action (Panel IV) have their own more distal antecedents, represented in Panel I. Historical, economic, and institutional factors have their impact on individual behavior—both by shaping the contexts in which socialization occurs and attitudes are learned (Arrow D) and as sources of the features of the immediate situations in which action takes place (Arrow E).

The broken arrows from Panel V reflect the *consequences* of political behavior, which may alter the situation in which it occurs (Arrow F), and cumulate across the many actions of many persons to modify the social environments that shape and support the attitudes of each (Arrow H), in the longer run constituting history and shaping institutions (Arrow I). Arrow G, leading back from behavior to personal dispositions in Panel III, represents the effects that self-committing behavior can have on attitudes. This is the phenomenon so much emphasized by Festinger (1957), which stands in its own right independently of dissonance theory. A political actor who adopts a position for expedient reasons may be convinced by his own rhetoric.

With the broad framework of the map clarified, we can now turn to the details. Consider first Panel III, personality processes and dispositions, working from right to left within the panel. We are concerned here with the inferred dispositions that the person brings to any situation that he encounters, and with their motivational basis. The problem is a dual one: to formulate how a person's attitudes come to bear on his political behavior and how these attitudes arise and are sustained in relation to their part in his ongoing psychological economy.

A first point that the map suggests is that we cannot take for granted just which of a person's attitudes will become engaged as a codeterminant of his behavior in a political situation. Political scientists are probably less naïve than psychologists about this. A citizen's vote for one or another presidential candidate depends, as we know (Campbell and others, 1960), not only on his focal attitude toward that candidate but also on attitudes toward alternative candidates, toward party, and toward issues. As Arrows M, N, and O are intended to indicate, the situation plays a dual role. It engages with certain of the person's attitudes and leaves in abeyance others that might potentially be engaged; and it serves as a codeterminant of behavior, together with the engaged attitudes. An example: On the floor of Congress, certain of a congressman's attitudes become engaged with the issue under discussion— different ones, very likely, from those that would be engaged in his discussion of the same issue with an important constituent. But what he *says* in either situation (and saying *is* behaving) will depend not only on his engaged attitudes but on what seems appropriate and instrumentally effective given the norms and contingencies of each situation.

These complex relationships give us no reason to suppose that people's political behavior should correspond to their attitudes on a single focal issue in any simple way. There are other technical aspects to the problem of the relation between attitudes and behavior (Fishbein, 1967); if the foregoing analysis makes sense, however, much of the puzzlement of sociologists and psychologists about the lack of clear correspondence between attitudes and behavior is pointless.

Moving to the left of Panel III, we turn to the problem of how attitudes are formed and sustained. Three functions of attitudes are proposed, slightly modified from Smith, Bruner, and White (1956).

Under *object appraisal* we recognize the ways in which a person's attitudes serve him by "sizing up" significant aspects of the world in terms of their relevance to his motives, interests, and values. All attitudes, not just prejudice, involve an element of "prejudgment": they are useful to the person in part because they prepare him for his encounters with reality, enabling him to avoid the confusion and inefficiency of appraising each new situation afresh.

A person's attitudes not only embody a provisional appraisal of what for him is significant reality; they also serve to *mediate* the kinds of *relationships* with others and the kind of conception of self that he wants to maintain. Is it important to the decision maker to think of himself as a liberal Democrat? Then his adopting a liberal position on an issue may contribute to his self-regard, as well as maintaining his standing with his political fellows.

Finally comes the class of functions to which psychoanalytic depth psychology has given the closest attention, here labeled *externalization and ego defense,* which underlies the theory of the authoritarian personality (Adorno and others, 1950). Here there is a covert agenda: the person's attitude is really less concerned with the avowed object than with containing some inner conflict that is analogically linked with it. McClosky's (1967a) data suggest a substantial ingredient of externalization in isolationist attitudes. Not only do isolationists tend to score high on scales of hostility, paranoia, misanthropy, and authoritarianism—content that suggests unfinished intrapsychic business—but they also show more contempt than others for weakness and more intolerance of human frailty. As McClosky notes, it may be logically inconsistent for an isolationist simultaneously to fear the demonic power of others and to scorn them for their weaknesses. The psychological consistency lies in the realm of externalization.

The arrows P, Q, and R raise the functional question about the motivation underlying any attitude. Different topics may be biased toward one or another function (think of the fluoridation issue, for example), and on the same topic people will differ in the balance of the functional mix on which their attitudes are based.

We have by now traced through enough of the map to place on it the distinctions drawn by Kelman (1958) in a widely cited article on three processes of opinion change. *Compliance* in overt behavior for the sake of rewards or punishments represents the impact of Arrow B— the predominance of situational pressures over one's own attitude in the resultant behavior. This is really *not* a case of opinion change, but of social influence on behavior. *Identification,* which "can be said to occur when an individual accepts influence because he wants to establish or maintain a satisfying self-defining relationship to another person or group" (p. 53), corresponds in my terms to influence governed by *mediation of self-other relationships. Internalization* "can be said to occur when an individual accepts influence because the content of the induced behavior—the ideas and actions of which it is composed—is intrinsically rewarding. He adopts the induced behavior because it is congruent with his value system. He may consider it useful for the solution of a problem or find it congenial to his needs" (p. 53). This formulation closely parallels my conception of *object appraisal*. As Kelman notes, the conditions and consequences of social influence are describably different for the three cases. The function of *externalization and ego defense* understandably falls outside his scheme, since it does not lend itself so obviously to deliberate social influence (his scheme really pertains more germanely to social influence than to opinion change). Attitudes strongly grounded in this function are likely to be held rigidly, but if they do change, the change is likely to be saltatory and irrational, to another attitude that is dynamically equivalent for the person, as in the conversion of a true-believing communist to a true-believing Catholic.

To return to the map, Arrows S and T, near the bottom of Panel III, reflect a different kind of relationship, which falls outside a strictly functional analysis. A person's attitudes and the way they engage with particular political situations bear the mark of his stylistic traits of personality as well as of the purposes that they serve him. Intelligence or stupidity, incisiveness or vagueness, zest or apathy, optimism or pessimism, decisiveness or hesitation—cognitive, temperamental, and behavioral traits like these have their own history and may perhaps partly be residues of the person's previous motivational conflicts, but their immediate relevance for his political attitudes and behavior is hardly motivational.

As we turn to Panel II at the left of the map, we now have a basis for identifying aspects of the person's social environment that are relevant to the development, maintenance, and change of his political attitudes. To the extent that *object appraisal* is involved, he should be responsive to the information that his environment provides about the attitudinal object or issue (Arrow U). The actual facts about it will be important in this connection only insofar as they affect the information that is socially available to him. The quantity and quality of this information will obviously vary widely from issue to issue and across the various niches that people occupy in society.

The information about a topic that reaches a person has a dual relevance, as the internal arrows in Panel II are intended to suggest: it feeds into his processes of object appraisal, and it also carries a second-order message about the social norms that prevail. When discussion of birth control began to percolate through Catholic channels, new grist was provided for object appraisal; and, in addition, the important news was conveyed that these previously taboo topics had become moot and discussable. As Arrow V indicates, the second motivational basis of attitudes—*the mediation of self-other relationships*—may then lead to a state of affairs in which it becomes safe to think in new ways. These relationships link reference-group theory (Merton, 1957, pp. 255–386; Kelly, 1952) to the functional analysis of attitude formation and change.

A person's life situation and socialization experiences may also predispose him —in general or in a particular topical domain—toward one or another of the functional bases of attitudes (Arrows W, X, and Y). What makes the rational man, in which the first function predominates? A good guess is that part of the story is rearing by loving and confident parents who give reasons for their discipline. In the shorter run, environments that sustain self-esteem and allay anxiety should also favor object appraisal. Research by the Witkin group (1962) on field dependence-independence and Miller and Swanson's work (1958, 1960) on child rearing and personality in entrepreneurial and bureaucratic families contain suggestions about the

sources of primary orientation to the second function, mediation of self-other relationships. As for externalization and ego defense, I would guess that conditions that
subject the developing person to arbitrary authority, that deflate self-esteem, that
arouse vague anxiety, that provoke hostility but block its direct expression are likely
sources.

To provide a useful simplification, any map leaves out complexities that it
does not attempt to handle. This one *assumes* the basic processes of motivation, perception, and learning rather than spelling them out. Thus, the threefold functional
classification sorts out the ways in which a person's attitudes are rooted in his underlying motives, whatever they may be, without spelling out a conception of human
motivation. As for perception, the map ignores the perceptual screening process that
intervenes between the environmental facts (Panel II) and what the person makes of
them (Panel III); likewise, between the immediate situation as it might appear to
an objective observer (Panel IV) and how the person defines it for himself. In regard
to learning, the present formulation makes the broad functionalist assumption (compatible with either a reinforcement or a cognitive theory of learning) that in general
people acquire attitudes that are useful to them. But it ignores the details of the
learning process and the persistence of learned structures beyond their original point
of usefulness. It also ignores incidental learning, according to which a person may
acquire much of the content of his political attitudes in an unfocused, only mildly
attentive effort to make sense of his world. At the time of learning there may be little
or no real payoff in object appraisal or mediation of self-other relations; yet should
the occasion arise, the basis for resonance to certain political positions rather than
others has been laid.

Political Attitudes and Model of Political Man

The functional view of political attitudes, as I have just illustrated it, fits a
view of man as a political actor who is guided in part by rational considerations of
how to advance his values and interests according to his lights, in part by the social
imperative to locate himself in relation to significant others, and in part by irrational
by-products of his symbolic ways of handling his inner conflicts. The quasi-teleologi-
cal phrasing embedded in the functionalist approach is in keeping with the view of
man as an actor or agent, not as a mechanism or "robot," which it seems to me is
essential if the realm of politics is to retain its legitimate human meaning. But is the
search for *determinants* of political attitudes and behavior, for which my map provides a scaffolding, compatible with the conception of man as a political actor?

V. O. Key (1966), the salty master analyst of American politics, thought not.
He saw the new empirical analyses of electoral behavior as adding up "to a conception of voting not as a civic decision but as an almost purely deterministic act"
(p. 6), and summarized his own counteracting view thus:

> In American presidential campaigns of recent decades the portrait
> that develops from the data is not one of an electorate straitjacketed by
> social determinants or moved by subconscious urges triggered by devilishly
> skillful propagandists. It is rather one of of an electorate moved by con-
> cern about central and relevant questions of public policy, of govern-
> mental performance, and of executive personality [p. 8]. . . .
> [There is] at least a modicum of evidence for the view that those

who switch [by crossing party lines from one presidential election to another] do so to support governmental policies or outlooks with which they agree, not because of subtle psychological or sociological peculiarities [p 104].

I am in no position to assess the extent to which Key's assertion at the end of the first quotation accords with the full data available, although there is apparently room for legitimate disagreement (see Sears, 1969). My concern is rather with Key's assumption that any account of political behavior in terms of social or psychological determinants is incompatible with the respectful treatment of "civic decisions." This seems to me to misunderstand the purport of sociological and psychological analysis (see Smith, 1968d).

Nobody has claimed that "sociological peculiarities" or "social determinants" exert their influence by any mysterious process of "straitjacketing" the electorate. Their influence lies rather in the fact that common experience and common social position yield similar perceptions of interest, and over time lead to the emergence of norms that reflect these perceptions. "Civic decision" is channeled, not abolished. It would be the less rational if it did *not* reflect social determinants.

Similarly with psychological determination, which is not to be equated solely with "subconscious urges"—the realm of externalization and ego defense. (Note, however, that political rationality in the aggregate is entirely compatible with the influence of "subconscious urges" as long as they are divergent or randomly distributed in the electorate. It is when blocs of voters start externalizing in tandem that a democracy is in trouble—for instance, from McCarthyism.) Decisions governed by object appraisal and the mediation of self-other relations *remain* decisions, potentially rational ones, even when their psychological determinants are displayed.

Skinner (1971), the humanists, and on this occasion Key (1966) appear to agree on philosophical or "metapsychological" premises according to which the scientific search for determinants of human behavior is incompatible with human freedom, dignity, and responsibility. These premises have recently been given a searching examination by Chein (1972), who makes a strong case that human freedom as we know it (of which political freedom is a special instance) depends on causal relations of the sort that science explicates, far from being incompatible with them. These abstract considerations need concern us here only insofar as they legitimize the scientific treatment of man as an agent.

Empirically, it is obvious that some people enjoy more freedom than others, whether we are concerned with political freedom (as cherished in normative political theory) or with inner freedom (to which psychological analysis is appropriate). Political man may be more an agent or less. A political psychology that seeks to contribute, as did Key, to a democratic politics that enhances human values should be particularly interested in the psychological determinants of political agency. Recent research and theory have made a promising start in identifying one set of these determinants, the sense of political effectiveness—a concept that lies at the boundary of the psychology of attitudes and of broader features of personality as treated by Knutson in Chapter Two. I cross this boundary with the justification of "hot pursuit," because my own theoretical interests have veered sharply in this direction from the traditional area of attitude psychology.

Almond and Verba (1963) showed that a sense of political efficacy on the part of the citizens appears as a central aspect of the "civic culture" of more effective democracies. Somewhat earlier, Douvan and Walker (1956) provided survey evidence that the sense of effectiveness in public affairs is at least loosely related to people's general feelings of competence. We appear to be dealing here with highly generalized *attitudes toward self and world* that are important partly because they tend to be self-confirming. A person who feels ineffective in politics guarantees his ineffectiveness by failing to participate. Conversely, a person who feels effective is more likely to participate in ways that actually make him so. The extent to which people's sense of effectiveness is generalized, the extent to which it is specific to particular types of situations or realms of concern, is of course an important empirical issue.

The work on political effectiveness seems to be dealing with a special case of much the same variable that Rotter (1966) studied under the concept "locus of control." With a rather crude pencil-and-paper scale that has since come to be widely used (called the I-E scale, for internal-external), Rotter found that people show consistent differences in whether they regard their significant outcomes as under *internal* control (resulting from their own skill and ability) or under *external* control (resulting from fate or chance). Their standing on this variable is related to whether they take an active or a passive stance in various contrived situations. From a different theoretical starting point, De Charms (1968) arrived at approximately the same distinction, between people who regard themselves as *origins* of social causation and those who regard themselves as *pawns*—and by virtue of this attitude act in ways to perpetuate their being so in fact. He is currently working with schoolchildren on methods for increasing their sense of being an origin.

Much work remains to be done to clarify concepts and measures in this area. Psychological research has unfortunately tended to freeze on the I-E scale because of its availability, much as it did on the F scale of authoritarianism two decades ago. Nevertheless, the line of investigation opened up seems likely to add to the empirical base for understanding, in a causal framework, how people can become more self-determining personally and politically. Since fundamental attitudes toward the self are involved, this research focus makes contact with the subtype of attitude-change theory that, in an earlier section, I noted as especially needing further elaboration and development: theories hinging on the self as a psychological construct. I am currently very much interested in both matters, so I am keenly aware that the functionalist map presented in Figure 1 has no convenient place to represent them.

A next agenda item, then, might call for refocusing the functionalist map to relate the psychology of attitudes more cogently to the acts of political actors (in keeping, in this respect, with the proposals for the study of politics made long ago by Lasswell and Kaplan, 1950). In the new focus, a kind of personality variable would be highlighted that differs from the unconscious motives of orthodox psychoanalytic theory and the stylistic variables of psychoanalytic ego psychology: attitudinal orientations that are constitutive of the self as actor and as reflexive object. Origin versus pawn is a good example. Perhaps in this new conceptual setting, the artificial barriers between a social psychology of attitudes and a personality psychology of motives and mechanisms may be dissolved. Such a development is fervently to be desired if we aspire to a scientifically more powerful and humanly more relevant political psychology.

4

PATTERNS OF POLITICAL BELIEF

Robert E. Lane

In the analysis of political belief systems and ideologies, the methods of many disciplines are germane and fruitful; this paper draws upon several of them: history and biography; psychology, anthropology, and sociology; and, more specifically, sociology of knowledge, phenomenology, and systems theory. Two special problems will be considered: the problem of constraint (that is, what causes beliefs to cluster in certain ways) and the problem of economizing (that is, the mangement of a belief system). Finally, I will discuss the ingredients of a core belief system.

Terms and Modes of Political Analysis

The language used to refer to the ideas under examination has such rich variety, such extreme individual variation, that the casual observer would hardly expect these terms to be dealing with the same kinds of things; yet they often are. A sampling of the various terms used to refer to political beliefs includes the following words: *analysis* (Dahl), *attitude* (Allport), *belief system* (Converse), *belief-*

disbelief system (Rokeach), *character* (Fromm, Inkeles, and Levinson), *codes* (Leites), *counter-ideology* (Johnson), *creeds* (Sutton, Myrdal), *culture* (Almond, Easton), *doctrine* (Oakeshott), *dogma* (Rokeach, Adams), *ethos* (Lewis), *heritage* (Elliott and McDonald), *idea systems* (Levinson, Lane), *ideals* (Chandler), *identity* (Erikson), *ideology* (Adorno, Mannheim, Lane), *image* (Barghoorn), *"isms"* (Ebenstein), *knowledge* (Mannheim), *lore* (Becker and Barnes), *mental products* (Merton), *mind* (Cash, Rokeach, Tucker), *miranda and credenda* (Merriam), *myth* (Cassirer, Sorel), *opinion* (Key, Smith, Lippmann), *personality* (Kardiner, Allport), *perspectives* (Lasswell), *philosophies* (Coker), *reflections* (Barker), *spirit* (Lynd, Beard), *theory* (Brecht, Hacker), *thought* (Coker, McIllwain, Rossiter), *tradition* (Hartz, Hofstadter), *value orientation* (Kluckhohn and Strodtbeck), *values* (Morris, Jacob), *view* (Owen), *utopia* (Mannheim, Lasswell), *weltanschauung, zeitgeist.*

At the same time that there is much overlap and confusion in these terms, there is also an intentional designation of different properties of ideas: cognitive emphasis (credenda, knowledge, belief system); evaluative, normative emphasis (miranda, ideals, values); distributional emphasis (culture, ethos, spirit); personalistic emphasis (personality, identity, character); implication of breadth and scope (philosophy, weltanschauung); implication of organized and coherent thought (code, belief-disbelief system); implication of probable invalidity (myth, lore); implication of official quality (doctrine, creed); historical emphasis (tradition, heritage).

The uses of the terms do not always reflect the indicated treatment, but they often do. It is the terms *thought, mind, theory,* and *ideology* that are particularly unhelpful in this respect. What is missing in this terminology are the words *argument, reasoning, thinking*—important concepts to be developed later.

But instead of looking at the terms employed, with their special emphases, let us look more closely at the kinds of subject matter treated. Twelve such classes of subject matter (with considerable overlap) emerge: studies of historical periods (Coker, 1934; Gierke, 1958); studies of political institutions such as political parties or the Supreme Court (McIllwain, 1910; Ostrogorski, 1902); close textual analysis of a particular work (Strauss, 1952); studies of a political philosopher such as Thomas Hobbes or a statesman such as James Harrington (Blitzer, 1960; Strauss, 1952); studies focusing on a particular issue or concept, such as justice or equality (Friedrich and Chapman, 1963; Tawney, 1926); studies of a particular political philosophy or ideology, such as liberalism or communism (Laski, 1927; Ruggiero, 1927); studies of events such as the American revolution or revolutions in general (Brinton, 1938; Rossiter, 1953); studies of political thought in an entire nation or in a community (Banfield, 1958; D. M. Brown, 1959; Merriam, 1929; Warner, 1949); theories of personality, such as the authoritarian or the psychopathic personality (Adorno and others, 1950; Lasswell, 1930); studies of a set of experiences (Lifton, 1961); studies in the sociology of knowledge (Mannheim, 1949; Merton, 1957); studies in the psychology of belief (Harvey, Hunt, and Schroder, 1961; Rokeach, 1960); analysis of opinion structures or belief systems (Converse, 1964; Lane, 1962.)

This is a sampling; it omits some studies of specific kinds of influencing and origins (as in the socialization studies), the communcation and persuasion studies, and some of the psychoanalytic studies (including biographies). Studies of belief systems inevitably overlap anthropological studies of culture, but these are not

included here. The list is intended to illustrate the richness of the field and the usefulness of variety, a usefulness that will be enhanced by current efforts at synthesis.

Ideological Production

What we have just seen is an inductive classification of the literature on
political thought and belief systems; other, more systematic, approaches have more
to do with ideology than with thought. One synoptic paradigm is suggested by the
following (Lane, 1962, pp. 415–416): "For any society, an *existential base* creating
certain *common experiences* interpreted through certain *cultural premises* by men
with certain *personal qualities* in the light of certain *social conflicts* produces certain
political ideologies." The terms, of course, are ambiguous, and controversy inevitably
attaches to whether ideologies imply action, veridicality, conflict, and so forth. I have
set forth some of these controversies in *Political Man* (1972, pp. 170-172) and take
the liberty of abbreviating and reorganizing that discussion here. The paradigm has
to do with shared experiences, thus referring to social, not individual thought.

Let us look first at the final term in the quotation—*political ideology*. Most
analysts think of ideologies as mixtures of empirical observation and mythology
(MacIver, 1948). Although some use the word *ideology* to refer only to ideas that
are embodied in action, such as those employed in social movements, most think of
ideology as selectively guiding action of all kinds (Bell, 1960; Sutton and others,
1956). Ideologies and belief systems are generally thought to be partly conscious and
partly unconscious; all ideologies have evaluative components, and most imply a
"telos" or goal reference (Billy, 1953; Parsons, 1951). Most analysts agree that in any
organization or society there is some compulsion to believe certain core elements of
the belief system (Parsons, 1951).

Let us now look at the other italicized terms in the quotation, taking them in
order. An *existential base*, a subject and term explicated by the sociology of knowledge, is the carrier or social vehicle of the ideology in question. For the ethos
literature—as reflected, for example, in Cash's *The Mind of the South* (1941)—a
people, community, or region is the vehicle of transmission and the source of nurturance. But for belief patterns more precisely termed ideologies, the vehicles are
variously said to be political parties, social classes, or occupations (Bell, 1960; Lowenstein, 1953a, 1953b; Mannheim, 1949).

Common experiences reflect thoughts—just as thought guides experience. The
term that perhaps best captures this relationship is *function*. As we shall see, common belief patterns are thought to be "functional" to organizations and societies (as
well as to individuals) in helping the members work together, in providing them
with rationales for their sacrifices and their relative social positions, and in maintaining their morale (Parsons, 1951).

Cultural premises are the common fund of values, epistemologies, and beliefs
of any particular culture; political belief patterns and ideologies draw upon these
premises. All ideologies have moral components, all imply epistemologies, all rely
upon causal theories available in the culture. The counterideology must selectively
employ the cultural beliefs of the established order to persuade members of a society
to criticize that order (Lane, 1972, p. 171).

Personal qualities are so intertwined with cultural premises that analytical separation is difficult, although personality and culture are separate entities. The importance of the separation for the analysis of belief patterns is emphasized later, in the discussion of *agency*. Without this separation, the analysis tends to be tautological or circular because the belief systems that are to be explained (explicandum) tend to turn up in the explanation (explicans).

Finally, without *social conflicts,* there is no change, no tension in the system, no consciousness of the beliefs in question. The beliefs are just "there." The important concepts of rationale; diffusion, persuasion, and other means of learning—even ideology itself—lose their meaning without the presence of conflict (Coser, 1956).

Sociology-of-Knowledge Paradigms

If we are interested in the sources of political belief systems, we might be guided by a sociology-of-knowledge approach, as reflected in Merton's (1957, pp. 456–488) paradigm. Merton puts his discussion in the form of questions about the where, what, how, why, and when of the mental productions that result in belief systems. His questions are useful but, as he himself goes on to show, require careful explication. Departing from his analysis here, we may note some implications of these questions.

Who produces the political ideas? Since ideas are mental products, the minds that produced them should be located. Among the important questions for analysis are the following. Are the ideas to be read in the contexts of lives and actions (statesmen, politicians, agitators) or in the context of other ideas (authors and their works)? Are the men important for their representativeness or for their deviance or because of the roles they occupy in society—or some combination of these? An important distinction in analytical modes is to be found in the analysis of the masses compared to the analysis of elites, with their superior information and, above all, their superior consciousness. If the distributed or shared quality of the ideas is important, analysis of the collectivity of which the "respondents" are members is essential.

When we talk about an individual's pattern of beliefs, compared to our discussion of group belief patterns, the meanings of the terms we use often change, and there is a shift in language and in the questions asked. Look, for instance, at the notion of the *stability* of political beliefs. Speaking of individuals, we might ask: Under what conditions will an element of a belief pattern change? In a hierarchically ordered system, what ideas dominate others? What are the functional equivalents of a given idea for a given person? Speaking of the stability of group beliefs, that is, the beliefs shared by the individual members of groups, we would ask: How will the pattern of individual changes affect the *net* support in various social positions for a given element of a belief pattern? What is the pattern of opinion changes in the collectivity (random, cyclical, constant)? Similarly, if we were exploring the idea of individual *conflict,* we would ask how an individual handles ambivalence, dissonance, logical inconsistency, psychic conflict. If we were concerned with social conflict, we would ask: How will persons with incompatible interests, needs, and preferences express and deal with these incompatibilities in different social and political contexts?

Other candidates for meaning change are the words *consciousness* (individual self-awareness versus collective or shared consciousness of group problems, group norms, and traditions) and *integration* (individual assimilation of ideas into a single belief structure versus collective assimilation of persons, with their various beliefs, into a single social unit). The meanings of some terms applied to individuals (for instance, *extremist, follower, other-directed*) are significant only wth reference to others. Finally, certain transformations of perspectives take place as one moves from analysis of individuals to analysis of collectives: individual *experience* becomes collective *history;* individual *thinking* becomes collective *policy making;* individual *choosing* becomes *collective choice;* individual *self-actualization* becomes *a free society;* individual *self-discipline* becomes *social control* or *order;* individual *conscience* becomes collective *moral norms.*

Where are the ideas located? In answering this question, we would have to consider (1) geography—distance and proximity, important because of communication nets; (2) societal location—roles, institutions, strata, communities, generational positions, social structures, nations; (3) ideational contexts—ideas placed in relation to other ideas, as suggested by the terms *modal, deviant, avant-garde, marginal, elite.*

What are the properties of ideas and their relationship to other ideas? For analytical purposes, the most important properties of ideas are relational. Specifically, we would want to know the relationship and the logical connections between one idea and another; the empirical ground on which the idea stands; the logical structure of premises, deductions, and inferences; the psychological basis for an idea (prejudice, dogma, obsession); the social basis for an idea (norm, convention, deviance); the style of thought reflected in the idea (fantasy, reason); the tenacity or stability of the idea; the evaluative component of the idea; the affective component of the idea (preference, desire); the mood component of the idea (hope, wish); the future (expectancy) reference of an idea (promise, threat); the demand component of an idea (request, order); and the conative component (will, plan, intention).

This suggestive list deals with the properties of a political idea, but we still do not know their actual referents, what they deal with. They have to be about something. Viewed traditionally, they are about the state; they answer the questions "Who shall rule?" and "By what principles shall the rulers rule?" From a distributive point of view, they deal ethically with distributive justice and practically with the answer to the Lasswellian (1936) question "Who gets what, when, how?" Institutionally, political ideas deal with certain structures and processes: executives, legislatures, judiciaries and the law, bureaucracies, parties and political cultures, and, of course, with ideologies. But viewed from another point of view, they deal with something much closer to the individual believer—namely, self in society (Lane, 1972, pp. 170–190).

Phenomena and Their Contexts

In some ways the paradigms that we have discussed fail to bring forth the basic framework of the questions that scholars and others are interested in. For the analysis of political beliefs, it seems to me that there are five basic questions: What are they? What caused them? What are their consequences (implications)? How shall we evaluate them (Are they true? Are they useful? Are they good?)? What shall we do about them?

In addition, there are four basic contexts, each of which adds meaning or new dimensions of understanding to belief systems: comparative (to set standards, give alternatives, reveal commonalities and differences); historical (to reveal change; give time perspectives; indicate antecedents; reveal standards, alternatives, commonalities, and differences); societal (to show institutional, cultural, and social settings and implications); personological (to show the relations of ideas to a man's experience, conflicts, behavior, and to his other ideas; Greenstein, 1969; Knutson, 1972a).

The description of a political belief system sometimes seems to be a straight-forward description of "what is there," that is, the analyst looks at the beliefs he wishes to describe and simply reports what he sees. But the processes of description and interpretation are more complicated than that. They involve three possible mis-understandings: those dealing with "objectivity"; those dealing with the very meaning of the term *is there,* that is the problem of the meaning of the term *is* or *is not;* and the misunderstanding of the relationship between an author of a work and the work itself, the text. These are difficult matters, but they are important because of the widespread confusion arising from a failure to understand them.

We said that the analyst may believe that he is simply looking at the beliefs and describing or analyzing them, just as a Rankian historian believes that written history is a record of "what actually happened" or the New Critic believes that he is simply analyzing "what is in the poem." But we know that perception is always selective and biased by what a person expects or wishes to see. This is especially true of Tocqueville (1856), Cash (1941), Banfield (1958), and others who describe whole cultural or community belief systems, however valuable their insights may be. The careful author seeks to correct for this bias first by an awareness of his own preferences, and second by reliance on evidence that is public and "objective," in the sense that others looking at the same evidence agree upon its character. The reader corrects for this bias by informed interpretation of the belief system of the author writing about the belief system of a given culture or community.

The second source of misunderstanding lies in the ambiguities of the language of description, especially the word *is* or more generally the verb *to be* or more generally still the concept of existence, a concept treated by metaphysics and logic. When an author says, for example, that "American belief systems are authoritarian," he may mean "all American belief systems," "some American belief systems," or "these American belief systems." "All" is clear enough, but "some" can mean "some and perhaps all" or "some but not all"; and "these," without precise specification, is notoriously ambiguous. Similarly, the problem of opposites or negations poses ques-tions, for they include contradictions ("American belief systems are not authori-tarian"), contrapositives ("Non-American belief systems are not authoritarian"), and contraries ("American belief systems are equalitarian"). Logic is important in the analysis of ideas, as we shall see, because this analysis often deals with the logical relationships betwen two concepts, especially when one idea is said to follow from another. In the same way, the analyst of ideas must employ the terms *either . . . or* with care since the statement "American beliefs are either ones of dominance or of submission" seems to (but may not) rule out the possibility that the same belief pat-tern might include both—which is often the case, as where a person is dominant toward the weak and submissive toward the strong. The same ambiguity inheres in the term *if,* which can, but need not, mean "if and only if," that is, a necessary *and sufficient* condition, one of the most important concepts in science. Finally, the reader will see the ambiguity of the term *certainly* in cases where objective and subjective certainty may be confused, as in the sentence "I am certain that the probabilities are equal that the electorate will choose the Republican or the Democratic candidate." The point is that descriptive clarity is impeded not only by observer bias but also by the very language of description.

A third confusion often arises between what was in the author's mind when he wrote his work and what a reader sees in the work (text) itself. Minds and texts are not the same thing, especially when one has an oral text, such as is provided by an interview. Understanding this point clarifies the problem of separating the author's meaning from the "plain meaning" of the text, usually through looking at the text in the light of other things the author has written or said. This is especially important in cross-cultural interpretation or interpretation of works written a long time ago since words change their meanings in translation, in different cultural contexts, and over time.

Now we shall deal with the first question mentioned above: What are they? That is, we shall deal with the explication and analysis of the belief patterns themselves.

In this connection, let us look briefly at various critical analytic methods often employed in phenomenological examinations of political beliefs.

Explication. Explication seeks to clarify ambiguities, confusions, or incompleteness in a textual argument; point out implications; and so forth. Although by no means the only method so employed, linguistic analysis such as that used by the British analytical school represents a form of explication. The tell-tale phrase is "What do we mean when we say. . . . ? Meaning is found not only in word and phrase usage but also in reference to historical events and in the conventions of the author's culture as well as statements in his other texts (see Weldon, 1953).

Exegesis. An exegesis is an analysis of the terms, metaphors, paradoxes, tensions in a work, especially to reveal hidden meanings, to compare one text with another, to show how the elements combine to state a message (Lane, 1961). Psychoanalysts (like the New Critics in literature) employ exegetical skills to discover latent meanings in a patient's oral texts.

Thematic Analysis. This type of analysis uncovers the latent themes or ideas in ambiguous material; finds an "ethos" in discrete opinions, an argument for capitalism in Calvin's *Institutes* or elements of Christian morality in *Das Kapital*. In contrast to the exegetical discovery of fresh paradoxes in each "poem" by the New Criticism, thematic analysis may find Jungian archetypes in every character. In thematic analysis there is an assumption that in the "ground" the figure or theme is there.

Classification and Typology. Sometimes there is a gain in understanding if a text is assigned to a "class" of things; the literary critic, for example, often asks whether a work is a good example of a particular genre and hence must answer the question "What is it?" To classify is, in one sense, to give genus and species or differentia; it helps to place a work. Thus, one asks, for example, whether a work is "fascist" or "authoritarian"; or whether a given constellation of ideas calls for a new concept, a new class, of which it is an exemplar. Typologies, often created in social science by the intersection of two or more variables (and sometimes by "substruction" of literary treatments), do not have hierarchical arrangements. They are useful as names for syndromes (properties that occur together). Where a belief system is ambiguous, explication will help to locate it in an established or novel set, class, or type.

Structural Analysis. Belief systems have forms; idea constellations have architectures. In *Political Ideology* (1962) I observed that the common men of Eastport developed their ideas in a relatively amorphous manner; there were few "stages," "points one, two . . . ," setting forth of premises. In structural analysis, *constraint* is an important concept, for it establishes "what goes with what" in a habitual fashion; it gives idea clusters and sometimes idea hierarchies.

Linguistic Analysis. Since language expresses meaning, the analysis of language often gives additional clues to meanings, lexically through word choice; stylistically through examination of mood, tense, and such rhetorical devices as hyperbole, irony, or metaphor; and through such literary devices as personalization, climax, and paradox.

Logical Analysis. Syllogisms, chain arguments, truth tables are difficult to apply to belief systems for a number of reasons. Because referents are imprecise, escape from the requirements of logic is possible in most instances by the lawyer's trick of distinguishing cases. Because identities are often not clear, because implication is vague, and because premises and propositions are almost never fully explicated, logical constraints are elusive. Thus, invalid arguments may be frequent (it does not follow that . . .), but the conclusions may be true and may be saved logically by new premises. The most important utility of logical analysis, then, lies in pointing out lacunae in the arguments, propositions that loosely (if not logically) imply opposing inferences, and various kinds of fallacies: fallacies of composition (what is true of the part is true of the whole), fallacies of division (what is true of the whole is true of the part), fallacies of accident (misapplication of a rule, often because of failure to specify quantities or degrees), equivocation (deliberate use of a term in more than one sense), ambiguity (unintentional equivocation), *non sequitur,* begging the question or arguing in a circle, *ad hominem,* and appeals to pity or prejudice or vanity or the like (Black, 1946, pp. 211–217).

Reconstruction. Since not every man produces a text, and since most literate societies provide for the scholar plural texts of ambiguous import and nonliterate societies provide only inadequately articulated conventions, inferences about beliefs and values must rely on behavior and artifactual evidence serving as text substitutes. From such patterned behavior as suspicion of strangers, propitiating prayer, child abuse, competitive social norms, the analyst must reconstruct the premises of a belief system. The anthropologist and the psychiatrist are familiar with this method; but imputation of analytical constructs to "natives" and patients depends on the analyst's imagination as much as on native behavior.

Systems Theory

So far, we have introduced three possible paradigms for consideration in the analysis of beliefs: the ideological-production paradigm, the sociology-of-knowledge paradigm, and the phenomenological paradigm. While the explication of these schema has been abbreviated, each has promised both some analytical results and some difficulties. Here we wish to set forth some of the possibilities of a systems-theory paradigm, also in abbreviated form.

The current popularity of systems theory is based upon its capacity to incorporate multiple considerations simultaneously; it lends itself to multidisciplinary use, as in ecological analysis; and it is compatible with complex computer simulation. But there are important differences between the application of systems theory to certain living systems (organisms, organizations, societies) and nonliving systems (markets, watersheds, communication networks). A systems analysis is applicable to both; but the living systems have what we may call the property of *agency*—that is, decisional units, or "regnant centers"—while the nonliving systems (and lower-order living systems like cells and organs) must rely upon programmed "decision rules" of some kind.

A belief system independent of the believers or some other unit of decision is a nonliving system. Although, as Converse (1964) has shown, there are some advantages in an analysis of belief systems independent of persons, personalities, or other "regnant centers," it seems to me that this mode of analysis gives up too much. What it gives up is the complex intrapersonal considerations that help to explain the resolution of conflict in an individual, and the play of forces in an organization or in a society that account for the resolution of social conflict. In the case of the individual, the analysis of beliefs apart from the individual's personality fails to take into account the individual's predispositions, his private "decision rules," the personal functions of a belief for his ongoing life strivings. In the case of mass belief systems, an analysis of beliefs that does not include social structure, decisional centers, leadership, and communicators, as well as communication nets, loses explanatory power. Social forces such as technological and economic change operate through people, and the people should be included in the analysis. The rule is not a dogma; it is an analytical algorithm designed to aid explanation. If followed, it would make beliefs the products of a system, with feedback into the system; or, alternatively, it would regard beliefs as elements of a system but not themselves a sufficient system. Perhaps the term *belief patterns* would be more appropriate, although in this chapter we occasionally slip into more common and looser usage.

With these considerations in mind, let us consider a paradigm for the analysis of belief patterns (or "systems"), both individual and collective, and discuss its uses for the analysis of political (and perhaps other) beliefs. The paradigm—an amalgam of various organization and systems theories (see Blau and Scott, 1962; March and Simon, 1958; Miller, 1972; Parsons and Shils, 1951)—employs the concept of "regnant centers," giving the system the characteristic of agency. Such a paradigm may be outlined in the following way:

A. Organization	1. Differentiated elements
	2. Related to each other in patterned ways with
	3. Some regnant centers of control and coordination and with
B. External Functions and Production Processes	4. Goals, problem-solving strategies, functions, needs, requiring
	5. Resources (external and internal) to

	6. Process inputs to produce outputs with
	7. Informational exchange (feedback) with the environment.
C. Internal Functions for Pattern Maintenance and Adaptation	8. Integrative (not task) mechanisms, combined with
	9. Selective admission, perception, and contact with the environment for
	10. System'-rewarding pattern maintenance and adaptation to environmental change.
D. Location and Limits	11. Boundaries distinguishing system and environment (marked, again, by effective interchange),
	12. Located in time-space-cultural settings.
E. Lawful, Routinized Behavior	13. Rules, laws, habits, conventions to guide element interaction, goal striving, product processing, and pattern maintenance and adaptation.

The paradigm has certain uses for the analysis of political (and perhaps other) beliefs which we now discuss.

First of all, in its organization this paradigm is made up of differentiated elements related to one another in patterned ways, with some regnant centers of control and coordination.

The *differentiated elements* of a belief system might be considered to be the separate beliefs; but that might imply a cognitive emphasis, which would exclude attitudes, values, and other less cognitive terms. Converse (1964) employs the term "idea-element"—partly, no doubt, to avoid this confusion. More simply, one could use the term *idea*. In order to embrace the thinker and the thought, it is necessary to conceive of these terms in a special way: they must be considered to be emergent from the thinker's experience; they must mediate that experience, express it, and prepare for additional experiences. In mass belief systems, or in culture itself, the units of analysis must likewise be considered to be linked by thought to what people have experienced and are trying to do. Harvey, Hunt, and Schroder (1961) employ the term *concept* for this purpose: "A concept is a system of ordering that serves as the mediating linkage between the input side (stimuli) and the output side (response)" (p. 1). These authors develop their theory of *Conceptual Systems and Personality Organization* in terms of "the nature and development of these subject-object ties and . . . facets and effects of variations in the kind of conceptual linkages between the individual and his world" (p. 1). There is no difficulty in also employing this mediation concept for mass belief systems.

There are some advantages in making the differentiated elements of the system do this work of mediation. All terms and their related public concepts have private meanings. In Eastport (Lane, 1962), the private meaning of "communist" for a packing house checker was "people who seek to bind me"; a young female clerk, reported in *The Authoritarian Personality* (Adorno and others, 1950) thought of "coercion" when she thought of government. Imagery is sometimes "tied"—that is, conventional; but sometimes it is intensely personal or idiosyncratic (Richards, 1954). Thus, unless the differentiated element in the analysis of political beliefs allows for variation created by personal experience and private meaning, the analyst may be misled by the standardized codes or words employed.

When we say these differentiated elements are *related to each other in patterned ways,* we refer mainly to the relationships involved in *constraint* and in *hierarchy* (or centrality). Constraint refers to "what goes with what," and to the sense of necessity experienced by the thinker (implying agency). Hierarchy deals with "what idea dominates or subsumes or forces change in other ideas under conditions of stress." Both of these concepts imply the agency of the thinking person; without him, ideas are inert. We shall deal with constraint in a later section; here let us discuss some problems of establishing hierarchy. We shall take an example from the ethos literature, as illustrated by Oscar Lewis (1960) in his account of the belief pattern in Tepoztlan. In this example we can see a variety of ideas or concepts intertwined, including the basic ones: I know (belief); I feel (attitude); I value—desire or consider desirable (value); I shall (conation—goal direction); You will or please do (demand).

One way to think of the hierarchical organization of the belief system of the Tepoztecans is to examine the interrelationships of the several elements. For example, the *belief* that people and the Gods are hostile and dangerous leads to an *attitude* of suspicion and to a *value* of independent self-reliance and work, which become moralized and thus embody both aspects of value (the desired and the ought); to *goals* of "accumulating property in land and animals"; and to *demands* that others not impose upon a person—but, more interestingly, lack of demands from government for aid and support. In this sequence of thinking, the belief element, the perception of the world as dangerous, seems to organize the other elements in the sense that these latter elements "follow" from the beliefs or are constrained by them (in a sense we shall discuss later). But belief and attitude are so intertwined that it is often difficult to assume priority. With equal plausibility one might say that early experience creates a hostility toward others (attitude) and thus leads, through various projective styles of thought, to a belief that others are hostile, that suspicion is justified, and therefore that self-reliance is required. Or one who values property—and moralizes it, as the Calvinists and others have done—might rationalize expropriative behavior with a perception of the world not unlike that of the Tepoztecans. Only a thorough knowledge of the society that produced and employs these beliefs will inform the analyst of hierarchical chains among such fundamental ideas. Just as the belief systems of individuals are best explicated in the context of their personalities, so cultural systems are accountable in terms of their host societies (Kardiner, 1945).

We have said also that our paradigm emphasizes *regnant centers of control and coordination.* In certain levels of living systems, such as cells and organs, these regnant centers may be difficult to locate; in nonliving systems, like markets or ecological areas, it might be said that the control is in "the program." But in individuals and societies, there *are* regnant centers, although their location is not always easy.

For the individual human organism, certain terms suggest the properties of this regnant center. The term that has sometimes been used to suggest the agent of political thinking, the *mind,* may be too heavily loaded with cognition. Murray and Kluckhohn (1949, p. 9), use the term *personality,* which, they say, "is the organization of all the integrative (regnant) processes in the brain." In the Freudian system, *ego* has the power of conscious control and direction, but ego may not be regnant over the impulse life of the individual or the monitoring minatory conscience. This line of thought leads quickly into two difficult puzzles, the mind-body problem and the problem of free will, both of them dealing with the regnancy of the mind, the self, the ego. More fruitfully, it raises other questions that are important because they affect the concept of agency in a functioning belief system.

The questions concern consciousness and control. Murray and Kluckhohn say that "regnant processes . . . have the property of consciousness"; but that explains little. Others use the metaphor of one computer monitoring another (Deutsch, 1963), but that does not explain selective consciousness—or unconsciousness. Freud gives some explanations in the concepts of repression and sublimation—unconsciousness for a purpose. The point is that the conscious mind may on occasion, like the queen of England, reign but not rule over political thinking. The point is further made by the concept of ego strength, representing the notion of a conscious mind with a somewhat larger domain in the personality, and a somewhat greater sense of mastery over the environment.

Fromm (1941) argues that at certain historical moments men find the burden of free choice too much for them and they *Escape from Freedom;* it has been said that historically the "impulsive Russians" look for outside controls to help them with their problems of self-control (Mead, 1951); Riesman (1950), among many others, has pointed to the abdication of the self in favor of control by group opinion. In my investigation (1962) of the political ideas of the common men of Eastport, an American urban community, I found that those with the weakest egos (the least control over impulsive drinking, eating, spending, and sexual expression) were most frightened by the idea of an extension of freedom. Further, they were the most likely to project a system of conspiratorial or "cabalistic" control on the world—largely, I thought, because they themselves had no experience of internal control and hence no understanding of pluralistic democratic controlling mechanisms (pp. 54–56, 124–26). Knutson (1972a, pp. 71–80) reports other findings with similar import. Thus, it seems to me, without the concept of agency and control, an analysis of belief systems or patterns is incomplete; with it, a whole new set of analytical problems, of which the above are only illustrative, emerges.

Societies, like organisms, are "living systems" (Miller, 1972); they have system properties in part because they too have regnant centers. To explain change in the opinions of mass publics, or in cultural values, or in policy positions, analysts employ a variety of theories of social change, but they cannot leave out reference to influential people in specified social positions. Thus, the "executive committee of the ruling class" or "the intellectuals" are assigned these deciding or influencing capacities in the sociology of knowledge (of whatever political persuasion). In the systems theories of Parsons (1951), Parsons and Shils (1951), and Easton (1965), the officers of political institutions serve as deciders under the influence of popular supports and demands. Controversies over the nature of community power—pyramidal or plural— reflect important schools of thought on the place and levels where values are implemented, policies formed, and agendas set forth.

A systems theory of mass opinion may consider, for any society, that the prime mover is something called "technology" or cultural diffusion or, perhaps, economic relationships; but in specifying the mechanisms whereby this "force" is translated into new values and new beliefs, the persons or the persons-in-roles who are responsible will be accounted for. Thus, two of the current important controversies dealing with *states* of opinion—the rise of consciousness in modern society and the decline of ideological thinking (Bell, 1960; Lane, 1966)—would be improved by discussions of whose consciousness has risen and whose ideological thinking has declined—and why certain people and not others have been affected.

In addition to a specific organization (with differentiated elements, patterned relationships, and regnant centers), our systems paradigm has specific external and internal functions. The external functions and production processes involve *goals, resources, process inputs,* and *informational exchange* (feedback) with the environment.

The common analysis of belief systems in terms of the functions they serve in the life of the individual treats these external functions primarily as those of reality guidance and social adjustment (Smith, Bruner, and White, 1956). In light of the individual's goals, purposes, or needs, how do his opinions help him to satisfy his needs and achieve his purposes and goals? As we shall point out in a later discussion, we can judge the "rationality" of an opinion only after we discover what the individual is trying to do. It may seem paradoxical, but opinions that do not follow the rules of logic can be "rational" in this sense. And, in a similar sense, ignorance may be more rational than knowledge.

The thinking that men do is here considered as the processing of information and other stimuli to produce outputs in the form of belief patterns. The resources are not only the information a man has at his command but his cognitive capacities; his capacity for moral reasoning, including empathic powers; and his capacity to eschew short-run gain at the expense of long-run disadvantages and costs. While this may be obvious enough, consider the utility of the "feedback" item in the paradigm. Illustratively, we may take the case of the common men of Eastport (Lane, 1962), framing their opinions about democracy. O'Hara, a factory mechanic, in answer to a question of what he thinks are the major problems facing America today, turns to foreign policy and indicates that the (then recent) Russian advances in technology and power threaten the United States, especially at a time when "everything started getting tight in this country." He blames the Republicans for the recession and therefore, in some measure, for the relative disadvantage of this country vis à vis the Russians. Under these circumstances, what kind of feedback will O'Hara get to correct or confirm such an opinion? His opinions on matters at the shop—and he has many such opinions—are subject to some kind of correction from the observation of the effects of different policies, effects on things that matter to him. But on foreign policy, or even on tax policy (his second major problem facing America today), the correctives from any kind of feedback are minimal. In discussions of the nature of opinion in mass publics, the limitations of feedback (designation of a policy, observed effects, and corrected policy) must be taken into account.

The external functions served by belief systems for organizations or societies usually embrace the following things. The belief system or ideology explains to its members why they are where they are and do what they do; it provides common goals for striving, reasons for collective success, and rationales for defeats or failures. It gives common codes for coordinate effort and common justifications for the distribution of rewards and punishments. It enlists morality in the service of necessity or at least of practice. In these ways it makes possible the use of resources to process matter/energy from inputs to outputs, and to process information into decisions and communications.

The functional arguments have difficulties, notably their implicit teleological themes, but the questions they seek to answer are important. Among others, these are: Of what use to the group are these beliefs? What rewards sustain these beliefs in the face of challenge? Who benefits and who loses through the adoption of these beliefs? What are the principal contending alternative beliefs that might serve similar purposes? How would they fit into other features of the belief system? Who would gain and who would lose what through change in the specified directions?

From such a functionalist perspective, both ignorance and knowledge, both orthodoxy and heterodoxy, derive meaning; that is, from analysis of their effects, inferences can be made about their "purposes" and functions and therefore about the forces that sustain them. Again the feedback problem is important, since organizations that do not receive information about their environments misjudge the reception of their efforts and risk decline.

Internal functions include integrative (not task) mechanisms, combined with selective admission, perception, and contact with the environment, for system-rewarding pattern maintenance and adaptation to environmental change.

For individuals, the internal functions of belief systems are various need gratifications, sometimes called "externalization" (Smith, Bruner, and White, 1956); that is, the treatment of the outside world in terms of the requirements of internal conflicts, self-justifications, and so forth. On the basis of a set of student ideological self-analyses, I (1969) tried to relate these students' beliefs to their need to be liked and to validate their likability, their need to make themselves seem important or strong (in their own eyes), their need to express and to control their own aggressive feelings, their need for a sense of their own morality, and their need to be autonomous from their own families or, alternatively, to identify with and carry on the family's political and social traditions. (Of course, their beliefs also had reality functions, especially to provide them with views that would help rather than hinder their careers, but also to express positions that would, if adopted, advance their own individual or group interests.) To these ends, from their own course work or, more important, from their reading and discussions, they heard and remembered and used those things that reinforced their beliefs, but with some tolerance for challenging, dissonant ideas. From the various theories that identify self with beliefs and personality with ideology, the uses of beliefs in maintaining identity may be inferred. The model alerts us to this with its reference to pattern maintenance, a useful way of thinking of identity.

For organizations and societies, the internal functions served by belief systems are those of integration, coordination, morale building, leadership legitimization, defining equity and justice within the system, and providing formulas for conflict resolution. With reference to the question of agency, in managing belief systems as in other matters there is often differentiation between beliefs associated with the tasks or the external functions and those concerned with the internal functions of morale and sense of well-being, but beliefs dealing with group loyalty or patriotism do double duty in these respects.

As with functional arguments dealing with external functions, the specification of gainers and losers, of needs gratified or group purposes served, gives clues to why beliefs are adopted, eroded, changed.

Our belief-system paradigm also includes *location and limits:* boundaries distinguishing system and environment (marked, again, by effective interchange) and time-space-cultural settings.

The individual's identity includes a social identity—a sense of group placement, of allies, of "people like me," in contrast to strangers and enemies. Here, then, we include group reference, which seems to guide opinion formation as much as anything does. It is this group reference that saves the individual from egoism; beyond this reference lies a broader human empathy; without group reference an individual is literally sick (Lane and Sears, 1964, pp. 90–91). Thus, for the individual as for the society, the belief system must help him in this placing function, defining roles and role behavior, status and status expectations, norms that are appropriate to the individual in these times, in those places. For most people, universality is a disadvantage, relativism, when a person needs guidance, a failure of directives.

For the organization and the society, for building a movement as for building a nation, the definition of boundaries is crucial; organizations and societies need both a "we" and a "they." Languages, customs, rituals, codes, histories, and myths help provide demarcations and, equally important, rationales for these boundary lines. Two considerations are most important here: the permeability between boundaries (for example, social class versus caste, or "the circulation of elites") and interchangeability of elements within boundaries (role specificity, division of labor). Inevitably the belief systems must provide guidance in these matters.

To analyze the dynamics of belief systems is to deal with the agencies of change within and between boundaries, to identify the persons or roles where decisions on boundaries are made and moralized, and to observe the traffic across boundaries, especially as this may be captured by the concept of "cultural diffusion."

Finally, our paradigm provides for *lawful, routinized behavior*—in the form of rules, laws, habits, and conventions to guide element interaction, goal striving, product processing, and pattern maintenance and adaptation.

What is lawful for the individual is that which does not violate his conscience or, more usually, his routinized habits and expectations. Although for every act there is an implicit or explicit belief to justify the act, the reverse is not true; not every thought, fantasy, image, or argument is reflected in behavior, especially since thoughts often rehearse alternative lines of behavior. The world of behavior, therefore, is smaller than the world of thought; the two worlds are not isomorphic. Further, as one moves along the concrete-abstract continuum, both for individuals and for societies, the lack of correspondence between thought and action increases.

Studying behavior patterns, one infers thinking and reasoning; studying thought patterns, one may infer behavioral consequences. Studying individuals, especially at the level of personality (conflict resolution, learning strategies, unconsiousness), one can synthesize behavior patterns and thought patterns—a synthesis made possible by the introduction of the powers of agency. Lawful, routinized behavior (codes, habits, and mechanisms) is the property of living systems at this level of the organism or person.

At the level of the organization or the society, the lawful regularities of the system that bear on its political beliefs are institutional practices; communication conventions; behavioral patterns, encapsulated in mores; and the cultural codes, often based on premises serving as answers to the questions "What is real?" (metaphysics), "What is true?" (epistemology), and "What is good?" (ethics). The intersection between systems of social behavior and social beliefs comes at the level of culture, but culture without society lacks agency; it is just there to be described (Benedict, 1934; Kroeber, 1944). Change acts through the agency of living men; thus, the dynamics of culture (value change, technological change) implies the interaction of society with culture. Here, then, lie the great questions: What kinds of social changes produce major shifts in belief systems? How does the change in property relationships alter moral values? What is the effect of the great increase in technology in modern society upon the epistemologies and values of mass publics?

Reasoning and Constraint

In this section I will deal in more detail with the idea of constraint, briefly touched upon in the preceding discussion. I shall rely upon, and criticize, the important discussion by Philip Converse (1964) in "The Nature of Belief Systems in Mass Publics" and shall contrast the concept of *constraint* with the concept of *reasoning*. Converse defines a belief system as a configuration of ideas and attitudes in which the elements are bound together by some form of constraint or functional interdependence. The constraint he has in mind is measured in the static case by predictability about other idea-elements, given any one or group of them, and in the dynamic case by the probability that a change in the status of any one idea-element would *psychologically* require some compensating changes in the status of others (pp. 207–208). One can quite easily measure constraints of this kind, given survey data and panel data; but, as Converse points out, the inquiry into *why* certain idea-elements go together is more difficult to conduct and offers less satisfactory answers.

Through the analysis of survey data, Converse shows that little use is made of broad economizing concepts such as liberal-conservative in the mass public; that political and policy information is rare among the 88.5 percent of the population who do not offer evidence of a liberal-conservative ideology; that such information is important in providing constraints of the kind mentioned; and that opinion change on a policy item in which the public has little interest is nearly random. Looking at "what goes with what," Converse shows that congressmen have much more predictable belief systems than the public. And the belief systems make more sense according to the liberal-conservative organizing principles. For the masses, belief systems are more likely to be organized according to attitudes toward social groups.

Any inquiry such as Converse's (that is, an inquiry about the relationship between various political ideas) is in my view, at least partly an inquiry into political *reasoning* and therefore requires an analysis of the ways in which people think about politics. In order to do this analysis, one must examine the thinking and reasoning *processes* as well as the patterns of association which these produce.

But the processes we have in mind are those of the subjects of the study, not those of the analyst. It is a nice question whether the concept of constraint as it is employed by Converse applies to the subject of analysis or to the analyst. With reference to the analyst he refers to "the success we would have in predicting [what idea-elements go together]." With reference to the subject of analysis Converse refers to the "probability that a change in the perceived [by the subject] status . . . of one idea-element would psychologically require [a change in the status of other idea-elements]" (p. 207). This concept of constraint on the capacity of the analyst to predict takes Bridgman (1928) literally: A concept is defined by the operations that measure the phenomena to be examined. But there is a looseness here that needs to be questioned. The phenomena to be examined are not merely the patterns of association of idea-elements and patterns of change; for, by definition, they include a subject's sense of necessary relationship ("psychological requirement") and thus a subject's experience of constraint, the sense that this idea *should* go with that one.

This confusion between reference to the subject and reference to the analyst would not be important if it did not have implications for the research findings that flow from the use of the concept. The most important of these implications is the priority this confusion gives to the analyst's role in setting forth the idea-elements *he* thinks are important, developing the conceptual framework that the analyst regards as most likely to "govern" the more specific beliefs (exemplars), and thus providing a guided opportunity for measuring association and change. Equally important, this focus on the analyst gives him, but not the subject, an opportunity for talking about the patterns of idea-element association. This is a substitution of correlation for cause and, as the analysis progresses, of cause for reason. Put another way, if one thinks of the term *constraint* in the less specialized sense of "to confine" or "to bring into narrower compass," the term should apply to the subject's experienced choice among idea-elements. He can explain why, for example, he feels constrained to say "yes" to the question "Are you in favor of leaving things like electric power and housing for private businessmen to handle?" His answer will be only part of such an explanation, but it is an important part.

The point can be made more specific. Among the working-class men I interviewed in 1957 (Lane, 1962), O'Hara, a factory maintenance mechanic, like every other person in the group of fifteen respondents, chose the statement "It would be better if mines and factories remained under private ownership" over the statement "It would be better if the government owned the mines and factories." Nevertheless, on the four discriminating items in Centers' (1949) liberalism-conservatism scale, he chose the more liberal answers: he generally sides with workers in labor disputes; he believes that management sometimes takes advantage of workers; he wants the government to guarantee jobs rather than opportunities; and he believes that workers should have more power. From his perspective, what are the constraints that led him to oppose the nationalization of the factories and mines? Some of them emerge from his discussion of big business. As a worker in a huge factory, he feels his own liberty more threatened by union decisions than by big business; he believes that big business should be credited for investing money into research; he fears monopoly (apparently including government monopoly); and he thinks an excess-profits tax will take care of the tendency of big business to cut back jobs and to grow even bigger through mergers. These beliefs, individual to O'Hara, constrain his views on the nationalization of industry; that is, they are the ideas that go with his opposition to nationali-

zation, that "prevent him" from supporting that policy, that would have to change if
he were to change his views. In a wider sense, there are, of course, cultural forces,
group pressures, information deficiencies, media discussions, authoritative statements
by respected leaders, and socialization limits that channel his thinking. He is not
aware of most of them; but as we examine "what goes with what" and why, his
reasoning is important. Even though he does not refer to a liberal-conservative continuum or use it as a "judgmental yardstick," and even though he is conservative on
"nationalization of industry" but is one of the two most liberal men in the group of
fifteen on the liberalism-conservatism scale, he has not thereby demonstrated a lack
of capacity to organize ideas. If, within a year or two, O'Hara were to find himself
unemployed, to blame this on a merger that he regards as monopolistic, and to change
his views about government ownership (perhaps at the same time that someone else
changes his views in the opposite direction), it would make little sense to call
O'Hara's changes "random"—that is, the product of many small forces of opposing
tendencies in society—even though the change process were to reveal to the analyst
a pattern resembling a random distribution. O'Hara would be then, as he is now,
basing his judgments on what he has known and experienced. There are political
philosophers, like Edmund Burke (1790), who would applaud this tendency.

Political reasoning is a term we may employ to refer to the ways in which
people justify or argue about their political beliefs. It bears the same relationship to
belief system that moral reasoning bears to morality and is discovered in the same
way: by finding out the grounds on which people base their beliefs. In the work of
Piaget (1965) and Kohlberg (1964), the ethical decision in moral dilemmas is not
so important as the ways in which decisions are made. Similarly, in logic, the important thing is the process, not the conclusion (which may be true but invalid);
fallacies are processual. Political reasoning is different from opinion formation, which
usually refers to external or unconscious forces that affect an individual's reasoning
process. Reasoning is not eliminated by stimulus-response sets or by conformity to
group pressure; these simply add new, if usually inarticulate, premises, such as "It is
better to agree than disagree" or "I have more to gain by making friends than by
defining new principles." These premises, it is true, impede the unraveling of the
reasoning by an observer, but an unconscious premise need not make the reasoning
illogical or ineffective or the object of forces properly described as "random." It is
just as well that it should be so, since we all have unconscious premises and for most
of us the most enduring political (or other values) are rooted in unconscious premises.
Much reasoning which seems illogical is seen to be logical as soon as the unconscious
premise is stated. In some ways, therefore, the injunction of logicians "Make certain
that all unexpressed premises have been included" (Black, 1946) is quite congruent
with the rules and practices of psychotherapy.

The view that there is something deficient about any political thinking that
does not employ the efficiencies of a "highly constrained system of multiple elements"
(Converse, 1964, p. 214) deserves examination. It may be true that "the idea organization that leads to constraint permits [the individual] to locate and make sense of
a wider range of information from a particular domain than he would find possible
without such organization." It may also be true that the liberal-conservative continuum offers economies of thought (and time and attention) and helps a person to
locate a policy and its implications in a set of ideas and values. But these advantages

by no means settle the case, for several reasons—among them the dubious value of economy, the fragile cohesion of ideology, and the weakness of logical constraints in ideological thinking.

Economy of thought is a value of uncertain priority; conformity and stereotypy also economize thought but are too costly of other values. Moreover, judgmental dimensions or yardsticks are often made up of disparate elements that cluster in people's minds. These elements may have no connection except that they are derived from a common intellectual source. An obsolescent tradition may be all that cements an ideology together.

Finally, it is not enough to say that elites "experience" ideologies as logically constrained clusters, if these bodies of thought are not, in fact, closely constrained by the rules of logic—which they are not. The next set of elites may have a quite different experience of logical constraint (the conservative of one era may believe that social security is incompatible with the premises of capitalism, while the conservative of the next era will find social security and capitalism quite compatible). While ideology is flexible over time, logical relationships should not be.

More specifically, one may agree with Converse (1964, p. 220) that conservatism consists of (1) caution in responding to new problems and reluctance to change, (2) resistance to welfare state programs and support for "free enterprise," (3) resistance to the expanding power of government, and (4) support for individualism and individualized solutions to social problems. This seems reasonable; it is compatible with the definitions of others (Huntington, 1957). But is there anything illogical or unreasonable in the following "nonideological" combinations: slow and cautious change in the direction of the welfare state; governmental intervention in society to give the individual more freedom from corporate control; accelerated change to restore capitalism to its former autonomy; enhanced use of governmental regulatory powers to make capitalism work.

Burke and Adam Smith do not necessarily go together. Violating conservative doctrine, a conservative president proposed a program of governmentally financed income maintenance; he also instituted price and wage controls. Experience makes clear what logical analysis could explicate: the reconstruction of arguments so that a chain of plausible (true?) propositions in proper form, with a set of distributed middle terms fulfilling the requirements of a logically valid chain argument, might be formed—with outcomes (inferences) that would embrace at least three of the four policies mentioned above. Yet they would be unlikely to be included together in a formal statement of ideology. As experience indicates, one can be quite logical in violating even conservative or liberal ideologies.

If we substitute *values* for *ideology*, referring then to *equality, community, piety, order,* and matters of that nature, do we discover a better set of constraints on individual policy choices? Operationally, if we know a person's values, can we predict his policy preferences? There are logical problems, psychological problems, and social problems in such prediction. One logical problem deals with the problem of degree. Thus, in the argument

The welfare of mankind is served by equality.

Equality is promoted by a confiscatory estate tax.

Therefore, the welfare of mankind is promoted by a confiscatory income tax.

the conclusion does not follow from the premises because it is not clear how much equality is included in the major premise. This kind of looseness is called the "fallacy of accident," and it is bound to plague any arguments involving values of unspecified degree.

A second logical problem, related to the problem of degree, stems from the plurality of values. Thus, it is plausible for a man who adopts the major premise above to argue as follows:

The welfare of mankind is served by high individual achievement.

High individual achievement is promoted by monetary rewards for achievement.

Monetary rewards for achievement are effective only if they accrue to the achiever's family.

Accrual to the family is denied by a confiscatory estate tax.

Therefore, the welfare of mankind is not served by a confiscatory estate tax.

Reasonable men do value both equality and the achievement motive; some also believe in the relationship of inheritable rewards as a stimulus to achievement. The apparent contradiction in the policy outcomes flowing from belief in these values is not likely to be resolved by abandoning one value for another. Instead, one might address the problem of degree ("great inequalities," not "modest inequalities," violate one's values) or adopt a belief that permits escape from the contradiction (inherited wealth is likely to be dissipated and hence does not lead to permanent inequalities; confiscatory estate taxes do not prevent gifts during the donor's lifetime). Values do guide policy conclusions; but as long as the degrees are not specified and the introduction of new causal connections is permitted, they do not, through the instrumentalities of logic, force a choice between values. (The usual escape of the equalitarians in such situations is to redefine *equality* to mean "equality of opportunity," but this was ruled out by our example. Nevertheless, redefinition of values to avoid self-contradiction is a standard escape from illogicality.)

The psychological grounds for evading logical constraints are reflected in the above illustration. Just as the person who is bound entirely by his ideology, so that experience does not have the power to change its elements, is an ideologue and unfree, so the person who governs all his policy recommendations by a single value is close to "obsession" or borders on "fixation" and is similarly unfree. The healthly person has multiple values, and he finds them often in conflict; his health is revealed in his toleration of the conflict and the means he chooses to reconcile the conflict, not in the way he makes all policy recommendations serve a single value, however economical that might be for him.

Since ideologies necessarily imply large causal theories, one may isolate causal theories for a brief examination. In what sense do they constrain idea-elements? The very largest ones—such as Social Darwinist theories of the survival of the fittest, Marxist theories on the necessary stages of history, and racial theories based mainly on genetics—all seem to dictate certain policy choices. Yet spokesmen for the National Association of Manufacturers, who adopt Darwinist views on domestic policies, also argue for protectionism in international trade; Chinese "Marxists" argue for abolishing intermediate stages and for moving from peasant (Asiatic) forms directly to communist forms; and racial theorists, upon finding Negro aptitude scores lower than Caucasian scores, may argue for differential education for the two groups but do not adopt their own "logic" upon finding that Japanese mathematical aptitudes exceed Americans'. Theories at this level guide policy choices, but one cannot say that they determine them; the constraint, therefore, is weakened by intruding considerations. Nor could one say that these intruding considerations weakened the rationality (as distinct from logic) of the policy preferences. On the contrary—at this level of theory, at least—societies are better served by employing them as heuristics rather than algorithms.

The mistake underlying reliance on the constraints implied by statistical clustering, scalar ordering, or acceptance of an idea cluster by an authoritative elite is based on the fallacious view that if some people see idea-elements properly clustering in a certain way, others should too. Such "constraints" or clusterings refer to neither logic nor rationality. Here it is important to repeat two points made earlier: (1) The uses of logic to constrain political thought may be weak (a) because mass publics do not understand or do not use the rules of logic and (b) because ideologies are rarely stated so as to permit close logical constraint. But in revealing the weaknesses of an argument, the employment of logical (critical) reasoning is crucial— especially for the critic of mass belief systems.[1] (2) Rationality is impossible to assess until the critic knows the ends pursued by the subject; only then may he judge whether means-ends rationality has been employed.

Connected to the concept of constraints is the tendency toward *contextualizing*. Most members of mass publics tend to fragment their views and to respond to issues or policies without regard to many other relevant considerations. Elsewhere I have argued that "one of the features of what is sometimes called 'understanding' is to grasp the context of an event; that is, temporally to know what went before and what is likely to follow, spatially to know the terrain, in human terms to see the play of the many motives involved. To understand an event in this way is to *contextualize* it; not to do this is to *morselize* it, to see it isolated from the surrounding features that give it additional 'meaning' " (Lane, 1962, p. 350). In examining this problem, I looked at three men representing three points between the morselized and the contextualized extremes of my sample. The issue was the discussion of Soviet-American relations—something rather distant from group interests that help many

---

[1] Even the classic case of the violation of logical constraint turns out not to have that property. McGuire (1960) performed some experiments, cited by Converse, in which persons who believe simultaneously in (1) expansion of welfare services, (2) cutting taxes, and (3) balancing the budget are deemed illogical. But the logic is not constraining for two reasons: each such person can argue for cutting something he does not care about and expanding welfare services and cutting taxes. Or, alternatively, he can argue, as did O'Hara, for a non-tax device to increase revenue—namely, a lottery. The constraint is in the middle-class ideology that does not think of lotteries as alternative government revenue devices.

people to locate themselves on an issue, but also not clearly guided by liberal-conservative organizing ideas, at least not any more.

Perhaps it might be said that another standard organizing "ideology" or quasi-ideology, internationalism-isolationism, might be helpful here. But, I believe, such a judgmental yardstick was as foreign to these men as was conservatism-liberalism. Nevertheless, there were distinct differences in the way they thought about Soviet-American relations—differences representing clear stages of development. These differences might be indicated by listing what the best contextualists do, in contrast to the morselizers. The contextualists include a time dimension (Russia "then," "now," and possible future changes); relate domestic and foreign policy; include various aspects of foreign policy, especially trade and military policy; look at the issue from the Russian side, especially possible Russian responses to American initiatives; refer to a theory or philosophy, such as the "philosophy of disarmament"; consider the effects of Soviet-American diplomacy on other nations (Lane, 1962, pp. 350–351).

Here the common man has gone beyond easy reference to his own experience, does not make any link to group interests, is not limited (by the interview situation, for example) to vague references to "the nature of the times," and does not clearly draw on ideologies or near ideologies. Yet, perhaps because he can be observed thinking and not merely responding, he cannot be said to be responding randomly and must be said to be constrained by values, information, and a modest understanding of other related events and issues. It is true that most of the men did not employ all of the contextualizing varieties of thought mentioned above, but almost no one employed none of them. If there was any one common judgmental yardstick employed, it was the degree of force or threat of force to be employed; by analogy it might be said that this way of looking at things did enlist personal experience (except that Russia is not easily personified as the man next door); but that particular yardstick (attitudes toward force, violence, war) escapes the subdimensions of the conservative-liberal yardstick the academic is tempted to employ. Something different from reference to an ideology, then, offers understanding and policy guidance; without standard ideological referents, these men were contextualizing a policy problem. In contrast, it might be argued, reference to an ideological posture would not only "constrain" policy thinking but would confine it. There are meanings of the term *ideology* that suggest defensive postures (Rokeach, 1960) such that the main objective of ideological policy thinking is to defend an ideological commitment, not to explore alternative policies as they affect values.

Finally some reference to the self-consciousness of an ideology is in order. It is true that most people can locate themselves on this dimension (only 4 percent of a national sample had "no opinion" regarding their own position on a scale running from "very conservative" to "very liberal"—American Institute Public Opinion poll, April 20, 1972), but many who do so have confused the two meanings of *liberal:* "generous," in one sense; "opposed to conservative," in another. I (1969) asked some sixty Yale students to explain in an ideological self-analysis what advantages they receive from their liberalism or their conservatism. In the process they had to set forth what they did believe. Typically they had great trouble in setting forth a coherent ideology. One of them, an extremely able young man who later spent five years in the Peace Corps expresses graphically what many others felt: "Trying to write this paper has proven to be a real bitch. I found that I don't really have any definite opinions, any logically constructed philosophy of life, not one of the way that society should be constructed or administered" (Lane, 1972, p. 127). One wonders how many "ideologues" captured in a survey net would, given the chance, have responded in the same way. And if that is true, it is problematic whether a judgmental conservative-liberal yardstick would prove to be an efficient economizing device for policy evaluation, however well it might predict "what goes with what" in a set of questions. One would, I think, prefer to see the political reasoning that employs these and other economizing central ideas, even if they are relatively unconscious, to arrive at policy decisions.

One alternative to the use of an ideology, like liberalism or conservatism, to guide a person in adopting an opinion is the use of reference to a group, like working class or Italian-Americans, for such guidance. A person using this group reference may believe that what is good for the group is good for him and substitute this reference for any further thinking about the matter. A generation of political scientists has developed the view that a group-reference or group-interest form of political guidance is not only the most common form but also the most fruitful and useful (Herring, 1940). They believe that the play of group interests in a free marketplace of interest groups produces a political balance benign for society. With qualifications, there is much to be said for this position. Since members of mass publics have only a dim and blunt perception of any political ideology that might inform their decisions, the group-reference solution may, indeed, not only be easier for them, but also guide them better toward decisions that are in their long-term interests. For these reasons one might differ from Converse's argument that reference to ideology makes for better opinions than does reference to group interest.

Economizing

The concepts that help a person organize his political ideas and that determine what ideas go properly together are not drawn primarily from some major judgmental dimension, such as liberalism-conservatism, but from more intimate sources, closer to the individual and the world he knows. Inevitably, if he has spent much time thinking about political-philosophical matters, he will employ the ready-made organizing concepts to be found therein. This practice is economical in the sense that it saves time and effort; it is efficient in the sense that these organizing concepts are designed to direct attention to policy implications. But most people have not spent much time on political-philosophical concepts; economy and efficiency for them require the employment of experience and reference to "contexts" closer to their own lives. We shall examine these contexts under the heading of a "core belief system" below, but first let us look more closely at the term *economizing*.

Among the dictionary definitions of *economy* are these: "the management or ordering of parts, functions, etc., in an organic or organized system; organization; also, a system or body so managed or ordered"; "thrifty administration"; "management . . . of an establishment . . . directly concerned with maintenance or productiveness." What, then, is economical political thinking? And what is the economy of the political mind?

One meaning or function of economizing in political thinking is *bookkeeping,* striking a balance between liked and disliked features of a political system. This has the important consequence of determining whether a person is, in sum, for or against the regime, the administration, a certain policy. Thus, people must manage their thinking so as to know where they stand on such large constructs as the following: (1) the constitutional order, the regime, the administration, and such various combinations of these as may be referred to as "the establishment"; (2) the net balance of costs and benefits flowing from the established order to the individual and the groups with which he identifies, compared to what he thinks he and they ought to have; (3) the net balance of influence the individual has, compared to what he thinks he ought to have.

Economizing also has a *consistency* function; that is, the management of the parts of the belief system in such a way as to bring together elements that have not been brought together before so as to reveal compatibilities and incompatibilities. These are of four kinds: (1) compatibility of ends—for example, the problems presented by simultaneous advocacy of individualism (the autonomy of the individual) and community (the familial model of common decision making and shared destiny); (2) ends-means compatibility—perceiving the relationship, for example, between welfare policy and preferences for "equal pay for equal work"; (3) means-means compatibility—that is, perceiving the way two policies complement or oppose each other (so that the economizing thinker would discover the difficulties in arguing at the same time for decentralized educational decision making and against revenue sharing); and (4) theoretical compatibility—for example, arguing for the overall principle of the inevitability of class warfare and for principles of mediation and arbitration in labor disputes.

Economizing, in this sense of managing the interrelationship of the parts, has a placing or *concept-attainment* (Bruner, Goodnow, and Austin, 1956) component; that is, the capacity to place the item into a set composed of elements whose shared properties are the important ones for the thinking at hand (thereby reducing the time and effort involved in appraising each item of an interrelated set of items individually). Thus, to know that TVA, Amtrak, and the Post Office are all examples of government public enterprise permits some economies of thought for those who support and those who oppose government ownership of the means of production. (For other purposes in the same general domain such concepts as *bureaucracy, public utilities,* and *service industries* are more useful.) The same economizing through assigning things (principles, events, policies) to concepts—that is, concept attainment —applies to such larger matters as strategic armament limitation treaties and the concept of the balance of power; reliance on unequal property taxes for educational financing and the concept of equality of opportunity; and licensing requirements for "subversives" and the concept of freedom of speech and of association. The economizing of course, takes place by relating principles to exemplars or genus to species.

Economizing takes place by recognition of the relationship of *part to whole.* In general, the stages of a process hang together because of their relationship to a set sequence: as cross-examination of witnesses may be related to due process in an adversary procedure, or as hearings may be related to the legislative process in American democracy. Or the part-whole relationship may be definitional; for instance, the court now says that "right to counsel" is part of "due process," arguing that the concept itself "logically" includes this protection. Things hang together as syndromes (spots and fever, for measles), with third-factor causes. Experience puts things together, as with conditioned reflexes or any kind of conditioning. Convention does this too, as in the sequence of phrases "thank you" and "you're welcome" or the defeated candidate's concession acknowledgment after an electoral defeat is apparent.

The economizing that links idea-elements to each other operates through (1) summation of good and bad and the consequent bookkeeping; (2) encouraging consistency (value compatibility, means-ends compatibility, means-means compatibility, theoretical compatibility); (3) discovering likeness in relevant properties (thus locating things in the same class covered by the same concept) and linking concepts or principles to their illustration or exemplars; (4) identifying parts and wholes—especially, for our purposes, parts of whole processes, but also parts of systems, organisms, syndromes; (5) employing the connections provided by experience, either conditioned or reflected upon; (6) definition, as may be established by an authoritative interpreter, like the Supreme Court or the supreme lexicographer; and (7) enlisting conventional arrangements, as in codes of behavior, linguistic usages, familiar juxtaposition, common origins. The mind, of course, must make the links to relate one idea-element to another; the thinking process may rest on observational acuity, interpretation of purpose or insight into function, free association (links provided by unconscious experience), analogical reasoning, conditioning, and/or inductive and deductive reasoning. But given these possible sources of relationships, it is too much to expect that the ordinary man, unused to the traditional judgmental yardsticks of Western political thought, would find these yardsticks the best or most economical way of relating idea-elements.

But there is another meaning of *economy*—namely, *thrift*—that is important. What is it that economical political thinking might be thrifty of, might save? I believe the answer is time and effort. (We will later examine the concept of economical as "efficient"—meaning economically productive of desired consequences.) I mentioned stereotypes above as economical of time and effort; so is a conditioned reflex. We need some criteria to decide what is a good use of thrift and what is a bad use. The criteria must rest first on alternative uses of one's time and effort; in this connection, some ideas from a recently published piece on the good citizen (Lane, 1972, pp. 299–317) may help to illuminate the problem.

For the concert pianist, who has no background in world events, little interest in public affairs, and a great and consuming love of music (and a social contribution to make there), the cost of developing a political philosophy and of relating this to a policy preference is high. For the Washington lawyer, with much interest, daily informational inputs, a capacity to employ experience and previously acquired skills in relating his idea-elements to each other and to their informing philosophies (values + causes), the cost is low. Thus, the thrift value of economizing on time and effort is very different for each person, even if the consequences (gains or losses) of a policy—say, a tax measure on identical incomes—are in many ways identical.

The calculations of cost and gain of political thinking are complex, as may be seen by the following formula (Lane, 1972, p. 311):

$$\text{Ratio of cost to gain in following the news on a chain of events} = \frac{\text{Cost of following and understanding the news} + \begin{array}{l}\text{Cost of modifying one's own situation according to an estimate of the impact of an event on the self}\end{array} + \text{Cost of any indicated effort to alter the course of history}}{\begin{array}{l}\text{Probable gain or loss implied by an event in the news}\end{array} \times \begin{array}{l}\text{Probability that the event will mature so that the indicated gain or loss will take place}\end{array}}$$

But even this set of calculations is more complex than at first appears. To every probability figure in the formula, one must attach a degree of certainty; that is, a weight indicating the confidence one attaches to the figure. Further, one must think in two different ways (as in statistical calculations) about the relative preferred risks in being wrong: Is it better to take action when one might be wrong, or not to take action when one might be right? Further, the costs of gaining the requisite information and calculating probabilities, certainties, and risks are greater than those involved in isolated reflection, for it is important to talk about these events and policies so as to rehearse one's ideas, receive criticism, anchor them in the judgments of others (Lane, 1962, p. 102). Thus, the time-and-effort cost figures run high.

But costs are to be evaluated as "high" or "low" not only according to the labor costs that may be calculated but also according to the benefits that flow from the "correct" decision. By what standard, then, might one judge a "correct" policy preference for a certain man? Marxists are willing to say that a working-class man who is not a socialist has misjudged his own interests, that he has a "false consciousness"; but history has not shown that even economically the working class is better off under socialist or communist regimes. In any event, the observer's judgment of the "right" and "wrong" policy preferences for a given person at a given time, with his plural values and multiple needs, rests upon shaky philosophical foundations and, I believe, flounders on the difficulties of interpersonal comparison that have given the economists such difficulties in comparing utilities of different persons.

The psychoanalysts have a better posture in determining what opinions and behavior are "right" for a specific individual. They seek to find out the complex needs and values that give enduring gratification to a patient, and then to guide him to give up coping patterns that provide short-term "secondary" or "neurotic" gain at the expense of long-term life satisfaction and to adopt behavioral and thought patterns that are expressive of *his* idiosyncratic enduring values. In the same way, one could say that a citizen adopts a correct policy preference when, after that degree of reflection indicated by the above formula, he expresses his long-term interests and values, whatever these may be.

This standard does several things. First, it avoids substituting the observer's values for the subject values, the mistake made by the Marxists. Thus, it permits an individual to prefer security over economic gain, popularity or respect of peers over class interest, freedom of choice over security, without the stigma of "irrationality," which such choices often provoke. Second, although this standard makes use of the individual's own enlightened self-interest as the criterion of right and wrong for his own preferences (and thus adopts a modified relativism), it does not strip the critic of his own judgment regarding the rightness or wrongness of an individual's policy preferences from another point of view, especially from the critic's own view of the public interest. It is not a totally relativistic standard; that is, it does not imply that everything is as good as everything else, according to whatever an individual or a culture may say is preferable.

In addition to the bookkeeping and consistency functions, then, economizing in political thinking takes into account the following calculations: (1) the costs of the time and effort in framing a policy and in participating in other ways; (2) the probability of making any difference in the world through this expenditure of time and effort; (3) the opportunity costs of the time and effort expended; and (4) the probability of adopting a correct policy, where "correctness" depends upon maximizing one's own enduring values and need gratifications.

These references to "making a difference in the world" and to "maximizing values" suggest that a political idea is a production good; it is instrumental in achieving other values. This is true in two senses. The first has to do with the societal product. From this point of view, the "correctness" of the idea does, indeed, depend upon information and social theories regarding ends-means relationships. In the second sense, the idea-element is productive of individual benefits in a person's social milieu: career advancement, popularity and friendship, family harmony or sense of independence from family. For these products, the correctness of the idea is to be judged not by what the world would be like if the policy were implemented but rather by the effects of the expression of ideas on other people. Like the calculations expressed in the formula above, the calculations here are complex: Group A is made happy to degree X, but Group B is made unhappy to degree Y; and these scores are multiplied in each case by the estimate of the importance of each group's degree of happiness to the holder of the opinion and summed in the bookkeeping operation described earlier.

But, as everyone knows, opinion elements are consumption goods as well as production goods; the mere expression of an opinion without further consequences has values: it may reveal to the spokesman his mastery of a subject, his own importance, his high moral posture. Opinions express anger, determination, depth of despair. The very expression of opinions is literally self-serving; it may provide the same gratification that a writer finds in writing for his secret file of unpublished works. But again, the calculations regarding the benefits gained are not simple; for the individual is both agent and critic, as the terms *guilt* and *sober second thought* imply. He may not be pleased with what he has said or even what he has thought. Consequently, it is a *net* benefit or gratification that must serve as the criterion. In sum, therefore, taking the individualistic point of view outlined above, we must estimate the correctness of an opinion according to both the societal and the social-production functions and according to the consumption function of an opinion. It is against these net benefits, weighted and summed, that the costs of an opinion must be assessed. Only then, it seems to me, does the term *rational* make sense.

Core Belief System

If the judgmental dimensions of Western culture are rather poor organizing principles for political thinking (on grounds of their elusive constraints on particular policy issues and their remoteness from the ongoing lives of individuals), and if social values are only little, if any, better, where shall we turn for such principles? What does constrain political thought? The clue to the answer, I think, lies in taking further the experiential and personalistic point of view outlined above and searching for ways in which ordinary individuals organize their political thinking. From this point of view, we need to know how a person thinks about *himself in society*. The answer to such a question is likely to be at the level of inarticulate axioms—inarticulate, at least, until we ask the right questions. The first of these terms, *himself*, may be conceived as an *identity;* the second term, *society*, we will examine as a universe of *human sets*.

To interpret the interaction of these two elements, the individual employs ideas that are the common man's analogs to the philosopher's several domains: What and who are authoritative? What values and goals are to be sought and worth seeking; what needs do these values and goals reflect? What is the individual's moral good; what is an appropriate moral code? What causes effect individual and social change; how shall we explain social events? What concepts of time and place are to be employed? What is it to "know"; what is true? How shall truth be discovered? If we know these things about an individual or group, we can predict his or the group members' policy preferences better than if we rely on the concepts of Western political thought. These personal-philosophic concepts are ingredients of constraint; it is these things that cause one idea-element to be associated with another in a political belief "system."

Identity. An identity (Erikson, 1956), of course, is the complex answer to the simple question "Who am I?" The answers are, in the first place, social; that is, placing the self in a social context of country, ethnicity, occupation, family. In this sense they link to the reliance on group reference that most studies find important in voting decision and in policy preference. In the second place, they are individual. Asked to describe themselves, the men of Eastport (Lane, 1962) mentioned such qualities as "imagination," "getting along well with people," "I don't blow my stack at the least little thing." Such concepts of individual identity can be linked to personality theory, with its concepts of conflict resolution, need achievement, approval motive, aggression, dependency, and so forth.

If the concept of identity is closer to the person than, say, "liberalism-conservatism," it seems more remote from policy preferences. But the links are there. A person's identity tells him something about his self-interest and, because it includes group reference, his group interests as well. Further, it tells him something about his proper role in political affairs, what he can and ought to do, what is appropriate for him. In some ways an identity gives information on what one "ought" to get from government, what one ought to give to government (am I rich or poor?), what rules are appropriate for "me." By its social reference, an identity establishes fault lines in society—indicating friends, allies, opponents, even enemies. These may or may not follow class lines; for most Americans they follow ethnic lines. And an identity, through establishing levels and orientations of trust and distrust (often by generalizing from the self), indicates a posture toward self-government and toward governmental reliability and responsiveness.

Human Sets. For the individual, society is made up of institutions and people; but the institutions, being generally remote, become personalized or at least identified with human groups who are thought to control, or benefit or suffer from, their operation. The common man is anthropomorphic. The human sets that people (including historians and social scientists) identify are these: families, cliques and associations, races and other ethnic groups, communities of region or place, nations, occupations, rich and poor and middle strata, religions and secular ideological groups, interest groups, parties. Stratified, these become castes and status groups, social classes, specialized elites.

In framing an identity, a person is likely to place himself among these human sets, and at least two general postures toward them are important. The first is the relationship of the individual to his set—his mobility in and out of the set and his capacity to dissent; in short, his individualism. The second posture is the relationship among sets: the lines of status, the terms of conflict, the nature of national and international community. The democrat believes in the plurality of sets, adjustment within them, and fluidity between them.

Authority. Authority is power plus legitimacy. Legitimacy was accorded to government by the men of Eastport (Lane, 1962) on three grounds: (1) the people (people like me) in the end control governmental policy; (2) the government is interested in us and is generally responsive to our needs; (3) the constitution is a legitimate source of power, and the rules laid down therein are sanctified, workable, and fair. Further, the means of selecting political authorities give us good leaders, kept good by their responsiveness to the people.

But these views do not give orientation on what to believe when opinion on a particular policy is divided. Asked whom they would turn to for advice, the people of Eastport were reluctant to name a person or a group or a leader; they wanted to vest that authority in themselves, whatever the reality of the case might be. Further, "experts" had to be challenged, for they might be interested parties. What is authoritative here, in the realm of political knowledge, is the *process of argument*— but not too prolonged, for too much talk is fatiguing. Charisma, the magical leader, is not eagerly sought.

Concepts of authority probably do give some constraint to mass belief systems but less than might be expected. Knowing whom an individual trusts might help to predict what idea-elements go together; but in their own terms the common men are selective shoppers, "buying" this idea here and that one there.

Values, Goals, Needs. Values are discussed in the language of philosophy and anthropology, needs in the language of psychology; but they come together, in some measure, as source and destination, motive and expression, cause and reason. They are not reciprocal, for although every need seeks a value, values do not always reflect needs—partly because values include both what is desired (needed) and what is desirable (preferable but not necessarily preferred). As mentioned above, generalized values tend to be weak constraints on political beliefs, but this is not true of needs.

It has been argued (Maslow, 1954) that needs are hierachically ordered in such a fashion that one must satisfy certain of them before one can consider others, and there is some evidence that this is true. Thus, a man must satisfy his physiological needs first; it is a condition of survival. The political belief systems of persons struggling with these needs (Knutson, 1972a) is short-term, egoistic, concrete; the test for a policy preference is "What immediate benefits in food, shelter, relief from sickness and pain does this policy offer?" The second-order needs for safety and security are little different. Both of these needs lead to subservience to the strong in exchange for food and protection—the patron-client relation the world over. At the third level is the need for affection and belongingness, sometimes expressed as love, sometimes as community, a form of generalized love. Deprivation of this need leads to hostility, prejudice, autism; those deprived adopt political beliefs reflecting these views in a generalized mistrust of others. Fourth, the need for esteem, generally latent as long as the more basic needs are unsatisfied, emerges as a stimulus to political activity—but also as an inhibition. The search for esteem to satisfy deficiency feelings in this respect need not give political orientation (left or right, authoritarian or equalitarian) but gives urgency to the search and indicates the rewards (recognition) that must be satisfied. Self-esteem and the expressed esteem of others are separate but related; both are important. Finally, there is self-actualization—the need that seems close to our concept of self-fulfillment. This need is sometimes expressed in the phrase "What a man can be, he must be." Like the highest stages of moral reasoning, embodying empathy and internalized conscience, self-actualization embraces others as well as the self. The self-actualized person, whether conservative or liberal, is humane, open-minded, present and future oriented, undefensive, cosmopolitan.

The theory embraces both an ontogeny, in the modified sense of the psychic evolution of the individual, and a phylogeny, in the sense of stages of history. Analysts have not had great success with stages of history, as Comte, Spengler, Sorokin, Marx, and now Charles Reich (1970) all bear witness. Stages of individual development have fared better—especially where there is no inevitability attached to the developmental theory. The theory of a need hierarchy has progressed beyond speculation, for several recent studies (Inglehart, 1971b; Knutson, 1972a; Simpson, 1971) reveal that a need-deficiency theory does help to explain political belief systems.

From my own investigation of the basis of political thinking in need gratification, examined through the instrument of student ideological self-analyses (Lane, 1969), it seems quite clear that liberalism and conservatism are themselves shaped by the uses to which an individual puts his opinions, their serviceability for what he wants to accomplish. Thus, the young men who expressed and revealed a need to be liked and a concern about their likeability tended, more than others, to bid for the affection of underdogs with a liberal "tolerance" and to require of the government the same kind of propitiation of others that they required of themselves. Those who were marked by aggressive needs might be either liberal or conservative; but those whose aggression was restrained largely by fear of the consequences to themselves were conservative, while those whose aggression was restrained by concern for the victims tended to be liberal (see also Thibaut and Riecken, 1955).

We are interested in what holds opinions together, making for clusters instead of isolates. As we have said, the deductive logic from, say, conservatism to a policy preference has only weak constraining power, but the logic of experience in gratifying needs may be more powerful. In *Political Thinking and Consciousness* (1969), I inferred some chains of reasoning for several young men who were particularly close to their families and wished to continue their familial identity, continuing roughly in their fathers' footsteps. The constraints represented by these internal arguments, first for a conservative and then for a liberal, help to show how certain idea-elements hang together. Gardiner, a moderate conservative from a prosperous home, "says" (here I interpret and paraphrase):

> Parental support and encouragement have led me to adopt the family ideology and model, and to accept my family's status and the value placed on status. I accept the status and status values. From them I receive a flow of benefits: ascriptive leadership, deference, indulgences, power. These benefits serve to validate my parental code and values, for they prove to pay off. Paying off in the present, these values become the basis of my future calculations, the basis for political argument and rationalization. Therefore: I am a Republican, a capitalist, a "moderate" conservative [p. 279].

McDonald, a liberal, makes explicit reference in his self-analysis to the analogy between the society and the family; he comes from a liberal professional home. He could be said to argue (as I reconstruct his argument):

> Society rewards and punishes like the family; the behavior and attitudes which are rewarding in the family are properly and naturally transferred to social behavior and attitudes. Control of aggressive and rebellious feelings and more or less compliant behavior toward paternal (good) authority is rewarding; it produces reinstatement of love and acceptability. Generalized social rules and norms are desirable, legitimate, not too constrictive; hence I accept them, and rebellion is unwarranted. Big business is bad authority, and hence criticism and challenge of it are not dangerous; socialist dogmatic authority is too constrictive, hence not acceptable (yet "something I intellectually need"). The Democratic party allows latitude for deviance, hence is acceptable and rewarding. Therefore: I follow social rules and norms; I am against the power of big business; I am not a socialist; I am a Democrat—and for the welfare state [pp. 281–283].

The point to be made here is that conservative and liberal ideologies are mediating concepts between the individual identity (with, in these cases, a need for continuing identification with the family) and policy preference.

Not moral axioms but moral reasoning is the clue to the relationship between morals and political beliefs. As with politics, one has a better understanding of what a man believes if one knows the way he thinks than if one has a map (or, more likely and less informatively, an inventory) of his beliefs. In the study of *Political Thinking and Consciousness* discussed above, we found some young men seeking, rather painfully, to reveal a high moral stance to the world and to themselves. Those who adopted a primitive moral reasoning based upon external rules turned out to be conservative; those who were guided by internalized consciences—on Kohlberg's (1964) scale those at stages 5 and 6—were liberal. Furthermore, for the middle-class person, an impression-management morality (stage 3) tends to produce a liberal orientation, probably because an expressed preference for a social arrangement providing some element of gain for groups other than one's own, the deprived and suffering, gives a better "impression" than would a preference for social arrangements clearly beneficial to oneself and others like oneself. For the working class, this argument would not hold.

Yet moral codes do not greatly constrain policy preferences—partly because moral prescriptions and premises must necessarily conflict; that is, one moral consideration is selected at the cost of another: efficiency (parsimony) at the cost of generosity, love at the cost of work, civic duty at the cost of familial duty, and so forth. This inevitable conflict is reflected in the moral apothegms of society: "Blessed are the meek" but "Fear God and take your own part"; "It is a fine thing for rich people to be philanthropic" but "Take heed for the morrow" (suggesting a more self-interested thrift). Prudence and initiative come into conflict in the familiar opposition: "Make haste slowly" or "Look before you leap" versus "A stitch in time saves nine" and "He who hesitates is lost." In morals as in the law general principles do not decide individual cases, for the life of the law (or of morality) is experience. And, as Converse (1964) found for most of his sample, general ideologies do not decide policy preferences; experience is more important.

Explanations of Events.   Policy preferences imply the beliefs that some governmental action will effect some preferred change; thus, they rely on theories of cause and effect. Lying behind the conservative ideology is a theory of the effectiveness of the market in achieving a just distribution of rewards; the liberal (in the American but not the European sense of the term) believes that governmental action can sometimes distribute rewards better, or at least can modify injustices or inefficiencies in the market allocation. Cutting across this explanatory principle is the principle of "cabalism" (Lane, 1962, pp. 113–130), the belief that small groups of powerful men or interests, either good or bad but always out of sight, decide things. These "cabals" might work through manipulating the market or through manipulating government, or most probably both. This is a kind of conspiratorial theory of cause; it relieves those who fear that no one is running things but frightens those who prefer to believe that things are pretty much what they seem.

Those who adopt great-men theories of cause may be conservative (the captains of industry are the great men) or liberal (the innovative presidents are the great men). But those who believe that some kind of organic process, perhaps beneficent but at least unchangeable, is at work in society—so that natural laws inscrutable to mankind are controlling our destinies—will most likely be conservative. These "organicists" hold that conscious human intervention, in the form of laws and programs, is impotent or, if not that, malignant in its ignorance of consequences. Conversely, those who have a "scientific" approach to society, believing that through informed inquiry we can discover the cause-effect relationships between human actions and their consequences, may be liberal, for the government can make things better, but they may equally be conservative, for it may be that private enterprise is a better and more beneficial agency of change.

But any great optimism about the constraining effects of the adoption of causal theories of these global character should be discouraged by consideration of the Marxist, the Christian, and the social scientific paradoxes. The Marxists believe that there is a historical inevitability to the dialectical process leading to the socialist society, but they also believe that dedicated communists are necessary to achieve their goal. The Christians believe that divine providence controls human events, but also that their own freely chosen actions are central to the guiding of human destiny.

And social scientists believe that there are no uncaused events, and yet they do not give up their own sense of undetermined choice. It is the old free-will dilemma, to which no solution is in sight.

Setting for Political Interpretation. The currently popular phrase employed to account for the malaise of the third world, "the frustration of rising expectations," reflects one way in which a sense of time may be out of phase with the maturation of events. In another sense, as the economists point out, the difference between preferences for money "now" versus money "later" is reflected in the interest rate; but since many individuals may discount the future at a higher rate, they may be improvident. A welfare society is designed to help such people through imposing mildly coercive social security tax provisions. But, of course, the main theme in time perspective, reflected in the value orientations employed by F. R. Kluckhohn and Strodtbeck (1961), is the differences among a past orientation (as revealed in the thinking of American Indians), a present orientation (Mexican American), and a future orientation (Protestant Americans). These orientations have constraining effects on policy preferences, as the very terms *reactionary* and *progressive* imply.

The constraints upon policy preferences and other political thinking made by a sense of "place" are often embedded in concepts of community. What is the relevant community to be taken into account: the village, the region (American South?), the nation, the Occident, the Afro-Asian world? The men of the Eastport study (Lane, 1962) clearly considered locality important in their private lives (because of family and familiarity), whereas in politics the nation was most important, for the media had nationalized the news. In the study of student orientation (Lane, 1969), on the other hand, localism was minimal; some of the students regarded the American nation as their theater of important events and their criterion of relevance, whereas for others the world order (in which the American nation was one important unit) was significant. By providing these criteria for attention and relevance, the sense of place and community guides policy preferences fully as much as any ideological posture toward liberalism or conservatism.

Epistemology. The main epistemologies go under the names *intuition, faith,* or *divine revelation; rationalism, empiricism,* or (a mixture of the last two) *scientific method.* All of them lodge somewhere on the abstract-concrete continuum. The emphasis in the preceding discussion—upon experience as constraint versus ideology as constraint—*seems* to argue, contrary to much informed opinion, that the concrete end of the continuum is more useful for opinion formation than abstraction. I do not accept that inference, for the reason that abstraction from experience, employing experiences comparatively and analytically, is a form of abstract thinking with as many credits as the deductive process of comparing case with principle and deciding accordingly. Similarly, a failure to compare, contrast, anticipate, or in other ways to rehearse alternatives in the light of experience, reduces the coherence and consistency (as described above) of a political belief system. Without the rehearsal of alternatives, order is given to responses by the sequences in which they are presented; they are dealt with in the terms presented, one at a time. This procedure gives over to "society" or "history" the power to give order or coherence to a belief system; the capacity to anticipate and to consider alternatives takes back this power for individual use.

The capacity to abstract the self from the environment, to see the self now and the self later as related but different, to hold in solution the emotional angry self while one deals with the problems of self and others in less angry terms—such a capacity gives to information a greater utility, and to reasoning a greater persuasive power.

These three capacities—relating event or problem to concept, rehearsal of alternatives, and separation of self from environment—are all capacities toward the abstract end of an abstract-concrete dimension. They are the products of maturation, education, intelligence; and they are informed by personal experience.

Other dimensions and concepts of knowledge guide the constraining functions in organizing belief systems. If one is not good at cognitive balancing, one tends to organize one's views by preference for message source rather than message content. If one is dogmatic, one organizes beliefs according to their utility in defending the dogma (and this is the risk implicit in the use of ideologies as constraining devices). Steeped in a philosophy of science, a man asks for causal chains and evaluative criteria before he decides—if, indeed, he ever does decide.

5

POLITICAL
SOCIALIZATION

Richard G. Niemi

Political ideas—like the consumption of cigarettes and hard liquor—do not suddenly begin with one's eighteenth birthday. The analogy does not stop there. For in their political habits—as in their consumption habits—young people are influenced by parents and other family members and by the schools. And yet the inculcation of traditional values and behavior is not completely successful; for whether it is in politics or in deciding what to smoke, new ideas and habits often come from the younger members of society. The analogy also pertains to the history of research on political learning and on learning about drinking and especially about smoking. While both politics and smoking have been around for a long time (sometimes simultaneously, as in smoke-filled rooms), only in the last fifteen years or so have serious efforts been made to understand the respective learning processes. Understandably, there is much to be learned—witness the naïve thought that stopping broadcasting advertisements of cigarette smoking would curtail the habit; but we have come a long way in a decade and a half.

I thank Roman Hedges for critically reading a draft of this chapter.

The present chapter, henceforth restricted to political learning, will survey much of the knowledge gained in recent years. But it will do so with an eye toward understanding the meaning and importance of specific research findings that have been uncovered. In addition, areas in which further research is necessary will be pointed out.

We will not try to provide a precise definition of the term *political socialization*. (For attempted definitions see Easton and Dennis, 1969, p. 7; Sigel, 1965, p. 2.) Greenstein (1968b, p. 551) properly indicates that socialization can be thought of either very narrowly—meaning, chiefly, civics classes in high school—or broadly—meaning "all political learning" (see also Greenstein, 1970a). To us the main feature of most socialization studies is that they involve learning at the preadult stage. Indeed, one contribution of the field of socialization is that it alerted researchers to the notion that political learning has roots deep in childhood. But we shall not confine our attention solely to preadults. We will on occasion draw from adult studies; and later on we will have to confront directly the question of the relationship between early learning and adult political life.

Youthful Political Learning

It is generally assumed that preadult political learning is important because what is learned early will have a significant impact on adult political attitudes and behavior. It is argued, for example, that one of the difficulties of managing a newly formed nation is that individuals bear no allegiance to those particular political boundaries. Instead, citizens of the new nation retain loyalties developed in the past and consequently have little interest in or loyalty to the new nation (LeVine, 1963). Similarly, when new and different regimes come into power in a nation, the new leaders often attempt to establish new modes of political thought—sometimes by reteaching adults (Fagen, 1970, pp. 318–320) but more often by changing the system of educating youth (Azrael, 1965, esp. pp. 257–258).

Even in established nations, the presence of "subcultures of discontent" (Greenberg, 1970c, ch. 5–8) is seen as potentially disruptive of stability and peace. Conversely, preadult attitudes favorable to the existing political system are often thought to be a major source of system stability (see esp. Easton and Dennis, 1969). Particularly in times of unrest and instability, the underlying support for a nation which develops early in life goes a long way toward explaining the maintenance of political systems.

Although the correctness of this assumption is a matter of utmost importance, and one we shall return to later, we will dwell on it here only long enough to make one further point. If, as seems obvious, youths do not suddenly develop political ideas at age eighteen, and if early learned attitudes are of cardinal importance, then it behooves us to seek the origins of political learning. But that implies not stopping with sixteen year olds or fourteen year olds, but studying children as early as they begin to develop political or politically relevant ideas—whenever that time is. We do know that children as early as first or second grade can articulate ideas about authority and about political figures. We also know that children's responses are sometimes unstable (Vaillancourt, 1970), which raises the question of just when *meaningful* attitudes take shape. In any event, the search for the origins of political learning has led to an awareness that children develop political or quasi-political notions at a very early age. Thus, the studies we cite below involve youngsters from from the first or second grade on.

At the same time that we recognize the consequences of political socialization for political systems, we should also recognize that political learning is important for the developing personality of each individual. Thus, for example, while we might be interested in political efficacy partly for its effect on the political system, we might be equally concerned with how a person's feeling of competence in dealing with the political world and society in general helps him meet his own needs and goals in life. (This subject is discussed at length by Smith, 1968b.) Similarly, we might wish to observe the development of moral judgment and behavior from the point of view of the society (to determine, for instance, how well a population obeys written and unwritten rules and laws); but we might also wish to consider a more individualistic point of view (to ask, for instance, why some individuals develop habits that deviate from conventional moral patterns and what happens to them as a result).

History

It is something of a tradition to note that writers ever since Plato have been concerned with the political socialization of youth. One writer (Connell, 1969) even delights in pointing out that Plato was far from the earliest author to concern himself with this matter. However, the era of serious academic attention is much shorter indeed.

In the area of general socialization, without a particularly political focus, studies have been done at least since the turn of this century. Such work has a long history and is still actively pursued today. Piaget alone has done research over a forty-year period. More recently, several journals, such as *Child Development* and the *Merrill-Palmer Quarterly,* have been devoted solely to this area. The political relevance of much of this literature is marginal or at least not clearly spelled out. But it is useful for gaining a wider understanding of child development and for placing political developments in a broader framework of general socialization.

Political socialization as such has some of its intellectual origins in educational research, which also goes back to the turn of the century. In particular, we might mention the scholarly study of formal aspects of civic training made in the late 1920s and early 1930s by Merriam (1931) and others. Another part of the intellectual ancestry of political socialization research is found in the studies of national character—studies undertaken during World War II and after (Inkeles and Levinson, 1969)—which attempted to specify internation personality differences and to understand their developmental origins. Finally, several scattered studies in the 1930s, the 1940s, and the early 1950s concerned political attitudes specifically. Many of these are summarized by Hyman (1959). In addition, there were studies of politically related attitudes, such as children's perceptions of social class and race (Hollingshead, 1949; Stevenson and Stuart, 1958).

The continuous and direct study of political socialization began in the middle to late 1950s under the impetus of three more or less simultaneous developments. First, Hyman's book *Political Socialization* (1959) reviewed much of the scattered literature that existed up to that point, and indelibly impressed upon political scientists and psychologists that political learning is indeed a challenging and worthy subject in its own right. The other two sources were studies begun under the direction of Easton and Hess at the University of Chicago and by Greenstein in New Haven. The rather surprising findings of these two studies about the idealization of children's political ideas have been a source of fascination and, with the college uprisings of the mid-1960s, a source of consternation. Ultimately, most of these findings were summarized in three works (Greenstein, 1965; Hess and Torney, 1967; Easton and Dennis, 1969). The New Haven and Chicago studies were both based on quasi-longitudinal research designs aimed at identifying the developmental path of political attitudes over the elementary school years. We will draw freely upon them in talking about children's views of authority.

In the mid-1960s another study, with a different research design and emphasis, was undertaken at the University of Michigan. In this study interviews were held with high school seniors and their parents, teachers, and school principals, with the purpose of more adequately determining the sources of young people's ideas. A major report of this study is forthcoming (Jennings and Niemi, 1974).

As with any emerging field of inquiry, texts soon appeared (Dawson and Prewitt, 1969; Jaros, 1972), along with several readers (Sigel, 1970; Greenberg, 1970c; Adler and Harrington, 1970; Orum, 1972; Dennis, 1973), review essays (Sears, 1968), and an extensive bibliographic effort (Dennis, 1971). These sources provide an overview of what has been done to date.

More recently, studies of political socialization have taken at least three new directions. First, there are studies of subgroups of the American population, especially groups likely to hold attitudes different from those of middle-class American whites. Examples include studies of Appalachian youths (Hirsch, 1971), studies of blacks (Lyons, 1970; Rogers and Taylor, 1971; Greenberg, 1969, 1970a, 1970b; Liebschutz and Niemi, 1972) and studies of Mexican Americans (Cornbleth, 1971; Garcia, 1972). Second, the host of studies of socialization in other countries indicate the degree of generalizability of some of the findings on American youths. Finally, the few methodological studies undertaken (Vaillancourt, 1970; Niemi, 1973) get at some of the serious methodological questions that must be considered when any new population, but especially a young population, is first studied.

Most of the findings cited below are based on survey research, although some studies using projective and semiprojective techniques (such as Adelson and O'Neil, 1966; Knutson, 1972b) and content analysis (Litt, 1963) have been used. (See also Chapter Fifteen of this volume.) Admittedly, survey research can be unreliable, especially when used with young children. Respondents may give unstable answers, may check substantive answers when "don't know" would be more appropriate, or may give what they see as socially acceptable responses. Moreover, closed-ended survey items often fail to bring out the way in which children organize their rudimentary political thoughts and the way in which their political ideas relate to nonpolitical (but politically relevant) orientations. Despite these possibilities, few psychologists, and even fewer political scientists, have actually used other methods, although there is a growing movement in that direction (Lane, 1969; Dennis, Billingsley, and Thorson, 1968; Greenstein and Tarrow, 1970; Merelman, 1971a).

Having now seen the rationale for and the history of studies of preadults, let us turn directly to what some of the studies have found.

Children and Political Authority

Do children think about political authority figures; if so, what do they think? The answer to this question is quite thoroughly documented in the Chicago and the New Haven studies. Both of these studies, along with the large number of pretests conducted in the Chicago study, were conducted in the late 1950s and early 1960s and were limited almost entirely to white, urban children. We shall have to return to the question of just how representative these results are of other times and other individuals. Moreover, both studies relied on survey responses, and it has been suggested on the basis of in-depth interviewing that survey responses may overestimate the extent to which children view authority favorably (Knutson, 1972b).

The Chicago study obtained questionnaires from second- through eighth-grade children and the New Haven study from children in the fourth through eighth grades. Thus, when we speak of early political learning, we have in mind children as young as seven or so. In fact, it has been suggested that some rudimentary political notions are brought to kindergarten by children, but it is difficult to establish this in any systematic way because of the problems of verbal communication about relatively abstract subjects at that age.

Easton and Dennis (1969, pp. 391–393) provide four terms to describe major features in the development of children's feelings about political authority: politicization, personalization, idealization, and institutionalization.

Politicization refers to the fact that young children fairly quickly learn that there is an authority above and beyond family and school figures. This politicization often comes about in rather simplistic ways—for instance, when a father obeys traffic laws so as not to run afoul of the policeman—but it is no less effective because of that. By the time children are seven or eight years old, then, they have become aware of an external force that demands some support, obedience, and (usually) respect. They may understand this external force only sketchily, and terms such as *government* may be foreign to them until they are older. But awareness of such a power makes possible the development of other political ideas from an early age.

Personalization refers to the fact that children first and most easily become aware of political authorities through individual men—most commonly, the president and the policeman. Collectivities such as Congress and the Supreme Court and other, more abstract concepts such as government are apparently less easily understood, although understanding increases throughout the elementary grades. It is significant that personalization should be found in a country such as the United States, where individuals are presumably subordinate to the constitutional system. This finding suggests that the young child's emphasis on individual personalities is due to cognitive limitations. To put it simply, it is far easier for the young child to learn about the president than about a group such as Congress.

A finding of particular interest to us older cynics is that idealization also characterizes children's views. That is, to most children political authority seems trustworthy, benevolent, and helpful. To a surprising degree children respond that the policeman and especially the president "would *always* want to help me if I needed it," that "they almost *never* make mistakes," that "they know *more* than anyone." Most children agree rather strongly that what goes on in the government is all for the best. Most agree with the blanket statement that all laws are fair. Such extremely idealistic responses soon fade away. But if indeed the earliest learned attitudes persist to some extent in later life, the child's idealization of political authority does help us understand the attitude, on the part of numerous adults, of unquestioned support for the government.

Finally, the development of children's viewpoints is characterized by institutionalization. Young children gradually learn to associate with depersonalized objects such as the government and Congress. In fact, they transfer to them some of the qualities previously attributed to the president and the policeman. This, of course, is a necessary step in a country in which allegiance is owed to constitutional authority rather than individual leaders.

As children get older, these images change quickly and dramatically. In part we have already described this development. They come to emphasize institutions more than individual personalities. They become aware of deficiencies in individual persons and inequities in the law. There is a growing differentiation between role and incumbent, so that, for example, the presidency remains highly regarded even if the incumbent president is seen as less than wholly praiseworthy. Interestingly, while teenagers' views of political figures are far more realistic (or less heroic and benevolent) than those of young children, they are still considerably more trusting and less cynical than those of adults. Clearly, the process of growing cynicism continues well into adult life, although at a slower rate than during the elementary and high school years (Jennings and Niemi, 1968a; 1974, ch. 10).

How generalizable are these patterns? Do they characterize today's children, and do they characterize the views of minority-group children and those of other groups in the society? The best available answer seems to be that the *patterns* described are highly generalizable, although the *level* of positive or benevolent views of political authority may often be lower than what was found by the earlier researchers. In other words, children today, when compared with older children and adults, still seem to be relatively favorable toward the government and specific authority figures. At the same time, their views appear to be somewhat less favorable than the views of the children in earlier studies.

Comparisons across time are difficult to make because of variations in the sample, in questions, and in methods of gathering data. Nonetheless, there are some suggestive results. Tolley (1972) found that President Nixon's actions regarding the Vietnam war received considerably less than full support from children. And in a study conducted in the late 1960s, Liebschutz and Niemi (1972) found that white students in Rochester, New York, were considerably less likely than the children in the earlier Chicago study to consider all laws fair. At the same time, these later researchers found the same overall pattern of much higher belief in the fairness of laws at the early grades. Thus, although more directly comparable data are needed, changes seem to have occurred in the level but not in the pattern of support for political authority over the past decade.

Among subgroups in the population, the most obvious group of children who might be expected not to share the developmental pattern described above are urban black children. We are speaking, of course, about young children and not adults, but the common viewpoint seems to be that young blacks very quickly learn "what the score is" and soon develop negative images of political authority. Interestingly, however, the data on this question are far from one-sided. Jaros (1967), for example, reports almost no differences in views of the black and white children in his sample in Detroit. Jennings and Niemi (1974, ch. 5), Rogers and Taylor (1971), and Kenyon (1969) found almost no differences in political trust between black and white students. In contrast, a number of studies (Dennis, 1969; Lyons, 1970; Greenberg, 1969, 1970a, 1970b; Liebschutz and Niemi, 1972) report fairly consistent differences in the expected direction. Reviewing these studies, Abramson (1972) made it clear that the explanation for these contrasting results lay in a rapid decline in political trust in the late 1960s, a decline especially notable among blacks.

Turning to contrasts between sexes and across social classes, we find some differences in the expected direction. For example, brighter children become politicized faster than those who are not so bright. Girls personalize and idealize political authority more than do boys. Lower-status children likewise have more personalized and more benevolent views of authority. More important, however, the pattern of development is again very much the same in every case: an early personalization and idealization followed by a decline in those features and a rise in other characteristic views, such as cynicism and a belief in the importance of institutions.

Just how generalizable are these patterns, then? Are there instances of real deviation from the development we have seen among most children in the United States today? Several of the key features we have pointed out are probably universal. Politicization, for example, must occur everywhere. Under some circumstances this process may unfold more slowly than in the United States (Pammett, 1971); in other instances it may occur very quickly. If children are raised by the state, so to speak, in communal groups organized or controlled by the central authority, they may very quickly learn about the transcendence of political authority. In fact, they may learn that political authority is the major outside source of authority—rather than the authority of family, of schools, of secondary groups, of religion, and so on. An attempt to bring about this kind of socialization process has in fact been made in the Soviet Union (Azrael, 1965) and probably also in China, with the collectivization of child rearing and with the centralization of the schools. It has not worked as well as political leaders might like it to because of difficulties in breaking down some authority relations—especially familial and religious authority; but it certainly has had some effect.

Personalization and institutionalization likewise are probably nearly universal, because, as mentioned earlier, it may simply be easier for children to grasp individual personalities first and abstract conceptions later. We would not go so far as to say that this pattern can never be reversed, but in the normal course of events it probably describes the development of most children.

Idealization seems to be the one concept that clearly is not universal. Some young children, in fact, grow up disliking political authority—evidencing "hostilization" (Easton and Dennis, 1969) rather than idealization. The one outstanding example of this kind of development was found by Jaros, Hirsch, and Fleron (1968) during research in the Appalachian region of eastern Kentucky. A few figures call attention to the sharpness of the contrast between their findings and those in earlier studies. When asked, for example, how hard the president works compared with most men, only 3 percent of the respondents in the Chicago study—but 41 percent of the children in Knox County, Kentucky—felt that he works less hard. Similarly, when asked their view of the president as a person, 8 percent of the students in the Chicago study, in contrast with 26 percent of the Knox County children, said that he is not a good person. What is perhaps most significant, however, is that the pattern of development itself is different among the Appalachian children. There seems to be little change in their responses by age, so that even relatively young children are not impressed by or are even cynical about political authority.

The extent to which idealization or hostilization characterizes young children in other cultures is a fascinating question. There are only hints of an answer. Hess (1963), for example, found that the degree of idealization is strongly related to age in the United States and Japan, while feelings about authority figures are virtually unrelated to age in Puerto Rico and Chile. His samples, however, were small and were intended only to be suggestive. There have been a number of suggestions that French children are relatively cynical about political authority (Wylie, 1964, esp. ch. 10; Roig and Billon-Grand, 1968; Abramson and Inglehart, 1970); but, as Greenstein and Tarrow (1969) note, sound empirical evidence is lacking. At the very least, then, we can conclude that idealization is less than universal and that there are probably significant instances of children who develop a hostile attitude toward political authority at a very early age.

We might well ask at this point just what the consequences are of the pattern of youthful development that we have surveyed. Since the extremely benign, and indeed naïve, views of early childhood are quickly replaced by more realistic and even cynical views of adulthood, are the early attitudes of any real consequence? In part this question is impossible to answer until we resolve the difficult issue of just how much constraint early learning places on later attitudes. Obviously, the childhood attitudes are rejected in favor of more realistic ones, but it may well be that the earliest learned responses are never totally forgotten and, moreover, that adults would be more cynical than they are were it not for the early idealization of authority.

If what is learned early in life is indeed influential in later years, the implications of early idealization may be of singular importance. That is, childhood views of political authority may be an important source of stability in the American political system (Easton and Hess, 1962; Greenstein, 1965). This point might be made most forcefully if we consider the possible consequences of altering the educational system to purposely instill in children at the earliest possible age a questioning attitude toward everything, including the foundations of political authority. A completely objective presentation might conceivably be made of the good and bad points of a variety of political systems. Individuals could be encouraged to make up their own minds about which system is best and about the proper means of bringing about that kind of system. Such an instructional program probably would bring about a gradual weakening of support for the present system and give rise to the probability that change would occur.

Whether such a program would be good from a normative point of view depends on one's attitude toward change and stability. Recently many young people in particular have argued that our political system is stagnant and that change is called for. If change is considered desirable, perhaps altering the socialization system in the direction indicated would help bring it about. But, of course, any subsequent system then established would be subject to the same forces for change. Instability of political regimes, as is common in many parts of the world, might be a far-reaching result. In contrast, the present socialization system, with its tendency toward early idealization, promotes stability in the political system, with the concomitant possibility of stagnation.

The point we are making is not that stability is more or less desirable than change, but that the socialization system plays a crucial role in the balance between stability and change. Alteration of the method by which we socialize children, whether accidental or planned, may very well have far-reaching consequences for the future of the political system.

We might point out in passing that the socialization of attitudes toward authority may also have serious consequences for individual well-being. One might wonder, for example, whether an individual is more likely to develop ego strength and a feeling of identity if he first learns that the political authorities in his country are extraordinarily good and only later is introduced to some of the complexities of making political judgments; or whether it is better from this perspective if he is trained from the beginning to have an open mind, to examine questions for himself, and to make his own decisions about what he considers best.

Before leaving the area of children's views of authority, we should call attention to one other type of study—namely, children's awareness of and understanding of national identity and foreign cultures. (A good summary of this work is found in Davies, 1968.) It has been found that children often have an egocentric view of the international system. A child can understand that children in other countries are "foreigners," but he finds it difficult to grasp that from the point of view of individuals in other countries he himself is a foreigner. In addition, certain geographical notions—for instance, that a city is within a state and that a state is within a country—are difficult to conceptualize (Piaget and Weil, 1951). Although strict stages of development may not be followed (Jahoda, 1963a, 1963b, 1964), certain viewpoints, along with an understanding of abstract concepts, generally do not develop before specified ages (Adelson and O'Neil, 1966, 1969). Finally, it has been documented that quite early in life children may develop unflattering stereotypes of other cultures and nations (Lambert and Klineberg, 1967).

Agents

Considerable effort in the study of political socialization has centered around the question of where children get their attitudes. Most of the work has focused on the family and the school, with proportionately less work involving peer groups, the media, and other sources of influence. Likewise we will concentrate here most heavily on the family and the school.

Family. Until recently one could easily summarize the academic and the popular stereotype of socialization in the family: "We are all like our parents, especially our fathers." Before more firm evidence was gathered, the reasons for this view seemed substantial enough. First of all, because the family is the earliest socialization agent, we can easily slip into thinking that it must therefore be the most important one. Second, since the young child is emotionally attached to family members, the considerable impact of family viewpoints would seem likely. Third, certain findings about partisanship, at least as they were typically interpreted, supported the notion that children generally adopt parental attitudes (Maccoby, Matthews, and Morton, 1954; McClosky and Dahlgren, 1959; Hyman, 1959, ch. 4; Campbell and others, 1960, pp. 146–149). Moreover, researchers were hard pressed to uncover significant amounts of adolescent rebellion regarding political matters (Nogee and Levin, 1958; Lane, 1959a; Middleton and Putney, 1963). Finally, it seemed obvious that fathers are more instrumental in passing along political views than mothers, although this viewpoint was probably due as much to male chauvinism as to empirical findings.

Since partisanship formed the primary empirical basis of the traditional stereotype, we might begin to summarize the empirical evidence that is now available by taking a close look at this attitude or orientation. (On the concept and measurement of partisanship or party identification, see A. Campbell and others, 1960, 1966.) Our discussion draws heavily on Jennings and Niemi (1968b; 1974, Part II), who interviewed a national sample of high school seniors and their parents. Some of the main results are also supported by an imaginative "sibling" study conducted by Hess and Torney (1967, pp. 97–99), in which the similarity between siblings was compared to that between matched pairs of nonsiblings. The results below are presented largely in terms of correlations. The use of correlations is intended to make the comparisons as comparable as possible across items differing in numbers of categories (so that percentage comparisons necessarily would vary widely).

Turning to partisanship, we find a correlation between parents' and students' partisanship not of .8 or .7 or even .6, as we might have expected, but of .47. How might we evaluate this particular correlation? From one point of view it is not too "bad" a correlation. It is certainly in the expected direction, and it is clearly much greater than zero. There *is* a definite similarity between parents and their children. Partisanship *is*, to a degree, passed on from generation to generation.

Some further understanding of the meaning of this particular correlation may be gained by taking a more detailed look at the underlying relationship. First of all, as a simple percentage table would reveal, there are not really very many families in which the parents are Democrats and the children Republicans, or vice versa. In fact, such families amounted to only 7 percent of the total in 1965. Hence, in this extreme respect there is considerable continuity in the American political system. On the other hand, if we divide the population into Democrats, Independents, and Republicans, we find that only about 60 percent of the student-parent pairs show identical partisan feelings. This means that if we consider the Independent category— and movement into and out of this category—more carefully, there is a greater degree of partisan fluidity than the previous comparison suggested. Among the Democrats, for example, one third of the students deviated from their parents at least to the degree of becoming Independents. Among the Republicans fully half of the students departed from parental ways, and among the Independents the figure was about one half. Thus, there is far from a one-to-one correspondence between parents and students in the matter of partisanship. With these percentages as a background, the .47 correlation seems to make considerable sense. It indicates only a small number of major deviations, representing movement all the way across the partisan distribution, but it also indicates a fair amount of shifting back and forth among narrower ranges of the partisan dimension.

Turning to other orientations studied, we find some additional surprises. There is no need to go through them all in the detail that we did with partisanship, but a few examples can be drawn upon to illustrate significant points. Consider, for example, the student-parent relationship for political cynicism. Cynicism is a general sort of dimension; it is not a response to one particular item or to a particular event but, rather, a generalized orientation toward the political system and toward political authority as a whole (see Aberbach, 1969, and the references cited therein). Thus, even if individuals' reactions to specific events and questions were to differ, we might expect a reasonably strong resemblance between the overall or generalized attitudes of young people and their parents. It is something of a surprise, therefore, to find that the correlation for this particular measure is only .12. Similarly, on a general measure of political interest—quite apart from particular manifestations of this interest, such as reading about politics or participating in politics—the correlation is only .12.

Having seen these results, we might turn instead to particular behaviors or attitudes toward narrowly defined issues in the hope that perhaps these would yield higher correlations. This hope is not very well fulfilled, it turns out. On some salient issues the correlation rises to as much as .3 or so. On certain other issues, however, it is even lower than the correlations cited for generalized orientations. Indeed, out of some twenty different orientations measured (Jennings and Niemi, 1974, ch. 6), there was only one—namely, presidential preference in 1964—for which the correlation rose above that observed for party identification. In the case of presidential preferences, the correlation was .59—still not of a magnitude sufficient to assume complete correspondence between parental and student preferences.

Some of the implications of these findings will be taken up later. Two other questions need to be confronted at this point. First, we might reasonably ask why the correlations are not higher than they are. Second, we might want to know whether the student-parent correlations are very high for certain types of students—for instance, those who are especially interested in politics. These questions might be answered in a number of ways, but here we will concentrate on a few of the major results.

One possibility is that the correlations would be higher if we used children's perceptions of parental attitudes rather than parents' own reports about themselves. That is, children may think they are more similar to their parents than they really are. The results of a whole set of analyses indicate that, for high school students at any rate, the student-"perceived parent" correlation is likely to overestimate the true student-parent correlation by about .1. Recall, for example, the true student-parent correlation of .47 for partisanship. The student-"perceived parent" correlation in this case is .58. Hence, as we would expect, the correlations involving perceptions are greater than the true student-parent correlations. However, the increase is not so large as to explain entirely why the actual relationships are no higher than they are.

Another reason that the student-parent correlations are not considerably higher is that other parental characteristics impinge upon the development of student attitudes. In other words, some family influence is not monitored by the student-parent correlations. Thus, for example, when a parent who feels that he is a Democrat votes in a particular presidential election for the Republican candidate, his children are much less likely to adopt his attitude than when his vote is consistent with his stated partisanship. Ironically, in such instances it is the parent's own behavior that leads students away from parental paths.

A third, glaringly important factor in explaining the degree of student-parent similarity and dissimilarity is the extent to which the parents themselves agree politically. For most political attributes, the fact of having similar parents raises considerably the probability that youths will follow in their footsteps. For example, whether the parents agree with each other seems to be more important than the family's degree of interest in politics, the compatibility of family members, demographic features such as region, or personal characteristics such as race and sex.

Even when the parents agree, however, student-parent agreement is far from complete. Most of the correlations reported by Jennings and Niemi are still below .40 (the highest being .57 for partisanship and .63 for presidential preference). Even when combined effects are considered, there are few sizable increases in the magnitude of the correlations reported. Even, for example, when the parents agree with one another, the parents and the child are both interested in politics, and family members get along well with each other, there are still many instances of student-parent disagreement.

A complementary point concerning parental influence involves children of parents who disagree with one another. Whether we look at the agreement of these students with their mothers or with their fathers or with some amalgam of the two parents, the typical student-parent correlation is far below what is observed when the mother and father agree. Thus, while there is a set of homogeneous parents whose children are more like them than overall comparisons suggest, a complementary group of students are frequently unlike their parents. This, then, is another factor that holds down the overall student-parent agreement rates.

There remains another question to be considered: the question of the father's influence on the children versus the mother's influence. Recall the stereotyped notion that politics is a man's business and that most socialization can therefore be traced to the father. This hypothesis, like so much widely believed but little-tested lore about the family, has proved to be resoundingly incorrect. The balance of influence between the parents appears to be remarkably even and, if anything, is tipped in the mother's favor. Evidence for this statement is found in a comparison of the student-mother and student-father correlations in families in which the parents disagree. Of some twenty comparisons made, the student-mother correlation was higher than the student-father correlation thirteen times, with three being dead heats and four showing at least minimal advantage for fathers. The differences usually were not very large, but the results clearly deny the one-sided influence of the father. The same conclusion was reached in a study of college-age children by Thomas (1971). Interestingly, another recent study suggests that in matriarchal Appalachia the influence of the mother is considerably stronger than that of the father (Hirsch, 1971, pp. 39–41).

Clearly, these conclusions about the evidently much smaller impact of the family than was previously thought deserve further consideration, for they have implications concerning the entire socialization process. Indeed, they are so important that we will come back to them after we have looked at other socialization agents.

Another factor that needs to be considered, especially by those well versed in psychological work, is the potential impact of family relationships. Psychologists, for example, have studied the effects on children when the father is gone for long periods of time (Tiller, 1957; Gronseth, 1957; Lynn and Sawrey, 1959; Burton and Whiting, 1961; see also references in Walter and Stinnett, 1971, pp. 81–82). Only a few political scientists have picked up this lead. Pinner (1965) suggests that parental overprotection leads to political distrust and disaffection. Langton (1969, ch. 2) suggests that children from maternal families are more authoritarian and less politically interested and efficacious than children from nuclear families. Lane (1969, ch. 14) has related identification with the family to political feelings of college-age students. Clarke (1973) finds that blacks in father-absent families are more cynical about politics than are those in two-parent families.

Studies of family relationships have not yet progressed to the point that outstanding and well-documented conclusions can be drawn from them in regard to politically relevant dimensions. But they clearly define an area in which future study is needed. They also call attention to the need for being cautious about concluding that the family in all its respects has little influence on the child's political development.

A second qualification to our earlier summary of parent-child similarity is the likely fact that there are significant differences across geographical and cultural boundaries. Butler and Stokes (1969, ch. 3) found that in many respects the pattern of political socialization is very similar in Great Britain and the United States. They note, however, that in one sense fathers are more important in the socialization process in Britain, because many of the British respondents could not recall their mother's political feelings; however, this inability to recall the mother's partisanship is declining among the younger voters. Converse and Dupeux (1962), in a classic article on France, point out that in that country many individuals do not know even their father's political persuasion. As a result, they contend, the socialization process is severely altered; specifically, partisan identification is considerably curtailed. Whether the relationship between socialization and partisanship observed by Converse and Dupeux will generalize to other countries remains to be seen, although there is suggestive evidence that it does not fully apply to Great Britain (Tapper and Butler, 1970). In any event, it is clear that various historical and institutional characteristics alter the development of party identification and of the influence of the family thereon (Converse, 1969; Dennis and McCrone, 1970).

So, too, there are cross-national differences in other characteristics of the family. Almond and Verba (1963, ch. 12) observed that participation in family decision making varies from one country to another. However, in all the countries that they studied, participation in family decisions is related to what they call *subjective competence* (political efficacy). Likewise, Langton (1969) notes that maternal families are much more frequent in Jamaica than in the United States, and while mother dominance of the nuclear family is found here, it is only a partial analog to complete absence of the father.

School. Trying to assess the role of the school in the political socialization process is a most fascinating if perplexing task. With all the resources devoted to the school and with the amount of time that children spend within school walls, we would like to think that we get some return on our collective investment. With our devotion to civics courses at certain grade levels, it seems only right that certain kinds of attitudes and orientations should be developed or strongly reinforced by this effort. And teachers naturally are frustrated if their efforts are not met with some development in the attitudes and behavior of their students.

Now in some ways there can be little doubt that the school has a significant impact. In sheer volume of knowledge possessed by an individual, whether it be knowledge of political or nonpolitical material, the school almost certainly plays a predominant role. And yet when it comes to political ideas and attitudes, it is far less clear just what role the school (grade school, high school, or college) plays. Let us begin by reviewing some of the conflicting research results.

Several well-known studies argue and/or show that the school or a particular course within a school has a significant impact on political attitudes. In most cases, however, a more or less serious qualification must be added to the statement of positive effects. Hess and Torney (1969, p. 101), for example, conclude unequivocally that "the public school appears to be the most important and effective instrument of political socialization in the United States." Yet their conclusion has been properly criticized (Sears, 1968; Niemi, 1969) on the ground that their evidence shows merely that significant changes take place during the elementary school years and that there is no necesary link between these changes and what actually goes on in the schoolroom.

One might also cite Newcomb's (1943) study of the effects of Bennington College on the students enrolled there. This is an excellent study, which convincingly shows that the college had a strong and real impact. And yet it is clear that this was an extreme result, not often to be duplicated; Newcomb's own study shows that several other colleges in the Northeast failed to have the same kind of impact on their students.

A number of other studies lend additional support for the impact of the school. Litt (1963) found that civics classes had a uniform impact on certain political attitudes and a significant effect on other attitudes under some but not all conditions. Patrick (1972) reported that an experimental course, entitled American Political Behavior, achieved some of the desired changes. Levin (1961) and Langton (1967) found that the partisan or class environment in the school had an effect on children's attitudes, although it should be noted that this was an effect of the informal milieu rather than of the content of the course work. One might also draw on studies of the college, which generally show "decreasingly conservative attitudes toward public issues" (Feldman and Newcomb, 1969, p. 326) between the freshmen and senior years. All of these studies together, along with many more casual observations, suggest that schools often make a significant impact on the development of political attitudes.

Nonetheless, the qualifications that we added to the above findings, in addition to a number of more negative results to be mentioned, indicate at a minimum that the effect of the school is far from uniform. A major study by Langton and Jennings (1968) found virtually no impact of civics courses on a cross-section sample of high school seniors, although these courses did have a meaningful impact on the black students in the sample. Although the results of this study must be qualified— since, for example, the study did not take into account the possible impact of other kinds of courses—the national scope of the sample, the variety of the effects looked for, and the utter absence of effects raise a serious question about the impact of civics courses.

One of the pretests reported by Hess and Torney (1967, pp. 8–10) suggests a broader conclusion. Questionnaire results revealed almost no changes between the freshmen and senior levels of high school in political interest, activities, and a variety of political attitudes. While these data can be countered with some positive findings of change (Hyman, 1959, p. 53; Jennings and Niemi, 1968a), the wide array of measures used by Hess and Torney weigh in their favor. Similarly, Merelman (1971b) comes to basically negative conclusions about the role of the school in students' civic training.

Some aspects of the informal milieu of the school have also been subject to question. Several studies have found little or no effect of participation in extracurricular activities, whether at the elementary school level (Hess and Torney, 1967, pp. 120–125) or at the high school level (Ziblatt, 1965).

Finally, although the results are by no means completely one-sided (Feldman and Newcomb, 1969, pp. 19–23), the various college studies lend themselves to the general conclusions cited above. Specifically, political science courses apparently do not increase political interest among students (Somit and others, 1958), and even presumably new and exciting ways of teaching about politics apparently do no better in stimulating interest and learning than do more traditional ways (Robinson and others, 1966).

Many of the same mixed findings pertain to studies done abroad (see Coleman, 1965a; Dawson and Prewitt, 1969). In new nations, for example, the schools allegedly bear an important part of the socialization of national identities (LeVine, 1963; Coleman, 1965a, p. 22). Presumably they are especially effective in countering the more traditional socialization of the family and can be manipulated to promote the interests of the new national unit. While this argument sounds convincing, a case study in Uganda (Prewitt and Okello-Oculi, 1970) suggests that manipulation and control of the education system does not work as easily in practice as in theory: "However attractive programmed political education might appear on paper, the political and administrative realities caution us not to expect significant results" (p. 620).

With all of these conflicting reports and conclusions, what are we to conclude about the school? One conclusion seems inescapable. The effects of the school are highly variable—depending at least on the quality of the teacher, the class material, the social and political composition of the school and classroom, particular circumstances of time and place, and even interactive effects such as the correspondence between what is taught in the classroom and what is informally taught outside of school. A second conclusion is more programmatic in content. It is suggested rather uniformly that extracurricular activities seem to have virtually no effect on students' political views, such as their feelings about democracy. While such activities might well be justfied on other grounds, it is difficult to support them on the basis of their supposed contribution to the development of democratic citizens.

The conclusion about the variability of the school's impact deserves further consideration. My own feeling is that the school has an enormous impact, but precisely what affects each student is so variable that it is difficult to measure the overall impact of any one component part. A particular course, for example, may have an important effect on two or three students because of their particular interest in the course, their precise stage of development at the time of the course, or the way the class material coincides with parental and peer influence. The same course may have no effect on the rest of the class. Similarly, a particular teacher, or a particular teaching style, may "turn on" certain students while at best not turning off the rest of the class. Effects may be even more specific than these examples suggest. A particular reading or a portion of a particular reading may have special significance for one person in the class while for the rest of the class it follows the proverbial path in one ear and out the other.

Thus, a particular teacher or a particular set of lectures or a particular set of readings or a particular class composition each may affect only one or two students in an entire class. Yet considering that during a three- or four-year period of high school and four years of college a student has a large number of classes, it is fully possible that every single student is affected in a serious way at least at one or two points during his schooling. The point is that if we measure the effects of individual components of schooling, and even of individual classes, we might find very little effect, even though over the course of four years nearly everyone is affected and some students deeply moved a number of times.

Such a view of the overall impact of the school has at least two consequences. The first concerns the way in which we look for school effects in future research. If we continue to look for the impact of a particular kind of teacher, or one particular class, or one particular method of teaching, and so on, we are likely to continue getting mixed results. Occasionally we will come upon a teacher or class or method that will have a broad impact on a group of students, but most often we will not. If instead we concentrate on analyzing individual students, trying to see what the effects of all the components of the school were on each of them individually, and only then aggregating across individuals, we might get a good estimate of the overall impact of school on young people. We might also be able to specify how many were influenced by teachers, for example, even though any one teacher may have influenced only a few students. An approach stressing the individual would also make fuller use of the gradations in development of children at the same age or grade level. Such variations have received little attention in the past, even though they no doubt help account for the variable impact of particular classes and of school curricula generally.

The second consequence of viewing the school in the way suggested is that it becomes much more difficult to evaluate curriculum and other school changes since it is clear that students will be differentially affected by any proposed changes. Some will be positively affected, some negatively, while many will not be affected at all. Nonetheless, we might in some ways be in an improved position. We might, for example, have a much improved estimate of what proportion of students was affected in what way by social studies courses."

Such a point of view admittedly might reduce or eliminate our ability to generalize about the effects of particular components of the school situation. It could likewise serve as an excuse to avoid procedures such as students' ratings of teachers, on the grounds that each teacher should be expected to reach only a small proportion of his or her students. This is not, of course, what we suggest. But we do feel that viewing the educational process in a more individualized or idiosyncratic fashion would allow us to estimate more precisely the overall effect of the school. In the long run, it might also help us design better tests of the effects of particular school characteristics.

Peers, Media, and Events. Families and schools have received by far the most attention of all socialization agents. Several other agents should be mentioned, however. There is a considerable literature on these agents, but most of it is not concerned with their effects on political views of young people.

Analysis of peer-group relationships is complicated by the variety of ways of defining and studying them and by the difficulty of carrying out adequate study designs. Thus, for example, while sociometric networks of friends have often been determined, seldom has the next step been undertaken—actually interviewing individuals *and their friends* in order to see just how homogeneous the friendship groups are and to make inferences about the influence of friends. One such study concluded that, outside the area of partisanship, students are more like their friends than unlike them and sometimes even resemble their friends more than their parents (Jennings and Niemi, 1974, ch. 9). Moreover, it is clear that similarity among friends is not an artificial product of social background similarities. In addition, the influence of friends seems evident from the finding that when friends and parents agree, student-parent similarity is enhanced, while when friends and parents disagree, student-parent similarity declines.

Other studies (Levin, 1961; Ziblatt, 1965; Langton, 1967) support the notion that informal peer groups are influential during and after adolescence. These studies suggest that the informal milieu is more important than participation in formal group activities. Studies of nonpolitical subjects (Hollingshead, 1949; Coleman, 1961) support this conclusion. The studies also indicate that peer influence increases over the adolescent years, although Hirsch (1971, pp. 71–77) has argued that this is not true in Appalachia because of its matriarchal culture.

An interesting cross-cultural perspective on peer influence is provided by two recent studies of child rearing abroad. Bronfenbrenner (1970) studied collectivized child rearing in the Soviet Union. He argues that in this system peers are very important in teaching and regulating behavior but that at the same time there is more adult direction and leadership than in our own country. Peers are also seen as important in Israel's kibbutzim, although again the setting provides adult leadership and guidance (Bettelheim, 1969). Although these examples may seem quite distant from our own culture, a substantial increase in day-care centers in this country would involve some of the same features as described in these two studies. It will be worthwhile for future researchers to pay close attention to the political and social ramifications of this kind of more collectivized child rearing. Interestingly, both Bronfenbrenner and Bettelheim conclude that there are valuable aspects of raising children in collectivized settings. Whether day-care centers can and should provide the same advantages (without even greater disadvantages) is an important and exciting new area for study.

In the modern world, where so much of our time both as youths and as adults is taken up by the mass media, one might expect the media to be a prime socialization agent. The last word on media influence is not yet in. As more and more sophisticated "packaging" is developed, the potential for massive, unidirectional influence is enhanced. Nonetheless, the media so far—instead of changing people's attitudes—seem primarily to reinforce attitudes formed elsewhere (see references in Dawson and Prewitt, 1969, pp. 198–199). Whether this situation will continue is uncertain. While increasingly sophisticated uses of the media may be developed, other factors may work against massive influence. Ironically, it is sometimes suggested that the large-scale development of cable television, with specialized channels for conveying news and public affairs in depth, will erode rather than add to people's political understanding. Presently, when all three major networks broadcast a particularly newsworthy item, such as the national conventions, people are forced to watch them or to abandon television completely. If at some future date such programs are carried only by specialized channels, many people may abandon political viewing in favor of westerns, situation comedies, and old movies.

Finally, we would be remiss if we did not point out the significance of political events to the socialization process. A commonly cited example is the so-called "Depression generation." The Depression and the images it helped form in people's minds played a dominant role in shaping American political party competition over the ensuing generation. And perhaps we now have a "Vietnam generation" of people who are more alienated, cynical, and uninterested in conventional party politics than the previous generation. There is no doubt that a major event affects the people who live through it—especially the people who are coming of age during that event (Beck, 1974). One readily observes, for example, the increasing proportion of Democrats among people who were in their twenties during the decade of the 1930s (A. Campbell and others, 1960, p. 154). Similarly, differences between political "generations" are readily observed in contemporary Britain (Butler and Stokes, 1969, ch. 11).

What is needed now are more precise measurements of just what constitutes a generation. For example, just how different are the attitudes of youths who came of age in the early 1960s and the late 1960s? How homogeneous are members of the Depression or the Vietnam generation? And especially, how and when do the effects of an event lose their impact? For example, to what extent will those who grow up in the 1970s be part of the Vietnam generation? Presumably they cannot escape some of the cynicism characteristic of the late 1960s, but the events of those days will probably have less impact than on individuals who lived through them. But just how to measure these differences has not yet been determined. Cohort analysis (Evan, 1959; Crittenden, 1962; Glenn, 1970; N. Cutler, 1970; Klecka, 1971), a relatively new type of study, may provide us with a far better understanding of the extent and the precise nature of the impact of events on the development of political attitudes. Clearly, this is a fruitful area for future study and for the development of new measures and methods of analysis.

Early Learning and Adult Political Life

To this point we have talked almost exclusively about preadult experiences. Now we must confront directly the question of how relevant these experiences are for adult political attitudes and behavior. There are at least two ways of approaching this problem. One way is to ask whether there is late as well as early learning or whether most political learning[1] takes place prior to, say, the adolescent years.

A few years ago it was reasonable to argue that almost all learning takes place

---

[1] We will not deal here with socialization into particular roles, such as that of legislator (Barber, 1965) and a variety of nonpolitical occupations (see the references and discussion in Brim and Wheeler, 1966).

during early childhood. It now seems clear that a significant amount of political learning continues well into adulthood.

If the patterns of political development in childhood are quite similar across social groups, however, they are quite different across social groups of adults. Education, above all, makes an important difference in the mode of development during adulthood. To take but one example, media usage continues to rise into late adulthood for people with less than an eighth-grade education. The same curve slopes upward more slowly as education increases, so much so that among college-educated people there is, if anything, a slight decline after the college years (Converse, 1971; Jennings and Niemi, 1974, ch. 10).

The greatest amount of change seems to take place relatively early in adult life, but it is surprising to us how much change continues into middle adulthood and even to retirement age (A. Campbell and others, 1960, p. 162; Easton and Dennis, 1969, ch. 14; Jennings and Niemi, 1974). What happens after retirement is only now being properly studied, with the increased awareness of and interest in what happens to older people generally. Whether people gradually disengage from political life or maintain their interest and awareness is a subject of some debate (Cummings and Henry, 1961; Glenn and Grimes, 1968; Glenn, 1969; Verba and Nie, 1972).

It is clear, then, that adult attitudes are not completely determined by childhood development. Of what significance, therefore, is early learning? There is, as one would suspect, not nearly enough evidence about this point, but the data that do exist support the notion that early learning does influence later development in important ways.

First, however, we must be clear about exactly what the question is that we are asking. Often the question is phrased "Do *early* or *later* experiences have a greater impact on the attitudes and behavior of adults?" Almond and Verba's (1963, ch. 12) comparison of family and the school versus job experiences suggests this formulation. The same point seems to be raised by the Prewitt, Eulau, and Zisk (1966–1967) study of whether early socialization or later political events make the greater difference in legislators' role orientations. It is to be expected, I feel, that correlations between present attitudes and those a short time ago (or related present attitudes or experiences) should be higher than correlations between present attitudes and attitudes from, say, twenty years ago. If this is what we mean by the attitudes of twenty years ago being less important, then this formulation and method of study would be appropriate. But such a result does not seem to me to mean that attitudes learned twenty years ago are unimportant or of no consequence.

We might more appropriately ask how high or low the correlation is between present attitudes and those of twenty years earlier. Only if we continually find very low or nearly zero correlations between early and later attitudes can we argue that socialization has no effect or is unimportant. (Even then we might still want to look for connections between early, basic values and later attitudes.) From this perspective I would not want to argue that early attitudes are less important than attitudes or events more closely related to the present time, although they are clearly less adequate predictors of current attitudes or behavior.

Only a few true panel studies exist (studies in which the same respondents were interviewed at more than one point in time) from which we can determine the similarity of attitudes at widely spaced intervals in time. Bloom (1965) summarizes a number of such studies. Unfortunately for our purposes, most of these studies deal with nonpolitical topics, although one deals with a "conservatism-radicalism" measure. Of five measurements over a fourteen- to twenty-year period beginning in early adulthood, the correlations were .22, .38, .53, .57, and .60. Obviously these are all of a sufficient magnitude to support the notion that what is learned by early adulthood acts as a significant constraint on subsequent developments.

The most extensive long-term, directly political panel study was carried out in the early 1960s by Newcomb and his associates (1967). Earlier we noted Newcomb's study of the tremendous affects of Bennington College on its students in the 1930s. In the early 1960s Newcomb located most of the women who were in the original sample and reinterviewed them. He then tested to see whether those who had been converted to a more liberal attitude in college had now reverted to their precollege views. Such a test is by no means trivial, for it is clear that what was liberalism and conservatism in the 1930s would not have the same connotation today. And, of course, one could not repeat precisely the same questions that were used in the earlier study. Nonetheless, Newcomb shows convincingly that Bennington did have a long-term effect on the women who attended it in the 1930s. Interestingly, Newcomb found that a surprising number of Bennington graduates remained in liberal social circles. This is perhaps another illustration of the effects of their having been converted. That is, they may have deliberately chosen liberal friends, hence finding support in their adult years for their newly found liberal views.

The pieces of evidence cited are, of course, far from adequate. In particular, none of the studies examines the continuity of attitudes from early or middle childhood to later years or over the critical period of late adolescence to early adulthood. Fortunately, a study of the later period is now beginning (under the direction of Jennings and Niemi). Nonetheless, in spite of the need for additional research, the presently available evidence strongly suggests that socialization at one point in time does have long-term effects. The assumption that early learning is an important factor in the developmental psychology of political attitudes does receive support.

Political Socialization and Social Change

Social events and political socialization research combined in the 1960s to create an intriguing intellectual puzzle. On the one hand, the point was made that if young children had benevolent attitudes about political authority during the late 1950s and early 1960s, then why did these same individuals react strongly against authority in the middle to late 1960s? Similarly, if we adopt the traditional view that children are much like their parents, then why was there a rejection of traditional values during the 1960s? On the other hand, if we accept at least tentatively the point of view that children are not much like their parents, then why is there sometimes little rejection of parental values, as in the 1950s? Or to put it all in a single question, can the process of political socialization explain both continuity and change in the social world?

The overview of the political socialization process that we have provided in this chapter gives some tentative answers to these questions (see also Jennings and

Niemi, 1974, ch. 12). The most relevant points can be summarized in the form of several general conclusions.

There is a large potential for malleability in young people's views of politics. Note that we say there is a large *potential* for change. Very often, as we argued, there is in fact a significant degree of similarity between attitudes of individuals at one point in time and at a much later point in time. Yet many attitudes, even partisan feelings, are not so firmly fixed that major changes are impossible. Indeed, the degree of change that has been observed in adults suggests that at least well into adulthood attitudes are not so firmly entrenched as has often been suggested. But particularly among young people, attitudes can change to a remarkable degree in a remarkably short period of time under the proper stimulus.

A major part of our understanding of this malleability in young people rests on the finding that children are often like their parents in the aggregate but not like their own parents. In numerous instances it was found that young people as a group were similar to parents as a group (or varied in ways wholly consistent with life cycle changes, such as having less cynical views). Yet even in these instances, the correlations between student and parent attitudes were low, suggesting that there were many compensating changes; some children were more liberal or more cynical or more cosmopolitan than their parents, while others were more conservative, more trusting, or more locally oriented. Hence, even when young children as a whole look very much like the older generation, we cannot conclude that most children are following in the footsteps of their own parents, with little possibility of change. To a greater extent than has been realized, children are forming their own political views. Thus, when social and political events capture their interest, young people are sufficiently free of parental influence that rapid changes in their attitudes are possible.

Children are often like their parents, we would argue, simply because of inertia. If there is nothing to push a child in one direction or another, it is easiest to be like his parents or at least like adults as a whole. Admittedly, it is difficult to predict when events will come along that will move young people. Also just what these events will be is perhaps unpredictable. During the 1950s, for example, "the bomb" seemingly had the potential for stimulating a radical alteration in young people's views, and yet it failed to do so. What we might do is to speak of probabilities of marked attitudinal changes. Presently we cannot, and perhaps we will never be able to, predict the exact occurrence of unstabilizing events. And yet the present socialization system in the United States arranges for what we regard as a relatively large potential for this kind of change.

This is not to make a value judgment about the present socialization system. Some would prefer more potential for change while others would prefer less. Again, the critical point is to emphasize the part played by the socialization process in determining levels of, or perhaps we should say probabilities of, stability versus change.

It should be obvious that none of what we have said denies the influence of families, schools, and other socializing agents. Families, schools, and most other agents do channel children along the same paths as adults; and, as we noted, in the absence of powerful forces children will turn out to be like their parents, at least in the aggregate. Thus, very often stability will mark the passage from one generation to another. And even when change and conflict are the order of the day, as in the middle to late 1960s, the instability would be even greater were it not for family and school influence.

What we have learned of the political socialization process thus contributes to our understanding of the likelihood of stability versus change and, more important, provides us with insight into the mechanisms underlying that balance. Tipping the balance toward greater change or stability involves ethical and normative questions, which go well beyond the scope of empirical political research. But such tough questions will have to be faced as we gain more and more knowledge about how to control our social as well as our physical environment. Political socialization research should allow us to face these problems with at least some knowledge of the consequences of the process, the rate, and the sources of political learning.

6

AUTHORITARIAN PERSONALITY IN CONTEMPORARY PERSPECTIVE

Nevitt Sanford

The day after Hitler came to power in Germany, Max Horkheimer, director of the Institute of Social Research in Frankfurt, moved from his home in the suburbs to an apartment close to the railway station. Within a few days he and other members of the institute staff were in Switzerland, where, against the likelihood of a Nazi takeover, they had set up a branch of the institute. How did it happen that these people were able to see the implications of what was happening and to take appropriate steps when most other German intellectuals and Jews clung to the belief that catastrophe could still be averted? (Psychoanalysts in Vienna were still carrying on their practices as usual, believing

The preparation of this chapter was supported by a grant (KO5-MH 12892-0151) from the National Institute of Mental Health.

that nothing serious would happen to them.) The reason was that they had carried out studies of political outlook in Germany and arrived at a very striking finding— namely, that whereas a great majority of working-class Germans expressed themselves as staunchly Social Democratic when asked polling-type questions, a significant number revealed themselves as highly authoritarian when asked questions that encouraged them to express indirectly some of their underlying attitudes and value orientations (questions that nowadays would be called "projective"). The conclusion of the institute staff was that Hitler probably would come to power and that if he did there would be no effective opposition from German labor.

This is probably one of the few cases in recorded history where social scientists were willing to stake everything on the truth of their research findings. But that is not the point here. The point is that much was known about authoritarianism and the other emotional appeals of fascism, much had been written about an "authoritarian character structure," before my colleagues and I started the series of investigations that led to our publishing *The Authoritarian Personality* (Adorno, Frenkel-Brunswik, Levinson, and Sanford, 1950). In America, probably the best-known work on this general subject in the early 1940s was Erich Fromm's (1941) *Escape from Freedom*. In this book Fromm, a former member of the Institute of Social Research, set forth his theory of the "sado-masochistic character" in relation to modern totalitarianism. His basic notion was that ever since the breaking up of the established authority of the Middle Ages, ever since the demise of what Walter Lippmann later called "the light and the leading" of the medieval church-state, men of the Western world have been ambivalent about the burdens of freedom and dignity, and their often unconscious wish to escape from these burdens renders them in various degrees susceptible to totalitarian propaganda. The individual in whom this susceptibility is strong has an emotional need, often unconscious, to submit to authority—in the first instance parental figures; at the same time, he has unconscious impulses of aggression toward these same figures, which impulses are often redirected toward outgroups such as ethnic minorities. Fromm thought of this psychodynamic structure as sado-masochism; but realizing that this term was commonly used in reference to perversion and neurosis, he used the term *authoritarian character* to refer to the same kind of structure in ordinary people.

Horkheimer and other staff members of the Institute of Social Research had already written up their study of German workers—in *Studien über Autorität und Familie* (1936), a volume containing a chapter by Fromm. Other European psychologists, most notably Reich (1933) and Erikson (1942), were writing about fascism and anti-Semitism from a psychoanalytic point of view. Probably Maslow (1943a) was the first American psychologist to join Fromm in discussing authoritarianism and in insisting that social attitudes serve important personality functions, although Stagner (1936) had earlier argued that fascist attitudes should be regarded as parts of an integrated system of outlook, beliefs, and attitudes.

Thus, the contribution of *The Authoritarian Personality* lay not in the new ideas it presented but in its empirical demonstration of the coherence of various beliefs, attitudes, and values associated with anti-Semitism and fascism and of the functional role of this ideological system within the individual's personality.[1] It

----

[1] "Demonstrate" may be too strong a word. Not all psychologists who have looked into the matter agree that these propositions have been demonstrated. But they would have to

accomplished what it did because of its way of combining psychoanalytic theory and American social psychology; more precisely, its authors found ways to test psychodynamic hypotheses through the use of interviews, attitude scales, projective techniques, and statistical methods.

In this chapter I want to summarize the general approach and the major findings of *The Authoritarian Personality,* paying particular attention to those portions that seek to convey something of the complexity of the personality processes forming the authoritarian pattern. This should prepare the ground for my discussion of how I see our work today and how my thinking about personality and ideology has changed since 1950. I shall also attempt to evaluate some of the research carried out by others since our work was published, and suggest what ought to be done now.

Our studies did not begin as an inquiry into authoritarianism or as an effort to test any specific hypothesis. They began, in 1943, when Daniel Levinson and I accepted a proffered donation of $500 for a study of anti-Semitism. We thought the place to begin was with the construction of a scale for measuring this form of prejudice. Scores on this instrument could then be correlated with a variety of personality and sociological factors. As devotees of psychoanalytic theory, we assumed the wholeness of personality and supposed that anti-Semitism has sources deep within the personality. And we were guided in part by psychoanalytic theory in composing items for the scale.

We carried out this study with the thought that it had to be complete in and of itself. Soon, however, the renewal of our grant, and further funding at a slightly higher level, made it possible for us to devise a methodology for the systematic study of anti-Semitism and personality. Else Frenkel-Brunswik and Suzanne Reichard now joined Levinson and me, and we all conducted interviews with subjects who had obtained extreme scores on the anti-Semitism (A-S) scale. These interviews, which ranged over wide areas of ideology and personal background, became the major source of our knowledge of the differences between people scoring high and people scoring low on our scale, and of the personality structure of people who seemed particularly susceptible to anti-Semitic and fascist propaganda. The interviews were supplemented by the Thematic Apperception Test, the Rorschach test, and "projective questions." It was our intention to conceptualize material from all these sources in such a way that it could be quantified and made the basis of questionnaires which could be administered to large groups of subjects.[2] It was our idea, in other words, to bring methods of social psychology into the service of concepts and theories from the dynamic theory of personality; we thereby hoped to make "depth psychological" phenomena more amenable to mass-statistical treatment and to make quantitative surveys of attitudes and opinions more meaningful psychologically.

We did not, however, in our quantitative work, go directly from anti-Semitism to personality dynamics. Instead, we asked about the relations between what subjects thought about Jews and what they thought about other people and other issues. Were the trends found in anti-Semitic ideology—its generality, stereotyped imagery, de-

---

admit that the weight of evidence is on the side of the propositions or, at the very least, that they are now reasonable. (See Brown, 1965, p. 525.)

[2] Funds for this work became available from the American Jewish Committee through the good offices of Max Horkheimer. Our cooperative arrangement with the committee also made it possible for us to welcome T. W. Adorno to our group.

structive irrationality, sense of threat, concern with power and immorality—also expressed in the individual's thinking about group relations and social issues generally? Accordingly, we developed scales for measuring generalized prejudice, or ethnocentrism (E) as we called it, and political-economic conservatism (PEC).

The E scale was made up of items pertaining to (a) Negroes and Negrowhite relations; (b) other minorities, including not only ethnic groups but minority political parties and religious sects, foreigners, "Okies," "zoot-suiters," criminals; and (c) patriotism—items dealing with America as an ingroup in relation to other nations as "inferior" outgroups. This scale of thirty-four items had a split-half reliability of .91, which we took as an indication of a very high degree of generality in ethnocentric ideology. The correlation of E with the anti-Semitism scale was .80, which led us to believe that anti-Semitism should be regarded as primarily an aspect of a broad pattern of ethnocentric ideology. Ethnocentrism was found to be related to political conservatism, the correlation of E and PEC being .50.

Two patterns of conservatism could be distinguished: a traditional laissez-faire conservatism and a "pseudoconservatism," in which profession of belief in the tenets of traditional conservatism is combined with a readiness for change of a sort that would destroy the very institutions with which the subject appears to identify himself. There was evidence that the pseudoconservatism items were the more largely responsible for the correlation between E and conservatism. The concept of pseudoconservatism has been followed up and amplified by Hofstadter (1965).

On the basis of our work with the three scales and the clinical procedures noted above, we proceeded to formulate the psychodynamic structure which we thought is expressed in ethnocentrism and in various opinions and attitudes associated with it. Since we assumed that action always depends upon the situation the person is in as well as upon personality, we referred to this structure as a *potential* for fascism, a *susceptibility* to anti-Semitic propaganda, a *readiness* to participate in antidemocratic social movements. In the remainder of the chapter I call this structure "authoritarianism," which is in keeping with current practice. It is worth noting, however, that in our work, in our early publications, and in the writing of *The Authoritarian Personality* we did not use this terminology. In our search for the correlates of anti-Semitism, we wanted to allow for the possibility that they embraced more than, or were constituted of something different from, the "authoritarian character structure" of Fromm (1941) and Maslow (1943). It was not until our book was finished that we thought of its title, which was intended to indicate our indebtedness to earlier writers and our concern with a pattern of personality organization.

It must be understood, however, that I am here discussing what nowadays is called "right-wing authoritarianism." As will be pointed out below, some of our subjects who obtained extremely low scores on the A-S or the E scale, particularly the "rigid" low scores, were observed to have something in common with the extreme high scores. In the years since 1950 a great deal of attention has been focused on "authoritarianism of the left" (see, for example, Rokeach, 1960), and much has been learned about certain characteristics that people at the two ends of the political spectrum have in common. The focus here, however, is not on these commonalities but on the distinctiveness and coherence of attitudes, beliefs, and values usually found on the political right.

The interviews and projective techniques which yielded the major specific hypotheses concerning the structure of authoritarianism also yielded some evidence favoring them—though their confirmation awaited the gathering of further data. For example, the interviews like some questionnaire material, showed unmistakably that a distinguishing feature of the highly ethnocentric subject is his tendency to glorify his parents. And the interviews also gave evidence of ambivalence in this subject's relationship with his parents. It was usually not long after the statements of glorification that a note of complaint or self-pity began to creep into the interview. How might one demonstrate that overt glorification of the parents is functionally related to underlying hostility toward them? One way would be to use a projective technique to obtain an independent measure of the latter and see if the two vary together. Unfortunately, this is not simple. What are the TAT signs of repressed aggression? Certainly not the frequency and intensity of aggressive actions by heroes of the stories. These seem to be, for the most part, indications of aggression that is accepted by the ego; it was more pronounced in the low scorers than in the high scorers on the A-S and E scales. But Betty Aron (1950) did conclude that there is more *ego-alien* aggression against the parents in the stories of high scorers, the indications being such things as the frequency with which parent figures are the victims of affliction or death and the frequency and intensity of aggression against parental figures on the part of characters with whom the storyteller is not identified.

Such conclusions as these still call for independent validation, and the same holds for the projective questions. The material elicited by this procedure is for the most part on the same level of personality as scale responses. Responses to the open-ended questions could easily be—and they sometimes were—translated into scale items. Thus, the projective questions yielded a large amount of material that independently confirmed scale findings on the difference between ethnocentric and nonethnocentric subjects. But, more than this, the material from the projective questions called for interpretation, for the conceptualization of underlying trends that would explain the pattern of overt expression.

Two of the projective questions read as follows: (1) "We all have times when we feel below par. What moods or feelings are the most important or disturbing to you?" (2) "There is hardly a person who hasn't said to himself: 'If this keeps up I'll go nuts.' What might drive a person nuts?" These two questions, like the six others used, brought out numerous differences between high and low scorers on the E scale. The "lows" are most disturbed by conscious conflict and guilt feelings, frustrations of love and dependence, consciousness of hostility toward loved objects; they suppose that people are "driven nuts" by inner psychological states or by a dominating environment. The "highs," on the other hand, are most disturbed by violations of conventional values by self or others or by a threatening or nonsupporting environment; they are also more disturbed by, and state that people are "driven nuts" by, what Levinson called "rumblings from below"—intimations that suppressed passivity, or anxiety, or hostility might break into the open.

Authoritarian Personality Dispositions

The major personality dispositions which, we concluded, largely make up authoritarianism may now be discussed in turn, with attention to their organization and their relation to anti-Semitism and ethnocentrism. This set of related tendencies will then be examined in the context of a more general psychodynamic theory of personality.

In our conversations with anti-Semitic subjects, we observed that most of their accusations against Jews were couched in conventionally moralistic terms. This theme was also pronounced in the original A-S scale items. These subjects, we believed, were revealing not so much bad experiences with Jews or an adaptation to a general climate of opinion as a need to adhere strictly to conventional, middle-class values, a disposition to feel anxious at the sight of or the thought of any violation of these values—something that could be attributed to instability in the individual's own value system. This disposition we called *conventionalism*. The term refers not merely to conformity with middle-class values but to rigid adherence to such values, to an *over*accent upon them, and to responsiveness to contemporary *external* social pressure.

Submission to authority, desire for a strong leader, subservience of the individual to the state had for some time been put forward as important aspects of the Nazi creed. It was thus not surprising that these themes were prominent in our interviews with highly prejudiced subjects. *Authoritarian submission,* as we termed the hypothetical generalized disposition of personality, was conceived of not as a balanced, realistic respect for valid authority but as an exaggerated, emotional need to submit. Here, as with conventionalism, the individual is assumed to be oriented toward external powers or agencies of control rather than under the direction of a conscience of his own.

Authoritarian submission is closely related, conceptually, to *authoritarian aggression*. Both attitudes, according to theory, spring from underlying hostility toward ingroup authorities, originally the parents. The individual strives to keep this hostility in check by overdoing in the direction of respect, obedience, and gratitude toward the ingroup authorities and by displacing the underlying hostility toward these authorities onto outgroups. This is the most essential connection between authoritarian aggression and ethnocentrism. But it appears that the tendency to displace hostility is more general than that seen in the common forms of prejudice; the greatest variety of people and actions are likely to become objects of condemnation. Moreover, the kinds of things for which the individual would punish other people are the same as those for which he himself was punished or for which he feels in his heart he deserves to be punished, in as much as he would like, unconsciously, to do these things himself.

In addition, our highly prejudiced subjects showed, both in the interviews and in some of the A-S and E scale items with which they heartily agreed, that they disapproved of a free emotional life, of the intellectual or theoretical, of the impractical. They tended to attribute these characteristics to their outgroups. And there was theory at hand to explain the relations of these attitudes to prejudice and to the personality trends just discussed. The individual who had had to repress hostility against his parents and others who appeared to be strong—and who was thus forced into submissiveness, which impaired his self-respect—would naturally be required to maintain a narrow range of consciousness. Self-awareness might threaten his whole scheme of adjustment. He would be afraid of genuine feeling because his emotions might get out of control, afraid of thinking about human phenomena because he might think the "wrong" thoughts. The term *anti-intraception,* borrowed from Murray (1938), describes such an individual—his general attitude of impatience with and opposition to feelings, fantasies, speculations, and other subjective or "tender-minded" phenomena.

This narrowness of consciousness is closely linked to two other tendencies noted in highly prejudiced individuals: *superstition* and *stereotypy*. Superstition indicates a tendency to shift responsibility from within the individual onto outside forces beyond his control; these forces then appear to the individual as mystical or fantastic determinants of his fate. Stereotypy is the tendency to think in rigid, over-simplified categories, in unambiguous terms of black and white, particularly in the realm of psychological or social matters. We hypothesized that some people, even those who are otherwise "intelligent," may resort to primitive explanations of human events at least partly because they cannot allow many of the ideas and observations needed for an adequate account to enter into their calculations; because these ideas are affect-laden and potentially anxiety-producing, they cannot be included in the conscious scheme of things. The assumption here is, of course, that many of the common phenomena of prejudice are superstitions or stereotypes.

As suggested above, when an individual is forced to submit to powers or agencies with which he is not fully in sympathy, he is left with a nagging sense of weakness. Since to admit such weakness is to damage self-respect, he makes every effort to deny it—sometimes by projecting weakness onto outgroups (according to the formula "I am not weak; *they* are") or by using the mechanism of overcompensation, whereby he seeks to present to the world an aspect of *power and toughness*. This "power complex" contains elements that are essentially contradictory. The power-centered individual wants to have power but at the same time is afraid to seize it and wield it. He also admires power in others, and is inclined to submit to it, but at the same time is afraid of the weakness thus implied. A common solution for such a person is to align himself with power figures, thus gratifying both his need to have power and his need to submit. By submitting to power, he can still somehow participate in it.

Although authoritarian aggression provides a very broad channel for the expression of underlying hostile impulses, many of our prejudiced subjects seemed to need still other channels. Possibly because of numerous externally imposed restrictions upon the satisfaction of their needs, they seemed to harbor a great deal of generalized hostility, which would come into the open whenever it could be justified or rationalized. Such rationalized, ego-accepted aggression (not including authoritarian aggression) we termed *destructiveness and cynicism*. The cynic, in our terminology, rationalizes his aggressiveness by attributing a similar aggressiveness to everybody else. In his view, it is "human nature" to exploit and to make war on one's neighbors. It seemed a fairly safe assumption that minority groups were often the victims of this undifferentiated aggressiveness.

The mechanism just described (and often alluded to in our discussion of authoritarian aggression and of superstition) is, of course, a form of projection. Indeed, projection has a crucial role in the whole theory of prejudice as a means for keeping the individual's psychological household in some sort of order. The most essential notion is that impulses which cannot be admitted to the conscious ego tend to be projected onto minority groups. We conceived of *projectivity* as a general feature of the personality, a feature that can be considered independently of the object onto which the projection is made. It is manifested mainly as preoccupation with "evil forces" in the world, with plots and conspiracies, germs, sexual excesses. (For a more detailed discussion of projection, see Chapter Fifteen.)

Concern with sex seemed to deserve special consideration, since our prejudiced subjects showed marked inhibitions in this sphere, and moral indignation over the sexual behavior of other people. Sexual immorality was one of the many violations of conventional values which they attributed to minority groups. This ego-alien sexuality is another characteristic of the typical prejudiced person.

We assumed, then, that these were the major personality dispositions under-lying overt anti-Semitism and ethnocentrism. We still needed to determine how these dispositions relate to one another and to the structure of personality as a whole. In our theoretical work on these questions, we leaned heavily on the Freudian con-cepts of superego, ego, and id. We considered that these features of the personality have characteristic modes of functioning in the highly ethnocentric subject. Speci-fically, the superego is strict, rigid, and relatively externalized; the id is strong, primitive, and ego-alien; the ego is weak and can manage the superego-id conflicts only by resorting to rather desperate defenses. According to this formulation, the first three of the personality dispositions just considered (conventionalism, authoritarian submission, and authoritarian aggression) all have to do with superego functioning. The strict superego demands—as a means for keeping unacceptable impulses in check—punishment of "wrongdoers" in the name of those authorities to whom the subject has submitted. Anti-intraception, superstition and stereotypy, and pro-jectivity may be regarded as manifestations of a relatively weak ego. Anti-intracep-tion involves the primitive defense mechanisms of repression and denial. Superstition shows an inclination to shift responsibility onto the external world, as if the ego were giving up its attempts to predict and control, while stereotypy is an attempt to deal with complex events by means of oversimplified categories. Projectivity is the con-sistent use of another relatively primitive mechanism of defense. Power and toughness, another manifestation of ego weakness, involves an overaccent upon the conven-tionalized aspects of the ego (for instance, the emphasis on "will power"); but this variable, like destructiveness and cynicism and sex, also expresses with a minimum of indirectness the activity of id tendencies.

A major hypothesis guiding our investigations into the origins of authoritar-ianism was that such central structures of personality have their beginnings in ex-periences of early childhood. By taking the many differences between the reports on childhood of subjects scoring high and those scoring low on the A-S and E scales, and considering these in the light of contemporary knowledge and theory of per-sonality development, we were able to put together a plausible account.

It may be helpful at this point to sketch very briefly the contrasting accounts of childhood by high and low-scoring subjects. High-scoring men more often de-scribed their fathers as distant and stern; the low-scorers as relaxed and mild. High-scoring women characteristically saw their fathers as hard-working and serious, while low-scoring women more often perceived their fathers as intellectual and easygoing. The mothers of high-scoring subjects, both male and female, were more often said to be kind, self-sacrificing, and submissive; the mothers of low-scoring subjects were more often described as warm, sociable, and understanding. High-scoring men tended to accent the mother's moral restrictiveness; low-scoring men, her intellectual and aesthetic interests. High-scoring women generally described their mothers as models of morality, restricting and fearsome; low-scoring women usually were able to offer more differentiated criticism.

In general, high scorers gave a rather undifferentiated picture of their parents, offering a somewhat stereotyped and idealized picture at the beginning of the interview and allowing negative features to make their appearance only when there was questioning about details. In contrast, low scorers more often undertook an objective appraisal, with good and bad features mentioned in their place. High scorers tended to deny that there was any conflict between the parents; the lows usually described some conflict in more or less realistic terms. High-scoring men usually described their homes as dominated by the father; low-scoring men more often described homes in which there was general orientation toward the mother.

Discipline in the families of the more authoritarian men and women was characterized by relatively harsh application of rules, in accordance with conventional values; and this discipline was commonly experienced as threatening or traumatic or even overwhelming. In the families of subjects low on authoritarianism, on the other hand, discipline was more often for the violation of principles, and the parents more often made an effort to explain the issues to the child, thus enabling him to assimilate the discipline.

In view of the more authoritarian subject's obvious inclination to put as good a face as possible upon his family and his childhood situation, we were inclined to assume that such negative features as appeared in his account were probably to be taken more or less at their face value; that is, to believe that the high authoritarians came, for the most part, from homes in which a rather stern and distant father dominated a submissive and long-suffering but morally restrictive mother, and in which discipline was an attempt to apply conventionally approved rules rather than an effort to further general values in accordance with the perceived needs of the child.

This account of the genesis of authoritarianism in the individual personality emphasizes early experiences in the family. It may well be asked, "What makes parents behave in ways that promote authoritarianism in their children?" We cannot merely say that they are authoritarian themselves, for this would be pushing the question of the origins of authoritarianism indefinitely into the past. Instead, we must consider that family life, within which personality largely develops, is constantly under the influence of various economic, social, and historical processes. We carried out no studies of such processes, as they might have affected the parents of our subjects, but we did offer some speculations; for example, that middle-class parents who have climbed rapidly and feel insecure about their new status are disposed to discipline their children in ways that favor the children's development of authoritarian tendencies. That is, people may consistently behave in authoritarian ways, or even develop authoritarian trends in their personalities, because of the social environment of the present as well as the past.

If contemporary social situations and processes help determine the behavior of parents toward their children, might they not also help determine the behavior of these parents toward outgroups? Many social scientists have thought so. Indeed, at the time we began our work contemporary economic and social factors and processes were generally considered the major determinants of ethnic prejudice. More inward, more individualistic factors, we thought, were rather neglected; and we were determined to give them their due. We assumed, however, that in the determination of ideology, as in the determination of all observable actions, there are situational as well as personality factors at work and that explanation requires the careful weighing of the role of each kind of factor. Accordingly, we studied anti-Semitism or ethnocentrism in relation to income and occupation; to membership in political, religious, and other social groups; and, of course, to those favorites of the social scientist, education and intelligence. Our methods, however, were not well calculated to give these factors *their* due, mainly because our 2099 subjects were drawn almost exclusively from the middle socioeconomic class, and were mainly white, non-Jewish, and native born.

We found no simple relationships between ethnocentrism and socioeconomic factors or social group memberships. There was only a slight tendency for higher incomes on the part of the subject's father to be associated with lower scores on the E scale. The offspring of Republicans were slightly less ethnocentric than the offspring of Democrats, the difference being significant at the 5 percent level of confidence. Subjects who had a political preference different from that of their fathers, however, were much lower on the E scale than were subjects whose political preference was the same as their fathers'. This permitted the kind of psychological interpretation we favored: having the same political preference as one's father may be an indication of submissiveness to ingroup authority, which favors ethnocentrism; having a different preference is a sign of critical independence, which favors freedom from ethnocentrism.

The story was much the same with religious group memberships. The religious denomination of parents did not prove to be significant for ethnocentrism. When the religious affiliation of the subject was considered in relation to his or her parents, however, interesting results were obtained. Subjects whose parents had the same religion were higher on E than subjects whose parents had different religions or differed in the sense that one was religious and the other not. Also, subjects who agreed with their mothers in the matter of religion were more ethnocentric than those who did not agree with their mothers. In sum, for religious subjects mere membership in a religious group is not as significant for ethnocentrism as the way in which religion is accepted or rejected: if its acceptance reflects conventional or authoritarian submission, we may expect to find some ethnocentrism; if its acceptance reflects the subject's own experience and independent thought, we may expect relative freedom from ethnocentrism.

Intelligence and education must be considered as factors in authoritarianism, even though we were not able to study them thoroughly or systematically. Scores on one or another of the standard intelligence tests were available for several groups, totalling 560, of our subjects, the great majority of whom had IQs of 100 or more. There was a low but dependable relationship between low intelligence and ethnocentrism. It was hard to tell which to accept more, the lowness or the dependability. It has often been remarked that prejudice is a form of stupidity in social matters. But does stupidity cause authoritarianism, or does authoritarianism cause stupidity? We believed that suggestibility and lack of discernment would favor acceptance of our E items, but we were inclined to see these traits as aspects of the total personality. It seemed hardly likely that subjects could free themselves from such psychodynamically determined tendencies as rigidity, concreteness and stereotypy of thinking, narrowness of ego bounds, and awkwardness in the face of psychosocial phenomena when they sat down to take intelligence tests. On the other hand, we thought of incompetence as a major source of low self-esteem and aggression and, hence, of ethnocentrism. We had to leave to future investigators the question of what would be the relationship between E and intelligence test scores in samples with wider ranges of IQ, and the question of how, ultimately, the interactions of native intelligence and psychodynamic processes were to be formulated.

Intelligence, of course, is correlated with number of years of formal education; not surprisingly, therefore, we found a slight negative correlation between ethnocentrism and amount of education. Since relatively few of our subjects had been to school less than eleven years, our samples were biased in the direction of higher levels of education. There was great variability, however, among subjects of the same educational level: being a highly intelligent college graduate is no guarantee against ethnocentrism.

F Scale

After the empirical and theoretical work described above had been done, we conceived the idea of constructing a scale for measuring potential fascism in the personality. We wanted not only a scale for measuring prejudice without mentioning the names of any ethnic minorities but a means for quantifying the fascist potential and estimating its strength in various groups of subjects. Our basic idea was that the personality dispositions expressed in anti-Semitism and ethnocentrism would be expressed in various other ways as well. For example, if a subject's tendency to attribute weakness to Jews springs from his own underlying fear of weakness, that fear might also express itself in an overaccent upon his own strength and toughness; hence we considered the item "An insult to our honor should always be punished" mainly an expression of the "power and toughness" dimension discussed above.

For every item in the new scale, which we called the F (for prefascism) scale, there was a hypothesis (sometimes several hypotheses) about its connection with prejudice. The major source of these hypotheses was, of course, the studies that had gone before, particularly material from the interviews and the Thematic Apperception Test; but, at the same time, we made use of the general literature, both empirical and theoretical, on anti-Semitism and fascism. Once a hypothesis of this kind had been formulated, a preliminary sketch for an item was not far to seek: something an interviewee had said, a phrase from the daily newspaper, a fragment of ordinary conversation. The item was then improved or made maximally useful to our purposes through successive trials with subjects.

Although the items could be classified as mainly expressive of one or another of our dimensions of authoritarianism in personality, most of the items were considered manifestations of more than one of these dimensions. Thus, in the item "An insult to our honor should always be punished," the idea of punishment, which would not have been necessary to an expression of overaccent on honor, was included because it was thought to express authoritarian aggression. Again, the item "Sex crimes, such as rape and attacks on children, deserve more than mere imprisonment; such criminals ought to be publicly whipped" seems a particularly good example of authoritarian aggression, but we thought of it as a combination of this disposition and our "defense against sex" dimension. This way of proceeding was in keeping with our notion that the several personality dispositions we had conceptionalized were dynamically interrelated, and largely constituted a structure—or "syndrome," as we called it. We wanted to develop a measure of the whole syndrome, and to do so in an economical way. To this end we packed as much meaning as we could into each item, trying to design it so that as many as possible of the facets of authoritarianism would be expressed.

We used the above-mentioned theory concerning authoritarianism and the total personality in the same way. According to theory the superego, the ego, and the id can be separated only by abstraction. In actuality, the functioning of any one of these agencies depends at any moment upon the activities of the other two; expressed attitudes and values are not readily classifiable as manifestations of superego, ego, or id but are to be understood as expressions of the relationships among these agencies. Consider the item "He is indeed contemptible who does not feel an undying love, gratitude, and respect for his parents." On the surface, this item expresses authoritarian aggression and authoritarian submission and, hence, might be classified as primarily a superego item. But the theory was that agreement with this extreme statement might well mask an underlying hostility toward the parents. In other words, we hypothesized that unconscious hostility toward the parents is a distinguishing feature of the highly ethnocentric person; our problem was to determine how this tendency might give itself away in an attitude scale. One answer was through signs of a reaction formation, this mechanism being a common one in the highly ethnocentric person. Thus, the present item had to do with an interplay of superego, ego, and id; an underlying unconscious, ego-alien tendency, coming mainly from the id, has led to anxiety of punishment (superego), which the ego seeks to ward off or reduce by transforming the forbidden tendency into its opposite. But this is not all. This is merely the authoritarian submission expressed in the item. "He is indeed contemptible" is an expression of authoritarian aggression. The ego must, so to speak, be doubly sure that punishment is avoided, and that the original id tendency finds some sort of gratification; hence, it joins forces with the punitive agency and imputes the "badness" to other people, who may then be freely aggressed against in good conscience.

It must be noted also that each item of the F scale is in the positive direction; that is, agreement with it is taken as an indication of potential for fascism. Here we followed a procedure that had served us well with the anti-Semitism scale (Levinson and Sanford, 1944). Setting out to study susceptibility to anti-Semitic propaganda in the midst of World War II, we used items that stated an anti-Semitic position and at the same time offered a "pseudodemocratic façade" or a rationalization for agreement: "There may be some exceptions but Jews . . ." The question was how far would a subject permit himself to be lured into agreement with antidemocratic sentiments. Interviews with subjects who obtained high or low scores on this scale satisfied us that our instrument was effective in identifying individuals who were relatively anti-Semitic and those who were the opposite. Items on the F and E scales, which were composed in the same way as the original anti-Semitism scale, were those that we considered fascistic in content (with varying degrees of explicitness) and that subjects might agree with without violating their democratic self-conceptions.

The F scale in its final form contained thirty items and had a split-half reliability of .90. The average interitem correlation was .13; the average item-total scale correlation, .33. The correlational analysis did not indicate that our hypothetical dimensions of authoritarianism were to any significant degree independent of each other. The items we had grouped together as mainly expressive of a given personality disposition tended to be intercorrelated (.11 to .24), but the items of one group correlated with one another no better than they did with numerous items from other clusters.

This last finding, taken together with the fairly high internal consistency of the scale as a whole, seemed sufficient justification for our thinking that the F scale measures *one thing*—in statistical terms a very general factor, which varies in amounts from one individual to another. At the same time, however, we thought of this one thing as something highly complex—a *syndrome,* as we preferred to say. A syndrome is a pattern of dynamically related variables; in the ideal case a change in one variable will bring change in all the others. Where a syndrome is fairly common in a population of individuals, its unitary character will be reflected in intercorrelations among its constituent variables.

We could not say that *all* the variables that make up the authoritarian syndrome are touched upon in the F scale; nor could we say with certainty which variables are the truly fundamental ones. It seemed clear, however (as will be documented below), that we had a measure that could make some highly significant differentiations among individuals.

According to theory (Murray and others, 1938; Sanford and others, 1943, pp. 20–22), the variables in a syndrome may be quite loosely held together. A variable which in one individual has a place in a given syndrome may in another individual appear in a different syndrome; and its nature may be somewhat different, depending on the context in which it is found. And, what is particularly important, syndromes themselves, though conceived as distinguishable patterns, have no true independence; their nature too will depend upon the still broader context of personality within which they have their being. Thus, individuals may exhibit the same syndrome in about the same degree and yet differ among themselves in numerous significant ways. No syndrome can ever totally embrace a person. Even when authoritarianism is pronounced, what emerges in behavior will depend upon what other syndromes are present. It is not proper, then, to speak of an authoritarian type of person. But one may speak of types of authoritarianism. Authoritarianism may vary from one individual to another, not only in quantity but according to which of the constituent variables are relatively pronounced, a matter which may depend upon what other factors are at work in the personality. Some of these variations in authoritarianism may be common in large populations.

Some varieties of high authoritarianism were labeled, by Adorno, *surface resentment, conventional, authoritarian, tough guy, crank,* and *manipulative. Surface resentment* refers not so much to any deep-lying tendency in the personality as to a state of affairs in which the individual is provoked to prejudiced and authoritarian modes of behavior by externally imposed frustrations. The *conventional* pattern emphasizes conventional values and determination by external representatives of the superego. The *authoritarian* pattern is similar to Fromm's conception of the sadomasochistic character. The subject achieves his social adjustment by taking pleasure in obedience and subordination, while remaining ambivalent toward his authorities. In the *tough guy* the accent, as might be expected, is on power and toughness and on destructiveness and cynicism. The individual is prepared to do almost anything to protect himself against what he perceives to be a hostile world. The outstanding feature of the *crank* is projectivity, with superstition and stereotypy also looming large. It is as if the individual has withdrawn into an inner world, where he concentrates upon self-aggrandizement and the protection of his self-conception by projective formulas. In the *manipulative* pattern anti-intraception is extreme. There is a marked deficiency of object cathexis and of emotional ties. In the extreme case people become objects to be handled, administered, manipulated in accordance with the subject's theoretical or practical schemes.

The patterns that seemed prominent among subjects low in potential fascism were labeled *rigid, protesting, impulsive, easygoing,* and *genuine liberal.* The *rigid* low scorer appears to have most in common with the overall high pattern. Here the absence of potential fascism, instead of being based on concrete experience and integrated within the personality, is derived from some general external ideological pattern. To quote Adorno and others (1950, p. 772), "We encountered a few subjects who had been identified ideologically with some progressive movement, such as the struggle for minority rights, for a long time, but with whom such ideas contained features of compulsiveness, even of paranoid obsession, and who, with respect to many of our variables, especially rigidity and total thinking, could hardly be distinguished from some of our high extremes." In the *protesting* low scorer the decisive feature is opposition to whatever appears to be tyranny. The subject is out to protect the weak from the strong; he can perhaps lead or at least be effective in revolts, but finds nothing to do once the revolt has met with success. In the *impulsive* pattern unconventionality is the outstanding theme. The subject is able not only to sympathize with what is different but to be different. The *easygoing* pattern is the opposite of the manipulative form of potential fascism. It is marked by imagination, capacity for enjoyment, and a sense of humor that is often directed to oneself. The *genuine liberal* is close to the psychoanalytic ideal, representing a balance of superego, ego, and id. Perhaps the outstanding features of this pattern are moral courage and a sense of personal autonomy. The subject in whom it is highly developed resists any interference with his personal convictions and beliefs, and he does not want to interfere with those of others.

Correlates of F Scale

If one knows personally individuals in whom one or another of the above patterns is pronounced, has carried out case studies of them, or has seen them in intensive psychotherapy, it might easily strike him as foolhardy to suppose that all this complexity could somehow be boiled down and expressed in a thirty-item scale. Although members of our research team had had these experiences, we persisted in our efforts to make "depth psychological processes amenable to mass-statistical treatment." The effort seemed worthwhile not only because of the light it might shed on personality organization and functioning but because American social scientists probably would not put much stock in our clinical findings unless we were able to render them in quantitative form.

It seemed to us particularly important to have an index of anti-Semitism and racism that made no reference to Jews or other minorities. Lowenthal and Guterman (1949), Adorno (1946), and others had shown that the fascist agitators of the 1930s, in America and elsewhere, made no mention of Jews. They contented themselves with negative terms like "international bankers," "bloodsuckers," "apostates," "vermin"; but when they said "Blood will have to be shed," their audiences knew full well whose blood. Thus, scales with items expressing hostile attitudes toward ethnic minorities not only risked being unfair to these minorities but also might not get at the full potential for racism and fascism.[3]

The F scale in its final form, however, seems to have served its purpose fairly well. Correlations with the E scale in various groups ranged from .62 to .87 and averaged .77. This should not, of course, be surprising, since, as indicated above, the E scale was thought of as expressing personality dispositions which, taken together, were supposed to be measured by the F scale. Consistent with this finding is the F-PEC correlation of .57.

The only data we had on our subjects' politically relevant overt behavior, as distinct from their verbal behavior, was their membership in the groups we approached in order to obtain responses to our questionnaires. As indicated above, we could not tell whether socioeconomic class as such is a determinant of ethnocentrism, but there was some evidence that membership in certain groups is an expression of an authoritarian outlook. Thus, it seemed consistent with our general theory to find that inmates of San Quentin prison obtained the highest mean F scale score of all the groups we studied, while psychiatric clinic patients obtained a relatively low score. This finding seemed, at the least, to express a difference between those who try to overcome frustration or resolve conflicts by striking out against the environment or blaming others as opposed to those who seek solutions within themselves. In general, the main difference between our low-scoring groups and our high-scoring ones was that the former in some way expressed liberal or progressive or humanitarian attitudes or thought; the latter did not. Thus, middle-class men recruited from the university and movie communities of Los Angeles, from the PTA, or from the laymen's league of the Presbyterian church were significantly lower on F than were members of a Berkeley service club, while working-class men who attended classes at the California Labor School or who belonged to a "militant" union were lower than other groups of working-class men.

Research Based on F Scale

Almost as soon as *The Authoritarian Personality* appeared, it became the object of vigorous criticism, both for its methodological shortcomings and for its neglect of "authoritarianism of the left."[4] The studies using questionnaires were said to be flawed most importantly by "acquiescence response set" (a general tendency to acquiescence) and by inadequate sampling, while the efforts to quantify interview

[3] Anti-Semitism is still the giveaway of the most dangerous political orientations. It is precisely because of their relative invisibility that Jews have projected onto them the most irrational destructive fantasies. And anti-Semitism is as hard to get at as ever. For example, Vice-President Agnew's "impudent snob" speech aroused a great deal of uneasiness and led to accusations that he was appealing to people's worst motives, but I could find few people who were struck by how much it was in the style of the fascist agitators of the 1930s.

[4] Useful reviews of *The Authoritarian Personality* and of research on authoritarianism, particularly research based on the F scale, have been published by Dicks, 1951; Christie and Jahoda, 1954; Sanford, 1954, 1956; Christie and Cook, 1958; Bay, 1958; Brown, 1965; Kirscht and Dillehay, 1967; Greenstein, 1969; and Knutson, 1971.

and projective material suffered from failure to rule out several kinds of observer bias.

As noted above, all items of the A-S, E, and F scales are in the positive direction. In reviewing this procedure for constructing the F scale, critics not surprisingly asked how we could tell whether high scores on the scale were due to authoritarianism or to response set. Cohn (1953) was probably the first to suggest that the F scale is in part a measure of acquiescence; but far more attention was accorded the work of Bass (1955), who composed reversed versions of the F scale items, administered both the original scale and the reversed scale to the same subjects, and obtained a correlation between the two scales of only −.20. Christie, Havel, and Seidenberg (1958) argued that Bass's reversed items were not in fact psychological opposites of the original items, and proceeded to show that the composition of such opposites is an extremely complicated business. As indicated above, each F scale item conveys a complex pattern of connotations. Nevertheless, Christie and his associates showed that an F scale with equal numbers of authoritarian and equalitarian assertions can be constructed. Numerous other studies, some of them highly ingenious, have been directed to finding out how much of the variance on the F scale is due to acquiescence. Conclusions have ranged from "virtually all" (Peabody, 1961) to "none worth bothering about" (Gage and Chattergee, 1960). Some writers agree with the authors of *The Authoritarian Personality* that acquiescence is an expression of "authoritarian submission" and that therefore the use of only F positive items increases the validity of the scale. Kirscht and Dillehay (1967, p. 25), in their valuable survey of research on authoritarianism in personality, sum up the controversy as follows: "Even after fifteen years of research, the influence of acquiescence on scores from the F scale is difficult to assess. This is due in part to mechanical problems in isolating acquiescence, but it is also due to the likelihood that the interaction between acquiescence and authoritarianism is complex." Couch and Keniston (1960) showed that the response set to agree ("Yeasaying") is a personality characteristic in its own right. It is not, apparently, a component or manifestation of authoritarianism, for these workers produced evidence that the two personality dispositions are independent. Rorer (1965), on the other hand, has pointed to the low correlations among different measures of acquiescence and thus questioned the conception of acquiescence as a unitary variable.

To readers who have worried about authoritarianism in the individual and in society ever since Horkheimer (1936), Fromm (1941), Maslow (1943), Reich (1933), and others drew attention to the phenomenon, and who have never felt there was any difficulty about recognizing it when they saw it, this controversy about response bias might seem trivial. To more than a few psychologists, however, the questions of how to formulate authoritarianism and how to resolve it into its constituent elements have seemed important, for these questions have considerable bearing on our understanding of the relations between authoritarianism and intelligence, education, socioeconomic background, and cognitive and emotional development.

Acquiescence, unfortunately, does not seem to be a very promising candidate for the status of component of authoritarianism. There are serious questions about what it is and how general it is; moreover, as Couch and Keniston (1960) suggest, its underlying determinants in the personality seem to be almost as diverse and complicated as those hypothesized for authoritarianism itself. Nevertheless, acquiescence response set is a factor in the F scale; therefore, correlations of this instrument with other scales made up of positive items—for instance, the A-S and E scales and Rokeach's (1960) dogmatism scale—are somewhat higher than they would otherwise be. This state of affairs has not, however, washed out any findings of the original study or created serious doubt about the generality of authoritarianism. Christie, Havel, and Seidenberg (1958) have shown that the F scale correlates with variables in which response bias is not a factor, and, as shown above, the conclusions from *The Authoritarian Personality* do not rest on findings from the use of this instrument but on the convergence of findings from various procedures. Future students of authoritarianism or similar personality structures, however, if they choose to use scales rather than some more revealing and trustworthy instrument, will probably be well advised to compose them of both positive and negative items.

Concerning sampling, Hyman and Sheatsley (1954) concluded from their masterful critique that the results reported in *The Authoritarian Personality* could not be generalized to any known population because of the unrepresentativeness of the people studied. Even today the problem of sampling is far from solved, for investigators still rely heavily on middle-class subjects, college students in particular. Nevertheless, during the years since 1950 the F scale (or shortened or equivalent versions of it) has been used with huge numbers of subjects of the greatest variety: Jews (Adelson, 1953; Himelhoch, 1950), blacks (Selznick and Steinberg, 1969; Kelman and Barclay, 1963), Lebanese (Prothro and Melikian, 1953), Germans (Cohn and Carsch, 1954), Japanese (Niyekawa, 1960), teachers in seven Western European nations (Levinson, 1958), Catholics (Brown and Brstryn, 1956), political leaders at the local level (Harned, 1961), people with low occupational status and little education (Martin and Westie, 1959), Washington lobbyists (Milbrath and Klein, 1962), and children (Lyle and Levitt, 1955).

F. H. Sanford (1950a) and MacKinnon and Centers (1956) used quota samples in greater Philadelphia and Los Angeles, respectively, while Janowitz and Marvick (1953) and Lane (1953, 1955) used national probability samples. Not all of these studies had to do directly with *The Authoritarian Personality*'s basic conception of personality and ideology, but none produced results inconsistent with it. As Roger Brown in his judicious review says, "On the level of covariation, of one variable correlated with another, the findings of *The Authoritarian Personality* seem to me to be quite well established. Anti-Semitism goes with ethnocentrism goes with anti-intraception goes with idealization of parents and self goes with a rigid conception of sex roles, etc." (Brown, 1965, p. 525.)

Many studies have served to widen the circle of covariation. For instance, high scores on the E or the F scale have been shown to be associated with high scores on various other attitude scales, such as scales for measuring rigidity (Gough and Sanford, 1952), misanthropy (Adelson and Sullivan, 1952), xenophobia (Campbell and McCandless, 1951), dogmatism (Rokeach, 1954), traditional family ideology (Levinson and Huffman, 1955), nationalism (Levinson, 1957), and a custodial orientation toward mentally ill patients (Gilbert and Levinson, 1957). These correlations afford confirming evidence of the generality of the authoritarian outlook.

Other studies—a great many of them—have used the F scale, or some variant or rough equivalent of it, as a prediction of overt behavior. For example, experiments have shown that authoritarianism is associated with mental rigidity, especially under conditions of anxiety (Neuringer, 1964); with suspiciousness and untrustworthiness in a two-person game situation (Deutsch, 1960); with conformity to group pressure (Crutchfield, 1955; Canning and Baker, 1959; Vaughn and White, 1966); with punitiveness toward people of low status (Roberts and Jessor, 1958); with autocracy in leadership roles and, in followship roles, readiness to be satisfied with appointed leaders (Haythorn and others, 1956a, 1956b); with obedience to an experimenter's authoritative commands (Elms and Milgram, 1966); and with resistance to efforts to change attitudes by educational means (Katz, McClintock, and Sarnoff, 1957). Other studies, focusing on behavior in natural situations, have shown authoritarianism to be associated with totalitarianism in clasroom teachers (McGee, 1954), failure to be nominated for leadership positions (Hollander, 1953), low ability to adapt to an unstructured educational setting (Goldberg and Stern, 1952), disinclination to participate in political affairs (F. H. Sanford, 1950a; Milbrath and Klein, 1962), tendency not to vote in elections (Janowitz and Marvick, 1953; Lane, 1955), and preference for candidates seen as conservative, regardless of party (Leventhal, Jacobs and Kudirka, 1964).

These findings have strengthened the argument in favor of a central and relatively deep-seated personality structure, which helps to determine behavior in a wide variety of situations. However, the findings are in the form of *general* relationships—correlations between variables in populations of people. Individual differences are large in all the studies, and factors other than authoritarianism clearly enter into the determination of all the kinds of behavior studied. As stated in *The Authoritarian Personality,* p. 36: "Specific social attitudes, if adequately measured, will undoubtedly be found to correlate with a variety of external and contemporary factors, and if one studies only specific attitudes he may easily be led to the belief that this is all there is to it. Consistent trends in the person can be revealed only by subjecting him to a variety of stimuli, or placing him in a variety of different situations, or questioning him on a wide variety of topics; then, according to the present hypothesis, consistent trends (that is, personality) will always be revealed."

An example of how far situational factors can go in determining what might be regarded as a specific form of "authoritarian behavior" is afforded by Milgram's (1963, 1965) experiments on what he called obedience. In what he described as a learning experiment, Milgram instructed his subjects, university students and townspeople, to pull switches which they thought would give severe and dangerous shocks to subjects who failed to supply correct answers to test questions. To Milgram's surprise, a large fraction of his subjects readily obeyed his instructions. Authoritarianism in personality may well have been a factor in determining obedience to the experimenter's words "You have no choice" (when they might have walked out); but the results of this experiment strongly suggest that ordinary decent people can be induced to carry out socially destructive acts in a situation embodying such features as a prestigeful university, a powerfully authoritative experimenter, the presumed requirements of science, and ignorance and confusion in the face of complicated technological products and arrangements.

The same line of thought has been used to explain why a great majority of professors at the University of California at Berkeley finally submitted to the imposition of a loyalty oath. Situational pressures, economic as well as social, became almost overwhelming (Sanford, 1953). In riots or massacres the role of situational factors seems even more crucial. As Sanford and Comstock and their associates (1971), in their analysis of events such as the My Lai massacre, and Hersey (1968), in his account of the Algiers Motel incident, have stressed, the actors in these incidents believed that they had some kind of permission to do as they did—partly because propaganda or cultural norms depicted the victims as beyond the pale; but in addition, they were all suffering from fatigue, fear, confusion, and momentary group pressures. All this is not to say that personality does not enter into the determination of such events. Authoritarianism, in particular, is a concept to explain the varying degrees of susceptibility in individuals to the kinds of situational pressures just described.

To work out the ways in which personality and the situation interact in single dramatic episodes is, of course, extremely difficult, for the necessary observations are hard to obtain. One can do better at the analysis of behavior in organizational or institutional settings, where the situational pressures on individuals are more manifest and durable. Levinson and his associates have probably gone further than anyone else in demonstrating some of the interactions between institutional characteristics and authoritarianism in personality. Studying staff members in three mental hospitals, they showed first that authoritarianism (F scale) goes with a "custodial" as opposed to a humanistic orientation toward the mentally ill. They then showed that the hospitals, and subsections of them, differed and could be reliably rated with respect to the degree of custodialism expected of their employees. Their major conclusion was that there is congruence between the policy requirements of a social system such as a hospital and the modal personality of its members. Authoritarianism in personality helps to determine who will select (and be selected for) a given organizational role and who will remain in it, while life in the role (with which an individual may identify himself) and in the organization (which may be oppressive or liberating) may increase or decrease authoritarianism in personality (Pine and Levinson, 1957; Gilbert and Levinson, 1957; Greenblatt, Levinson, and Williams, 1957). Levinson and his associates offer what appears to be the right approach to the study of institutional racism or sexism or other forms of antidemocratic corporate behavior. The individual occupants of an institution's diverse roles may be replaced without changing that institution, but the study of the personalities of individuals who live or work there is necessary to a complete understanding of their behavior and of the meaning of corporate actions. Such study is also necessary to an understanding of the impact of organizational life upon individuals and of how and why some individuals are able to resist organizational pressures (Howard and Somers, 1971).

Situational factors (or, one might better say, a range of nonpersonality factors) help to determine not only overt social behavior, individual and collective, but also one's responses to any item of an attitude scale. The F scale item "Obedience and respect for authority are the most important virtues children should learn," for example, was acceptable to almost everybody in Prothro and Melikian's (1953) sample of Arab students and in F. H. Sanford's (1950a) representative sample of greater Philadelphia. It certainly seems fair to say that most of these subjects, in agreeing with this statement, were merely expressing a cultural norm rather than coping with an unresolved conflict of personality. Again, on all occasions when I have discussed the details of the F scale with groups of people who were not psychologists, someone has protested, "But I agree with item X because it is true." No doubt each item of the F scale has an aspect of objective truth for some people, in the sense that it reflects more or less accurately the real world in which they live or in the sense that they find it rational or practically adaptive to act as if the statement were true. Indeed, it has been argued with some persuasiveness—for example, by Miller and Riessman (1961) and Campbell and others (1960)—that "working-class authoritarianism" is mainly to be explained on this basis. And again, an "authoritarian" response to an F type of item might be a matter of simple ignorance. Hyman and Sheatsley (1954) in their methodological critique aptly point out that the authors of *The Authoritarian Personality* simply were not justified in attaching psychodynamic or even ideological significance to a subject's mentioning George Washington or General MacArthur as his most-admired person when they had not established whether the subject knew the names of any other great men or women.

We were aware of these and various other possible determinants of response to particular scale items, for example, a subject's discussion with his friends shortly before he filled out our questionnaire, but we relied on the trend of response in the scale as a whole—behavior in numerous, varied microsituations. (It is unfortunate that the studies of national samples mentioned above used very short versions of the F scale, for this raises questions about whether their measure of authoritarianism was accurate and whether they were measuring the kind of authoritarianism we were talking about.) And we relied, for support of our psychodynamic hypotheses, upon the correlations of the F scale with other variables. But Hyman and Sheatsley (1954) had an important point when they said that since we had not studied samples in which nonpsychodynamic factors might loom large, it could not be said that our main hypotheses was proved by the data we presented.

This kind of criticism has been the taking-off point for many studies of the determinants of authoritarianism, mainly studies in which the F scale or some variant of it has been the dependent variable. Some of these studies have tested some of our hypotheses concerning the origins of authoritarianism in childhood in the setting of the family. Harris, Gough, and Martin (1950) found that ethnic prejudice in children was associated with an accent on obedience, strict control, and inculcation of fear on the part of their parents. Frenkel-Brunswik (1954) reported that prejudice and associated personality characteristics in children were found most often in families where relationships were "characterized by fearful subservience to the demands of the parents and by an early suppression of impulses not acceptable to adults." Lyle and Levitt (1955) found that scores on a children's antidemocratic scale were correlated with parental punitiveness as measured by a sentence-completion test. Baumrind (1967), on the basis of careful observational studies of nursery school children and their parents, distinguished three patterns of parental behavior toward children: authoritative, authoritarian, and permissive. She concluded that the authoritative pattern is most favorable to the development of desirable traits in children, while the authoritarian pattern tends to give rise to distrust, withdrawal, discontent— traits that may be thought of as forerunuers of authoritarianism.

But studies of this kind have been few. Much more interest has centered on finding determinants of authoritarianism in culture, socioeconomic class (SES), and low educational status. Culture comes very much to the fore when the F scale, properly translated, is used in different nations. Workers in Germany (Cohn and Carsch, 1954) and students in Lebanon (Prothro and Melikian, 1953) and South

Africa (Pettigrew, 1958) obtained significantly higher F scale scores than do their counterparts in the United States. And, speaking of students, the F scale has been administered to many large samples of students, in all classes, in various higher educational institutions. According to the summary of this work by Feldman and Newcomb (1969), authoritarianism is significantly reduced over time, that is, is lower among seniors than among freshmen, in most colleges, a phenomenon that might be largely explained as adaptation to campus culture. What seems quite clear is that culture is a main determinant of the fact that F scale scores differ, in all classes, from one institution to another—being higher, for example, in church-related colleges than in secular ones, higher in vocational institutions than in those in which the liberal arts are accentuated.

Findings concerning the role of SES are not so clearcut. Lipset (1959) marshaled evidence from various studies, including *The Authoritarian Personality,* to show that authoritarianism is more pronounced in the lower than in the middle classes. Miller and Riessman (1961) took strong exception to Lipset's conclusions, which, however, were soon to receive support from Lipsitz's (1965) analysis of data from three surveys of opinion. The difficulty here seems to be that different types of authoritarianism have to be considered and that when large samples of lower-class people are brought into the picture cultural, or subcultural, differences become highly important.

Low education apparently is a major factor in authoritarianism and is largely responsible for correlations with low SES as well as with certain culture patterns. Selznick and Steinberg (1969) have brought together evidence from various studies of the relations of education to prejudice and authoritarianism—including their own —and have advanced more completely and effectively than anybody else what is by all odds the most important criticism of *The Authoritarian Personality.* They start by recognizing that the *findings* of the original study are largely intact; it is the *theory* to explain the findings that has to be called into question. The original theory, in their view, is not so much wrong as unnecessary since an alternative theory can better explain the facts we now have. The alternative theory is, roughly, a cognitive theory, in the tradition of Hyman and Sheatsley (1954), Rokeach (1960), and McClosky and Schaar (1965). The most essential idea is that authoritarianism can be explained as resulting from a lack of cognitive development, without recourse to psychodynamic or "ego defensive" theories. As Selznick and Steinberg (1969, p. 141) write, "What is at issue is not the face meaning of F beliefs but the reasons they are accepted. Does acceptance of F beliefs have psychological sources and intellectual consequences, as the original study claimed? Or does acceptance of F beliefs have intellectual sources and psychological consequences, as their relation to education strongly implies?" These authors go on to argue that Western society contains at least two cultures, the common and the enlightened, and that anti-Semitism and other forms of prejudice are simply aspects of the common culture. The question then is not why people *accept* anti-Semitic views but why some do not (p. 169). Selznick and Steinberg are not simple-minded about the ability of just any sort of formal education to reduce prejudice (p. 191); they say that "at its best, education involves a total belief system of a fairly general and abstract nature"; some people are less "receptive" to it than others, and some apparent freedom from prejudice in the upper middle class is simply "conformity."

A discussion of this thesis requires that we ask what education is. And what is culture, and how is it transmitted? To consider culture first, Kroeber and Parsons (1958) define it as "transmitted and created content and patterns of values, ideas, and other symbolic-meaningful systems." According to a major anthropological tradition culture is transmitted mainly by the family rather than by the school, and it becomes incorporated by personality not only through conformity or routine learning but through a variety of psychodynamic processes including unconscious identification with parents. The individual personality is not a mere carrier of culture; each assimilation of a social element is a product of something from the culture and something already in the person. Patterns of upbringing vary from one culture to another, but within a given culture they have enough generality and enough impact on personality that we may discuss a modal personality for that culture. Personality is not so fixed or durable, however, that it may not at any time of life change under the influence of cultural change. And individuals may, at any time, contribute to culture.

It follows that differences in F scale scores from one culture or subculture to another do not by any means contradict or downgrade the role of personality in authoritarianism. Selznick and Steinberg, however, would leave personality out altogether, relying simply on the learning of cultural norms or elements as an explanation for authoritarianism. No doubt such learning, or nonlearning, influences F scale scores and may even be largely responsible for high scores in the "surface resentment" type of authoritarianism and the "rigid" type of low authoritarianism. But any alternative theory of authoritarianism must explain the major finding of the original study—the patterning of the component dispositions. Why should anti-Semitism be associated with anxiety about sex, with self-glorification, with submissiveness toward authority? To say that this is "in the culture" or is due to a general lack of enlightenment (as Selznick and Steinberg do) is not an explanation. Why should the dispositions go together in a culture? I would argue as we did in *The Authoritarian Personality,* that they go together because they constitute a dynamic system, in an individual or in a social group. In any culture the common emotional impulses of individuals are shaped through shared experience in the social group, and ways of controlling these impulses are developed in the individual and in the group, thus forming and favoring cultural values. In any culture some individuals accept prevailing values and social codes without necessarily needing them for defensive purposes, but such individuals most quickly adopt the cultural elements they *do* need for such purposes; and any individual may develop methods for coping with the problems of life in the same way they were originally developed in his culture. Culture and personality continuously interact, in mutually supporting ways.

Although Selznick and Steinberg do not invoke personality theory to help explain the origins and working of the common culture, they at least assume individual differences in receptivity to enlightenment; and here, as noted above, they give the intellectual the primary determining role. On this point they have received a great deal of support from psychologists. Rokeach (1954, 1956, 1960) has taken the lead in arguing that the best way to conceive of authoritarianism—in his view "authoritarianism of the left" as well as authoritarianism of the sort so far discussed in this chapter—is not in terms of psychodynamic processes or even psychological content but in terms of cognitive style, most importantly the "open and closed mind." Rokeach states that his main intention has been to arrive at a conception of authoritarianism that is "more general." His conception is indeed more general; but it is also emptier. Anti-Semitism, or the tendency to ascribe all manner of evil to enemies foreign and domestic while thinking only good of ourselves, is expressive of a man's deepest passions, most certainly his basic needs and inner conflicts, not just his style of thinking. We were right, I believe, when we searched for the appeals of fascism in the 1940s, to study personality comprehensively and in depth, with attention to the interaction of cognitive and psychodynamic factors; and I would advocate the same course in the study of destructive ideologies today. What matters most in the study of prejudice and violence is who the victims are, how they are conceived, and who sanctions, by what means, the attacks upon them (Sanford and Comstock, 1971). It makes a big difference, and to a great many people, whether the victims are hippies at home and Asians abroad, with violence sanctioned by government agencies, or policemen and "the establishment," with sanctioning by a small and intimate group of true believers. To say that the actors in both cases are dogmatic or violent, without specifying what they are dogmatic about or violent against, is not enough, and to imply that it is enough is to skirt the real issues. Established authority reserves the right to say what is dogmatic and what kinds of violence are legitimate while exempting itself from any such categorization. Government-sponsored studies of violence, initiated in connection with the political activism which began in 1964, have been directed to violence per se or objectless violence, and, where the individual was concerned, they have been carried out according to the popular assumption that for this "ill" there must be a cure, such as a pill or an operation. These studies carry the implication that it is out-group violence that is bad, while our violence is, if not good, at least necessary, there being so much violence to contend with.

It is hard to make the argument for the primacy of cognitive style hold water. Kirscht and Dillehay (1967, p. 132) strongly support Rokeach. But then they go on to say, "Certain domains of belief often serve as foci for the close-minded style" (p. 133). Seeking to explain this statement they fall back on precisely the sort of formulation in psychodynamic terms that pervades *The Authoritarian Personality*— that is, that mental rigidity comes largely from anxiety, which comes from the arousal of impulses such as sex and aggression, which might be expressed in ways that run counter to powerful cultural demands.

Such formulations as this rode the crest of the wave in psychology during the 1940s, and *The Authoritarian Personality* participated in this trend; thus, one can appreciate the concern of some psychologists to give the cognitive a fair chance (Sanford, 1970b). But they don't have to go overboard or risk driving the whole boat onto the rocks. In the foregoing discussion, unfortunately, it has been necessary to speak of personality and culture and of the psychodynamic and the cognitive as if they were sharply separated opposites, in competition for the distinction of being the more important. That was not in the spirit of *The Authoritarian Personality*, which, though it gave most of its attention to dynamic theory of personality, also showed awareness of the intricacies of personality-culture and psychodynamic-cognitive relationships. Thus today, although I find little in the facts or theories of *The Authoritarian Personality* that seems fundamentally wrong, I have no difficulty in urging that we now stress the *interaction* of personality and culture, of psychodynamic and cognitive processes.

The last comes directly into focus when we consider education, which I as well as Selznick and Steinberg consider the essential counter to authoritarianism. But what is education? Selznick and Steinberg—in company, it seems, with most adherents of our enlightened culture—seem to assume that education is a matter of learning content and training intelligence, while I see it as a means for developing the whole personality. When my colleagues and I began to study education at the college level in 1952, we asked ourselves how authoritarianism might be reduced through education. We soon realized that the reductions over time in E and F scale scores that regularly occurred in a liberal arts college were not solely a matter of adaptation to campus culture, for correlations began to accumulate between degree and direction of change in scale score and a wide range of factors and processes within the academic environments. Since 1952 my colleagues and I have published many articles and several books treating this subject in detail (D. Brown and others, 1956; Sanford, 1957, 1958, 1959a, 1959b, 1960a, 1960b, 1961, 1962a, 1962b, 1963, 1964a, 1964b, 1966a, 1966b, 1967, 1968a, 1968b; Katz and others, 1968; Axelrod and others, 1969), and the trend in college studies that we started has resulted in an outpouring of publications relevant to the fate of authoritarianism in college. (For summaries of this work, see Webster, Freedman, and Heist, 1962; Katz and others, 1968; Chickering, 1969; Feldman and Newcomb, 1969.) Unfortunately, psychologists, sociologists, and political scientists are prevented by the norms of academic culture, which virtually prohibits their having anything to do with education, from reading any of this literature. (I could find only one reference to it in the dozens of papers, books, and monographs consulted in the course of preparing this chapter.) It is not possible adequately to summarize it here. The main point is that freedom from authoritarianism increases with education—not only because of exposure to enlightened culture, not only because of intellectual development, but because personality itself changes under the impact of well-directed education. Various features of the college environment work, or can be made to work, to reduce authoritarianism in personality: governance that helps the student become his own authority, course content that helps him become aware of his own impulses, teaching that challenges preconceptions and gives practice in criticism, faculty members who are models of independent thinkers, and a general climate of freedom and respect for the individual.[5]

In all this we deal with interactions, often very subtle, between the cognitive and the psychodynamic. For example, I know of one young woman whose system of primitive, right-wing authoritarian ideas was changed through a class in psychological statistics. She could not maintain her rigid mental compartments in the face of

---

[5] Several writers have called attention to the irony in the fact that when our study of anti-Semitism and fascism was published in 1950, the Cold War was on and national attention was focused on communism. There is irony also in the fact that at about the time our work on the college experience (its potentiality for liberating students through developing broader perspectives, relativity of values, self-insight, the courage and knowledge to challenge authority, and so forth) was beginning to catch on among educators, national attention became riveted upon students who were already "liberated." Of course, as the Feldman and Newcomb (1969) survey shows, the students involved in "protest" or "activism" were never more than a small minority of college students in the country at large. This does not downgrade the significance of student activism in the 1960s, but it does remind us that the great educational challenge was, and remains, how to help students develop beyond authoritarianism.

knowledge about variability, probability, and so forth. Her instructor found her crying in the corridor after a class, and her complaint was "You are ruining everything I ever believed." But I would argue that instruction in statistics would not have been so effective had this young woman not loved her teacher.

If this kind of change occurs in college, what, we may ask, about the schools? I have not been able to find any relevant longitudinal studies of junior high and high school students, but I would hypothesize that some relatively unprejudiced children become more prejudiced and some relatively prejudiced children become more liberated as they go through school—depending on the kind of school environment they encounter at different stages of personality development. Adelson (1971) has reported a highly significant study of the development of political ideas. He found that early adolescents are highly authoritarian, with significant reduction occurring in middle and late adolescence—largely because of cognitive development. For example, the early adolescent's relative inability to think abstractly or to cope with the relativity of values is highly favorable to his acceptance of authoritarian stereotypes. But the early adolescent's extraordinary bloodthirstiness toward deviants of all kinds must have to do with the problems of these young people in coping with their own impulses and with the authorities around them. Which comes first, the cognitive failings or the inner conflicts? Is it necessary to ask this question about processes so intimately bound up together? Certainly the problems of adolescents are the more difficult the less well the individual is able to think, but abstract thinking and relativity of values can be taught—though probably not to children who are afraid of their teachers or by teachers who cannot think abstractly themselves. Adelson has opened up a rich area for future research.

What To Do Now

The trouble with research on authoritarianism is that it has been research on *The Authoritarian Personality*. Instead of following the lead of this work—adapting its comprehensive, exploratory, empirical approach to the study of other problems, such as the appeals of communism or the new populism—personality psychologists have shown an obsession with the F scale. This preoccupation is not due just to laziness or a lack of imagination; it has to be understood in the light of the recent history of psychology and the politics of research. Since the early 1950s we have witnessed a gradual downgrading of the concept of the person and the growth of a kind of puritanical future orientation, expressed as a concern for building an eventually useful science on the model of nineteenth-century physics. In addition, there has been mounting pressure within—and from above—university departments for more and quicker publications. As a result, and with the full support of governmental funding agencies, a virtual ban has been placed on comprehensive inquiries into personality, on case studies, on naturalistic and exploratory studies—in short, on virtually everything necessary for the discovery of anything.

We should now launch a whole new attack on the problems of personality and politics, aiming at psychological understanding of the issues and the patterns of thought and action observed today. If we proceed in the way the authors of *The Authoritarian Personality* went about their work, the results cannot fail to be exciting and important. This fresh approach should take into account the fact that authoritarianism of the sort we studied in the 1940s is a psychohistorical conception—it owed much of its content and structure to the period in which it was observed and formulated. Indeed, its particularity in this respect accounts to ·a great extent for the value of the concept.

Max Horkheimer, in his foreword to our book, referred to the potential fascist we studied as "a new anthropological species," a person in whom the ideas and skills typical of a highly industrialized society were combined with irrational or antirational beliefs. According to this view, we could not hope fully to understand authoritarian leadership of the 1930₃ through studying Oliver Cromwell or Cotton Mather; and, by the same argument, the study of prefascist personalities in the highly industrialized society of the 1940s cannot be expected to tell us all we need to know about right-wing extremism in the postindustrial society of today.

Indications of change in the content and structure of what we called fascist potential are not hard to find. For one thing, many users of the F scale have called attention to out-of-date items: items that make direct reference to events of the time ("It is best to use some prewar authorities in Germany to keep order and prevent chaos") as well as items that seem to require a different interpretation today in view of changed circumstances or changes in the general climate of opinion—items, for instance, that make reference to work, science, authority, and sex.

Again, scale items that were once considered expressions of personality now have ideological significance. Recently a student asked me about personality measures that might be predictive of ideological trends among college students. I suggested, among others, the social maturity (SM) scale, developed by my colleagues and me in the early 1950s (Webster, Sanford, and Freedman, 1955), which now has a place in the Omnibus Personality Inventory (Heist, 1960). Our idea had been to produce an ideology-free instrument for measuring the F syndrome, by using items from established personality inventories such as the MMPI (Hathaway and McKinley, 1951). Our product, a scale comprising 123 items, had a reliability (KR-20) of .88 and correlated .74 with the F scale in large samples of Vassar freshmen. The student was back the next day to say that he could not use this instrument because it was loaded with ideology. An examination of the scale showed me that he was quite right. Items that in the 1950s could be regarded as expressive of such generalized personality dispositions as punitiveness, conformity, sex-role preference, or cynicism would surely be identified by today's students as middle class or as expressive or Consciousness I or II (Reich, 1970).

We have to consider, too, that personality dispositions which in the 1940s belonged to the F syndrome today belong to something else, or may indeed be different in meaning or in underlying source. Consider, for example, anti-intellectualism, which we saw as an important feature of potential fascism. In what we then called anti-intellectualism, theory was rejected in favor of "the facts"—the tangible and objective; intellectual activity, considered as a source of pleasure or meaning, was rejected in favor of keeping busy with practical affairs or throwing oneself into action and adventure; intellectual activity as a source of insight or as a guide to living was rejected in favor of external authority, religious faith, or the conventional wisdom. Anti-intellectualism was associated with opposition to feeling and, it seemed to us, lack of capacity for feeling. It was our view that in the high scorers on the F scale both thinking and feeling were inhibited, and consciousness constricted, because of a fear of impulses.

All this seems a pretty far cry from the anti-intellectualism among middle-class college students, which has been the subject of much comment in recent years. There is little interest among these students in the old issue of the things of the mind versus the practical, and recourse to authority of some kind as the source of truth and knowledge seems to have been replaced by recourse to feeling and intuition. Thinking (disciplined thinking, at any rate) and feeling are separated and set in opposition, the former being rejected apparently because of its association with "big science" or that super-rationality (thinking separated from feeling and value?) that has got us into so much trouble as a nation—uncontrolled technology, Vietnam, and so forth. This way of sorting things out favors the expansion, or perhaps the altera-tion, of consciousness and the direct expression of impulses. This new anti-intel-lectualism may have something in common with the old: both may be ways of coping with a world that becomes increasingly hard to understand or to do anything about. But we cannot really tell without carrying out, today, theoretically based clinical studies of the kind reported in *The Authoritarian Personality* and summarized above.

The argument here is that personality itself—not just issues and ways of regarding them—changes with the times. The prototypic right-wing authoritarian of the 1930s and 1940s now seems a bit quaint; and as we look to the future, it seems that we have to worry less about old-fashioned dictatorships than about domination by corporate systems that nobody seems able to control. And if the "authoritarian family," the one presided over by a father whose sternness and rigidity increased as he lost his grip on affairs in the larger world, is changing or disappearing in pace with the liberation of women and the decline in the birthrate, we can certainly expect change in the type of personality we saw developing in this sort of family.

When I say that personality changes with the times, I do not mean that the general laws governing its functioning will have to be rewritten or that we must abandon our sense of kinship with the ancient Greeks or the neurotic personalities of Freud's time. There are universal human dilemmas, such as how to gratify basic emotional impulses in ways that do not violate the norms of one's culture, and there are, apparently, universal laws governing the ways in which inner conflicts are re-solved: for example, the conditions under which one or another defense against a proscribed impulse will be chosen. Naturally, we expect little historical change in these basic functions.

A given child's ways of coping with inner conflicts bear great similarity to those of many other people in his society, and we arrive readily enough at the notion of a major pattern of culture. We know from anthropologists that patterns of culture differ from one society to another, and we can conclude from the same kinds of observations they have made that culture patterns may change from time to time in the same society. As early as the 1930s American psychoanalysts were complaining that they could not find among candidates for their treatment any "simple hysterics" of the type Freud described; and they were soon to learn that such patients had become rare in Vienna too. To explain how and why this change took place would take us too far afield. The point for us here is that we have to deal in such instances with highly significant change—not, to be sure, in human nature itself, but in processes that are central to the functioning of personality; specifically, such processes are observable in the ways in which sexual and aggressive impulses find guilt-free overt expression and in preferred types of defense against proscribed impulses: for example, repression in 1890, as contrasted with the separation of behavior from feeling, or acting as if one had no problems today.

Changes of this kind are reflected in instruments like the F scale. This instrument does, to be sure, rest on some assumptions concerning universal, or nearly universal, human ways: for example, that parents cannot bring up children without frustrating them and thereby arousing hostility, and that hostility against parents is a potent source of anxiety. We must, however, allow for the possibility of historical change in respect to who does the punishing, the kinds and severity of punishment, and the ways in which hostility and anxiety are managed; and we should expect changes of these kinds to be expressed in political behavior and ideology.

Rokeach (1960), in seeking a more general conception of authoritarianism, may have been concerned about the time-boundedness of our syndrome and was seeking a conception of personality characteristics—cognitive style—that would be predictive of political extremism in all times as well as in various places. But cognitive processes are not immune to historical change; in any case, they are bound up with psychodynamic processes that most certainly change over time. The political behavior that we really worry about is usually particular, like the fascism and the communism of the 1930s and 1940s or our Manichean foreign policy in the Cold War period and the Vietnam policy of the Johnson-Nixon administrations. The rightist authoritarian we studied in the 1940s participated in and was shaped by, even as he helped to shape, the life of his times; and we should expect the same of political man today.

Although a man's personality and his politics are all of one piece, the two can be separated, by abstraction, for purposes of study. We must bring to bear upon contemporary political behavior and thought all the knowledge we have of personality and its development. Political scientists have to find a "human basis for the polity" (Knutson, 1972a), and the best candidate, surely, is personality theory. We can build on the kind of theory of human functioning that went into *The Authoritarian Personality* and on that work's demonstration of the clustering of attitudes and opinions, of the intimate relations between cognitive and psychodynamic process, and of the importance of irrational factors in the determination of political outlook. Even more important, we can build on its way of studying personality and ideology—not the specifics, which have their shortcomings, but the general approach. And we can build on some developments in personality research that have occurred since 1950.

How shall we look at personality today? I should say that dispositional structures of personality, such as rightist authoritarianism, are less closely related to behavior, less fixed or durable, and owe less to early childhood experiences than the authors of *The Authoritarian Personality* supposed. Particularly important, from the point of view of personality theory, is the notion—barely touched upon in *The Authoritarian Personality*—that personality structures, even "deep" or "central" ones, are sustained by the social system in which the individual lives and can change when that system changes. Study of the loyalty oath controversy at the University of California at Berkeley (Sanford, 1953) showed that situational pressures can be of crucial importance in determining behavior and may, when sustained, bring about changes in personality itself. Forced by overwhelming pressure to go against con-science in signing a special loyalty oath, individuals suffered a change in the structure of the superego and in the relations of the superego and the ego. What happened within a relatively short span of time then may also happen very gradually, as when a dean over the years comes to identify himself with an authoritarian social role. By the same token, authoritarianism in personality can be reduced in college, and quite probably in other kinds of organizations. Adelson (1971) says it is reduced in high school. He suggests that such reduction is mainly a maturational process, and per-haps it is. When high school students have been studied as much as college students have, however, we may find that certain school experiences reinforce adolescent authoritarianism and that other experiences speed up the developmental process.

The personality syndromes most useful in understanding and predicting politi-cal behavior will surely embrace both cognitive and psychodynamic factors. It is interesting to note in this connection that the potential for fascism we described in 1950, by definition a highly complex phenomenon, has never been satisfactorily re-solved into measurable components. The F scale resists satisfactory factor analysis—largely, I think, because each of its items is complex, designed to be expressive of more than one of the theoretical components we conceived of. I suggested in 1954 that "in place of further analysis of the present F scale, one perform the [factor] analysis with an instrument three or four times as long. . . . A greatly lengthened F scale could easily be composed of items we discarded or items suggested by our later clinical findings, and this is to say nothing of the large number of items written by other workers in the course of constructing scales that correlated with F" (Sanford, 1954, p. 24). Harold Webster, Mervin Freedman, and I had this very much in mind when we set about developing the 123-item "nonideological" social maturity scale mentioned earlier (Webster, Sanford, and Freedman, 1955). The simple and straight-forward items of this scale fell readily into classes that made sense, but we never got around to a formal factor analysis.

O'Neil and Levinson (1954) had much the same idea that we did. They performed a factor analysis using eight items from the F scale, eight items pertaining to enthnocentrism, six to religious conventionalism, and ten to traditional family ideology. Four factors were extracted: religious conventionalism, authoritarian sub-mission, masculine strength facade, and moralistic control. The last three of these factors correspond to hypothetical dispositions considered in the construction of the original F scale. Factor analysis of a greatly lengthened scale might provide more empirical support for our original formulations, or it might give a different and more adequate picture of the dimensions of authoritarianism.

Robert Holt (1972) is addressing himself to this same problem. He wants to "dimensionalize, in an area that has been dominated by typological concepts." And he takes the same view of the F scale that I have been trying to put forward here: "The method by which the scale was constructed, relying on the fact that the various types of items did in fact covary, froze into an instrument and into an operational definition of a concept a particular configuration of attitudes that existed at a partic-ular time and place in history, partly for extrinsic reasons." His further work will, of course, take into account the likelihood that the prevailing pattern of authoritarian attitudes has shifted. It will also take into account recent progress in personality research. About the time *The Authoritarian Personality* was published, Jane Loevinger suggested to its authors that the authoritarianism we studied was best conceived as a stage of ego development. *The Authoritarian Personality* had a great deal to say about ego weakness and ego strength, finding many apparent manifestations of the former among the high scorers on the F scale, many apparent manifestations of the latter among the low scorers. Loevinger proceeded to view the whole matter in a developmental perspective. On the basis of data gathered by means of a sentence-completion test, she defined six stages of ego development: (1) the presocial and symbiotic, (2) the impulsive, (3) the conforming, (4) the conscientious, (5) the autonomous, (6) the integrated. If one reads her *Measuring Ego Development* (1970) in conjunction with *The Authoritarian Personality,* it is easy to come to the conclusion that the first three stages are more characteristic of high scorers, the last three of low scorers on the F scale. This study, it seems to me, is a nice example of the way to make progress in personality research: to proceed from a vague and global notion to a set of differentiated and measurable variables. Anyone about to study personality and politics today would do well to include among his instruments for measuring personality the Loevinger sentence-completion test.

But, of course, in such a study we should not wish to limit ourselves to possible components of the 1950 version of right-wing authoritarianism. Jeanne Knutson, in undertaking her comprehensive study of personality in relation to political participation, leadership, and socialization, looked far and wide for relevant personality variables before settling on the following scales: security-insecurity (Maslow, 1941–1942), anomia (Srole, 1956), manifest anxiety (Taylor, 1953), status concern (Silberstein and Seeman, 1959), esteem (Milbrath and Klein, 1962), faith in people (Rosenberg, 1954), dogmatism (Rokeach, 1960), intolerance of ambiguity (Budner, 1962), threat orientation (Martin and Westie, 1959), the F scale, and her own measures of the needs in Maslow's hierarchy (Knutson, 1972). She began this work in 1967. A few years later she very probably would have included Loevinger's sentence-completion test (Loevinger and Wessler, 1970) and the Kohlberg (1971) measures of moral development.

There is, of course, a lot of intercorrelation among these measures, and the question of what are the basic factors must be left open. A correlational analysis of all the items of these scales and Robert Holt's proposed dimensionalization of everything that goes into contemporary right- and left-wing authoritarianism might very well yield a similar set of factors.

The scales and other measures mentioned here, with the exception of the F scale, seem heavily weighted on the side of what the psychoanalysts call ego psychology. The personality psychologists may be missing a bet. The F scale, for all its faults, at least considered that man is a whole, that he is alive and filled with passion. Maybe the troubles of the F scale scared the psychologists away from trying to get at man, so conceived, by means of objective and quantitative methods. As far as I know, the only scale developed in recent years that is based on psychodynamic theory is the Fromm-Maccoby scale for measuring "love of life" versus opposite tendencies (Fromm and Maccoby, 1971). This instrument has already been called, by a leading psychologist (Smith, 1971b), worse than the F scale in its methodology, and I agree; but it has demonstrated an extraordinary capacity to predict political behavior— for example, in separating McGovern from Nixon supporters in August 1972 (Comstock and Duckles, 1972). Apparently the only thing it has going for it is the fact that it works. Duckles, Comstock, and others are now developing a more elaborate scale based on the Fromm-Maccoby theory. I should like to see the instrument for studying destructiveness (Sanford and Comstock, 1971) supplemented by instruments for characterizing and measuring self-conception, unconscious sex identity, and unconscious fantasy, and then used in the study of various kinds of political behavior and outlook, including images of and attitudes toward ethnic minorities, females, and males.

What are the political problems and patterns that most invite study today? I am willing to leave this largely in the hands of political scientists, though I would suggest that they look again at the types of highs and lows described in *The Authoritarian Personality.* The differences between surface resentment and other types have been explored to great advantage by D. Katz and his associates (Sarnoff and Katz, 1954; Katz, McClintock, and Sarnoff, 1956, 1957; Katz, 1960), and by Pettigrew (1958) and Smith (1965), all of whom have made a distinction between "cognitive" and "ego-defensive" authoritarianism. The "rigid low" calls attention to what people scoring at the two extremes on the F scale have in common. "Left-wing authoritarianism" has so far been poorly conceived and poorly investigated. I have insisted elsewhere (Sanford, 1956; Sanford and Comstock, 1971) that the F scale and Rokeach's (1960) dogmatism scale are flimsy vehicles for carrying the enormous weight of left-wing ideologies. The role of personality in such ideologies still awaits thorough study, as do other patterns suggested by our types of high and low authoritarianism. In studying such patterns I would proceed in much the same way that we did in the studies leading to *The Authoritarian Personality;* and I would be guided, today, by some principles of "action research."

Let us start with naturalistic observations of, and interviews with, likely subjects, covering a wide range of possibly significant factors. Let us then observe what goes together and form hypotheses about these coherences, check these hypotheses in more directed interviews and with the use of projective techniques, and carry out some case studies to reveal something of the organization of relevant processes in individuals. *Then* we can define some variables with precision and develop measures of them, which can be put into appropriate research designs.

The subjects of this kind of research must also be its clients; that is the first principle of action research (Sanford, 1969, 1970c). Suppose we want to know about personality patterns in black consciousness, the new left, or the women's liberation movement. We would not proceed by asking questions whose implications were unknown to our subjects or by inducing them to take part in experiments whose purposes were concealed. We would instead ask, in our own way, questions that *they* want answers to, and that have a relevance to their purposes, and they would be the first to receive a report of our findings. We, as scientists, put the pursuit of truth at the top of our value hierarchy, and nobody will object to that. But since what we do in the name of this value has practical consequences, we have to decide whether we are content merely to be neutral (which means that our "facts" become available, almost exclusively, to those who already have everything) or whether we are committed to building a more humane and more rationally organized society. If the latter, few of our prospective subjects, or subject-clients, will refuse to work with us.

The other day I was talking with a student about his study of different white image patterns of black people in relation to more general political orientations. He asked, "How do I get reactionary subjects?" That is the question—the question for research. If he can find out how to persuade reactionary subjects to take part, on the basis of their own knowledgeable choosing, in a psychological inquiry, he will know a great deal about how to reduce the paranoid style in American politics. Since that is what we really want to know, why not go about finding out directly, by approaching subjects in the spirit of action research?

"Reactionary subjects" can be approached directly. They are, after all, law-abiding citizens who openly favor quality education, scientific inquiry, and decency in interpersonal relationships. The first thing to do is to quit stereotyping them (as I have perhaps just done) and then to see if one can keep one's head while engaging them in a discussion of politics. The stereotyping is a serious matter. It follows almost inevitably from our delineation of types of personality and politics. We must force ourselves to remember that this "reactionary," this "high scorer," who makes us a little anxious, is still very much of an individual and not all that different from ourselves. Like everybody else, he can further develop his personality; and to help him and others do that is the ultimate aim of all our work with him.

7

ANOMIE, ALIENATION, AND POLITICAL BEHAVIOR

J. Milton Yinger

It is scarcely surprising, in a period of almost continuous conflict within and between nations, that students of politics should devote a major share of their attention to the sources of disorder, of disaffection, of political negativism. This attention matches a widespread concern among other observers of the contemporary scene.

The prevailing images of our culture are images of disintegration, decay, and despair; our highest art involves the fragmentation and distortion of traditional realities; our best drama depicts suffering, misunderstanding, and breakdown; our worthiest novels are narratives of loneliness, searching, and unfulfillment; even our best music is, by earlier standards, dissonant, discordant, and inhuman. Judged by the values of past generations, our culture seems obsessed with breakdown, splintering, disintegration, and destruction. Ours is an age not of synthesis but of analysis, not of constructive hopes but of awful destructive potentials, not of commitment but of alienation [Keniston, 1965, p. 4; see also Sykes, 1964].

171

In such a context, which is by no means new in human experience, certain terms acquire unusual salience. Critical words are revived or new ones are invented that seem to help us deal, both emotionally and intellectually, with the flood of disturbing experiences and observations. If we are not careful, a few "big" concepts become the code words of an intellectual tradition and are used as explanations rather than as labels for complex situations that require explanation. Our vocabularies become involved in the desire to simplify our enormous problems—whether of action or research. Use of key words becomes the mark of the sensitive person, a demonstration that he is *au courant,* if not *avant garde.* Under such conditions, these words take on a great variety of meanings, as they spread from their original base to one related phenomenon after another. In the end they may refer to vast problem areas; they may be more indicative of a mood of the times and of an intellectual tradition than of a specified referent.

Anomie and *alienation* are among the code words of contemporary intellectuals. If we do not use them with care—subjecting them to linguistic and methodological analysis—we may, unwittingly, illustrate the truth of Walter Kaufman's appraisal: "As it becomes more and more impossible to keep up with developments in different fields, most people feel a growing need for bargain words that cost little or no study and can be used in a great variety of contexts with an air of expertise" (in Schacht, 1971, p. xlix). This risk is the greater because our key terms have both value-laden and objective components; they are critical appraisals of society and of individual tendencies at the same time that they are attempts to describe. John Horton (1964) may exaggerate when he writes that anomie is "basically a utopian concept of the political right," focused on the need for social control, while alienation is "a utopian concept of the radical left," focused on domination; but he makes clear the need for keeping alert to the critical and evaluative connotations of the words as we explore their descriptive and analytic uses.

Despite the great frequency with which alienation and anomie are used in research and in critical writing, there have been relatively few attempts to subject the concepts themselves to analysis. (For exceptions to this statement see Keniston, 1965; Merton, 1968; Schacht, 1971; Seeman, 1959.) In his article on Durkheim in the *International Encyclopedia of the Social Sciences* (1968), Talcott Parsons states that "Anomie has become one of the small number of truly central concepts of contemporary social science." Yet there is no article on anomie in this encyclopedia or in its 1931 predecessor. Parsons refers to the concept only briefly, as do a few others writing for the *Encyclopedia.* There are articles on alienation in both encyclopedias, but the earlier one refers only to its economic-legal meanings and the latter mainly to its historical uses.

We are left, then, with highly significant words of broad and open-ended meanings. Some of our attention will have to be given to questions of usage and definition as we seek to assess the importance of anomie and alienation for politics.

Anomie

Although anomie (or "anomy," in an English spelling) was used at least as early as the sixteenth century to refer to a condition of disorder, doubt, and uncertainty (Merton, in Clinard, 1964, p. 226), it nearly disappeared from view until revived by Durkheim in *The Division of Labor* (1893) and, much more fully, in *Suicide* (1897). There is some ambiguity in Durkheim's usages, but the predominant meaning is clear: *Anomie is a state of society in which norms have lost their power to regulate behavior.* A literal translation of the Greek source might read "no laws" (*a nomous*). It is deregulation. There is, in Parsons' phrase, a lack of structured complementarity in human interaction. Thus defined, anomie is a property of the cultural system; it is not a quality of individuals. It is a near equivalent of anarchy, if government is the referent, where no group or political system is granted sufficient legitimacy to govern.

Although Durkheim used *anomie* most commonly to refer to a quality of groups with low levels of agreement on norms and values, he occasionally used it to refer to lack of integration in functions. An industrial crisis, for example, would be an indication of anomie insofar as the various activities of a specialized work force did not combine in ways to achieve mutually accepted goals. If the two meanings are combined, we would say that a society is anomic when it exhibits a low degree of consensus and a low degree of integration. Merton (1968) has suggested, however, that a special kind of dissensus, in a context of low integration, characterizes anomic societies. He notes that industrial societies particularly have encouraged their members to strive for newly accessible goals; at the same time, less attention has been paid to teaching respect for, or furnishing opportunities for, culturally approved means. Anomie, in Merton's sense, exists when agreement on goals is not matched by agreement on appropriate means to those goals, or when many persons are caught in circumstances where approved means do not yield expected satisfactions (pp. 185–248). In Merton's words, "An extreme cultural emphasis on the goal of success attenuates conformity to institutionally prescribed methods of moving toward this goal. . . . Norms are robbed of their power to regulate behavior" (p. 223).

My own preference is to consider this a particularly important kind of anomie in industrial, and probably industrializing, societies, but not to use it as a definition of anomie. It is perhaps too culture-bound to be useful as a general description of the phenomenon of deregulation, of the absence of pattern in the mutual expectations for social action.

Anything approaching an objective reading of the extent of anomie has proved difficult to achieve for two reasons. First of all, the implicit critical and evaluative element in the concept allows each of us to load our own perspectives onto the reading process. Second, deregulation as a quality of social systems is intrinsically difficult to measure. Each of these requires brief comment.

Problems in Definition. Almost all commentary on anomie (see, for instance, DeGrazia, 1948b) assumes that it is an unfortunate quality; but such an assumption implies a comparison with some other social arrangement that is preferable. When specific values are stated, anomie can take on a desirable connotation. "There was probably a high level of anomie in the American colonies in 1775—a necessary aspect of the disengagement from the British Empire. Perhaps increase in anomie is an inevitable part of the process whereby old tyrannies are broken and new values given a field for growth" (Yinger, 1965, pp. 189–190). Even so, anomie is undoubtedly associated with chaos and human suffering under some conditions. What we lack, however, are clear indications of the consequences of given levels of anomie, experienced by specified populations or subpopulations, under particular circumstances. In the absence of such indications, values and fears play a large part in our assessments of the extent and the effects of anomie. Violence, discord, and deviation are highly visible and readily seen as clear indexes of anomie. In a somewhat nostalgic *Gemeinschaft-Gesellschaft* tradition, we may tend to compare contemporary societies with partially imaginary models of small, smooth-running, integrated rural societies, where all members agreed on goals and means and were well socialized to their positions.

In my judgment, the extent of anomie in a society is a crucial variable for the student of politics and of other social processes. It will become a powerful concept, however, only if we can learn to measure it reliably and validly, overcoming our ideological readings of the evidence. The tendency today may be to overlook signs of consensus and integration, to forget the invention of various techniques of mediation and arbitration, to disregard the emergence of new norms out of conflicts that weakened the old norms. Since many periods in history characterized by sharp value disagreements and conflict have been followed by periods of greater consensus and integration, there are clearly norm-building as well as norm-destroying processes in human societies (Becker, 1960). Were this not the case, we would have to think in terms of an analog of the second law of thermodynamics, with social systems inevitably running down from some presumed aboriginal state of integration. We will be wise to think of existing levels of anomie and the trends as qualities of society to be studied, not assumed. References to the reciprocal quality, integration, can be of great value in identifying anomic situations (Freedman and others, 1956, pp. 170–203).

Problems in Measurement. There are strong tendencies, as we shall see, to reduce anomie to a psychological term. (We will examine such uses in the next section, since they are conceptually closer to alienation than to anomie as originally defined.) Even among those who have kept a strictly structural meaning, however, measures of levels of anomie have been only poorly developed. Research on the effects of anomie on politics (or of politics on the level of anomie) will remain rudimentary until more adequate measures have been designed. Doubtless some combination of direct measures, indexes, and individual items aggregated into group measures can produce a valuable scale of anomie.

Durkheim used international and economic crises and family instability as indicators of anomie. Crime rates and other forms of "deviation" have been used as indexes. (One should not be surprised that anomie thus measured is associated with deviation. And any inference of causation, running in either direction, is unjustified when such a procedure is followed.) Data on the size and cost of "social control" structures—police forces, for example—may produce a useful index of anomie. Records of the availability and use of mediation and arbitration procedures are valuable. They indicate arrangements for preventing value disagreements from spiraling into more serious forms of conflict. They could be read alongside records of group conflict.

Anomie may be more characteristic of societies with heterogeneous populations; it therefore could be "measured" by data on cultural origins; ethnic identity; religious, racial, and lingual diversity; and other demographic information. A related dimension is the group structure of a population. Cross-cutting memberships that increase communication, contact, and shared perspectives across important lines of social distinction may well signify low anomie; the lack of such memberships indicates, at least under some conditions, high anomie.

Various forms of collective behavior may be good indexes of anomie. It may be high, for example, in societies where religious sects or cults are proliferating, where revitalization movements express efforts to recapture a lost sense of cultural identity, where third-party or other "splinter" political groups indicate a reduced sense of allegiance to the traditional or established political processes.

Measures of individual attitudes and values—if they are clearly recognized as indexes of anomie, not manifestations of it—are likely to be among the simplest ways to assess the extent of deregulation. Levels of alienation, as we shall see, are often used in this way. In contrast, the extent of tolerance, as a value or expressed in behavior, might indicate the degree to which members of a society share a cultural perspective. A good index, of course, changes in close correlation with the variable it indexes—as a column of mercury rises or falls in a glass tube when temperature changes. Psychological and social indexes are seldom so valid; they must be used in conjunction with other measures.

More direct measures would go beyond the aggregation of individual attitudes or other tendencies to study the extent to which a group of interactors live in a similar cultural world. This procedure has been followed by Jessor and his associates (1968) in their study of a tri-ethnic community. A sample of the community's members were asked to indicate whether they thought that certain activities were prescribed, permitted, or proscribed. The modal answers and the variances were calculated. The higher the proportion of responses in the modal category and the smaller the variance, the lower the level of anomie. By this process Jessor and his associates were able both to define the concept operationally and to treat it as a variable, with a range of possible scale values (see especially pp. 244–258). It may be well to repeat that this is a group measure; it represents a loss of pattern in mutual expectations for social action. Where the modal category is small and the variance around it large, anomie is experienced even by those in the very center of the mode as well as by those who are distant from it.

If Merton's (1968) somewhat narrower definition of anomie is used, measurement requires, as he notes (p. 229), the combination of several sets of data: information on exposure to cultural goals and to norms that regulate efforts to achieve those goals; acceptance, within various segments of a population, of those goals and norms; the extent to which the goals are accessible—the jobs, schools, and other supports in the opportunity structure; and the extent of discrepancy between accepted goals and their accessibility.

These references to problems of measurement may help to explain why anomie has been poorly developed as a research concept. Most studies use a few individual characteristics or attitudes as an index of anomie, or even let the distinction between a group and an individual property slip away entirely. An adequate social psychology of political behavior is blocked by this process, for what we need are clear analytic distinctions among elements, a clear designation of individual and group levels, and then studies of the results of their various combinations. This procedure is followed in the study of many social scientific problems. We have no difficulty distinguishing between the group fact of a wealthy society and a particular individual's wealth. It is clear that to be poor in a wealthy society is a different experience from being poor in a society characterized by poverty. The same distinction, though often disregarded, is essential in studies of anomie and alienation. In most cases it is more difficult to measure a structural property than an individual property. More data are required; problems of reliability are greater. Any one or two measures are likely to yield an incomplete picture of the social structure. Perhaps a combination of several of the sets of data I have suggested above, however, can begin to produce an adequate measure of anomie. Such a measure remains, several decades after Durkheim, a primary research need.

It is important not to confuse anomie with possible responses to it. Perhaps the most frequently cited part of Merton's work on anomie is his analysis of types of responses. Upon experiencing the disjunction between means and ends which Merton defined as anomie, a person may act in a number of different ways. His response depends upon the severity of the experience, his other inclinations, his social location, and other variables. Merton (1968, pp. 193–211) lists five possibilities: A person may continue to accept the culturally approved means and ends as best he can; he may "innovate" in means (for instance, he may steal to try to achieve a culturally urged standard of living); he may act ritualistically by accepting the means, even if the ends are thus denied; he may retreat into apathy or neurosis, trying to solve the contradiction by inaction; or he may rebel, in an effort to create a new pattern of means and ends without the contradictions. Although this paradigm has great relevance for politics, it has not been systematically applied to political behavior. It has been most intensively used to examine the varieties of delinquent behavior, a topic we cannot explore here (see Clinard, 1964; Cloward and Ohlin, 1960; Cohen, 1965); but Merton's scheme is valuable because it requires a clear distinction between anomie and behavior and thus encourages us to search for individual factors—alienation among others—that must be brought into the system of explanation.

Alienation

In a few hours' time, one can identify hundreds of articles and books that use the term *alienation*. Its roots go back hundreds of years in theological work, at least to Hegel in philosophy and to Marx in political and economic thought. It is prominent in existentialist writing, both religious and secular, in some forms of psychoanalysis, in social science, in literature, and in many polemical and critical studies of modern society. Perhaps its currency in the United States today can be shown by noting that three of the five persons giving nominating speeches at the 1972 Democratic party convention referred to alienation.

Since the boundaries set by this word, broad as they are, are indistinct, we must also note the great frequency with which other terms are used to refer to similar phenomena. There are various degrees of overlap in the meanings of alienation and the meanings attached to pessimism, powerlessness, cynicism, "ressentiment" (as discussed by Max Scheler), despair, feelings of external (in contrast with internal) control, existential anxiety, authoritarianism, lack of efficacy, distrust, credibility gap, apathy, necrophilia, meaninglessness, normlessness, self-estrangement, and isolation. To make our task even more complicated, we must add the words *anomia, anomy,* and *anomie* (like Mark Twain, social scientists have no sympathy for ignorant people who know only one way to spell a word), which are currently used more often to refer to a property of individuals than of groups. We are not likely to be much better off if we shift to German and compare the overlapping meanings of Hegel's *Entäusserung* renunciation, surrender), Marx's *Entfremdung* (estrangement, alienation), and Weber's *Entzauberung* (disenchantment, discovery of the senseless quality of the world).

In the face of such complexity and confusion, perhaps the wisest thing for the writer—or at least the reader—is to turn quickly to the next chapter. But there is something about the word *alienation* that will not let go of the modern mind. It draws us into a huge and indefinite but highly significant aspect of the human situation. Whether as a critical and polemical term or as an analytic construct, we cannot set it aside. It would simply reappear with a different spelling. Although it seems impossible now to get a reasonably precise definition of alienation that would be widely accepted, we can at least sketch its meanings as a "sensitizing" concept. The tasks of research, then, are to take some segment of the concept, to design ways to measure that segment, to study its relationships to other segments, and to examine the ways in which the various forms of alienation are expressed in particular contexts. Only gradually will we discover which of the many individual tendencies that various authors have chosen to identify as forms of alienation actually "belong together," on the class if not the species level (in the sense that the bat, the whale, and the lion belong together as mammals).

Much of the contemporary interest in alienation stems from Marx. His emphasis was on the work situation but spreads easily to politics, religion, and other elements of the "establishment." "What constitutes the alienation of labor? First, that the work is *external* to the worker, that it is not part of his nature; and that, consequently, he does not fulfill himself in his work but denies himself, has a feeling of misery rather than well-being, does not develop freely his mental and physical energies but is physically exhausted and mentally debased. The worker, therefore, feels himself at home only during his leisure time, whereas at work he feels homeless" (Marx, 1844, pp. 124–125).

Fromm, another major source of attention to alienation, focuses somewhat more on the individual experience than the external force, but his definition is not inconsistent with Marx's: "By alienation is meant a mode of experience in which the person experiences himself as an alien. He has become, one might say, estranged from himself. He does not experience himself as the center of his world, as the creator of his own acts—but his acts and their consequences have become his masters, whom he obeys, or whom he may even worship" (Fromm, 1955, p. 120).

There is clearly a polemical quality in the use of alienation by Marx and Fromm. Alienation is bad, and it is largely the product of bad institutions. In trying to asess its value as a concept for political psychology, however, we perhaps ought to remind ourselves that most of us applaud certain alienations. We can evaluate them only in terms of their influence on the attainment of stated goals; "if most men are mere caricatures of what they might be, it is quite possible that in order to become more humane they must first become more estranged. This notion finds support not only in Hegel but also in some of the world's great religions" (Kaufman, in Schacht, 1971, pp. liv–lv).

Alienation, as I shall use the term, implies a time dimension: one experiences the loss of a relationship or value. One cannot be estranged without having been attached. The term is useful only if that from which one is alienated is specified. The politically alienated feel estranged from political structures and processes that formerly were accepted as valuable means to desired goals. This is a rather severe limitation of the concept, but I think it is essential. If the feeling of powerlessness is an aspect of alienation, we must distinguish it from the experience of powerlessness as an endemic fact of life. The causes and consequences of alienative powerlessness and endemic powerlessness are quite different.

It is important to ask whether alienation is a diffuse condition, unrelated to new structures and goals, or whether it implies a kind of zero-sum situation, in which alienation from one group or set of standards implies integration with others. Most commonly, alienation is thought of only in the first or total sense. Alienated persons are said to be without goals, negativistic, distrustful. Keniston (1965) found that the extremely alienated young men whom he studied wholly distrusted any affirmation. "Theirs is an ideology of opposition, and the world offers so many targets for their repudiation that they have little energy left for the development of affirmative values" (p. 69). This we might call acute alienation. We are dealing, however, with a variable, not an attribute. Few people are cut off from all group attachments and goals. One who is alienated from an established church may join a sect—or a golf club. The politically alienated may join protest movements. Some of the alienated young see themselves as sharing a contraculture or achieving integration through "Consciousness III." In short, measures of distrust, lack of efficacy, and the like, should always refer to particular structures and values. Efforts should be made to discover the strength and nature of the attachments that alienated persons do have. If there are none, this is a special case that requires separate analysis of its causes and effects.

Alienation, then, is the experienced loss of a relationship and of a sense of participation and control, with reference to prevailing social structures. It may or may not be associated with new attachments designed to counter the loss. Self-alienation is not a different phenomenon but is an internal view of the same loss; for central to self-definition are the attachments to the interpersonal and institutional world that surrounds each person.

Sources and Dimensions. It would take us too far from the study of the political implications of alienation to review the literature dealing with it as a general concept, but three questions require brief comment: What are various explanations of the origin or sources of alienation? What are its several dimensions or forms? And how may these be measured?

Two traditions, which we can somewhat inexactly call the Marxian and the Freudian, furnish many of the explanations of the sources of alienation. In the first, an oppressive economic or political structure produces the sense of estrangement. Many recent studies document the relationship, if not the exact causal connection (Blauner, 1964; Lipsitz, 1964; but see also Seeman, 1971). Using a somewhat broader sociological frame of reference, many authors see alienation as a result of frustrations produced by the social strucutre or as a consequence of its anomic qualities (Parsons, 1950, pp. 256–267; Etzioni, 1968; Fromm, 1955). Those in the Freudian tradition emphasize the interpersonal, and particularly the childhood experiences as sources of alienation. If a child feels severely cut off from necessary emotional supports as he moves into new and more complicated personal relationships, he may attempt to handle his "exile" by interpreting *his* condition as the human condition. Having projected one's own feelings of anguish onto "society," one cannot afford to permit any attachment, any trust of others, because this might expose the true location of his difficulties. Keniston (1965, pp. 53–54, 61) describes the situation well:

> In all young men and women the advent of adulthood releases immense new energies and potentials, which in most are centrally involved in establishing new intimacies with the opposite sex. This new learning is seldom smooth; but when it is severely blocked by unresolved needs and frustrations from the past, it takes but a slight catalyst—and often no catalyst at all—to transform these energies into rage, scorn, and aggression, often symbolically directed against those who have stood in the way of full adulthood. . . . The alienated prefer to maintain that the world is a dark and gloomy place rather than to say simply that they are pessimistic. Psychologically, it is important that they see the world, the state of the universe, as *causing* and justifying their own pessimism.

The structural and the interpersonal sources of alienation are not, of course, mutually exclusive, and many authors (Barakat, 1969; Keniston, 1965) emphasize their interaction. On an analytic level, nevertheless, the distinction is important, for the balance of sources in particular cases may critically influence the strength and direction of behavior—including political behavior—that expresses the alienation.

The great complexity and diversity of phenomena that have been labeled alienation have prompted a number of scholars to describe its several "dimensions." Such an effort is often based on the assumption that some unity underlies the several forms. It is not enough, of course, that they happen to be called by the same name to affirm this unity. A number of factor analytic, correlational, and scaling studies have investigated the question empirically, with helpful if not definitive results (see Middleton, 1963; Neal and Rettig, 1963, 1967; Pearlin, 1962; Simmons, 1966; Streuning and Richardson, 1965). In my judgment, however, we are still at the stage marked by an intuitive feeling that certain individual tendencies are somehow related: they come from the same causes, they reinforce one another in many instances, and they are manifestations of the sense of exile that some people experience.

Whatever the outcome of efforts to find an underlying unity, it is clear that the term *alienation* is now used to refer to a wide variety of different tendencies. In a seminal paper, Melvin Seeman (1959, pp. 784–790) has described five logically distinct meanings in the literature on alienation: *Powerlessness* is "the expectancy or probability held by the individual that his own behavior cannot determine the occurrence of the outcomes, or reinforcements, he seeks." When experiencing *meaninglessness*, "the individual is unclear as to what he ought to believe." *Normlessness* is "a high expectation that unapproved behaviors are required to achieve given goals." Individuals are *isolated* "who assign low reward value to goals or beliefs that are typically highly valued in a given society." And *self-estrangement* "means to be something less than one might ideally be if the circumstances in society were otherwise."

These terms have been used frequently in later research and commentary; but unfortunately, precisely shared meanings have not evolved. Powerlessness, for example, which is perhaps the critical variable for the student of politics (or at least the most researched), is defined in various ways. Political alienation, to Thompson and Horton, is the *reaction to* perceived inability to influence events—not, as defined by Seeman, as perceived inability itself (Horton and Thompson, 1962; Thompson and Horton, 1960). Despite such differences, the identification of several aspects of alienation is a step toward understanding the complexity of the phenomena encompassed by the term.

Measurement. Another necessary step is the development of reliable and valid measures for each aspect, or a scale of some combination of aspects. We can only illustrate the work being done along this line. Dozens of measures have now been developed, through the use of intensive case studies (Keniston, 1965); content analysis (Taviss, 1969); and especially questionnaires, in which a number of respondents are asked to express their degree of agreement or disagreement with statements believed to indicate some element of alienation (Dean, 1961; Finifter, 1970; Mizruchi, 1964; Seeman, 1959; Srole, 1956). (For a discussion of psychobiography as a method, see Chapter Eleven in this volume.) Some studies simply record the answers to a series of questions. The Harris poll, for instance, notes that, in 1972, 50 percent of a national sample agreed with the statement "People running the country don't really care what happens to people like me"; in 1968, 36 percent had agreed and in 1966, 28 percent (*Plain Dealer,* June 19, 1972, p. 18-B). Other questions in the poll were "The rich get richer and the poor get poorer," "What I think doesn't count very much," "I feel left out of things going on around me," "People who have the power are out to take advantage of me." When answers to these questions are combined into an index, 47 percent of the 1972 national sample were recorded as alienated, compared with 40 percent in 1971. It is interesting that among supporters of President Nixon the percentage was 36; among Senator McGovern's it was 53.

Several authors have designed scales and tested them for unidimensionality. Middleton (1963) found that answers to questions dealing with several of the meanings of alienation isolated by Seeman fell into a Guttman scale, with a coefficient of reproducibility of .90. Those who agreed with the normlessness statements, for example, were likely also to agree with statements referring to work estrangment, social estrangement, powerlessness, and meaninglessness. Since the number of items used in preparing the scale was small and the sample was drawn from one city only, we cannot be certain of the general usefulness of this scale; but it represents a valuable step toward more adequate measurement.

As noted, a number of writers (Davol and Reimans, 1959; Lowe and Damankos, 1968; McClosky and Schaar, 1965; Nelson, 1968; R. A. Wilson, 1971) have employed *anomie* as a rough synonym for alienation or, more precisely, have taken a term that originally referred to a property of groups and used it to refer to an individual, psychological property. It seems appropriate to discuss the use of anomie (or anomia or anomy) as an individual quality here, in a section dealing with alienation, in order to distinguish such use from anomie defined as a quality of groups. This redefinition of Durkheim's term happened first, perhaps, in somewhat incidental references by Robert MacIver and David Riesman; but the usage became widespread only after the presentation, and later publication, of a paper by Leo Srole (1956). In his terminology, anomie (changed to anomia in the published version) refers to an individual's "self-to-others alienation."

Before we comment on the scale that Srole developed, it may be helpful if we examine possible confusion resulting from such word transpositions. This shift occurred, in all probability, because of the frequently observed, if not well-measured, correlation between anomie and alienation. Anomic settings produce alienation; and/ or alienated individuals increase the level of anomie. To some degree, one can be used as an index of the other. The closeness of this relationship, however, makes the drawing of careful analytic distinctions all the more necessary. Some of the most important questions arise in connection with nonalienative behavior in highly anomic situations and with alienation among those who live in relatively eunomic settings, characterized by strong normative agreement.

In fields where one term is used as an index of another, and where measurement is, in any case, imprecise and conceptualization shaky, there is a risk that the index will be confused with the variable it is used to measure. Since anomie as a structural fact is difficult to measure, we run the risk of losing sight of it when we use the same word for a psychological variable. To be sure, Srole used a different spelling; but in a large share of the papers that use his scale or discuss it, the spelling reverts to *anomie* or *anomy*. In what turns out, after the first paragraph, to be a valuable paper,[1] McClosky and Schaar (1965, p. 14) write: "Almost all work on anomy to date has employed 'sociological' explanations to the virtual exclusion of all others. This paper claims that the standard sociological theory of anomy has serious conceptual weaknesses and cannot satisfactorily account for many of the relevant facts." This is a curious statement, lamenting that a sociological term has been used sociologically. In point of fact, it seldom has been. Reduction to individual measures; often without explicit intentions of aggregating into a group measure, is far more common. Thinking of an analogous problem in the physical sciences, I doubt that one is likely to find in a journal of organic chemistry a paper by a physicist lamenting that chemists have been studying the molecular properties of various combinations of C, H, and O without at the same time studying their individual atomic properties. Nor will we find such a journal using the same word for carbon and alcohol (or oxygen and sugar, for the teetotalers). Of course, sociological theorists cannot account for many of the facts of behavior by studying anomie alone, although some sociologists are likely, following Durkheim, to forget the analytic quality of the discipline. Psychological factors must be brought into the interpretation. At this stage, though, I wish that lexicography were more highly developed among social scientists. It might lead to the use of alienation as a general "focusing" concept, referring to feelings of estrangement within individuals, and to the use of anomie to refer to a condition of deregulation, of loss of pattern in member interactions, within groups. This wish stems from no passion for order (in this somewhat disorderly fellow) but from a passion for conceptual clarity that will help us go about our business of understanding human behavior.

To return to Srole's (1956) scale of alienation (anomia), we may be wise to list the questions used, for they have been employed in many studies. The scale is composed of only five statements, and respondents are asked to express their agreement or disagreement with each statement: "There's little use writing to public

---

[1] But see the comments of Srole (1965) and Nettler (1965), with the response from McClosky and Schaar.

officials because often they aren't really interested in the problems of the average man." "Nowadays a person has to live pretty much for today and let tomorrow take care of itself." "In spite of what some people say, the lot of the average man is getting worse, not better." "It's hardly fair to bring children into the world with the way things look for the future." "These days a person doesn't know whom he can count on."[2]

It is not clear just what this scale measures, and Srole included no tests of validity. It has not fared well under methodological examination (see, for instance, Carr, 1971; Meier and Bell, 1959; Miller and Butler, 1966; Proctor, 1971). Because the items are simple and clear, however, and because many researchers have agreed with Srole's estimate that they seem to have "face validity," the scale has been widely employed. The relationships of "anomia" to social class (Bell, 1957; Mizruchi, 1960; Nelson, 1968; Simpson and Miller, 1963) to prejudice (Angell, 1962; Hamblin, 1962; Lutterman and Middleton, 1970; Roberts and Rokeach, 1956; Srole, 1956), and, as we shall note in a later section, to politics have been extensively studied.

Another widely used scale that is in the alienation domain, although the term is not explicitly employed, has been developed by Rotter (1966). He uses a twenty-item scale (six of the statements are "filler" items) to measure what he conceptualizes as a generalized expectancy for internal or external control. This expectancy is judged important because reward and reinforcement, in the psychological sense, are influenced by the degree to which a person perceives them as "contingent on his own behavior or independent of it." Respondents are asked to choose between two statements in each of twenty-nine sets. For example: "Many of the unhappy things in people's lives are partly due to bad luck" or "People's misfortunes result from the mistakes they make." Four of the pairs of statements deal with politics. For example: "The average citizen can have an influence in government decisions" or "This world is run by the few people in power, and there is not much the little guy can do about it."

The concept of "internal-external control" is mentioned here because, like scales of "anomia," it measures one aspect of alienation as I have defined it. Its meaning is close to that of powerlessness. Rotter himself notes: "The concept of alienation . . . does seem related at a group level to the variable of internal-external control. The alienated individual feels unable to control his own destiny. He is a small cog in a big machine and at the mercy of forces too strong or too vague to control" (p. 3). The internal-external scale, or variations of it, has been used in studies of responses to discrimination (Coleman, 1964b, 1966a; Gurin and others, 1969); in studies of learning (Bullough, 1967; Gurin, 1970; Seeman, 1963, 1967a); and, as we shall note later, in studies of politics.

Space limitations prevent discussion of the many other scales of alienation. We

---

[2] In a more recent version, four items have been added to the scale; but these have not yet been widely used in research. Since the new questions are also all stated in the same direction (with agreement indicating anomia), the scale has not avoided problems of response set. The four additional items are: "Most people really don't care what happens to the next fellow." "Next to health, money is the most important thing in life." "You sometimes can't help wondering whether anything is worthwhile." "To make money there are no right and wrong ways anymore, only easy and hard ways." (See Survey Research Center, *Measures of Social Psychological Attitudes,* 1969, p. 175.)

shall mention only one more, a scale designed to measure political alienation. Drawing on the work of Seeman, but modifying his list of types of alienation, Finifter (1970, pp. 390–391) posits four forms of alienation toward the polity: powerlessness ("an individual's feeling that he cannot affect the actions of the government"); political meaninglessness ("political decisions are perceived as being unpredictable"); perceived political normlessness ("the individual's perception that the norms or rules intended to govern political relations have broken down"); and political isolation ("rejection of political norms and goals that are widely held and shared by other members of a society"). Using the data from the national probability sample employed by Almond and Verba for *The Civic Culture* (1963), Finifter found twenty-six questions related to political alienation. When factor-analyzed, twenty-one of these questions fell into two distinct clusters—a powerlessness dimension and a perceived normlessness dimension.

Finifter's work is a useful construction of a specifically political alienation scale. Our predictive power is increased by thus designating a precise referent for respondents' alienative attitudes, rather than dealing with alienation in general. One of the critical problems for research is to discover the conditions under which various forms of alienation converge and when they diverge. When such information is combined with measures of the separate modes of alienation, we have a way of avoiding a picture of alienation as a uniform and simple tendency (Seeman, 1972). Martin and Bengston (1971) set five basic institutions (political, economic, educational, religious, and familial) against the five modes of alienation designated by Seeman. Using this twenty-five-cell matrix, one is able to compare, for example, feelings of political with educational powerlessness, or perceptions of normlessness across the five institutions. For all three of the age groups into which Martin and Bengston divided their respondents, political alienation (accumulating the five modes) was highest; economic alienation was second. Of the five modes, powerlessness was highest and meaninglessness second, again for all three age groups. Such findings might not be repeated with different samples, using different measures; but the procedure is a valuable way to speed the "mapping" of alienation. It helps us avoid the assumption that the tendency is uniform and pervasive—an easy assumption among those for whom alienation is more a polemical than a descriptive term. It seems impossible— and probably unwise, even if possible—to remove the critical element from the concept. What we need is a parallel in use in which alienation is measured in sufficiently objective terms that its use in research can be strengthened.

Only with improved measures will we be able to discover how much projection there is in the persistent theme of alienation. If a person does not know who *he* is, where he belongs, what he believes, he may try to deal with the resulting discomfort by declaring that alienation is widespread. If such declarations of alienation occur, then other persons—perhaps less alienated themselves, but hearing from many articulate people that modern man is alienated—seek to explain the presumed widespread alienation. They believe that they ought to believe it is there, since many fervent voices have told them so. (And among the ambiguous signs of human behavior, perceptions can be selective to produce the necessary result.)

I do not know that this is true but am simply emphasizing the importance of measurements that persons from different perspectives can agree upon. There may be a general underestimate of alienation and anomie in the contemporary world—a tendency to see order where it is lacking, of feigning meaning and coherence where they are in fact weak. Or, even if some "oversensitive" persons exaggerate today, they may be alerting us to nascent, latent, but powerful trends leading to more alienation and anomie. Such warnings may help to set reverse processes in motion. In either case, it can be argued that one of the key functions of the intellectual—and the artist —is to anticipate serious difficulties and help to set self-negating prophecies in motion. We need also to know, however, when the opposite occurs, when overestimation promotes self-fulfilling prophecies. It seems likely that the most effective policies will be based on accurate appraisals.

A Field-Theoretical View

Despite the large number of valuable studies of alienation and anomie, we have still, it seems fair to say, some distance to go before we achieve clarity of definition and precision of measurement. We are even further from research that combines the two in order to examine behavioral outcomes under a range of conditions. Alienation is not behavior but a tendency. Even those who are strongly alienated do not lack other predispositions that can be activated in some contexts. Anomie is not a uniform fact but varies in its implications for behavior, depending upon the tendencies—including the levels of alienation—of those who experience it. It is not enough, of course, that we combine only these two variables into a system of explanation, for there are many contextual facts besides anomie and many individual facts besides alienation. In a formal research design that is still too simple but may illustrate the necessary multivariate approach, we might combine four variables, each dichotomized. As Figure 1 shows, there are sixteen possible outcomes (of individual political behavior or of religious response, for example) from such a system. Knowing that a person is high or low in alienation is only a start toward understanding or predicting his behavior. A highly alienated, upper class person in a wealthy society, for example, might be apathetic toward politics; a similar person in a poor society might be deeply involved in a counter-revolutionary movement.

There are few problems with the methodology of such an approach. Regression analyses, multiple-classification analyses, and the like, can be applied to much more intricate designs. What we lack are adequate data. "There is not a single empirical investigation of anomie and deviant behavior," Merton wrote a few years ago, "that has succeeded in mouting a research design that *systematically,* rather than impressionistically and qualitatively, includes simultaneous analysis of collectivity, subgroup, and individual attributes in relation to deviant behavior" (in Clinard, 1964, p. 240). That statement is not literally true today. For illustrations of studies that combine individual and group measures, see Jessor and others (1968) on deviation; Warner and Defleur (1969) on discrimination; Rushing (1971) on class differences; Finifter (1970) and Kirby (1971) on politics. There is, however, still a shortage of systematic social-psychological studies that examine the independent and interactive influences of anomic settings and alienative tendencies.

For our purposes in this chapter, it may be adequate to consider alienation and anomie as independent variables. Our attention is directed toward their separate and combined influences on politics. In fact, of course, their sources also require explanation. Among these sources are various influences that flow from the conse-

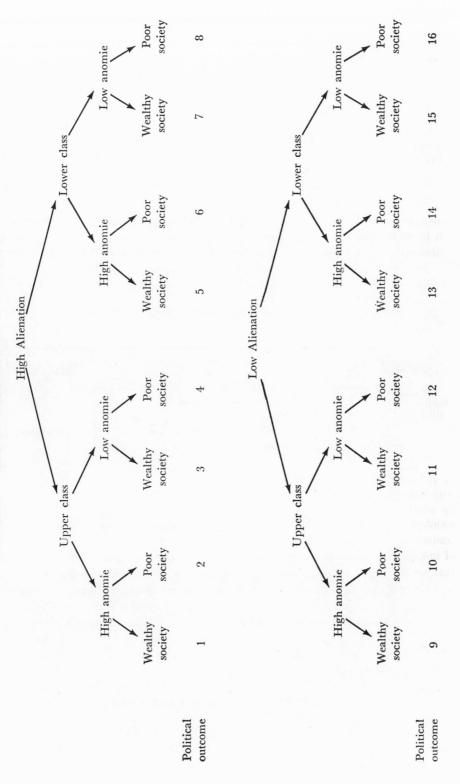

FIGURE 1. A MULTIVARIATE APPROACH TO POLITICS

quences of anomie and alienation. The effects of anomie and alienation become causes in a feedback process. Thus, in an analysis of an evolving system, we might designate rapid social change (especially when it is experienced at different rates), growing social heterogeneity, persistent war, and the rapid expansion of wants as some of the sources of anomie. Alienation may spring in part from these causes (just as it may contribute to them) but also from stressful socialization. Shifting focus, we see anomie and alienation as the independent variables. They lead to various outcomes, depending upon various intervening conditions. These outcomes, in turn—be they opposition, apathy, withdrawal, or other "responses"—feed back into the system out of which they came. One of the most important and difficult questions relates to the conditions under which the behavioral outcomes heighten or reduce the alienation and anomie from which, in part, they flowed. This field can be sketched as shown in Figure 2, with the $\pm$ on the return arrows indicating that "consequences" can either increase or decrease their own "causes." (A political or religious movement springing from an anomic setting among alienated persons may "cure" their alienation by reducing the normlessness of the environment, or it may divide a society further and compound the frustrations of its members.)

FIGURE 2.   A SYSTEM APPROACH TO ANOMIE AND ALIENATION

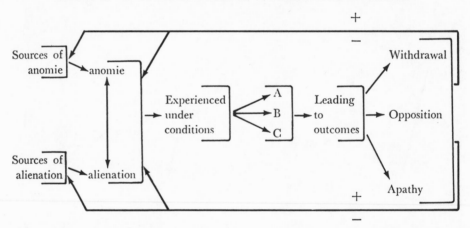

Studies of the relationship of politics to alienation and anomie seldom can be put into such a system, since most of them deal explicitly, and appropriately, with some small part of the field. As long as we recognize the level of abstraction on which they work, we can heighten our understanding of the psychological and sociological sources of political behavior. However, if we try to see them in the context of this larger field-theoretical statement, perhaps we can avoid "the fallacy of misplaced concreteness" that Whitehead warned aginst. It is rather easy to forget that one has abstracted from a complex system.

Political Effects of Alienation and Anomie

If the preceding discussion has not sharply delimited the meanings of anomie and alienation, it may at least have alerted us to the cautions necessary in applying these concepts to the analysis of politics. We turn now to that task. This section is entitled "Political Effects of Alienation and Anomie," but that topic cannot be sharply separated from its counterpart, "alienative and anomic effects of politics." Some of our attention therefore will be directed toward research in which political institutions and processes are treated as the independent variables.

There is much more empirical work dealing with alienation than with anomie defined as a structural fact. It is sometimes possible, however, to infer measures of or references to anomie from analyses of alienation. A study of powerlessness, for example, may give indications of the lack of opportunities to achieve culturally approved goals, which is anomie in the Merton sense. A study of disenchantment and the withdrawal of legitimacy, a second major form of political alienation, may note the general normlessness of the social environment, that is, its anomic qualities in the Durkheim sense. We will call attention to these references or inferences when they occur, even if the explicit subject of a study is political alienation.

Among the many questions that might be examined with reference to the political effects of alienation and anomie, several seem of special importance: In what ways are political effects related to religious or other possible effects of alienation and anomie? How do alienation and anomie affect political participation? How do studies of mass society contribute to our understanding of the interactions of politics, anomie, and alienation? To what degree can political deviation, to the left or to the right, be accounted for by alienation and anomie? Each of these questions deserves extended examination. Our hope will be, in the limited space available, to state the issues in a way that will help to clarify their discussion and promote further study.

Religion or Politics for the Alienated? With a little change of language, the following description could be applied to many different kinds of movements at many different times in history.

> Once upon a time of great turmoil, people came together sharing their outrage over the evils and corruption of the world. Together they read the works of a prophet of a century before, discoursed upon them and added their own commentaries. Rejecting the venal luxury of the exalted, these elect, seeing the true light, embraced a life of poverty. The present age must be coming to an end so they dedicated themselves to ending it, thus ushering in the coming Last Age in which the pure would be united in brotherly communion and the present rulers chastised, punished, and, if necessary, eliminated. The teachings spread. Multitudes were fired with the new faith. Established powers pronounced against the dangerous new teachings and persecuted the heretics. The believers, in turn, heightened their fury against the authorities and sharpened their determination for apocalyptic change. They must actively bring about the New Order [Endleman, 1972, p. 3].

This description appears in a review of a book dealing with contemporary crises in American universities, but it refers to thirteenth- and fourteenth-century sectarian movements in Europe. In the prevailing interpretation (see Yinger, 1970, ch. 14–15), religious sects are seen as expressions of alienation, as protests against societies experienced as frustrating and anomic, although "loss of faith" and "deprivation" are more likely to be the terms used. "The last root of all sectarianism lies in the alienation of some group from the inclusive society within which it has to carry on its life" (Stark, 1967, vol. 2, p. 5).

If alienation can be among the sources of either a political or a religious movement, additional evidence must be brought in to determine when one or the other will occur. To be sure, a movement may be a mixture. Whether one is referring to the seventeenth-century English Levelers, for example, or to the post–World War II Soka Gakkai movement in Japan, or various aspects of the current Black Power movement, both religious and political elements are apparent. In some contexts, however, they are competitive, or at least mutually exclusive. H. Richard Niebuhr attributed the relative absence of sectarian protests in the West during the last century to the availability of radical political movements. It is significant that in recent years there have been radical sectarian protests, particularly among American blacks, who feel relatively powerless politically. There has also been some conservative religious revival among those alienated from the trends of contemporary life. In a recent study, as yet unpublished, I found that university students in Japan, Korea, Thailand, New Zealand, and Australia consider religious activity more effective than political activity in dealing with man's most serious problems. In the sample of 850, 51 percent and 46 percent responded favorably to the two questions dealing with political efficacy; 65 percent and 79 percent responded favorably to the two questions dealing with religious efficacy.

Such items leave us with the question: When will the alienated turn to religious, when to political, and when to other kinds of activity (or inactivity)? We can give only a general answer to the question, based on three kinds of information. Political action is more likely when there are extensive channels of communication to political groups, when the values of the surrounding culture and subculture are expressed strongly in political terms, and when the individual involved has acquired tendencies that sensitize him to political cues. Religious structures, cultures, and tendencies, of course, promote different modes of expressing one's alienation. ·

References to religion as a response to anomie and alienation, perhaps as an alternative to a political response, are less common than discussions of alienation *from* religion (Pin, 1962) and religion as a source of alienation, generally based on the contention that the religious establishment contributes to the support of unjust social arrangements (May, 1949). Undoubtedly these conditions are common, particularly in societies undergoing rapid social change. One consequence is likely to be increased support for "apocalyptic" political movements that promise to cure the society of normlessness and to lift the burden of the feelings of alienation. "In France, for example, ecological studies which contrast degree of religious practice with communist strength show that the communists are most successful in regions in which the 'anticlerical' wave had previously suppressed much of the traditional fidelity to Catholicism (Lipset, 1963a, p. 530).

It is important to know, of course, what conditions lead to a political movement that is, in part, an expression of alienation from an established order, including the religious order; and what conditions lead to a religious movement that is, in part, an expression of alienation from the secular order. Moreover, one expression of alienation may develop into another. A critical problem for future research is to specify more fully the conditions that transform religious manifestations of protest into political forms or political movements into religious sects. Different aspects of alienation are made operative in the two situations. And religious and political movements are often quite different in their implications for society and for their own members.

Despite these differences, however, there are also important similarities. The protest movements emphasize the normative breakdown of the social order; they seek to increase the sense of alienation of their members from that social order. And then they promise the *way*—the way to a new arrangement of things here or hereafter and to a source of meaning and power.

Political Participation. It is sometimes assumed, perhaps too quickly, that estrangement from political structures, personnel, and policies, or a high level of normlessness among the members of a society leads to apathy, political withdrawal, and a low level of political participation. Yet it is also observed that the politically estranged may be swept up in enthusiasm for a political movement. Also, in some societies at least, periods of political crisis (one element of which is low normative agreement on political matters, or anomie) produce extraordinarily high political participation. Here, as elsewhere, the need is for a careful specification of the conditions under which these two different effects occur.

The results reflect, in part, different meanings of the term *political alienation*. Olsen (1969), for example, distinguishes between political incapability and discontentment. Lane (1962) sees a syndrome involving three attitudes: I am the object, not the subject, of political life; the government is not run in my interest—it is not my government; I do not approve of the way decisions are made—rules of the game are unfair. Finifter (1970) hypothesizes four dimensions of political alienation: powerlessness, meaninglessness (political decisions are perceived as being unpredictable), normlessness (perception that the rules intended to govern political relations have broken down), and political isolation (rejection of the political norms and goals widely shared in the society). Factor analysis of questions related to political alienation, however, revealed only two distinct dimensions: political powerlessness and perceived political normlessness. This is close to Olsen's distinction; it is also close to Lane's distinctions if the last two attitudes he lists are combined.

However we finally subdivide the concept of political alienation, we need to recognize its complexity in two senses: its own internal structure and its relationships to other forms of alienation. We cannot assume, for example, that there is a close association between feelings of political powerlessness and other forms of powerlessness. There is doubtless a close connection in many cases; but the relationhips require specification. Some persons who have strong feelings of efficacy in one setting—owners of a small business, for example—may experience feelings of powerlessness in politics precisely because they cannot match the degree of control there that they have in their occupations.

Although it furnishes valuable guidelines for the study of the relationship between alienation and political participation, we cannot review the extensive literature dealing with more general questions of participation. This much, however, needs to be said: The earlier affirmations of a high negative correlation between alienation and participation have been extensively qualified by the more recent research. When the relationship is specified by type of organization, by level of mobility orientation

of the respondents, by education, by ownership versus managership, and other variables, the simple corrrelation is reduced and sometimes disappears (Cutler, 1969;
Neal and Seeman, 1964; Nelson, 1968).

A primary task of studies dealing with political participation is to design
reliable and valid measures. Although no one scale has emerged as the definitive one,
there is substantial agreement on the items to be included. Olsen (1969), for example, has measures of media exposure, frequency of political discussion, voting, and
political involvement (reading party literature, giving money, doing volunteer work).
Erbe (1964) has combined many of the same items into a scale, using modifications
of a procedure developed by Julian Woodward and Elmo Roper: "(1) frequency
of informal political discussions ('frequently,' two points; 'occasionally,' one point);
(2) role in informal political discussions (atempts to dominate, two points; equal
role, one point); (3) attempts to influence public officials (on two or more issues,
two points; on one issue only, one point); (4) personal political campaigning (two
points if any in last four years); (5) financial contributions (one point if 'yes'); (6)
number of times voted in last four years (six or more, three points; three to five times,
two points; once or twice, one point)" [p. 202].

Further work is needed on such scales of political participation to discover if
all the appropriate data have been included, weighted in a reasonable way, measured
accurately (not simply dependent upon memory), and otherwise refined. They represent a substantial foundation, nevertheless, for empirical work to build upon.

What, then, are some of the findings relating levels of political participation
to various forms of alienation? Using a sample from three small midwestern towns,
Erbe (1964) found a simple correlation between alienation, measured by Dean's
(1961) scale, and low political participation. The relationship disappeared, however,
in a partial correlation employing socioeconomic status and organizational involvement. It was the association of alienation with these latter variables that produced the
original simple correlation. Using his two measures of political alienation—incapability and discontentment—Olsen (1969) found in another midwestern city a small
but significant negative correlation between political participation and his alienation
measures. In one out of eight possible comparisons, the relationship was not significant: those high in discontent were no less likely to vote. This finding should be
put alongside the fact that, when education is controlled, the business and professional
respondents had the highest rates of discontentment. *Their* alienation does not dis-
courage participation in the form of voting. It is important to emphasize, however,
that they were characterized by discontentment, not by powerlessness, emphasizing
the importance of this distinction between types of political alienation. Aberbach
(1969) found that a related distinction—between lack of trust and feelings of in-
efficacy—helped to interpret the 1964 election. Political trust was negatively associated with the Goldwater vote. Interpersonal trust was not, nor was political or
personal efficacy.

The importance of the distinction between types of political alienation is
clearly shown by Finifter's (1970) analysis of a national probability sample. The
political participation index was formed out of answers to six questions. The political
powerlessness index was derived from answers to eleven questions, which strongly
intercorrelated in factor analysis. The perceived political normlessness index was
derived from the answers to ten questions. There was a high negative correlation

between powerlessness and participation, with many other variables being controlled; but there was no correlation between normlessness and participation. This second form of political alienation was most powerfully associated with lack of faith in people, a variable that explained only a small part of the variation in political powerlessness.

In the face of such findings regarding the various forms of political alienation, it is clear that we shall have to use any single-factor indexes with care. They may obscure important relationships.

A number of studies have specified the political participation–political alienation relationship in various ways. Using a probability sample of Berkeley residents, Templeton (1966) found that alienated persons, as measured by a modification of Srole's scale, tended to withdraw from national politics but not from local politics. When channels for the expression of discontent are readily available, as is more likely to be the case on the local level, the alienated, on the basis of this evidence, take part. On occasions, of course, such channels are available on the national level. Approval of George Wallace has often been interpreted in this way, although seldom with substantial empirical support.

Because Templeton did not distinguish between powerlessness and normlessness as forms of political alienation, we cannot say how emphasis on one rather than the other might affect the direction of political participation in his sample. A number of other useful studies of community politics (for example, Horton and Thompson, 1962; McDill and Ridley, 1962) also combine several questions into one alienation measure, leaving open the question whether or not feelings of political powerlessness affect political behavior differently from feelings of distrust or normlessness.

In a study of the associations between political knowledge, organizational memberships, and political alienation in Sweden, Seeman (1966) limits his discussion to one type of political alienation, powerlessness. Through a number of controls, he found that those with strong feelings of political powerlessness were less likely to have knowledge of political affairs.[3] They were also less likely to be interested in the discussion of politics or in keeping up with international affairs. (See also Levens, 1968.) Although it is difficult to establish the time order of these relationships, Seeman argues cogently for the interpretation that powerlessness (low expectation for control) inhibits the learning of political information and interest in political affairs. It would be interesting to know whether there are cyclic reinforcements to such patterns, from powerlessness to low levels of knowledge back to powerlessness. It would also be valuable to know whether such cycles might be reversed. Some evidence for a reversal is found in a study (Gottersfeld and Dozier, 1966) of sixty-two persons being trained as organizers for a community-action program in East Harlem. When they were measured by Rotter's internal-external scale, those who were experienced as organizers felt less powerless than newcomers to the program. There is no reason to think that alienation need always be the independent variable.

Mass Society and Politics. Questions of anomie and alienation reverberate through the discussions of mass society. Although these terms themselves are not always used, descriptions of normlessness and estrangement are common, with implications that their intensity has created a fundamentally new kind of society, *gesell-*

---

[3] Recently, Seeman (1972) has reported similar findings for France.

schaftlich in the extreme. Louis Wirth's (1948, pp. 2–3) description of a generation ago is relatively more objective than most. Mass societies, he wrote, are characterized by great numbers, widely dispersed, with heterogeneity of interests, values, and power. Since the members of these societies, though exposed to the same media, know few of their fellow recipients or the producers of the contents, there is continuous experience of anonymity. The mass is relatively without leadership or a program of action. There are few common customs; hence, the population is open to suggestion, to currents of collective behavior. Individuals are substantially unattached; their memberships are largely for special interests, where part of self is expressed, in contrast with the wholeness of experience in the primary groups of more communal societies. Durkheim would not have been uncomfortable with Wirth's description as an account of anomie.

More recently, psychological qualities believed to be characteristic of those who experience mass societies have been given more attention. Mass man is often regarded as a poor participant in a democratic society: "The psychological type characteristic of mass society provides little support for liberal democratic institutions. The mass man clearly is available for mobilization by mass movements, since he lacks a strong set of internalized standards and substitutes standards of the mass. Therefore, in the absence of an acceptable self-image, the individual seeks to overcome the anxiety accompanying self-alienation by apathy or activism" (Kornhauser, 1959, p. 112).

We cannot undertake to trace here the lineage of these ideas, back to the ancients, the church fathers, or even to Tönnies and Durkheim. The contemporary reader will recognize them as attempts to account for the *Escape from Freedom* or *The Lonely Crowd*. There is some nostalgia in the descriptions of modern urban life; and ideology sometimes interferes with observation. "Everyone is against atomism and for 'organic living.' But if we substitute, with good logic, the term 'total' for 'organic,' and 'individualistic' for 'atomistic,' the whole argument looks quite different" (Bell, 1960, p. 27). It would be foolish, of course, to disregard the differences in human experience produced by the immensely expanded network of communication, the greatly increased mobility, industrialization, urbanization, and the other critical elements of modern life. The cultural "blueprints for action" and the character structures more or less shaped to work with those blueprints are severely strained, just as they have been in earlier periods of drastic transition—from food gathering to settled agriculture, for example. The task is to examine the contemporary situation, in our case in terms of its politics, without comparing it with an imaginary past.

Interpretations of mass society, as Kornhauser (1959) points out, are of two major types. Most nineteenth-century and some more recent commentators lament the loss of standards, the destruction of cultural elites, the loss of liberty in an effort to attain equality. Mankind has moved into an "era of crowds" characterized by the "sovereignty of the unqualified." Opposed to such aristocratic interpretations are the interpretations of democratic critics of mass society. They characterize it in these terms: "(a) a growing atomization (loss of community); (b) widespread readiness to embrace new ideologies (quest for community); (c) totalitarianism (total domination by pseudocommunity). In this universe of discourse, mass society is a condition in which elite domination replaces democratic rule. Mass society is objectively the atomized [anomic?] society, and subjectively the *alienated* population. There-fore, mass society is a system in which there is *high availability of a population for mobilization by elites*" (pp. 32–33).

A critical quality of mass societies, according to most interpretations, is the relative absence of intermediate groups that can serve as buffers between the indi-vidual and the total society with its powerful governmental structure. A pluralistic society, in Kornhauser's terms, has a structured heterogeneity that differentiates a society but does not divide it. Dividing lines do not reinforce one another; therefore, they serve as channels of allegiance to the total society rather than as a substitute allegiance. But war, depression, rapid urbanization, and other shocks to the social order destroy such intermediate groups. As a result, according to this line of argu-ment, several resources brought to society by such groups are lost. They satisfy some needs and hence lower the reliance on politics; they serve as channels for communi-cation to the decision makers and hence lessen the need for or likelihood of direct intervention; they serve as checks on one another; they reduce the alienation of individuals by giving them meaningful attachments and some feeling of control over their lives; and their leaders often help support the larger system into which their own authority is bound.

We have noted that the evidence for such effects is anything but decisive. Some groups may be the expressions of alienation without affecting its intensity; others heighten it by giving it a vehicle for expressions; many are associated with lower alienation. We are still in need of differentiated research that will help us dis-cover how particular groups influence persons of given levels of alienation in specific contexts.

Political Deviation.   One of the best ways to study how anomie and aliena-tion influence politics in contemporary societies is to study political deviation. There are risks involved in such an examination. It may seem to support the assumption that mass societies are uniformly riddled with anomie and alienation and peculiarly vulnerable to antidemocratic political movements. In fact, however, *some* of the forces influencing politics in such societies (tendencies toward equalitarianism; the universalistic standards of bureaucracies; the production of a deeper national, as contrasted with a local or class, culture and experience) lend support to democracy (Gusfield, 1962; Mann, 1970). Another risk is that studies of deviation tend to focus on extreme deviation. Until we learn to measure anomie and alienation more pre-cisely, only the more extreme varieties show up on our recording instruments. We will therefore miss the possible reformist sensibilities and activities of the slightly alienated, and we will overlook the flexibility and freedom that may require a small dose of anomie. This is another version of the ancient problem of freedom and order.

Despite the risks, the student of alienation and anomie has much to gain by studying political deviation, both of the left and the right. Before turning to that task, we need to note the current difficulties in defining deviation. The defining process itself is being sharply examined and challenged. Many scholars and activists declare that those with the power to label (whether the labeling refers to criminality, mental illness, level of intelligence, or political legitimacy) rather than consensual standards determine who is deviant. This current debate is itself a sign of anomie.

Were standards fully shared, there would be little difficulty in knowing when they were being violated.

DiPalma and McClosky (1970) resolved the issue of definition by designating as deviant those who disagree with a statement that is accepted by 70 percent of a population under study. By summing answers to a series of questions, one can design a scale of deviation. Their questions dealt mainly with political values and traditional rights, not specific political issues. For example (the deviant response is given in parentheses); "Our freedom depends on the private enterprise system" (disagree), "We need a strong central government to handle modern economic problems efficiently" (disagree), "To bring about great changes for the benefit of mankind often requires cruelty and even ruthlessness" (agree). DiPalma and McClosky found a steady increase in rates of alienation and anomy (an individual measure in their usage) as the rate of deviation increased. This was true of both a Minnesota state and a national sample. There were, it should be noted, a number of interaction effects that qualify this general relationship. Among the college-educated sample, alienation and anomy scores vary much less drastically between conformers and deviants than they do among noncollege respondents. Among the latter, nonconformity was associated with particularly high alienation and anomy scores. From the data at hand we cannot tell which came first, the alienation or the deviation, or whether they were mutually supportive. And there is no clustering of the deviation answers around specific political movements and activities; hence, the importance of the relationship for political behavior can be determined only by further study.

DiPalma and McClosky used a purely objective definition of deviation: disagreement with a majority (70 percent) view. In a time of deregulation, however, the majority view, the traditional answer, and the standard speech pattern are subjected to criticism; the customary labeling process is exposed. I once heard an American scholar give a learned lecture on the Far East. During a question period, an Asian demolished the speech with a gentle inquiry: "Far? Far from what?" Today, we hear the same question with regard to many issues, although the inquiries are often more strident. "Welfare mothers," who in the past have simply been assigned (or denied) help, now enter the political arena to fight for their checks and to try to increase them as a matter of right. How far are they from "legitimate" political activity? On this anomic issue, our society does not know whether to class them with chiselers or as minor-league colleagues of the five cotton farmers who, in 1970, were paid over one million dollars each for not planting cotton. The majority, I would guess, see them as deviationists—taking a position beyond legitimate political debate. A few label the cotton farmers that way also; but since the farmers were dealing with a law passed by Congress and signed by the president, it is more difficult to make the label stick.

In a time of stress and change, deviation thus becomes politicized, with various minorities demanding the right to resolution of issues through political processes. And political debate becomes "deviationized," with the protagonists and antagonists trying to brand their opponents as beyond the political pale (Horowitz and Liebowitz, 1968). This process is not yet well understood but is beginning to get careful study, particularly with reference to protest activities. Even a cursory study of commentary on riots, for example, will reveal that some observers interpret them simply as a series of individual criminal acts; others regard them as elements in a rebellion or revolution—designed to destroy the social order, not to communicate with it; and still others define them as protests, as a more or less legitimate form of communication, a desperate shout trying to get above the noise pollution of our civilization to demand change.

It is clearly of great political importance how a protest movement is defined by various segments of the public. According to Turner (1969), "Five theoretical perspectives can be used to predict when the protest interpretation will be made: (1) events must be credible as protests; (2) an optimal balance is required between appeal and threat; (3) protest interpretation is often an aspect of conciliation to avoid full-scale conflict; (4) protest interpretation can be an invitation to form a coalition; and (5) protest interpretations can be a phase of bargaining by authorities" (p. 815; see also Olsen, 1968).

Political Deviation to the Left. With these problems of definition in mind, we can profitably examine some of the many evidences that political deviation stems, in part, from higher than normal levels of alienation and anomie. (Once again, this is not a valuative statement. I would personally lament some and applaud other forms of political deviation.) Radical deviationists are those who want to push ahead to a hoped-for new world. They have never "had it good"; or, seeing some objective improvement now, their aspirations have been drastically raised, and they want to continue the direction of change. Reactionary deviationists want to go back to a previous (real or imagined) world in which they and those with whom they identify were better off; or where their present high levels of income and influence seem less likely to be threatened by "upstarts." These statements are insufficient definitions, however. In a democratic polity, far right and far left are also defined in terms of their unwillingness to grant legitimacy to the existing political processes. Extreme rightists see the society in which people like themselves prospered (or so they believed) disappearing, and they see no way within the system to restore it. Extreme leftists see their hope for a new society frustrated, and they see no way within the system to attain it. Seeing themselves as perpetual minorities, they cannot accept temporary electoral defeat; they promote polarizing strategies designed to change the system.

These political outcomes, whether of the left or the right, are products of interaction among the objective situation, particular individuals' places in the system, and their tendencies to interpret their circumstances in a given way. Research seldom specifies these ingredients; hence, we are left with probability statements. Studies of communists and ex-communists in noncommunist societies speak of "loss of faith," neurotic tendencies, feelings of emotional and social rejection, which overlap to some degree the concept of alienation (Almond, 1954; Cantril, 1958; Ernst and Loth, 1952). Although they do not generally demonstrate that these are more characteristic of their subjects than of the general population, this seems a reasonable deduction from the evidence presented. Whether or not these people live in more anomic settings, they experience their social worlds as anomic and respond by seeking a new normative system, a faith that will help them overcome their sense of meaninglessness and powerlessness (Grossman, 1949).

More recent studies of leftist political deviation have dealt with protest movements among students, or young people generally, and among Negroes. Remembering the problems associated with defining both deviation and protest, we can profitably examine a few of these studies. Questionnaires given to a sample of students at the Berkeley and Los Angeles campuses of the University of California revealed only low and insignificant correlations between "personal powerlessness" and participation in a protest demonstration (Kirby, 1971). Agreement with the "social powerlessness" items, however, was significantly correlated with participation in protests. (Among the statements used were "The average citizen can have an influence on the way the government is run" and "Real decision-making power in this country is in the hands of a few men who make up a power elite.") Kirby argues that this relationship is in part the product of a counterculture which recruits support from alienated and nonalienated alike. Activism is not associated with expressed feelings of loneliness or personal powerlessness but with sharing the views of this counterculture. He emphasizes, in our terms, the anomic setting—the availability of sharply competing normative systems—as a source of protests.

In their widely cited books, Roszak (1969) and Reich (1970) give a somewhat different interpretation. Their descriptions of technological rigidity—of disorder, corruption, and loss of self—are severe. The protests they see among the young, however, are basically apolitical. In Roszak's view, "the alienated young are giving shape to something that looks like the saving vision our endangered civilization requires" (p. 1); but the vision is an emphasis on psychic and cultural rebuilding—indeed a counterculture—not on politics. This is also Reich's view: "There is a revolution coming. It will not be like revolutions of the past. It will originate with the individual and with culture, and it will change the political structure only as its final act" (p. 2).

These are, as I read them, essentially "religious" books, describing one road to salvation and proclaiming that alienated young people have started down that road. Just as the Quakers pulled away from the intensely aggressive political and economic interests of the Levelers in seventeenth-century England, some current humanistic (I would not call them secular) sect movements emphasize withdrawal and noncooperation with a harsh world, to the end not that political power can be seized but that politics will be transformed. Roszak cites the founder of the Quakers, in fact, in describing his view of how best to deal with the crises of modern life:

> The process of weaning men away from the technocracy can never be carried through by way of a grim, hard-bitten, and self-congratulatory militancy, which at best belongs to tasks of ad hoc resistance. Beyond the tactics of resistance, but shaping them at all times, there must be a stance of life which seeks not simply to muster power against the misdeeds of society, but to transform the very sense men have of reality. This may mean that, like George Fox, one must often be prepared not to act, but to 'stand still in the light,' confident that only such a stillness possesses the eloquence to draw men away from lives we must believe they inwardly loathe, but which misplaced pride will goad them to defend under aggressive pressure to the very death—their death and ours [p. 267].

No doubt this is one response being made to politics by the alienated. Alongside it we must note the continuation of protests and radical opposition. Comparing members of the radical Students for a Democratic Society with members of the conservative Young Americans for Freedom, Westby and Braungart (1970) found significantly higher levels of alienation—as measured by responses to questions dealing with attitudes toward parents, school, and religious leaders—among the former. These measures are rather weak, however, and we are left by such studies with the task of sorting out the varieties of political response that can flow from various levels and types of alienation. Using her two dimensions of political alienation, Finifter (1970) suggests that when both are low, conformative participation is a common response; when powerlessness is high but perceived normlessness low, apathy is the modal response; with the opposite combination, one finds a reform orientation—protest groups working within the system; when both are high, there is likely to be extreme disengagement—separatist and revolutionary movements, complete withdrawal. This is a useful way to structure the problem; but the fourth category leaves undetermined the conditions under which either withdrawal or revolutionary protest occurs. Additional structural and psychological variables need to be introduced into the system to differentiate between these two contrasting responses.

Additional variables are used in some of the research dealing with protests movements among America's black population. Various forms of alienation are among the forces influencing these protests, with the six designated by Fendrich and Axelson (1971, p. 251) being a representative list. Black political alienation, as they describe it, has these dimensions: distrust of white authorities, whom they regard as incompetent and biased; rejection of a public philosophy that pays only lip service to justice, equality, and opportunity; a positive black identification—a set of attitudes that foster a separate social psychological identity; support for leaders and organizations that reject traditional reform and advocate drastic change; favorable sentiments for political and social separation; and support for the use of violence. Although this is a useful list, it requires some modification. Except perhaps for the first two dimensions, the reference is to responses to alienation and the environment in which it is experienced, rather than an account of various aspects of alienation. It leaves out powerlessness, one of the most thoroughly studied dimensions.

In examining the relationship of alienation to protest movements among blacks, we must not forget that alienation is probably much more widespread than participation in protest activities. It may be a necessary cause of protest, although it clearly is not a sufficient cause. Blacks may resort to protest because they are relatively powerless and lack political resources (Wilson, 1961), or protest may appeal to a wider "third party," thus creating a political resource in the face of powerlessness (Lipsky, 1968); but many who experience powerlessness have not been involved in protests. Conditions that promote extensive communication of shared feelings of alienation and encourage the formation of groups contribute to protest activities (McPhail, 1971). They have been carried on, it should also be emphasized, in a strongly anomic environment. Rioting and other forms of protest are sharp challenges to the legitimacy of existing economic and political structures at a time when opposition to traditional educational procedures, national war policies, the civil rights movement, and other aspects of national life have made normlessness highly visible.

We have few direct measures of the anomic situation in which protest activities occur. Thinking of anomie in the Merton sense, however (a gap between the culturally approved goals and the structurally furnished means), we do have a good index of it in measures of perceived relative deprivation. Real gains in income, for example, can increase discontentment if they are experienced as psychological losses, because they do not represent any closing of the gap separating one from a comparison group. Using an instrument designed by Cantril, Crawford and Naditch (1970) divided a sample of Detroit-area residents into those who saw a low discrepancy between their present situation and "the best possible life" and those who saw a high discrepancy. The latter consistently scored significantly higher on attitudinal questions dealing with militancy. For example, 54 percent thought that riots help the Negro cause, compared with 28 percent of those who perceived low discrepancy.

Unfortunately, various indicators of external structural discrepancies have not been added to measures of perceived discrepancy between goals and means. Individual perceptions do not determine the structure within which behavior occurs, the supportive or challenging behavior of others, or the levels of satisfaction and cost attached to given decisions. Psychological research tends too easily to overlook the distinction made by H. A. Murray and others between an *alpha* and a *beta* press: "The former are those elements in the objective environment, as seen or inferred by the trained observer, that can affect behavior. They need not necessarily be easily observed; in fact, perceived factors are often rationalizations. The beta press is made up of the forces acting upon an individual or group as perceived by them" (Murray, 1938, pp. 126, 290).

Lacking direct measures of anomie, of discrepancy between goals and means, Crawford and Naditch (1970) used their measure of perceived discrepancy in a helpful way. They cross-tabulated it against the Rotter internal-external control measure. Using data gathered by Ransford shortly after the Watts riot, they found that only 12.6 percent of their respondents characterized by internal control and low perceived means-ends discrepancy expressed a willingness to use violence to obtain Negro rights. In contrast, 57.1 percent of those characterized by external control and high means-ends discrepancy indicated a willingness to use violence. Of those who were "cross-pressured" (external-low or internal-high), 25.5 percent expressed a willingness to use violence.

The importance of this combination for politics is shown in further cross-tabulations with reference to other questions. Crawford and Naditch (1970) used a large sample drawn for the United States Civil Rights Commission from Negro men and women in metropolitan areas of the North and West. Among other questions, subjects were asked: "Have you ever taken part in a civil rights demonstration?" Those who were high in internal control (the highest third) and high in perception of means-ends discrepancy (again, the scale was divided into thirds) were most likely (28.2 percent) to answer yes. Those high in external control and low in means-ends discrepancy were least likely (3.8 percent), with the two "cross-pressured" groups falling in between (15.5 percent and 17.1 percent).

In comparing responses to these two politically relevant questions, one might speculate that an increase in the sense of internal control, as a measure of low alienation, increases the likelihood of participation in a civil rights demonstration. On the other hand, an increase in feelings of means-ends discrepancy, as an index of anomie, raises the likelihood that a person will express a willingness to use violence. The two measures are doubtless correlated, so that firm statistical deductions are not justified.

The importance of multivariate interpretations is shown in a number of other studies. Gordon (1972) found that participation in the Newark riot was most likely to occur among those who were low in political trust but high in political efficacy—not among the more fully alienated, those low in both. Ransford (1968) combined three variables to produce a valuable interpretation. Interviews with a sample of 312 Negro male heads of households secured information on social contact with whites, as well as on feelings of powerlessness (the internal-external scale) and racial dissatisfaction. Although he treats isolation as a measure of alienation, it might well be regarded as an anomic element in the structural sense, since it involves facts regarding interaction across the race line, not perceptions of separation. All three variables are significantly associated with answers to the question concerning willingness to use violence to secure Negro rights. There are a number of interaction effects among the variables. Perhaps the most interesting is that among those who are isolated from contacts with whites, powerlessness and racial dissatisfaction are particularly strongly associated with violence proneness. Isolation is less decisive in its influence among those who are low in powerlessness and dissatisfaction. Such multivariate analysis may help to reconcile the somewhat contradictory findings concerning the alienative qualities of segregated neighborhoods (Bullough, 1967; Wilson, 1971).

The combined effects of the three variables measured by Ransford are decisive: Respondents low in contact, high in powerlessness, and high in dissatisfaction contrast sharply with those who are low in alienation by these indicators. Sixty-five percent of the former, but only 12 percent of the latter, are willing to use violence.

Of the many other studies that explore the relationship of various alienation measures to protest activities among blacks, we will comment on only one more. Reporting on a Detroit-area sample, and using a five-point scale of political trust, Aberbach and Walker (1970) indicate that 54 percent of those lowest in political trust (and only 17 percent of those highest in trust) answer "yes" or "maybe" to the question "Can you imagine a situation in which you would riot?" This relationship is particularly strong when cross-tabulated by reported experiences of discrimination.

Because we are dealing with extremely complex relationships, the patterns are by no means clear. We are beginning to sort out, however, the kinds of alienation and the levels of anomie most closely associated with political—or politically relevant—protest movements among American Negroes. The great need in future research is to achieve a more systematic combination of structural and psychological variables. When the whole field of forces is the unit of analysis, interaction effects among individual and group factors will receive the attention they deserve.

With reference to the general topic of the effects of anomie and alienation on radicalism, we should emphasize that the relationship is not determinative. To some degree, radicalism is simply the expression of cultural training. Matza (1961) argues persuasively that student radicalism, far from being contracultural, is an expression—perhaps an exaggerated expression—of values and beliefs rooted in the dominant culture. Populism, visions of a transformed society, and evangelistic fervor are scarcely inventions of rebellious youth. Organizational effects must also be taken into account: Unionized unemployed Negro workers are more militantly class-conscious than the unorganized (Leggett, 1968, ch. 5). In addition to such cultural factors, deprivation influences the degree of radicalism. Although the idea that deprivation by itself leads to radicalism seems inadequate, certainly many forms of *relative* deprivation heighten the sense of injustice. Use of the concept of relative deprivation modifies the Marxian interpretation considerably, and it helps to account for the fact that the strongest protests and the most severe revolutionary trends occur among those who have experienced a period of steady gains but who see those gains against even more rapidly rising hopes and envisioned opportunities (Davies, 1962; Edwards, 1927; Simpson and Yinger, 1972, pp. 715–719; and Chapter Nine below). This argument, however, brings us back toward Merton's theory of anomie. It is easier for a society to lift goals and hopes than it is to revise systems of opportunity. Riesman once spoke of the difficulties involved in trying to "ration dreams." One might say that many contemporary societies are highly anomic because they do not distribute dreams as unequally as they distribute income and power.

Political Deviation to the Right. There are many similarities of environment and of alienation between those who deviate to the political left and to the political right. Both see a rapidly changing world where guidelines to action have become problematic; both tend to feel estranged from that world. There are subtle differences, however, in the nature of that estrangement. One might say that those on the far right see a glass that is half empty, and they fear that it soon will be entirely empty unless present trends can be stopped and reversed. Those on the far left see a glass that is half full, and they fear that it never will be entirely full unless present obstacles to change can be removed. The reality component of these feelings may be fairly small, but it is seldom lacking from the equation. A political movement that can emphasize the shared discomfort of the left and the right may, for a time, combine the left and right in expressions of populist discontent. When the reality of the situation is examined, however, the shared component proves to be too weak, and the movement breaks apart.

Certain structural conditions and cultural training lead more to the rightists' fear of loss than to the leftists' frustrated hopes for continued change. These conditions are found in greater than average amount among those groups who have received fundamentalist training, whether Protestant or Catholic; those clinging to traditional white supremacy; those in small businesses who feel the constant threat of loss of freedom of action; those whose money is "new" and not entirely "justified" by cultural standards; those trained to old-fashioned military notions, rather than to long-range strategic planning intricately connected with diplomatic issues. When several such influences converge on a person, the kind of life he sees as essential is so severely threatened no amount of activity within the system seems capable of reversing them. When he is moved to action, it is characteristically to try to stop something (to repeal, to impeach, to get out), not to accomplish something new.

Empirical support for these propositions is extensive but not entirely consistent. We can examine only a small part of the research on the far right that uses the concepts of anomie and alienation (Abcarian and Stanage, 1965; Bell, 1963; Hofstadter, 1965; Sokol, 1968). In this research, sensitivity to the questions used (most of this research is based on interview or questionnaire data), the samples selected, the historical period, the society, and other contextual factors is high. This helps to account for the inconsistencies; it also requires that one speak tentatively.

McClosky's (1958) well-known work on this topic is more a study of conservatism as a political philosophy than of right-wing political movements. After several checks for reliability and validity, he produced a twelve-item conservatism scale, which contains many of the themes in a wide range of material describing the conservative image of life. Sample statements are "Duties are more important than rights," "No matter what the people think, a few people will always run things anyway," "People are getting soft and weak from so much coddling and babying." Extreme conservatives (those who scored between 7 and 9 on his twelve-point scale) tended to be in the high ranges of his "anomie" (an individual measure) scale. Fifty-nine percent fell in the top third, compared with 30 percent of the moderate conservatives, 16 percent of the moderate liberals, and 4 percent of the liberals (0-2 on the conservatism scale). The same pattern appears in connection with the measure of alienation, with the following percentages falling in the top third of the scale as one moves from extreme conservative to liberal: 45, 27, 20, 11.) McClosky is careful to note the necessary qualifications in interpreting these findings. The sample is drawn wholly from Minnesota; there is inadequate use of various controls that might help to separate types of conservatives; the relationships may be simply correlational, disguising the underlying causal influences of additional variables; and, in particular, his "extreme conservatives" are not identical, granted his scale of measurement, with "right-wing authoritarians," although he does not describe precisely how they differ.

That modes of measurement are crucial is shown by comparison of the results of studies that use different scales. Schoenberger (1968), for example, identifies conservatives as those belonging to the New York Conservative party. On most personality measures they do not differ significantly from members of the Republican party. Some of these measures—for instance, authoritarianism and misanthropy—overlap the domain of alienation, although the term is not directly used. Schoenberger believes that his findings contradict those of McClosky; but until similar measuring processes are used, we must reserve our judgment. It seems likely that membership in a large, well-organized party is a quite different phenomenon from selecting the conservative response to a variety of questions. With such widely differing measuring instruments being used in the two studies, it is particularly important to control for other variables (education, income, residence, and the like) before comparisons are made.

In a study of a Northwest sample, Rohter (1970) distinguished between the rightists and nonrightists on the basis of group memberships (for instance, the John Birch Society and the Liberty Amendment Committee), content analysis of letters to the editors in several newspapers, and various attitude measures. His four-question scale of alienation does not distinguish among various themes but seems to tap the sense of powerlessness most fully. There is a significant relationship between the degree of "radical rightness" and the level of alienation. Nine percent of those lowest on the radical-right scale are high in alienation, compared with 40 percent of those high on the radical-right scale. Of those low in alienation, only 8 percent are high on "rightness"; 36 percent are low on "rightness." Rightists and nonrightists also differed significantly on a three-item sense of powerlessness scale. None of these relationships is decisive. Clearly many other factors are involved, as Rohter emphasizes. But the study brings further supporting evidence to the proposition that right-wing political beliefs and activities express deep-seated feelings of alienation. We need simply to emphasize again the need for distinguishing between the sense of alienation that comes from a belief that things have changed for the worse and alienation based on a belief that things have failed to change sufficiently rapidly or in the correct direction to prevent deterioration.

A full exploration of the association between anomie, alienation, and the radical right would require a comparative study. A comparison of American right-wing politics with, for example, "baasskap" in South Africa, Action Française, ultra-nationalism in Japan, and Nazism would help to reveal the various mixtures of individual psychological factors and the structural-historical factors that can lead to extremism on the right. Equally valuable would be a study of anti-Semitism; for as a political movement—if not as an individual, culturally taught prejudice—it has been a vehicle for the expression of negativism, of opposition to the emergence of the modern world, of resentment over the directions of change, and of deep-seated estrangement in many lands. We cannot explore the vast literature on anti-Semitism here (see Simpson and Yinger, 1972, ch. 9–10) but recommend it as invaluable to the student of the political right.

Conclusion

Having used the space available for this chapter, we must summarize its argument briefly. Our understanding of political behavior is enhanced by the introduction of measures of anomie and alienation. These phenomena, although highly interactive, require separate measurement and analytic treatment. Each is a complex variable, with its boundaries not yet well established; hence, many more years of effort will be needed to design reliable and valid scales. In particular, there is a great need for the addition of behavioral to verbal measures of alienation and of direct to indirect measures (aggregations and indexes) of anomie. Because the two phenomena are so close empirically, there is particular need to study their interactions and their separate influences. A high association between alienation and some form of political behavior, for example, might be interpreted as a causal relationship if the possible prior influence of anomie on both had not also been examined. In a more likely relationship, the reciprocal influences need to be explored. Finally, it is important not to emphasize the impact of alienation and anomie to the exclusion of more old-fashioned factors. Cultural influences, class location, party memberhips, occupational subcultures, and many other variables affect political behavior. Although these interact with alienation and anomie under some conditions, they are analytically and often empirically separate from them. Even among the politically "deviant," where the evidence for alienative and anomic factors is strongest, many other influences are at work. Development of the kind of social-psychological interpretation expressed in this chapter will best be promoted by keeping it in continuous relationship with the larger theoretical system of which it is a part.

8

PATTERNS OF
LEADERSHIP

Daniel Katz

The first bridges between psychology and
political science were built around the relationships of personality variables to political events and often around the psychopathological aspects of personality. The
great pioneer in the bridging of the two disciplines, Harold Lasswell (1930, 1948),
has convincingly described the role of personality factors in political behavior, with
special attention to compensatory and defensive syndromes. Moreover, he has suggested that the theoretical approximation of the political type of leader would be the
one in whom power is the primary goal—specifically, one high in authoritarianism.
This early linking of psychology and politics deserves closer investigation.

Its major weakness is that it ties psychological processes to the irrational in
political behavior. If people and their leaders behave as one expects them to, it
implies that a psychological explanation seems unnecessary. If, however, outstanding
leaders meet with reverses or if poorly regarded leaders meet with success, or if their
behavior seems to follow an irrational model, then psychology is invoked to provide
answers. If a leader like Hitler behaves like a psychopath and if people, instead of
incarcerating him, enthusiastically support his craziness, then psychologists and, even
better, psychiatrists need to be called in to explain the cruel nonsense. Even less

dramatic examples can be cited to show the attempts to use clinical psychology for the political leader who does not meet our ideal expectations. There is the instance of Woodrow Wilson's ill-fated attempts to persuade "the small group of willful men representing no opinion but their own" to accept his warlike policies and later the League of Nations. Wilson's actions have inspired volumes, which attribute to him an intellectual coldness and contempt toward his colleagues, supposedly growing out of a childhood tyrannized by a sarcastic father (George and George, 1956).

Now, we do not object so much to the attempts at psychoanalyzing key figures at a distance as to the emphasis upon the defensive mechanisms of a single character in the drama. With perhaps unbecoming ingratitude the social psychologist asks about the less dramatic incidents: Are these not also motivated actions? Why limit psychological study to the irrational and unexpected? The answer that there is no problem in the latter case is not a good answer. Sometimes men act rationally and sometimes irrationally. What factors are at work in one case and not another? And the boundary between the rational and irrational is not always that easy to draw.

A psychological approach to political science is not a study of psychopathic personalities in politics or even of more general personality factors related to political decision making. Rather, a psychological approach is a different level of analysis, which studies the behavior of people in political settings, whether the behavior is situationally induced or whether it derives from childhood socialization practices. It is the microapproach to social sciences—dealing with the perceptions, cognitions, expectations, and motivation of people. In contrast, the more traditional political science approach, at the macrolevel, is concerned with collective outcomes and their relation to institutions. The political culturologist is just not interested in psychological explanations, whether clinical or social for he is dealing with the broad sweep of patterns of events, which for him have their own logic. At the microlevel, the political behaviorist, however, frequently can join forces with the social psychologist in a common research enterprise. They enter such undertakings not as representatives of unique disciplines but as behavioral scientists. The recent sourcebook in political psychology edited by Greenstein and Lerner (1971) attests to the interdisciplinary character of this field, with papers from political scientists, historians, sociologists, social psychologists, and clinical psychologists.

Though such joint ventures in political psychology have made great progress in recent years, they have been largely confined to electoral behavior, political socialization, and citizen involvement in political affairs. The study of political parties and leadership within the party and in governmental structures is not very far advanced as an interdisciplinary science.

General Leadership and Political Leadership

Leadership is the process by which one individual consistently exerts more influence than others in the carrying out of group functions. If all members are equipotential and substitutable in determining group outcomes, the group will continue to function in some fashion even if it loses a particular member. If all members are equipotential in function, then there is no need for the concept of leadership. As McFarland (1969, p. 155) puts it: "The leader is the one who makes things happen that would not happen otherwise." Moreover, a leader influences others through more than a single action, or two or three such actions. That is, there must be some degree of constancy or predictability in the leader's influence over others. Finally, a leader is someone who influences an entire group—not just one other individual.

Can political leadership be distinguished from other forms of leadership—for example, from business or educational or religious leadership? One can, of course, regard the differentiating characteristic of political leadership as its occurrence in certain settings, such as a political party or a government office. This definition does not furnish a generic difference with respect to the social psychological processes involved, and in fact such differences are difficult to identify.

The major difference between political and other forms of leadership is the target against which influence is exerted. Two targets are political in nature. One is the reformulation or change in group goals, as in the reform or overthrow of existing systems or, conversely, the mobilization of forces to resist system change. The other is the allocation of resources and rewards which may or may not involve system change. Politics, then, has to do with decisions about policies and about resource allocation. Political leadership is concerned with affecting such decisions and is of course found in other settings than the political party or the government. Two areas of leadership would, then, be excluded from our conception of political leadership. One would be the application of existing rules by bureaucrats; here, no policy change and no shifts in the distribution of resources among people are involved. The members of Congress, in passing tax bills, are engaging in a political process, but the internal revenue officers who carry out the provisions of such legislation are not acting politically if they follow their prescribed roles. They may have power over people in enforcing the rules, but they are not exercising political leadership. If they were to go beyond their duties and utilize their position to favor one group over another, then they would become political. In some forms of eastern bureaucracy it is not uncommon for bureaucrats all along the line, from top to bottom echelons, to exploit their positions and become political figures.

The second area that lies outside political leadership is what French and Raven (1959) call expert power—influence exerted in collective task accomplishment because of superior knowledge. We do not speak of the technical expertise of the engineer as political, even though it is influential. He may increase group output, but he does not have anything to say about how this increased product is to be distributed. He is nonpolitical. He is not concerned with changing the social system (the power relationships between people) but is oriented toward the task and toward people as objects for task accomplishment.

The chairman of a meeting, in following parliamentary procedures, can assume the role of expert or the role of political leader. If the chairman is there because he is a knowledgeable parliamentarian and because he plays his role impartially, political leadership is not involved. If, however, he uses his chairmanship to recognize his friends and to gavel down his opponents—in other words, if he becomes a partisan—he is exerting political influence. In the first case he was facilitating the outcome of the group process and giving heavy priority to the rules in running the meeting. In the second instance he was intervening in the ongoing activity and giving priority to outcomes which he favored.

We are saying, then, that following the rules of the game in general does not require political leadership even though the follower of the rules is in a role that carries authority. The rules may be inequitable, but it is their formulation and extension or modification, not their execution, that is political.

In excluding from political leadership the administrative skills for carrying out policies and the technical expertise for task accomplishment, we are recognizing that not all system functioning is political in nature. Parsons (1960) distinguishes between the technical, the managerial, and the institutional subsystems of social structures. The technical (or production) is concerned with the task, whether producing automobiles or teaching a foreign language; the managerial, with decision making about and control of people; the institutional, with relationships to other social systems. The production subsystem is thus not basically political in nature. This is an old but neglected distinction in social science. Oppenheimer, in his classic volume *The State* (1914), distinguished between two means of acquiring wealth: the economic, by producing it; and the political, by getting possession of the title to it. Weber (1922), less interested in class conflict, formulated his bureaucratic model without regard to its political functioning and saw its roles filled by those chosen for their competence for their tasks. His was an engineering approach to social organization. Though the theoretical distinction between political and nonpolitical influence has long been recognized, there are practical difficulties in its application, since psychological distinctions do not always follow formal organizational patterns. The engineer can exploit his technical expertise to influence company policy in nontechnical matters. As long as the system operates mechanically, on the basis of an accepted reward structure, political processes are minimally involved. In practice, there is always a mix of the political and the nonpolitical; but we have been suggesting areas and conditions in which the dominant feature of the mix may be more political than nonpolitical.

One domain of particular interest with respect to this distinction is that of decision making in organizations. In democratic societies participation in decision making is seen as a rewarding process in itself, in which people should share. Many people thus may regard anyone above them not merely as an administrator following rules or a technician employing expertise but as a power figure. When subordinates challenge the legitimate authority of superiors, they are attempting a change in the structure of the situation. As they join the issue, the situation becomes political.

What differences are there in the social psychology of political leadership compared to nonpolitical leadership if we accept the above criteria concerning targets of influence? These criteria, it will be recalled, have to do with exerting influence in two directions: to affect the allocation of rewards and to change the existing social structure or to prevent such change. For one thing, the political leader is either a partisan representative of his group or an ideologist or formulator of policy (politician or statesman). As partisan representative he seeks prestige, privilege, or power for some group in an attempt to advance its cause or protect its interests or some combination of both. He may internalize the values of his client group, or he may represent it without personal convictions, as does the lawyer representing a client. This in fact may be one of the less obvious reasons why political leaders in all Western democracies are drawn so heavily from the ranks of the legal profession. Lawyers outnumber the members of any other profession in the parliaments of European democracies, in the American Congress, and among the governors of states in the United

States (Blondel, 1963; Milbrath, 1965). Even the militant left and minority groups are interested in seeing more of their young people trained as lawyers.

The lawyer role has some interesting differences compared with the role of the ideologist or policy formulator. The man who influences people through his conceptualization of goals is not as avowedly partisan as the lawyer pressing the claims of his client. The ideologist moves toward a broader rationale. Though he seeks reforms or revolutionary change, he usually speaks in general terms so that conversion to the cause is possible. The ideologist, then, tries primarily to appeal to people's values and to their basic trust in the sincerity of his own beliefs, whereas the partisan pleader is expected to manipulate the situation to the advantage of his followers and to seek compromises for their benefit.

Not all ideological leadership is political in nature. To the extent that the leader formulates policies which energize and direct some group to achieve its objectives in competition or in conflict with other groups, he is a political leader. If, on the other hand, his ideology embraces all of mankind, so that there is no outgroup or enemy, his leadership is more religious than political. Thus, Mahatma Gandhi was a religious leader in his humanitarian philosophy, his egalitarianism, and his ethic of nonviolence. On occasion, when he departed from his own broad ethical principles in practical situations to a more limited tactic of winning concessions from the British rulers, he moved in the direction of political leadership.

A second characteristic of political leadership is that the representative of partisan interests becomes involved in a constant process of social exchange between his followers and other competing groups. He obtains concessions and in turn persuades his people to yield some ground. In this interaction he often becomes an interested party in his own right. He needs power of his own to operate effectively as opportunities arise, and part of his reward is the possession of power. His followers grant him some freedom to act for them, and in return he secures benefits for them. Hence, a triple set of social exchanges develops: between groups, between the leader and his followers, and between leaders. In the leader-follower relationship, the leader obtains favors and exacts concessions for his following, and they in turn are expected to support him as leader. In this continuing exchange process, the leader faces the challenge not of "What have you done for me?" but "What have you done for me lately?" Many of the bosses of political machines in American cities had their positions undermined when federal patronage and federal programs supplanted the local spoils system.

Because of his insecure position in this social exchange relationship, the leader seeks to buttress his own position by extending his power beyond the immediate situation. He needs to build up some reservoir of obligations to himself, both from those below him and those above him in the social structure. He seeks to increase his control of rewards and sanctions and to make many people beholden to him. Hence, he devotes time and effort to acquiring power for the future as well as for the present to carry on his group functions effectively. Power seeking, however, can readily become an end in itself. The empire building of the political leader is often construed as indicative of the seeking of power in and for itself. Basically, power seeking is built into the political process, although the political leader may not have this as his only personal motive. The leader who finds a concern with power personally uncongenial, however, will find politics a difficult and rough road. Many leaders do show a mixed pattern of motivation, with power seeking as only one of the drives involved.

The manipulative politician, who intervenes as the wheeler and dealer in the political process, fits the pattern just described. But how about the consensus seeker, who attempts to adjudicate competitive claims? The political compromiser, however, does not play the role of impartial arbitrator as in a labor-management dispute. He does not stand above the scene or outside the scene, but is part of it; he is an active protagonist, if not of some of the parties, then of the solution he favors. Moreover, he seeks acquiescence not by bringing antagonists into communication with one another but by keeping them apart. In third-party intervention to help resolve conflicts, the role of the third party is to restore communication between the conflicted parties, find common goals, and have the parties reach some solution through a full under-standing of their own motives and those of their antagonists. The political leader, however, plays a more active role, and the competing parties direct their pressures toward him to exact concessions in their own favor and at the expense of their rivals.

Controversy Concerning the Great-Man School of History

If we describe leadership as the differential influence exerted by a particular person, is not the logical extension of this view an acceptance of the great-man school of history? According to this doctrine, history is synonymous with the biog-raphies of great men. The Reformation was the story of Luther, Calvin, and Zwingli; the French revolution, of Voltaire, Robespierre, Danton, and Marat; the Russian revolution, of Lenin, Trotsky, and Stalin; fascism, of Mussolini and Hitler. The school of cultural determinism rejects this great-man approach to social explanation as a misplaced personality cult. Leaders, say the cultural determinists, are produced by historical forces and are constrained in their roles by ongoing social processes. Thus, Presidents Eisenhower, Kennedy, and Johnson, though different personalities and subscribing to different value systems, followed the same foreign policy in Eastern Asia. Richard Nixon, the ardent supporter of free enterprise, instituted peacetime controls over prices and wages. It is the situation, not the actor, that determines the outcome.

Both approaches suffer from their emphasis upon one aspect of the leadership process. The cultural determinists are preoccupied with the situation, and the great-man proponents are preoccupied with the characteristics of the leader. The fact is that leadership by definition is a relational process, involving both the leader and the people led. J. F. Brown (1936) perhaps has presented the clearest exposition of this relational character of leadership. In two propositions—(1) the leader must have membership in his group and (2) the leader must come from a region of high potential in the social field—Brown calls attention to the characteristics of the leader as they relate to the social field (that is, he must be high in values, temperamental qualities, and intellectual abilities esteemed by the group). The cultural determinists assume that social fields are so tightly structured that there is no room for movement or maneuvering by the leader, and they also assume that social conditions have created a number of people of equipotential for assuming leadership positions. This position is like the thesis of W. F. Ogburn (1922), who showed that many great inventions and discoveries are hit upon by more than one person at approximately the same time. Historically, however, these two assumptions (about the structure of the field and the presence of a number of people of approximately the same abilities) are frequently not realized. Just as every football team is not three-deep in star quarterbacks, so a group or a nation may at times lack the great men who could help to determine its destiny. Part of leadership ability, moreover, is the vision to see when and where there are gaps or weaknesses in the social structure to permit movement and redirection.

Sidney Hook (1943) has carried the argument further in a personalistic approach to heroic leadership. He hypothesizes not only that the decisive outcome can be attributed to a particular individual but also that no other person could have functioned in similar fashion. Without Lenin, for example, the czarist regime would have fallen, but the successful Bolshevik revolution would not have occurred. Hook's method in determining heroic leaders is to use a probabilistic reconstruction of history, to examine past situations and look at probable outcomes without given key figures.

The great-man school, in concentrating upon the personality of the leader, does not seem to recognize that a leader's personal characteristics and values must fit the needs and aspirations of his following. Outstanding leaders often lose their supporters and drop out of sight—not because they have changed but because the pattern of wants and desires of their followers has. Winston Churchill, the great war leader of Britain, whose eloquence, wit, and courage made him an almost legendary figure, was rejected by the English electorate in the first election after World War II.

We can still accept the definition of leadership as differential influence without joining the great-man school of history. Personality can at times be the critical factor, but individuals may exert influence for a number of other reasons. They may have special expertise about the issues in question, they may have command of special resources, they may be in positions of importance. If we think of acts of leadership, moreover, rather than a personality mystique, we will be in a better position to relate acts of leadership to situational forces. This is not to deny that there are occasions when charismatic leadership assumes critical importance. But this is a matter of recognizing that for the followership the leader possesses quasi-magic qualities. The task of the scientist is not to attribute these qualities to the leader but to examine what it is about his behavior or his personality and what it is about his followers that produces these attitudes of devotion.

Leadership Orientation and Behavior

If there is one clear and compelling finding in studies of leadership, it is the discovery of two fundamental types of leadership orientation and behavior, the task-oriented and the social-emotionally oriented. In laboratory studies of small groups without formal leaders, Bales (1958) reported that leaders did emerge. Some individuals gave direction to the group through their suggestions about the task itself, others through their supportiveness of their fellows. Few leaders combined both patterns, though there were some who did.

Many writers have called attention to these two major dimensions in group functioning. One of the first was Barnard (1938), who distinguished between the *effectiveness* of a group in getting a job done and its *efficiency* in providing a return to its members in personal satisfactions. On the basis of her empirical studies Jennings (1943) described two types of groups: in one type, relations among members are based primarily upon their working together on a common task; in the other, intermember associations are the main reasons for the group's existence. Jennings recognized that most groups are not exclusively of either type but represent some mixture of these patterns. Deutsch (1949a) has similarly written about task functions and group functions, and Homans (1950) about internal systems (concerned with person-oriented reaction) and external systems (concerned with the survival of the group in its environment). Though Cattell (1951) takes a different approach to the study of groups, in his distinction between maintenance synergy and effective synergy he is in agreement with other theorists; for maintenance synergy is the energy expended to keep the group in being, and effective synergy is the total energy used to solve or complete a task.

The extensive research of Fiedler (1967) does raise the question of whether leaders themselves have to carry the operation of both task and supportive functions to ensure effective performance. He has found that group performance can be negatively related to the socioemotional supportiveness of the group leader, for instance, the leader who maintains psychological distance between himself and his men has a more productive group than the man who is personally close to his subordinates. In most of Fiedler's field studies, however, the supportive function was operative in other ways, either through an informal leader or the assistant to the leader or the fact that there already was a high level of positive intragroup relations. His contingency model examines four sets of variables: (1) the structured versus unstructured character of the task, (2) the power position of the leader, (3) the quality of leader-member relations, and (4) the psychological distance of the leader. Where leader-member relations are already good *and* the supportive function taken care of, then the leader who is personally close to his men can detract from group output. Where leader-member relations are poor, then personal closeness is positively correlated with performance, provided that either the task is structured or the power position of the leader strong. Fiedler's work, though not in political settings, is the most systematic research on leadership and group effectiveness in its measurement and control of a number of important variables.

The task and supportive patterns are not commonly found in the same person, since concern for objective task accomplishment can preclude concern for affective interpersonal relations, and vice versa. Furthermore, it is difficult for the task master to be perceived as a warm supportive person by those whose work may receive critical attention. This distinction can become exaggerated and take on additional dimensions when organizations deliberately add leaders who are yea sayers to balance the nay sayers or the reverse.

Position in Organizational Hierarchy

We believe that the distinction between task and supportive functions is fundamental in leadership patterns—both in small groups and in large organizational structures. The most common settings for the exercise of influence are social systems with definite power structures. The structure generally assumes the form of a pyramid and confines those at the lowest level to very little participation in decision making. In everyday life we are fully aware of the limited rule of the precinct leader compared to the governor or president, but in the social science literature on leadership we tend to ignore these critical institutional settings. Table 1 shows the development of the two main leadership patterns (task-oriented and socioemotionally oriented) at different levels of the organizational hierarchy. At the lower levels in social and political structure (for instance, the precinct captain or ward boss in the political party or the first line supervisor in industry), the area of freedom for decision making and leadership is narrowly circumscribed. The task is given, and so too are most of the procedures for carrying it out. The leader at this level can develop technical competence, which we would regard as nonpolitical even though he operates within a political party. Political leadership enters, however, as the precinct captain or first line supervisor encourages his people to contribute more to the group effort than they otherwise would. The skill of the leader lies in assessing what constitutes positive reinforcement for the different members of his group. In summary, the leaders at the lowest echelons in social systems exert influence in their skillful use of existing structure. They are not in a position to elaborate or modify system requirements.

At intermediate levels in the organizational structure, the scope for the exertion of influence expands greatly. Task orientation can now go beyond the completion of a given job and can take the form of extending and developing the organizational structure itself. To the mastery of technical know-how is added the special skill of initiative and of innovation. A specific example of such supplementing of structure occurred in the Democratic party in the state of Michigan on the part of a county chairman. Her county was one of four comprising a congressional election district. The county itself was well organized and the county organizations geared nicely into the state system. But there was practically no enduring organizational structure for the congressional district in question. The county chairman proceeded to contact her fellow county chairmen in the same district to set up an appropriate board, which could be tied both to the counties at the lower level and to the state and the nation a higher levels. In business organizations a department head may similarly develop additional structures to piece out gaps in the existing system.

When intermediate levels of management, whether in political or other organizations, introduce *and implement* changes of this character, we would consider it an act of political leadership. For the implementation requires more than calling on old rules and describing the need for the change; it requires promises, persuasion, and bargaining. Most organizational blueprints neglect this reality of organizational life. The model as originally devised does not automatically keep spinning on the basis of prescriptions of procedures and invoking of rules. Changes are always necessary in the formal structure, even if they are only extensions or the filling out of old structures. Such changes, to be accepted and to be effective, call for political leadership, which basically follows a bargaining or negotiating principle. Failure to realize the psychological requirements for change has been a frequent cause for the breakdown of otherwise well-conceived administrative reforms.

Even when intermediate levels attempt little change in existing structure, they have considerable freedom in developing the social-emotional function of adjudication and the engineering of consent. Claims and demands from the subsystems they

Table 1. HIERARCHICAL LEVEL AND LEADERSHIP PATTERNS

Hierarchical Level in Structured System	Type of Leadership Process	Related Task Orientation	Related Socioemotional Orientation
Lower Levels	administration; use of existing structure	(a) technical expertise (b) knowledge of rules (nonpolitical)	concern with equity for subordinates
Intermediate Levels	extending, supplementing, and piecing out of structure	(a) insight into organizational problem (b) assessment of bargaining possibilities	complex human-relations skills in integrating primary- and secondary-group relations
Top Echelon	origination and change of structure; formulation and implementation of new policy	(a) system perspective (b) originality and creativity	charisma (a) symbolic (b) authoritarian (c) functional

Source: Adapted from Katz and Kahn (1966), p. 312.

manage have to be met in some fashion that will ensure the loyalty and effective support of the various groups involved. This is not the role of the judge in assessing guilt but of the compromiser who wants to keep the system functioning.

In the political system the problem of maintaining loyalty is even more pronounced in that the consent of the governed is a critical variable. In fact, politics has been defined as the art of compromise. The engineering of consent is based upon compromise, and herein lies the dilemma of political leadership. Compromise is well suited to labor-management disputes over economic issues. Each side gives a little, and the conflict is settled. But moral and ideological disputes do not provide the same easy resolution. One cannot give a little on a moral principle. The baby is still illegitimate even though a tiny infant. The art of the politician, then, is to select for negotiation and bargaining those issues that do not involve moral principles or to redefine moral issues so as to deal with certain specifics that are not precedent setting. For example, black pressure for quotas to ensure more black representation runs counter to egalitarian principles of treating human beings without regard to race. The leader meets the issue not by conceding the principle of quotas but by accepting it as a temporary expedient in the interests of redressing past injustice.

The managers or politicians at intermediate levels also have as a major function the socioemotional problem of integrating primary- and secondary-group relations—that is, of encouraging interpersonal relations that will be supportive of the formal structure. Formal patterns of role relationship are impersonal and by themselves produce deprivation of social reinforcement; they also reduce spontaneity of expression and confine the individual to prescribed and often fragmented forms of activity. Hence, they need to be modified to permit more freedom for social interaction and greater scope for individual effort. The lowest echelons lack the authority to develop such modifications, but at the intermediate level the effective leader can maintain organizational objectives and yet encourage modifications that will permit more social interaction and greater group cohesiveness.

One procedure for the officer at intermediate levels is to develop a two-way orientation in the system, so that he can be representative of those below him and yet accepted by his superiors. If he relates only in an upward direction, he may be favored by those above him, but he will not be supportive of his own followers and hence will lack their support. If he relates only to those below him, he may be known as a good guy but not as an effective leader, since he lacks the support at upper levels to accomplish things for his followers. In an old study in a public utility, Pelz (1951) found that the foremen who were valued by their men were those who could be effective in going to bat for them up the line. The members of work groups were not as favorably disposed toward the foreman who was friendly and democratic in manner as by the foreman who could back up his friendly stance through effective action in their behalf.

When we reach the top echelons in a social system, the area of freedom for the exercise of influence is greater than at any other level. This is almost a redundant statement if the hierarchical organization is completely authoritarian in its formal structure. But in a democratically based system the authority structure can be changed by the electorate. Policies can be validated or rejected. Leaders can be re-elected or turned out of office. The authority structure then is not really pyramidal in form, since the large electorate is at times the top of the structure; the system therefore is more accurately represented as a pyramid within a circle. Hence, top leaders often feel that they are under many constraints from the subgroups comprising their public, and thus their margin of decision making is greatly reduced. One university president, after taking office, stated frankly that he could not hold his position very long unless he carefully observed the limits beyond which his behavior would alienate any one of four groups: (1) his board of regents; (2) his faculty; (3) the student body; and (4) the people of the state, especially their representatives in the state legislature. Since the four subgroups placed different constraints upon him, he felt that his area for decision making was restricted to a narrow band of the total spectrum.

Nevertheless, in general there is more opportunity for policy formulation and its implementation at higher than at lower levels. At times the field of forces may be tightly structured, and the responsible officials may have little room for movement. But those below them who seem to have more freedom in reaching decisions are not making decisions as far-reaching in scope. Moreover, the perception of constraints by the official may underestimate his real freedom. President Johnson probably thought he had no alternative to continuing the war in Vietnam—a policy supported by two previous administrations. It was almost axiomatic that a national leader in office should not take actions that could be attacked by his opponents as destructive of national honor, national prestige, and national interest. But there had been changes in nationalistic forces, and Johnson and most of the Democratic leaders had missed the significance of these changes. On the other hand, President Nixon, in spite of his lack of charismatic leadership, did not allow misperceptions of the situation to deter him from embarking upon bold new policy courses toward China and Russia.

The two dimensions of leadership again can be seen at this level of leadership, but they assume rather different forms. Task-oriented leadership now becomes the conceptualization of collective goals and the formulation of policy. This can in its fullest extent mean the initiation of new structures. Franklin Roosevelt formulated new domestic policies and new international policies which implied structural change. He followed through, moreover, to implement new policies—not only by naming new personnel but by setting up new governmental agencies and creating new governmental posts. Some leaders are content with espousing ideological changes, others with modifications in formal structure; but the outstanding leader attempts both.

The qualities necessary for leadership at the top levels of complex organizations are heavily conceptual and intellectual. The political system, mediating the demands of other systems, calls for cognitive skills of a high order, as many business leaders have discovered in their assumption of government office. Mann (1964), on the basis of his studies of industrial organizations and governmental agencies, maintains that at upper levels in the structure the conceptual abilities of the manager far outweigh his technical expertise and his skills in human relations. Katz and Kahn (1966, p. 313) have used the concept of *system perspective* to refer to the ability of the leader "to see, conceptualize, appraise, predict, and understand the demands and opportunities posed to the organization by its environment." The necessary frame of reference goes beyond the problems of the day to the complex internal functioning of the system in relation to the historical direction of external events. Open-system theorizing is relatively new in behavioral science, but the outstanding political leaders have long been system theorists at a practical level. Motivational aspects of leadership can be less significant than intellectual attributes when we deal with policy formulation and implementation. There is some controversy about the extent to which Franklin Roosevelt sought power as against ideological goals. The discussion is interesting but may be of minor moment. What is major is Roosevelt's deep understanding of historical trends and his keen appreciation of internal and external system forces.

Roosevelt's masterful uses of self-directed networks of intelligence and of self-determined timing of decision making are well described by Arthur Schlesinger (1959) and Richard Neustadt (1960). Upon assuming office the president of the United States can be overwhelmed by the huge, complex bureaucratic structure; and if he does not rise above it, he can become little more than a confused office boy. Roosevelt seized upon two basic dimensions of organizational operations, to which he could not allow himself to become a captive. One was the information system, which necessarily filtered and reduced enormous inputs into usable capsules but filtered them according to the needs of the bureaucratic structure and its personnel. Roosevelt persistently checked information from official sources with as many private, informal, and other channels as possible, utilizing his wide acquaintance with people from many walks of life as well as his wife's discerning reports from her variety of contacts. The second trap Roosevelt avoided was that of bureaucratically imposed deadlines for decisions. If the president accepts the time schedule imposed upon him, he is under such constant pressure that the decisions are hardly his own. The unrelenting time pressure is what many high-ranking officials report as their most trying experience in government, since they do not have an opportunity to give adequate consideration to major problems. Roosevelt saw this clearly and became the "master of the self-created deadline," to use Neustadt's (1960) expression. Neustadt goes on to say:

> Not only did he keep his organizations overlapping and divide authority among them, but he also tended to put men of clashing temperaments, outlooks, ideas in charge of them. Competitive personalities mixed with competing jurisdictions was Roosevelt's formula for putting pressure on himself, for making his subordinates push up to him the choices they could not take for themselves. It also made them advertise their punches; their quarrels provided him not only heat but information. Administrative competition gave him two rewards. He got the choices and due notice, both.
>
> As a result he also got that treasure for a president, time to defer decision. By and large, his built-in competitions forced the choices to him early, or at least made him aware that they were coming. He, not others, then disposed of time to seek and to apply his own perspective" [pp. 157–158].

The socioemotional pattern at top levels can be one of charisma. At lower levels the socioemotional leader is sympathetic and supportive of his immediate associates and in fact is seen as one of the group. In some respects, the charismatic leader is close enough to the group to permit identification with him, but he is also perceived as having a magic about him that makes him a superior figure. It is precisely this combination of membership character and high potential (noted by

Brown, 1936) that enables people to attach themselves to his personality and then soar to accomplishment beyond their everyday expectations. A comparison of Truman and Roosevelt is interesting in this connection. Both men espoused the cause of the common people vigorously and built up links of identification with them. But with Truman the process did not go much further. The common man was satisfied that in Truman he had someone like himself who would fight for his interests. In Roosevelt, however, he had a leader whose power to achieve great things was almost unlimited.

To move the concept of charisma closer to operational measures, two criteria can be utilized. The first criterion is the degree of emotional arousal among the followers, as in the reception accorded the Kennedys compared with other Democratic leaders. Charismatic leaders are reacted to emotionally by both their adherents and their opponents. The wild enthusiasm of the one group is matched by the deep hatred of the other. The operational test for the charismatic political figure might be a well-defined U-curve of affectivity toward him, with very few people assuming intermediate positions. The second criterion is the wide scope and great efficacy of the leader in the perceptions of his followers. The portrait is global and not discriminating. Specific weaknesses are neglected in this great figure. Weber (1922), to whom we owe this concept, talked of this second characteristic—namely, the magic aura that people attribute to their hero—as the basis of his definition.

What leads to such high emotion and such exaggerated beliefs about a leader? On the negative side, one of the first conditions is some degree of distance. Day-to-day intimacy destroys illusions, as in the valet-nonhero relationship or in romantic love affairs. This is one reason why there is little charisma at lower levels in the system. The man or woman above you whom you see every day may have strengths, but he also has obvious weaknesses and no charisma. But the leader whom you see on great occasions and under special circumstances is sufficiently remote to arouse charisma.

Much more than psychological distance is necessary for charisma, of course. Three types of interpersonal relations can be distinguished. First, the leader may have charisma because he symbolizes the followers' wishful solutions of internal conflicts. Instead of acquiring insight into their deep-lying motives, people seek some release from their conflicts by projecting their fears, aggression, and aspirations onto some social objects which allow a symbolic solution. The charismatic leader provides the symbolic solution, both through his personality and his program. He does not analyze the complex causes or true history of people's frustrations but echoes their feelings about the issue and justifies their acting out their impulses against the enemy. The advantages of the solution are psychological, not rational. There is temporary release of tension. Since the symbolic solution does not necessitate any digging into causes, the individual can eat his cake and have it too. Since the solution is social and not idiosyncratic, people have the support of some of their fellows. Part of their conflict generally involves the superego, and some degree of social support helps to counteract superego forces. Hitler had charisma for the German people, who—with their lower-class and middle-class origins and with their deprivations after World War I—found in his arrogant rhetoric the power they thirsted for. The psychology here is very much that of compensatory defense mechanisms as described by Adorno and his colleagues (1950). The repression of childhood hostility by the insecure is not the end of such hatred. It appears in attacks against minority groups, to whom the undesirable characteristics of their attackers have been attributed, especially under conditions of social support.

A similar account of charisma, with some added complexity concerning social identity, is described by McFarland (1969) in his interpretation of biblical history. For the Hebrews wandering in the wilderness Moses provided a new social and personal image. McFarland writes: "Thus in times of value strain, a charismatic hero may appear whose psychological processes are paralleled by his public actions, perhaps in a widely appealing resolution of a personality identity crisis that provides the critical decisions and values for a new social identity, thereby leading to social change through the establishment of new social structures infused with new ideology" (p. 175). This account applies as much to Hitler as to Moses, in that the Germans were under a value strain and Hitler provided them with a new identity as members of a superior race with appropriate ideology and with new social structures to provide properly for their new status.

Charisma involving the symbolic solution of internal conflict is much more common among the leaders of social movements than among the officials of established structures. The latter are too tied to existing practices to furnish convincing ideological appeal for the dawn of a new day when the meek shall take over the earth.

A second form of defensive charisma is less complex. It involves no new ideology but is a continuation of dependence upon the father figure or, more accurately, an identification with the aggressor. The two conditions for such identification (Sarnoff, 1962) are the possession of overwhelming power by the aggressor and the inability of the person to escape the exercise of such power. Hence, totalitarian regimes are the most likely structures to breed such charisma. They do this by concentrating power at the top of the structure and by making it difficult if not impossible for people to leave the system. A literal example of the latter device was the building of the Berlin wall. Identification with the aggressor also is likely where home and school training have been authoritarian; an emotional dependence then is readily perpetuated in adult life toward leaders in a position of authority.

A third type of charismatic process, which is not the product of internal conflict, should be noted. People can magnify the power of their leader because they perceive in him some attributes that can advance their interests. They may not be searching for a new identity, and they may not be driven by internal conflicts. Fully aware of the goals they seek, they may be emotionally excited about an able leader who might help them toward their objectives. They are not seeking a symbolic solution, but they have an emotional attachment and a wish-thinking exaggeration of the leader's abilities. Eugene McCarthy, for many of his followers, was a charismatic leader of the first type in symbolizing a wishful solution of internal conflicts; Adlai Stevenson was a charismatic leader of the third type.

Pye (1961) uses Erikson's (1958) description of identity crisis to explain the role of charismatic leadership in the political development of emerging nations. Old customs lose their meaning, and old structures which bound people together crumble. People grope for a new collective identity. The leader who has achieved his own personal integration and can articulate it for others becomes a charismatic figure. His ideological appeal is not merely for agreement on political forms and measures but represents a shared orientation on a deeper level—that of personal values.

These forms of charisma should be related to the types of frustration and deprivation which leave many people dissatisfied with things as they are. The one type is a general frustration: people lump together their many personal, family, occupational, and social grievances, with little discrimination or analysis of what the problems are or what the solutions could be. This frustration is more anomic than revolutionary and is accompanied by general feelings of distrust and unwillingness to cooperate with one's fellows. The second type of frustration is more of a thwarting of specific needs; for instance, workers wanting better and more secure jobs. There is some analysis of the problem and some knowledge of alternative solutions. There is distrust of those on the other side but a willingness to cooperate with those experiencing a similar fate. The general frustration can lead to counterrevolution and to our first type of charismatic leader. The populist forces behind George Wallace could well reflect the generalized distrust of the powers that be. The more particularized distrust may have been important in the nomination of George McGovern. Here people with specific problems were moving toward specific solutions as articulated by their leader. To lump together the antiestablishment forces as a populist revolt, and thus account for the strength of the following for these two figures, is to miss important differences in political leadership.

The concept of charismatic leadership has received so much attention in recent years that the foreign term *charisma* appears in the public prints. This attention is probably related to the value conflicts in our society, to present as well as anticipated shocks, and to some of the palpable malfunctionings of old institutional practices. Conventional bureaucratic leadership promises more of the same, and one would predict the emergence of charismatic leaders in the years ahead.

Both policy-making and charismatic leadership have greater opportunities for expression at the top echelons of a social system, and they can complement one another in the great leader. The new conceptualization of goals needs some charismatic pattern to secure acceptance. Woodrow Wilson initiated new structures and formulated new ideology for international relations but lacked the charisma within his own country to secure support for the League of Nations. But abroad he did have such charisma, and his doctrine of self-determination for small nations changed the map of Europe.

We have referred in passing to the social movement as a more ready place for defensive charisma to appear than the established social structure. In our discussion thus far we have given little attention to other variables than position in the hierarchical structure of the leader. Let us turn, then, to a more adequate account of social settings before commenting on some of their special characteristics in relation to leadership practices.

Social Settings

If we see leadership as a relationship between the leader and his followers and carry through the logic of this position, then we are bound to examine the patterning of the followers and the ways in which leaders and followers communicate and interact. If the followers are some aggregate of unorganized individuals, we have one context; if they are well organized in a role structure the leadership relationship takes on a different form. We would suggest four major dimensions of social settings in which leadership occurs:

1. *Degree of structure or role-determined behavior of people in relation to one another.* At the one extreme would be a highly organized role system like the army or like a hospital. At the other would be aggregates of people comprising a public or potential public with some common characteristic such as age or occupation. A social movement would occupy an intermediate position in that it is no longer an unorganized aggregate but a mobilization of people around known objectives and known leaders; nevertheless, its common values are still not precisely defined by implementing norms and its role system is on the primitive side.

2. *Primary and secondary relationships.* A related but not identical dimension is the degree to which primary relationships support or oppose the secondary relationships. The aggregate of individuals may become aware of one another and interact with one another in local settings, and thus the aggregate can be mobilized in a public opinion process. This could occur without primary-group involvement, but most studies indicate that people move toward acceptance of ideas from the remote leader through the mediation of local influentials with whom they are in contact. Similarly, the social movement without much formal structure requires the support of primary-group participation. Without mass meetings, demonstrations, and informal sessions, social reinforcement would be minimal. In fact, the vitality of the movement owes a lot to the opportunities for primary-group involvement.

3. *Relationship of group or unit to other systems.* Some groups and organizations are relatively independent of other structures; some are intimately associated. Political systems by definition are integrators of other systems and hence show a great deal of interdependence with them. In addition to the degree of interdependence is the character of the interdependent relation. It can be one of mutual interaction or social exchange; or it can mean a superordinate-subordinate relationship, in which an organization is a subsystem highly dependent upon a more powerful structure. It can be one in which there is economic cooperation but ideological conflict, or vice versa. Intersystem relationships have not been systematically identified let alone studied, so that we can furnish only a few examples of their bearing upon processes of political leadership. One reason they come to the fore in considering political leadership is that the political figure frequently has to relate to his own subsystem, to other organizations, and to some aggregate of publics.

One implication of looking at the contextual setting in terms of interorganizational relationship is the identification of a boundary role as opposed to internal roles. The leader occupying a boundary position in which he must relate to other structures will carry out different functions than the leader embedded in the system with little contact with external groups. It has been said of Lyndon Johnson that his experience and knowledge as a political figure was confined to the domestic scene. Hence, when he assumed the Presidency, he was not well quipped for his boundary role of dealing with other nations.

4. *The mix of democratic versus authoritarian institutions in the system* (varying from the dominantly direct democracy of the kibbutz to the centralized bureaucracy of a totalitarian society). The strength of the kibbutz leader lies in his powers of persuasion and skills in interpersonal relationships; the strength of the

totalitarian leader, in his use of coercive power in the maintenance of dictatorial control.

Social Movements and Revolution

The leader or official in a structured institutional setting has many built-in advantages over the leader of a relatively unorganized aggregate of people or even of a social movement. The organized structure already has some cohesion based upon interdependent roles or common norms or common values, or some combination of these three elements. For the unorganized aggregate or semiaggregate setting, a sustained basis for integration has still to be developed. In the organized structure the leader has formal legitimacy for his position of authority. In the developing social movement the legitimacy rests upon the development of an ideology. With established legitimacy go sanctions against noncooperation with the leader—sanctions not available in the aggregate setting.

In the organized structure the leader is in a strategic position of advantage because he has better access to mass media, greater resources and staff, and many dependent subgroups. Most leaders in established systems have engaged in a social-exchange process over time and have people who are obligated to them as well as people to whom they are obligated. Other officers and members of the organization thus have an investment in their leaders. That is why it is so difficult for newcomers to move into the system and assume direction of it in short order. Michels (1915), in his study of political parties, formulated his iron law of oligarchy because he saw these tendencies toward entrenched power as overriding in strength even in formal democratic systems. He argued that officials are bound to be more knowledgeable about problems than the rank and file; they have more experience in organizational procedure and can give more time to determining policies and maintaining power than can the rank and file.

Outside the established structures, leaders have to start almost from scratch to build a following, to achieve unity within it, to maintain it over time, and to give it direction. Critical situations arise which create fairly widespread dissatisfaction with existing institutions—economic crises, an unsuccessful war, some obvious malfunctioning of the system. The emerging leader can base his appeal upon these common frustrations and also can find some support from a general dissatisfaction with old institutions. There are also the slightly disturbed, the borderline paranoiacs, the cranks, and the misfits who may rally around a new cause. The older radicals themselves are afraid of this lunatic fringe and attempt to build their movement around a dependable core of those with genuine ideological commitment.

Noninstitutional leaders have certain distinct advantages. They have more freedom of movement in two senses: they lack the many commitments to existing groups and power figures; and their legitimacy resides in a new ideology, which they can interpret as they will within very broad boundaries and which has not become clarified through many specific tests of application. The established leaders, because they do not want to radicalize the discontented, are often reluctant to use their power to squelch the opposition. Hence, their challengers can justify any action on the part of their own followers and yet hold the established leaders to the restrictions of law and order. They have the advantage of making the authorities play the game according to known rules while they themselves are free to make up their own rules as they go along.

In addition to this greater freedom, the leader of a social movement has the advantage of the vitality of a new cause, a new forumlation of goals. The ideas of the established order seem trite, and people are habituated to the old appeals to the point of virtual indifference. People may move back and forth between a longing for security and a desire for novelty. When the old way of life meets needs and expectations, people's wishes for novelty are overshadowed by their wishes for security. When the old pattern no longer meets their needs, they are heavily attracted both by the promises of the emergent leader and by the novelty of his proposal. For certain key groups—namely, for artists and writers—novelty has an even greater appeal, since these groups seek new ways of perceiving life and new conceptions of man in relation to his fellows (Lipset, 1960). Hence, as Brinton (1938) has pointed out, every revolution is preceded by the desertion of intellectuals from the establishment to the radicals.

Ideology and charisma are more important for the social movement than for the leadership of the ongoing organization. In the ongoing institution, ideological leadership can be significant, but it is more a clarification and extension of existing goals than the formulation of new doctrine. Social movements, lacking as they do the consistent supportive inputs of established organizations, depend much more upon the appeal of the great cause and the charisma of the new Messiah. To sustain a social movement requires either the continuity of the same charismatic leader or a well-developed ideology embodying a program of social change geared to specific causes of discontent. Traditional Marxists have realized this in their programmatic approach, which provides both a social philosophy and a practical strategy and set of tactics for social actions. Thus, the movement can suffer some reverses, but there remains a consistent body of positive doctrine to give stability to the cause. The new left has not learned this lesson, and its quasi-anarchism provides no stabilizing force. It has its appeal for overthrowing the older system but no program for replacing it, since it is antisystemic in its approach. Hence, like crisis management it operates by the seat of its pants. It may be strong in one emergency and weak in the next, and it fails to build power as have Marxian revolutionary movements in the past. Moreover, with no clearly formulated goals, its followers can even be co-opted into the system.

The classic account of revolutions and their changing leadership is that of Crane Brinton (1938). He describes common characteristics of the French, American, English, and Russian revolutions, with the French revolution as the basic prototype. Preceding the revolution there is a division of society in which the underprivileged develop power. It is not a period of severe depression and repression but, on the contrary, a period of increasing prosperity and rising expectations. The intellectuals desert to the revolutionary cause. The old regime meets the rising expectations very poorly and is in fact characterized by a decadence of leadership. It shows no understanding of the depth, extent, or nature of popular discontent. It is indecisive and vacillating in its use of power. Thus, when the revolt breaks out, the old regime is overwhelmed by the tempo of events and offers concessions that would have been adequate a short time before but are no longer adequate. It essentially plays yesterday's ballgame.

With the actual revolutionary outbreak, moderate leaders come to the fore, the Kerenskys and the Mirabeaus. They link the new with the old and attempt real reforms in the structure. Again the timing of events is against them, since by now the people are demanding more complete change. More radical leaders, whose promises are consistent with current needs, emerge. A double feedback cycle is set in motion, with competitive leaders reinforcing the demands of their following and in turn having to move to more extreme positions to maintain their leadership. Moderate leaders cannot show sufficient action or progress to maintain their position and are displaced by the extremists.

The extremists attempt to achieve the revolutionary changes explicit or implicit in the ideology of the revolutionary movement. The easy change is the liquidation of old rulers and old oppressors. The Russian revolution was successful in removing and dispossessing the old elite. The French revolution was not as thorough in spite of its reign of terror. The more difficult change is the building of new social institutions to replace the old. The extremists are better at liquidating their enemies than at rebuilding society. They have to meet the aspirations of the people for a better way of life. As this becomes difficult, their hold over their followers becomes shaky and a "Thermidor reaction," a swing to the right, sets in. Thus, in France a new conservative leadership arose, with Napoleon as the charismatic figure.

Brinton's anatomy of revolution may not apply to all successful rebellions as precisely as the analogy to the anatomy of living structures suggests. For example, in the Russian revolution (although Stalin did replace Trotsky and opted for building communism in one country rather than for world revolution), the Thermidor reaction hardly paralleled the conservative turn in the French revolution when the rising bourgeoisie took over. Nevertheless, the Brinton framework provides a useful tool, which with modifications and additions can be applied to revolutionary social movements. It calls attention to a number of factors in political leadership to which reference has already been made.

First of all, leadership is clearly a relation between followers with needs and wishes and leaders who conceptualize, symbolize, satisfy, or promise satisfaction of these needs. Brinton shows that leaders can be quickly displaced when their old techniques are inappropriate to rapid changes. What is not fully developed in Brinton's account is the basis of common needs in the economic and political structure of the society. We need to identify the lines of divisiveness in a society, the groups with common sources of frustration. The lines may be economic, according to ownership of property; they may be religious; they may be ethnic and nationalistic; or, as in French Canada or Northern Ireland, they may be a combination of sources. A group of people with a common set of grievances can become a significant social force if able leaders come to the fore. We cannot divorce a study of political leadership from a study of social structure. According to Trotsky (1932), there was no full-fledged Thermidor reaction in Russia because czarist Russia had been moving from feudalism to large-scale capitalism, with few small businesses, and hence had no sizable small bourgeoisie.

Brinton's dynamic conception of social process, in which he sees acceleration of a movement through feedback, is congruent with modern system theory. Leaders in certain periods must either become more militant or be replaced by those who are. Their very militancy, however, only reinforces the extremism of their followers.

Killian (1962) has described this process in his discussion of desegregation leadership. As the civil rights movement gathered momentum, old accommodating leaders were often replaced by revolutionary leaders. When formal leaders were not replaced, they moved to some degree in a radical direction but were not even perceived by the people in the community as speaking for the blacks.

In one Florida city a study (Killian and Smith, 1960) revealed a complete turnover in leadership. In 1957, during a bus boycott, panels of white and black leaders—including some who might have been involved in the boycott and some who had occupied positions of liaison in the past between the white and black communities—were interviewed. The emergent leaders in the bus controversy were of the protest type, with not a single holdover from the accommodating leadership of the past.

Sooner or later—since most people do not sustain their drives toward remote goals—there is some falling off among followers in their support of extreme leaders. These leaders can misperceive the situation because the vocal people may still talk aggressively but may be a small minority of their potential backing. The problem becomes clear when specific action programs calling for mobilization and demonstration receive less support than anticipated. The militant leaders may then assess the situation and move toward a more moderate position. Thus, in the early 1970s some militant black leaders—who felt they were getting out of touch with their own communities and some of the older organized groups, such as the church—took a somewhat less militant position.

The Brinton thesis of decadent elites, their replacement by the moderates, the swing to extremism, and finally the Thermidor reaction is suggestive of equilibrium theory. The old leadership, out of tune with social change, represents an unstable equilibrium. The extreme move to the left produces change but also the threat of too much change and insecurity. Stability is restored with the swing toward the center. Hence, according to equilibrium theory, in spite of some change the social field has tendencies toward a steady state. However, the fluctuations in social process and in leadership effects do not really balance out one another. Even after the Thermidor reaction, the social pattern cannot be said to have returned to its former state.

Also explicit in the Brinton analysis is the importance of psychological deprivation as against material deprivation. Revolutionary movements gather steam under conditions of economic improvement. Once people experience some improvement in their own lot, they raise their sights for further improvement, as in Lewinian research on level of aspiration. Only, then, when this increasing expectation encounters sharp disappointment do people become frustrated and rebellious. This is the thesis of Davies (1962), who combines conceptions of de Tocqueville and Marx in pointing out that economic setbacks have revolutionary implications when preceded by periods of rising aspirations.

Another necessary condition for rebellion is the realization that one changes things for the better through getting together with those experiencing a similar fate. Turner and Killian (1957, p. 31) emphasize this aspect of revolutionary action and hold that in addition to conditions of frustration "there must also be a belief in better conditions which can be brought about through collective action. . . . As conditions are improving for a group . . . the members . . . develop an image of an even better state of affairs, as their early gains give them hope."

Similarly, Gurr (1970), in his elaboration of the frustration-aggression hypothesis to account for rebellion and revolution, sees relative deprivation as basic. Relative deprivation for him is the discrepancy between *value expectations,* or goal objects to which people feel they are justly entitled, and *value capabilities,* or positions which people see themselves as capable of attaining. The leader of the social movement, or revolution, would play his role in part by making clear to people the discrepancies between their expectations and capabilities and would suggest ways of joint action to realize their capabilities.

Totalitarian Versus Democratic Structures

To the anarchist and to the romanticist, all organizations may look alike in that they supposedly stifle the human spirit. But organized structures, like cities, can differ; and one key to their understanding is the source and exercise of legitimate power. The source of power can be at the top of a hierarchical structure, with some delegation of its exercise down the line. Or its source can be in the people and its exercise delegated to elected officials. In large democratic societies, there can be some mix of these patterns, since the administrative bureaucracy is not only hierarchical but also remote from the control of the electorate. To make officials more responsive to the needs of the people is a top-priority issue for large modern democratic nations. Nonetheless, the social structure in which leadership is exercised in good part determines the nature of that leadership. In democratic structures the leader is concerned with the engineering of consent, with a social-exchange process among groups and between himself and his followers, with negotiation and compromise, and even with an integration of conflicting elements in the society. No matter at what level he operates, he knows he is answerable sooner or later both to his general electorate and to specific subgroups. In contrast, the totalitarian leader is not concerned with a social-exchange process in which he maintains a favorable balance but with preventing the exchange process from becoming operative. His orientation is not to meet the needs of people but to prevent those needs from becoming articulated and channeled into collective expression and action.

The totalitarian leader has at least three critical continuing problems. First, all institutions must remain under the control of a single authority system. Not only is there a single political party, but the schools, the press, the church, and even organized sports and recreational groups should answer directly to the political state. Any organized group with a fair degree of autonomy can become a means of mobilizing people against the regime. Soviet Russia's treatment of Jews is less a matter of old Russian anti-Semitism and more a matter of totalitarian policy, which finds it dangerous to admit any pluralism into the system.

A second problem is that contact and communication with the outside world must be heavily restricted. Internal totalitarian control gives potential rebels no chance to organize, but they can get a foothold in other countries and keep alive some opposition. More important, communication with the outside world can contribute to economic and social change and can provide new standards and make problems for dictators. Totalitarian regimes need a closed society. The Spanish dictatorship may over time be undermined through opening its doors to tourists and especially to economic investment. Motor transport and technology may change Spanish society radically in the next decade.

Finally, in a society of any size, the totalitarian leader must delegate some power to his subordinates. The greatest threat to his rule may come less from social movements within his nation than from a palace revolution—for instance, from one of his lieutenants exploiting some of his delegated power. Stalin's long period of dictatorship, involving many contradictory actions on his part, can be understood as his personal interpretation of external and internal threats. In the beginning Soviet Russia faced external threat and the need for internal restructuring to provide a viable economy. Stalin's policies were directed at these difficulties, but his perception of Russia's needs was readily identified with his own need for personal power. Consequently, he turned his attention from the preservation of the revolution to the liquidation of fellow Bolsheviks who might threaten his own domination. Thus, systemic forces set the stage for Stalin's dictatorial role, but his reign of terror was less a response to system needs than a function of his own paranoid personality (Nove, 1964; Tucker, 1965).

Totalitarian leadership, then, moves toward making its control as thorough and tight as possible. Its target of preventing rebellion and counterrevolution expands to the persecution of anticipated personal competitors for power. Stalin is a textbook case of this pattern, as is Hitler. A dramatic exception can be cited in Marshall Tito of Yugoslavia, under whose regime the nation shifted from a centralized bureaucracy to something of a decentralized system, and the borders of the country became increasingly open both for natives and foreigners.

This exception calls attention to two objective factors so far neglected, as well as to Tito's systemic perspective and charisma. In the first place, we have not mentioned the dependence or independence of a system as a limiting condition on the totalitarian leader. National states in the modern world are not self-sufficient; thus, Spain, in spite of its geographical position and history of exclusiveness, could not achieve the status of a closed society. Tito had the choice in 1948 of becoming a Russian vassal or moving toward the West. By choosing to open channels to the West, he increased the power of Yugoslavia as a third force in world politics.

In the second place, we have been discussing an ideal of totalitarian society, where there are no power groups outside the official political party and where the official party leadership dominates all phases of life. But even when there are no formal structures to support the interests of various factions, power still may build up in military cliques, among technical experts and professionals, or among functionaries. In Yugoslavia there was another potential in affecting national decision making—namely, the ethnic identification of the component subgroups, such as the Serbs, the Croatians, the Macedonians, and the Slovenes. These groups had a strong consciousness of kind (their own kind) and little affection for some of the other ethnic groupings. The centralized bureaucracy of the federal system had not destroyed these divisions and in fact had too many other difficulties, such as its eastern inheritance, to function well. By decentralizing down to the level of community and work place, Tito reduced the strength of the ethnic groupings. Lesser leaders would have lacked the penetrating insight of Tito into the system forces, both within his nation and within the world community. He had breadth of perspective and an appreciation of trends of events over time. Moreover, he had the decisiveness of mind to take the appropriate actions at the appropriate time.

Finally, Tito enjoyed a charisma based upon an unusual combination of factors. He had been the strong, courageous military genius who had led the common people against the invading Italian fascists and German Nazis. He helped create the new nation. He symbolized the people's cause in rebelling against their own nobility, landlords, and plutocrats. He was the George Washington, the Abraham Lincoln, the Napoleon of Yugoslavia, and still alive and vigorous. He could confront powerful Russia and rally the Yugoslavs against the threat of foreign domination. Sidney Hook, in making his case for the heroic leader, could well take Tito as one of its clearest examples.

In countries that historically have lacked strong voluntary or semivoluntary associations of people, the totalitarian leader can more easily control organized internal opposition. The colonels in Greece were able to bring off their coup and to remain in power because Greece had weak labor unions, poorly organized political parties, frail professional organizations, and in general no strong secondary associations. Few, if any, organized structures stood between the individual and the state. The colonels, then, needed no real popular backing when they seized power, nor did they need it to remain in power. Individuals, no matter their number, are powerless without organization to summate and integrate their efforts. Totalitarian leaders can maintain themselves for long periods without meeting the needs of their people for a better way of life.

The role of secondary associations, of voluntary and semivoluntary associations in mediating between elites and masses, is central in Kornhauser's (1959) thesis of mass society. He holds that two sets of factors predispose a society toward totalitarian movements. One is the autonomy of the elite, the access to it through free elections and equal opportunity in the educational system. The other is the availability of the masses to manipulation by the elite. In a society where there are few and weak organizations intervening between the state and the citizens, the masses are readily available to persuasion and direction by elite leaders. Mass society, in Kornhauser's theory, represents such a condition of ready manipulability of people; in addition, in mass society elite positions are accessible. Such conditions can give rise to a mass movement led by demagogues who can convert the society into a totalitarian regime by establishing themselves as rulers and then freezing the elite structure. Greece would be an example of such a series of events.

Demagogic leadership not only fails dismally to keep its promises to the masses but clearly never intended to keep them. The leader of the mass movement who promises a more equitable society while planning to take power himself is clearly in this category; but many leaders in a democratic society also are often guilty of some degree of deception. The many subgroups with diverse and even conflicting demands make it difficult for the candidate, who needs the support of all of them, to present a frank program. However, when there are strong voluntary associations of various occupational, interest, and factional groups, there is a check upon the sellout of political leaders. They have to keep the faith to remain in the game. Almond (1963) has approached this problem from a somewhat different angle in showing that the function of political parties and their leaders in a democratic system is to articulate and aggregate the interests of the various subgroups in the population. In this way the interests of the people get translated into governmental action. The aggregation of interests by political leaders requires some compromise and even allows for some integration. In Almond's model, democratic leadership involves the social-exchange paradigm of Blau (1964) and suggests a dominantly rational decision-making process by the leaders.

There are problems, however, in the use of the concept of social exchange in trading favors and obligations in the political arena. Not only is too rational a decision-making process suggested, but we know little about the identity of all the agents in the transaction. We do know from careful empirical study that such national political leaders as members of Congress do not receive votes from their electorate in return for the policies they support. Stokes and Miller (1962), in a thorough study of congressmen and their constituencies, found that the electorate knew little about their congressmen and their actions in Washington. In fact, over half the voters did not even know the names of their representatives. At the presidential level there may be more accountability, and Gamson (1968) has used the social-exchange model to suggest that a president can build up political credit through past behavior but then may exhaust it, as Lyndon Johnson did in his policies toward Vietnam. It is interesting, however, that in 1956 President Eisenhower was not evaluated on the basis of his policies or actions as chief executive; his great popularity was a personal popularity, based upon his being perceived as a nice man, a man of integrity, sincerity, and warmth—a good family man. This was the well-documented finding of the Michigan researchers (A. Campbell and others, 1960) who reported that favorable references to Eisenhower "already strongly personal in 1952 became overwhelmingly so in 1956" (p. 56).

The exchange process between elected officials and their constituencies probably occurs in much more limited contexts than even politicians believe when they so carefully attempt to get mileage out of issues. It does occur for small segments of the population, special interest groups who are more knowledgeable about what is going on in Washington. Numerically they do not count, but they may be in a position to influence others. It also occurs when a problem—such as the Vietnam war or the busing of children—becomes critically salient for many people. On the whole, however, the exchange process is much more common between leaders than between leader and electorate.

The complexities of leadership in a democracy are well summarized by Neustadt (1960, p. 179) in his study of Franklin Roosevelt, Harry Truman, and Dwight Eisenhower: "Effective influence for the man in the White House stems from three related sources: first are the bargaining advantages inherent in the job with which to persuade other men that what he wants of them is what their own responsibilities require them to do. Second are the expectations of those other men regarding his ability and will to use various advantages they think he has. Third are those men's estimates of how his public views him and of how their publics may view them if they do what he wants."

Motivation and Personality of Leaders

Though different characteristics of leaders may appear significant in different contexts, are there some general motivational attributes that distinguish leaders from followers? The distinguishing aspect could be the nature of the motivational pattern or the general level of motivational arousal—leaders might have different motives or they might be more driven than others no matter what motive possessed them. In discussing motives, some writers tend to equate activities and motives. Just as bankers are assumed to have an affinity for financial affairs, politicians are said to be motivated by a love for power. This in fact was an early thesis of Harold Lasswell (1948). And one can cite many instances of political leadership that support this thesis. Neustadt (1960) though an admirer of Franklin Roosevelt, describes his life as a romance with power, with the White House as his natural home and the American people as his extended family. Biographers of many outstanding political leaders present similar portraits. Hargrove (1966) does suggest, in his account of six presidents, that only the presidents of action (Wilson, Theodore Roosevelt, and Franklin Roosevelt) were power driven, while the presidents of restraint (Taft, Hoover, and Eisenhower) were not so motivated. Again, this seems more of an equation of behavior and motivation than a systematic psychological analysis. And there are instances of leaders whose other values are much more dominant than their power drives—who do not choose to run for reelection or who risk defeat because of their stand on issues. And those, like Lasswell, who favor a power hypothesis modify and qualify their position to include other motives. Even Wolfenstein (1969), who argues that "leaders crave, relish, and have confidence in their own power and authority" (page 33), also speaks of the need for "a feeling of the rectitude or legitimacy for themselves and the cause they serve" (page 13).

Greenstein (1969) carefully analyzes the relationship between personality factors and political outcomes in showing the three sets of linkages involved: (1) Deeper levels of personality are linked to political beliefs, but the association is imperfect in that the political belief is not a simple reflection of a deeper need. (2) Beliefs in turn are linked to behavior, but again the relationship is not one to one. (3) The behavior of individuals aggregates in ways that are often not additive. Thus, we cannot predict directly from a depth personality factor to a political decision. But Greenstein urges that instead of dismissing personality study we follow along the complex set of linkages to provide adequate information about the whole process.

Most social behavior, it is clear, has more than a single determinant, and the reward structure of organizations and social movements provides other incentives for leaders than the possession of power. In ongoing systems there are many sources of reward for leaders: higher income, prestige, affiliation and interaction with one's fellows, a sense of accomplishment from tasks completed. Barber (1965) found that state legislators showed wide variation in motivation and behavior. He was able to reduce the diversity of their activity to four patterns—each combining temperamental traits, personality style, motives, and skills.

Social movements, especially in their early periods, do not afford a variety of incentive of established structures for their activists. Two forms of motivation are likely to come to the fore: power and ideological goals—either power-hungry individuals or fanatics devoted to a cause or some combination of the two patterns. Sometimes a single leader can be possessed by both motives and can handle the contradiction by cloaking his own goals as the justified aspirations of his people. Harold Lasswell (1930), in his pioneer work in personality and politics, made this process central to political leadership. According to Lasswell, when private motives are displaced onto public objects and rationalized in terms of public interest, the result is political man.

At lower and intermediate levels in social structure, in our view, power is not necessarily the dominant value for most leaders, but it does assume more importance at higher levels. There is some empirical support for this hypothesis. A study of precinct and higher-level leaders in the Detroit area found such differences (Eldersveld, 1964). About 25 percent of those in the higher echelons (compared to only 1 percent of the precinct leaders) reported that economic and political gains were their sources of satisfaction from their party activity. Over half of the precinct leaders (compared to about one fourth of the higher-level leaders) emphasized social satisfactions such as working with congenial and like-minded people and friends. Unfortunately, the very top levels of the party structure were not represented, so the evidence is incomplete. A study of precinct leaders in a Norwegian community gave very similar results (Valen and Katz, 1964). At this level in the party structure, leaders seem to obtain their substantial gratifications not from satisfying some power drive but from being involved with like-minded colleagues in meaningful and interesting activities. More direct questions about career goals in a study of legislators in New Jersey, Ohio, California, and Tennessee showed an even more inflated emphasis upon altruistic-contributive as against selfish-exploitative objectives (Eulau and others, 1961).

We are concluding, then, that some generalizations can be made about the motives of political leaders but that these generalizations have to specify social settings and have to be statements of a probabilistic character. When we examine the question of motivational arousal, there can be no question that political leaders are more internally driven than their followers. They work longer, they endure greater hardships, and they seem inexhaustible in their physical energy. Some of this drive, of course, may be not a matter of motivation but a constitutional factor of sheer physical energy and endurance. Long before American politics had reached its present strenuous character, and even before he himself had reached the White House, Woodrow Wilson (1908, pp. 79–80) wrote: "Men of ordinary physique and discretion cannot be presidents and live, if the strain be not somehow relieved. We shall be obliged always to be picking our chief magistrates from among wise and prudent athletes—a small class." The political leader must have not only an extraordinary physical constitution but also a high degree of internalized motivation. To react to the immediate situation, to be a counter-puncher, is not enough.

In addition to his physical endurance, the political leader survives the demands upon him because these demands feed his own patterns of motivation. The man eagerly seeking election may be reinforced by having to make one speech after another to different groups. An important motive in democratic political systems, then, seems to be the need for affiliation, the love of social contacts: The need for affection "probably accounts for a major part of the membership of political clubs and interest groups and, to a lesser extent, the civil service and legislatures" (Knutson, 1972a, p. 46). Psychobiographic accounts have made a good deal of the need for affection in helping to account for the behavior of such important leaders as Wilson (George and George, 1956), Trotsky (Wolfenstein, 1969), and Stevens (Brodie, 1966). One study noteworthy for its direct attack upon the problem by measuring the affiliation needs of local officials and ward chairmen and nonpoliticians (businessmen) reported higher need affiliation scores for the political leaders in the more noncompetitive jobs (Browning and Jacob, 1964). The same investigation found no significant motivational differences between politicians and nonpoliticians in power and achievement motivation. The level of position was more important in giving high scores on these needs than the political distinction versus the business distinction. The need for affection is closely related to the trait of sociability, and most studies of sociability (for instance, Milbrath, 1965) report very significant correlations between participation in politics and the need for social contacts. This relationship persists even when socioeconomic status is held constant. Thus, "sociability should be called a necessary but not a sufficient condition for entering politics. Many sociable persons do not become active. The reverse is not true, however; a nonsociable person has a barrier to participation in socially interactive political behavior" (Milbrath, 1965, p. 75).

The higher drive level of political leaders relative to followers may be true of outstanding performers compared to the rank and file in all walks of life: surgeons, engineers, scientists, teachers. Other things being equal, the highly motivated person should exceed the poorly motivated in any field of endeavor. It remains for empirical studies to test the degree of internally sustained drive in political leaders compared to other groups in the population. We have the tools for such studies of leaders in depth interviewing, projective measures, and sampling methods; but so far no one has combined these techniques in systematic research. Sampling is often the greatest weakness, so that we cannot generalize beyond the few cases generally selected to meet the conveniences of the researcher. In other words, there are no basic methodological roadblocks to studies of differential value and motivational patterns of leaders in various levels in the political structure and in other organizations as well.

Earlier we did not restrict political leadership to those in formal political roles (party position or public office) since the same psychological processes of exerting influence can be found in other organizational settings. Studies that compare formally designated politicians with the rest of the population are thus not definitive in identifying the characteristics of political leadership. In the United States, industry or the military may offer as attractive opportunities for the politically oriented as do the political parties and government. Nonetheless, the comparison of political participants with nonparticipants should give a crude measure of relevant characteristics. When positive differences are found, they merit careful consideration. Negative differences tell us little. There should also be differences between elected and appointed public leaders, in that the former have to seek validation of themselves and their policies in different fashion than the latter. Hollander and his colleagues have begun an interesting research program on such differences, and their findings furnish hypotheses for field research (Hollander and Julian, 1970). Their research, for example, suggests that immediately after election, when their credits are high, leaders are more confident of themselves and willing to deviate from the group; whereas later, if their credits are on the wane, they are particularly sensitive to group opinion.

Barber (1972a) has made a bold attempt to combine level of motivational arousal and type of motive in his analysis of presidential character. He selects activity-passivity (the amount of energy invested in the presidency) as one dimension and positive-negative feelings about one's own activity as the second dimension. The combination of the two dimensions provides four character types: active-positive, active-negative, passive-positive, and passive-negative. These four character types possess qualities that further differentiate them from one another. For example, the active-positive type emphasizes a rational mastery of problems and therefore may fail to take into account the irrational in politics. Active-negative people are compulsive characters suffering from a perfectionistic conscience. Passive-positive people are low in self-esteem and feel generally unloved; although they have some positive feelings toward their none-too-great involvement, these feelings are superficial and their capacity for enjoyment fragile. Passive-negative people are in politics only because they feel it is their duty to be there; they lack flexibility and tend to withdraw or leave the field.

The following presidents are regarded as falling into these four character types: *active-positive*—Thomas Jefferson, Franklin Roosevelt, Harry Truman, John Kennedy; *active-negative*—John Adams, Woodrow Wilson, Herbert Hoover, Lyndon Johnson, Richard Nixon; *passive-positive*—James Madison, Howard Taft, Warren Harding; *passive-negative*—George Washington, Calvin Coolidge, Dwight Eisenhower.

The argument, then, runs that such a character typology has predictive power for decision making and effective policy formulation of given presidents. Woodrow Wilson's failure to secure Senate acceptance of the League of Nations can be related to his compulsive righteousness, which did not permit compromising or negotiating with his Republican enemies. Hoover's inability to cope with the catastrophic Depression during his administration is similarly accounted for by his stubbornness, self-righteousness, and moralism. Finally, the tragic decisions on Vietnam in the Johnson administration were the result of Johnson's rigidity and his belief that the war was a matter of national honor and criticism of our involvement in it immoral.

Barber's typology may well stimulate theoreticians and researchers in the field because it is so incomplete and contains so many unproved assertions. In the first place, the theoretical framework is fragmentary, although some of his insights could lead to the development of a theoretical model. Why his two dimensions, activity-passivity and positive-negative affect, should generate the properties attributed to his four character types is far from clear. These properties derive neither from any set of logical propositions nor from careful account of the psychodynamic processes assumed.

In the second place, there are no well-designed criteria for assigning presidents to the four categories. Wilson, Hoover, Johnson, and Nixon are placed in the same positive-negative category, characterized by a struggle to achieve power though hampered by a perfectionistic conscience. The impediment of a perfectionistic conscience somehow does not seem to be on target as the major character syndrome of Johnson or Nixon or even Hoover. Since the two dimensions of activity and affect are supposedly responsible for placing people in these categories, we again need specific criteria for the content analysis of documents, speeches, and records for measuring degree of activity and amount of positive and negative affect. Moreover, these measures need to be taken over time and related to dependent and independent variables. Johnson, for example, may have enjoyed his exercise of power on the domestic scene, and a negative evaluation of his activity on the international scene may have been the result of his failure in that realm rather than the cause of it.

In the third place, though the subtitle of the book is predicting performances in the White House, this is post hoc explanation. Because the author was dealing with historical materials, he did not predict future behavior for most of the presidents considered. He did, however, venture the prediction that Nixon, possessing the in-flexibility of the active-negative personality, would adhere rigidly to a failing line of policy. In fact, however, Nixon has been the most pragmatic of all recent presidents and has pursued a liberal foreign policy in more open relations with China and Russia and adopted the Democratic line on wage and price controls. On other domestic issues he has taken a stand close to the position of the majority of the electorate.

It is possible to make predictions when dealing solely with historical materials, where knowledge is lacking about patterns of relationship. One can predict that if given variables are operative, then other specified variables will also be present. But both sets of variables need to be specified and criteria for their measurement devel-oped. For example, Child, Storm, and Veroff (1958) theorized that there would be a relationship in primitive societies between achievement motivation and economic enterprise. They used achievement themes in folk tales as a measure of motivation and the presence of entrepreneurs as a measure of economic activity and found the predicted relationship. The Barber thesis, however, lacks such operationalization of its variables and does not carry us much beyond the traditional intuitive approach. Nonetheless, it may spur other workers to formulate hypotheses and develop measures for their testing.

In most treatments of power drive and political leaders, there is scant recogni-tion of changing patterns of motivation as societies move from preindustrial through industrial to postindustrial stages. Knutson (1972a) relates such societal shifts to Maslow's motive hierarchy (1954) and political participation and leadership in the future. She calls attention to Aronoff's findings of intergenerational differences in psychic need satisfaction in a West Indian community as evidence of motivational changes which can well affect the political scene. Her penetrating analysis suggests that with satisfaction of lower need levels the citizenry can become more self-actualiz-ing and that leadership in a truly democratic society may be based not in compensa-tory power needs but in self-actualizing tendencies. She optimistically suggests that some 60 percent of Congress and party officials are minimally self-actualized and uses V. O. Key's (1966) description of political influentials as support for her position. Key noted the consensus among the influentials that public opinion should prevail and that democratic processes should be observed.

Interpretive Summary

In this account of political leadership we have attempted to achieve some balance between personality and situational approaches to political influence. It has been widely recognized that both terms of the relation known as leadership—both the behavior of the key actors and the social setting—need to be described and studied. Nevertheless, little has been done to set forth the characteristics of social settings and their relationships to leadership patterns. We have called attention to five major dimensions of the relevant social environments: (1) degree of formal role structure; (2) relative autonomy or dependence of system in which leadership is exercised; (3) the mix of primary and secondary relationships; (4) the totalitarian versus the democratic character of the authority structure; (5) position of the leader in the hierarchical structure.

We have also attempted to relate patterns of leadership to three of these dimensions. A pattern represents not a single motive but a characteristic set of actions resulting from motives, personality style, and cognitive skills. It is our conviction that progress in this field will come not from attempts to link a single motive or a single personality syndrome to leadership achievement, but from a more thorough search for consistent leadership patterns as they relate to general but identifiable characteristics of the social environment. The personality-trait approach to leadership of a past generation of psychologists proved barren. It was replaced by an emphasis upon personality syndromes or types. This in itself is not enough in that there is a neglect of intellectual skills and other aspects of leadership behavior as well as the relation to social settings. When our research and theorizing become more sophisticated, we may abandon the notion of leadership as a linear relation and describe it as a circular process in which there are cycles of events mutually affecting one another.

With the development of methodology in the social sciences and its increasing application to practical and theoretical problems, it is difficult to account for the slow research progress in the field of political leadership. The importance of content analysis, of measurement, of specification of variables, of research design should no longer be a matter of dispute in the behavioral sciences. Moreover, a number of investigators have demonstrated with considerable ingenuity how research methods can be applied to historical materials. Part of the answer may be that we are in too much of a hurry and want complete answers even if they turn out to be fictitious. Because of the phenomenal success of natural science in recent years we forget the laborious, careful years of effort that precede seemingly spectacular outcomes. But there is no reason for believing that the problems of social science are so simple compared to natural science that we can jump the steps of careful observation, of the development of measures, of sampling design, of hypothesis testing, of theoretical development, and of analysis procedures.

9

AGGRESSION, VIOLENCE, REVOLUTION, AND WAR

James Chowning Davies

In the first Christian century a prophet named John wrote what he said was the revelation, to him from Christ, of the end of the world. It was imminent and it was horrible, and all the evil people were going to be destroyed. In the twentieth Christian century both evangelical and scientific prophets have been predicting, for decades, the same thing. The end is imminent (since the end of World War II the clock on the cover of *The Bulletin of the Atomic Scientists* has variously read five or eight or twelve or seven or two minutes to twelve), and everything on earth will be destroyed. The fact that the end has not yet come—at least by the time the reader reads this—is altogether ignored. The ancient and modern reasons for the inevitability of Armageddon are stated and

234

restated. They invariably imply or assert the moral notion of mankind's innate wickedness or the scientific notion of his innate tendencies to violence.

These predictions are based on knowledge that no one really possesses about the roots of violence in the nature of men. It seems quite reasonable to suppose that all men have in common certain basic tendencies to behave in predictable, ordered ways. It does not seem quite reasonable to suppose that these tendencies invariably include an innate desire to do violence. Rather, as I will later argue, it seems more reasonable to suppose that violence is a *response* to the frustration of desires that indeed are innate in all humans.

We cannot make definitive assertions about the certainty or even the high probability of total annihilation, but we can diminish the muddle of thought about violence and its causes. To do this, we have to consider factors originating in men's nature (their organisms) and in their environment. But since the commonest assertions about violence imply or assert things about men's nature, those factors will here be most carefully considered that originate within men, in their central control systems—that is, in their nervous and endocrine systems. These two parts of men's anatomies will be discussed first psychologically and then physiologically.

Some Definitions

Much of the emotional wordage about violent behavior results from the failure of people to make clear what they are talking about. So let me state rather precisely, at the outset, how I use the terms *aggression, violence, revolution,* and *war.*

Aggression is a tendency to engage in hostile and intentionally destructive acts —purposive acts whose consequence is injury to other living objects (usually people) or damage to things that pertain to other living objects.[1]

Violence is the characteristic of acts that are successfully injurious or damag-

---

[1] Intent and purpose are here regarded as synonyms and defined very elementally. They include acts ranging from a clam feeding itself to a bear scratching itself to human beings doing either of these things and in addition making love or war. Purpose is not here regarded teleologically in the philosophical sense but only as goal-*orientation*. Purpose is regarded as emerging out of the activation of wants within the organism and as indicating a tendency to act in a way that can satisfy those wants.

Most interaction between persons and between persons and objects is here deemed to be intentional, purposive. Whether intent is conscious is a matter I do not intend here to discuss. If a clam uses its muscle to open its shell to get food, I am willing to infer intent without raising the issue of *conscious* intent. Many of men's actions are such that one can suppose a person knew what he was doing but was unable to control his action. Whether a person is able to control his action—that is, to *decide* whether to do a purposive (goal-oriented) act is another question to which neurology may sometime provide some answers. Too many mentally ill people knowingly commit violent acts for us to say that these (often consciously) intended acts are controlled.

The factors of intent and conscious control nevertheless have to be considered to avoid assuming that human beings have either total control or no control over their actions. If the distinction is not made, every traffic fatality would send every surviving driver to prison. The legal distinction between willful and accidental homicide remains both necessary and ill-defined. And the legal concept of willful negligence is a semantic paradox: negligence implies that one failed to be reasonably aware of the consequences of his action; willful implies intentional action. (For an earlier discussion of these definitional problems, see Davies, 1970.)

ing. It is one consequence of an aggressive tendency. Sometimes aggressive tendencies produce violent—that is, destructive—acts. Sometimes, when sublimated, aggressive tendencies produce acts that are constructive, creative, or nurturant. Sometimes, when one is overwhelmed by threat of injury or damage to one's possessions, he may suppress aggressive tendencies, and thus they may not lead—at least immediately—to violent acts.

To avoid pedantic repetition in the discussion that follows, the phrase *aggressive acts* sometimes appears as shorthand for "acts that are the result of aggressive tendencies." But it is important to separate the inferred tendency from the observable act because not all aggressive tendencies do end in violent acts and not all inferences about aggressive tendencies are accurate.

One more ambiguity about aggression requires clarification: the easy verbal habit of not distinguishing between the broad category of assertive acts and the sub-category of those assertive acts which are distinguished by the intent to injure or destroy.

Assertiveness is a tendency to interact voluntarily, forcefully with animate or inanimate objects, which together compose the environment. This tendency leads to acts that often, though not always, involve observable contact with persons or things. The contact need not be physical: it may range from waving a hand or shaking a fist from a distance to shaking hands and saying "hello" to a person next to you—or, alternatively, hitting him. All these actions are here deemed assertive. Those whose intent is hostile and destructive are deemed aggressive.

Opposite to assertiveness is a tendency to be indifferent to the environment—either withdrawing from it without affect or letting it act on one without approving or disapproving, liking or disliking. During anesthesia, a person being surgically treated on an operating table is indeed observably indifferent to the surgeon's non-violent actions. But a person, perhaps a serf or a slave, who is spat upon by a gentleman may appear to be indifferent or passive without actually being so. He may later, to his own and the gentleman's surprise, set fire to the gentleman's house, an obviously purposive, violent act stemming from an aggressive tendency that follows being spat upon and appearing to be indifferent. We later consider what it is within men that spitting on them frustrates.

Revolution is here defined as a substantial change in the power structure of a society—a change accompanied by substantial violence. If the change is substantial but is not accompanied by much violence, it seems more appropriate—particularly in an analysis relating revolution to aggression—to call it substantial or even radical change but not revolution. If the change is not substantial but there is much violence in the society, it is turbulence but not revolution—and certainly should be seen by rulers as a very ominous sign that if they do not allow or welcome a change in the power structure, a revolution will very likely take place. A rebellion is here defined as an attempted but abortive revolution—that is, one that seeks to change the power structure by violence but fails to do so.

Examples of revolutions—according to this definition—are the French, Russian, and Chinese revolutions and also the Nazi revolution. Examples of substantial changes in the power structure that have occurred without substantial violence are the Jeffersonian and Jacksonian epochs in American history, both of which substantially broadened the power base of the American polity; and the agitation surrounding the Reform Acts of 1832 in Britain, whose consequences were comparable in substance to the Jeffersonian and Jacksonian epochs in America. Examples of rebellions, of revolutions that aborted, are these: the Peasants' Revolt in Germany in 1525, Dorr's Rebellion in Rhode Island in 1842, the Civil War in America in 1861–1865, Antonio Conselheiro's rebellion in Brazil in 1896–1897, and the Boxer Rebellion in China in 1900.

War is definable as a concerted, coordinated effort by two large societies to oppose each other in mortal combat. The aggressor in war may be defined as the warring party that crosses the frontier of the other, but this is a less central issue than the intention of both parties to the conflict to injure and kill each other as much as is necessary to win—or at least not to lose—the conflict. *Conflict,* the generic term, refers to the total class of antagonistic interpersonal acts (both nonviolent and violent), ranging from a "violent" argument between brothers to a war between two nations.

In this chapter our problem is to seek explanations for aggression, violence, revolution, and war—not *all* interaction, *all* change, and *all* conflict. The discussion therefore sadly lacks the drama of talking about the war between the sexes, the revolution in fashion, the violence of starvation, and about violent argument between two people. But what this chapter loses in the raising of adrenalin levels, perhaps it gains in clarity.

Some Rather General Explanations

The ancient urge to understand ultimate causes is so strong that most people sooner or later find it impossible to wait for the truly final statement of ultimate causes. They produce such a statement—or adhere to one that someone else has produced. It is not only evangelists and ideologists who have stated ultimate causes and responsibilities. Learned men, a subcategory of people, have also produced such statements. Scientists, including psychologists, have also produced such statements. It should therefore not logically be a surprise, but probably is a surprise psychologically to note the distinguished and/or famous company to which the syllogism applies.

Freud, Einstein, and May on Aggression. At the age of seventy-four, Freud (1930) expressed his notion of a dualism of warring instincts. These instincts, in Freud's thought, are forces of which men are only rarely conscious.

One of these instincts is Eros, the force that compels people to procreate sexually and, when sublimated, to create in other than sexual ways. It is the instinct that seeks life, that provides (or *is,* Freud sometimes said) the energy for the continuation of life and the development of culture. The other is the death instinct, the force that seeks to destroy life, to return all living matter to the inorganic state. We can call it the psychological parallel of the Second Law of Thermodynamics, the law stating the tendency of all energy states to achieve homogeneity and therefore uniform and minimal activity.

Overseeing this conflict between life-energy and death, in Freud's system, is the ego, the rational set of forces that occasionally succeeds but usually fails to control the conflict between Eros and the death instinct. The role of the ego was at one time compared by Freud to a rider on a rather wild horse; but whether the rider seeks to protect the horse from death or to drive it to death is not to my knowledge clearly discussed by Freud. The ego gets most of its energy from Eros and plays a sometimes constructive role in the struggle that ultimately ends in destruction—the triumph of death. The kinship of Freud's systematization to the simpler and philosophically immortal dichotomy between emotion (manifestations of instincts) and reason (the ego) is clear.

From this dualism of Eros and the death instinct, Freud developed what to him was a necessary sequitur: aggression is innate in men; one of their two basic instincts is to kill others and finally themselves. A part of them wants to cancel out all the tension that life amounts to, all its frustrations, and to erase life—their own and that of others—forever.

In a public exchange of letters with Albert Einstein, Freud stated explicitly what was not quite clear in his earlier writings: Man is instinctively aggressive. In this exchange of letters, Einstein raised the question: "Why can men be so easily aroused by their leaders to wage war?" He then answered it by saying: "because man has within him a lust for hatred and destruction" (Einstein and Freud, 1932, p. 18). To this Freud (pp. 40–41) replied: "I entirely agree with you. I believe in the existence of this instinct. . . . We [psychoanalysts] assume that human instincts are of two kinds: those that conserve and unify, which we call 'erotic' . . . or else 'sexual'; and, secondly, the instincts to destroy and kill, . . . the aggressive or destructive instincts." And he added: "The death instinct becomes an impulse to destruction when, with the aid of certain organs, it directs its action outwards, against external objects" (p. 45). With a notable—and characteristic—self-consciousness, Freud said: "All this may give you the impression that our theories amount to a species of mythology and a gloomy one at that! But does not every natural science lead ultimately to this—a sort of mythology? Is it otherwise today with your physical science?" (pp. 46–47).

Part of Freud's solution for the conflict between the life and death instincts sounds much like Plato's reliance on guardians: "That men are divided into leaders and the led is but another manifestation of their inborn and irremediable inequality. The second class constitutes the vast majority; they need a high command to make decisions for them, to which decisions they usually bow without demur. In this context we would point out that men should be at greater pains than heretofore to form a superior class of independent thinkers, unamenable to intimidation and fervent in the quest of truth, whose function it would be to guide the masses dependent on their lead" (Einstein and Freud, pp. 49–50).[2]

It now seems self-evident that Freud was on solid ground in exploring the unconscious determinants of human behavior and in asserting that sex impulses, or life-energy itself, are major determinants of a variety of actions—some of them relating to war and to aggression; that is, to the tendency of people to injure and destroy. It is not at all self-evident, however, that Freud's clinical observations and his observations of World War I were adequate to support such a confident assertion of the innateness of aggression. His theory (and that of his successors) was (and is)

---

[2] Roazen (1968, chs. 4 and 5) discusses Freudian and post-Freudian psychoanalytic ideas about how society and government not only inhibit but also facilitate, both control and liberate, men from what Freud called their innate aggression (and other instincts).

at least decades if not centuries ahead of the evidence. It was more evangelical than scientific: It was "a sort of mythology."

May (1972) presents a synthesis of psychological ideas on the origins of aggression that is more broad and reasoned than was possible in Freud's time. There have been more wars and violence to reflect on since Freud wrote. May defines aggression as "a moving out, a thrust toward the person or the thing seen as the adversary" and the goal is "to cause . . . a restructuring of power" (p. 148). He places what I have called assertiveness and aggression into the same broad category and then distinguishes between constructive and destructive aggression. His analysis of its causes emphasizes the various demands which can produce a thrust toward the adversary when they are frustrated. The desire to establish self-esteem, to count for something both as an identity and as an active force in society, and to actualize oneself—all are demands which make one move against others. His analysis is clear and specific, and it directly attacks, in his own well-defined terms, the stubborn adversary of our ignorance of our constructive and destructive actions in a turbulent, violent epoch.

Lorenz and Ardrey on Aggression and Sin. We can here consider only two of the most celebrated of the recent writers who have undertaken to probe into the hidden causes of men's open destructiveness. These are two ethologists: Konrad Lorenz, the Austro-German student of animal behavior under (largely) natural circumstances, and Robert Ardrey, the forceful American synthesizer of the work of other ethologists.

Lorenz says that aggression is an innate tendency. It is the product of evolution, of the natural selection process whereby those genetic mutations that are viable under given environmental circumstances tend to flourish. That is, aggression is "phylogenetically programmed," "autochthonous," "endogenous," and "spontaneous." Lorenz does not always distinguish between acts that involve quick and close contact but lack the intent to injure or destroy and those acts that are destructive. But he does argue that men, like many other vertebrates, engage in destructive action toward other persons and things. That this is so is too manifest to question. That the causes for such universally observable acts are phylogenetically determined and endogenous is not too obvious to question.

Scattered clues in *On Aggression* show Lorenz's uncertainty about whether aggression is an initial drive or a response to threat. At one point (1967, p. 104) he mentions what he calls "the allegedly irresistible drives of hunger, fear, or sex." At another (1967, p. 94) he mentions what he calls " 'the big four'—hunger, love, fight, and flight." The relationship between these drives and aggression, at least in *On Aggression,* remains unclear. It is possible, within his system, to suppose that the frustration of these drives produces the universally observable manifestations of aggression, but Lorenz does not systematically consider the relationship between each of the drives or between them and the aggressive tendency. He is by no means opposed to the concept of instincts and indeed argues at one point that they are not as such dangerous. He says (1967, pp. 228–230) that the danger of annihilation arises not from men's instincts but from their ability to think conceptually, abstractly, *without* understanding the roots of human behavior. This theme recurs, as we shall see, in Arthur Koestler's analysis.

Lorenz does not quite leave us with such an inconclusive conclusion. After presenting a massive, exciting array of data and an uncertain set of drives, he then proceeds optimistically to exhort. His prescription on the verbal level includes these phrases, used conjointly and more or less interchangeably: "rational morality," "reasoning morality," "rational responsibility," "responsible morality" (Lorenz, 1967, pp. 232, 245, 286). In short, an appeal to right reason. The basis for "good" behavior, in Lorenz's view, lies in the nature of men. Any categorical imperative, then, is not really Kant's imperative (arising spontaneously from somewhere outside the nature of men) but man's. He must act in accordance with his nature. Man should know himself, including both his constructive (affiliative) and destructive (agonistic) instincts. Man must realize his little-tapped potential for affiliative identification (love) with an expanding circle of human beings and his enormous capacity for disguising in the langauge of virtue the act of destruction.

Robert Ardrey (1961, 1966) has also put forth a well-known theory. It is that "the passion for territory is inborn, its borders learned" (1966, p. 266). Ardrey does not equivocate; he does not qualify; he does not say that social territory is simply one kind of territory. He insists that people (and other vertebrates) have an innate passion for space—land, water, and air. Territorial passion, in fact, is stronger than sex in holding people together, the attachment between males and females is based more on territory than on sex, and the rules governing the use of territory are "more permanent than sexual opportunity" (1966, p. 100). This passion for territory, in Ardrey's view, seems to come ahead of anything else, except possibly food.

What this passion for territory is itself based on is not quite clear. It is not based on amity. In fact, amity is the product of enmity, emerging when two or more people turn their enmity onto external objects as they join in defense of their children, their marriage, their home (1966, pp. 271, 273). Ardrey does mention a set of basic drives—for security, stimulation, and identity (1967, pp. 170, 333)—and all these are satisfied by territory. Identity may be linked to solidarity, which may be linked to action, but, as we have noted, amity develops as one turns his enmity away from those with whom he shares his territory and becomes aggressive against outsiders who attack it. Territory is the categorical imperative. Everything else appears to be secondary—not just to his analysis but to his belief about the fundamental wellsprings of human interaction. The relationship between the territorial and other lesser passions remains unclear. Only the struggle for territory goes on, and from it springs war.

What does become clear is Ardrey's intense moral tone. We must recognize, by whatever terms, that we are all endowed with original sin. What we lack and need is "a biological morality." The imperative moral criterion should be the welfare of the population, which overrides the welfare of the individual. Biological morality restrains the individual to the ultimate benefit of the species. It is the survival of the species that matters, not the accidental fact of individual lives. Whatever helps man survive, then, is good. Whatever does not is bad. The virtue is in survival. Because of man's innate vice, there must be strong controls, in the interest of survival of the species Homo sapiens. The criteria for controls (other than survival) and for controlling the controllers he does not consider.

Ardrey's popularity, like Lorenz's, is in small part a consequence of his remarkable writing ability. The large part is that, like Lorenz, he fits a mood of deep anxiety about the fate of the world when so many people in our turbulent century see it as being in the hands of man, uncontrolled by either natural laws or supernatural forces. Ardrey also fits the mood of profound worry that man is not naturally good but naturally evil. He jokingly confesses that he has his own small sins and roars at the sinfulness of man. The fit is precise: men are generally sinful, I am a little sinful, and if we all don't straighten up and do right—if we don't act contrary to our violent nature and in accordance with our innate territorial demands —then the world is doomed and in some vague way it's our fault, or more exactly, the fault of the other fellow. (For a recent critique of Lorenz and Ardrey, see Alland, 1972.)

Regarding the conclusions of Lorenz and Ardrey, we can appropriately raise the question that Freud raised with Einstein: Does not every natural science ultimately lead to a sort of mythology? Two facts remain indisputable: first, no one yet knows as much as such writers claim to know about human nature and, second, humanity has thus far miserably botched the job of committing suicide, of truly fulfilling its hypothetical death wish.

If the generality of mankind and its leaders had taken seriously enough during the last twenty centuries the evangelical and "scientific" assertions about innate tendencies to violence, we would long since have committed total collective destruction, human racial suicide. It is perhaps fortunate that illiteracy is still high enough that literate arguments postulating violence as an inborn drive are not more widely read. It is surely unfortunate that along with illiteracy go the profound frustrations that turn many poor people to violence, once they have the chance. In any case, Hitler succeeded in both genocide and suicide to a frightful degree; the rest of us have for the most part failed. Why have we not expressed ourselves naturally, in one glorious, irradiated, cosmic few seconds of deliberate or accidental total destruction? Just possibly because it is not our nature to do so.

Koestler on Selflessness. The words of ethologists who speak with tongues which individually are pointed but collectively forked are confusing. An even newer thesis, contradictory to the aggressiveness argument of Lorenz and Ardrey, is rather confounding. And for its supporting evidence it shifts from the observation of animal and human behavior in real-life situations to some basic theory and research in psychology and neurophysiology.

Arthur Koestler (1967, 1969) does not trace man's aggressiveness back to an innate tendency to destroy just for the fun of it. Instead he supposes it to be derived from the urge to dedicate oneself to a cause, a leader, an ideology, and then to proceed to sacrifice one's fellow men if possible and oneself if necessary to that cause, leader, or ideology. As evidence for this "urge," he cites such occasionally massive popular movements as crusades, wars, and revolutions. And then his explanation becomes neurophysiological: it derives from his belief in the inability of the forebrain, the cortex, the reasoning part of the brain, to control the midbrain (the hypothalamus and related structures linked to the forebrain). Indeed, Koestler argues, the emotional part of the brain, which has been called the limbic system, crucially controls and enslaves the reasoning part, the forebrain. The limbic system is "the ghost in the machine." Translated into philosophical language, it is the old argument that emotion outweighs reason.

Koestler sees the problem which threatens man's doom by the bomb as an imbalance between what he calls the integrative and the self-assertive tendencies. (In ancient China, it might have been called Yang and Yin.) Selfless dedication to cause, leader, and ideology reflects an excess of the integrative tendency. And this excess, of course, is the consequence of the failure of the forebrain of man to control his limbic system. We return later in this chapter to a discussion of the physiology of violence.

The reductionism with which writers from Freud to Koestler have treated aggression suggests another reductionism: that the main barrier to our understanding of aggression lies in the tendency to dichotomize. When explanations and prescriptions are posited in terms of unreason against reason, emotion against reason, limbic system against cortex, hate against love, nature against nurture, man's natural virtue in a vicious society or his natural vice in a virtuous society—if these pairs are posed in one form or another, then analysis becomes futile and endless.

Quincy Wright on War. It is refreshing to note that a man who has concentrated his lifelong intellectual endeavors on the study of war has avoided such reductionism. Quincy Wright (1964, p. 108) comes up with four categories of cause of war: technological, legal-rational, sociological, and psychological. These causes, in his view, somehow emerge from the interaction process between nature and nurture— although Wright generally tends toward a neurophysiological, ultimately biological orientation: "Cultures are but abstractions of common psychological elements in aggregates of human beings" (p. 112). He talks about "general tension level" as an abstraction which relates to war as an outcome of individual's tensions and as a product of various frustrations. These frustrations, or "apprehensions," relate back to a system of "primitive drives."

The main primitive drives are food, sex, dominance, self-preservation, home territory, activity, independence, and society (pp. 26–27, 320). These are somehow related to processes involved in pursuing satisfaction of other primitive "mechanisms" like identification, rationalization, repression, displacement, projection, and the scapegoat. And these things transform "natural human affections, annoyances, ambivalences, and frustrations into group hostilities" (pp. 320–321). The listing of primitive drives is not quite clear, nor is their relationship to other phenomena. Indeed, at one point Wright even includes among man's "biological instincts" "aggressiveness and sadism" or "the love of aggression and dominance" (p. 267).

In Wright's view, war is "inevitable in a jungle world; peace is an artificial construction" (p. 105). War is "natural" in the sense that it is a response to "internally generated interests and motivations"; peace is "artificial" in the sense that "its maintenance depends on a general desire to maintain it, on a correct image of the world as one whole, and on the guidance of political decisions and actions by sound . . . knowledge" (Wright, 1968, p. 466). He does not make clear whether this general desire is a wholly artificial product of culture or partly a product of the primitive social drive.

Wright hopes that this sound knowledge ("psychological, sociological, political, economic, and technological") will enlighten "national hubris" with "rational themis." But rational themis in his system must be a part of men's natural endowment along with primitive drives. At some points he seems to regard it as the endowment of intellectuals only. He does not, however, consider the paradox that man's (limited) ability to gather, assess, and use such knowledge is a derivation of man's possessing a highly developed forebrain and that this forebrain is part of man's nature, physiologically considered, just as much as primitive, basic drives are part of his nature, psychologically considered. He refers repeatedly to the thesis contained in the charter of UNESCO that it is not in external circumstances but in the minds of men that the origins of violent social conflict are to be found. But he does—however uncertainly—conceive war to be the outcome of an interaction process between innate demands and an environment that fails to meet these demands. And in all his studies he never abandoned his etiological pluralism or forgot the need to analyze environmental forces. And he altogether rejected the reductionist tendencies of other students of the origins of conflict.

One need no longer believe, I would argue, that the aggressive tendency and violent acts are the direct, unmediated product of an innate tendency or that they are the simple product of environment. One can assert that innate tendencies, discoverable by psychological and neurophysiological research, bear the same indirect, mediated relationship to environmental circumstances that genes do to the total organism. And one can assert that aggressiveness develops when innate tendencies are frustrated. The environment by itself cannot produce the organism without the genes; the genes cannot construct an organism—not even an aggressive or territorial organism—out of themselves.

However, it is not the environment but the genetic structure that produces form out of the disordered environment. Correlatively, it is the human central control systems (the brain and the endocrines) which integrate behaviors that are paradoxically both constructive and destructive, integrative and disintegrative. It is reductionism to say that the central control systems do this all without enculturation, without training and even conditioning. It is also reductionism to argue, as environmental or sociological monists have argued, that whatever structure and order there is in human behavior is altogether the product of environmental inputs. Wright did not very systematically integrate into his writings—perhaps could not do so in his time—either psychological or physiological research. He nevertheless avoided the reductionism of most social scientists, who see at the roots of violence only the environment—and the social environment at that. And he shunned the simplism of the Social Darwinists and their preoccupied descendants, who can see only man's nature—and a destructive nature at that.

The polemics of ethologists have, in an anxious era, focused our attention on aggression but have not increased our knowledge of its causes. Wright's open and nonpolemical work did not focus a broad reading public's attention on aggression, but—unlike the polemics of ethologists—did increase our knowledge of it.

Sophisticated Psychological Explanations

An early major assault on the intractable problem of explaining aggression was undertaken in 1939 by a group of Yale psychologists. In their classic pioneering work, *Frustration and Aggression,* Dollard and his associates stated a set of theoretical relationships which now appear oversimple but remain a logically and psychologically elegant proposition of great, though not ultimate, explanatory value. We will first state their basic proposition and then indicate how some people have modified it.

The theory is stated on the first page of the book: "Aggression is always a consequence of frustration," and "the existence of frustration always leads to some form of aggression." The authors thus posit a direct one-to-one relationship between frustration and aggression: if cause *A,* then effect *B;* whenever effect *B,* then cause

A. They do not quite say that aggression is the only consequence of frustration but that aggression is always a consequence of frustration. In other words, frustration will inevitably produce aggression, although it may also produce other reactions.

The tightness of the logic contrasts markedly with the sloppy thought of those who had struggled with the causal problem before—and who have struggled with it since. But the Yale group's theory of frustration and aggression is not fully developed. They are quite willing to include within aggressive responses to frustration the kinds of aggression that are turned inward: self-hate, self-punishment, obsequiousness toward threatening persons. But they do not consider that people may make a nonaggressive response, including the response that Freud and others have labeled positive identification with the aggressor—not obsequiousness toward the aggressor but identification with him. A common example of such identification is the anti-Semitic Jew. Another is the "Uncle Tom," the black who identifies with whites and rejects blacks. Rather obviously, identification with the aggressor involves the hostile elements of both self-rejection and rejection of one's group; but it stretches the categorical statements of the Yale group to say that identification with the aggressor, arising from frustration, is aggression and only aggression.

The Yale group allows in principle for this kind of reaction by talking about factors that inhibit the expression of aggression, most notably the fear that expressing it will be met with punishment of some sort. They do allow for a reaction which is turned against (displaced, in Freudian language) some object other than the source of the frustration, for a reaction in which the object may be self or other persons or things. A frustrated person may physically or mentally beat his wife after the boss in the factory or office has frustrated him. This action lies within the Yale group's range of aggressive responses to frustration, as would a response of self-punishment.

But their analysis leaves out two things of great significance. One is the organic aspects of the frustration; that is, what internally causes the person to be frustrated. The other is a full consideration of alternative responses to frustration.

The Yale group mention almost nothing about what it is, internally, that is frustrated. That is, they talk very little about specific demands of the organism which, when blocked, produce frustration. They use the term *instigation* but—with the shyness of stimulus-response psychologists—talk little about what instigations are, except as they may be inferred from overt behavior. To the extent that they talk about organic demands that are environmentally frustrated, they say that a child who wants an ice cream cone and does not get one is frustrated, rather than that a child with an activated hunger drive will be frustrated if he is denied food. They tend to say that someone disappointed in love will become aggressive rather than that there is an innate need for love which, when denied, will produce aggressive action. *Need* in the language of the Yale group becomes the ambiguous phrase "goal response." They thus avoid saying that there are any innate needs and sidestep the tricky problem of purpose and intent. The focus of attention remains relatively shallow and close to the surface of observable acts.

A major leap forward in the reciprocal interaction between theory and research was made in 1962 by a University of Wisconsin psychologist, Leonard Berkowitz. He clearly defined aggression as "behavior whose goal is injury of some object," although he later reintroduced an unnecessary ambiguity in talking about "instrumental" aggression, the kind whose "goal [is] other than doing injury" (Berkowitz, 1962, pp. 1, 31).

Berkowitz markedly clarified and quantified the relationships between various parts of the aggression process. He pointed out the relationship between the strength of the forces that are frustrated, the strength of the frustrating force, and the resultant frustrated behavior. He examined how individuals weigh the alternatives of weak or strong response, and of response that is directed toward the source of the frustration or deflected away from it. And he was more specific than the Yale group about what the drives ("instigators" or "goal responses") are, including both physical and self-esteem needs. He pointed out that aggressive acts may also satisfy an acquired motive, may reduce internal conflict. They may also restore self-esteem.[3]

More significant than any such accretions to our understanding of aggression is Berkowitz's emphatic assertion that frustration does not always produce aggression, even in sublimated or displaced or internalized form. He mentions not only the withdrawal alternative to aggression—as when a person is unable to fight back against that which frustrates him or fears worse consequences by aggressing than by not aggressing. He also mentions something that Freud emphasized in his *Civilization and Its Discontents,* the alternative to aggression that may variously be called sublimation or constructive action.

A person may, because of frustration (and several other factors, including his particular talents and training), engage in creative acts which only in the most tenuous sense can be deemed aggressive against other persons or objects or against self. Such would be the case of Beethoven, who was at times forced into practicing on musical instruments by his mercurial and often drunken father and then became a composer. Presumably Beethoven's prime purpose in composing was not to get back at his father, but perhaps some of the intensity of Beethoven's efforts is attributable to a childhood-established pattern of work to avoid punishment by father. Such also would be the case of Lincoln, who said that his father taught him how to work but never taught him to like it, and who did not go to see his father when he was dying. Despite his hostile feelings toward his father, Lincoln sublimated his frustrations by activity that made him a success.

The situation that we have arrived at with the help of the above psychologists may be summarized thus: (1) Frustration tends to produce aggression. (2) Aggression is a common but not inevitable consequence of frustration. (3) The concepts of frustration and aggression, to the extent that they are related to each other and neglect the *internal* causes of frustration, probably focus too exclusively on the immediate and concrete rather than the more ultimate and fundamental causes of violence. (4) Frustration may be one of the factors producing action whose effect is not to injure or destroy but to create.

Explanations by Social Theorists

Major social theorists, from Marx onward, who have concerned themselves with the causes of revolution lend increasing support to an interaction theory of violence—the interplay of forces within the organism and the environment. Marx

[3] The rise in self-esteem that may follow aggressive action was put in poignant political context by Frantz Fanon (1968). What Sorel (1908) called "the sentiment of glory," which is fulfilled by combat, seems similar to what is here called self-esteem.

(1849) talked about the gradual degradation of the masses as a major step in the sequence leading to revolution and the development of class consciousness as a necessary step between degradation and revolution. Tocqueville (1856) said almost the opposite: It is when circumstances are improving that men turn to revolution. Both writers concentrated heavily on the socioeconomic environment. They implied much but said relatively little directly about intraindividual dynamics.

Writing in the twentieth century, when psychological knowledge had begun to develop, the sociologist Pitirim Sorokin (1925, p. 33) did mention human impulses: individual self-preservation, alimentary, sexual, group-defense, and self-expression. Violent social outbreak is likely when "the 'cramped' hereditary impulse begins to put pressure on the 'brake'—that is, on habit."

Lyford Edwards (1927), deriving his list of basic human "wishes" from W. I. Thomas (1923), said that when these wishes for new experience, security, recognition, and response are frustrated, people feel balked in their expectations and revolution becomes likely. George S. Pettee (1938) developed further Sorokin's idea of the "cramp" that faces people whose expectations are frustrated and emphasized the need to measure quantitative changes over time in order to analyze violent change systematically.

These separate tributaries have, more or less systematically, jointly contributed to the establishment of a broadening river of theory and research on the causes of aggression, violence, revolution, and war. What is most exciting is that few workers on the subject of violence and revolution any longer have the brashness to assume that they can ignore the central congeries of forces that operate within the central nervous and endocrine systems of the human organism as these interact with forces originating in the environment. What was the good sense and precocious judgment of Quincy Wright is now relatively universally accepted by all those interested in theory of public violence. It is less appreciated by many of those who have done research in the problem, as we shall see.

Recent Theory

What Ted Robert Gurr (1970, p. 6) called "the renaissance of systematic theoretical and empirical work on political violence by political scientists" began in the 1960s. The "renaissance," implicitly or explicitly, was the product of a broad range of prior writing, perhaps most centrally derived from the work of the historian Crane Brinton, whose work in turn was developed from a variety of sources, including Tocqueville, Edwards, and Pettee. The first case of the rebirth of this systematic study, on historical, sociological, and psychological grounds, was an article of mine entitled "Toward a Theory of Revolution" (Davies, 1962). I presented the idea of a J-curve of rising expectations and gratifications followed by a period during which there is a short, sharp reversal in gratifications (see Figure 1). In this brief period the gap widens between what people want and what they get, and the probability of revolution increases greatly. The sociological basis for the development of the theory lies in the conflict that develops in a society, when major segments of the society see themselves as acutely suffering from this sudden "subjective" deprivation, typically occurring during an economic downturn. The psychological basis lies in

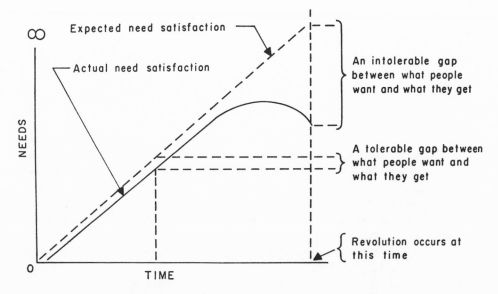

FIGURE 1.   NEED SATISFACTION AND REVOLUTION

the frustration of basic needs, a frustration induced by the sudden reversal in gratifications. My list of basic needs was derived mainly from the need hierarchy of
Abraham Maslow: deprivation of "adequate" amounts of "food, equality, or liberty"
among people who "differ in their degree of objective, tangible welfare and status"
(Davies, 1962, p. 607). (For a more fully developed statement of the broad political
relevance of Maslow's need hierarchy, see Davies, 1963, ch. 1-2; and Knutson,
1972a.)

Somewhat later (Davies, 1969), I broadened and tried to make more explicit
this theory that violence occurs when a period of rising expectations and satisfactions
is followed by an intolerably growing gap between the two. That is, the theory was
made more explicit by emphasizing that violence becomes increasingly likely when
any kind of basic need which has come to be routinely gratified suddenly becomes
deprived. For purposes of joining in political violence of the concerted sort that
produces riots, rebellions, and revolutions, then, the frustrated aristocrat who is
denied access to his career aspirations (perhaps by military service in a war he
deems supportive not of good principles but of an elite that governs the economy,
the army, and the polity) can readily join with his usual class enemies, with working-
men distraught by inflation, with upwardly mobile people whose education is interrupted by depression or war or the like. The conjoining factor is the common
state of mind: the profound frustration that develops when the environment in the
form of culture, society, and government denies the opportunity for basic needs to
get fulfilled.

In an ingenious combination of the time-sequence theory of Crane Brinton
(1938) and of some alienation theory, David Schwartz (1971) has stated a set of
sequential relationships between the individual and the political system as he and
his values become alienated from it; he forms revolutionary organizations, carries

out a revolution, and then becomes changed himself as his alienation is replaced by the establishment of his values.

A new integration of psychologically based theory of violence has been presented by Gurr (1970). He establishes as his basic proposition the concept of relative deprivation. Karl Marx had said in his *Wage Labour and Capital* (1849) that "although the enjoyments of the workers have risen, the social satisfaction that they give has fallen in comparison with the state of development of society in general. Our desires and pleasures spring from society. . . . Because they are of a social nature, they are of a relative nature" (p. 94). Building on this and more specifically psychological foundations, Gurr emphasizes the inadequacy of the frustration-aggression nexus and argues that revolution occurs when substantial segments of a society feel relatively deprived. They feel so when they perceive a discrepancy between their "value expectations" and the "value capabilities" of their environment. Put more simply, people feel deprived when there is a gap between what they want and what they can get.

A major difference between the J-curve and this theory is the strong emphasis of the former on the crucial dimension of time—of comparisons between expectations and gratifications as they change over time. Another difference is that Gurr emphasizes the Marxian kind of comparison not just over time but as between the differing rewards of various social groups. Another difference is that the J-curve theory argues that there must be not just a gap but one resulting from a *downturn* in gratifications. Although theoretically the gap may result in other ways, as when both expectations and gratifications rise but expectations increase more rapidly than gratifications, it is hard to find a case of *rebellion* or *revolution* that does not involve a downturn in gratifications. Part of the downturn before the 1789 French revolution was a set of economic reversals. Part of the downturn before the Black Rebellion of the 1960s in America was the use of dogs and firehoses by law enforcement officers in Birmingham, Alabama, in April 1963—after black people had come to expect that the days of wanton violence perpetrated against them (as in lynchings) had passed (Davies, 1969, pp. 720–723, 727).

Gurr's theory is founded also on a set of basic value expectations (welfare values and deference values) derived from Harold Lasswell and Abraham Kaplan (1950) and related to Maslow's (1943b) hierarchy of basic needs (the physical, security, affectional, self-esteem, and self-actualization needs). But Gurr's integration of Lasswell-Kaplan and Maslow so changes the latter's need hierarchy that it becomes a randomly ordered list. Nevertheless, Gurr's emphasis on relative deprivation is indeed a significant forward step in synthesizing theory about public violence. Among other side benefits, his explanation for why men rebel provides a thorough and scholarly summary and systematization of the work of others. His empirical evidence that real-life revolutions occur in the absence of the J-curve kind of time-sequential relative deprivation is less persuasive.

Quantitative Research

The troubled decade of the 1960s has indeed, as Gurr indicated, seen a renaissance of concern, not just for theory but also for research. Among the earliest, perhaps the earliest, new pioneers are Ivo and Rosalind Feierabend and their associates (1966, 1969, 1972), who combined the frustration-aggression hypothesis of the Yale group with later developments of theory on the gap between expectations and gratifications. From Lipset (1959) they borrowed statistical measures of development (including gross national product; caloric intake, telephones, physicians, newspapers, and radios per capita; literacy, and urbanization). From Lerner (1958) they borrowed a threefold classification of traditional, transitional, and modern societies. And they developed their own indicators of political instability on a seven-point scale ranging from 0 (change following a regularly scheduled election) to 6 (civil war or mass executions). The product of their work has been a massive correlation of degrees of stability with Lipset's measures and Lerner's stages of development. With statistical and classificatory precision, the Feierabends have established that nations in transition are the least stable and that modern nations are generally more stable than traditional ones. They have not yet been able to deal adequately with the more difficult research problem of integrating their data with psychological theory and with patterns of relative deprivation.

The political scientists doing empirical research in violence and revolution have already shown an ability to analyze empirical data and, more often than not, a lack of psychological knowledge. Tanter and Midlarsky have conjoined various indicators to the J-curve (Tanter and Midlarsky, 1967; Midlarsky and Tanter, 1967); and Tanter (1969) has conjoined various indicators to a classification of sources of conflict between and within nations. In an ingenious analysis on a statistical and theoretical base, Russett (1964) has related the land-tenure system in various nations to their political stability. Bwy (1968) has combined psychologically based theory with extensive statistical data to produce a thorough synthesis of knowledge about Latin American political turbulence. In what promises to be a very long-range project, comparable in duration to Quincy Wright's extended and extensive research, Singer (1963, 1968, 1972) has established the research base for long-term trend analyses of the antecedents of war. His research to date, however, shows a reluctance to work with any kind of motivational analysis. Singer does not seem to deal adequately (if at all) with a relationship deemed essential by Wright—the relationship between war and the wants of men. If Singer should turn to the manageable task of measuring these wants by various indirect indicators (as the Feierabends, for instance, have done), then his work should be a great contribution.

The interviewing technique used in survey research has begun to be fruitful for studies of political discontent. Lloyd Free (1971)—following the seminal work of Hadley Cantril's *Pattern of Human Concerns* (1965), which deals less specifically with political violence—employed an ingenious and promising mode of interviewing. It deals less with overt political violence and attitudes toward violence and more with its roots in social and individual discontent. Free successfully interviewed segments of the population in five countries, to find out whether they expect things to get better or worse for them in the years to come. He used a ten-point vertical "self-anchoring scale," wherby the people interviewed could point to where they are now and where they will be in the future—higher or lower on the scale. Applying the technique to Brazil, Nigeria, Cuba, the Dominican Republic, and the United States,

Free found that his data correctly predicted political violence in three of the five nations.

Toward Fundamental and General Analyses

The study of violence (both political and nonpolitical) is subject to the same problem as that faced by the legendary drunk who looked for his lost keys under the street light because that was where the light was brighter. The study of violence by social scientists is being undertaken where the data are visible. The data that are examined are gross data about such trends as population growth, urbanization, occupational mobility, immigration, and gross national product. The implications of such data are by no means yet exhausted, but the tendency to look for the keys where the light is brightest is very often undertaken unsystematically, without any theory to make the search systematic. Meanwhile, there is an ever increasing and little-exploited opportunity to analyze violence in plain psychological daylight.

When crudely conceived empirical research is conjoined with sensationalism, the work tends to become ever more quixotic and its durability ever more ephemeral. When a social scientist, laden with computerized data, asserts conclusive evidence to prove that ghettos cause violence, one is entitled to wonder what caused and causes violence in middle-class suburbs and on middle-class campuses. When a social scientist, inclined to even bolder generalization, says that overcrowding causes violence, one is entitled to query why such heavily compacted cities as Tokyo and Rio de Janeiro, instead of blowing up, continue to grow into megalpolises. Or to query why violent crimes in recent years are reportedly at least four times as numerous in New York as in Tokyo. Or to query why there was such mammoth and concerted violence by the hordes of Genghis Khan and Alexander the Great. Were their troops fugitives from the ghettos of Peking or Athens or Cairo?

If a serious cause of violence is the symbolic stuff on television, why does it produce violent tendencies among such a tiny fraction of those who watch the cops beat the robbers or vice versa? More to the point, did those who watched the real violence of the Vietnam war, as reported symbolically on television broadcasts, show an increase or a decrease in their desire for American continuation of the war?

In short, if ghettos are eliminated, big cities dispersed, and all television showing of violence removed, how much fundamental assurance will either social scientists, political leaders, or general publics have that they have attended to the fundamental reasons for violence? Perhaps little more assurance than a person who jumps into a rowboat has about eliminating the causes of floods and storms. With good luck and more effective use of the innate potential for long-range memory, he may survive to build dams and levees. Or survive to explore the headwaters of frustration and not just stare at the flash floods of overt violence. With bad luck, he remains an evangelist in scientific disguise (or the victim of one), and an evangelist (or victim) who prefers shouting in the darkness because he fears to find in the daylight that his great discovery is only a rivulet.

If indeed—as is too obviously the case—violence, both by private citizens and by public officials, has occurred in a wide range of circumstances over both human history and prehistory, it is then indeed appropriate to consider the common characteristics of those who commit destructive acts and the common circumstances in which potentially everyone commits violent acts. This calls for an extension of the beginnings undertaken by such social scientists as Sorokin and Wright.

Some Integrating Principles. A basic premise of my analysis of everything I have here discussed is that *all* behavior is a product of (a function of) the *inter-action* of the organism and the environment. $B = f(OE)$.[4] If students of violence start and end in the environment, they will consider only one of the two fundamental variables on the right side of the equation. If, as ethologists seem to be doing, they start in the organism and end with an analysis of only the most visible evidence of organic determinants—in which environment plays a maximally evident role, which they ignore—they will only replace the forthright, clear, and holistic conclusions of environmental determinists like Marx, Pavlov, and Skinner with a newly muddled set of errors.

Many social theorists and researchers depreciate both the existence and the activation within the organism of its basic demands as they develop from infancy to maturity. This leaves them free to make any generalizations they wish about the inherent violence of men. If they deny or if they fail to see or recognize the central relevance of basic demands, then indeed violence, in their thought, becomes not a means of satisfying such demands but something that is engaged in for its own sake and is therefore indeed innate in just the same sense that the demands for water, food, and—I would argue—dignity are innate.

Let me summarize some basic hypotheses. Violence is always a response to frustration, but violence is only a subset of a still-undefinable total set of responses to frustration. Violence as a response is produced when certain innate needs or demands are deeply frustrated. If these needs are met by a nurturant environment, the organism usually is "healthy." If they are not, it never fully develops. It withers and dies after a brief time of flowering, or it turns to violence to gain need satisfaction. It never realizes the potential that is innate within it. The human potential is reduced to that of primates, lower vertebrates, or crustaceans.

Let me state the relevant motivational hypothesis—a modification of Maslow (1943b). There are four substantive needs, in descending order of prepotency: the physical, social-affectional, self-esteem, and self-actualization needs. In the day-to-day social interaction of every individual, any one need may dominate his attention, but whenever any lower need (like the physical need for food or rest) becomes active, it will overpower the activity of the central control system that has been responding to any higher need (like the self-esteem of self-actualization need). A person may be activated to revolt by any one or a combination of need deprivations. The poor man is most likely to be activated by physical deprivation—which if it is *very* severe will *de*activate him politically. The person of high status and skill is more likely to be activated to revolt by deprivation of his self-actualization need to pursue an occupation suitable to his talents and training. But if he is actually hungry, the high-status

---

[4] For a fuller explication of this premise, see Davies (1963, pp. 1–6). In the present chapter I substitute E (environment) for S (situation) used in my earlier version. A similar and prior discussion of this premise is to be found in Lasswell and Kaplan (1950, pp. 4–6). They use the terms *acts, nonenvironmental determinants* (or *predispositions*), and *environment.*

person may be activated to revolt by physical deprivation as well as career deprivation.

In addition to these four substantive needs, I postulate three closely inter-related implemental needs: security, knowledge, and power. Each person has some innate tendency to gain minimal satisfaction of each of these implemental needs, but he pursues their satisfaction in the course of seeking means of satisfying one or more of the substantive needs. That is, a hungry and unemployed workingman may exert power by breaking into a bakery. A (substantively) career-frustrated university graduate may seek an (implemental) explanation for his plight by reading and adopting an ideology that argues the origins of misery within a particular social system.

The basic phenomenon of violence covers a wide range of overt acts, whose related antecedent events we may call causes. This range covers cases in which there is a great difference between the relative contributions of organic and environmental causes. Here are four examples of this range, indicating the varying proportions of organic and environmental cause: (1) Some outbreaks of violence may be caused by brain abnormality—resulting from such things as abnormal cells in the amygdala or a tumor surrounding and destroying part of the hypothalamus; in such cases, the abnormality is great enough to produce violent action following only the slightest environmental stimulus. (2) Other violent outbursts may be statistically rare overt responses to very traumatic early childhood experience—as when one of three siblings becomes a killer, all being raised in a family where the father regularly beat the mother and in a neighborhood where violence was common. (3) In individuals with no evident brain abnormality and no evident childhood trauma, violence may result from intense situational incitement to violence, like that facing soldiers in combat. (4) Finally, in a person with normal brain development and normal childhood experience, violence may be a response to chronic circumstances that are profoundly frustrating but not like the violent matrix in which a soldier or a ghetto inhabitant acts violently.

These four categories are designed to discriminate between relative degrees of contribution of the organism and the environment to the overt violent behavior. In *each* of the four categories there is an interaction between organic and environmental forces. For example, in the first category, a person suffering from brain tumor or other abnormality acts violently on some cue, however slight, from the environment. Perhaps it is the mere presence of a wall or of a person. The organism's role is dominant. In the last category, which includes most of those who get involved in war or revolution, the environment frustrates demands of the organism that are altogether normal. To reiterate, from the first to the fourth category the oganism and the environment both are necessary parts of the interaction process. In the first case, the organism is overreacting and the environment is not "objectively" frustrating. Cases in the second and third categories represent a mix of less-to-more normal organism and less-to-more frustrating environments. In the fourth category, the environment is extremely frustrating.

Political violence is here regarded as falling into the fourth category, for most of those who participate in it. Most (but not all) military and revolutionary leaders, and most of those among the general public who join in such violent action, have normal organic behavioral tendencies. The circumstances of such American military and revolutionary leaders as George Washington, Thomas Jefferson, Andrew Jackson, and Dwight Eisenhower were such as to make their aggressive response to perceived political threat, from within or without the country, a reasonable or normal one. Similarly, though under quite different circumstances, the traumatic experiences of Vladimir Ulyanov in his adolescence (the death of his father, his brother, and his sister for reasons attributable to the tsarist government) are necessary parts of an explanation that regards Lenin's intensively hostile and vicariously violent actions against the regime to be normal reactions. In the same general category of normal reactors to profoundly frustrating environments may be included such leaders as Trotsky, Danton, Cromwell, Castro, and Mao Tse-tung.

All such normal reactions to profoundly frustrating environments—whether the reactors be leaders or ordinary citizens—are, on the dimension of time, relatively infrequent, for at least two reasons. One is that among normal human beings there is a wide range of tolerance for frustrating circumstances. Seen from present-day perspective, it is nearly incredible that slaves in the Middle East and in North and South America tolerated or even endured their wretched environment. It is likewise quite incredible that serfs in Western Europe and particularly in Eastern Europe tolerated serfdom until as late as 1861.

Another reason is that, in the perpetually continuing dialogue between demands of the organism and gratification of these demands by the environment, there is often (perhaps usually) enough flexibility in the customs, laws, and power structure of societies to provide minimal satisfaction of the demands made at any one point in time. It is when the expectations of people to live *more* than an animal life of primitive survival and consociation are aroused and when these basic human expectations are frustrated that revolutions and wars occur.

These new demands and expectations arise in the minds of people more or less unconsciously. When a revolutionary leader advocates that the oppressed rise against their oppressors, he is only verbalizing a response for which the predisposition has been long developing within him because of his own frustrated expectations. The new demands develop first and are articulated later. A person typically experiences hunger pangs before he says he is hungry. A person first experiences sexually mature love longings in adolescence, after a long sequence of organic developments that start in the pituitary. Only *after* the organic changes and the longings have generated within his body will he turn his attention to a girl and say "I love you."

At this point it would be possible to veer off into some kind of full-fledged (and premature) statement of revolution and war on a psychological base. This would surely slake the thirst that the intolerance of ambiguity about violence amounts to and might conceivably be enlightening. But it is more appropriate first to describe psychologically the sequence of organic and environmental events that ends in violence and then to mention some of the research that is the basis for describing such a sequence.

The *first* step in the sequence of events leading to violent action is *the activation* of some innately rooted demand within the organism. The resulting state of tension calls for release by or in the environment, which contains the means of satisfying the demand. When a person is thirsty, the environment can provide water. When a person is tired, the environment can provide rest. When he feels lonesome, the (human) environment can provide him company.

The *second* step in the sequence is *the frustration* of one or more demands of the organism. This can take such forms as a failure to provide water (frustrating a person's thirst) or quiet, dark, and comfortable surroundings (frustrating a person's demand for rest).

The *third* (preaction) step in the sequence is *the mental process of seeking and deciding* how to overcome the frustration which the environment places between the individual's demands and their gratification. This mental process can take various forms: effort to find a path around the blockage; effort to find a substitute object for the one initially demanded (as in sublimation); effort to deny or suppress the demand (as in displacement); or effort to destroy the blockage.

The *fourth* step is the one in which *the individual acts.*

With respect to the elemental demand for water: a path around the blockage might be for a thirsty man to decide to look for a well not controlled by the man who refuses to give him water; a search for a substitute might become a search for wine; denial or suppression of the demand might take the form of fantasizing bubbling streams; an effort to destroy the blockage might be the decision to overpower the man denying water.

During the third step—seeking and deciding—tension builds up and becomes available for extreme physical effort. If the demand is actually met, the tension is released and the person relaxes. But any mental effort or any subsequent physical effort that falls short of actually fulfilling the demand will at most release the tension momentarily. Whether it be fantasizing babbling brooks or listening to comparable political orators, whether it be deciding to kill (or, in the action step, actually killing) the man who owns the well or the ruler who controls the government, such effort in itself is of only momentary, mediate, and not ultimate consummatory effect. That is, thought—and even action, whether nonviolent or violent—*which does not actually produce satisfaction of the basic demand* will not release the tension that builds up when the demand became active. This point is a very crucial one for the theses developed in this chapter.

Following the third step of deciding how to overcome the frustration comes the fourth, the action. In the action step, the effort shifts from mental to physical. The individual makes a move, more or less blindly, which has as its purpose consummation of the basic goal, satisfaction of the basic demand. When it is a matter of water, the action usually is not very blind. When it is a political matter, having to do with rearranging the power structure of the society, the action is usually almost blind. The actors who demand political change have a very clear idea of what they do not want and a very unclear idea of what they want. Their opponents, the established ones, are sure they want things (notably power relationships) to stay as they are and are not sure *why* things should stay as they are.

Both the unestablished who want to become established and the presently established have inefficient notions of how either to effect or to block change. Fantasy is not the exclusive treasure of either of these groups. Violence-oriented thoughts and images and even violent acts may be (but are not necessarily) fantasies, escapes, processes that have little to do with effecting or blocking change. One example is the victory over tsardom that killing Nicholas II produced in Russia and the continued victory of tsardom that Stalin's rule amounted to. Another is the popular assumption that if the ground troops can be replaced with the use of carefully controlled massive bombing, then responsibility for effecting or blocking change—in Europe in the 1940s and Asia in the 1960s and 1970s—can be avoided.

Physiological Research. There is not adequate research to confirm or disconfirm the four-step sequence from activation of a basic need, to its frustration, to the mental process of searching and deciding, and then doing it. But there are some seemingly fragmentary pieces of research which such a statement of sequence helps to make coherent.

One line of experiments with laboratory rats has shown what happens when they are faced with frustration of the need to be free from bodily harm (specifically, electric shock). In these experiments (Payne, 1968; Berkowitz, 1968) rats are placed, alone or in pairs, in cages with an electrified grid floor. When a rat is alone, it tries to escape from the situation and becomes intensely restless but does not attack the walls of the cage or itself. When two rats are placed in the cage and shocked, each will attack the other. This experiment may be regarded as a classically elemental instance of what Freud called displacement. When a substitute figure—some kind of doll—is placed in the cage, an animal undergoing shock will attack it, though not so readily as it will another rat. In whatever variation, the experiments show the sequence of arousal of the physical need to be free of pain from the environment, the frustration, the search, and the violent act. Another experiment (Lamprecht and others, 1972) found that rats immobilized two hours a day for twenty-eight days fought more than a control group of rats did. The report also indicated various chemical changes that took place following the immobilization, which is one form of physical deprivation.

In another and now famous line of research, Harlow and his associates (1958, 1962, 1970) examined the effects of environmental deprivation of the nonphysical need for affection among monkeys. In these experiments, neonate monkeys were denied interaction with all other monkeys, including mother and age mates. Under such conditions, the researchers found, even the regular provision of milk from a fake mother contrived from wire, hardware cloth, and terry cloth does not provide the measure of emotional warmth necessary for normal growth. Monkeys so raised are not capable of normal play, normal sex, or any other normal social interaction. When the females that are so raised and thus are uninterested in sex are involuntarily impregnated and produce offspring, their treatment of their own offspring is abnormal and usually brutal. What is more immediately relevant to understanding violence is that such abnormally raised monkeys tend to oscillate between extreme withdrawal and fierce rage reaction to those approaching the cage. Sometimes in a period of rage they bite their own arms, tearing the flesh away from the bone.

A similar phenomenon was observed by René Spitz (1949) in his work with children raised in a foundling home, where they had minimal contact with nurses and none with mothers. These children, like some of Harlow's monkeys, also often showed a shift in mood from withdrawal to rage. The sequence following separation of a child at about age two from its mother is described by Bowlby (1969, pp. 27–28) as (enraged) protest, despair, and then detachment.

The deprivation in the Harlow, Spitz, and Bowlby studies is not physical in the usual sense, though body contact is part of it. The frustration of the nonphysical need for affection, or what Bowlby calls attachment, is so crucial as to produce, sooner or later, a rage reaction. Rage and violence may thus be products of either physical or nonphysical deprivation. Violence comes from frustration, but frustration comes from many kinds of deprivation.

The strong influence of social ties in inducing violence is also indicated positively in another experiment. In it there was no radical loss of all social ties but merely the threat of the mild social loss that disapproval amounts to. In a contrived situation Milgram (1963, 1965) found that subjects threatened with the forceful command of the authority figure in the form of the experimenter were willing to administer what they were falsely told was a near-lethal shock to helpless victims, stooges of the experimenter, who loudly protested the shock. The experimental situation was not a real-life one, but there is ample evidence from combat behavior to indicate that people threatened with the loss of the approval of their crucially important military associates are capable of "voluntary" killing of helpless civilians.

The Nerves. Traditional psychological research has been done with intact animals and people, leaving only reasonable inference as to what actually goes on within the "black box" of the central nervous system when some need of the organism is frustrated. However, under various names like psychobiology and physiological psychology new research and new findings are appearing that already have shed some light on the sequence of neural events. In a book with the appropriate title *The Physiology of Hostility,* Moyer (1971) has gathered systematically the findings of many others and himself. The direct political applicability of such research is yet to come. But the research does demonstrate that violent behavior is the result of a stimulus applied from the environment to the organism. The neural and endocrine control systems produce violence, but only upon external stimulus.

In a striking experiment, two German researchers (Holst and Saint Paul, 1962) showed what happens to chickens when an electrode is inserted into a particular part of the brain and then a tiny electric current is passed through. Chickens that knew and were friendly toward the experimenters became suddenly extremely hostile, seeking to fly at and peck their faces. This research follows a long line of investigations into the effects of cutting away, damaging (by cauterization or otherwise), or merely stimulating various parts of the brain. Walter Cannon and associates found that removing all of the brain in front of the hypothalamus (the main part of the midbrain) in cats produced animals that were almost spontaneously fierce (as in step 1 of the four-step sequence) but unable to direct an attack at the perceived source of threat. Other investigators found that merely cutting a nerve tract between the hypothalamus and brain areas in front of it (that is, toward the forebrain, the cortex; "behind" would mean toward the brain stem and spinal cord) produced fierce animals which directed their rage specifically at the source of the stimulation.

The amygdala, a prominent part of the brain structures lying between the midbrain and the forebrain, contains some substructures that increase rage and others that produce placidity. That is, when parts of the amygdala are electrically stimulated, the animal becomes enraged; when other parts are stimulated, it becomes placid. Removal of the entire amygdala has produced placidity in some animals. Electrical stimulation at various points of the amygdala has produced rage and placidity in human beings hospitalized with a history of epileptic seizures and violent behavior. In some of these cases surgical lesion (by electrolysis) of part of the amygdala stopped the violent behavior (Mark and Ervin, 1970).

Other research has been done on cases in which little or no environmental stimulus provoked the violent response. Rabies, the disease whose symptoms include a tendency to attack violently, shows the effect not of ablation or electrical stimulation but of a virus. The rabies virus attacks a particular part of the hippocampus, which is part of the limbic system. Olds(1965) summarizes research in which a rage response was produced by nonviral, nonelectrical, nonmechanical stimulation. Potassium chloride was placed on the surface of the hippocampus through a tiny glass tube (a cannula). When two rats so treated were placed together, they adopted the posture of attack.

In a long and still-developing line of research with primates and other high vertebrates, Delgado (1969) at the Yale Medical School has made experiments with electrodes permanently implanted in various parts of the brains of monkeys and of a fierce bull, the electrode being remotely activated. And he has been able to stop aggressive behaviors of dominant monkeys so effectively that monkeys which were on the top of a social hierarchy became docile and moved down the hierarchy. When a switch was then placed in the cage, the monkeys lower in the hierarchy learned to switch off the aggressiveness of the top monkey.

Other research has provided some kind of mirror image of the effects of various kinds of interference that has elicited or inhibited violent responses. In the now famous research in which electrodes were implanted in the "pleasure centers" of the midbrain, Olds (1956, 1958; Olds and Olds, 1962) produced the opposite of aggressive reponses. While not directly relevant to understanding the physiology of violence, Olds' research shows the high specificity of various parts of the midbrain as they respond to external stimuli.

This growing body of neurological research demonstrates that there are many specific parts of the brain which, when stimulated, produce violent behavior. It also demonstrates that such behavior occurs only when there is internal lesion (as in a tumor) or external stimulation. No research demonstrates the spontaneous occurrence of violence.

The Endocrines. All this neurological research says nothing about the other part of the central control system—the endocrine glands, from the pituitary on down —that induces or inhibits violent behavior by secretion of tiny amounts of hormones into the bloodstream. The three most significant endocrine glands affecting violent behavior are the bean-sized pituitary (also called the hypophysis), the adrenal, and the sex glands. The pituitary, responding to signals from the brain as it develops, secretes various hormones at various times to both the adrenals and the sex glands. The sex glands, on command from the pituitary, develop and in turn secrete into the bloodstream such hormones as the androgens and estrogens in quantities that vary by sex. More androgens than estrogens are secreted by male sex glands; more estrogens than androgens are secreted by female sex glands. Androgen levels have been found to correlate positively with aggressive, including violent, tendencies. Despite the efforts of some people by verbal means to make males and females identical in all ways, there remains a difference in degree in aggressive and violent tendencies between men and women. Part of the difference is attributable to endocrine secretions that are not very responsive to verbal commands or ideologies (Guyton, 1966, ch. 56, 72).

Perhaps the major endocrine function involved in producing our end product, violent behavior, is performed by two distinct but similar hormones. The hypothalamus, operating not through the pituitary but through the sympathetic nervous system, triggers not only the sympathetic nervous system itself but also the inner part (the medulla) of the adrenals which secrete two hormones whose role in the body's response to threat is crucial. These two hormones are adrenalin (epinephrine) and noradrenalin (norepinephrine). The nerve endings of the sympathetic nervous system also secrete adrenalin and noradrenalin, but in tiny amounts whose effects last only a few seconds; the amounts secreted by the adrenal medulla are larger, and their effects last for several minutes.

Some of the effects of adrenalin and noradrenalin on body tissues are the same; some are different. Both hormones are critical factors in behavior that may become violent in the total psychosomatic effort to protect the body from threats perceived (or misperceived) by the visual, auditory, and other sensory parts of the forebrain. Noradrenalin causes constriction of the blood vessels in the skeletal and visceral muscles; it causes acceleration of the heartbeat; it causes relaxation of the intestines; and it releases sugar into the bloodstream. Adrenalin does all of these things but has less effect on the constriction of blood vessels in skeletal muscle tissue, produces more acceleration of the heartbeat, and much more effect in increasing the metabolic rate of the whole body (including the brain), which thereby becomes more active and excitable. One simplified way of describing the difference in effect of these two hormones is to say that noradrenalin tends more to prepare the individual for physical action in response to threat, whereas adrenalin tends more to produce an internally aggressive response, one form of which may be to attack oneself.

The proportions of adrenalin and noradrenalin secreted by the adrenalin medulla vary in different species. In man, the secretion is about 75 percent adrenalin to 25 percent noradrenalin; in lions, somewhat more noradrenalin secretion than adrenalin; and in whales and chickens, about 80 percent noradrenalin to 20 percent adrenalin. In behavioral terms this comparison suggests—but by no means demonstrates—that man's endocrine system, more than that of other vertebrates, disposes him to respond to threat by partially internalized and deliberative activity. Other species are more likely to respond immediately to threat by skeletal muscle activity, including physical fight or flight behavior.

These are some quite tentative inferences from research in neurology and endocrinology. Perhaps the major distinction between Homo sapiens and other species is the complex of neural and endocrine factors which incline him to deliberate and control his responses to the frustration of his basic needs. In man, that is, step 3 (the seeking and deciding step) is much more significant in the sequence from the internal activation of needs to the ultimate response in overt action. The complicated circuitry of the cortex, the forebrain, and the endocrines has a greater role in man than in other species in deciding how to respond to stimuli, including those perceived as gratifiers of what people want and those seen as frustrators of what they want. Vertebrates lower than man—including primates and other high vertebrates—do not have the amount of cortex that gives them time to sort out and appraise stimuli so carefully. So they respond more immediately and skeletally—and less cerebrally.

A Resume of the Roots of Violence

None of the research or theorizing on violence has yet provided anything like an adequate basis for definitive statements about the causes of revolution and war—whether on a historical, sociological, economic, psychological, or physiological basis. In defense of even the most pessimistic ethologists (like Ardrey) and psychologists (like Freud), it can be said that their pessimism may have the sobering effect of diminishing unenlightened optimism. Nevertheless—in my opinion at least—men's violence is not the direct product of an innate violent tendency. Violence is a response to the extreme frustration of one or more innate substantive needs that range from the physical, affectional, dignity, to the self-actualization needs and a response to the extreme frustration of one or more of the instrumental needs—security, knowledge, and power—which provide the organic part of seeking satisfaction, in the environment, of the substantive needs.

It is in the analytical area between innate tendencies and overt behaviors that both theory and research are most uncertain. Environmentalists, including stimulus-response psychologists, find man to be almost entirely the product of the shaping given him by his environment. Hereditarians, including those whose view of genetic determinants is based altogether on their field observations of overt behaviors (visible acts), find man to be altogether the product of his genes and maintain a studied aloofness from microbiology and from neurophysiology. Their interest in the contents of the black box does not extend to opening it.

What is, nevertheless, more frustrating even than the tunnel vision of both environmentalists and hereditarians is the reluctance of physiologists to consider man as having any motivations except the simplest physical and emotional ones. Physiological research has typically had to do with the physical demands of the organism for water, food, sex, affection, and freedom from pain. Work is particularly needed on the nonphysical demands of the organism if we are to find out why men turn to violent, aggressive political action in war and revolution. It is absurd to assert that such violent behavior does not involve specific responses to specific stimuli that threaten people when they lose their sense of dignity. There is of course no dignity gene, no dignity part of the limbic system or of the cortex; but wars have been fought and people have fought to the death for reasons that have little to do with survival and a great deal to do with liberty, equality, fraternity, and the dignity of man.

We know that the limbic system, the "emotional brain," has some kind of intermediary role between the forebrain and the brainstem. If there is any one research area that remains largely unexplored, it is the neural links, the nerve-fiber links, between the limbic system and the cortex. When these and a few other major unknown systems are explored, we will then know better why a degraded serf will burn down the mansion of his lord, why a black man who has never been beaten by a white man will turn against him for reasons that appear to have little to do with the physical well-being of the black man. Meanwhile, if we continue to believe that the impulse to violence is a basic drive, we might as well discontinue our analysis of the roots of aggression, violence, revolution, and war because then nothing short of total collective suicide can really solve the problem of violence. If the impulse to violence is derived from frustration of basic drives, then analysis that seeks to satisfy basic drives of people in all circumstances becomes appropriate, and the diminution of violence becomes feasible.

10

ASSUMPTIVE FRAMEWORKS IN INTERNATIONAL POLITICS

Herbert C. Kelman

Alfred H. Bloom

The study of international politics typically has taken the nation-state as its unit of analysis. It is difficult to challenge the view that, in the current international system, nation-states are the central and most powerful actors. The assumption that they are the *sole* actors, however, can be and has been challenged (cf. Wolfers, 1959; Singer, 1961; Alger, 1963). One could gain considerable leverage on the analysis of international political processes by focusing on a variety of other actors, including individuals. The relevance of individual actors becomes apparent when we recall that it is individual human beings who make the decisions and carry out the actions that shape the course of political events; that it is individual human beings who perceive and misperceive, who give and withhold support, who compete and cooperate, who kill and die; that it is the fulfillment of the needs and interests of individuals across the world that constitutes the ultimate task of international politics. Clearly, the inputs of these individual human beings—their perceptions, interpretations, assumptions, and reactions—help to shape political outcomes. These inputs represent the locus of analysis of the social psychologist and the source of his potential contribution to the study of international politics.

Social-Psychological Study of International Relations

Since the mid-1950s, there has been an increasing volume of systematic research on psychological aspects of international relations. A variety of empirical studies, theoretical formulations, and policy analyses, focusing—directly or indirectly —on international conflict and other issues in international politics, have made use of psychological (particularly social-psychological) concepts and methods. These activities are part of the larger evolution of two new and highly overlapping intellectual traditions—the peace research movement and the "behavioral" study of international relations—which have drawn on theoretical orientations (often, though not exclusively, in the form of mathematical models), on procedures of data collection, and on techniques of measurement and data analysis developed in the various social sciences. Research in these traditions, which has become a rather vigorous international enterprise in the past decade, represents the convergence of at least two major interests: an interest among an increasing number of international relations specialists in developing their field as an empirical social science discipline; and an interest among an increasing number of psychologists, sociologists, economists, anthropologists, and other social scientists in applying their skills and knowledge to problems of war and peace.

The interest of psychologists in problems of war and peace and other aspects of international relations certainly antedates these more recent developments (see Kelman, 1968b). Beginning at least in the early 1930s, a series of empirical studies explored attitudes toward war and peace, toward aggression, toward international relations, and toward one's own and other nations. (For reviews of the earlier work, see Klineberg, 1950; Pear, 1950.) There were also various theoretical examinations of the causes of war, within either a psychoanalytic or a general psychological framework (for instance, Durbin and Bowlby, 1939; May, 1943; Tolman, 1942). Whatever the merits of individual findings or hypotheses produced by these efforts, however, they did not add up to a systematic analysis of the psychological aspects of international politics. The empirical research was carried out largely within the context of the general study of social attitudes, with little explicit reference to the

This chapter is a product of a research program on social influence and commitment to social systems, supported by U.S. Public Health Service Research Grant No. MH17669-04 from the National Institute of Mental Health. The chapter draws on several earlier publications by the senior author (see Kelman, 1965, 1968a, 1969, 1970, 1971, and 1972). Work on the chapter was completed during his tenure as Visiting Fellow at the Battelle Seattle Research Center.

processes of foreign policy making or international interaction. The theoretical formulations tended to view war and peace from the perspective of individual motivation—often emphasizing aggressive motives and psychopathological manifestations—without sufficient recognition that the role of individual motives can be understood only in the context of the societal and intersocietal processes that culminate in war or peace.

In contrast to the earlier work, recent psychological studies are more likely to start at the level of international relations itself, rather than extrapolating from individual or interpersonal behavior. To be sure, some research or writing in this area still can be criticized for its tendency to "overpsychologize" political phenomena. There is, in fact, no consensus among current scholars about the role to be assigned to aggressive motives in the causation of war, or about the extent to which one can properly generalize from interpersonal (or intergroup) conflict to international conflict, or about the significance of central decision makers' personality characteristics in the foreign policy process. Nevertheless, it is probably fair to say that the mid-1950s mark a qualitative as well as a quantitative change in the study of psychological aspects of international relations. Since that time, conceptualization and measurement of psychological inputs into international relations have increasingly started out from an analysis of international political processes (and domestic foreign policy processes) at their own level. Research in the area has increasingly taken place in an international relations context or utilized the archival residues of foreign policy decision making and diplomatic interactions. Writings have shown increasing theoretical and methodological sophistication, with greater awareness of the complexities one encounters in moving across different levels of analysis. And, most important, two groups of specialists have emerged and interacted closely with one another: students of international relations, with a political science background, who are thoroughly grounded in social-psychological concepts and methods; and social psychologists (as well as students of other disciplines outside of political science) who have systematically educated themselves in the field of international relations.

We shall not attempt a comprehensive review of social-psychological research on international relations, but a brief listing of the types of studies that can be subsumed under this rubric may be helpful at this point. To illustrate these different types of research, we have deliberately selected recent publications (after 1965). Reviews of and references to many of the earlier publications can be found in Kelman (1965). We shall divide the studies into two major categories: studies focusing on attitudes relevant to international relations held by various groups of individuals; and studies focusing on psychological and social-interactional factors in international politics and foreign policy decision making. As a rough approximation, one might describe the first category as studies in which psychological factors constitute the dependent variables and the second as studies in which they serve as the independent variables.

In speaking of attitudes, we have in mind a whole range of dispositional variables, variously referred to as attitudes, beliefs (see Chapters Three and Four in this volume), values, images, perceptions, expectations. Thus, in the most general terms, studies in this category are concerned with the ways in which individuals relate themselves to their own nation and other nations, to the international system as a whole, to problems of foreign policy, and to the broader issues of war and peace.

What is the structure of attitudes and images in these domains, what are their determinants, and what are the conditions of their change? Three subcategories of studies can be distinguished:

1. *Attitudes toward foreign policy and international affairs.* The focus here has been on general orientations toward foreign and military policy and toward war and peace, as well as on opinions on specific foreign policy issues, such as the Vietnam war. Often studies in this genre have centered on the dimensions of belligerent versus conciliatory and nationalist versus internationalist orientations. A review of many of these studies can be found in Eckhardt and Lentz (1967). Among the determinants of general foreign policy orientations, research has explored both personality variables (see, for instance, McClosky, 1967) and demographic variables (see Galtung, 1967). A recent study by Modigliani (1972a), using public opinion surveys conducted during the Korean war, tries to tease out the structure of public opinion toward the war and to explore the relationship between policy preferences and social class. A number of recent studies (Verba and others, 1967; Brickman, Shaver, and Archibald, 1969; Granberg, 1969) have explored opinions toward the Vietnam war in the American population and in various special subpopulations.

2. *National and international loyalties.* The focus here has been on the relationship of the individual to the national system—the sources, the nature, and the exclusivity of his commitment to it. Several analyses of nationalism from a social-psychological perspective have recently been presented (Fishman, 1972; Kelman, 1969; Tajfel, 1969). Empirical studies have also explored the meanings of national identity (Herman, 1970; Schwartz, 1967), the different ways in which individuals may be integrated in the national system (DeLamater, Katz, and Kelman, 1969), and the relationships between loyalty to the national system and loyalty to subnational units (Klineberg and Zavalloni, 1969). Another potentially important focus for research is the relationship between loyalty to the national system and loyalty to transnational or supranational units such as regional organizations, international organizations, or the global community. Such studies might throw light on the conditions for the development of wider loyalties and the coexistence of multiple loyalties. A recent study by Kerr (1973) represents a contribution to research on this problem. It is also unique in that it is based on interviews with an elite sample, centrally involved in at least one aspect of international relations, and that it explores changes in their attitudes as a function of their direct participation in international political processes.

3. *Images of other nations.* There is a long tradition of research in this area, focusing particularly on ethnocentric attitudes and associated positive stereotypes of one's own nation and negative stereotypes of other (especially "enemy") nations. Recent studies have been concerned with multidimensional scaling of such images (Robinson and Hefner, 1967; Wish, Deutsch, and Biener, 1970), with the development of images of foreign nations among children (Lambert and Klineberg, 1967), and with the impact of international contacts on the images of own and other nations (Kelman and Ezekiel, 1970). Of special interest are studies that trace the development and change of mutual images in the course of international political interactions. Druckman (1968) explored this process in the context of the Inter-Nation Simulation, a laboratory simulation of the international system developed by Guetzkow and his collaborators (1963).

Attitudes related to international affairs held by various groups of individuals are a legitimate research interest in their own right. How relevant such research is to an analysis of international political processes depends on one's conceptualization of foreign policy making and international politics. Most analysts would probably agree that attitudinal factors play some role in the process and would therefore regard research into them to be of at least tangential relevance. For example, even those who assign minimal importance to public opinion in foreign policy making would no doubt agree that the moods, expectations, and reactions of the public are part of the context within which the decision makers operate. Similarly, even those who look to geopolitical, economic, or organizational factors to account for the course of interaction between two nations would probably concede that mutual attitudes of trust or distrust and perceptions of the other party's intent are likely to have some bearing on the outcome. The political relevance of any particular attitude study depends on its closeness to the actual context of foreign policy making and international politics. Thus, the relevance of a piece of research is more readily apparent if, as in Modigliani's (1972) study, it examines public attitudes in terms of the nature and sources of support that decision makers can expect for various foreign policy moves; or if, as in Kerr's (1973) survey, the sample consists of participants in an international political enterprise; or if, as in Druckman's (1968) simulation, images are explored as they emerge from and feed back into political interactions. These studies, in fact, are closely related to the second category of research that we have identified: research on psychological and social-interactional factors that enter into the processes of international politics and foreign policy making.

This second category of research focuses directly on international political processes. It is concerned with such political outcomes as the type of foreign policy pursued by a given nation, the nature of the decision reached on a specific foreign policy issue, the reduction or expansion of conflict, the means used for pursuing or containing conflict, the development of peaceful and cooperative relationships, and the formation of alliances, of regional organizations, and of transnational institutions. These outcomes are explored in terms of some of the psychological or social-interaction processes that may help to shape them: for example, the dispositions and role behaviors of various relevant actors; the leadership and influence patterns of decision-making units, and the internal and external pressures under which they function; the mutual expectations and perceptions of the interacting nations; the psychological atmosphere within which the interactions are carried out; and the threats, inducements, and other bargaining strategies and tactics that are utilized. In these studies, then, social-psychological factors generally serve as independent and mediating variables to account for political outcomes. This statement is somewhat oversimplified, however, in that analysis often focuses on social-psychological factors as part of an ongoing, chainlike process. Thus, for example, research on the role of mutual perceptions in international conflict is concerned not only with the effects of perception on action but also with the way in which action (one's own and the other side's) generates and modifies perceptions, which in turn influence subsequent actions.

We shall again list the research in this area in three subcategories:

1. *Public opinion in the foreign policy process.* The focus here is on the role that the moods, expectations, perceptions, and sentiments of the public, or of various special publics, play in the foreign policy process. The shape of public opinion deter-

mines the population's readiness for various national actions, its interpretation of and reaction to international events, its degree of support for various foreign policy moves—and thus the freedom and constraint within which decision makers operate. It may be best to refer to this category of research more broadly as "domestic sources of foreign policy," to use the title of a book edited by Rosenau (1967). The various chapters in his volume deal not only with the orientations of the citizenry toward international affairs but also with the group and organizational processes through which these orientations are articulated and with the ways in which they are brought to bear on decision makers. The study by Verba and his associates (1967) on public opinion toward the Vietnam war illustrates the use of public opinion data to assess the population's readiness for certain foreign policy directions. By probing more deeply than the typical public opinion poll, these authors were able to challenge the assumptions, apparently held by many decision makers, about the kinds of policies that the public would or would not support. White (1968), using a variety of sources (including some public opinion data), analyzed the perceptions of the Vietnam conflict by various groups in the United States and in Vietnam—including their perceptions of their own and the other side's attributes, goals, and prospects. He concludes that the perceptions of the different groups are, to varying degrees, distorted and traces the psychological and social processes that generate such misperceptions, which in turn account—at least in part—for the onset and continuation of a war that "nobody wanted." One final development that should be mentioned here is the use of aggregate data to infer psychological states prevalent within a population. Feierabend and Feierabend (1966), in a cross-national study, developed an index of systemic frustration (discrepancy between social wants and social satisfactions) from a number of national indicators, and related it to the incidence of domestic political violence. Such aggregate indices of public moods could be related, in similar fashion, to the incidence and nature of international conflict.

2. *Decision-making processes in foreign policy.* Research in this category focuses on the foreign policy decision makers and decision-making units within a given country and explores the psychological and social interaction processes that culminate in state action. A number of writers have used intensive case studies of major foreign policy decisions as the raw material for analysis. Thus, Paige (1968) presents a detailed analysis of the United States' decision to enter into the Korean war, utilizing the Snyder, Bruck, and Sapin (1962) framework for the study of foreign policy decision making. Joseph deRivera (1968), working with the Korean decision and with several other foreign policy actions, emphasizes the role of the decision maker's construction of reality—which in turn is influenced by personality, group, and organizational variables—on the choices he makes. Janis (1971, 1972), in analyzing several critical decisions, traces the effects of group pressures toward uniformity and ingroup loyalty within a small decision-making unit on the cognitive processes of the participants and hence the quality of the decisions reached. Allison (1971), in a detailed account of the Cuban missile crisis, contrasts the classical model of the decision maker as rational actor with two alternative models, viewing decisions, respectively, as *"outputs* of large organizations functioning according to regular patterns of behavior" and as "a *resultant* of various bargaining games among players in the national government" shaped by "the perceptions, motivations, positions, power, and maneuvers" of the various players (p. 6). The Cuban missile crisis also

provided the data for a study by Holsti, Brody, and North (1969), using content analysis of documents authored by key United States and Soviet decision makers during a critical ten-day period. Their analysis focuses on the relationship between decision makers' perceptions (particularly of the other side's intentions) and their actions. They compare the Cuban missile crisis to the events leading up to World War I, on which their earlier research had focused, pinpointing some of the perceptual factors that may account for the very different outcomes. A study by Robinson, Hermann, and Hermann (1969) illustrates the use of simulation and gaming techniques in research on foreign policy decision making. The study investigated the effects of crisis conditions on the amount and type of search behavior in which decision makers engaged. A very different type of research in this general area focuses on individual decision makers or on decision-making units, rather than on specific decision occasions. Such research might explore the personality styles or the assumptions and perceptions of key decision makers, or the operative goals and decision processes of organizational units with foreign policy responsibilities. Glad's (1969) psychobiographic study of Senators Borah and Fulbright provides one illustration of this type of research (see also Chapter Eleven in this volume).

3. *Interaction processes in international conflict.* Social-psychological analysis is particularly relevant to the study of interactions between nations or their representatives. Many kinds of interaction can be subsumed under this rubric; for example, international communication in its various forms, normal diplomatic contacts, or collaboration within the framework of international organizations. Major emphasis in social-psychological research, however, has been placed on the handling of conflictual relationships—on the ways in which conflicts are pursued, managed, and resolved. Interest has focused not only on observing the microprocesses involved but also on discovering the conditions conducive to various outcomes; for example, the conditions under which conflict is expanded or contained, under which it takes violent or nonviolent forms, under which it is terminated because one party has prevailed at the expense of the other or because a cooperative solution has been worked out. A large experimental literature has developed in recent years, based on the use of the Prisoner's Dilemma (see Rapoport and Chammah, 1965) and similar bargaining games for the study of conflict. These studies are considerably removed from the level of international conflict, but they often try to incorporate some of the crucial variables involved in the interaction between nations. (For a recent discussion of the logic of such gaming research, see Rapoport, 1970; see also Chapter Fourteen in this volume.) The various chapters in a volume edited by Swingle (1970b) bring together many experimental findings on such determinants of the course and outcome of bargaining and negotiation as the type of bargaining strategy selected by the different players, the type of influence attempt (including threats and promises) used, the personality characteristics of participants, and the situational context of the interaction. Games have also been used to test the effectiveness of specific strategies, as in the Pilisuk and Skolnick (1968) study, which was designed to assess Osgood's (1962) proposals for deescalation. Closer to the level of international conflict are such laboratory procedures as the Inter-Nation Simulation (Guetzkow and others, 1963), in which participants play the roles of national decision makers in an environment programmed to represent major parameters of the international system. The possible uses of this procedure are illustrated in a study

by Raser and Crow (1969), which explored the effects of a deterrence strategy based on the capacity to delay response on the process and outcome of interaction in the simulated world. A recent paper by Guetzkow (1969) reviews the various uses of simulation in international relations research. Another approach to the study of interaction processes in international conflict is represented by some recent "action research" programs, bringing together representatives of conflicting national groups for face-to-face communication in a controlled environment (Burton, 1969; Doob, 1970; see also Kelman, 1972). The procedure represents a special form of third-party intervention (see Young, 1967), with social scientists acting as the intermediaries. It provides unusual opportunities for observing the dynamics of conflict and exploring some of the conditions for its resolution (see Fisher, 1972). Finally, an entirely different approach to the study of international conflict is taken by Gamson and Modigliani (1971) in their work on the Cold War. On the basis of a content analysis of newspaper accounts, they developed a chronology of the interactions between the two parties to the Cold War for the period from 1946 to 1963, coded in terms of several descriptive dimensions. These data were used to test competing theories of the Cold War, each of which yields different predictions about the way each side ought to be reacting to various actions by its antagonist.

Before concluding this brief overview of social-psychological research on international relations, we call attention to the multiplicity of methods that it employs. The sources of data range all the way from laboratory experiments to national population statistics. Between these poles we find simulation studies, sample surveys, interview or questionnaire studies with selected populations, psychobiographies or personality assessments, group observations, organizational analyses, ethnographic field studies, action research programs, and content analyses of historical documents or newspapers. This methodological diversity gives witness to the inherently interdisciplinary character of this area of research.

Sources and Nature of Individual Contributions

The varieties of social-psychological research that we have outlined aid in the study of international politics by focusing on individual actors and the interaction between them. We see this effort not as an alternative approach to international relations but as a contributory one. The goal, in our view, is to develop not a complete and self-contained social-psychological theory of international relations but a general theory of political behavior at the system level in which social-psychological factors play a part, once the points in the process at which they are applicable have been properly identified. To focus attention on the individual actor does not imply that such an analysis can provide a total picture of international political processes. Certainly, every participant in both the national and international systems, at whatever level he makes his contribution, is heavily influenced by the political, ecnomic, and social realities that surround him, and acts within the constraints and procedures of institutional structures. Moreover, once an individual actor has developed a point of view, made a decision, or taken a politically relevant action, he has contributed only one of the many and varied inputs that shape every political outcome. There is no substitute for analysis of the structural mechanisms and systemic processes that select among the myriad of individual inputs and mold them into final policy decisions. In examining the sources and nature of individual contributions to international political functioning, therefore, we are merely focusing on a particular nexus in this larger process, in the hope that such an analysis may lead to creative reconceptualizations of some old issues in the theory and practice of international relations.

One can distinguish three principal groups whose individual inputs may eventually influence outcomes on the international level: decision makers, national leaders, and wider publics.

National decision-making elites and the elites of international organizations clearly enjoy some degree of influence on the choice of policy alternatives and thus ultimately on outcomes in the national and international systems. The extent of direct personal influence of any one member of these elites, however, would depend on such factors as his position in the hierarchy of his national government or international organization and the degree of latitude he is permitted, by virtue of his position, in decision making within the particular area under his jurisdiction. Added to these factors are the implicit limits imposed on his choice of alternatives by the expectations of his fellow decision makers, of the larger organization for which he works, and of the public at large, to whom his organization is at least in theory responsible.

Second, one can generally identify a powerful element outside of governmental structures, capable of exerting substantial influence on the outcomes of nationally and internationally relevant decisions. Its influence is in part due to its control of such means as financial or editorial support that the decision maker needs to retain his position and/or successfully execute his policies in the short or long run. Much of its power, however, stems from its relationship to public opinion. Rosenau (1963, p. 6) refers to this source of influence when he speaks of national leaders as opinion makers—that is, "those members of the society who occupy positions which enable them to transmit, with some regularity, opinions about foreign policy issues to unknown persons." By virtue of their positions, these leaders can impede or facilitate achievement of consensus. They perform, in Rosenau's terms, a "veto-support" function; decision makers are constrained by their opposition and turn to them for help in the mobilization of popular support.

Public opinion, both domestic and international, represents a third source of individual inputs into the international political system. The moods of the general public and their broad orientations toward national and international affairs are an essential part of the climate in which national policy makers operate. In part, these moods and orientations within the population exert a directive influence on the process of policy formulation, in the sense that they impel decision makers toward perceptions and actions that reflect public sentiments. Often decision makers are not only influenced by these pervasive moods but actually share them with the rest of the population. In fact, these moods may originate in the very elites from which the decision makers are recruited and then spread among the rest of the population, so that it becomes difficult to specify who is influencing whom. Moods and orientations within the population also exert a constraining influence on the policy-formulation process. Even though the decision maker may have a great deal of latitude on any given foreign policy issue, he usually has to operate within certain broad limits set by the population.

In this regard, the existence of widespread political apathy and malleability in a population does not imply that public opinion is irrelevant to the policy process. Rather, a climate of apathy represents a special state of public opinion—a situation in which the national leadership can assume that it is free to formulate policy within the confines of very broad limits set by public opinion without the risk of losing popular support. President Nixon's appeal to the "silent majority" in support of his Vietnam policy is an interesting example of an attempt by a national leadership to actually use a state of apathy (or of presumed apathy) as a resource in the political arena. Furthermore, indications are that even a silent majority, to whatever extent it does or can exist, will impose implicit limits on the acceptability of the policy alternatives chosen by their national leaders. The silent majority's support may have been specific to what they perceived to be the President's policy of disengagement in Vietnam and probably could not be transferred indiscriminately to whatever policy he might choose.

As long as the decision maker adopts policy alternatives that lie within the implicit limits acceptable to the relevant population, he may encounter no difficulty in mustering support for the chosen alternative or for his own reelection. On the other hand, if he violates certain pervasive popular assumptions governing the range of acceptable alternatives, he may be risking not only electoral defeat but also a loss of the popular backing needed for the achievement of the domestic and foreign policy objectives of his party or nation (Rosenberg, 1965a).

Any one of these individual actors, whether he be a member of the foreign policy decision-making elite, a national leader, or an informed citizen, responds to a wide variety of macrolevel factors whenever he forms an opinion or decides on a course of action. Implicitly or explicitly, he will be influenced by ecological considerations, such as the geographic position of his country and the basic resources that it has available; economic considerations, such as the productive activities upon which the economy is based, the general standard of living and level of technology characteristic of the society, and the current point in the business cycle; political considerations, such as the nature of the regime, the stability of the government, and the extent of its involvement in international conflicts; and considerations of military strategy and international diplomacy, such as his country's involvement in power blocs, military alliances, and regional organizations. These considerations—which are at the heart of the traditional discipline of international relations—form the context in which opinions are formulated and decisions are made, but they do not explain how the individuals involved perceive, interpret, or react to that context. The mediating variables that enter at the level of perception, interpretation, and reaction—that is, at the level of individual functioning—may prove to have substantial impact on the outcomes of interaction and at the same time provide potential leverage for implementing change.

Social-psychological investigation, as we have noted, has focused on the different types of variables that may affect individual functioning at the levels of perception, interpretation, and reaction. Among others, these include personality dispositions, situational pressures, and psychopolitical assumptions.

Personality Dispositions. A wide variety of personality factors—authoritarianism, xenophobia, extrapunitiveness, need achievement, and self-esteem being just a few of many examples—are potentially relevant to the political process. (For reviews of relevant studies, see Raser, 1966; Terhune, 1970.) The dispositions that characterize important decision makers and opinion leaders may have a direct impact on the decision process. (Hermann and Hermann, 1967, provide some suggestive evidence on this point in an interesting simulation of the outbreak of World War I.) Dispositions that are widely shared within a society or at least among its major elites may play an indirect, yet often pivotal, role in the process.

The impact of the idiosyncratic dispositions of prominent decision makers and opinion leaders depends on the relevance of a given personality factor to decision-making behavior; on the centrality of the particular decision maker's position in the decision-making structure; and on the nature of the decision involved—for example, as Wolfers (1959) proposes, whether it is a decision in response to a perceived opportunity rather than to a perceived threat to national survival. In general, personality dispositions of important decision makers are probably less likely to have an effect on the overall direction of a decision than on its qualitative characteristics, such as the style in which the decision is communicated and carried out. These qualitative characteristics, in turn, may have a wider impact by affecting the way in which the decision issue is conceived by the public, since major political leaders often serve as models in the formation and change of public attitudes.

Perhaps of greater importance to the foreign policy decision-making process than the idiosyncratic dispositions of major decision makers and opinion leaders are those personality dispositions, developed through similar socialization experiences, that are shared by a large segment of the society. Such shared dispositions are likely to affect the overall approach to foreign policy of the decision-making apparatus. Furthermore, they have a bearing on the way in which the general population perceives the society's needs and interests and interprets the intentions of other societies, and on its preference for certain means over others in the pursuit of societal goals and in the response to domestic and international challenges.

Situational Pressures. A second set of social-psychological variables involves the pressures that individuals feel at the point of politically relevant decision or action, pressures deriving from the demands of the immediate or larger situation. Even such a seemingly insignificant factor as an overheated or crowded room may enter importantly into the final outcome of a negotiation by triggering a spiraling process of misperception and misattribution. One negotiating team's irritability, caused by the condition of the room, may be perceived as hostility by the other team and lead to a reciprocally hostile reaction. As a result, a cooperative atmosphere—though perhaps desired by both parties—may fail to materialize during the session, and both sides may find it difficult to assume a cooperative stance in future negotiations. (For a discussion of situational effects on bargaining, see Sawyer and Guetzkow, 1965.)

In their simulation studies, cited earlier, Robinson, Hermann, and Hermann (1969) found evidence to suggest that in a crisis situation decision makers tend to abandon the search for new alternatives and instead direct their energies toward a search for new information about the alternatives that are already on the table. At the same time, crisis tends to lower their confidence in whatever alternative they finally select. Janis (1971, 1972), in his analysis of several major foreign policy decisions, uses the term *groupthink* to describe the mode of thinking that dominates in a situation in which a cohesive group of decision makers, insulated from outside influences, is engaged in a stressful decision process. In such a situation, loyalty to the decision-making group tends to become the dominant consideration, and pressures toward conformity and consensus override critical thinking. Another source of pressures is the presence of authorities or symbols of authority, which often discourages individuals from personally appraising the issues and pushes them in the direction of adhering to the prescribed interpretations and role definitions.

At the level of the general public, situational pressures may also play a major role in the formation and expression of opinions on foreign policy issues. An atmosphere of national crisis, for example, tends to engender widespread reluctance to engage in independent political thought and action. Such reluctance is often reinforced by deliberate attempts on the part of political authorities—concerned with maintaining an image of national unity—to impose a narrow definition of proper political attitudes and behavior and to equate dissent with subversion.

Psychopolitical Assumptions.   Individuals—whether they are national decision makers, opinion leaders, or involved citizens—bring to the political arena a complex of underlying assumptions, conceptual frameworks in terms of which they formulate specific opinions and arrive at decisions on issues of international politics. Often these assumptions represent an unanalytic acceptance of the givens of national and international systems and an undifferentiated view of the various actors in these systems. One of the consequences of such assumptive frameworks is to impose unnecessary limits on the range of alternatives considered in the formulation and execution of policy. An analysis of assumptive frameworks, therefore, offers a unique opportunity for those students of international relations who are particularly concerned with reconceptualizing and changing the processes of foreign policy making and diplomacy.

Many common assumptions in international relations, if left unanalyzed and unchallenged, present obstacles to peaceful resolutions of international conflicts and to creative responses to new global realities. Because they often assume that public support for foreign policies depends on their conformity to certain static principles that are (presumably) widely held and deeply felt—such as the national interest, the national honor, national superiority, or military strength—decision makers may underestimate their freedom to pursue innovative, peace-oriented policies or overestimate their freedom to engage in militarist adventures, arms races, or expansionist policies. Because they often assume that international conflict consists entirely of a series of competitive moves and countermoves, whose outcome depends on the relative military strengths of the antagonists, decision makers may select ineffective and dangerous influence strategies, and miss opportunities for conflict resolution based on a more differentiated model of conflict. Because they often assume that the nation-state is the paramount—indeed the only relevant—unit in the international system, decision makers may arrange for the needs of their populations (for example, in the areas of military security or economic development) in less than optimal ways and block the evolution of a more functional, peace-prone global system consisting of multiple, cross-cutting units. As long as we fail to subject these assumptions to critical analysis and to question their validity and appropriateness, they may continue to have a pervasive and often deleterious effect on international politics.

Social-psychological concepts and methods can make a valuable contribution to identifying these assumptions and to increasing our understanding of the processes by which they are developed and maintained. Since the individual is the locus of assumption making, a social-psychological approach, which takes the individual actor as its primary unit of analysis, can illuminate the assumption-making process itself. Furthermore, it permits a more differentiated view of the actors (the foreign policy public, the parties to an international conflict, or the operative units in the international system) that these assumptions tend to homogenize; it also permits a more detailed examination of the interaction processes that these assumptions often ignore.

In the remainder of this chapter, we shall attempt a social-psychological analysis of three types of assumptive frameworks in international politics, to which we have already alluded: assumptions concerning the role of public opinion in foreign policy, the nature of international conflict, and the structure of the international system.

Role of Public Opinion

Most students of public opinion in the foreign policy process would probably agree with Etzioni's (1969, p. 576) formulation: "While public opinion does not participate effectively in many specific foreign policy decisions, it does serve as *a context that sets significant limits* on the maneuverability of the national decision makers." The decision makers' freedom of action, therefore, is less dependent on the distribution of public attitudes toward the specific issue than it is on the broader context within which the issue is perceived and to which the specific attitudes are linked. As Etzioni (p. 577) points out:

> We would expect the elites to have considerable freedom of action but only within the limits of established contexts, and only so long as their specific actions do not disorganize these contexts or create a countercontext. Thus Kennedy was relatively calm about the 1961 Cuban fiasco (and public opinion in his support even rose after the crisis), but he also realized in 1962 that another fiasco, this time in the missile crisis, might associate him with an appeasement or "soft" context. . . . When a new event occurs for which there is no ready context, such as Soviet expansionism in 1946–1947 or Soviet orbiting of a satellite in 1957, the national decision makers seem relatively free to interpret it. But once a bit is placed in a context or a context is established, the public feeds it back to the leaders . . . who, under most circumstances, are boxed in or are compelled to invest much effort to alter it.

Decision makers often seem to assess their freedom of action by reference to the distribution of public attitudes on the specific issue under consideration, thus underestimating or overestimating the freedom they actually enjoy. Many decision makers, however, are quite aware that the limits within which they operate are broad and that public reactions to a specific issue may vary with the context in which this issue is presented. Yet even these decision makers tend to make some questionable assumptions about the *nature* of the contexts within which the public judges foreign policy actions. While they recognize that public views on specific issues may change—and that they, as decision makers, can facilitate such changes—they usually conceive the contexts to which specific attitudes are assimilated as largely static entities. These contexts, in their view, are formed by certain basic underlying principles to which the public expects foreign policy actions to conform; any deviations from these principles would be unacceptable. Specifically, they assume that the public expects its national leaders to be militant in protecting the national interest and upholding the national honor; to maintain a superior military, diplomatic, and economic posture; and to expand their political and ideological influence throughout the world. As we shall try to show, this assumptive framework is based on an incomplete analysis and an undifferentiated view of the way in which public opinion on foreign policy issues is formed.

Static Model of Public Opinion. Decision makers who assume a static public opinion, which judges foreign policy actions on the basis of their militancy, may well misread the mood of the public to conform with their particular model. Thus, they may overestimate the public's support for belligerent and expansionist moves and underestimate the public's readiness to accept more conciliatory policy alternatives. Such misreading can easily occur because decision makers may be biased in selecting the pronouncements that they regard as truly representative of public opinion; because public reactions are generally formulated within a limited set of officially recognized alternatives; and because the meaning of these reactions and the depth of commitment they represent are rarely explored.

The standard public opinion polls often reinforce faulty readings of the public mood. For one thing, because of their methodological shortcomings, polls may create a false impression of the stability and content of opinions on a specific issue. As Rosenberg (1965a) points out, both the motivation to please the interviewer and the motivation to appear to one's self as a politically involved citizen cause poll respondents to exaggerate the extent to which they actually hold opinions on the issues raised and the fixity of those opinions, and to bias the opinions they express toward what they perceive to be the socially acceptable consensus. The perceived consensus usually reflects the decision makers' own expectation of a preference for a militant posture. Furthermore, opinion polls present respondents with a limited set of options, usually consisting of the alternatives formulated by the decision makers themselves. Thus, the polls generally describe opinions that are already "processed" to a considerable degree, in that they are expressed in terms of the options formulated by the national leadership and with an awareness of what the leadership considers the proper response. Such processed opinions are hardly an independent source of information about what the public expects and prefers. Certainly they do not indicate what alternative courses of action, not yet entertained, might be acceptable to public opinion. A related and major limitation of the standard opinion poll is that it ascertains only the percentage who approve or disapprove of a particular policy action without exploring the meaning these opinions have for different respondents, the context within which they are held, and the depth of commitment they represent. Thus, if a poll shows, for example, a high rate of approval of a given policy, the decision maker is provided no perspective for gauging the significance of this finding. If it conforms to his assumptive framework, he is likely to misread it as representing stronger public support for the policy and less willingness to consider alternatives than it does in fact.

The misreading of the public mood concerning the war in Vietnam during the Johnson administration provides a case in point. In their survey of American attitudes toward the war, conducted in 1966, Verba and his associates (1967) probed more deeply into the public's feelings about the war than the earlier polls had done. The results indicated a more differentiated and in a sense more flexible orientation toward the war across both elites and the mass public than would have been expected on the basis of previous poll data. Although 61 percent of the respondents approved of President Johnson's handling of the situation in Vietnam, the data, reminiscent of the Patchen (1964) findings on attitudes toward China, suggested that a good part of that 61 percent had answered affirmatively out of a commitment to the President rather than a commitment to his specific policies. This would in turn imply that public opinion allowed the President much greater freedom to alter his course of action in Vietnam than the previous poll data had presumably indicated. This conclusion is further substantiated by data showing considerable openness (as long ago as 1966) to various moves to negotiate a settlement of the war: 88 percent of the American people were willing to negotiate with the Viet Cong; 54 percent agreed that free elections should be held, even if the Viet Cong might win; and 52 percent were willing to accept a coalition government including the Viet Cong (p. 320).

The misreading of the public mood on specific foreign policy issues illustrates one of the drawbacks of the static model of public opinion: It exaggerates the fixity of the context within which the public is likely to judge a particular action, assuming that people will support an action if it shows "strength" and reject it if it shows "weakness." In reality, however, there is no one-to-one relationship between the apparent militancy of an action and the public's reaction to it. How the public reacts depends on how the particular action is defined—in what context it is placed. This is a dynamic process, in which the national leadership plays a decisive role. If we grant for the moment that decision makers are constrained by the broader contexts within which the public views foreign affairs, their ability to define and redefine the context of specific issues often gives them greater flexibility than they realize or admit. To be sure, as our earlier quotation from Etzioni (1969) indicates, the context they set at one time may limit their freedom at a later time.

Most decision makers, of course, do not take a passive stance toward public opinion. They may argue, and actually believe, that they are constrained by public opinion when these alleged constraints are in keeping with their own policy preferences. On the other hand, when they perceive public opinion to be opposed to or insufficiently supportive of their preferred policies, they do engage in efforts to change it. These efforts themselves, however, usually conform to the static model of public opinion assumed by most decision makers. If public opinion does not provide sufficiently strong support to certain militant foreign policy moves, decision makers normally try to appeal to the set of static principles that they assume to be important to the public: the need to protect a vaguely defined national interest, to uphold the national honor, to maintain national superiority, or to expand national influence. If they are worried about public support for certain conciliatory foreign policy moves, they try to redefine the context within which these policies are placed —showing that these are, indeed, consistent with the national interest, the national honor, or the nation's global power position. In either event, decision makers are working within an assumptive framework that exaggerates the fixity of the principles that serve as the context for public reactions to foreign policy actions.

The assumption of a static public opinion, favoring militant postures, ignores two major considerations: (1) Public adherence to doctrines of national interest or superiority is not universal or stable and certainly not inevitable. These principles derive from the nationalist ideology that characterizes the modern nation-state. This ideology is fostered by the national leadership and, in established nation-states such as the United States, is widely accepted in the population—albeit with considerable variations in intensity and precise content. Decision makers assume that "the national interest" and national superiority represent important concerns to the public, in large part because they are important to the decision makers themselves and because they offer them a relatively flexible basis for regulating public responses to foreign policy issues. Very often these concerns are indeed important to major sectors of the public—to some because of their own ideological commitments, to most because they are told by their national leaders that they are important. The extent to which people attach importance to these principles, however, and the depth of their commitment to them vary widely for different groups and at different points in time. (2) The formation of public attitudes toward a specific issue is a dynamic process, in which the interaction between individual citizens and decision makers plays a major role. The shape of public opinion emerging out of this interaction depends very heavily on the nature of the relationship of various segments of the population to the national system and to its current leadership. If the public supports militant actions promoted by the leadership, it may do so more because of its underlying trust in the leadership than because of a commitment to principles of national militancy. In the absence of trust, the leadership might find it difficult to mobilize support for militant actions; given a basis of trust, they might be equally successful in mobilizing support for conciliatory actions.

The static model may be a good predictor of public reactions under many, perhaps most, circumstances. Decision makers often succeed in mobilizing public support by appealing to the principles of national interest, honor, and superiority, and they may maintain themselves in power by affecting a militant foreign policy posture. The model cannot, however, account for those occasions in which anticipated public support for a militant policy breaks down (as in President Johnson's Vietnam policy) or earlier anticipated public opposition to a conciliatory policy fails to materialize (as in President Nixon's China policy). It cannot account for the successful efforts by citizen groups to mobilize American public opinion against fallout shelters and in favor of the test-ban treaty (Etzioni, 1969, p. 578). Above all, it limits the exploration of potential innovative approaches to foreign policy, which might provide alternatives to existing policies.

At the policy level, as we have already pointed out, the static model introduces a systematic bias toward overestimating existing and potential public support for militant actions and underestimating support for conciliatory ones. It may thus encourage decision makers to persist in policies that the public will not back up and to reject prematurely alternatives that the public might well have supported. Moreover, insofar as the static model ignores the role of trust in the leadership as a central determinant of public support, assigning greater weight to the appearance of militancy, decision makers may be inclined to risk their credibility in the pursuit of militant policies and thus forfeit long-run support (which is apparently what happened to President Johnson in 1968). Failure to give proper weight to the ongoing relationship of the citizenry to the national system may also lead to a neglect of some potentially effective means of mobilizing support for foreign policy innovations.

Determinants of Foreign Policy Orientations. To analyze public opinion in foreign policy as a dynamic process, one must explore the ways in which different individuals and groups within a population relate themselves to broader foreign policy issues. These orientations, in turn, have implications for the possibility of mobilizing their support for various foreign policy actions—whether on the basis of appeals to the national interest and superiority or on the basis of other appeals— and for the conditions under which such mobilization can take place. A first step toward a more dynamic analysis of public opinion is to identify and account for different foreign policy orientations. How do different orientations fit into and vary with an individual's general personality dispositions, his position in society, and— perhaps most important—his relationship to the political system?

An illustration of the link between foreign policy attitudes and general personality dispositions is provided by McClosky's research (1967a). McClosky sampled over 5000 individuals in an effort to arrive at a more differentiated understanding of isolationist orientations toward United States involvement in world affairs. He found isolationism to be part of a cluster of attitudes, including classical and welfare conservatism, radical doctrines of the right and left, and attitudes critical of democratic beliefs and practices. This cluster of attitudes, in turn, is linked to a characteristic cognitive style and underlying personality dispositions.

> Despite its strong chauvinistic overtones, isolationism is frequently associated with feelings of disappointment in one's own society and disaffection from the political institutions of one's country. The isolationist orientation parallels closely other forms of belief that rely heavily upon dichotomous thought processes, that lack breadth of perspective, and that seek to exclude whatever is different, distant, or unfamiliar. . . . Like other deviant orientations, it signifies for some of its proponents a failure of socialization and an inadequate internalization of the norms. It is more common among those who are, by any criterion and for any reason, parochial and less common among those who are open to experience and cosmopolitan in their perspective [McClosky, 1967a, p. 107].

Isolationists and nonisolationists respond very differently to a variety of specific foreign policy issues, such as immigration, foreign aid, level of tariffs, participation in NATO, and defense spending. Though these specific opinions may shift in the face of different pressures, the general pattern of findings suggests quite clearly that individuals and groups differing along the isolationism-nonisolationism dimension (and the broad cluster of attitudes and personality dispositions that it represents) are likely to differ in their readiness to support various types of foreign policy actions.

Starting from a more sociological perspective, Galtung (1969) attempted to link the cognitive processes underlying an individual's foreign policy orientation to his social position. He distinguished between a gradualist approach to foreign policy (characterized by a stable, inductive, pragmatic, means-end intellectual style; a differentiated acceptance and rejection of the status quo; and a gradual orientation to change) and an absolutist approach (characterized by a volatile, deductive, moralistic, subsumptive intellectual style; a total acceptance or rejection of the status quo; and an all-or-nothing orientation toward change). Individuals who operate at the center of the system enjoy, by virtue of their position, easy access to important communication channels on foreign affairs. They are thus able to gain a more differentiated picture of the international situation and the practical alternatives available to their nation; and they tend to develop a sense of the utility of pragmatic action in the field of foreign policy making. It is these individuals who, according to Galtung, assume a gradualist approach to the foreign policy process. By contrast, individuals at the periphery of the system remain cut off from the immediate flow of information and are denied the opportunity for personal experience with the world of international relations. The result is that a moralistic ideological thinking style combines with secondhand informational inputs (see Katz and Lazarsfeld, 1955) to produce what Galtung has labeled the absolutist orientation toward the foreign policy process. The two groups differ markedly and predictably in the types of foreign policy actions they are inclined to accept or reject (Galtung, 1967).

Personality dispositions and social position take on special importance because they affect the individual citizen's overall relationship to the political system. The nature of this relationship, as we proposed earlier, greatly influences the conditions under which the individual will provide or withhold support to various foreign policy moves, the kind of support he will give, and the kinds of appeals from decision makers to which he will be responsive. Thus, the patterns of relationship to the system and its current leadership that characterize different segments of the population are a crucial determinant of who can be mobilized (and when and how) to provide what kind of support for various policy options.

In earlier work (Kelman, 1969), we presented a framework distinguishing different patterns of personal involvement in the national political system. This framework illustrates one approach to the determinants of foreign policy attitudes in terms of the interaction between individual citizens and the national leadership. Such an analysis should be particularly helpful in illuminating major changes in public mood vis-à-vis foreign policy issues and in assessing the potential of alternative policy choices and of new approaches to the foreign policy process.

Model of Personal Involvement in National System. As summarized in Table 1, the model distinguishes six patterns of personal involvement in the national system. The rows represent two sources of attachment or loyalty to the system—sentimental and instrumental. The columns represent three means of integration of the individual into the system—ideological, role participant, and normative. In other words, the rows distinguish, essentially, two types of motives that lead the individual to cathect the system. The columns, on the other hand, distinguish three components of the system via which members may be bound into it.

An individual is sentimentally attached to the system when he sees it as representing him—as being, in some central way, a reflection and extension of himself. For the sentimentally attached, the system is legitimate and deserving of his loyalty because it is the embodiment of a group in which his personal identity is anchored. An individual is instrumentally attached to the system when he sees it as an effective vehicle for achieving his own ends and those of other system members. For the instrumentally attached, the system is legitimate and deserving of his loyalty because it provides the organization for a smoothly running society in which indi-

Table 1

PATTERNS OF PERSONAL INVOLVEMENT IN THE NATIONAL SYSTEM

| | | *Manner of Integration into the System* | | |
		Ideological	Role Participant	Normative
Source of Attachment (Loyalty) to the System	Sentimental	Commitment to cultural values reflective of national identity	Commitment to the role of national and its associated symbols	Acceptance of demands based on commitment to the sacredness of the state
	Instrumental	Commitment to institutions promotive of the needs and interests of the population	Commitment to social roles mediated by the system	Acceptance of demands based on commitment to law and order (principle of equity)

Source: Adapted from Kelman (1969), p. 280.

viduals can participate to their mutual benefit and have some assurance that their needs and interests will be met. Each type of attachment may be channeled in three different ways, depending on the manner in which the individual is integrated into the system (as shown in the columns of Table 1).

An individual who is ideologically integrated (first column in Table 1) is bound to the system by virtue of sharing some of the cultural and/or social values on which the system is based. He supports the system because—and to the extent that—he sees it as consistent with these values, which he has internalized and incorporated into a personal value framework. This value framework generally defines for him the range of political alternatives he is willing to accept and provides the basis upon which he evaluates and decides in the political arena. Ideological integration, then, manifests itself in a more or less rational and abstract evaluation of policies and institutional arrangements—an evaluation based on their effectiveness in expressing the identity of the population and in providing for its needs and interests. The cognitive processes involved in such evaluations are probably quite similar, regardless of whether the ideological integration is sentimentally or instrumentally based. The values against which policies are judged are more specifically ethnic-cultural values in the former case and more universal values in the latter case, but these may often be fused among ideologically integrated individuals. (It should be noted, in general, that sentimental and instrumental attachments are not mutually exclusive, although in some individuals one or the other may predominate.)

In one sense, ideological integration implies a highly conditional form of support for the system. The ideologically integrated individual expects the system not only to conform to a set of basic values in its institutional structure and its approach to policy issues but also to evolve new institutions and approaches as these values confront changing circumstances. For example, an ideologically integrated American may feel that a laissez-faire conception of the role of government may have been quite consistent with the society's basic values in the 1880s but that—in light of changes in economic conditions, social needs, or government resources—such a conception is inappropriate for the 1970s. Thus, to assure the continuing support of the ideologically integrated individual, the leadership must provide for a periodic renewal of the system's commitment to its underlying values.

In another sense, however, ideological integration can be seen as the most stable basis of support to the national system. Since commitment in this case rests on basic values rather than on the sanctification of specific norms, procedures, or symbols, the individual is prepared to support novel procedural and institutional alternatives as long as he perceives them to be in line with system values. Moreover, he is likely to extend trust to the regime during transfers of power, as long as the incoming administration is (in his eyes) committed to maximizing the system's values, regardless of its charismatic appeal or its relationship to a previous charismatic leader. Ideologically integrated individuals may thus play an especially important role in what Weber refers to as the institutionalization of charisma—the attempt by national leaders to channel, upon the death of a charismatic leader, the loyalties that had developed toward the man into loyalties to a continuing national system.

At the other extreme, the normatively integrated individual (third column in Table 1) does not take it upon himself to evaluate policies and institutional arrangements in terms of their consistency with a set of basic values. He is bound to the system by virtue of his unquestioning adherence to its rules. He accepts the system's right to prescribe the behavior of its members within a specified domain and has learned, through his socialization and life experiences, to regard compliance with the system as a highly proper and valued orientation. If his attachment to the system is primarily sentimental, his acceptance of the system's right to unquestioning obedience is most likely based on a commitment to the state as a sacred object in its own right. If his attachment is primarily instrumental, his obedience most likely reflects a concern with preserving law and order as a necessary condition for the efficient and equitable functioning of society.

The normatively integrated individual usually obeys demands from legitimate authorities automatically, without analyzing their value implications. His readiness to comply may, however, depend on the extent to which these demands are authoritatively presented as the wishes of the leadership or the requirements of law. One primary indicator of the authoritativeness of a particular demand would be the existence of clearly visible and specified sanctions to ensure proper behavior.

Ironically, the very readiness of the normatively integrated individual to comply with system demands may at times impose serious constraints on the flexibility of decision making within the national system. He is inclined to accept without reservation the authorities' definition of what is a proper and an improper national posture, particularly in the foreign policy domain. Having accepted this definition, however, he is likely to resist basic changes in national policy, since such changes would disrupt his sense of propriety and order and threaten his integration in the system. Since, as Galtung (1969) has pointed out, there is generally a lag in communication of basic foreign policy orientations from the center to the periphery, the normatively oriented individual (who typically resides at the periphery) may finally adopt a conception of the "proper" foreign policy stance that the elite was propagating earlier just when the elite itself has abandoned this conception in favor of a new approach. Under these circumstances, rather than deviate from what he still considers the normatively required posture, he may question the legitimacy of those who advocate the new approach.

Normatively integrated individuals may also withdraw their support when they feel that the authorities have failed to fulfill their part of the bargain on which the individual's relationship to the system is founded, and that the basis of their integration is therefore threatened. A recent study of public reactions to the trial of Lieutenant Calley (Kelman and Lawrence, 1972) suggests that normatively integrated individuals may have been particularly indignant about the Calley conviction because they considered it unfair to hold a man personally responsible for actions taken in obedience to orders from legitimate authorities. They accept the obligation to obey orders without question, but, in return, they expect the authorities to take full responsibility for the consequences of the actions they ordered.

Role-participant integration (second column of Table 1) falls somewhere between the ideological and the normative orientations. Individuals integrated in this manner resemble the normatively integrated in that they do not measure system performance against a set of basic values. They are closer to the ideologically integrated, however, in their sense of "ownership" of the system. They are bound into the system by virtue of their personal identification with roles within the system. These roles enter significantly into their self-definition, and they thus have a personal stake in maintaining them and in living up to their requirements. They are inclined to give ready support to the system provided the relevant role is made salient in the situation in which that support is elicited. The supportive behavior is essentially a way of meeting the expectations of a personally significant role—the role of good national citizen or some subsystem (occupational, organizational, community) role mediated by the national system. In meeting role expectations, the individual reaffirms his links to the national system and confirms the self-definition anchored in that relationship. An individual integrated via role participation is likely to maintain his allegiance unless he feels that the regime is systematically undermining the integrity of the roles to which he is committed.

Individuals integrated via role participation are likely to react differently to certain specific policies depending on the source of their attachment to the system. Sentimentally based role participation involves a strong emotional identification with the role of national and its associated symbols; the individual sees the national system as the collective expression of his personal identity. Under the circumstances, he tends to regard that system as the exclusive protector of his needs and interests and to conceive international conflict in competitive, zero-sum terms. He is thus suspicious of any arrangements that might imply an erosion of the autonomy of the national system (for instance, by relinquishing control to a supranational organization), and he favors a militant posture in relations with other nations. By contrast, instrumentally based role participation involves a personal commitment to various social roles whose effective performance depends on the national system; the individual sees the national system as a useful framework within which to pursue his economic and other personally significant interests. He is thus quite willing to support policies that improve the system's effectiveness in meeting his needs and interests, even if these policies entail some reductions in national autonomy or some concessions to other nations.

Some empirical findings relevant to the distinction between sentimentally and instrumentally based role participation can be gleaned from the study by DeLamater, Katz, and Kelman (1969) of national role involvement in an American community. This study distinguishes three types of commitment to the national system—symbolic, functional, and normative—two of which bear on the distinction made in the present scheme: Symbolic commitment corresponds quite closely to sentimentally based role participation, and functional commitment corresponds to instrumentally based role participation. Data were obtained through intensive interviews, consisting of a variety of questions about the respondent's conception of his national role, as well as a series of attitudinal and demographic items. A scale measuring each of the three types of commitment was constructed out of items that were theoretically relevant to that orientation and that also seemed to hang together statistically. The scale for symbolic commitment included eight items that tapped the respondent's emotional involvement with national symbols—his personal attachment to these symbols and his sensitivity to any indication that they are being slighted. A respondent would receive positive points on this scale if he indicated that (1) anyone who criticizes the government in time of national crisis is not a good American, (2) anyone who does not stand during the playing of the national anthem is not a good American, (3) he owns an American flag and displays it on national holidays, (4) the American public pays insufficient respect to the flag, (5) he disapproves of Americans who take no pride in America's armed forces, (6) he would consider it an insult if a foreigner laughed at the Peace Corps, (7) he would be insulted or angry if a foreigner criticized racial segregation in the United States and attacked the free enterprise system, (8) he is "first, last, and always an American." According to the present conceptual scheme, a high score on this scale would indicate a strong sentimentally based attachment to the national system, channeled through identification with the national role and triggered by the presentation of national symbols.

The scale for functional commitment included six items that tapped the respondent's orientation to the economic benefits of American society and his emphasis on citizen participation. A respondent would receive positive points on this scale if he indicated that (1) the things that particularly remind him of being an American include factors relating to opportunity, (2) to be a good American a person ought to participate in public affairs, (3) apathetic persons are among those whom he regards as "not good Americans," (4) people refer to affluence and related matters when they talk about "the American way of life," (5) one of the most important things that makes America different from other countries is its level of opportunity, (6) one of the most important things that makes America different from other countries is its level of affluence. In terms of the present conceptual scheme, a high score on this scale would imply a strong instrumentally based attachment to the national system, channeled through the person's entanglement in various social roles that depend on the effective functioning of that system.

Comparisons were made between respondents with high scores on one of the three types of commitment and low or medium scores on the other two. The "high symbolic" group and the "high functional" group turned out to differ on many dimensions. The functionally committed were younger than the symbolically committed, were better educated, had higher incomes, were more often in professional or technical occupations, had fathers who were better educated and more often in professional or technical occupations, were more likely to describe themselves as "middle class" (rather than "working class"), and were more bureaucratically oriented. The symbolically committed were more likely to have grown up in farming families, to have lived on a farm for ten years or more, and to have lived in the area for ten years or more. The two groups also differed on a variety of attitudinal items. The functionally committed showed greater openness to other cultures and systems, greater tolerance for deviant political positions, and greater support for liberal causes. The symbolically committed tended to favor a more militant stance in American foreign policy and were much less willing than the functionally committed to turn over power to international organizations.

These findings are nothing more than first approximations, since the study was not designed to test the present model. Yet they are generally consistent with our view of the differences between instrumentally and sentimentally based role participation and thus suggest the usefulness of further empirical investigation of the model with the use of indices specifically tailored to its parameters.

The type of model of personal involvement in the national system that we have outlined should make it possible to specify the nature of the policy moves that individuals and groups of each modal type can be expected to favor or reject, and the most likely conditions and means for mobilizing their support. The support of the ideologically integrated individual for a specific foreign policy alternative should depend on the value implications of that alternative, defined by his vision of the appropriate national goals within the international system and his assessment of the policy's probable consequences. In the long run, ideologically integrated individuals provide the firmest support for the system, but at any given point they may call for a reappraisal of national priorities in terms of certain basic cultural and social values. In the short run, the most reliable support comes from the normatively integrated individual. He is likely to accept any foreign policy move without question, as long as he perceives it as reinforcing existing authority patterns. His support is most readily mobilized by appeals that link demands for action to legitimate sources of authority. Finally, role-participant integration provides support that is more active and enthusiastic than that based on normative integration but less selective and conditional than that based on ideological integration. The support of an individual who is integrated via sentimentally based role participation can be mobilized by the introduction of national symbols, which heighten emotional arousal, and by implied threats to national sovereignty. Support of an individual integrated via instrumentally based role participation can be mobilized by co-opting his subsystem roles in the service of the national system. He should be responsive to appeals directed at his economic and other subgroup interests and ready to accept a wide variety of policies (militant or conciliatory, supportive of or antagonistic to international organizations) that appear to promote these interests.

From the point of view of national leaders, each type of integration represents a unique set of resources for mobilizing public support. They can draw on ideological commitments to support major policy reorientations and novel institutional arrangements; on role-participant commitments to elicit special efforts and sacrifices in periods of national crisis or of rapid economic development and social change; and on normative commitments to assure the smooth operation of the system in periods of relative calm and to reassert their traditional authority in periods of social unrest.

Considerable research is needed to clarify and refine the different patterns of personal involvement in the national system distinguished by the present model; to identify the foreign policy orientations characteristic of each pattern; and to explore the role that these different orientations, in turn, play in the articulation, mobilization, and impact of public opinion on foreign policy issues. As research based on this and related efforts to probe the dynamics of public opinion in the foreign policy process accumulates, we will be in a better position to predict the degrees of freedom of decision makers on various foreign policy issues, the most probable sources of support for and resistance to different actions, and the repercussions these actions are likely to have among different segments of the population. It should also become possible to specify the kinds of long-term efforts at public education that would help to build a public opinion more favorable to innovative, constructive approaches to foreign policy.

Nature of International Conflict

Like the common model of the role of public opinion, the assumptive framework with which decision makers and the public commonly approach major international conflicts often stands in the way of cooperative modes of conflict resolution. Conflict as a process tends to be viewed entirely as competition between two rational parties, the one seeking justifiably to protect its interests and the other engaged in a "diabolical" effort (White, 1968) to prevent the first from realizing its goals. Pruitt and Gahagan (1972) have labeled conceptual approaches of this type as the "aggressor-defender models" of conflict.

Aggressor-Defender Model. According to this model, "one party (the 'aggressor') is assumed to be the originator of the conflict and the major contributor to its continuation. His behavior is typically explained in terms of the *motives* and *emotions* satisfied by the conflict and the failure of *deterrents* against aggression" (Pruitt and Gahagan, 1972, p. 19).

Ralph White's (1968) analysis of misperceptions in Vietnam suggests that the war was continued at least partly because both sides operated within this undifferentiated assumptive framework. Decision makers on each side tended to project an exaggeratedly diabolical, aggressive image of the other while at the same time maintaining, by means of rationalizations, an exaggeratedly self-righteous perception of their own conduct. According to White's analysis, each side affected a virile national self-image, disguising its own desires for power, prestige, and self-aggrandizement, and subscribed to a distorted view of the situation in Vietnam and of its own military capacity. The resulting black-and-white conception of the conflict precluded the formation of more differentiated images of one's own and of the adversary nation; obscured areas of common interest, in which cooperation would be feasible; and inhibited the development of mutual trust. Within this context of lessened sensitivity, it was extremely difficult to arrive at a peaceful and lasting solution to the conflict. Since, moreover, according to the aggressor-defender model, the outbreak and perpetuation of conflict are entirely due to aggression on the part of one's adversary, the only appropriate way to settle the conflict is by physically stopping him or deterring him, by whatever means available, from further aggression. The possibility that the types of interactions generated by the conflict may themselves be contributing to its escalation and perpetuation is rarely if ever considered in the planning of succeeding policy moves. Rather, each side assumes that it must concentrate its efforts on projecting an image of strength, backed by a visible display of military power, thus lending credibility to its threats and deterring its adversary from continuing in his "aggression."

More generally, the aggressor-defender model promotes the view that the only viable means of guaranteeing international peace is the maintenance, on the part of each major power, of a military force of sufficient strength and preparedness to deter any would-be aggressor. A substantial amount of effort in recent years has focused on testing the validity and examining the implications of this view. (For more comprehensive discussions of the psychology of deterrence, see Deutsch and Krauss, 1960, and various of the chapters in Pruitt and Snyder, 1969, and in Swingle, 1970b.) Schelling and Halperin (1969) call attention to the irony of a deterrence strategy in a world whose weaponry is capable of overwhelming destruction. The existence of offensive weapons with the power to destroy the retaliatory capacity of another nation-state puts a marked premium on being the first to attack or, as Schelling and Halperin put it, at least "a close second." Thus, if a nation even remotely suspects that another nation is building up its capacity for a possible attack, it will feel pressured into at least contemplating a preemptive act of aggression in order not to lose the distinct advantage to be gained by attacking first. Similarly, any hesitation in reacting to what is thought to be an indication of aggression may involve an enormous loss of comparative advantage. The net result is that the use of the deterrence strategy may very well increase the chances of preemptive or accidental war rather than the chances of a reduction in international conflict.

In light of this drawback of a mutual-deterrence strategy, Raser and Crow (1969) suggest that one way of restraining international conflict might be a retaliatory force that is not vulnerable to initial attack by other nation-states. In order to test this hypothesis, they employed multiple runs of the Inter-Nation Simulation, in which one nation, "Omne," was provided with the capacity to withstand any attack and to retaliate decisively. The results indicate that providing Omne with this retaliatory capacity did indeed reduce the incidence of preemptive war, but at the same time it encouraged Omne to assume a more belligerent and aggressive stance, thus causing a complementary increase in the occurrence of strategic war. Although generalizations from a simulation study to the real world require great caution, the study points to at least one possible unintended psychological consequence of a deterrence strategy, even under the conditions of an invulnerable retaliatory force. Swingle (1970a) suggests two additional unintended reactions to deterrence, with potentially hazardous consequences. If the capacity to punish, especially in the case of bilateral punishment, is extremely strong, "an opponent may not believe a threat to use such punishment" because "it is not in the interests of the threatener to execute the threat at any time. This, in turn, gives rise to a policy of encroachment in which each infraction is not large enough to justify the execution of the threat." Furthermore, "severe threat tends to put a premium upon antagonists acting as though they are irrational, since the appearance of irrationality increases the credibility that the threat might actually be executed" (p. 248).

Conflict-Spiral Model. One of the consequences of the aggressor-defender model is a conception of international conflict as a zero-sum game, in which one side's gains are matched by the other side's losses. Various social science writings have challenged this assumption, reconceptualizing international conflict as at least potentially a positive-sum game, permitting outcomes that leave both sides better off. Basic conflicts of interest between the parties may, of course, exist; but even when they do, there are often some bases for cooperation that would accrue to the mutual benefit of the parties. The question is: Why do parties in conflict usually find it so difficult to discover these positive-sum solutions?

To answer this question, we must analyze the dynamics of the conflict process itself: What is it about the conflict situation that blocks the discovery of mutual interests, and by what means could these be made to surface? The aggressor-defender model is not at all useful here. Not only does it obscure the possibilities of cooperation between the conflicting parties, but—since it analyzes conflict entirely in terms of the motives of the antagonists—it ignores the ways in which conflictual interactions themselves may reinforce and enlarge the conflict. To correct for these shortcomings of aggressor-defender models, social scientists have developed models focusing on the dynamics of the interaction between the conflicting parties. Pruitt and Gahagan (1972, p. 23) have labeled these the "conflict-spiral models": "The basic assumption of these models is that conflict develops and is perpetuated through vicious circles in which each party's conflictual action is a reaction to the other party's recent behavior. This reaction may be punitive or defensive; but regardless of which, the other party then reacts with more conflict behavior, continuing the circle." Perceptions of one's own nation and of the other nation play an important role here. *A* may arm for what it considers legitimate reasons of defense; *B,* convinced of its own peacefulness, perceives *A*'s action not as a defensive move but as evidence of *A*'s aggressive intent; *B* therefore arms in defense against possible aggression from *A; A,* in turn, perceives *B*'s action as further evidence of *B*'s aggressive intent and therefore proceeds to increase its own level of armament; and so on. Conflict-spiral models have been central to a number of recent analyses of international conflicts and approaches to conflict resolution. (For fuller discussions, see Richardson, 1960; North, Brody, and Holsti, 1964; Pruitt, 1965; Shure, Meeker, and Hansford, 1965; Osgood, 1962, 1969.)

Perhaps the best-known proposal for conflict resolution based on a conflict-spiral model is Osgood's GRIT strategy (Graduated and Reciprocated Initiatives in Tension Reduction). The strategy starts with the assumption that solutions acceptable to both sides can best be discovered in an atmosphere conducive to the development of open channels of communication, mutual trust, and the mutual extension of empathy. Osgood proposes the use of unilateral conciliatory steps, preceded by explicit announcements of intent, as a means of fostering the desired atmosphere and thus triggering a gradual deescalation of tensions and ultimately a deescalation of military investments. Although these initiatives entail some sacrifice for the nation that takes them, they do not involve a significant impairment of its military capacity. Initial steps are small, but they are gradually expanded as the other side reciprocates with tension-reducing actions of its own. Essentially, this strategy is an attempt to reverse the conflict spiral: Conflict is escalated as each party's aggressive moves are recipro-cated by the other; Osgood proposes to deescalate it through the initiation and reciprocation of conciliatory moves. In short, the strategy addresses itself to the dynamics of conflictual interaction, which are often responsible for expansion of the conflict and for the difficulty in discovering cooperative solutions.

Osgood's analysis has received some support from laboratory studies. In the context of the Inter-Nation Simulation, Crow (1963) demonstrated the success of a GRIT strategy both in reversing a trend toward escalation of tensions and in inducing an initially hostile and hesitant nation to reciprocate the conciliatory ges-tures of the initiator of GRIT. Pilisuk and Skolnick (1968), using an extended ver-sion of the standard Prisoner's Dilemma task (see Komorita, 1965; Rapoport and Chammah, 1965), found that the combination of a conciliatory strategy with honest prior announcement of moves can be effective in inducing reciprocal cooperation. The effectiveness of the GRIT strategy in these two rather different laboratory situations gives added weight to Osgood's proposals, although one must, of course, keep in mind the limitations of generalizing from the laboratory to the international system.

We concur with Pruitt and Gahagan's (1972) assessment that the conflict-spiral approach represents a definite improvement over the more commonly held assumptive frameworks about the nature of conflict. As a dynamic and two-sided model, it corrects for some of the major limitations of the various aggressor-defender models. At the same time, it has some limitations of its own. Pruitt and Gahagan point out, for example, that it tends to be *over*symmetrical in its treatment of the two conflicting parties; that it treats the parties as undifferentiated units, ignoring the composition of each party and the possibility that this may change over time; and that it does not account adequately for the observation that conflict, once begun, often perpetuates itself even in the absence of immediate provocation. As a result, this type of model seems "overly optimistic about the possibility of reversing conflict processes once they get started" (Pruitt and Gahagan, p. 27). Another limitation of the con-flict-spiral model is that it views the conflictual interaction entirely in terms of alter-nating actions and reactions—moves and countermoves—by two independent parties, ignoring the possibility that in some respects the two parties (or at least segments of each) can be viewed as a single system, with a shared definition of the situation. As a result, this type of model may overlook conflict-resolution approaches that rely on a redefinition of the relationship between the parties and of the nature of their conflict.

Structural-Change Model. A family of approaches that correct for some of the limitations of the conflict-spiral model is described by Pruitt and Gahagan (1972) as "structural-change models." These models assume that "certain changes take place in one or both parties that tend to perpetuate the conflict well beyond the initial motives or escalative sequence that began it. These changes may occur in the social structure of the parties; in images, attitudes, motives or feelings; or in the salience of issues or commitment to their solution" (p. 28). Thus, for example, the conflict may create or bring to the fore organizational units, social movements, or population groupings that have a vested interest in the conflict itself and thus contribute to its perpetuation. Similarly, the conflict may engender new goals, or sharpen negative images of the adversary, or bring new issues into focus, which give it a life of its own, independent of the initial precipitating incident.

Structural-change models are not necessarily inconsistent with conflict-spiral models. Often the processes highlighted by these two approaches work simultaneously and in conjunction with each other (Pruitt and Gahagan, 1972, pp. 35–36). For example, at various points in a conflict-spiral process, B's escalatory response to A's provocation may be accompanied by structural changes in B: a particular faction within B may gain prominence as leader of the struggle; new attitudes toward A may become crystallized. These structural changes may have a multiplier effect on the conflict, increasing its intensity and duration to levels beyond those produced by the spiraling processes themselves.

What implications does a structural-change model have for conflict resolution? In stressing the self-perpetuating nature of conflict, this model reminds us "that conflict is very hard to reverse once structural changes have begun to take root" (Pruitt and Gahagan, 1972, p. 34). It is important, therefore, to introduce tension-reducing steps early enough to prevent the emergence of new social and psychological structures. On the other hand, Pruitt and Gahagan's assessment of efforts to reverse conflict processes may be unduly pessimistic. It seems reasonable to propose that such efforts at deescalation as the GRIT strategy may produce structural changes in their own right, just as escalatory steps do. Thus, systematic conciliatory moves, announced and initiated by A, may bring a peace-oriented faction within B into prominence and may help to improve A's general image within B. These structural changes may have a multiplier effect on conflict-resolution processes, accelerating them beyond B's specific reaction to A's specific initiative.

Even at best, however, once structural changes have occurred, unilateral initiatives cannot resolve the conflict; they can only contribute to creating an atmo-sphere in which conflict resolution becomes possible. As for conflict resolution itself, the structural-change model has two general implications for the development of effective strategies.

(1) To overcome the organizational and psychological commitments to the perpetuation of the conflict, an effective strategy of conflict resolution must take specific account of these commitments. Thus, selection of participants for any uni-lateral, bilateral, or third-party effort at conflict resolution must be based on a differentiated view of the composition of the parties, recognizing that some elements within each party are more amenable to resolving the conflict and others more committed to its perpetuation. It may be easier to reach agreements by working with the former, but more difficult to actualize such agreements if the latter are ignored. Furthermore, efforts at conflict resolution must provide a context in which the con-flict-induced structural changes within each party can be explored and counteracted. That is, each side must be able to gain some understanding of and address itself to the new images, attitudes, and goals that the conflict has generated on the other side, as well as the different types and degrees of investment that various groups within the other nation have made in the continuing conflict.

(2) To reverse the structural changes that reinforce perpetuation of the conflict, an effective strategy of conflict resolution should aim toward creating struc-tural changes of its own, in the form of organizational and psychological commitments to the resolution rather than the perpetuation of the conflict. Both the form and the

content of the interactions constituting resolution efforts need to be designed in ways that allow such structural changes to occur *within* each side. That is, they need to provide inputs that generate new attitudes toward the other side, new images of possible relationships between the conflicting parties, and new goals that depend on resolution of the conflict; and they need to foster the emergence of organizational units with investment in conflict resolution. Of even greater potential significance, perhaps, is the promotion of structural changes in the relationship *between* the two conflicting parties. The dynamics of conflict often create a symbiotic relationship between the conflicting parties (or between certain subunits of them), whereby both sides join in a shared definition of the conflict as intractable and in a shared commitment to its perpetuation. It may be possible to direct conflict-resolution efforts toward the creation of a new joint system, involving both parties in a shared definition of the conflict as a common problem and in a shared commitment to collaborative efforts at solving this problem. Such structural changes would not eliminate the competitive relationship between the conflicting parties; rather, they represent a shared commitment to collaborative problem solving that exists alongside the competitive interests causing the conflict. Structural changes of this kind depend on the development of contexts and procedures for conflict resolution that place a premium on adopting a collaborative role and a problem-solving orientation.

The structural-change model does not provide ready-made formulas for effective strategies of conflict resolution, but it does offer some conceptual guidelines for the discovery and evaluation of such strategies. Though we cannot point to full-blown strategies derived from this model, recent experiments in conflict resolution incorporate some of the insights of the structural-change approach. Notable among these are the exercises in "controlled communication" of John Burton (1969) and his associates at the Centre for the Analysis of Conflict at University College, London, and the Fermeda Workshop, organized by Leonard Doob (1970, 1971) and his associates at Yale University. In both of these efforts, representatives of nations or national (ethnic) communities involved in an active conflict were brought together for face-to-face communication in a relatively isolated setting, free from governmental and diplomatic protocol. Discussion, following a relatively unstructured agenda, took place under the guidance of social scientists—knowledgeable both about group process and about conflict theory—and were designed to produce changes in the participants' perceptions and attitudes and thus to facilitate creative problem solving.

One of the exercises organized by Burton (held in a university setting in London over a one-week period in the fall of 1966) dealt with the conflict between the Greek and Turkish communities in Cyprus. Top decision makers of the Greek and Turkish Cypriot communities selected two representatives to the exercise, but the representatives participated essentially as private citizens rather than in an official capacity. The relatively unstructured discussions were designed basically to encourage the participants to share their definitions of the conflict, their perceptions of the goals and actions of both sides, and their assessments of the costs and benefits of various alternative approaches to conflict resolution. A panel of social scientists intervened periodically in an attempt to move the discussion away from mutual accusations toward a behavioral analysis of the causes of conflict, its escalation, and its perpetuation, as well as toward exploratory efforts at possible solutions.

The Fermeda Workshop focused on the border disputes in the Horn of

Africa, between Somalia and its two neighbors, Ethiopia and Kenya. Six nationals of each of the nation-states involved were invited to participate in the workshop, held in a Tyrolian resort hotel. Unlike their counterparts at the London workshop, they were mostly academics with no direct involvement in the foreign policy process. Although some time was spent at the Fermeda Workshop in discussing theoretical models of conflict and illustrative cases, these topics received much less attention than in the Burton exercise. By contrast, greater attention was given to the ongoing process of interaction and interpersonal behavior in an effort to enhance the members' self-awareness and communication skills, thus providing the tools and the atmosphere for a problem-solving approach to the conflict.

These approaches are, in various ways, consistent with a structural-change model. For example, in defining the appropriate participants for a controlled communication exercise, Burton recognizes the different interests and commitments represented by different elements within each of the conflicting parties. Thus, the exercise is focused on elements most immediately involved in the conflict on a day-to-day basis (for example, the Greek and Turkish communities in Cyprus), rather than those more remotely involved (for example, the governments of Greece and Turkey). Both Burton and Doob try to create an atmosphere that permits mutual understanding and exploration of each side's perceptions, intentions, and goals, and of the psychological and organizational commitments generated by the conflict. Such exchanges provide a sounder basis for determining the barriers to conflict resolution and for testing the potentialities of various moves toward resolution. Furthermore, these approaches are designed to reverse structural-change processes conducive to perpetuating the conflict (just as the GRIT strategy is designed to reverse conflict-spiral processes conducive to the perpetuation of conflict). They create an atmosphere that increases the participants' access as well as their receptivity to inputs that may generate new attitudes and goals. Above all, they provide a normative context and use a set of techniques that encourage participants to move from a combatant role to a collaborative role and to engage jointly in a process of conflict analysis and problem solving. Thus, at least within the context of the workshop, a new relationship between the conflicting parties may emerge, with a shared commitment to a common effort and to a redefinition of the conflict.

Workshop approaches can be expected to produce changes in perceptions and attitudes among the participants; for example, participants may come away with a better understanding of their own side's contribution to the conflict and of the goals and intentions of the other side. There is evidence that the London and Fermeda efforts were successful in producing such changes. There is considerably less evidence that these workshops were successful in producing innovative ideas for resolving the conflict, but there are good theoretical reasons for proposing that workshops are in principle capable of such outcomes. The real question is when and how the products of conflict-resolution workshops—in the form of changed attitudes and innovative solutions—can be transferred to the policy process. The problem of transfer represents the most serious limitation of the workshop approach. (For a fuller discussion of this issue, see Kelman, 1972, pp. 195–200.) In general, it is reasonable to assume that feedback from the workshop to the policy process is greatest if the participants are close to the center of decision making, as in Burton's model. It can be argued, however, that the ideal candidates for participation are individuals who are at some *intermediate* distance from the decision-making apparatus. Those who are *closest* to the locus of decision making may be less able to shed their official roles; they may be less likely, therefore, not only to experience substantial changes in attitude but also to inject changes they do experience into the policy process. To assess the value of workshop approaches, analysis and research must identify the points in the international political process at which individual perceptions and attitudes have major impact, both on short-term decisions and on long-term trends, and to specify the types of individuals who are located at these points and the nature of their contributions to the policy process. Such information would provide a systematic basis for determining the occasions on which workshops may contribute to conflict resolution and for selecting the participants appropriate to a given occasion.

Even at best, problem-solving workshops are merely inputs into a more complex resolution process. They are not alternatives to diplomatic and political negotiations, but supplementary or preparatory to them. They do, however, represent a promising approach to breaking down the social and psychological structures that perpetuate conflict and to redefining the nature of the conflict and the relationship between the conflicting parties.

Structure of International System

In opening this chapter, we referred to the assumption of the nation-state as the sole actor in the international system. We pointed out that this assumption can be and has been challenged. Indeed, our entire discussion is based on the view that one can enhance the study of international politics by focusing on other actors, including individual actors. In closing the chapter, let us return briefly to this issue, which lies at the heart of the potential contributions of social psychology to the analysis of international politics.

Nationalist Model. Both national decision makers and their constituencies largely approach the international system with an assumptive framework derived from nationalist ideology. According to this framework, the nation-state is *the* relevant and legitimate unit in the international system, in which paramount and ultimate power is vested. It stands at the pinnacle of power and is entitled to overrule both smaller and larger political units. It is commonly perceived as a natural unit, and its exercise of final authority is regarded as self-evidently right. The cognitive and affective dominance of the national system in the minds of national leaders and populations makes for an excessively narrow conception of the structure of the international system. The organization of the world as a set of paramount nation-states has such a powerful hold on our thinking that we find it almost impossible to think— and particularly to think creatively—about alternative structures.

The perspective of the nation-state dominates our thinking to such a degree that even professional students of international relations are generally unable to escape it. They tend to use the nation-state as the basic unit of analysis and as the primary actor in the international system. Even those whose observations are based on the behavior of decision makers tend to assume that the nation-state is *the* decision-making unit and that the decision makers speak for it. These assumptions are often justified; but if we build them into our conceptualization, we are unable to discover the conditions under which an alternative set of assumptions for organizing the global system would be equally or more appropriate. Thus, our very way of studying the international system is a major factor in determining and reinforcing its character.

The pervasive and refractory assumptions of the nationalist model have been particularly inadequate in view of the important changes that the nature and functions of the nation-state have been undergoing in recent years. To conceptualize the international system as operating entirely through autonomous, supreme nation-states does not fully conform to current reality, nor does it provide an adequate model for meeting many of the needs of the world's population.

There is no doubt that the nation-state remains the dominant unit in the international system. After all, this is the basic assumption on which the international system is organized, an assumption that is constantly reinforced by national and international institutions. This does not mean, however, that the typical nation-state is as independent or self-sufficient as the ideal model of the nation-state would imply. There is increasing penetration of national states by other states and by international organizations (Rosenau, 1966). Even powerful states are constrained, not only in their international activities but also in their domestic affairs—in the political, economic, and social realms—by events and reactions in other countries. Regional groupings are playing a larger role in the affairs of component states. Inter-governmental agencies, staffed by international civil servants, carry out various important nonpolitical functions (for instance, in such areas as health and welfare or economic development), at least for smaller states.

In many important ways, therefore, both national governments and their individual citizens function in a transnational society, or a series of transnational societies. This reality is also reflected in the trends toward the development of a genuine world community. Especially among the youth of all nations a common universal culture, with a common set of values and tastes, seems to be taking shape. Furthermore, because of common problems and increased facilities for cross-national communication, such phenomena as student rebellions spread rapidly over a number of societies. International contact for many segments of national societies is extensive and—particularly in professional fields, such as science, medicine, the arts, and various areas of scholarship—national lines have become increasingly meaningless for organizing the business at hand.

In addition, the nation-state is no longer capable of serving some of the functions that it was designed to serve. Foremost among these is the function of military security, which no state—no matter how powerful—can fulfill on a unilateral basis today. Newer and poorer states, in particular, cannot entirely rely on their own resources to carry out the functions of economic development and of meeting the health and welfare needs of their populations. Higher education, scientific research, and technological development are among those functions that will probably have to be organized on a transitional basis to an increasing degree. It should be possible to test empirically whether some of these functions can be discharged more adequately by national or by transnational arrangements.

A major implication of the new developments is that we are living in a world that, in important ways, deviates from the nationalist model of the international system. Already, various societal functions are being organized and cultural values and tastes are being expressed on a transnational basis, even if the extent of this phenomenon is not fully recognized. Other important functions seem to require transnational organization if they are to be effectively fulfilled, but this necessity has not been translated into action. In either event, an assumptive framework that views the nation-state as the only operating unit within the international system and as the only natural and self-evident basis for organizing and carrying out the functions of a society does not appear adequate to current realities and necessities.

Functionalist Model. An alternative model of the international system takes as its starting point the concept of a global society, in contrast to the conception of a world consisting of so many sovereign nation-states. There is no implication here that, in an empirical sense, the world functions as a single, integrated social unit. Rather, for analytical purposes, the model treats the world as a total system, consisting of various interdependent units organized in different ways to fulfill a variety of functions. It makes no prior assumptions about the relative power of different units and about the manner in which their functions are carried out. Analysis focuses on the whole range of actors in the international system, including not only the nation-states but also the many individuals, groups, and corporate bodies—subnational and transnational, governmental and nongovernmental—that are engaged in global interactions. This model thus puts the nation-state into perspective. It permits a functional analysis of the global system, revealing the functions that are and those that are not being adequately met by nation-states and interstate units, the functions that are already being carried out by a variety of transnational units that have developed alongside the nation-state, and the functions that seem to call for new forms of transnational organization.

It seems appropriate to refer to this alternative framework as a functionalist model, not only because it is based upon a functional analysis but also because it overlaps considerably with the various functionalist theories of international integration. (For fuller discussions of such theories, see Mitrany, 1966; Haas, 1964; Burton, 1972. Haas also presents a detailed case study of the International Labor Organization, to explore whether and how a functional international organization contributes to international integration.) Functionalist theories are guided by a normative and prescriptive orientation as well as an analytical one. Essentially, they start with a critique of the nation-state as an effective vehicle for meeting the social and economic needs of the world population, and with the assumption that these needs can best be met through functional (nonnational) rather than political (national) organization. They do not propose to mount direct attacks on nationalism and national sovereignty, but rather to build transnational functional institutions concerned with specific human tasks. It is assumed that, as the number and significance of such institutions increases, new loyalties—toward the specific institutions and toward the new world order they represent—will gradually take shape. Whether or not such developments would eliminate the nation-state, they would certainly reduce its paramountcy, and they would be conducive to a more peaceful world order—peaceful not only in the sense of preventing war but in the sense of actively working to eliminate the roots of war.

To develop functionalist alternatives to structuring the international system, we must first abandon an assumptive framework that postulates an international system entirely composed of sovereign nation-states. Of course, the functionalist model in turn makes a series of assumptions that need to be carefully examined, both theoretically and empirically. Central among these are the assumptions (1) that multiple loyalties can coexist, (2) that new loyalties emerge out of functional involvements, and (3) that cross-cutting commitments and loyalties promote the integration of a social system. There is considerable support for these propositions at various system levels, but there is a great need for empirical research to explore their validity at the level of the international system as such. Such research must take account of the special character of loyalty to the national system as it has evolved in the modern world.

The development of functional, transnational institutions does not require a displacement of national loyalties, but it does imply a tolerance for multiple loyalties, for permitting the existence of transnational loyalties alongside the national ones. There is no necessary conflict between the two. Multiple sets of loyalties are, in principle, completely compatible with one another, as long as the groups to which these loyalties are directed serve different functions and apply to different domains of a person's behavior (see Guetzkow, 1955). According to nationalist ideology, however, loyalty to the nation-state enjoys an exclusive status; therefore, many segments of a national population are inclined to view national and transnational loyalties in competitive terms—particularly when loyalty to the nation-state is rooted in sentimental attachments (as discussed earlier in this chapter).

Whenever a situation is viewed as a competition between national and transnational loyalties, the latter almost invariably lose out. Transnational institutions typically lack legitimacy because they are not supported by important sentimental and instrumental links for most individuals. They do not have at their disposal the kinds of mechanisms of concerted socialization that are available to the nation-state, in which major societal institutions collaborate from the very beginning in building loyalty to the system. Educational efforts geared to "world citizenship" are distinctly limited in their capacity to create sentimental attachments and cannot substitute for the emotional conditioning and the many-sided reinforcements that underlie national loyalty. Deliberate efforts to develop international symbols and to create a sense of international identity are unlikely to succeed in the face of the power of national symbols and national identity; in fact, they may intensify national commitments if they are perceived as threats to national integrity. Similarly, transnational institutions do not have at their disposal—given the structure of the international system— mechanisms for entangling individuals in social roles and for creating functional interdependencies. Thus, for most individuals, international authority (as epitomized, for example, by international law) is an abstract, artificial construct; in contrast, national authority has for them a concrete and existential meaning. The comparative disadvantage of transnational institutions does not represent merely a quantitative problem. It is not only that national commitments are stronger; they are in a qualitatively different position from other kinds of commitments, both to larger and smaller units, or to units organized on a cross-cutting principle.

Under these circumstances, what are the conditions under which loyalties to transnational institutions are likely to evolve? Along with the functionalists, we would hypothesize that such loyalties are most likely to emerge out of involvement in transnational organizations, designed to fulfill specific functional purposes. Such functional involvements are less threatening to the sense of national identity than a direct appeal to internationalist sentiments might be, and they are less subject to interpretation in competitive terms. According to our model of personal involvement in the national system, openness to functional transnational involvements should be greater to the extent that loyalty to the national system is rooted in instrumental attachments. Such attachments are compatible with a more pragmatic approach to the organization of societal affairs. Thus, individuals who are instrumentally attached to the national system should be ready to support transnational institutions if these are seen as having functional value—as, for example, pragmatic bureaucrats in Western Europe were prepared to support the European Economic Community because they saw it as an effective vehicle for carrying out their economic functions. Once individuals become functionally involved in transnational institutions, loyalty to these institutions—and to the world order they represent—should spontaneously evolve in due course.

We would further hypothesize that international integration is likely to increase as more and more important segments of national societies become entangled in a network of transnational commitments that are relevant to some of their vital needs and interests. The best example of such entanglements is the participation of individuals in transnational organizations that enable them both to enact their professional roles in a personally meaningful way and to work for the benefit of groups with which they are positively identified. The nature of these organizations may vary widely: they may be concerned with problems of business, labor, agriculture, health, welfare, education, science, literature, the arts, or religion; they may range from intergovernmental agencies, such as those linked to the United Nations, to private organizations set up on a completely nonnational basis; they may be, at one extreme, highly organized and formal (such as an international mechanism for conflict resolution) or, at the other extreme, totally unofficial and unorganized (such as the worldwide youth movement that serves to express the common concerns and values of the emerging generation). What is critical in all of these organizations is that they create, for their participants, strong functional ties to a global society. Participants become committed, in one area of their lives, to a transnational definition of the world, because such a definition is instrumental to meeting specific needs and interests that have personal significance for them.

From the point of view of international integration, these functional commitments are important because they represent a principle of organization that cuts across the division of the world into national units. In making these commitments, individuals are not expected to transfer loyalty from a smaller to a larger unit but to entertain multiple loyalties in keeping with their multiple roles in a variety of cross-cutting functional systems. Such loyalties to functional, cross-cutting entities can more readily bypass the dominance of the national system. They can counteract the polarizing effects of a world system in which all relationships are subordinated to a single basic cleavage along national lines. Finally, they can reinforce the development of a broader, more realistic, and more imaginative assumptive framework, which recognizes the possibility of various ways of organizing the global system to meet the needs and interests of the world population.

11

CONTRIBUTIONS OF PSYCHOBIOGRAPHY

Betty Glad

Psychobiography is, essentially, any life history which employs an explicit personality theory—that is, a perception that individual behavior has an internal locus of causation as well as some degree of structure and organization (Levy, 1970, p. 56). The specific theoretical framework employed may be a traditional psychoanalytic one, growing out of the work of Freud, or it may be based on the writings of theorists such as Jung, Horney, or Sullivan. I will not attempt here to choose between these possible frameworks but rather will deal generally with all forms of depth psychology—those conceptions of personality that contain a theory of unconscious motivation. Despite certain brilliant achievements, psychobiography as a research form is just now beginning to win general acceptance in political science. After a short history of its development, I outline and then evaluate several assumptions which have reinforced this scholarly skepticism. The main purpose of the chapter is to show that a better understanding of the approach will enhance its possible contributions to political science. Furthermore, I argue that the problems of data collection and interpretation which face the psychobiographer are in no sense unique but are shared by biographers with other predilections as well as by social scientists in general.

History

Victorian biographers were concerned mainly with getting the facts. They gathered together a mass of details and arranged them chronologically, purporting to reproduce, without bias, a man and his times. Thus, Pierce, in his four-volume *Memoir and Letters of Charles Sumner* (1878–1893), attempted to document his subject's every act and gesture, as Sumner himself observed them. Similar efforts are evident in works such as Monypenny and Buckle's life of Disraeli (1913–1920), Morley's life of Gladstone (1903), and the ten-volume work by Hay and Nicolay on Abraham Lincoln (1886). (For histories of Victorian biography, see Johnson, 1912; Nicolson, 1927; Garraty, 1957.)

Replicating the past, however, is not simple. Even the most scrupulous of the traditional biographers had to rely on some frame of reference in selecting and interpreting their data. Although the principles of selection and organization might be implicit, the biographer's approach was governed, generally, by conventional notions of what is important in a life history and how it should be presented (see, for example, Hartman, 1922–1923; Schneider, 1937; Langer, 1958). In the typical treatment of a great man, for example, there was usually an introductory chapter on his ancestry, in which his greatness was traced to his inheritance (Johnson, 1912). The simplest laws of heredity were distorted in a frantic "cytological search for famous chromosomes" (Tozzer, 1933). In recounting his subject's childhood, the biographer also looked for—and usually found—signs of his future greatness—some indication that his destiny was determined at an early age (Johnson, 1912; Fuess, 1933).

Personality descriptions, moreover, were intuitive and ad hoc; and the interpretations based on them were conventional and unsystematic. In presenting his subject's character, the biographer generally accepted the idealized self-image offered by the subject himself and supported by his closest admirers (Johnson, 1912; Jones, 1932). The subject was almost always portrayed as rational and high-minded; and any actions based on narrow self-interest were either ignored or justified in lofty moral terms (Langer, 1958). And if the subject experienced an emotional breakdown, it was attributed ordinarily to "overwork" (see Bain, 1927, p. 37).[1]

In the works of Lytton Strachey (*Eminent Victorians,* 1918), however, another kind of biography was attempted. (For a history of earlier attempts at in-depth biography, see Guedalla, 1939; Trueblood, 1939.) Strachey and his followers, no longer content with "depicting the shell of outward events" (Mumford, 1934), pulled aside the public masks of their subjects, revealing the complex and contra-

---

[1] Many contemporary biographies retain these tendencies toward the use of ad hoc, impressionistic principles for selecting and interpreting data. As Howard (1969, p. 12) points out in his survey of judicial biographies, the authors make rather conventional interpretations of personality: "No Freudian inferences jar these pages, though we know that Daniel suffered melancholia, Doe hypochondria, and Barbour insanity."

dictory human beings underneath (Jones, 1932; Fuess, 1933; Josephson, 1940). Rejecting the multivolume commemorative biography, Strachey (1918, p. v) suggested a more subtle technique. The wise biographer, he explained, "will attack his subject in unexpected places; he will fall upon the flank, or the rear; he will shoot a sudden, revealing searchlight into obscure recesses, hitherto undivined. . . . He will row out over that great ocean of material, and lower down into it, here and there, a little bucket, which will bring up to the light of day some characteristic specimen, from those far depths to be examined with a careful curiosity" (cf. DeVoto, 1933).

In some hands, this new form deteriorated into the "debunking" biography. Woodward (1926), for example, took pains to point out that George Washington's ancestry was undistinguished; that he dealt in slaves and indentured servants and ejected squatters from his lands; that he started wearing false teeth in 1789; and that he had no children, possibly due to an earlier attack of mumps. Such an approach, however, distorts the complexity of character as much as the idealization it seeks to replace: "Seeking to deflate . . . the extravagant reputations of the past, [these biographers] often completely neglected the realities upon which they were founded. Besides, they lost an important clue. The mask itself is as important an aspect of a life as the more devious tendencies it conceals. To tear off the mask and to throw it away was a little like tearing off the face of a clock on the hypothesis that if one wanted to tell time correctly one must get nearer the works; it abandoned the very part of the instrument that recorded the action of the works" (Mumford, 1934, p. 7).

Psychobiography, which was developing concurrently with these other forms of the "new biography," showed similar characteristics—toward deeper analysis but with tendencies to accentuate the negative. It differed in that an explicit personality theory was used. Initiated in 1910 by Freud in his analysis of Leonardo da Vinci, psychobiography at first was used mainly by psychoanalysts. Typical were Abraham's study of Amenhotep IV (1912), Jones' work on Louis Bonaparte (1913), and Hartman's study of the abolitionist William Lloyd Garrison (1922–1923). Shortly thereafter, several full-length psychoanalytically oriented biographies appeared—for example, Johnson's *Randolph of Roanoke* (1929) and Clark's *Lincoln* (1933). (For surveys of this literature, see Dooley, 1916; Fearing, 1927; Schmidl, 1962; Kiell, 1964.) Lasswell (1930) went beyond these works in his attempt to use depth psychology for the development of social theory. Through in-depth studies of several political actors, he sought to demonstrate that "political movements derive their vitality from the displacement of private motives upon public objects" (pp. 202–203).

Political scientists, however, did not build on these early beginnings for some time. An occasional political biography—for example, DeGrazia's 1948 article on Gandhi—drew upon the Freudian framework (compare McConaughy, 1950); but the systematic use of psychobiography for the exploration of the interface between personality, attitudes, and political behavior did not really begin until 1956, with the publication of the Georges' book—*Woodrow Wilson and Colonel House*—and Smith, Bruner, and White's *Opinions and Personality*. There were followed by the works of Lane (1962), Gottfried (1962), Rogow (1963), Barber (1965, 1972a, 1972b), Glad (1966), and Wolfenstein (1967). Similar work has been done by historians such as Mazlish (1972) and psychologists such as Erikson (1969) and W. C. Langer (1972).

Prevailing Assumptions

This early neglect of psychobiography as a research tool may be partly explained as a reaction against the somewhat cavalier attitude of earlier biographers toward documentation (Garraty, 1957, pp. 139–145). More important, however, are certain closely connected assumptions that have governed the thinking of proponents as well as critics of the psychobiographic form. They have generally taken it for granted that personality theory is useful primarily for explaining pathological or irrational behavior; that analyses of individual pathologies should be followed by proposals for therapeutic interventions on either an individual or a societal basis; that psychobiographic studies necessarily deal with the idiosyncratic traits of individuals; and that the approach is an alternative to the political and sociological explanations of political behavior and, as such, is competitive with them. These trends can be seen in several recent psychobiographic studies, as well as in the literature dealing with these studies.

The emphasis on pathological behavior is evident in several major works. Alex Gottfried (1962) sees in Anton Cermak's drive to power in Chicago an underlying dependency, for which Cermak compensated with action of an overaggressive and independent nature. Edinger (1965, p. 297) attributes Kurt Schumacher's failure, in his political competition with Konrad Adenauer in postwar Germany, to compulsive strivings "to relieve inner personality tensions by means of adaptive mechanisms that had proven effective in the past for maintaining the equilibrium of his personality system." Wolfenstein (1967) holds that Gandhi, Trotsky, and Lenin carried into their adult lives unresolved conflicts with the parental generation (each man struggling with a primitive image of authority). Forrestal's performance as Secretary of Defense, according to Rogow (1963), was much influenced by severe inner conflicts and guilt feelings, due to his earlier relationships with a dominant mother and an indulgent father. Fred Israel (1963, p. 132) suggests that Key Pittman's growing alcoholism during his years as chairman of the Senate Foreign Relations Committee was due to "promotion depression"—his responses to advancement to a position that he felt incompetent to handle. Alexander and Juliette George (1956) attribute many of Woodrow Wilson's adult role failures to his youthful unhealthy relationship with his exacting father; conflicts over that relationship contributed to Wilson's breakdowns whenever his most intensely held commitments were challenged.

Although the foregoing biographers have dealt with subjects who showed strong unconscious conflicts, each has also looked at his subject's strengths and skills. Other studies, however, have been almost totally denigrative. For example, Zeligs (1966) in his analysis of Whittaker Chambers seizes on every error and every lapse of memory to prove that Chambers was a pathological liar, a cheat, and probably an overt homosexual. Freud and Bullitt (1967) in their analysis of Woodrow Wilson make certain that "little Tommy" gets away with nothing (Erikson, 1967). There was, apparently, something contemptible in Wilson's desire to be respected and in the breakdowns that he suffered. His achievements are belittled (he had to become a statesman in order to be a "man"); and the views of contemporaries who found him gracious, or a warm and inspiring teacher (for instance, Allen Dulles, 1966), are simply ignored.

This assumption—that personality theory is specifically a tool for the study of the pathological—is made explicit by Rogow (1968; see also Merriam, 1925; Fearing, 1927): "While most political leaders neither require nor merit a psycho-biography, the form is particularly appropriate when we are dealing with odd or deviant political careers" (p. 605). Rogow goes on to suggest that the approach be applied to left- and right-wing political extremists, alcoholics, suicidal types, "born losers," individuals with psychosomatic illnesses, and individuals who make erratic political shifts.

Many psychobiographers have also felt obligated to supplement their analyses with proposals for therapeutic intervention. For example, this is a salient theme in Rogow's (1963, pp. xv) work on Forrestal: "Forrestal's illness and suicide were not inevitable; the illnesses and suicides of other world leaders are not inevitable; and it is not inevitable that the world community become ill and commit suicide. But there will be other Forrestals and other wars if attempts are not made to prevent, detect, treat, and cure those illnesses that affect rational mental processes in decision-making environments." To this end Rogow suggests a change in public attitudes—a recognition that public office imposes considerable strain on an individual and that mental illness may be an occupational hazard. To keep the obviously ill from holding high office, he also recommends psychological tests as a condition of employment; to keep them from breaking down while serving, he recommends early diagnosis and therapy (see also Lasswell, 1948, ch. 6; Klineberg, 1964, pp. 65–66).

Related to this emphasis on psychopathology, but somewhat distinct from it, is a third tendency—the equation of the "individual" with the "idiosyncratic." Thus, Morton Kaplan (1964) has written that the extent to which psychological explanation will apply, even marginally, to international politics "will hinge on the psychological reactions of particular individuals with particular personalities in particular political roles in particular political circumstances." Even Fred Greenstein (1971) seems to be governed by this assumption. In an excellent essay that clears away many objections to the use of personality theory in the analysis of political behavior, he highlights those factors that make idiosyncrasies count. Thus he holds that personality factors are relevant only in situations where personal differences might have an impact—for example, in the actions of a top political leader in a crisis situation. Joining this with the first assumption above, he assumes that the "individual" is also likely to be pathological: "Wherever the circumstances of political behavior leave room for individuality, the possibility exists for ego-defensive aspects of personality to assert themselves."

The equation of the "individual" with the "idiosyncratic" takes a somewhat different form in the writings of Henry Kariel (1967). For him the unique individual is likely to be creative and forward-looking. Thus, he sees the psychiatrist's objective as the freeing of the individual from all formulas. The implication is that the mature person is unique in the sense that he is free—that is, undetermined and unpredictable. "By nature, man is obstinately in rebellion against social constraints. He is therefore to be comprehended as an irreducible phenomenon, as existing ultimately independent of all circumscribing systems, classifications, or blueprints. He is a being in process, always unfinished, a being of only partially expressed potentialities. His mental health consequently is to be defined in the infinitely varied terms of the individual himself—that is, in reference to his own possibilities. His ego is to be understood as creatively integrating internal needs and external demands" (p. 337).

There is, in short, a tendency in the psychology and politics literature to assume that personality theory is applicable only to the atypical. Though such atypicality is ordinarily associated with the pathogenic—the deviant who is judged "neurotic"—in some instances the deviant may be especially strong, possibly a "hero of history." But even here personality theory may be viewed as having little predictive value, merely proclaiming that the subject is free and therefore able to make his own choices. For general discussions of the issue of free will versus determinism, see Fromm (1947, pp. 221–227), Garraty (1957, pp. 5–7), and Holt (1961b).

The fourth assumption—that the psychobiographic approach is an alternative to more traditional political and sociological explanations—is evident in several works. Lasswell (1930) set the stage for the competition between the two modes of explanation in his use of psychoanalytical methods to show that political movements cannot be understood in terms of manifest political intentions, deriving, instead, their vitality from the displacement of private motives upon public objects. Wolfenstein (1967), though he explicitly rejects this form of reductionism, tends to ignore the social and economic factors that led to Trotsky's revolutionary role choice—that is, that Jews were restricted to a certain territory, could not own land, were forbidden to enter certain professions, and were limited by quotas in the universities.

Today, however, it is mainly the critics of psychobiography who are guilty of this form of reductionism, often ignoring explicit disclaimers from the authors. They assume that if other relevant factors can be demonstrated, personality examinations are not required. For example, James Q. Wilson in his review (1962) of Gottfried's *Boss Cermak of Chicago* ignores the sophisticated political analyses in that work, concluding that the explanation of the transformation of Democratic party politics in Chicago will "require more than a clinical look at the boss's bowels" (an emphasis that Gottfried explicitly rejects). Morton Kaplan (1964) questions the whole use of psychological explanation in political science: "Did Churchill project his own hostility onto the Germans when he urged Britain to oppose Nazi aggression? To pose the question is to demonstrate that adequate analysis requires a political analysis of the elements of Nazi policy. That is, one must know whether Germany was probably genuinely aggressive or Churchill probably genuinely hostile. And, if one makes such analysis, the policy consequences will generally be elucidated apart from psychological analysis."

The preceding quotations from outspoken critics of psychobiography reflect a more widespread attitude among political scientists—an assumption not only that institutional or environmental analysis is an alternative to individual psychology but that it has greater explanatory power. Even the literature dealing with leadership shows this bent. As Tucker (1965; see also Rutherford, 1966) has pointed out, there is a tendency to assume that the American political system selects individuals for high public office who will perform their function in accordance with the requirements of the situation; pathogenic types are sorted out because they are unable to build sufficient social support to get to the top. A discussion of individual characteristics, it follows, is not required for most political explanations. Even the litera-ture on totalitarianism is influenced by this point of view, with Arendt (1951) and others arguing that this phenomenon can be explained in bureaucratic terms rather than by an individual leader's pathology (Gilbert, 1950; Tucker, 1965; Rutherford, 1966). In short, as Edinger (1964, p. 437) has said, when we consider conduct to be the result of political environment, "the behavior and personality of the individual tends to be all too often obscured—if not factored out."

Critique

The conceptions of psychobiography discussed in the previous section have limited unnecessarily the utility of this form for the analysis of political behavior. Reflecting the close connection, historically, between personality theory and clinical practice, these assumptions are based on a neglect of contemporary ego psychology, as well as of certain scientific commonplaces. The source and nature of these mis-understandings may be delineated and certain clarifications made along the following lines.

The assumption that the psychobiographic form is especially suited to dealing with the pathological or the irrational subject has its roots in clinical psychology. Depth psychology, traditionally, has been concerned with the neurotic, whose self-defeating tendencies can be traced back to unresolved emotional conflicts of his early years. It is this tradition from which most psychobiographers have drawn. As Edel (1961, p. 465) has aptly observed: "I do think that certain papers in applied psychoanalysis have lost much of their value because their authors have enjoyed their underwater snorkeling to such an extent that they never once looked up to see the great glittering exposed mass of iceberg. . . . To be sure, the submerged part deter-mines the shape of what is above. Nevertheless, it is the visible shape which confronts the world . . . and it is the relationship between the submerged and the exposed which is all-important."

Contemporary ego psychology, however, offers a conceptual apparatus for dealing with the entire human being, a way of looking at the connections between the submerged and the more visible aspects of personality. Though it does not ignore the more primitive drives, ego psychology is concerned with the mature, the rational, and the adaptive or creative response to contemporary situations. Erikson (1963), for example, has emphasized the synthesizing function of the ego in developing stable conceptions of the self through a series of stages that extend throughout life. Maslow (1954) has been concerned with the characteristics of the "healthy," creative human being. And Kubie (1961, pp. 58–59) has pointed out that neither a rigid insistence on rationality and control nor the mere projection of unconscious impulses into action leads to creativity; only when the formerly unconscious impulses are touched by and reorganized by the rational faculties are new solutions found. Such a process is possible only for an individual who can afford to risk the unknown, to engage in the "freely searching, scanning, shaking-together process which we call free associa-tion."

Recent psychobiographies reflect the influence of revisionist ego psychology. Erikson's works on Luther (1958) and Gandhi (1969), for example, show that the strengths, and not merely the weaknesses, of great men must be considered if these men are to be really understood. Barber (1965, pp. 252–253) sees certain "law-makers" as especially productive and well-adjusted personalities. In my work on Charles Evans Hughes (Glad, 1966), I show that his early development of certain ideological structures and skills was significant in preparing him for his very success-ful career in American politics. His political life cannot be viewed as the displace-ment of infantile needs into the public arena; rather, it must be seen as an expression of a basic personality structure which was well geared to his chosen field of action.

The therapeutic slant of some of the literature may be dealt with quickly. Although personality theory has historically been wedded to medicine and its proofs dependent upon specific clinical responses, therapeutic intervention is not a requisite of its use as an explanatory framework. Indeed, Freud himself attributed greater significance to psychoanalysis as a science of the unconscious than as a therapeutic procedure (see, for instance, his letter to Jung, Dec. 6, 1906, in Jones, 1955; see also Greenacre, 1955; Hitschmann, 1956). In the social sciences generally, an under-standing of the relationships between variables does not obligate the investigator to control a given social system as a demonstration of the validity of his ideas. Scientific investigation requires only that the variables be isolated and manipulated in the laboratory or through comparative studies and that hypotheses be checked against a broader framework of scientific knowledge. In short, the application of personality theory to the histories of political actors does not obligate the author to put his sub-jects onto the couch and solve their problems or even to propose ways to keep them from infecting the broader society with their neuroses.

The equation of the "individual" with the "idiosyncratic" is also based on a misunderstanding of the nature of the clinician's emphasis on subjective experience in the therapeutic situation. It is true that each person uniquely (that is, subjectively) experiences his own anxieties, dreams, and fantasies. Further, his emotional fixations and defenses can be traced back to specific encounters during the formative years with his family, peers, and teachers. Moreover, any basic change in his personality may require a specific type of encounter with one psychoanalyst—an encounter enabling him to recall and relive those specific emotional experiences that led to repressions and symptom formation.

These experiences and adaptations, however, are not singular but are more or less patterned (Trueblood, 1939; Dollard, 1935; Fromm, 1941, pp. 277–299). All human beings have some common emotional and intellectual structures and poten-tials—for example, a capacity for affectionate attachment and an ability to learn through abstract symbols. These in turn are shaped by some common human ex-periences, such as a long period of dependency on parents or other adults and the gradual construction of an identity through the learning of symbols and the recogni-tion of boundaries between self and others. These experiences may be specific, in some respects, to an individual's culture or subculture—for example, the quality of affection given or attitudes toward food and sex. Indeed, the precise structure of the family, its values, its conflicts, the techniques by which it socializes its members, the acceptance or rejection of various defenses against anxiety—all can be viewed as embodiments of a particular culture. But whether universal or culturally specific, the adaptations and subjective experiences of each individual, important as they are to him, follow more general lines. His inner life and his relations to his family—the private realm—are patterned to a considerable extent and are therefore predictable.

It is true, of course, that the *arrangement* of human and culturally specific traits in any one individual is in some sense distinctive. His personality, like his thumbprint, has certain unique swirls. These differences, however, usually are much less significant than the similarities; the truly unique aspects of personality ordinarily consist of only minor variations on a few basic patterns. The very development of depth psychology is predicted on the assumption that the most basic human characteristics are widely shared. Indeed, personality theory would be impossible were this not so. (For the debate between "ideographic" and "nomothetic" views see Allport, 1938; Beck, 1953; Eysenck, 1954b; Holzberg, 1957; see also Chaper Two in this volume.)

The emphasis on the "individual" in psychoanalytic thought, then, should not be equated with the study of the atypical. Each person is seen, more appropriately, as an exemplar of all human life at one level of abstraction, and of specific cultural or subcultural characteristics at another. The distinctive aspects of this configuration for most individuals are apt to consist of only minor variations.

The assumption that the psychobiographical approach is competitive with more traditional political and sociological explanations is based, in part, on the misconceptions just discussed. But it is also related to the emphasis which depth psychology has given to unconscious motivation and to its consequent tendency to underplay situational variables.

This emphasis on the unconscious is in some respects legitimate, based as it is on a recognition of the processes of externalization, whereby the neurotic masks his own self-defeating tendencies by attributing his failures to outside forces. But this emphasis also reflects a tendency among clinical psychologists to generalize from their experiences with a relatively select clientele to human beings in general. The anaylsand generally comes from the upper middle class and is impeded in his goal attainment by his own buried conflicts and self-defeating defense mechanisms rather than by such factors as poor education, lower-class status, poverty, or serious physical ailments. Cure, it follows, depends less on social reform or a lucky change in individual circumstances than on new subjective experiences—that is, on an ability to bring to consciousness emotional conflicts repressed by the individual early in his life and expressed through symptom formation.

There is a tendency, then, to see the analysand's problems as isolated from the social and economic crises of the day. Lynd (1965) provides an example from a case cited by Elisabeth Hellersberg. An intelligent young man who had been a left-wing social critic in college later developed a serious mental illness. His recovery was manifest in a decrease in his radical interests and in his ability to get a raise. One day he simply lifted the telephone receiver and asked for an appointment with his superior, which he was immediately given. The result was an instant salary increase of 100 percent. As Lynd wryly comments: "The implication seems clear: the healthy, adjusted person does not need to question the society; he can demand and get whatever economic support he needs from it."

More recently, Coles (1967) has concluded that a similar middle-class bias made it difficult for him to understand southern black children who were going through mobs in order to attend previously segregated schools. He was puzzled by his failure to find any "psychopathology" in these children. The truth was finally brought home to him by one of the mothers, who explained: "Well, I think they just went ahead and did it, because it was there for them to do. And their spirits, they held up because they knew they was doing something good, and it made a lot of sense to them."[2]

Even a demonstration that certain political behavior has its roots in infantile fixation does not negate the need for political explanation. Wilson's bargaining behavior at Paris cannot be evaluated solely in terms of his unconscious needs; the political results of this bargaining style must be judged in political terms. Forrestal's (Rogow, 1963) inclination to take rigid bargaining stances may also be understood in terms of his pathology, but these stances served him well when, as Secretary of the Navy, he had to negotiate with Air Force Secretary Symington over the establishment of the Department of Defense. Even the demonstration that the Soviet threat had become a central theme in Forrestal's paranoic symptomology does not tell us much about the reality of that threat to the United States. And, as Gottfried (1962) has shown us in his study of Boss Cermak, the very pathology that is damaging to a man personally may prove useful in his career as a power seeker and have significant, perhaps even constructive, political results.

In short, the emphasis on unconscious motivation in traditional personality theory has sometimes led to a depreciation of the importance of situational (economic and political) variables for human behavior and their outcomes. Though the importance of unconscious motivation and infantile fixations cannot be denied, political scientists must also look at structural variables within which an individual acts and must weigh their impact on his behavior.

The presumed conflict between psychological and environmental analyses can also be traced to confusions in our scientific thinking—the failure to take into account developmental sequence and to distinguish between explanation at different levels of analysis (Greenstein, 1967). It is true that personality is largely shaped by prior environmental forces and it is to these that the social scientist usually refers when he speaks of "social characteristics." But though social characteristics can cause psychological characteristics, they do not eliminate the significance of the latter, as some political scientists have assumed. Rather, the characteristics at these two levels continue to interact with each other.

The confusion is due, in part, to the inappropriate application of certain standard techniques for the elimination of spurious correlation, controlling for third factors.

Unless one reached the *most primitive* original cause that initiated the sequence that led to the independent variable under study, one would always be able to find at least in principle an antecedent condition that really was responsible for the effect. In this sense, all demonstrations of

---

[2] When a social scientist relates individual economic and political failures and "stress" to individual pathology, he is apt to go on and equate the healthy personality with the successful one. This may account for the reluctance of many social scientists (Rutherford, 1966) to admit that pathogenic individuals may get to positions of power in society. Actually, the paranoic type of personality may well work his way into positions of considerable political authority, as Devereaux (1955) and Tucker (1965) have pointed out.

relations . . . are spurious. Now in practice one can never reach the original cause in the developmental sequence. . . . But in addition, the concept of spuriousness cannot *logically* be intended to apply to antecedent conditions which are associated with the particular independent variable as part of a developmental sequence. Implicitly, the notion of an uncontrolled factor which was operating so as to produce a spurious finding involves the image of something *extrinsic* to the . . . apparent cause. Developmental sequences, by contrast, involve the image of a series of entities which are *intrinsically* united or substitutes for one another. All of them constitute a unity and merely involve different ways of stating the same variable as it changes over time [Hyman, 1955, pp. 255–256].

But how does the analyst determine which antecedent conditions are intrinsic parts of a developmental sequence? Hyman (1955, p. 256) suggests the following guide: "Instances where the 'control' factor and the apparent explanation involve *levels of description from two different systems* are likely to be developmental sequences. For instance, an explanatory factor that was a personality trait and a control factor that was biological such as physique or glandular function can be conceived as levels of description from different systems."

Another way of clearing up this confusion is to look at sociology as the study of stable patterns of behavior between individuals within a group and psychology as the study of the intrapsychic systems of individuals. Psychology is useful in predicting either the responses of different types of individuals to comparable stimuli or the responses of similar types of individuals to diverse or changing stimuli (see Smelser and Smelser, 1965). The emphasis in political science up to this point has been on the former concern—for instance, how different individuals might react to a particular political candidate or issue. Of equal concern, however, should be such matters as the use of terror in political rule or the impact on individuals of traumatic events such as atomic warfare (Beradt, 1968; Lifton, 1968).

Briefly, then, psychoanalytic explanations are not competitive with economic, sociological, or political analyses. All human behavior is the result of multiple causation, and explanation can be sought at several levels of analysis (see Chapters Three and Twelve in this volume). The human psyche is involved in all political behavior—including routine and conformist responses. The psychic makeup of any individual is the result of his physical heredity and his earliest encounters with the culture. His behavior at any one moment is the result of his psyche as it has evolved to that point in time, as well as those factors in the environment with which his psyche interacts. It is at this juncture that psychology connects with sociology and political science.

The argument to this point might be summarized as follows: Psychobiography has been generally restricted to the explanation of pathological and idiosyncratic behavior, often slighting the environmental factors that influence behavior and sometimes recommending therapies at the societal level which are politically naïve. With these misconceptions cleared up, however, the approach may prove to have a broader utility. Psychobiography may well go beyond the usual concern with the idiosyncratic and pathological behavior of individuals to explore the impact of modal and rational personality structures on the political process. And this can be done in a way that is complementary rather than competitive with the other social sciences.

Scientific Utility

Given a proper understanding of the psychobiographic form, one can see its potential for theory building in political science. It should yield a deeper insight into historical events and, in addition, should promote empirically based generalizations about the connections between political and psychological phenomena. This potential, only partially realized now, may be outlined in general terms, as follows.

Depth psychology is likely to yield more significant interpretations of the personality structures of political actors than does traditional biography. For example, the circumstances under which Woodrow Wilson's "stubbornness" would be evoked, and the specific form it would take, can best be elucidated through the usage of concepts from depth psychology dealing with compulsive behavior (George, 1971). Anton Cermak's hostility, suspiciousness, and doggedness (Gottfried, 1962, pp. 336, 373) take on a deeper meaning in the light of Franz Alexander's theory of organ neurosis. With the knowledge of Cermak's colitis, Gottfried was able to impute to Cermak (and to verify in other ways) attributes of the typical colitis patients studied by Alexander—underlying feelings of weakness, dependence, and helplessness, to which the ego reacts with feelings of shame and guilt. Karen Horney's (1950) model of the perfectionistic personality helps to explain Charles Evans Hughes' apparent self-confidence and high levels of performance along with his fits of depression, defensiveness, and avoidance of intimacy with others (Glad, 1966, pp. 112–114). Only in the light of Horney's model do all of Hughes' characteristics fit together into one conceptual framework. And Hitler's "strength," as W. C. Langer (1972) points out, was fundamentally a reaction formation created to cover the weakness he despised in himself.

The psychobiographic approach has another advantage. Relying on an explicit conceptual framework, it enables an author systematically to compare one individual with another. Traditional political biographies, with their ad hoc and impressionistic interpretations, make such comparison impossible, as Howard (1969) discovered in his survey of judicial biographies. By way of contrast, Wolfenstein (1967) was able to make meaningful comparisons between the lives of his three subjects (Trotsky, Lenin, and Gandhi) because he used an explicit conceptual framework. It helped him to isolate in each man those key personality traits that might have had relevance for revolutionary leadership. Others using explicit personality theories in comparative biography include Smith, Bruner, and White (1956), Lane (1962), Barber (1965, 1972a, 1972b), and Glad (1969).

The psychologically oriented biography also lends itself to a holistic approach —that is, to the study of the complex entity that is an individual life. As Alexander and Juliette George (1956, p. 318) have said: "The variety of ways in which given personality factors may express themselves in a political leader's behavior . . . emerge only when the career as a whole, not merely a few isolated episodes from it, is examined in detail." This type of biography has been explained in detail by Edinger (1964, pp. 668–669):

For our purposes, a holistic approach to the dynamics of personality development and expression—which gives consideration to antecedent as well
as contemporaneous events, . . . to the "inner man" as well as the impact of sociopolitical "outside" variables in the patterning of behavioral
characteristics—seems most appropriate. . . . In considering the psychological development of our subject, we must seek to examine not only
formative childhood experiences but personality development through
adolescence and adulthood to the point of any particular political act,
including traumatic experiences and other personality crises which may
have significantly influenced subsequent behavior. Nor must we neglect
the impact of socialization on personality development, the continuous
process by which the individual adopts patterns of adjustment and responds to his social and political environmental stimuli.

Psychobiography also lends itself to the study of political cultures. Survey
methods have been used to study isolated attitudes, personality traits, and their connection to specific political acts such as voting. The psychobiographic approach, however, is better suited to the exploration of *systems*—organically connected institutional
and psychic variables in an ongoing political culture. It provides a manageable research entity—the individual and his career—for analyzing these complex relationships. Starting with the subject's psychic system and empirically exploring the past
and present relationship of that psyche to environmental inputs and political outputs
(that is, his personality and career in relationship to a particular milieu), the investigator is able to cut into a complex set of interacting variables—to remove and
empirically examine a slice of culture (see, for example, Dollard, 1935, p. 4; Aberle,
1961; Holt, 1962).

My work on Charles Evans Hughes (Glad, 1966) is a case in point. American
foreign policy failures since World War I have been attributed to the "American
approach"—that is, to the tendency to view concrete problems through a moral-
legalistic framework, which has often distorted reality and courted political failure.
Impressionistic surveys drawn from many sources might have been used to substantiate this charge. Scientific inquiry, however, requires a more systematic approach to
data; yet the topic must be kept sufficiently narrow to remain within the grasp of
the researcher. Psychobiography is one such approach. A study of the "American
mind" through Hughes—the major foreign policy decision maker of his day and a
representative of the official culture—provided the limits necessary for a specification
of the subject matter, as well as a proper subject for the inquiry. After establishing
through an analysis of Hughes' personality and career that he was a man of his times,
I was able to explore the complex connections between his policies and thought as a
key to the nature of these connections within the broader American culture.

Psychobiography is particularly useful in formulating hypotheses about the
interactions between social structure and psychic mechanisms. These hypotheses can
then be validated by more rigorous forms of investigation. But it is also possible to
generalize to broader political phenomena from the experiences of a single individual.
The general guidelines for the appropriate use of the case-study method in science
need not be repeated here (see, for example, Campbell and Stanley, 1963; Horst,
1955; Becker, 1968). The particular problems encountered in generalizing from the

biographical study of one political actor to broader political patterns, however, can be dealt with as follows.

Insofar as it can be demonstrated that an individual is typical (in important respects) of a "class," generalizations to other members of that class can be drawn from his biography. These initial classifications, of course, are difficult to make. As indicated earlier, the psychic makeup and the career of any individual is in certain basic respects typical of human beings in general and in other respects typical of others in his particular culture. (For discussions of typological analyses see Hempel, 1965; Lasswell, 1968.) But subcultural variations also occur. In a complex society the proliferation of social classes, social roles, and ethnic groupings creates subcultures which can lead to wide variations in career and personality structures. Furthermore, some individual idiosyncrasies will manifest themselves. Any mobile individual in a complex social structure such as the United States encounters ideas and values that he ignores or rejects because they appear unworkable, create anxiety, or promise him no satisfaction. Nor can the creative leap of the "new hero of history" be ignored. For better or worse, Napoleon, Bismarck, Hitler, and others fused together various cultural strains in a way that bore the imprint of their unique personalities.

There is a problem, then, in distinguishing between idiosyncratic and modal personality and career patterns, and between characteristics of human beings in general and characteristics of subcultures. (See Chapter Twelve in this volume.) But if a biographer is to generalize, he needs to know what his subject might typify. Proofs, then, must be devised to enable him to make these distinctions.

The problem of the idiosyncratic is minimized when the individual chosen for study is neither a psychotic nor a creative genius—a charismatic leader who breaks old molds. It is easier to generalize from the experience of a moderately successful leader who was widely esteemed as embodying the virtues of his day (Trueblood, 1939). As Lovejoy (1936, pp. 19–20) has pointed out, it is on these sensitive souls of less than the greatest creative power that contemporary ideals record themselves with clarity.

We may assume that an individual is an exemplar of his culture or subculture if we can show that he has the following qualifications: (1) He is performing with wide acceptance in a high-status role to which he has had routine or easy access. (2) This success was obtained without great psychic costs to himself; in other words, he is an adjusted personality within his culture. (3) His basic values are also manifest in key institutions which he has encountered in the socialization process. (4) He has been rewarded from many different sources on the basis of these values. (5) His associates (teachers, colleagues, followers) hold similar values and also fit easily into the culture, performing in influential roles and being rewarded by others in the culture. These constitute proofs that the individual has been successfully integrated into his culture or subculture and that his personality and career embody at least some significant aspects of the culture.

The individual or subcultural idiosyncrasies that such a person may maintain can be empirically explored through comparative biographical studies. Thus, the researcher can contrast one subject's personality and career with others who have had different social experiences and perform different social functions. Trait clusters can then be delineated—some overlapping, some discrete, some characteristic of men in all cultures, some shared by the individuals of one broad culture, some specific to particular class, ethnic, regional or religious groupings, and a few, perhaps, altogether unique.

Specific Contributions

At this point, it might be useful to outline specific areas where the psycho-biographic method has been employed in political science and to suggest possible contributions in the future. The following areas of investigation will be discussed: role performance and recruitment; the nature and consequences of political attitudes; the relationship of attitudes to background characteristics and socialization processes; the psychic foundations, in general terms, of political ties.

Psychobiography has been most fruitful in the analysis of role-performance characteristics. Barber (1969, 1972a, 1972b), for example, has shown that subtle differences in aspects of presidential role-performance style (types of rhetoric used, ways of relating to significant others, techniques of decision management) can be related to underlying personality characteristics. Wedge (1968) has done a similar analysis for Khrushchev, as has Mazlish (1972) for Nixon.

Furthermore, overall performance may be evaluated in terms of the fit between role expectations, individual style, and personality. Edinger (1964) has explored some of these relationships. There are leaders, he notes, whose personality characteristics drive them to behavior that is dysfunctional for their office. Driven by unconscious goals or the desire for immediate gratification, they unconsciously invite defeat. Woodrow Wilson and Kurt Schumacher, Edinger suggests, were two such individuals. Adaptive role performance, he continues, requires other personality characteristics: "Men like Franklin Roosevelt and Konrad Adenauer . . . have in common a keen sense of 'reality' which enables them to adjust their behavior to the expectations of their salient counterplayers and thus to acquire and exercise political leadership. Their personality characteristics apparently permit sufficient outward orientation to satisfy their personal needs as well as the expectations of those who could facilitate or block their desire for political leadership" (p. 655).

Edinger also recognizes another possibility—one in which the role player meets the expectations of others and at the same time influences the very definitions of his office and its outputs. The great leader, he says, handles some of his own inner problems by adapting to the expectations of others and by changing his surroundings. "Striving to find his own identity, he strikes out against his environment and succeeds in stimulating a satisfying response in the public arena because he is the right man at the right time" (p. 666).

The various possible responses of a political leader to his office may be characterized as adaptive, maladaptive, or innovative (Glad, 1969). In the adaptive response, the officeholder successfully meets the work, self-control, and other requirements associated with the office; in the maladaptive performance he falls short of these expectations. In both of these responses, the traditional conception of the office and of its proper political output remains intact. In an innovative adaptation, however, the officeholder is sufficiently sensitive to the expectations of others to maintain his following, while simultaneously employing new strategies and ideas to change the output of the office. His purpose may be to articulate and integrate new demands into the political system or to expand his own power.

My work may be used to illustrate these considerations. As Secretary of State, Charles Evans Hughes (Glad, 1966) met both his personal needs and the expectations of significant others (for instance, the president, congressional leaders, subordinates in the department, leading journalists, and foreign ambassadors). He was not able, however, to direct American foreign policy along the substantially new paths suggested by the radical changes in the international situation of the United States after World War I. A successful leader in terms of traditional values and definitions of his office, he was not a "hero of history," not a man capable of manipulating the political situation to produce creative solutions to new political problems.

Borah and Fulbright (Glad, 1969), unlike Hughes, grappled with the boundaries of their offices (as chairmen of the Senate Foreign Relations Committee), employing new strategies and ideas in order to change policy outputs to meet (in their terms) the requirements of a changing situation. Both men, with quite different personality structures, exhibited a certain independence from the opinions of others. But Borah's independence was based on an emotional detachment from others and an ability to externalize conflicts. Insensitive to the reactions of those about him, with no conscious doubt about the correctness of his position, he was able to integrate his energies around one core device—political attack justified as moral superiority. And this ability to stand alone on strategic and ideological matters—untroubled by moral doubt and seemingly unaware of external political complexities—was the key to his success. Fulbright, on the other hand, appreciates the ambiguities of the political situation and has a measure of sensitivity to the opinions of others. Unlike Borah, he does have doubt and ambivalence, which may slant his blows and deter him from the maneuvers that might give him more immediate impact. Yet his role as dissenter has been less compulsive than was Borah's and is based more on his perceptions of changing political realities than on inner compulsion. In other words, Borah's style seems to have been based on a somewhat rigid ego structure and a need to dissent, while Fulbright's seems to have its source in a relatively flexible and reality-testing ego.

Aside from suggesting interesting connections between personality and role performance, studies such as the above are helpful in developing theories about leadership. My study of Borah and Fulbright, for example, suggests that stress situations can elicit innovative leadership from at least two different personality types. The analysis also supports Hollander's (1958) thesis that any leader has a limited idiosyncratic credit against which he can trade. Insofar as he performs well and meets expectations in certain areas, he gains a kind of credit, an ability to deviate elsewhere. But if he deviates from role expectations too often, he may lose the support of others in his political environment.

Psychobiographic sketches also have been useful in dealing with the selective recruitment of personality types for specific political offices. Analyses of the careers of Woodrow Wilson and Anton Cermak, for example, support Lasswell's (1930, 1948) hypothesis that politics is likely to attract power seekers who are compensating for underlying feelings of weakness. Wolfenstein's (1967) biographies of revolutionary leaders suggest that the choice of a revolutionary role is related to psychological traits. Repressed aggressive feelings toward the father may find a suitable target in the repressive authoritarian regime which permits the individual to "externalize his feelings of hatred." Other work could be done along these lines. For example, one could compare and contrast the personalities of bureaucrats with party leaders, diplomats with generals, crisis with noncrisis leaders, or middle- with high-level political managers (see Smelser and Smelser, 1965, pp. 255–322).

Psychobiography has also been used to explore the relationship of personality to political attitudes. Through in-depth analyses of ten men, Smith, Bruner, and White (1956) showed that the relationship between opinions and personality is a very complex one. Support for or opposition to the publicly formulated alternatives on current issues appeared "in the guise of final common paths"; that is, individuals could arrive at common policy points from diverse private routes. Intellectual and temperamental traits were related (Smith, 1958), however, to politically relevant items such as cognitive style. Personality seemed to be most clearly related to differences in concreteness or abstractness of thinking. "More extensive appraisals can be envisaged . . . of the degree to which the attitudes prevalent on the topic in a defined population serve one or another of our three functions [the management of emotional conflicts, social adjustment, and reality testing]. Such partial but extensive inquiries into opinion dynamics look particularly promising as avenues to the understanding and perhaps prediction of *shifts* in public opinion in response to events and to different styles of leadership or manipulation" (p. 16).

Personality and ideology may also be related to background characteristics. Thus, Levy (1948) found that anti-Nazi Germans, as contrasted to typical Germans, had escaped rigid and conventional family structures. Lane (1962), in his biographies of fifteen working-class men in "Eastport," attempts to explain the sources of the ideology of the "common man" in terms of his culture and experiences. Furthermore, much of the current work on political socialization (for instance, Greenstein, 1965) could be tested and extended via in-depth biographies.

Psychobiography's greatest potential may reside in the testing of several theories that deal with the emotional bases of the political bonds between people and a delineation of the meaning of "political culture." The character of the charismatic tie has been studied through analyses of charismatic leaders and their supporters or subjects (Gilbert, 1950; Tucker, 1965; Willner, 1968, 1969; Stark, 1968, 1969). Sereno's (1962) views on the leader-follower symbiosis and his skepticism regarding the very possibility of decision making and myth making by an elite could be investigated through analysis of the relationship of a "hero of history" to selected individuals in his life. Perry's theories (1957) of national identification might be explored through comparative biographies of traitors and patriots. (See Chapter Ten in this volume.) The psychological bases of the perception of and response to an enemy could be studied through the comparative analysis of parochial and cosmopolitan leaders (cf. Holsti, 1969). The impact of "national character" on policy making has been investigated through the analysis of "typical" policy makers (Glad, 1966); and the dynamics and political consequences of cultural lag have been investigated through the analysis of individuals socialized in one historical period and exercising political responsibilities in another (Glad, 1966).

There is also much to be learned through an analysis of the behavior of individuals in extreme situations. Such an examination helps to define the conditions of behavior so ordinary as to be assumed "natural" (for instance, compliance behavior or passivity in extreme situations). Thus, the efficacy of fear and torture in demoralizing and ruling a subject population might be extended beyond Bettelheim's

(1960) pioneering studies based on his concentration camp experiences (see Beradt, 1968; Dicks, 1972). And the nature of panic behavior could be further explored through the analysis of individuals who have faced sudden and severe public crises (Stanton and Perry, 1951; Langer, 1958; Lifton, 1968).

Data Collection and Analysis

In addition to the traditional problems in obtaining data, the psychobiographer faces special difficulties. As one historian has noted, "It is almost impossible to reconstruct his subject's inner life and at the same time remain true to the fragmentary evidence available" (Duberman, 1967; see also Kiell, 1964, pp. 14–21). The psychobiographer, ordinarily, cannot verify his interpretations by giving his subject projective tests or scientifically designed interviews, nor can he get his subject on the couch or place him in small-group experiments. If the subject is alive and in power, he will probably be less than candid in interviews, and he is not likely to consent to any serious probes into his psyche or his political strategies. And if he is dead, as Rogow (1968) points out, he has literally taken "his dreams and fantasies, his Oedipus complex and identity crisis, with him." If he has been a major public figure, he has also taken care to erase the traces of his secret life. Politicians, as Rogow states it, "are a notoriously secretive lot, and any inkblots they had inadvertently left behind are usually wiped clean by their loyal posterity."

Yet one can gather from the traditional biographical sources sufficient information on an individual to warrant a psychological explanation. Memoirs, letters, speeches, artistic productions, public documents, newspapers, interviews with associates, and oral histories can all provide clues to the subject's personality which the astute observer can then piece together into an explanatory framework (Allport, 1942).

Aside from the usual handling of these data sources, the psychobiographer might find it useful (see Edinger, 1965) to apply such tools as content and factor analysis to speeches, letters, and other personal documents. Through the usage of such techniques, a subject's basic ideology may be more clearly revealed. An interaction analysis of the subject's immediate entourage may also yield a new perspective on his personality and leadership qualities. Furthermore, the biographer might choose to observe a contemporary subject in action by observing his behavior at press conferences, on the platform in public hearings, and in legislative bodies. Through direct observation, the biographer can document, for example, the subject's gestures, his speech habits and bearing, and his responses to stress. On occasion, researchers also have been able to administer projective tests to their subjects (Lasswell, 1930; Smith, Bruner, and White, 1956; Gilbert, 1950), although influentials are not likely to submit to these procedures. In some instances the subject's artistic productions— his writings, paintings, compositions—may be used in lieu of the foregoing (see, for instance, Freud, 1910; Mumford, 1934; Allport, 1942; Edel, 1961). And though seldom available, medical and psychiatric records may be used. Rogow (1963) and Weinstein (1967) have shown how such documents can be used for interpreting the inner life of a subject.

Armed with personality theory, the biographer will find significance in data that the traditionalist will often ignore as too private, too personal, or simply irrelevant. Thus, Cermak's colitis became central to Gottfried's (1962) interpretation of Cermak's personality. In my work on Hughes (Glad, 1966), several "unimportant" items proved crucial in interpreting his personality: for example, his attitudes toward an old schoolmate in financial need, his devotion to Swoboda's exercise regimen, his ordering of clothes from Brooks Brothers, his desire and ability to take mountain-climbing vacations by himself, and his defensive response to A. Lawrence Lowell and George Wickersham when they attacked his reversal on the United States' entry into the League of Nations. Similarly, certain details in Fulbright's public presenta-tions during the summer of 1969—for instance, his handling of his own mistakes, including lapses in memory, and his misuse of psychological terms, which showed a relative lack of defensiveness—were useful to me in interpreting his personality and role-performance style (Glad, 1969).[3]

"Much of this may appear to be 'nit picking,' " as Rogow (1968) has pointed out, "but it is well to keep in mind that it is the nits in psychoanalysis, the seemingly trivial episodes to which, at the time, little importance may be attached, that often supply the principal clues to personality development."

In collecting and analyzing biographically relevant data, some researchers have emphasized the need for objective measures and quantitative techniques (Bald-win, 1942; Dollard and Mowrer, 1947; Holsti, 1969). In terms of scientific rigor, the approach has much to recommend it, but as a research technique it is likely to have a limited use in psychobiography. In covering an entire life, the biographer is required to draw from a wide variety of sources; intuitively, he may discover that some are more important than others (Garraty, 1957, p. 219; Holt, 1961). In the Hughes study, for example, themes apparently unimportant by quantitative measure (for example, the number of references to "reason" in his speeches) were shown—through an investigation of the teachings of his parents, church, and school author-ities—to be the keystone of his ideological system. This finding could not have been determined by any formula for collecting and handling the data announced at the beginning of the project; it was based, instead, on an interplay between theoretically based "hunches" and flexibility in the choice of trails leading to data. Furthermore, in comparative biography one may have to rely on data types that are not compar-able in quantitative terms. Any available source must be used when one is trying to capture relevant but slippery facts about diverse individuals, who may have left quite different trackings behind them.

This concern for getting the data wherever it might be found was the basis of my decision to approach Borah and Fulbright in different ways (Glad, 1969). In Borah's case, I was able to obtain relevant data from his letters and scrapbooks in the Library of Congress and from certain interviews in the Oral History Collection at Columbia University. Though this kind of material was not available for the study of Fulbright, he and others in his environment were available for interviews

---

[3] Boder (1940), Baldwin (1942), and Dollard and Mowrer (1947) have shown that quantitative techniques can be used to make interpretations from such items as theme se-quences or adjective-verb usages. For general discussions of the relevance of minor details to personality interpretation, see Mumford (1943), Guedalla (1939), Garraty (1957, pp. 113–146), Bushman (1966); cf. DeVoto (1933) and Boyd (1932). Boyd, in criticizing what he considers to be an overemphasis on sex in psychobiographical works, quotes George Bernard Shaw to prove how unimportant the matter is. This is an attitude that any psychobiographer would explore further in a study of Shaw.

and direct observation. Thus, I followed an analysis of relevant published materials (interviews, biographies, the *Congressional Record,* newspaper stories, speeches, committee hearings) with my own observations of Fulbright's public appearances (in the summer of 1969) and interviews with Fulbright and significant others in his political environment.

There are problems in this approach, of course. When the processes of data collection and interpretation cannot be systemized in accord with specific criteria and quantitative measures, the observer's own characteristics will influence the data he gets. This is evident in both interview and direct-observation techniques. The status, age, and sex of the interviewer will affect his ability to gain access to influential persons, as well as their willingness to be candid with him (Dexter, 1970, ch. 6; Gorden, 1969, pp. 127–137). The kinds of data obtained will also depend on how the interview is conducted. The old notion that the interviewer should be as un- obtrusive as possible can be questioned (Dexter, 1970, pp. 24–29). If he plays a neutral role, he may get only neutral, guarded responses. For example, in my inter- views with decision makers for the Borah-Fulbright project (Glad, 1969), I sometimes drew routine and uninformative responses. In these circumstances, I occasionally asked provocative questions or suggested interpretations in order to evoke unguarded responses. This tactic often yielded new information—bringing forth anecdotes and attitudes which had been absent earlier in the conversation. Similarly, in direct- observation situations, the observer's own personal and intellectual characteristics are relevant to what he sees and hears. The ability to perceive slips of the tongue and changes in voice tone or speech patterns, for instance, is based on a capacity for sensitive perception and an understanding of the implications of nuances.

Furthermore, any biographer is bound to have an attitude toward his subject —often positive but sometimes not (Edel, 1961; Erikson, 1968; Roazen, 1968). The psychoanalytic profession has long been concerned with the negative effect which biased practitioners might have on their subject, developing procedures for its mini- mization. Recognizing this problem, some psychoanalysts have suggested that only experts in their profession are qualified to engage in psychobiographic studies (Hitsch- mann, 1956).

This proscription, however, is founded on a basic confusion. The psycho- biographer is not engaged in therapy (Edel, 1961). Though there may be aspects of countertransference in his perceptions of his subject, an intimate relationship is not established with the subject, making the usual procedures for controlling transference and countertransference somewhat irrelevant. Rather, the psychobiographer is en- gaged in historical and scientific endeavors; and if the usual scientific methods are followed, interpretations about personality and role performance will be subject to the usual tests that govern social and political science (Garraty, 1957; Edel, 1961).

Because the psychobiographer may attend to some unusual and varied data forms and because his personality may influence what he can get and how he inter- prets it, it is particularly important that he follow traditional rules for data collection and management. In interpreting data which is often fragmentary and sometimes internally contradictory, he is well advised to follow guidelines such as those sug- gested by Allport (1942) in his "Use of Personal Documents in Psychological Science." (See also Malone, 1943; Gottschalk, Kluckhohn, and Angell [n.d.]; Garraty, 1957, ch. 8.) Equally important is the requirement that his sources be given, so that the credibility of his sources and his relative objectivity in employing them can be checked.[4]

Some psychobiographers have not met these standards, showing an almost cavalier attitude toward facts (as noted by Garraty, 1957, pp. 128–135; and Langer, 1958). The Freud-Bullitt (1967) book on Wilson is a very good example of what not to do in this regard. The details of authorship are unclear; indeed, Erikson (1967; see also Hofstadter, 1967) finds it hard to believe, on stylistic grounds alone, that Freud could have written almost any portion of the work as published. Bullitt's informants were anonymous; and, in addition, statements are made which no biographer could possibly substantiate—for example, that "little Tommy" never had a fist fight in his life. Freud has been criticized also for his reconstructions of Leonardo da Vinci's life (Garraty, 1957, p. 114), as has Phyllis Greenacre (Wyatt, 1956) for her work on Jonathan Swift and Lewis Carroll. Greenacre, in particular, shows an open disregard for the usual tests in authenticating her "facts," using the psychoanalytic framework to originate data. Childhood wants, she argues (1955, p. 107), can be "reconstructed from known characteristics, problems, and repetitive actions supported by memory traces." Indeed, "the experienced psychoanalyst knows just as definitely as the internist observing later sequellae of tuberculosis . . . that the deformity is the result of specific acts upon the growing organism."

This kind of retroactive reasoning, which gives up any independent verification of data, ignores certain important differences between therapy and history. In the therapeutic situation, interpretations are derived from the free association of the subject and verified by his concurrence in them and by his subsequent emotional growth as he comes to accept them. When this form of verification is given up, as it must be outside the clinical situation, the only checks left on the inquiry are those used, generally, in the historical and social sciences.

Another kind of problem arises when one is dealing with sensitive topics, as psychobiographers frequently do. Access to sources is often granted on the condition that certain kinds of information not be used. Garraty (1957, p. 171) cites several instances where prominent biographers were confronted with this kind of problem. Robert T. Lincoln, for example, withheld his father's papers from a series of biographers, including Ida Tarbell and Senator Beveridge. A single exception was made for his father's secretaries, John Hay and John G. Nicolay, but even here he exercised "plenary blue-pencil power" over sections of the work in no way related to the Lincoln papers. The italicized sections in the quotation below represent one such deletion at Robert Lincoln's request: "Thomas, to whom were reserved the honors of an illustrious paternity, *appears never to have done anything else especially deserving of mention. He was an idle, roving, inefficient, good-natured man, as the son of a widow is apt to be according to the Spanish proverb. He had no vices so far as we can learn but he also had no virtues to speak of*. He learned the trade of a carpenter *but accomplished little of it*. He was an easy-going person."

---

[4] To check against possible bias in case studies Paige (1968) has suggested that analyses be kept separate from data presentation, the language in the latter being "decontaminated" through the deletion from the account of words rich with connotations. Aside from a possible scientific loss from such usage (the loss, for example, of "subtler" data), there are obvious aesthetic costs. Most biographers think it important to evoke moods through their selection of details and choice of words. See Fuess (1933), Malone (1943), Hughes (1964), Garraty (1957, ch. 10), and Kennan (1959).

Aside from these practical problems, the biographer may be restrained by his own moral and aesthetic standards from revealing all the private peccadillos of his subject. Dumas Malone (1943) experienced such problems in his work on Thomas Jefferson. In the course of his research, he came across certain "lurid" stories about Jefferson's personal life, most of them emanating from an editor who had turned upon his original benefactor. Jefferson, moreover, had admitted the truth of one such story. What should the biographer do? Malone dealt with the problem by trying to depict the situation as honestly as possible, while at the same time not accentuating it. "Much depends on the length of the biography I am writing, but at all events I must try to depict the man in the proportions which I have perceived." Similar standards, Malone also points out, were used in dealing with potential entries into the *Dictionary of American Biography,* each case being judged on its merits. Insofar as there was any rule at all, Malone contends (pp. 135–136), "it was that dereliction in matters of public concern was more important than private morality."

In dealing with these problems, Guedalla (1939, pp. 932–933) suggests that the standards of good taste are primary and that these standards vary with the subject.

> That which is relevant to the portrait you are trying to paint, even if it is grotesque . . . is not vulgar. If it is irrelevant, it is unpardonable comic relief of a music-hall order, and then you are behaving in an inferior fashion. . . . Let me give an example. If what you are trying to write is the life of a lyric poet, his emotional life is of the very core and center of your theme. In that case it is material . . . which young lady, seated upon which stile . . . was the first young lady. If, however, you are writing the life of a governor of the Bank of England . . . such matters as these are irrelevant and unpardonable comic relief; and telling us about them, that is no proper part of your business.

This distinction between men in different roles is too simple a distinction for the psychobiographer. Even a governor of the Bank of England has a personality which influences his role performance. And insight into his personality may be gained by going into matters such as his love life. Affairs of the heart should be given their proper proportion, it is true; but if their relevance to significant aspects of personality is obvious, they should be included in a biography (cf. Boyd, 1932).

Certain special access, coverage, and documentation problems in interview techniques might be discussed at this point. The grapevine approach is useful in procuring access to interviewees. In my work on Fulbright and Borah as chairmen of the Senate Foreign Relations Committee, for example, the initial interviews in Washington were arranged through two key Senate aides, and from those initial interviews over fifty others were arranged. Approximately 80 percent of the individuals contacted in this manner responded favorably to a request for an interview (see also Dexter, 1970, pp. 28–36).

A questionnaire is of value in conducting interviews because it provides for the efficient and systematic coverage of the items to be discussed and ensures some kind of comparability in the data collected. However, questionnaires also have disadvantages. If rigidly adhered to, they are likely to lead the discussion into topics about which the interviewee is either ill informed or unwilling to talk, thereby leaving his special knowledge and possible contributions untapped. Furthermore, a set format may create a stilted atmosphere in which sensitive information is not likely to flow (see Gorden, 1969, pp. 51–57).

In attempting to resolve these problems in my Borah-Fulbright project, I used open-ended questions concerning the work, style, and other role-performance characteristics of my subjects. To promote spontaneity and candor in the subjects' responses, I memorized these questions before each interview and brought them up in a conversational manner at an appropriate time in the interview. Furthermore, adjustments were made for the special interests and knowledge of each interviewee. One staff member of the Senate Foreign Relations Committee, for example, whom I had asked about Fulbright, turned out to have anecdotes to tell about Borah and Key Pittman, which proved most useful.

There is also an inherent conflict between gaining information and documenting sources in interviews, and the weighting of these concerns will influence how one makes and keeps interview records. Tapes have obvious advantages, since the diversion of note taking is avoided and documentation is nearly perfect. Because of these advantages, my original intent in the Borah-Fulbright project was to tape the interviews and deposit them in the Oral History collection at Columbia University, to be opened under conditions specified by the interviewee. I soon discovered, however, that most interviewees felt inhibited by the tape and preferred not to use it. It seemed, then, that I had to take notes. To retain spontaneity and information flow in the interviews, however, I decided not to take notes during an interview. Instead, each exchange was reconstructed from memory immediately after the interview through dictation into a tape machine (cf. Garraty, 1957, pp. 208–210).

The information was often given to me with the understanding that it was not for attribution, and in some instances the material was "privileged." To provide a means of documenting these sources, I devised the following compromise. Attributions in the final paper were made not by name but by code letters which indicated in general terms the role and the political inclination of each individual. These code letters also referred to the typescripts, now in the University of Illinois library, which gave all the details of the interview.

Interpretations

When approaching a biographical study, the researcher may choose from a number of psychological frameworks (Jones, 1932). The choice should be governed by the nature of the available research materials, the purpose of the study, and the feasibility of validating the conclusions (see Trueblood, 1939).

If information about the subject's childhood is available, the Freudian principles might be employed. Diaries or other autobiographical reports, information from the subject's parents and others about their educational techniques, psychoanalytic or medical records where available—all lend themselves to this kind of analysis. When these reports contain information about the dream and fantasy life of the subject, the biographer is doubly fortunate. For contemporary subjects, published sources may be supplemented with interviews, and in some rare instances projective techniques may be used (see Chapter Fifteen in this volume). Gilbert (1950), for instance, was able to use projective tests on certain Nazi leaders, because they had lost a war, were in prison, and were required to accept Gilbert as their psychologist.

The neo-Freudian frameworks of Erik Erikson and Karen Horney may be better suited to studies where little is known about the dreams, fantasies, or childhood experiences of the subject. It is somewhat easier to describe character structure, with its reality testing and ego-defending mechanisms, than to attempt an analysis of unconscious material (see, for instance, Glad, 1966; cf. Bushman, 1966). Relatively traditional sources—letters, statements by coworkers, public speeches—all can be used to show how the subject manages power, handles his work, and relates to others. Analysis of the subject's speeches is particularly useful in this context, since it reveals his tacit assumptions about reality and the ideological prisms through which he views the world. The extent to which ideological structures are deeply rooted in the personality system has been pointed out by Schilder (1936), who has made "ideological analysis" a part of his therapeutic work. Interviews also can produce information about the public aspects of character structure. More sensitive questions about the subject's relationship to his mother or wife or about his sex life are likely to yield defensive and unproductive responses rather than useful information.

Although there is some data loss in this kind of analysis—the etiology of the psychological mechanisms observed and their connection with specific fantasies and emotions—this loss does not present a problem of major proportions. The ego-defense or ego-integrative aspects of behavior, as observable in adult functioning, are the immediate cause, in personality terms, of adult political behavior.

Maslow's (1954) description of the self-actualizing person may be useful in explaining those who manifest in their careers some form of creative accomplishment, including unusual leadership ability. Rather than veiling the great leader in the hero-of-history mystique, these theories provide explanatory frameworks, perspectives from which political performance can be analyzed in terms of its style and situational components (cf. Holt, 1961). Thus, the capacity for innovation may be related to a certain kind of psychic development (Maslow, 1954; Kubie, 1961), while the ability to create in a political context may require, in addition, a special way of relating to people (Edinger, 1964). The innovative leader must have a sensitivity to the expectations of others in order to maintain a following, and an ability to stand alone in order to try new methods or see new solutions to problems. The essential features of a leader such as Abraham Lincoln are more likely to be caught in networks such as these, rather than in a worm's-eye view (such as that of Clark, 1933) that emphasizes his infantile fixations, ego-defensive maneuvers, and his "immature" religious beliefs.

In addition to personality theory, the biographer may also use conceptual models from sociology dealing with such matters as the socialization process, role-performance expectations, and organization theory. The breadth and depth of the analysis, as well as the choice of research techniques, will depend on the researcher's primary concern. When the objective is to relate a specific political characteristic to key emotional conflicts or to ego-defensive maneuvers, it may be best to focus on select and more obviously relevant aspects of the careers and personalities of several key individuals. On the other hand, if the objective is to weigh the emotional, ideological, and situational concomitants of an individual's role performance, then a broader analysis of his life and self is called for. A biographer can use the entire conceptual apparatus of the social sciences to relate his subject's political position to the subject's personality, physical and intellectual makeup, and current and past environmental influences.

In choosing conceptual frameworks, the biographer should be aware of certain problems in timing. An early decision to employ a particular theoretical system can provide focus and a kind of efficiency in information gathering; it may help the researcher more quickly to separate significant from insignificant data. If a conceptual framework is chosen prematurely, however, the investigator may try to force the data into inappropriate categories. As a check against this, the biographer must remain flexible enough to be able to "break set" should the data so require (Trueblood, 1939; Guedalla, 1939). (For a criticism of Freudian rigidity along these lines, see Wyatt, 1956; Schmidl, 1962; Hughes, 1964, pp. 44–53.)

For example, I initially perceived of Charles Evans Hughes as a political realist. In rejecting the principles of collective security and in emphasizing the primacy of American national interests, he seemed to fit Hans Morgenthau's model very well. Given this perception of him, I was puzzled by his dogged commitment to projects such as the World Court and the Pan-American Arbitration treaties. Then I began to notice the references in his speeches to the rule of reason and to perceive his tacit assumption that reason is in some way related to evolutionary change. It was after I had gone back to the writings of his father and his favorite teachers that I began to see connections. Only then did Hughes's basic tenet—that only evolutionary political change is rational—become clear. A commitment to collective security, then, with its assumption of a radical reordering of human institutions and values, would be irrational. Modest change, as reflected in proposals for the establishment of the World Court, however, could be supported as a development in accord with reason and guaranteed by history.

The worth of the interpretative framework used in a psychobiography can be judged by its efficiency and economy in ordering a wide range of significant data as well as by its prior scientific standing. In other words, the interpretative framework must explain the given details in an economical, consistent, and meaningful way that accords with depth psychology as well as with the general body of social science data and theory. (See Knutson, 1972.) This test, which Farber (1950) calls plausibility, is described as follows: "For a scientifically trained person plausibility probably involves some swift mental manipulations which attempt to fit the hypothesis into accepted frames of reference, thus roughly testing it, and finding that it does violence to none of these frames and indeed fits some fairly well." But there is another factor making for plausibility. *"That is, that a single concept appears successfully to subsume a number of discrete social phenomena, or at least to interrelate them."*

In this sense, then, the evaluation of psychobiographic interpretation differs in no substantial way from those for any broader-gauge theory in political science. The psychobiographer is simply borrowing an explanatory framework from another field in order to explore causal factors which have been hitherto slighted but are of considerable importance to the analysis of political behavior.

Conclusion

In disposing of certain key assumptions—common to psychobiographers and their critics alike—psychobiography will have a greater utility for political science. Revising his assumptions to take full account of contemporary ego psychology and scientific philosophy, the psychobiographer is able to go beyond the usual concern with the idiosyncratic, the pathological, and the therapeutic to explore the impact of modal and rational (adaptive, reality-oriented) personality structures on the political process and to do it in a way that is complementary rather than competitive with sociological and political explanations.

As a form, psychobiography has scientific merit. Not only is it likely to provide a deep and systematic study of personality; it also permits a holistic approach to the personality and politics field and the building of political generalizations. Through it, insights can be gained into such phenomena as the relationship of personality to background characteristics, role-performance characteristics, political attitudes and perceptions, and patterns of behavior in panic and crisis situations.

Though the psychobiographer cannot eliminate elements of subjectivity in his work, certain restraints and principles of validation should govern his approach. Depth psychology, for example, may direct him to details, many of them quite elusive, which are ignored in traditional studies; nevertheless, he must be guided by the usual tests for documentation followed in history and the social sciences. The sources of his data must be given, so that his facts are susceptible to an outside check; and his explanatory framework should be explicitly presented, so that it may be judged by other scholars in terms of its ability to handle the data in an economic and internally consistent way that accords with the broad body of social science theory and data.

12

SURVEYS IN THE STUDY OF POLITICAL PSYCHOLOGY

Herbert H. Hyman

Omnipresent and omnipotent, if it were not idolatrous, might be an apt description of the survey method in political psychology. McClosky (1967b, p. 65) hails it as "the most important procedure in the 'behavioral' study of politics" in a review of survey research in political science. His reference to "the handful of large-scale voting surveys that have in three decades taught us more about the act of voting than was learned in all previous history" (p. 71) surely gives a sense of the method's awesome powers.

McClosky is but a single judge, perhaps prejudiced in our favor; but a careful reading of his decision will show how well documented it is and how truly versatile survey research can be in illuminating the problems of modern political science. Yet, to be precise, he is writing about the "behavioral study of politics," not about "political *psychology*." Some subtle shades of meaning may attach to these vague, undefined terms, and perhaps surveys are not so all-powerful in whatever special realm is political psychology.

An essay by Katz, in the same volume with McClosky, reduces this ambiguity. According to Katz (1967, p. 149), "survey and field research can contribute heavily to the development of a more adequate psychology." Furthermore, "a naturalistic description of the behavior of human beings in various social contexts is a prerequisite for the understanding of man" and is readily provided by survey but not by laboratory methods. Katz's argument is persuasive and documented by many examples that enlarge and elevate psychological thought. The title of his essay indicates that Katz is describing the "*potential* of survey methods in psychological research" as well as "the practice" of surveys in current psychology. These methods may not be omnipresent or omnipotent as yet, but the paper certainly fills one with expectations of the better psychology that could be founded upon the creative use of survey methods.

Evidence from so judicious a psychologist as Katz cannot be construed as special pleading. However one might define the particular field of "political psychology," it surely is located at the intersection of political science and psychology. Thus, the McClosky and Katz essays taken jointly suggest how powerful survey methods can be for political psychology specifically, and we shall draw freely on their many ideas in this paper.

The skeptic may still reserve judgment. He might argue that McClosky and Katz, as contributors to a volume on survey research in the social sciences, necessarily presented the method in too prominent a light. Then he should weigh the evidence in David Sears' chapter on political behavior in the *Handbook of Social Psychology* (1969). That assignment did not compel any special attention to survey research. The essay is a substantive presentation of findings on electoral and public opinion processes treated from a social-psychological perspective. Yet Sears remarks, "Almost all the studies cited are *survey* studies rather than experimental studies" (p. 316, italics added). The past accomplishments of the method, its proven power to illuminate the field, compelled his attention. A sense of the historical growth of survey method and its intimate relation to the development of political psychology is provided by comparisons of the three editions of the *Handbook of Social Psychology*, spanning more than a thirty-year period. The 1954 edition contained a chapter, "The Psychology of Voting: An Analysis of Political Behavior" (Lipset and others, Vol. 2, pp. 1124–1175), which also leans heavily, but not exclusively, on evidence from surveys. The first edition, published in 1935 (K. C. Murchison, ed.), contained no chapter whatsoever on "political behavior" although it did contain a classic essay on attitudes by Gordon Allport. In part the discipline was oriented then toward different substantive problems, but any attempted chapter would have had little empirical evidence to draw upon, since the rise of the modern sample survey (in the late 1930s) postdates that edition.

One should ponder the next passage in Sears' preface: "Experimental research on political behavior is quite feasible, and has been attempted on occasion. It is to be hoped that those occasions will become more frequent" (p. 316). A chorus of readers may well chant: A paradox, a paradox, a most ingenious paradox. If experimental research on political behavior is "quite feasible," why has it been so occasional in the past? Perhaps the mystery is easily solved. Perhaps it is so far from feasible in its classic laboratory form that most scholars do not attempt it, and those that do often produce something trivial or grotesque. A reading of the essay by Katz (1967) will suggest the inherent obstacles to a laboratory-based and experimentally oriented *social* psychology. His analysis is equally applicable to a political psychology. In his words, "Many psychological problems do not lend themselves to laboratory manipulation, either because of the time dimension, the complexity of variables, or the power of the social manipulation" (p. 150). But the roots of the difficulty, in his judgment, lie deeper yet—in the classical experimentalist's fundamental conceptions, which lead him to emphasize purity and aridity of formulation and to disregard variations in subjects and problems of sampling people and their environing conditions. No doubt it is these many obstacles that account for Sears' inability to find many useful experimental studies to draw upon.

Sears indirectly sharpens our awareness of a singular virtue of survey research on political psychology—its feasibility. The virtue, of course, could be a vice if political psychologists become enticed by the sheer feasibility into the habitual and excessive use of a method for which they were inadequately trained or which itself suffered from serious deficiencies. Such dangers cannot be ignored. There have been many surveys that were poorly conceived but all too easily undertaken and badly executed. However, such studies as *The American Voter* (Campbell and others, 1960), *The People's Choice* (Lazarsfeld, Berelson, and Gaudet, 1944), *Negroes and the New Southern Politics* (Matthews and Prothro, 1966), *The Responsible Electorate* (Key, 1966), *Union Democracy* (Lipset, Trow, and Coleman, 1956), *Personality and Social Change* (Newcomb, 1943), *Communism, Conformity, and Civil Liberties* (Stouffer, 1955), *The Development of Political Attitudes in Children* (Hess and Torney, 1967), *Children and Politics* (Greenstein, 1965), *The Civic Culture* (Almond and Verba, 1963)—and these are only a small selection—surely establish that the method does not suffer from severe inherent deficiencies. As we shall argue, in concurrence with the three judges and as these vivid exhibits convey, surveys are indeed powerful weapons. They are omnipresent because their feasibility and desirability make them attractive to many scholars.

Nature of Surveys

Exactly what has been adjudged so powerful? Survey research seems to rule the realm of political psychology. Perhaps this is only an illusion arising from a looseness of definition, the accomplishments that properly belong to other methods being credited to a "survey" because we have assimilated them all under one broad and false label. By a detailed and restrictive definition of a survey, we shall appraise its powers better.

A survey is an inquiry of a large number of people, selected by rigorous sampling, conducted in normal life settings by explicit, standardized procedures yielding quantitative measurements. It belongs to the larger class of field methods and is in sharp contrast to the experiment carried out in the artificial setting of the laboratory. It is the total *constellation* of features of this particular field method that makes it powerful. All work together to ensure the desirable property, and all of them are essential.

The ability to study large numbers of people in their varied and normal life settings yields that "naturalistic description of the behavior of human beings in various social contexts" that Katz stresses as important for the growth of psychology. The rigorous sampling, plus the large numbers, permits one to generalize about the population or universe under study with a minimum of error. Although the universe can be a specialized, *relatively* homogeneous, and geographically concentrated population, often it is a widely dispersed, heterogeneous mass of people. Under these conditions rigorous sampling is essential if only to make it possible to cover the multitudes efficiently, economically, and accurately. Even with the economies introduced by sampling, it usually is a large and costly enterprise. The large numbers also permit one to refine or differentiate the descriptions, to break down the mass and describe the varied patterns in different social contexts and groups, and to use further modes of analysis developed for examining the processes and causes underlying phenomena.

To approach large numbers of people spread far and wide in their normal settings, the investigator must employ a large field staff—each with his own idiosyncrasies and remote from central control. Consequently, the procedures must be explicit and standardized—partly to make the unwieldy apparatus operate efficiently but mainly to instruct and ensure the proper functioning of the staff. The standardization of procedures also reduces uncertainty, ensuring that all know the operational definitions of the entities being studied and that the original and other investigators can subject the same problem to repeated study, thus providing confirmatory tests and evidence on processes of change over time. The standardization of measurements on the individuals in the single or repeated surveys ensures that one can evaluate comparisons unambiguously, confident in his judgment that any differences are real and not artifacts of varied procedures applied to the contrasted persons.

Any study of a large number of individuals is bound to generate a large volume of data. But surveys typically study many variables or characteristics for each unit, ensuring a multifaceted description and tests of the multiple and complex causes of a phenomenon. The volume of data increases geometrically. Quantitative measurement is essential if only to compress the bulky material into comprehensible and manageable form, but it also makes for exactitude of description and permits a great many statistical and analytic procedures to be applied.

What about methods that lack some of the specified features? If they are conducted in a natural setting, they certainly are "field methods." They have that much in common with a survey, but they should be labeled accurately—for instance, as case studies, community studies, or field experiments. By our definition, they are not surveys. A study with so few cases that it is almost an invisible entity might be called a "minisurvey" but it is really no survey at all, just as a miniskirt at its best is almost no skirt at all. A field study involving substantial numbers of cases but lacking the rigor of sampling or standardized procedure or quantitative measurement might be called a "quasi-survey," but if it is devoid of all such safeguards, it is really no survey at all and should be labeled a "pseudosurvey."

Minisurveys and quasi-surveys, even pseudosurveys, may lead to discoveries. Indeed, history documents the lasting contributions that such methods, on occasion, have made to political psychology. Lasswell's pioneering study *Psychopathology and Politics* (1930) provides a vivid example. At best it was a minisurvey of some unknown but small number of cases, but it was a work of discovery and deep exploration. By our stringent definition, the contributions of all such field methods to political psychology cannot be credited to the accounts of the survey method. But the deficiencies of such methods should be acknowledged. That they are surrounded by uncertainty and risk cannot be doubted, and the safety and generalizability that accrue only when the true survey in its entirety is operated should be recognized.

Those who launch their own small voyages of discovery and exploration, equipped with inexpensive and flexible methodological tools, might liken the survey to a giant fishing expedition lumbering across the sea of humanity, creaking along on a regimented inexorable schedule. The fishing net might seem so gross and crude that much would slip through its grid and be lost to science; strung so close to the surface that nothing at a subterranean depth would be caught; stretched so rigidly along a predetermined course that it could never be cast in some new direction to make an important catch that had been unexpectedly sighted. A master fisherman despite limited resources might spot some promising little pool in that great sea, drop a line to a deeper depth, and with patience, flexibility, and skill make a great scientific catch.

In terms of the image, Lasswell was a master fisherman. Indeed, an ardent fisherman can move from pool to pool, enlarging the richness and variety of his catch. Riesman and Glazer (1952) in their case studies of character and politics did just that—fishing for a while in Vermont, then in the backwaters of Chicago, and then off the East River at 99th Street in New York City. A diligent and patient fisherman can even return again to the same little pool, spending hours exploring its deeper depths. Lane (1959a) in his case study of political belief did just that, spending fifteen hours with each of fifteen men drawn from a special pool in an eastern industrial city which contained only white, married, native American, working- and lower-middle-class men.

The metaphor, however, conveys too rosy a picture of these other methods. In 1930 no one knew in what exact pool Lasswell had done his fishing and how he had drawn and caught the fish. No one could anchor his findings. They simply floated somewhere in the great sea of humanity, and only through the accident of an "After-Thought Thirty Years Later" (Lasswell, 1960) do we obtain some vague clues to their social location. His little pool of cases was only a drop in the ocean of humanity. What if he had fished in other waters?

Minisurveys and pseudosurveys are at best suggestive. Whether they are deep and wide explorations that yield true discoveries must be confirmed by more rigorous methods. That crude methods can stimulate ideas—some of which later prove to be good and others misleading—and that minisurveys should be buttressed by major surveys are the points to be noted.

Variety of Surveys

The genuine survey should not be seen in terms of one stereotyped image. Much latitude and a great variety of surveys are possible. The size of sample, the nature of the universe, the research design, and the instruments can all be chosen so as to create that one special inquiry best suited to one's purse and purpose. One is not limited to a *single* survey. A set of surveys, varied in character so as to complement each other or phased over time, may form the component parts of a larger inquiry. Nor is one limited to surveys alone. Other methods and surveys can be combined into a multiform inquiry, yielding the combined advantages of the several methods and attenuating the errors peculiar to each. Consider some of the possibilities.

The inexpensive minisurvey and the costly giant survey on an entire nation are but two polar types. The national survey—better yet, the survey of several national populations—approaches the study of mankind in all its generality, describes humans over the widest range of social contexts. Thus, it is a form of inquiry to be cherished. But if one cannot afford five thousand cases, a national survey limited to a sample of one thousand may be more than adequate for one's purposes and within one's means. If one's resources are too meager for that, but the problem calls for only a few measures, the institution of *the amalgam or caravan national survey* now provides a practicable approach. One buys only a little piece of the periodic national surveys that the major agencies conduct, paying only a small portion of the total cost, which is divided among the several parties who have amalgamated their interests.

If one cannot afford the out-of-pocket costs for a piece of a new national survey, or if one's problem is not amenable to that design, the strategy of *secondary analysis* provides an even more economical solution. Within the thousands of surveys already conducted and conveniently accessible in various archives—many of them national in scope—may be contained the data appropriate to one's problem, and the costs of fielding a new survey are completely obviated. But those investigators who are forced or wish to conduct a new minisurvey or larger survey of a specialized group may also profit greatly by combining their narrower study with the secondary analysis of national surveys, a design that one might label *semisecondary analysis,* since it blends the old and the new together. The national data provide statistical norms for evaluating one's crude or limited sampling and empirical points of comparison that stop the investigator from making *pseudocomparative* inferences, simply using his imagination to fill in the cell that is contrasted with his own cases but that he has not in fact studied.

Old surveys may also provide sampling frames for the selection of individuals from what would otherwise be a most elusive population to locate and sample on one's own. By using the old surveys as such a "locator device," one may sometimes incidentally obtain measurements over time for a panel study, the first wave of measurements costing one nothing. By these and other applications of semisecondary analyses, the lone, poor scholar can use old surveys to strengthen his own studies. (See Hyman, 1972a.)

The riches of the archives far surpass most investigators' dream of wealth. Make the extreme assumption, however, that none of the *old* surveys can provide the particular sampling frame or statistical norm or empirical point of comparison that an investigator needs. Then (as mentioned above) the scholar can buy into an amalgam survey, "piggybacking" the few questions at little cost just to create the special sampling frame or norm or empirical point of comparison he needs.

Strategic Universes. The national survey—whether old or new, giant or medium in size, financed in one way or another, used exclusively or as an auxiliary— is but one large class of surveys. A genuine survey, just like a minisurvey or case study, can be sharply focused on a narrow geographical area, a community, or a specialized population of individuals, whether concentrated or spread throughout the body politic. One then studies his problem in its most strategic site but by the rigorous methods of a survey. Everyone who knows that classic survey *The People's Choice* (Lazarsfeld, Berelson, and Gaudet, 1944) remembers the findings and the panel design employed, but few recall or ponder the fact that it was restricted to several panels of about six-hundred individuals living in Erie County, Ohio (mainly in the little city of Sandusky), in 1940. What an odd choice. What strategy was behind it? "This county was chosen because it was small enough to permit close supervision of the interviewers, because it was relatively free from sectional peculiarities, because it was not dominated by any large urban center although it did furnish an opportunity to compare rural political opinion with opinion in a small urban center, and because for forty years—in every presidential election in the twentieth century—it had deviated very little from the national voting trends" (p. 3). The findings were strengthened by the large sampling and rigorous methods applied to this strategic universe. Nevertheless, the investigators were concerned about their generalizability beyond that narrow place and point in time. So they chose a second restricted universe, Elmira, New York, and surveyed its population in 1948 (Berelson, Lazarsfeld, and McPhee, 1954). If one large-scale survey has that much vulnerability, we must recognize that a minisurvey would be even more vulnerable.

If we accept the risk of narrowing our findings in order to sharpen them, there are many possibilties for surveys of restricted but strategic universes. Depending on the availability of the sampling frames, the geographical concentration of the units, and their accessibility, the costs of inquiry may be modest. One example will make the case in its true complexity. Jaros, Hirsch, and Fleron (1968) conducted a survey of a sample of 305 children drawn from the universe of rural public school children in grades 5–12 in 1967 in Knox County, Kentucky. Certainly the individuals within the scope of the inquiry were geographically concentrated, easily accessible, and measured by simple means that were most economical: standardized paper-and-pencil instruments administered in the classroom by the teacher. Indeed, to make it feasible, "a few schools, not accessible by road, did not participate. . . . The cost of including them would have been very high" (p. 566n). Cheap it was, but what an exotic choice of universe. What commended it was that it typified the isolated, rural, impoverished region of Appalachia, a subculture sharply contrasted in its family structure and ideology with majority America; there, the investigators expected to find a pattern of political socialization at variance with those earlier reported—a pattern with a much more "malevolent" content. The further restriction to the children in the area was apposite with the developmental concerns of the study.

For the sake of the argument, turn history back and assume that this survey had been done ten years earlier, *prior* to the time when Greenstein (1965) studied the political socialization of children in New Haven, or Hess and Easton (1960) studied it in Chicago, or Jennings and Niemi (1968a, 1968b) studied it in national sample surveys. Then, however strategic the universe and rigorous the survey, the restriction to the one site with its emphatic cultural tone would have created the risk of a pseudocomparative conclusion, in which the investigators filled in the other cells with imaginary data, much more "benevolent" in tone. Or, conceivably, they might have run the risk of overgeneralizing their findings, seeing Appalachia as the microcosm of the nation and projecting upon the nation as a whole the malevolent patterns they had documented in one area. The existence of the other surveys was what protected them, and they properly located their findings by reference to the statistical norms provided.

One might point the moral that the best time to start a restricted survey is only after someone else has provided a norm. Scientists who pioneer in surveying limited, however strategic, universes—if they are conservative—would seem to have to wait to generalize until they extend their own surveys, or until someone else subsequently does it for them. But they can also follow the strategies already mentioned—creating their own norms through piggybacking, or finding them through diligent searching of the archives and secondary analysis. Indeed, much evidence on the political ideologies of children, based on nationwide sampling, did exist years before this survey and had, in fact, been used in an early secondary analysis of political socialization (Hyman, 1959).

One restricts a survey to one geographical site often with the intent to describe some political-psychological pattern in a strategic group and then to relate that pattern to its sociocultural context by supplementary observations of the community. In this respect, such a study combines the rigor and breadth of a survey with some of the depth of the classical community study. The inquiry partakes of the kind of political social psychology or the political anthropology one finds, for example, in Banfield's (1958) study of the culture and politics of an Italian community, although the observations are not based on a prolonged period of field work. Indeed, a community survey that does not provide such an interpretive background is not exploiting its full advantages. So, for example, the changes among the individuals surveyed in Elmira could be seen not only in terms of the larger temporal context of the 1948 presidential campaigns, as revealed by the panel design, but also in the context of the local institutions, as revealed by conventional field work in the community (Berelson, Lazarsfeld, and McPhee, 1954). A survey researcher has much to gain by this particular multimethod design. In this particular form, however, the single-community survey leaves one uneasy and for the very same reasons as does the conventional community study. The connections are simply woven together by the discerning analyst into a plausible pattern. It is proof by juxtaposition, and really another example of the *pseudo*comparative design, since the analyst is making the assumption that the behavior of the individuals located in a contrasted cell or community which he has not studied would be different.

The empirical survey of a second community, or a third, would make it truly a comparative design, and the scientific gains would certainly repay the increased costs. But if the investigator cannot afford the expenditures for such a semirestricted inquiry, there are ways to operate the single-community survey so as to strengthen the tests of sociocultural factors. *The* community is a whole only because the investigator has perceived it that way. Look at it another way. It is composed of neighborhoods, each with its distinctive institutions and subculture. And since any survey involves a large sample, the population of each type of little community within the larger community has presumably been sampled adequately, or by proper planning can be. The investigator really has a series of surveys; by collecting the background information on each smaller context, he can thus conduct the comparative tests required. In this fashion, Katz and Eldersveld (1961) examined the influence of the precinct political organization and of the ethnic and class composition of the neighborhood on political behavior in a single survey restricted to Detroit. The example is chosen advisedly, since such a conglomerate as Detroit obviously contains many contrasted communities and is perceived as a unity only because of the grossness of our vision and the narrowness of our focus on a few overarching institutions.

The amount of background information required may seem to make this design too costly. But it can be carried out in an efficient and relatively economical way: the same interviewers who conduct the survey can function as a large crew of field workers to collect the background data on their respective neighborhoods. And if one chooses his community wisely, all the background information on the neighborhood units may already be available in convenient form, and no costs or labors for special collection of the information are involved. For example, a wide array of such information for small neighborhoods in Los Angeles County is now on file in the UCLA Political Behavior Archives (Marvick and Bayes, 1969). Indeed, the existence of such information makes a particular community a strategic site for a survey, apart from any theoretical preconceptions about its being a fruitful place to examine some problem. Both the practical and the theoretical are coordinates for locating strategic sites for community surveys.

Just as one can reorganize his perception of a single-community survey, one can perceive a nationwide survey in a new light. It is not only a single survey of one giant collectivity but also many surveys of the series of smaller collectivities contained within it—of sixty counties, six giant cities, or fifteen or thirty largish cities. By subdividing and then regrouping these territorial units into types, one has many cases for testing contextual hypotheses and a wide range of values on the contextual variables. The background information on the different places can be collected efficiently by the regular crew of interviewers from local documentary sources, observation, or from interviews with key informants (see Hyman, 1945), or may already exist in some convenient compendium about the nation and its subdivisions. By sensitivity to such possibilities, W. Miller (1956)—simply by subdividing national survey data already in hand by county units—was able to demonstrate that the political behavior of individuals with the *same personal characteristics* varies according to the party that dominates their particular environment. Such tests can now be accomplished economically and efficiently by secondary analysis for contextual units of particular size and for particular characteristics of such units. Turk's (1969, 1970) "Large City Data File" at the University of Southern California contains information on over 300 variables that characterize 130 American cities with populations of over 100,000. The archives of the Interuniversity Consortium for Political Research contain information on all counties in the United States, including their historical characteristics over the last 150 years. The national survey may thus be regarded as doubly desirable. It can describe patterns with utmost generality, over the broadest kind of environment, and it can also serve to examine the way processes operate in varied smallish environments. The restricted survey can be subdivided also, but there is no magic by which it can be made to grow beyond its limited boundaries.

The survey of the restricted site does, however, have one hidden advantage for the political psychologist, if only he is sharp enough to note a subtle feature of the design and to exploit valuable data that are normally buried within such a survey. Without benefit of small-group research, he can study small-group interactions within his narrow survey. Since the *large* sample of one *small* community tends to saturate the population with interviews, by chance he has probably sampled many interacting individuals in that community, several members of many of the primary groups. Automatically he has evidence from the parties in such social transactions, if only he meshes the data from those who are in fact partners. By contrast, in a national survey, no matter how big the sample, the cases are spread too thin to catch many partners. One may feel that even in a community survey the yield of partners is likely to be too few if simply left to chance. Special sampling designs, however, have been developed for increasing the yield (Coleman, 1958) from a given size of sample. The instruments and coding must also be designed so as to locate the partners, and can be sharpened so as to enrich the evidence on the relations between such individuals and their perceptions of one another.

Sometimes investigators restrict their surveys to one or more communities not in order to see the psychological patterns in the population from the perspective of particular environments but for the opposite reason: to see some community event or occurrence against the background of the population's psychological patterns. For example, the fifteen cities included in surveys sponsored by the Kerner Commission had had varied experiences of recent civil disorders, and the surveys were quickly set in motion to reveal some of the psychological forces that had created these events—although, to be sure, the longer *prior* history of each community was also used as context to explain the patterns in the population (Campbell and Schuman, 1968).

Thus far, our illustrations of strategic universes for study have been in terms of their geographical extent and location. Obviously, other principles guide one to a strategic universe. A few illustrations suggest both the variety of other possibilities and the ways in which a survey can be focused on a specified group. A political scientist comes naturally to the thought that the power a group exercises make it a strategic universe for a survey. Surveys of political elites seem more consequential than are surveys of ordinary men, and the *political,* as well as the theoretical and the practical, provides a principle for locating strategic universes. One can easily make elites the *exclusive* object of attention in a survey (see, for example, Hunt, Crane, and Wahlke, 1964), but such an approach then relegates the rank and file to an object worthy of *no* attention from surveyors. Sensibly, the two groups are often incorporated into the same large inquiry, the findings about each being regarded as *complementary parts* of the total picture. Thus, Stouffer (1955) surveyed political intolerance in the 1950s, not only in a sample of about five thousand ordinary Americans, representative of the national adult population, but also in a sample of about fifteen hundred individuals who held offices in the local governments and major voluntary associations in each of the cities where his rank-and-file sample lived. In the analysis, the two groups often were compared, just as the children of Appalachia were compared with children in New Haven and Chicago. But the implicit model is somewhat different. It is not as if two surveys of *independent,* contrasted groups had been done, simply for some informative test. The elite and the mass in the same town presumably interacted with each other, complemented each other, in some complex way that jointly determined the patterns of intolerance manifested in the 1950s. Surveys of complementary samples thus have a similarity to community surveys of interacting partners, although the former can be operated on a grand scale across very wide geographical universes and the interactive processes under study do not necessarily operate through the same direct intimate relations.

Other vivid exhibits show the varied models of complementarity that can shape the design. Shortly after the 1958 election, using a national sample of all constituencies, Stokes and Miller (1962) conducted a survey of the electorate and complementary surveys of the incumbent congressman and other major party candidates from the same set of districts. The model is explicit: "Through these direct interviews with the persons playing the reciprocal roles of representative government, this research has sought careful evidence about the perceptual ties that bind, or fail to bind, the congressman to his party and districts" (p. 532).

A national survey of the Turkish peasantry (Frey, 1963) provides an exotic example of the general design. Within each of the approximately four hundred villages from which the peasant sample had been drawn, four elite individuals were chosen and surveyed: the secular official who headed the village and his wife; the religious head and his wife. The implicit model was one of influence and interaction that flowed through several channels, women being linked to the elite mostly via other women, and men and women being influenced by both the religious and secular elites.

A last and somewhat different example is provided by the national surveys of political socialization (Jennings and Niemi, 1968a), where—in addition to the main sample of high school youth, complementary *sub*samples of the teachers, fathers, and mothers of the children, elites of a sort, were also surveyed. Thus, both the subjects and the agents of socialization were studied, and the several sets of findings could be dovetailed to provide a more comprehensive understanding of the process. By drawing unbiased *sub*samples of the various complementary groups, rather than samples of equal size, the investigators introduced an economy into the design without jeopardizing the conclusions.

These several studies, particularly Stouffer's survey, suggest a valuable set of distinctions and will lead us to a fourth principle for choosing strategic universes, and to even more general matters of research design and questionnaire construction. Although Stouffer's leaders were elite (since they exercised control over many other individuals and large organizations, and since they possessed unusual competence), instructions and questions put to them did not cast them symbolically into a performance of their public roles or a rendition of their knowledge about governmental and other institutions and constituencies in the community. They were reporting on themselves, about their *private* feelings and thoughts and preferences. Admittedly, they were also asked about their *perception* of the world; but this, like the other variables, was treated as psychological stuff, not as objective information. By a strict interpretation of these data, one must say that we have learned only about private character, not public performance. To be sure, this is in no sense unimportant evidence. It was an advised research decision to seek out this level of data. Certainly, as Lasswell suggested long ago, the psyches of these very important persons must in some degree be irrepressible and invade their public life; but it is also true that "good" people can be inhibited and corrupted by the social forces pressing on them when they have to function in some public arena. The tolerance toward nonconformity of Stouffer's elite might have been quite different if the entire inquiry had been structured so as to make the public part of their lives salient to them.

Stouffer's elite also had unique and prolonged opportunities to observe many other local people and the organized life of the community, and in some degree were very superior persons (gifted, educated, trained to be sensitive) and had unusual access to recorded sources of information. If the inquiry had been structured differently, they could have been cast in the role of *informant,* not respondent, instructed to tell as objectively as possible—even with the aid of their records—about others rather than about themselves. Admittedly, the investigator can end up on somewhat shaky ground. One can easily establish that humans are fallible observers and that perceptions are guided by need. But one can validate such reports in surveys in four ways: by choosing as a strategic universe those whose credentials establish some special competence and history of opportunity to acquire the requisite knowledge; by drawing large samples of informants, whose reports can be consolidated and used as checks upon one another; by creating the mental set toward objectivity through the line of questioning; and by using internal tests of the degree to which these inform- ants' reports are correlated with measures of their psychic dispositions, rather than informed by their respective levels of competence (see, for example, Hyman, Levine, and Wright, 1967).

Surveys of informants remind us that the method is flexible enough to be operated in ways that resemble the classic procedure of anthropology and com- munity study, although the informants are drawn by a rigorous sampling design, their number is much larger, and the investigator's contact with each informant is briefer. There is no survey that does not contain at least some minimal element of the role of informant. But the role is rarely maximized in survey research. Even in surveys of elites and populations that have some special competence, the respondent role is generally made to predominate. Parents and teachers in surveys of political socializa- tion could be construed as competent informants about the children, about the transactions in the family unit or in the classroom, but more frequently are treated as respondents whose *own* ideologies are measured. One could, of course, have a different mix within each interview in such surveys, or one could use separate *sub- samples* as informants and respondents respectively. For example, Hess and Torney (1967) drew a complementary sample of about four hundred teachers of the classes from whom the children were drawn, and their "attitudes were measured to com- pare their responses with those of their students and to assess [inferentially] their influence on the attitudes of the younger subjects" (p. 237). In addition, a subsample of 169 teachers were cast as *informants,* and the "role of the school in socializing children" was determined by a "curriculum questionnaire," which contained such questions as how much time was spent on each of a series of topics, whether the teaching was planned or incidental, or whether flags and other patriotic symbols were displayed in the classroom, the reports implicitly being accepted as factual descriptions of the schools.

The last example will also suggest some additional valuable distinctions. Sur- veys are usually conceived of as studies that focus on *individuals,* taken singly or in great numbers. But the individuals sampled may be only the vehicles of the study, carrying us toward an ultimate *target* universe which has never been directly meas- ured. That target universe may be another population of individuals, or it may be a set of *collectivities* (family units, organizations, or institutions), as in the example of the classroom and the schools. The use of informants as vehicles permits surveys to describe collectivities. The sampling of respondents who are members of a collectivity permits us, by addition, to describe it, if we use the model that it is an aggregation.

Instruments. The discussion of the role an individual assumes in a survey brings us directly to the topic of questionnaire design. Although our definition re- quires that every survey incorporate explicit standardized procedures that yield quantitative measurements, there is still room for great variation in the instruments employed. No one should be misled by the stereotyped image of a "poll," in which only a few questions in fixed-alternative form are asked. Not all surveys are that rudimentary. Although there are limits to the patience of people, it is common and practicable for surveys to include sixty to one hundred questions, some with sub-questions. By the power of words and memory, the respondent's past, present, and view of the future can be encompassed in the lavish list of questions. Different realms of experience—the cognitive, affective, conative—can be explored and many variables studied simultaneously. If one question will not suffice for valid and reliable measurement of a variable, a battery or scale can be constructed. Our definition calls for quantitative measurement but does not demand that *all* the data be translated into that form. Surveys commonly supplement quantitative description and analysis with qualitative case materials—background reports by interviewers, comments, protocols, brief profiles, illustrative quotations from individual questionnaires—to enrich the findings. The questionnaire can combine various procedures. Some questions may be closed and force all respondents to express their individuality in terms of the few alternative categories provided, but some are open-ended and supplemented by probes so as to allow individuals to express their views in depth and detail and in their very own words and style. The survey researcher of long ago who invented that classic opener "What you are about to say interests me very much" was being witty, but he was also making a serious point. The stimulus clearly is standardized but sure leaves plenty of room for individuality. The responses could even be quantified or counted under categories, although it would be hell to build the code.

A single interview with an elaborate questionnaire can be long and searching, but recall also that some designs involve more than one encounter with a respondent. We tend to think of the *seven* interviews with the panel of respondents in Sandusky as discrete points of comparison over time, but if we add all seven together it makes one very lengthy unified inquiry into a person's views. We tend to focus on the *core* inquiry in Almond and Verba's *The Civic Culture* (1963), in which about one thousand respondents in each of five countries were asked almost one hundred questions, not an insubstantial instrument. But we may forget that small subsamples of about one hundred respondents in each of the countries were *re*interviewed at a later date and asked an additional 130 questions in a "political life-history interview." Although a survey researcher must make his procedures explicit and standardized *for his interviewers,* they do not have to be uniform over the *grand total* of all respondents. They should be uniform over those subclasses whose measured characteristics will be compared, so as to reduce ambiguity in the inferences. As long as the investigator prescribes what variations will be introduced when, he can safely interpret his findings. There is flexibility, but it is controlled by him. By their design, Almond and Verba reached the depths they sought, but economically and without burdening all respondents. They needed only a small staff of skilled depth interviewers to cover the subsamples.

Survey researchers have been unusually creative in inventing or adapting instruments for use with large samples of ordinary individuals. The political psychologist should borrow liberally from what is already available, thereby saving himself the hard labor of instrument design and getting in the bargain an instrument whose properties have already been established plus statistical norms from other times and populations. Many verbal instruments are listed, critically reviewed, and findings therefrom summarized conveniently in a set of three handbooks developed by Robinson and his associates (1968, 1969).

The following examples illustrate the variety of *verbal* instruments that can be incorporated into surveys of the general population. Thorndike and Gallup (1944) developed two parallel forms of a steeply graded, multiple-choice, twenty-word vocabulary test which they were able to use on a sample of 3000 adults as a measure of verbal intelligence. Morgan and his associates (see Robinson, 1968, pp. 154–158) developed a thirty-five-item composite instrument, containing four subscales, to measure "a modernism syndrome" or a "concern with progress." Stouffer developed a fifteen-item Guttman-type scale to measure tolerance of political nonconformity (Robinson, 1968, pp. 163–164). McClosky (see Robinson, 1968, pp. 170–178) developed a sixty-five-item composite instrument, containing subscales, to measure a syndrome of "democratic or antidemocratic attitudes." Matthews and Prothro developed a Guttman-type scale to measure political participation; this scale was used in a survey of eleven southern states (Robinson, 1968, pp. 429–430). Campbell and his associates developed four- and five-item scales to measure sense of citizen duty and political efficacy; these scales have been used in a series of Michigan national surveys and thus provide many norms (Robinson, 1968, pp. 459–462). Short versions of the F scale to measure authoritarianism, based on from four to ten items, have been used successfully by the Survey Research Center and also the National Opinion Research Center on a series of surveys (Robinson, 1969, pp. 262–270). Finally, Christie's "Machiavellianism" scale has been adapted for use in national samples (Robinson, 1969, pp. 506–516).

Survey researchers, however, have not limited themselves to conventional verbal instruments. All sorts of other approaches have been applied successfully. Vicary (1948) adapted that classic instrument the word-association test; by giving his test to subjects a second time, he was able to assess stability of performance. The ancient tradition of constitutional psychology inspired Stapel (1947–48) to obtain interviewer ratings of body type, and corollary ratings of temperament, on six national surveys in the Netherlands. The estimates were highly stable from survey to survey, and the ratings of temperament were not biased by the interviewer's own temperament. Although this is an unusual example, the use of interviewers to make all sorts of observational judgments and ratings of the respondents is exceedingly common, and represents an assessment based generally on many clues, verbal and behavioral, in the course of the interview. By contrast, survey researchers sometimes base such ratings on the overall reading of the entire interview after it is turned into the office, treating it as a kind of clinical protocol but without benefit of first-hand observation. An unusual example of the joint use of both "holistic" rating methods can be found in the surveys of the German population at the end of World War II, where they were employed successfully in the assessment of the respondent's identification with Nazism (Peak, 1945).

Robinson and Hefner (1968) applied a procedure reminiscent of classic concept-formation tests in experimental and clinical psychology to a large sample in Detroit. Subjects were given a list of nations and asked to group together those that they judged to be similar, thus describing the ordinary man's "perceptual map" of the world. By supplementary questions and inference, the investigators established the dimensions or concepts underlying the groupings. Various forms of the instrument, listing different nations, were rotated over a series of *equivalent* subsamples. This split-ballot design has many useful applications. When contrasted types of respondents are examined, procedures (as earlier noted) must be uniform. Otherwise, both instrument variation and respondent variation confound the interpretation. But if respondents are made equivalent, varying the ballot provides an unambiguous test of the contribution of the instrument. This one methodological use of the general procedure is enough to suggest that the measuring instruments in surveys can be calibrated.[1] In this same study, and in many other surveys, the Semantic Differential (Osgood, Suci, and Tannenbaum, 1957) was also found to be applicable in surveys of the general population.

For use in a national survey, Veroff and his associates (1960) adapted the Thematic Apperception Test for assessing need for achievement, affiliation, and power. Greenstein and Tarrow (1970) used a story-completion method in a cross-national survey of political socialization. Graphic materials (for example, in the shape of thermometers or ladders) have been used to obtain ratings and judgments of magnitude. Pictorial materials have been used, sometimes as projective tests (see Chapter Fifteen in this volume) but also to reduce ambiguity surrounding an ordinary question, to present an otherwise ineffable stimulus to the average respondent or a complex concept to a verbally unsophisticated population, and to test aesthetic preferences (see, for example, Hess and Torney, 1967, pp. 234–235; DeFleur and DeFleur, 1967; Noelle and Neumann, 1967). Aesthetic preferences may seem remote from our topic, but such preferences for given kinds of pictorial stimuli could serve as an index of cultural modernity, of "bohemianism," or of ethnic identity, which would be useful to the political psychologist.

The split ballot creates opportunities for designing another kind of projective test, as illustrated in a study by Haire (1950). A brief shopping list of groceries was presented to subsamples of respondents, all being asked to describe the woman shopper who had supposedly made the list. The lists were systematically varied over the different but equivalent subsamples, a given commodity being rotated in and out of a list and other commodities being constant over all subjects. One is reminded of Asch's classic experimental studies of impressions of personality. The paradigm might well be used not with shopping lists but with a list of attributes or actions of nations or government officials, the subjects being asked to assess the importance of one component in the total impression.

This partial list of examples will suggest the many ways in which survey

[1] Other designs than the split ballot can, of course, be used to assess the quality of survey instruments. Panel studies, for example, provide automatic evidence of repeat reliability. Although opinions are changeable, some characteristics (such as age, place of birth, past education) are by definition unchangeable. Repeating the face-sheet items on a second wave of a panel thus reveals the amount of error in such measures, and such studies in the literature provide comforting evidence. On a single-shot survey, an investigator may deliberately reinterview a small subsample after a very brief interval of time, in order to estimate the stability of response, making the assumption that attitudes and other psychological characteristics, although changeable over *long* intervals, should not be subject to capricious short-term fluctuations. Following this design, Hess and Torney (1967) retested a 10 percent subsample of their original twelve thousand children after an interval of from four to fourteen days, and computed stability coefficients.

instruments can explore the psyche of the ordinary man. One should not think, however, that a survey has to be excessively psychologistic or that the measurements must be exclusively subjective in origin. As has already been noted, in designs that are contextual *objective* information on the individual's environment obtained from independent sources can be merged with his subjective reports. And in surveys that sample strategic populations of known character (for example, government officials, school children, registrants in particular parties, members of organizations) objective information on each individual sampled, known from records or simply by virtue of membership in the specified universe, can also be merged with his subjective report.

The examples presented are not typical of the routine, unimaginative survey. But in the hands of ingenious investigators, the survey is an instrument that is most pliable. There are constraints, however. It should be stressed that the ability to intrude upon ordinary people in the course of their normal lives and to elicit the measurements is dependent on consent and cooperation. (In only very rare instances —such as the United States Census, and even here the sanctions are very rarely applied—are respondents legally compelled to participate. Thus, one might define almost any survey as "an inquiry involving voluntary cooperation.") There are limits to what the people allow, and ethical constraints on what the surveyors should attempt or perpetrate.

What is allowed varies with time and place and topic but does set limits on the power of survey methods to explore particular problems. A recent report, somewhat far afield, provides an example. For attempting a survey among university students in Madrid to discover what young people know about sex, Nicholas Caparros was accused of conducting a "shameful survey," subjected to a police investigation, charged with creating a public scandal, and then faced trial and a six-month jail sentence (Rome, *Daily American,* December 15, 1971, p. 4:7). Such a case is perhaps irrelevant to the progress of *political* surveys, but consider a more relevant datum. In their cross-national inquiry, Almond and Verba (1963, pp. 117–118) found that 32 percent of their sample of Italians interviewed in 1959 refused to report how they had voted in the last national election, and 31 percent refused to report their "usual local vote." The refusals were distributed about equally in all social strata, suggesting a prevailing societal norm. By contrast, in the American sample the magnitude of such refusals was between 1 and 2 percent. Fortunately, on the many topics of central interest other than voting, refusals were rare; and the refusals to report voting preferences could even be exploited to shed indirect light on one matter of central interest, the emotion and suspicion pervading Italian political culture. But those political psychologists who focus their surveys on voting would no doubt see such a situation in a gloomy light, and should treat it as a cautionary example.

Surveys as Experiments.   In reviewing the variety of surveys, although they have often been compared with other field methods, we have made no reference to field *experiments.* However, surveys can be incorporated into an experimental design, even though they take place outside the laboratory. Panel or trend surveys may be spaced deliberately around some major event, thus providing a *natural* experiment on a complex, prolonged, and powerful set of variables whose effects are inferred from the changes measured in the successive surveys and from collateral evidence reported by the respondents. Where the "treatment" is sufficiently circumscribed (for example, a local information campaign), a companion survey can be conducted in another untreated community, which functions as a control group, or available trend data from national surveys can be exploited for control group estimates.

Occasionally, surveys may even be incorporated into true *field* experiments, when some powerful agency deliberately manipulates some set of independent variables or program of social intervention in collaboration with a researcher who is geared to measure the effects by his surveys. The treatment may be allocated in some special arrangement, so that experimental and control or comparison groups are created, all to be surveyed as part of an elegant experimental design for measuring the net effects of manipulation. Indeed, evaluations of programs of social intervention might well be described as field experiments combined with survey measurements.

In these two ways, an experimentally oriented surveyor can test major *contemporary* variables which are beyond his personal powers of manipulation. But his control over the apparatus of the survey itself provides a *direct* way to create his own experiments within the course of a survey. A classic mode of manipulating variables in experimental social psychology is by verbal stimuli and instructions presented to the subjects. Surveyors occasionally employ the very same vehicle within a split-ballot design, applying variant stimuli to equivalent subsamples, communicating a passage of text to one group but not to another, introducing a proposition with the name of a prestigious and credible source in one group but not in another. The split ballot, although usually employed for methodological experiments on the influence of question wording (Noelle-Neumann, 1970), is readily converted to such substantive experiments. But although the approaches of the experimentalist and the surveyor can converge, in usual practice the surveyor moves in an opposite direction, exploiting his method not for an experiment but for its unique advantages: for discovering things he had never dreamed of, obtaining reliable and generalizable descriptions of the endless variety of social, psychological, and political patterns, and weighty, if not final, evidence on the processes moving through long courses of time and complex chains of causations that explain the patterns he has described.

Now consider the ways in which surveys can be exploited specifically for the study of political psychology.

Individual Differences and Total Political Character

Political psychology, however one might elaborate the details of the field, surely must mean the study of politics from the perspectives of psychology. The distinctive concern of psychology has always been the individual. Indeed, whole branches of the discipline (differential psychology, psychometrics) have been erected simply on the basis of the study and measurement of individual differences. Then it must follow—whether we realize it or not—that we are engaged in political psychology a great deal of the time when we conduct surveys, since they automatically yield reliable evidence on the distribution of individual characteristics.

The individual differences described in surveys do not necessarily have political relevance or psychological significance. For their own good reasons, some have surveyed individual differences in the taste for fancy cars or rock music; in belief in the devil, the malevolence of scientists, or the frailty of women; in preference for daylight saving time, pets, southern cooking, football, or hunting; in such behavior as buying on the installment plan or going to church. These examples and thousands more in no way deny the argument. If the political psychologist points his survey in the right direction, then it will describe individual differences that are relevant. Moreover, a great many completed surveys that seem devoid of political-psychological content should not be dismissed too quickly. The theorist who pauses long enough over them may sense some hidden significance and make a contribution to political psychology by the secondary analysis of what are trivia to less thoughtful minds.

The individual differences described by any inquiry are obviously dependent on the sample that is measured. With small or biased samplings and restricted or downright peculiar universes, an investigator may underestimate the variability in the population, judge something to be common when it is truly rare, or regard something as aberrant when it is truly ordinary among common men. He may miss important clues about its social location and correlates and spin out theories and research that are misguided. The survey, by virtue of its rigorous and large-scale sampling of the general population, automatically yields accurate evidence on the shape of the distribution of individual differences, on the extent of variability, on the modal pattern in the large and the differentiated patterns in various social contexts.

The *instruments,* of course, are as essential as the sample to the accurate description of individual differences. The mode may be displaced by a biased instrument, and the variability that can be documented is limited by the insensitivity of the measurements—people seemingly all the same or cut on a few models simply because the instrument cannot register the fine differences between them. But survey instruments are not as unrefined as some might think. Inspect the distribution of political activity among American adults, described by Woodward and Roper (1950) from a national survey more than twenty years ago. The scores, shown in Table 1, represent a composite of voting, membership in political organizations, communication with public officials, political-party campaign activity, and talking politics with friends. The instrument clearly distributes the population by fine gradations, and the obtained national distribution says a good deal about the nature of political man in America at mid-century.

Classic psychology, however, has concerned itself with man's *enduring* nature, although some branches are concerned with man's changeability. Political psychologists, whether guided by the one or the other concern, would follow the same line of inquiry, using their instruments on repeated surveys spread over time. What is stable and what is changeable are but the two sides of the same question, and the answer is readily bought with the same methodological coin. Table 2 presents partial distributions for various discrete political activities obtained in American national surveys conducted by the Survey Research Center during four presidential campaigns. Apart from the suggestion of a tiny secular trend, such data reveal that low levels of political activity are indeed a *stable* feature of modern American man. Such a finding also was implicit in the Woodward-Roper survey and was bought for less coinage than trend surveys demand. The question asked in a single survey can have a much broader temporal referent than the moment of inquiry. Thus, for example, Roper's respondents were asked whether they had *ever* communicated with a public official, not whether they had communicated only during that particular month.[2]

---

[2] We gloss over important questions of the reliability and validity of such measurements. An investigator who broadens the temporal referent of a question must, of course, ponder the risk that memory error is introduced. And any form of questioning presents

Table 1. DISTRIBUTION OF POLITICAL ACTIVITY OF
AMERICAN ADULTS BEFORE 1950

	Score on Woodward- Roper Scale	Percent
High Activity	12	.1
	11	.3
	10	.7
	9	1.2
	8	1.6
	7	2.4
	6	4.
	5	6.5
	4	10.3
	3	15.6
	2	19.
Low Activity	1	19.1
	0	19.2
		$N = 8000$

Psychology also has long been concerned with *universal* man, although, here again, such branches as social psychology are especially concerned with the way society and the group modify man. Again, these are but two sides of the same question. Cross-national surveys readily provide the comparative distributions needed, although such surveys are very expensive. By way of illustration, Table 3 presents contrasted distributions for one discrete form of political activity, "talking politics," in another society, Germany, based on many surveys by the Institute for Demoscopy. These data are not strictly comparable with the American findings, because of variations in the instruments, but are presented because the long time series provides an unusual illustration of the stability of these distributions. Despite all sorts of vicissitudes in German society and politics in the years 1952–1964, this feature of German political man persisted. As he entered the 1970s, however, a substantial change seems to have occurred, judging by the one recent point in the time series. Whether political conversation will remain at this new higher level is an empirical question that can be answered only by future surveys, although other evidence suggests to the analysts that a new political climate has emerged.

It is possible to show the contrast in national distributions from truly compar-

general problems of appraising error. Certainly the stability of the data in Table 2 suggests high reliability and little sampling error. The dangers of a bias toward the systematic inflation of reports of such "socially desirable" behavior have also been subject to empirical study. They are far less than one might have thought; and, for some modes of analysis, constant errors do not distort the inferences. (See, for example, Campbell and others), 1960; Cahalan, 1968.)

Table 2. POLITICAL ACTIVITY AMONG AMERICAN ADULTS SINCE 1950

	1952	1956	1960	1964	1968
			Percent		
Belong to Civic or Political Organization	2	3	3	4	3
Worked in Campaigns	3	3	6	5	6
Attended Political Meetings	7	10	8	9	9
Talked Politics with Friends	27	28	33	31	33
Votes	73	74	74	78	76

Source: Robinson and others (1968, p. 591).

Table 3. POLITICAL TALK AMONG GERMAN ADULTS OVER A TWENTY-YEAR PERIOD

	Often	*Occasionally*	*Hardly Ever*
		Percent	
1952—April	17	37	46
July	19	41	40
October	16	38	46
1953—September	18	44	38
1955—May	15	41	44
1956—March	17	37	46
June	13	38	49
1957—August	14	41	45
1958—June	13	41	46
1959—May	16	41	43
1960—July	14	39	47
1964—December	19	43	38
1972—March	28	45	27

Source: Noelle and Neuman (1957, p. 45); Noelle-Neumann, personal communication.

able surveys. For example, in Almond and Verba's (1963) inquiry into *The Civic Culture,* a question about the frequency of talking about public affairs was asked in five countries. In June 1959, 39 percent of their German sample answered "never." (This is a more extreme position than provided in the question used by the Institute for Demoscopy and thus likely to be characteristic of a group smaller than those who "hardly ever" talk politics, found to be 43 percent in the May 1959 entry in Table 3.) In contrast with their 39 percent in Germany, Almond and Verba found that only 29 percent of the British sample and 24 percent of the American sample, but 66 percent of their Italian sample, "never" talk politics (p. 116).

These differences were obtained from *one* set of surveys describing the respective populations at that particular time, although the question clearly has a much broader temporal referent. This safeguard may not satisfy those psychologists who are interested in national political character and who therefore wish to distinguish between differences that for sure are enduring and those that are transient reflections of the circumstances in a society at a given moment. Note, therefore, the crucial finding in Table 3. In twelve different surveys between 1952 and 1964, the proportion of Germans who "hardly ever" discuss politics *never* reached as low a figure as Almond and Verba reported for England and the United States, nor as high a figure as they obtained in Italy. Ideally, cross-national surveys should be replicated over time; but since that is extremely expensive, a single comparative inquiry can be buttressed by available surveys, another instance of the utility and feasibility of semisecondary analysis. Indeed, the German time series through 1960 was available for all to exploit, conveniently compiled in the periodic handbooks of the Institute for Demoscopy.

The findings, even though extended over time and space, are nevertheless fragmentary in describing only one feature of man, his level of political activity. Thus, they may not satisfy those who are interested in the *total political character*. The characteristic involved, however, refers to a broad domain of activities. The single dimension along which individuals are scored is already an abstract and general one, and the distribution on this variable is critical for all sorts of theorizing. Contemplating such distributions in the course of his trade, Roper (1957) was led to distinguish, within the American public, the "politically inert" and the "participating citizen"; and Almond (1950) was led to his formulation of three political strata: the "mass public," the "attentive citizen," and that rarefied group given for its excellence the title "opinion elite." The statistical norm obtained routinely from such a distribution—far toward the pole of inactivity—differs sharply from what is defined as normative in traditional theories of democracy. That finding has either supported radical critiques of democracy as incompatible with man's political nature or has led to a revised and more realistic conception of the requirements for democracy (Berelson, Lazarsfeld, and McPhee, 1954, ch. 14; Almond, 1950).

It is a quick and easy step in survey analysis to break down the aggregate distribution into a set of differentiated distributions and thus describe the patterns in different social groups. Inactivity is not randomly distributed but located predominantly in the lower social strata. Thus, applied political psychologists with a bent toward reform are helped to see where and how they might work to ameliorate the situation. Other political psychologists, who might be too quick to conclude that inactivity represents willful neglect, are forced to see that it reflects social disadvantages and to look for its roots in the right places.

Still other political psychologists, from inspecting such national distributions and juxtaposing them against their observations of the political system, are forced to consider what Greenstein (1971) has called the problem of "aggregation." How some political systems can operate at all or as well as they do under the burden of the pattern that prevails in the population is hard to understand if one sees the polity as the simple sum of the characteristics distributed in the general population. To determine collectively the functioning of the system, therefore, one is forced to develop more subtle models of the way individuals are aggregated. The differentiated distributions for various social groups are very helpful in this connection. Perhaps a rare pattern typical of only a particular small group in the population is effectively multiplied because of the great weight that group has in the governmental process. Thus, when Key (1961, pp. 536–537) "frets with the puzzle of how democratic regimes manage to function," he locates the "missing piece" in "the upper layer of activists" and in the peculiarity of their "subculture" rather than "in the qualities of the people that may be thought to make democratic practices feasible." This model suggests an obvious agenda for research and underscores some of the points already made. It calls for a series of surveys of elites and analyses of the obtained *distributions* to see whether they are both distinctive and homogeneous enough to support the notion of a peculiar subculture characterized by certain themes.

There are other models. Perhaps a pattern that is exceedingly rare within a certain group but essential to their political survival becomes weighty because it is multiplied by the vast population size of that group. Thus, for example, when Woodward and Roper (1950) reported the distribution of political activity, they also were able to engage in the following political arithmetic: While the individuals on the level-A economic level were three times as likely to have a "very active" score as those on the level-C economic level, 54 percent of the active people came from level C and only 13 percent from level A. The poor made up by their numbers (far more than 3:1) for their relative inactivity and thus could make their weight felt.

One may try to build these models by armchair theorizing, but it is a most difficult mental exercise. Instead, one may start inductively and empirically searching for clues by inspecting the distributions within and between societies obtained from many past surveys. It may turn out that very different polities exhibit aggregate distributions that are much the same in many respects, and different only in some particular parameter; or it may be that the difference inheres only in the distribution obtained for some particular subgroups. How far one can go with *aggregate* distributions from *one* society is suggested by Key's (1961) treatment of the "patterns of distribution." Building on conventional descriptive statistics, plus the classic insights of Floyd Allport, Key examined such patterns as bimodality and a J-curve and determined their implications for the functioning of the American polity.

Relevant Variables and Political Character

Although surveys of single characteristics and their distributions may not gratify some psychologists, for all the reasons mentioned they deserve considerable inquiry. But what particular variables are especially relevant and important? We shall list some of the general areas within political character and suggest fruitful lines of exploration.

Political Action. It is self-evident, even without recourse to our earlier examples, that the *action* of individuals produces, if anything can, some effect on the political system. Political psychology must either begin or end its inquiries at this point if it is to have true relevance. The level of general political activity and the frequency of specific classes of acts warrant the most careful description and attempts at explanation. Properly, these variables have been the focus of a great deal of survey research.

Given the prevalence of inactivity that the distributions document, those actions that bring inactive and active strata into contact, and thus provide for the arousal of otherwise passive individuals, assume special importance. Similarly, actions that enlighten otherwise ignorant individuals are important in light of the widespread political ignorance that has been documented. Thus, the substantial literature on personal influence or opinion leadership or the diffusion of information is of critical significance for understanding some of the dynamics of political behavior (see, for example, Lazarsfeld, Berelson, and Gaudet, 1944; Berelson, Lazarsfeld, and McPhee, 1954; Katz and Lazarsfeld, 1955; Bell, Hill, and Wright, 1961; Rogers, 1962). American *national* surveys of these patterns are still needed, however, since many of the classical inquiries are limited to particular communities where the process and magnitude of such influences may well be peculiar. Comparative surveys in other nations might also reveal different findings. Acts of influence might well vary in character and magnitude depending (1) on ecology and the opportunity for contact; (2) on the hierarchical structure of the society, making some influentials more visible and notable but perhaps more distant and unapproachable; (3) on the sense of trust that pervades interpersonal relations; and (4) on the presence of specialized institutions that formalize and channel communications.

Two forms of leadership, the *responsive* and the *self-propelled,* should be sharply distinguished in the questions used and should not be neglected in the analysis. In *The People's Choice* (Lazarsfeld, Berelson, and Gaudet, 1944), these respective forms of leadership were measured but not distinguished. That is, each respondent was asked whether he had ever been *asked* for advice and also whether he had ever *tried* to convince someone else politically. Individuals who had engaged in either act were treated as "opinion leaders" without any distinction, and nowhere in that analysis can one even find the intercorrelation between the two activities. But from Robinson's (1952) subsequent factor analysis of these data, we know it to be for Sandusky a mere .17, the one behavior hardly predicting the other (see also Agger and Ostrom, 1956).

In a subsequent major study of personal influence (Katz and Lazarsfeld, 1955), conducted in Decatur, Illinois, the indicators of political influence were confined solely to measures of the "responsive" pattern, respondents reporting whether they were asked for their advice at all and, if so, how frequently. When those respondents were then asked, "Do you know anyone around here who keeps up with the news and whom you can trust to let you know what is really going on?" "about *half,* in fact, were unable or unwilling to name anyone within their acquaintance whose competence and trustworthiness in public affairs they accepted" (p. 140; italics supplied). Almost identical findings were obtained in a subsequent study of a Wisconsin community (Lowe and McCormick, 1956). Truly passive people, it appears, will not bother to solicit advice. Indeed, they might avoid it (Wright and Cantor, 1967). Even if they felt impelled to seek advice, they might be too ignorant to know where to turn for it or might well seek it in the worst quarters. Such factors seriously limit the role of the responsive leader. The self-propelled leader, by contrast, could be a persistent force and even make a public nuisance of himself by penetrating into places where he was not wanted and without any invitation.

As one contemplates the many surveys in which opinion leadership of one type or another has been studied, a most obvious line of inquiry seems to have been neglected. No one seems to elaborate upon the initial questions by probes so as to describe the content of the transactions. "What, specifically, did the advisees ask?" "How long did you talk?" "What did you say to convince him?" The format of an initial question followed by probes is a common and feasible procedure; if one is overwhelmed by the cost or thought of coding so much open-ended material, an adaptation of Schuman's (1966) random-probe technique could be employed. The probes could be applied to only a subsample of the instances or different probes allocated to different subsamples.

Political Affect. The variables of political action and, as we shall soon see, political attitudes have been incorporated in endless surveys. Ironically, surveys of political *affect,* descriptions of the distributions of various kinds of emotions and sentiments that accompany political thought and behavior, are almost completely absent. So fundamental a category of experience, one of such classic interest to psychologists and one that may well either arouse people to action or inhibit their activity, seems to have been singularly neglected. To be sure, there are some pallid indicators of an investment of some kind of emotion into politics in routine questions about interest or attention, but the kinds of data presented in Table 4 from Almond and Verba's (1963) comparative national surveys exist in almost splendid isolation. Respondents were asked how often they felt each of a series of emotions. The statistics tabled contrast those who report such feelings any of the time and those who

Table 4. FEELINGS ABOUT VOTING AND ELECTION CAMPAIGNS
IN FOUR NATIONS IN 1959

	United States	England	Germany	Italy
	Percent			
Sometimes find election campaigns pleasant and enjoyable	66	52	28	18
Sometimes get angry during campaigns	57	41	46	20
Sometimes find campaigns silly or ridiculous	58	37	46	15
Never enjoy, and never get angry, and never feel contempt during campaigns	12	26	35	54
	970	963	955	995

Source: Almond and Verba, 1963, table 13. Reprinted by permission of Princeton University Press.

never have them. Almond and Verba use the last construct in the table as an index of political *apathy*. They define apathy as the absence of all *feeling* rather than as inactivity, the definition implicitly given to it in much survey research. Some inactive people may have strong feelings of disgust, despair, fear, and the like, about politics and in that respect may be far from "apathetic."

The questions used by Almond and Verba dealt specifically with the affect accompanying elections, certainly a moment when emotions might be temporarily heightened. The good example of Almond and Verba could be followed and extended to many other political spheres and times by the construction of appropriate questions and the use of other instruments. Every interviewer of long experience can recall those rare encounters where a respondent literally exploded with moral outrage or some other violent passion when some political question was put to him, but he can also recall endless conversations on the most earthshaking questions that remained utterly bland in tone. Interviewers' ratings of affect could readily be collected on a systematic basis, and their spontaneous observations codified.

The study of political affect may also contribute to our understanding of self-propelled opinion leaders. They seem so essential and yet have been found to be too few in numbers, in the occasional studies, to manage the magnitude of their assignment in the body politic. Unless they are motivated by hope of gain, or recruit themselves from the ranks of aristocrats who have both the leisure and the altruistic and moral impulse to elevate the mass, or are recruited and trained as professional cadres, they would have to spring from the ranks of *agitators,* those who are propelled to act unceasingly because of the depths of their own passions. Lasswell (1936a, p. 488) reminded us long ago that the "agitator has come by his name honestly, for he is enough agitated about public policy to communicate his excitement to those about him." Apart from old case studies, we know little about modern agitators or their numbers because we have not charted the distribution of emotions in political surveys, nor singled out those at the extremes for special study.

The study of another dimension of affect, although not anchored in the immediate political environment, would add to our understanding of influence processes. As earlier noted, individuals may be deterred from seeking advice not only by passivity or ignorance but also by the fears and suspicions that may pervade interpersonal relations. Indicators and scales for the measurement of such variables have been found practicable and applied on a national scale and comparatively.

In their comparative study, Almond and Verba (1963) applied a scale for the measurement of "faith in people" previously developed by Rosenberg (1956, 1957). Rosenberg found that scores indicative of "misanthropy" predicted anti-democratic and anti-internationalist attitudes, but his results were based only on samples of American students. Almond and Verba found that distrust was much more characteristic of the German and Italian samples in 1959 than of the British or American samples. Such feelings, of course, can be aggravated or allayed by circumstances. In 1948, for instance, a sample of German citizens were asked whether, in their opinion, people can be trusted (NORC, 1948). In those most threatening times, distrust was almost universal among Germans, only 6 percent expressing trust. By 1959 trust had risen considerably, to the level of 19 percent. Nevertheless, a dramatic difference between Germans and Americans persisted. By semisecondary analysis, the combination of old data obtained incidental to the original inquiries and new primary surveys, Almond and Verba obtained evidence on the more enduring features of German national character and on the situational determinants of such sentiments. Now, if one were to juxtapose the time series on trust that has become available from a series of national surveys by the Survey Research Center, one could document empirically that the distinctive American pattern is also an enduring one (Robinson and Shaver, 1969, pp. 529–532; Campbell, personal communication).

Other dimensions of affect have direct relevance for political psychology, and the distributions can and should be plotted regularly. Long ago, for example, Almond (1950) asserted that Americans are subject to wild swings of mood in relation to foreign affairs. Since there is no stable investment of feeling in that realm, policy-makers have only a shifting base of support on which to rely. It should be noted that the original formulation and a subsequent critique many years later (Caspary, 1970) were both based on secondary analysis of national surveys.

Political Knowledge. Men are also guided, if only imperfectly, by their cognitive processes and levels of knowledge. This region has been subject to a great deal of research. Sears (1969, pp. 324–329) provides a convenient summary and secondary analysis of such findings. Although some items of information are more readily absorbed than others, political ignorance is widespread and applies to many topics. Further analysis, however, has mapped the distinctive social geography of the pattern. There are persistent concentrations of ignorance in certain places—notably, among those with little education. By intercorrelating the answers to long batteries of questions, the analysis also speaks to the problem of the generality or specificity of knowledge. There appear to be "chronic know-nothings" politically and those who "know it all" (Hyman and Sheatsley, 1947). In some degree, these respective types of persons are socially determined, being prevalent in particular social groups, but the analysis also suggests that idiosyncratic factors are involved. The problem is important to the welfare of democracies as well as to political theorists and psychologists. Further survey research of a somewhat distinctive design could sharpen our understanding.

Obviously, life has made it easy for some people to learn almost anything, whereas for others learning has been made exceedingly difficult. That is what the basic analysis underscores. But the surveys also yield instances of deviant individuals who despite their advantages end up as know-nothings, and of other deviants who surmount their handicaps and become know-it-alls. The surveys, if we only take note, routinely function as locator devices to obtain unbiased samples of such specialized, rare, and otherwise elusive types, and yield them in sufficient numbers, if need be by slow accumulation and the pooling of many surveys. Subsequent intensive surveys of these special groups would be strategic for theorists and practical men.

Political Beliefs and Attitudes. Since men's political acts are guided not only by knowledge and feeling but also by their conceptions of and orientations toward features of the political environment, this vast region of the political psyche has been the subject of endless and varied surveys. To be sure, in only a few realms can the individual's inner directives be directly translated into specific individual acts toward the objects in question (for instance, toward nonconformist neighbors or toward minority groups in his town). With respect to the distant and overpoweringly important features of the political environment, actions are reserved for those in power, and ordinary men can express their orientations and beliefs only by voting their preferences or supporting some policy stand. In this connection, it should be noted that many findings in this realm are bound to be confusing and paradoxical. The irony of the ordinary man's fate is that he may have but few and unsatisfactory choices to make for the political representation of his attitudes and beliefs. All sorts of men must stand under the same political banner simply because that is the only one available and though a poor representation of their views, the best they can find. Given these circumstances, one must expect to find some heterogeneity among fellow partisans and low correlations between partisanship and single attitudes since men cannot find anything or anyone to represent their total *constellation* of attitudes and must sacrifice some preferences to advance other desires.

Within this broad region, surveys have been employed not only to describe the content of beliefs and attitudes but also other formal dimensions—for example, the intensity with which beliefs are held. One such dimension that helps bring order into this domain, and is of special interest to political psychologists, relates to the matter of *structure*. Are specific beliefs and opinions and attitudes of common men part of larger constellations, perhaps even organized so thoroughly and elaborately that they form total *belief systems,* coherent ideologies about the entire world of politics? Alternatively, are they discrete, so that there is no consistency in an individual's attitudes across related situations and toward features of the environment that in fact have much in common? (See Chapter Three and Four in this volume.) This is one of the classic problems of psychology and is obviously of special interest to political psychologists, either because they believe that there is some unity to the person or because they see politics as the clash of ideologies or as devoid of ideology. As empirical researchers, they would find their task greatly simplified if they could count on the existence of comprehensive attitude structures or belief systems. Then they would not have to engage in endless itsy-bitsy measurements and could simply locate individuals along the few major axes that define the basic structures within which the specific entities are contained. Alternatively, if there were a great deal of specificity, they might be urged to caution in testing theories about personality determinants of political attitudes, since so much would then seem to be determined by the situation rather than by the inner man. And they would have to move in the direction of many measures of attitude in the hope of transcending the specificities and finding some thread of unity to tie on to their personality measures.

That the level and nature of mental organization do vary in different universes has been empirically documented. Thus, surveys of the problem in the general population are especially welcome and fairly plentiful. For example, by intercorrelational methods, sometimes carried to the point of factor analysis, applied to a series of heterogeneous attitude measures, G. H. Smith's (1948a, 1948b) early finding that there are "*two* kinds of liberalism" has been confirmed; there may be even more than two (Allinsmith and Allinsmith, 1948; Williams and Wright, 1955). For sure, in America in the 1940s there was no total ideological system in the common man that disposed him toward liberalism or conservatism of every kind. But there was a considerable degree of organization: domestic economic attitudes clustered into a consistent pattern of liberal or conservative views; and attitudes toward foreign affairs and noneconomic domestic matters, such as civil liberties and the treatment of minorities, formed a liberal or an illiberal cluster. In Smith's studies, at the level of ecological correlations, the linkage between these two systems was negative, the more educated strata being peopled by noneconomic liberals and economic conservatives, and the lower strata showing the opposite profile. In subsequent studies (Hero, 1969; Campbell and others, 1960) the two basic clusters of foreign policy attitudes and domestic economic attitudes have been isolated repeatedly, but the two spheres seem almost independent of one another, linked by only the most feeble of correlations. In perhaps the most definitive of such studies, Hero, by the secondary analysis of national surveys spanning a thirty-year period, does document, however, that the linkage between the spheres has varied over time and that there are a few narrower patterns of attitude whose contours do cross both domestic and foreign issues.

The structures revealed by statistical methods applied to arrays of measures necessarily have a somewhat abstract, intangible character. The elements do intercorrelate, hang together within the sample; but the investigator has no sense of the psychic cement that binds them. He does not find a visible constellation of belief and attitude in a concrete person. Some investigators therefore have adopted a more clinical approach, examining the answers of each respondent to see how he articulates the connections between his ideas and to determine whether there is an explicit patterning. By such an analysis of surveys conducted during the 1956 presidential election, Campbell and his associates (1960) concluded that only a small minority of Americans, perhaps less than 10 percent, exhibit an ideology in the sense of a structure formulated in terms of some modestly *abstract set of concepts* that political scientists and sociologists of knowledge would accept as ideological.

Such an approach tells us a good deal about the clarity and style of political thought of the common man. It does not deny the existence of attitude structures and belief systems, but it sharpens our realization that such structures are cemented not by abstract ideas but in some other ways. Indeed, statistical analyses replicated over the 1956 and 1960 elections (Campbell and others, 1960; Converse, 1964) revealed the two main subsystems of attitude found by the other investigators. This clinical approach also bears on the larger question of intellectual functioning and presents us with a paradoxical problem. Ideologies, being pushed and sold by ideologues and elites, pervade the political environment; judging by the 1956 findings, however, the common man shows little receptivity or capacity to absorb such ideas. Perhaps the explanation is that few such ideologies were being pushed during that particular bland period. Field and Anderson (1969) had this very hypothesis and tested it with surveys conducted in 1964, when Senator Goldwater was a dramatic symbol of conservatism and stimulated a sharp clash of ideologies. Ideological thought had expanded to about one third of the population by then; but about two thirds of the population still did not function in this way, despite the fact that the scoring for "ideology" was lenient and the stimulus most compelling.

Such findings permit us to study a few relatively broad systems of political beliefs and attitude, to locate and describe individuals along a few general dimensions. But we are not *instructed* by the studies of structure to ignore narrower topics for inquiry in the region of political attitudes. Little subsystems of belief, even discrete attitudes, may be of critical importance and strategic objects of investigation to which we may wish to devote whole surveys or strings of surveys. Beliefs about and popular support of war, beliefs and attitudes relating to civil liberties for political nonconformists, attitudes about the president and the way he performs his duties—these are examples of such specifics. Indeed, these very examples have been studied through surveys and often accomplished simply through secondary analysis (see Mueller, 1970, 1971; Hamilton, 1968, Hyman and Sheatsley, 1953; Lipset, 1964; Lipset and Raab, 1970).

A last set of beliefs deserving of special study are the beliefs about other people's beliefs and attitudes. Floyd Allport (1924) and Katz and Schanck (1938) talked long ago of *pluralistic ignorance,* the false ideas that many of us have about each other's ideas. In mass society, the barriers to correct knowledge may be great; but pluralistic ignorance is also found in the little community. It may even be found among those who are members of the same association (Breed and Ktsanis, 1961). All sorts of whimsical or tragic processes may flow from pluralistic ignorance, with consequences for politics. Those suffering from what Allport called the "illusion of universality" may fight on, encouraged by the belief that they have an army of millions behind them—in fact, a phantom army—and may validate their own views by a consensus that is only the product of their fantasy. Others, suffering from another variety of pluralistic ignorance, may surrender their position in the false belief that no one shares their views, when in fact they are quite an army.

Political Character. By the systematic description of the characteristics of individuals on these major types of variables, we arrive ultimately, adapting Katz's phrase, at a "psychological taxonomy of political behavior." Along the way, to achieve comprehensiveness, we may explore within our surveys new regions and plot additional specific dimensions in greater detail. For example, some may wish to study a special region of political *values.* Whatever one might add to ensure the realization of the taxonomy, survey methods can provide the descriptions of the populations for many times and places. Yet some psychologists might find the ultimate product unsatisfying. They might regard it as only a catalog or inventory of *parts* of men, in no way describing the whole man, the separate characteristics never being joined together to form the political character. Yet this would be to underrate the degree of synthesis that can be reached in survey analysis. When we present a description of a general variable, a *composite* index of political knowledge, or political activity, or liberalism, or ideologically flavored thought, we have already reached a halfway stage between the description of a discrete characteristic and the total political character. We can move still further toward complex description, toward typological constructs which convey a profile or combination of the different political features of a man. Instead of locating individuals along one dimension, to produce a univariate distribution of the population, we can locate them by reference to scores on two dimensions (producing a bivariate distribution) or by reference to three dimensions (producing a multivariate distribution).

To cite one example, the Survey Research Center developed scales of "citizen duty" and "political efficacy," to measure two dimensions of belief that underlie political activity, and described the *separate* distributions of the American population on each of these dimensions over time. Eulau and Schneider (1956) simply combined the two scales into a superscale of "political involvement." This approach yields a more comprehensive description of the forces that affect an individual's actions, and we are then in a position to isolate interesting types for further study. An individual with little efficacy who is nevertheless impelled by a high sense of duty is a very different moral type from the individual who despite his feeling of efficacy has no sense of duty to participate. The former is truly the "high-minded citizen," since he believes he has nothing to gain from his participation.

Consider as another example the joint distribution created by measuring political knowledge and political attitude. We arrive at some estimate of those who might be labeled the "political irresponsibles" (people who hold a strong position in the absence of knowledge) and of the "political Hamlets" (people who know a lot and yet have lost all sense of where they want to go politically). In these ways surveys can provide a many-faceted and comprehensive description of the individual.

Explanations of Political Behavior

Surveys can describe the politics of men, but the task of explaining their behavior still remains and may appear to some to be beyond the powers of survey methods. It should be noted immediately that one really has moved far in the direction of explanation when one has achieved adequate description. Catching the right hypothesis is half the battle; testing it in the right way is only the second half. Obviously, it is much better to catch it quickly rather than to find it only after a long string of negative tests of fruitless hypotheses.[3]

How shall one catch the right hypothesis and put it to a good test? We are all familiar with the contribution of serendipity to the growth of theory. That needs no review, but the special relevance of surveys to the experiencing of serendipity does deserve brief mention. Anomalous observations would seem to be chance occurrences that rarely come our way. Yet by casting the wide net of a descriptive survey over a total population, the investigator is more likely to capture such anomalies, and in turn catch a good hypothesis.

Katz remarked that "a naturalistic description of the behavior of human beings in various social contexts" is a prerequisite to understanding. The ability of a survey to work as a *locator* device helps in many ways in hypothesis catching. The distributions in the aggregate, over time, and for major social groups provide a large *set of statistical norms* for locating a particular pattern and sensing what it means. Knowing that it is deviant or normative in the population at large and in specified groups, persistent or transient, parallel to other patterns or a discordant feature of a larger profile, we are less likely to concoct arbitrary assumptions and wild theories, and more likely to move in the direction of sound hypotheses. If one is still confused, the initial surveys can serve to locate unbiased samples of individuals who exhibit the mysterious entities for subsequent deeper exploration, leading ultimately to clarification.

Within the ordinary survey, the analysis usually involves both description and explanation. Ironically, the mix these days is all in the direction of explanation; description, despite its utility, is regarded as pedestrian and only a lowly exercise of the powers of a survey. A special methodology, elaborated for testing causal hypoth-

---

[3] This is not to deny the value of eliminating hypotheses by successive disconfirmations and the possibility in some instances that a negative finding indirectly supports another hypothesis, which is the only alternative explanation. For such possibilities in survey analysis, see Hyman (1955, pp. 226–241).

eses with survey data, is codified in easy steps in the literature (Glock, 1967; Rosenberg, 1968; Hyman, 1955). Whatever hypothesis may guide each political psychologist to measure some favorite independent variable, all, as survey analysts, can follow these steps toward tests that are logically sound and built upon the solid foundations of good sampling. Because the single survey is a spacious vehicle that can carry many variables, no analyst need risk his whole inquiry on an exclusive and possibly misguided hypothesis. By a kind of benign Parkinson's Law, he is led to fill the vehicle to capacity with many variables, and thus is guided naturally toward complex models of causation. He can examine one or more individualistic determinants of some phenomenon, but observe how their influence is modified in different social contexts. He can examine influences out of the distant past, but as they have been overlayed by recent stimuli. He can trace political behavior back to its deeper roots in some fundamental motive or cognitive or affective entity, some style of personality or intellect—and not just to a single such source; but he can also trace the links in the long causal chain that connect the private and political spheres. Some of the variables previously presented only as ways to describe the political sphere indeed may be treated as just such causal links—for example, political beliefs and attitudes as underlying political action, and political knowledge as shaping beliefs and attitudes.

Initial surveys, as earlier noted, can also serve to locate unbiased samples of rare and elusive groups who exhibit a set of *independent* variables implicated in some hypothesis, whose influence is then tested. In this connection, one may suggest the rare potentiality for locating individuals whose particular political and psychological characteristics at a much earlier stage of their lives were measured by surveys out of the *distant past* and whose subsequent long-term development is traced by impaneling them in a new survey years later. Ethical and technical difficulties stand in the way, but designs involving such *selective experimental impaneling* should be regarded as a real possibility. (See Hyman, 1972a, pp. 58–61; see also Chapter Two of this volume.)

In these specialized ways, surveys can move from description toward explanation, toward good hypotheses and good tests. But it may also be argued that one already has arrived at an explanation when one has established securely the *differentiated* descriptions of political characteristics. For example, the contrasted distributions of political activity among young and middle-aged people or poor and middle-class people—distributions described time and again by dozens of surveys in many countries —establish that age and class are *causes* of political activity. Some analysts would find such a notion of "cause" too crude and not psychological enough for their taste; but it is a perfectly legitimate assertion as long as it is protected against spuriousness, and that is readily done in survey analysis. If one wishes, however, to move beyond this gross level, refinement is easily achieved. One can easily test the effect of combinations of social characteristics working simultaneously to reinforce each other or to create cross pressures; or he can test the effects of status sequences, movements over time from one social position or milieu to another.

Some might still find this level of causal analysis too "social," seeking instead to isolate those psychological factors that regularly accompany a status or follow from it, or those that impinge in no socially ordered fashion upon individuals and "truly cause" a process and an effect. What they would regard as pure social description, nevertheless, can help them locate the psychological causes and links and bring those to ultimate tests. A recent monograph illustrates the sequence. Reed (1972) established by the secondary analysis of many surveys that there are enduring differences between southerners and northerners in political and other respects. One might say that being southern is a powerful determinant of behavior; but one might ask, as he did, exactly what it is about southern life that causes the patterns. By multiple standardization—in effect, the simultaneous control of a set of variables—he established that the differences cannot be explained away by the relative lack of industrialization, urbanization, and education in the lives of southerners. Multiple standardization, defined more precisely, yields the hypothetical distribution that describes what southern behavior would be like if southerners had the same amounts of urbanization, education, and industrialization as northerners. In one sense it is description, but it also constitutes an explanatory test of a complex of causes and, in this case, led to the conclusion that some other subtle and residual features of southern culture are the true causes. Reed then theorized that the South is a cherished normative reference group and that patterns of socialization help perpetuate its distinctiveness. He was then able to make direct tests to support these social-psychological hypotheses.

The paradox that groups often do not produce the patterns one would expect in most of their members was a major stimulus to the rise of reference-group theory. Differentiated descriptions, the distributions for various social groups yielded by surveys, provide a continuing source of nourishment for the theory by showing how much variability exists within a group and how much uniformity between groups. One may conceive of the variability within a group as stemming not from the fact that some individuals adopt strange reference groups but simply as the product of their varied *multiple* memberships. But, as already noted, surveys can classify individuals along multidimensional lines and then document how much variability persists. And special measures of the normative and comparative reference groups that individuals select are readily incorporated into surveys, and the effects of such psychological variables put to direct test (for such examples, see Hyman and Singer, 1968).

In these various ways, descriptive surveys lead toward explanations of political behavior. Some political psychologists may be creative enough to catch a good hypothesis right out of their own imagination or from out of some prior body of theory. Then, of course, they can move immediately to an explanatory survey containing measures of the appropriate variables. There is, however, still another avenue to explanation that can be explored in survey research: the study of processes of learning and development as explanations of political behavior. Nothing could be a more central concern of psychology than learning and development, the way individuals are altered by experience over the course of their lives and naturally grow and change and decline. Surveys can reveal such processes over the long course of time and often also isolate their sources, although, as always, there are causes behind causes.

The many surveys of political socialization need no review here (see Chapter Five). Clearly, the young are a population strategic for study. Special surveys of samples at various "early" age stages are readily conducted and provide a quasi-longitudinal picture of an important segment of the longer process of political development—although, of course, there are technical difficulties in conducting conventional surveys among the very young and in sampling young adults, who often are inaccessible in such institutions as the army and residential colleges.

Surveys among adults always enumerate age. This datum provides the basis for quasi-longitudinal analysis of a long segment of the process, either in a specially conducted inquiry or through the secondary analysis of a great many surveys. Some investigators may reconstruct features of the distant past and even try, as Almond and Verba did, to obtain entire political life histories—producing, so to speak, a complete longitudinal inquiry. These several approaches do present technical difficulties. Problems arise in the interpretation of comparisons between age groups drawn from within the same survey, in deciding whether the differences reflect the general aging process or the particular experience of different generations. But these problems are not insurmountable. Ironically, the secondary analyst often is in a much better position than the primary analyst, since he can draw together a larger body of data from different time periods. Sometimes, he can apply the method of cohort analysis to a series of available trend surveys, producing definitive evidence on the general process of aging, and also on the influence of the specific experiences of different cohorts or generations (For a summary of such studies, see Hyman, 1972a, ch. 7.)

Some may find such approaches too inferential and too fraught with technical difficulties. It should be noted that truly longitudinal surveys, special panel studies of the changing politics of adults, have been maintained over periods as long as five to six years, providing evidence on a fairly lengthy segment of process (see, for example, Campbell and others, 1966). By the strategy of selective experimental impaneling, it would be possible to bring an even longer segment under scrutiny.

It is ironic that special surveys of the *very old* are very rare, while surveys of the young are fashionable and multiply every day. The old are an equally strategic population for the student of learning and development. They too should be surveyed despite the technical difficulties in sampling the full population, some of whom are contained within institutions, and in interviewing those who are feeble and handicapped. Here, too, it is comforting to note how much can be accomplished through secondary analysis by highly skilled investigators, and one can only hope that more investigators will explore these farthest reaches of time.

This chapter has reviewed the many ways that surveys can describe and explain the political behavior of individuals and in turn help us to understand the political system. That is enough of a contribution. But we cannot conclude without mentioning a rare contribution that surveys can also make.

Examining politics from the perspective of psychology is somewhat like the task of the subject in old-fashioned experiments who was shown a picture where figure and ground kept reversing themselves in his perception. The political psychologist faces a similar situation, although it has not been so apparent to him. He too can reverse his normal rigid perspective. Instead of looking at politics only as the figure against a background of psychological variables from which it emerges, he can focus on the psychological as the figure against a background of the political system that has shaped it. The study of the relation between psychology and politics can move in both directions. Indeed, it is likely that the empirical relations we demonstrate and quickly interpret in a unidirectional fashion may sometimes reflect a process moving in the opposite direction. A political system can invade and alter our psyches, just as it can reflect our prior dispositions. A legal system can legitimate our highest or basest impulses, and it can reflect them.

We emphasize the reverse perspective not just to urge caution in our interpretations but to elevate neglected problems to a higher place in our research agenda. We would then revive a great, if uncommon, tradition in psychology and a classic concern of political science. Recall Lewin's interest in the effects of authoritarian leadership and the memorable questions that political theorists have asked about whether a given political system is bad for men. Recall that Lasswell (1960), who had dealt with the psychological *sources* of political behavior in *Psychopathology and Politics,* finally remarked that "the purpose" of psychological analysis "is to reveal the significance of any institutional practice . . . for human values," to appraise it "in terms of importance for man" (p. 276). Psychological data in abundance in ordinary surveys tell us of man's sensitivities and satisfactions under a particular political order. Trend, and comparative contextual, and cross-national surveys could systematically document the psychological effects that varying political institutions produce. We could and then would deal with noble problems.

13

EXPERIMENTAL RESEARCH

John B. McConahay

For most of its history, political psychology has relied almost exclusively upon the sample survey and the in-depth interview as its chief empirical methods. However, recently we have seen an awakening of interest in a method dominant in other branches of psychology for years, the controlled experiment. A few examples of this emerging interest are the establishment of a laboratory for political research at the State University of New York at Stony Brook; the founding of a new scholarly journal, *Experimental Study of Politics;* the popularity of the experimentally oriented Program of Advanced Training in Psychology for Political Scientists, now in its fifth year at Yale University; the increasing number of "experimental" articles appearing in established political science journals (see S. R. Brown, 1970); and the appearance recently of symposia devoted to experimental research in political science (see Laponce and Smoker, 1972). In the

Work on this chapter was supported in part by USPHS training grant 5 TO 1MH11526, Advanced Training in Psychology for Political Scientists, to Yale University, J. B. McConahay, Director. The author wishes to thank Diane Straus and Shirley F. McConahay for their research assistance and Noreen O'Connor for typing multiple drafts of the manuscript.

hope of further advancing this trend to incorporate experimentation into political psychology, this chapter is written with a very definite readership in mind: those behavioral scientists interested in political psychology who wish to add experimental techniques to their repertoire of methodological skills.

Because of space limitations, not every aspect of experimental design and execution can be covered. Therefore, those that are covered in detail represent aspects of experimental methodology which (in my opinion) need the most emphasis for the above readership, given the current state of the experimental art in political psychology. Readers wishing more details about certain aspects should turn to Campbell and Stanley (1963), Aronson and Carlsmith (1968), Kiesler, Collins, and Miller (1969), and Winer (1971). Readers should be warned, however, that after reading this chapter and the above works, they will not yet be good experimenters. To learn to be good experimenters, behavioral scientists must start *doing* experiments.

A Sexy Illustration

We turn immediately to an illustration from a realm which older generations saw as nonpolitical but which has recently become the subject of much political debate (see Millett, 1970; J. Q. Wilson, 1971) and even served as the topic of a presidential commission study (Commission on Obscenity and Pornography, 1970).

In their monumental studies of sexual behavior, Kinsey and his colleagues (1948, 1953) found that 77 percent of the males and 32 percent of the females in their samples reported being aroused by "photographs, drawings, motion pictures, and other portrayals of sexual action." Kinsey used a self-selected or volunteer sample and "in-depth" clinical interviewing techniques, which involved open-ended questions with multiple probes. Using a national probability sample of adults and straightforward "survey interviewing" techniques, Abelson and his associates (1970) found that 23 percent of the males and 8 percent of the females were aroused by sexual materials. Finally, Berger, Gagnon, and Simon (1970) found in a sample survey of American college students that 46 percent of the males and 14 percent of the females were aroused by exposure to "pornographic photographs, drawings, comic books, movies, and writings." The results of these surveys—using three different types of samples, two different types of sampling techniques, and two different methods of interviewing—appear quite consistent with Kinsey's conclusion that men are more likely than women to be aroused by sexually oriented materials.

When males and females were exposed to such materials under experimental conditions, however, a different set of findings emerged. Jakobovits (1965) found that males and females are equally aroused by erotically "realistic" stories and that females are significantly more aroused than males by "hard-core" stories. Similarly, Sigusch and his associates (1970) found that women are more aroused on the average than men by exposure to pictures of heterosexual intercourse.

These data illustrate two of several pitfalls of a political psychology based exclusively upon the sample survey as a method of research and two of several valuable contributions that experimental procedures can make to the discipline (other gains will be discussed later). First, the findings of survey research may simply reflect widely held myths about human behavior or the sample's consensus about what the socially desirable answer to the interviewer's question should be.

Thus, when asked if he is aroused by sexually oriented materials, a male respondent might say "yes" because he believes that most males are aroused by such stimuli or because he thinks that the interviewer or researcher will regard him as less than masculine if he responds that he is not aroused. Similarly, a woman might answer "no" when asked the same question because she believes that women in general are not aroused or she fears that the interviewer will regard her with contempt for admitting to a response that nice girls and nice women are not supposed to have.

A second pitfall is that the results might be interpreted as reflecting basic laws of political psychology when they merely reveal a picture of the way people are currently behaving in response to existing political and social stimuli. Thus, in our example, the differences between men and women in the various surveys might have resulted from the fact that pornography (until very recently) was an exclusively male domain. It was produced by men for male entertainment. Hence, to both male and female respondents, the terms *sexually oriented* or *pornographic* might have suggested pictures of nude females, striptease shows, and the Playmate of the Month. Such materials would arouse heterosexual males but have very limited impact upon heterosexual females. Consequently, even without the distorting effects of mythology and social desirability, males would report having been aroused by such materials while females would remember being unaroused.

The laboratory experiments overcame both of these difficulties by using physiological as well as self-reported or subjective measures of arousal and by presenting pictures or stories intended to arouse heterosexual women as well as men. The physiological measures, in addition to providing an independent check upon the arousal level of the males, called the attention of both males and females to their physiological state and made them less likely to give false levels of arousal on self-reported scales. (The subjects may have thought the investigators would know how aroused they were anyway.) The pictures of nude men and the stories about nude men and heterosexual intercourse were sexual stimuli that the women would rarely have encountered under commercial or "natural" circumstances. Hence, they reached heights of arousal from these materials that they would never have achieved looking through the pages of *Playboy*.

Need for Multiple Methods

The point of this long illustration is not that experimentation is the answer to all research problems in political psychology. Other methods—for example, projective techniques, corrections for social desirability, and cross-cultural surveys used as additional techniques—might have helped Kinsey, Abelson, Berger, and their associates to avoid their pitfalls. Furthermore, sample surveys are indispensable for developing a picture of the ways in which people are currently behaving in our political or social culture. Perhaps the greatest contribution of the survey researchers has been the *destruction of social myths* about the ways people conduct their sex lives, make up their minds about electoral choices, and participate in urban violence (Sears and McConahay, 1973).

Experimentation, then, is not the answer to all research problems in political psychology, but it is an indispensable additional approach. As many of the contributors to this volume emphasize, behavior in a specific instance is a joint function of *both* psychological predispositions and the stimulus properties of the immediate situation. Survey research, though conducted in "natural" settings, is rarely able to take into account the specific context of the behavior reported by interviewed subjects. Hence, one might overlook the contexts controlling respondents' various reports of their behavior and, as in the above example, conclude that women are not as aroused by erotica as men in *any* and *all* contexts. Experimental research, though frequently conducted in "artificial" settings, makes the environmental setting quite explicit and examines the ensuing behavior on the basis of the joint effect of both environmental and predispositional factors. If we are going to make theoretical and empirical advances in political psychology, we must take both factors into account and consequently must use both experimental and survey methods (along with others).

Experiment Defined

We have so far used the terms *experimental* and *experiment* rather freely, but what exactly do we mean by them? In this chapter, we shall use the terms *experiment* or *experimental design* to mean a situation in which certain variables are manipulated in such a way that the subjects cannot choose or select the level or type of treatment they receive; then the results of these manipulations upon other variables are observed. This definition is quite similar to that of others (Brownlee, 1960; Campbell and Stanley, 1963; Cox, 1958; Edwards, 1960; Fisher, 1925, 1935; Winer, 1971) except that most of the others, writing in the agricultural or laboratory psychology tradition, assume that the experimenter controls the independent manipulation and determines which subject receives what level or type or treatment. While this pre-experimental equalizing of treatment groups by random assignment is often possible in political psychology (and, as a technique for equalizing, is superior to matching on one, two, three, or n dimensions), the researcher does not always have this power. There may be occasions when God, a bureaucracy, or fickle fate assigns subjects to treatment conditions while the researcher bravely takes advantage of these ongoing experiments to collect data and share the results with his or her colleagues. The essence of an experiment in this chapter, then, is not that the experimenter (E) controls and randomly assigns the treatment (X) but that some random or chance mechanism beyond the control of the subject (S) is used to achieve pretreatment equality of experimental groups upon the relevant dependent variables. Therefore, *experimental* in this chapter is not synonymous with *laboratory,* since the random assignment of subjects to treatment conditions may occur in a laboratory or in a field setting.

Where pretreatment equality of groups is attempted or assessed by some means other than random assignment, we shall, after Campbell (1968; Campbell and Stanley, 1963), refer to the research design as quasi-experimental. These designs are not ideal but may be the best available and may yield valid data to a sensitive researcher.

Previous Studies

Researchers wishing to do experiments in political psychology will either have countless or very few examples to guide them, depending upon the criteria for selection. Since all of psychology is important for understanding political behavior, the political psychologist could start with studies of psychobiology, animal learning, and autonomic conditioning. Indeed, the laboratories for political research at the State University of New York at Stony Brook are among the finest physiological psychology facilities at any university.

Of more direct relevance, perhaps, are the studies by psychologists which have rather obvious political implications even though their authors were not necessarily interested in pursuing these implications. Here we might include (among many others) the classic studies of attitude change and mass communication (Hovland, Lumsdaine, and Sheffield, 1949; Hovland, Janis, and Kelley, 1953), the studies of selective exposure (Freedman and Sears, 1965), the social-psychological studies of leadership (Fiedler, 1965), the experiments in violence and aggression (Berkowitz, 1969), and the work of Christie and Geis (1970) on Machiavellianism.

Special mention should be made of the work on obedience by Milgram (1965) and on deindividuation by Zimbardo (1969). Milgram found that Yale students (and later, ordinary people off the streets of Bridgeport, Connecticut) would give supposedly lethal levels of electric shock to persons simply because they were ordered to do so by an authority figure. Zimbardo found that people, when deindividuated, would give increasing levels of shock even to persons they liked, once others started doing it. The implications of these experiments for a political psychology of the military and for an understanding of My Lai are obvious and frightening. (See Chapter Six for a discussion of some of these implications.)

Political psychologists wishing to learn from experiments with manifestly political content will, at present, have few examples to guide them. Some field studies of campaign techniques or propaganda and electoral choice (Blydenburgh, 1971; Hartmann, 1935) are not experiments by our definition (even though they have the words *experiment* or *experimental* in their titles). They tend instead to be quasi-experiments, since they do not use random assignment to determine levels or types of treatment. Other studies (for instance, Barber, 1966) are sometimes loosely refered to as experiments but are more appropriately designated as simulations (Abelson, 1968b). Finally, many studies did incorporate some form of random assignment into their designs but failed to have sufficient replications (Reback, 1971) or used the wrong number of degrees of freedom in their data analysis (Gertzog, 1970).

Three experiments have been chosen somewhat arbitrarily for review here because they are all in one field, electoral behavior, and are among the best-executed experiments in any field. The first, a study by Eldersveld and Dodge (1954), attempted to assess the effects of different propaganda techniques upon voter turnout and preference. In 1953, subjects in three wards in Ann Arbor, Michigan, who had previously expressed ignorance of or hostility toward a proposed city charter revision were assigned at random, and as individuals, to receive one of three treatments: (1) mail propaganda, (2) personal contact by students posing as campaign workers in support of the charter revision, and (3) no mail or personal contact by the research team. The data, gathered in postelection interviews, suggested that both mail and personal contact will increase voter turnout (*turnout effect;* see Kramer, 1970) and make voters more likely to vote in the advocated way (*preference effect;* see Kramer, 1970). Furthermore, personal contact produced a greater turnout effect (statistically significant) and a greater preference effect (marginally significant) than did the mailed propaganda (both statistical tests based upon my calculations from their data).

In the second experiment, Eldersveld (1956) replicated this turnout effect for propaganda and also explored several alternative techniques of propaganda. In this experiment, conducted in 1954, residents of Ann Arbor who had voted in national and state but not local elections were exposed to different types of propaganda urging them to vote in an upcoming local election. This hard core of five hundred local election apathetics were assigned at random to one of six experimental groups or to a control group. The experimental groups received the following propaganda treatments: (1) personal contact by students, (2) personal contact by party canvassers, (3) telephone contact, (4) contact by students and by mail, (5) "rational" appeals sent through the mail, and (6) "moral" appeals sent through the mail. The control group was not contacted at all. The results (based upon a check of the city clerk's records to see who actually voted) replicated the turnout effect for personal contact, which differed significantly from both the noncontacted groups and from the mail-contact groups. Mailed propaganda did not produce a significant turnout effect as it had in 1953. Although one might find some fault with certain aspects of the experimental techniques used in these two experiments, they still stand as well-executed experiments and are even more awe inspiring when one considers the state of the experimental art in the mid 1950s.

The third "true" political psychology experiment executed before 1970 is the work of Kamin (1958). His dependent variable was voting not in an actual election but in a fictitious electoral contest. That is, Kamin took advantage of the low level of information in most mass publics (Hyman and Sheatsley, 1947; Converse, 1964; Sears, 1969) to present his subjects with a choice between fictitious candidates for a fictitious office in the guise of asking opinion-polling questions. The subjects were English and French Canadians, and the fake opinion poll asked for their choice of candidates in an election that pitted candidates with French surnames against those with English. The party affiliations of the two fictitious candidates and the position of names on the ballot were also varied at random. The results showed that, in the absence of party labels, the English preferred English candidates and the French preferred French but that names last on the ballot (regardless of ethnicity) were preferred least. When party labels were present, both English and French subjects preferred the candidate of their party regardless of the candidate's ethnicity. A procedure somewhat similar to Kamin's was used in 1966 by Lorinskas, Hawkins, and Edwards (1969) to study ethnicity and party identification among urban and rural voters in Illinois with Polish surnames. It is not reviewed here because of certain difficulties in the urban-rural comparisons and because of errors in their data analysis.

Despite the valuable contributions of these experiments to political psychology and the success of some social-psychological experiments in illuminating certain processes important for a theoretical understanding of aspects of political behavior, in recent years a number of manuscripts reporting upon experimental studies were rejected (quite unfairly, in the opinion of many investigators) by the established political and behavioral science journals. Thus, to provide an outlet for further research into political phenomena and to stimulate further experimental research in this field, a new journal, *Experimental Study of Politics,* was founded in February 1971. The appearance of this new journal means that those interested in experimental approaches to political psychology will not be forced to publish only in psychology journals, where the study of politics is considered an applied rather than a basic research field. Furthermore, researchers will now have an outlet that might catch the eyes of more persons concerned with "nonpsychological" aspects of politics.

The articles thus far published in *Experimental Study of Politics* (*ESP*) are not yet as methodologically sophisticated as those in the established psychology journals (*Journal of Personality and Social Psychology* and *Journal of Experimental Social Psychology,* for example), but they are improving with each issue as political scientists learn to do experiments by doing them, and they are not as sterile as articles in the established psychology journals either.

Advantages and Disadvantages

As Sears (1969) has pointed out, there is no reason in principle why experimental studies of political psychology should not prove fruitful. Yet, as we have seen, very few experiments have been attempted in political psychology or more general political behavior. Perhaps political scientists and sociologists simply are unfamiliar with experimental techniques; or perhaps academic psychologists—fearing that they would be thought of as applied psychologists by their academic colleagues—have shied away from studying political behavior; or perhaps the subject matter of political psychology simply does not lend itself to experimental study. Most probably, however, existing political-psychological theories have made experimentation inappropriate to this date.

As with any other research technique, the experimental method has both its advantages and disadvantages. The productive researcher should choose a technique that best suits his problem, one whose advantages in that specific situation outweigh its disadvantages. What are the advantages of the experimental approach? Advocates of experimental methods usually agree upon the following advantages, summarized by Aronson and Carlsmith (1968, p. 10): "In sum, the major advantage of the laboratory experiment is its ability to provide us with unambiguous evidence about causation. Second, it gives us better control over extraneous variables. Finally, it allows us to explore the dimensions and parameters of a complex variable."

Aronson and Carlsmith, writing for an audience primarily composed of true believers in the experimental approach to social psychology and of those who would soon be socialized into the state of being true believers, could get away with making what other observers might regard as an exaggerated claim for the experiment's ability to settle questions of causation. In theory an experiment may be able to provide unambiguous evidence of the direction of causation; but social science studies, using any technique, rarely provide completely unambiguous evidence, and in many if not most complex social and political interactions the direction of causation is rarely one way. Nevertheless, as compared with correlational and observational techniques, the experiment does allow for relatively more control of extraneous variables and does permit detailed exploration of complex variables. In short, experiments are invaluable tools for theory building and theory testing. As indicated, surveys and other correlational techniques are great for discovering and documenting things as they currently exist or changes as they take place, but their utility diminishes as we attempt to explain why and to examine possibilities that have not yet occurred. Middle-range empirical theories are an aid to both of these tasks. Unfortunately, most of the theories in political psychology are not middle range but are global and generally untestable by any technique. (For an exposition of this problem in the area of democratic theory, see Cnudde and Neubauer, 1969.) Without middle-range theories, both psychologists and political scientists have sensed that the disadvantages of the experimental approach outweigh the advantages.

The major disadvantages usually cited by critics of experimental approaches to psychology and politics are the artificiality of the manipulations; the unrepresentativeness of the samples studied; the impossibility of generalizing from the controlled, bivariate or trivariate laboratory to the multivariate world; and the cost of overcoming this artificiality, unrepresentativeness, and isolation by moving toward field experiments or bigger, more elaborate, better-staged laboratory experiments. (For the details of these criticisms, see Chapter Twelve in this volume.)

These criticisms are generally but not entirely valid when applied to laboratory experiments. Moreover, the charges of artificiality and isolation are frequently based upon a misunderstanding of what the laboratory experimenter is trying to do, a confusion of "mundane" with "experimental" realism (see Aronson and Carlsmith, 1968). Furthermore, experimentalists are not the only researchers who are guilty of making theoretical leaps from possibly artificial or weak empirical operations. The survey and correlational studies of alienation provide a classic case in point, as their critics have pointed out (Keniston, 1960; Kraut and McConahay, 1971; Seeman, 1971). Finally, the high cost of overcoming these difficulties by moving toward field experiments or bigger, more elaborate, better-staged laboratory experiments is also a factor in correlational research. A sample survey of adults in the United States or even south central Los Angeles is a very expensive task. Consequently, many correlational analyses use dubious operationalizations of theoretical concepts imposed upon somebody else's questions, which are then reanalyzed and reinterpreted. And many correlational analyses combine the worst of both worlds by giving paper-and-pencil questionnaires to captive audiences of college students or other unrepresentative samples. Thus, the problems of social desirability, face validity, and unrepresentativeness of subjects are combined with the inability to untangle questions of causation.

The principal advantages of an experimental approach to the study of political psychology may be summarized as follows: (1) The experimental approach permits greater confidence in causal inferences than with other procedures. (2) There is greater control of extraneous variables. (3) There is better opportunity for precise exploration of the dimensions and parameters of a complex variable, so that one can study process as well as outcome. (4) The approach affords greater control of social desirability than with other procedures. (5) In conjunction with appropriate theories, one is able to create, explore, and evaluate conditions that have not yet evolved or developed "naturally" in the existing political and social world.

The disadvantages of an experimental approach to political psychology may be summarized as follows: (1) The manipulations and settings, especially of laboratory experiments, appear artificial. (2) The samples used are generally haphazard (Kish, 1965) and unrepresentative of any specifiable population. (3) The control of extraneous variables (deemed an advantage above) introduces bias, which limits the generalizability of experimental findings to the multivariate "real" world. (4) Experiments that might overcome the above disadvantages are impossible in some cases and impossibly expensive in most others.

When we have appropriate middle-range empirical theories to test, the advantages of experimentation will, I believe, frequently outweigh the disadvantages. As yet, however, we do not have an abstract formula for deciding when an experiment is appropriate. The complete and flexible researcher should be familiar with more than one technique, so that he does not have to formulate every problem or theoretical model to fit one procedure. Just as social psychology suffered in the past because experimentation was viewed as the only path to truth, political psychology will be retarded if we behave as if only sample surveys, only multiple regression, or only introspection is the path to truth.

Basic Methodology

In this section, we shall examine some of the basic methods and issues common to all experiments involving human subjects. The approach will be mainly intuitive and expository rather than mathematical. There are a number of good mathematical treatments of this subject (Fisher, 1925; Hays, 1963; Winer, 1971), and the would-be researcher should have an understanding of the mathematical foundation of this field; but there is a large gap between knowing the mathematics and being a good experimenter. In addition, since much of the mathematics and statistics of the experimental design are a special case of regression analysis, I assume that most aspiring political and social scientists already are familiar with the general if not the specific mathematics involved.

Internal and External Validity. Following the tradition of Campbell and Stanley (1963), we shall distinguish between the internal and external validity of empirical studies. Internal validity refers to the question "Did in fact the experimental treatments make a difference in this specific experimental instance?" (Campbell and Stanley, 1963, p. 175). Internal validity, then, is necessary if an experimental study is to be causally interpretable. External validity deals with the question of generalizability: "To what populations, settings, treatment variables, and measurement variables can this effect be generalized?" (Campbell and Stanley, 1963, p. 175). As with other inductive inferences, the question of external validity can never be answered completely. Though complete closure is impossible, some designs will approach external validity more closely than will others. Generally, with a large number of specific exceptions, psychologists are more concerned about the internal validity of a research design while political scientists are more concerned with the external validity.

Campbell has identified nine classes of extraneous variables which threaten to confound all experiments (Campbell, 1957a, 1969; Campbell and Ross, 1968, Campbell and Stanley, 1963). We shall examine each quite briefly here. A thorough discussion of the first eight factors may be found in Campbell and Stanley (1963); the last factor is discussed in Campbell and Ross (1968).

History, any specific event that may occur between the observations on the dependent variable, is the first threat to internal validity. A president may be assassinated, a war may escalate, a political scandal may occur; any one of these events might affect an experimenter's dependent variable quite independently of the experimental manipulation. As the time increases between measurements and as isolation from the real world decreases, this threat becomes more and more of a reality. The specific events within a single session, intrasession history, may also become a serious threat to internal validity if all the subjects in a single session receive the same experimental treatment.

Maturation, processes at work in the individual which operate independently of any historical or experimental events, poses a serious threat to political socialization studies. Included here are aging or maturing, fatigue, increasing hunger, and the like.

Testing the effects of taking a test the first time upon responses the second time, can be a real threat to attitude and opinion research (see especially the discussion in Kiesler, Collins, and Miller, 1969). Familiarity with the questions may increase performance on proficiency tests (reading, mathematics, grammar), or the mere act of giving an opinion or a response to an attitude question may set into motion cognitive and emotional processes which produce a change in behavior quite apart from any "communication" or other manipulation introduced by the experimenter.

Instrumentation changes pose a special threat whenever human judges are called upon to rate subjects on a set of behaviors or dimensions. For example, the first few subjects might not have appeared nearly so radical to the judges after the judges had been exposed to the entire sample of subjects.

Statistical regression occurs as a result of the random error inherent in any existing psychological measuring device (personality scale, attitude scale, intelligence test). It should not be confused with regression analysis (Blalock, 1960) or with regression in the psychoanalytic sense. Because the measuring instruments are imperfect, persons who score extremely high or extremely low on an instrument the first time have had their extremity from the mean accentuated by random error. Hence, second measurements using the same or correlated instruments should find these extreme scorers moving back, regressing, toward the mean, since the randomly distributed errors are now operating in another direction. Since researchers in political psychology are usually interested in groups or persons with varying degrees of some psychological property (self-esteem, need for power, authoritarianism, conservatism), a confounding of the experimental effect with regression effects is a very potent danger. Therefore, the rule of thumb should be to look out for regression effects whenever subjects are chosen because they are extreme on some measure and the dependent variable is an identical or correlated measure.

Selection biases occur whenever subjects can choose the treatment condition they will be in. This is true even when the subjects do not know that they will be in an experiment at the time they make the choice. For example, people who choose to attend early-morning classes (as well as those who teach them) are different in many ways from those who choose to attend afternoon classes. If the experimenter assigns one treatment to the morning classes and another to the afternoon, then he confounds the differences between morning and afternoon people with his treatment difference.

Experimental mortality, a differential loss of subjects between treatment groups or treatment and comparison groups, is a major threat whenever the study covers a long time period or whenever subjects leave an experimental group after it is established. For example, as Kelley (1967) has noted, the somewhat counterintuitive dissonance effects produced in forced-compliance studies (Festinger and Carlsmith, 1959; Carlsmith, Collins, and Helmreich, 1966) are trivial if many subjects have refused to emit the counterattitudinal behavior in the low-reward condition. Because they were aware of this, researchers in this field have always taken great pains to keep subjects in their experiments.

Selection-maturation interaction, biases introduced by differential rates of maturation or other autonomous changes across treatment groups, can occur whenever subjects are selected by the experimenter for treatment conditions on any basis other than random assignment. For example, if the special participatory democracy course in a political socialization study is given only to students in the fourth grade while students in the fifth grade are used as the control, the resulting differences may be a function of the different rates at which fourth- and fifth-grade students mature.

Finally, instability in the data—resulting from the unreliability of measures, fluctuations in sampling of subjects or units, and other spontaneous or autonomous errors in repeated or "equivalent" measures—may also bias the results. This is the only threat to internal validity to which statistical tests of significance are applicable (Campbell and Ross, 1968; Campbell, 1969).

In true experimental designs, random assignment to conditions by the experimenter or some other generator of chance assignments will effectively neutralize these threats to internal validity. Other confounds resulting from the experimental manipulations themselves will require more complex designs based upon random assignment (Underwood, 1957).

Any number of factors could affect the generalizability of the results of a study and hence its external validity. Only the six discussed by Campbell (1969) will be reviewed here. Other threats to external validity will be discussed later in this chapter.

The reactive or interaction effect of testing, a major threat to external validity, may increase a subject's sensitivity to the treatment or independent variable so that one cannot generalize from pretested to unpretested individuals. This effect, which is an interaction between the testing and the experimentally manipulated independent variable, is a threat to external validity and should not be confused with the simple effect of testing, which is a threat to internal validity. For example, if an experimenter wanted to test the effects of a certain antiwar communication upon a certain population, he could control for the simple effects of giving the pretest by pretesting attitudes toward war in the entire sample and then dividing them at random into an experimental and control group. Since both groups were pretested, differences between the two groups could not be attributed to testing; internal validity would still hold. At the same time, exposing subjects to the pretest might have made them especially sensitive to the communication delivered to them, so that they paid closer attention to the message than they normally would have. Thus, it would be very difficult to generalize from pretested to unpretested subjects. Though internal validity was high in this example, external validity was threatened. This sort of threat can be handled by making the pretest disguised, removed in time, unobtrusive, or otherwise nonreactive (Webb and others, 1966), or by use of a posttest only or of an experimental design that does not involve a pretest or that has a means of assessing the distortion due to pretesting (Campbell and Stanley, 1963).

The threat to external validity most frequently cited by political science critics of experimental research is the potential interaction between the subjects selected and the experimental arrangements. In other words, our manipulations might work on college students and white rats, but they may not work on people.

There is virtually no way to deal with this threat except by drawing a random sample from the population of interest (adult Americans, adult Americans and Western Europeans, adults from all over the world, all peoples) or by successive replications in various subsamples of all peoples.

External validity is further threatened by the reactive effects of experimental arrangements, generally known as the Hawthorne effect (Roethlisberger and Dickson, 1939). People who know that they are in an experiment may respond differently from those who do not. One solution to this problem is to experiment upon people who do not know that they are in an experiment, but such a procedure runs into serious ethical problems.

Multiple-treatment interference is a threat to external validity whenever subjects are used who have participated in other experiments. This is an especially significant hazard when researchers use college students or students from university-affiliated "laboratory" elementary and secondary schools or when advertisements in the newspaper attract a number of professional subjects, who earn or supplement their income by participating in studies of every sort—from tests of new drugs to political psychology studies.

The final two threats to external validity result from the complexity of the measures and treatments involved in social and political experiments. The measures that we use are not "pure" but contain systematic as well as error components which are irrelevant to the dimension we wish to measure. Statistical tests can allow estimates of the distortion due to errors, but the irrelevant responsiveness of components of our measures may produce results that are mistaken for experimental effects. Similarly, irrelevant components of the experimental treatments may produce replications (or failures to replicate) that bias our understanding of phenomena. Therefore, we need multiple measures with as little in common as possible except for the theoretical variable they are supposed to measure, and we need experimental replications that are equally diverse. As Kiesler, Collins, and Miller (1969) urge, we need a "heterogeneity of irrelevancies."

Control of Independent Variables. In the typical laboratory experiment, whether in the biological, agricultural, or physical sciences, the experimenter has virtually complete control over his independent variable. The experimenter decides which rat gets the severe shock, which plot gets the hybrid grain, and which combination of chemicals gets the calcium phosphate. As a consequence, direct causal inferences are relatively easy to make and the experimental designs need to be made complex only to increase efficiency (Campbell and Stanley, 1963; Fisher, 1925, 1935). In the typical laboratory experiment involving human subjects, the control is less and the designs must become correspondingly more complex; but there is still more control than one has in correlational research, where the control is only a mathematical approximation at best.

To illustrate why control is so important, we shall examine the problems raised by a study of campaign or propaganda techniques. Let us suppose that we want to do a piece of research dealing with some aspect of local-level campaign activity (such as voter registration or personal contact or mailed leaflets) upon voter behavior. If we attempt to use straight correlational techniques in our study, as has been done frequently (see, for instance, Crotty, 1971; Cutright and Rossi, 1958; Cutright, 1963; Kramer, 1970; Price and Lupfer, 1973; Wolfinger, 1963), by assessing the type or level of activity and then correlating it with voter turnout or voter preference, we are left with the nagging possibility that either the direction of causation is opposite to that which we wish to infer or that some unknown or unanticipated third, fourth, or fifth factor or combination of factors caused both the high turnout or preference effects and the level or type of campaign activity.

For example, the campaign managers, unable to propagandize every district or person in their electorate, might have chosen the high-turnout or high-preference wards, precincts, or individuals for special contact because they knew that they would get results there; that is, the high turnout and preference rates in these wards caused them to be propagandized. A more complex three- or four-factor interaction might also be responsible for producing a turnout or preference effect in the propagandized wards. For instance, the ethnicity, ideology, life styles, or other personal characteristics of the campaign directors or available volunteer workers might have made them choose certain wards, precincts, or persons to propagandize and exclude others because the campaign personnel were more at ease with some groups or more concerned about the interests of some groups than others. Here the control might flow from certain issues or candidate styles, which produced *both* the turnout and preferences of the campaign workers *and* the voters in the target wards.

In the campaign-activity literature, there have been some brilliant attempts to introduce statistical controls which rule out reversals or third factors in the causal relationships. (See especially, Crotty, 1971; Kramer, 1970.) Regression or analyses of covariance using previous election results can shed light on the direction of causality, and various controls for plausible third and fourth factors can rule them out or assess their effect. However, these mathematical controls have their limitations. First, the investigator can control or rule out only those factors that he recognizes as potential threats. Usually these are the most obvious social and demographic factors and a few structural variables for which data were available. Second, the researcher may be able to think of other potential factors, but he cannot deal with them because the data were not gathered or were not available or because his sample was so limited that he has used up his degrees of freedom with the controls previously introduced. Finally, as Simon and Rescher (1966) have demonstrated formally, no correlational method can resolve the causal question.

In experimental studies of campaign techniques (Eldersveld, 1956; Eldersveld and Dodge, 1954) there is no question of the direction of causality. The experimenter controlled who got the contact, the leaflets, the emotional appeal, or the telephone calls. Hence, he or she caused the voting effects; the voting effects did not cause the experimenter (as opposed to the party chairman) to choose a given ward. While the *direction* of causation in quasi-experimental studies of voting techniques (Blyden-burgh, 1971; Gertzog, 1970; Reback, 1971; Gosnell, 1927; Hartmann, 1935; Orbell, Dawes, and Collins, 1972) is also usually clear cut, *differences between the groups* caused by third and fourth factors are not so easy to rule out as in true experiments because the matching or analysis procedures may still leave possible factors which cannot be eliminated or assessed. As with mathematical controls in correlational studies, the researcher can assess or rule out only a limited number of factors in a quasi-experimental design. On the other hand, true experiments—using randomization or chance mechanisms to assign treatment units to conditions—can rule out all possible third- or fourth-factor correlations because the randomization process automatically makes all other variables orthogonal or uncorrelated with the independent variable. Thus, in the true experiment the researcher controls not only for those factors that he or his colleagues thought were *plausible* (before or after the data were gathered) but also for all *possible* third- or higher-factor correlations with the independent variable: those which his critics might dream up and those which research fifteen years later reveals to be of crucial importance.

In many instances this distinction between all *possible* correlated factors and those that are *plausible* might appear impractical. We might be able to advise a political candidate to invest his money in personal or telephone contacts rather than emotional mail appeals without being certain that all possible artifacts had been ruled out (see Campbell, 1969). Nevertheless, when we wish to move toward the construction of rigorous empirical theories, we should at least strive for the perfection that experimental control gives us.

Randomization. In the preceding discussion, the term *control* was used in two related but somewhat different senses. First, it referred to the power of the experimenter to determine the fate of the subjects or treatment units with regard to the application of the independent variables (or to the lack of power of the subjects or treatment units to determine or self-select their fate). It also referred to the ability of the researcher to rule out other factors related to both the independent and the dependent variables. The first type of control could be exercised in either experimental or quasi-experimental designs (although in some quasi-experimental designs the subjects' power is much greater than in others or in true experiments). The second meaning of *control* is present only in true experiments, because random or chance mechanisms for assigning treatment units to conditions is necessary if *all* possible third- and fourth-factor correlations between independent and dependent variables are to be controlled or ruled out.

When we speak of randomization, two possible misinterpretations may occur, depending upon the background of the reader. For those unskilled (or at least unschooled) in the techniques of survey research, random assignment may be interpreted to mean haphazard or even sloppy. This is not the case at all. As we shall see, the procedure is explicit and exact, quite the opposite of haphazard, careless, or sloppy. For those readers approaching political psychology from a survey research background, randomization in assignment to treatments may be confused with the procedure for drawing the sample or selecting the levels of the independent variables. Random selection of samples and treatment levels is important in experimental as well as survey research. The samples used in experimental research may be equal-probability samples (Kish, 1965; Young, 1966), in which case randomization is an integral part of the selection procedure; or the samples may be haphazard, convenient, or not even a sample at all, as in cases where the total population of interest is used in the experimental design. The nature of the sample affects the external validity of the study but does not affect the control of independent or third-factor variables.

The procedure for choosing the levels of the independent variable affects the mathematical or statistical model chosen for data analysis (fixed versus random, finite versus infinite). The nature of the appropriate model determines the size of the error term used to test the significance of the effects and also influences the external validity to some degree; but, again, it does not affect the control of extraneous factors. (For discussions of the mathematical models required for tests of significance in experimental research, see Cornfield and Tukey, 1956; Ferguson, 1959; Stanley, 1956; Winer, 1971.)

In order to achieve control over extraneous factors, a random or chance procedure is a must. Just as random selection is necessary to ensure that a sample is drawn from a population in which every subject or unit was equally likely to have been drawn, so random assignment is necessary to ensure that every subject or unit is equally likely to be given any treatment or combination of treatments.

When subjects or units are randomly assigned to treatments, the following benefits accrue to the researcher. First, all third- or fourth-order correlations between the independent and dependent variables are eliminated. Second, the treatment groups are equated on all dependent variables at the time of randomization. Third, postexperimental differences between groups can be tested for significance by the appropriate mathematical models developed to estimate the expected values of the error variation in dependent variable scores.

When the analysis of variance model, based upon random assignment, can be used for assessment of significance, smaller sample sizes are generally required than in correlational work to achieve the same statistical confidence levels in the differences between treatment groups. This is because, as S. R. Brown (1971) pointed out, the estimate of variation due to error in correlational work is a theoretical valued based upon sample size. Hence, in correlational work, error is reduced principally by increasing sample size. In experimental work, using the analysis of variance model, the estimation of variation in dependent variable scores due to error is an empirical matter. Although error can be reduced in experiments by increasing sample size, it can also be reduced by manipulating other factors directly under control of the experimenter in the concrete situation. While this reduction may represent an artificial magnification of the experimental effect, reducing external validity and introducing a hazard rather than a benefit, I think that it is a benefit to have the estimate of error determined empirically in each situation and that the option of devoting resources (time, money, effort) to aspects of the research other than the procurement of subjects is also a benefit.

Matching on one, two, or more dimensions is the method of assignment to treatment conditions usually posed as an alternative to randomization. This procedure has several drawbacks, however. First, as we have indicated repeatedly, though the researcher might match on a large number of dimensions, he cannot match on all dimensions except by randomization. Second, it is frequently impossible to match on certain combinations of dimensions. For example, Hartmann (1935) matched his wards on population density (38.44 versus 37.28 persons per acre) but then discovered gross inequalities in wealth in the wards ($2070.12 versus $871.72 mean assessed value per capita). Although modern multivariate techniques can reduce some of this bias, they cannot eliminate it. Third, matching on other extraneous variables, even when possible, does not ensure that the experimental groups are matched on the most important variable of all: the dependent variable.

As an illustration of this last point, let us consider two studies, one quasi-experimental (Clausen, 1968) and the other experimental (Kraut and McConahay, 1972), of the effect on subsequent voting behavior of subjects interviewed by poll-takers. Clausen compared the voting turnout rates reported by respondents in two different independent national samples: one drawn by the University of Michigan's Survey Research Center and interviewed both before and after the presidential election of 1964; the other drawn by the United States Bureau of the Census and interviewed only after the election. By some very clever analyses, Clausen was able to rule out noninterview biases and response invalidity as explanations for the 3.5 percent larger turnout reported in the SRC sample over the Census Bureau sample. Hence, he concluded (tentatively) that the preelection interview had stimulated people who normally would not vote to vote in the election that followed. Nevertheless, Clausen (and his readers) could never be certain that the turnout rates of the two samples would have been equal had they both received either preelection and postelection interviews or postelection interviews only. The samples were drawn by different organizations, were of different sizes, were intended to represent two different populations (all voters versus all adults), and therefore might have differed in their turnout rates even without the preelection interview. Clausen's quasi-experimental design provides suggestive evidence of the stimulation effect of a preelection interview, but it is weak evidence to use in starting a chain of theorizing about psychological mechanisms to account for this stimulation effect.

An experiment by Kraut and McConahay (1972), planned and executed in blissful ignorance of Clausen's work, provided much less ambiguous evidence that the interview effect is real and rather powerful in low-salience elections. In this study, an equal-probability sample of registered voters with Italian surnames was drawn from a middle-class ward in New Haven, Connecticut. The experimenters divided the entire sample in half by assigning every other name on the alphabetical list of persons in the sample to group A or group B. Then, by flipping a coin, they designated group B as the experimental group and group A as the control group. Subjects in the experimental group were subsequently contacted and interviewed by graduate students. (The subjects knew that the interviewers worked for Yale but were unaware of their status as graduate students.) The interviews involved a modified version of studies (Kamin, 1958; Lorinskas, Hawkins, and Edwards, 1969) in which subjects were asked some standard party-identification and political-efficacy questions and then given a series of hypothetical electoral choices pitting candidates with Italian and Anglo-Saxon surnames against one another. When additional subjects were needed to meet the requirements of the ethnicity study (because some experimental subjects had moved or died) ; a new probability sample of Italian-surnamed subjects was drawn. This sample was twice as large as needed for the ethnicity study and was split on an even-odd basis into two groups, which were then assigned to experimental and control conditions by the flip of a coin. Party officials (unaware of who was an experimental and who was a control subject) identified the persons in the total sample who had voted in an election two weeks after the interviews (May) and three months after that (August). In both elections, interviewed subjects voted at a higher rate than noninterviewed subjects.

Noninterview biases and response invalidity, the two major alternative explanations for Clausen's findings, were handled automatically by randomization in the Kraut and McConahay experiment (1972). Differences in turnout rate due to differences between the experimental and control groups in the number of persons who were incapacitated, dead, or absent from the community were ruled out because these persons were equally likely to have been assigned to either group, and the turnout rates were computed on the basis of the entire experimental and control groups— not simply on the basis of who was actually contacted. Similarly, response invalidity was not a possible rival hypothesis because errors in recording and/or deliberate tampering with the voting records were as likely to have happened for subjects assigned to the control as for those in the experimental group. Finally, there could not possibly have been any subtle, undetected, unthought-of, or unexpected differences between the experimental and control samples in the second study (differences that might have made for differences in turnout rates even without an interview) because the experimental and control subjects were drawn as part of the *same* sample, using identical procedures from an identical population.

The Kraut and McConahay study illustrates one method that can be used for making random selections. There were two treatment conditions; and since there was no reason to suspect that an alphabetical list of Italian surnames would have a systematic pattern of variation which coincided with the choice of every other one for group A, this method of systematic assignment was chosen. However, one must be careful in using this or other systematic procedures. As Kish (1965) has pointed out, a monotonic trend or an unfortunate systematic fluxuation among subjects in the sample may bias the assignment. For example, if an experiment were being conducted in a California housing development where two basic styles of "uniquely individual" houses were available, one costing $20,000 and the other costing $30,000, an assignment procedure placing every other house on a list of street addresses in the experimental group might bias the assignment if the developer had used a similar procedure to intermix his "deluxe" and "superdeluxe" houses. Thus, much to the experimenter's chagrin, he might later discover that the experimental subjects were more affluent than the control subjects.

This type of bias could also occur if subjects were coming to a laboratory setting at various times of the day and the experimenter decided to assign all the morning subjects to one treatment condition and all the afternoon (or even worse, all the evening) subjects to a second condition. He might think he had avoided the problem by assigning the 10, 12, 2, 4, and 6 o'clock subjects to one condition and the 9, 11, 1, 3, and 5 o'clock subjects to the other. However, he is in trouble if he does not realize that ROTC meets only on the even-numbered hours. Thus, his "pro-military" communication (given during odd-numbered hours) might get, on the average, an especially sympathetic reception for reasons having nothing to do with the "emotional" quality of its arguments.

The moral, then, is that systematic assignment by a procedure of every nth subject or unit is a relatively easy and straightforward technique provided the researcher has thought about possible confounding trends in the sample.

The best, most elegant, and only slightly more inconvenient procedure is to use a table of random numbers (for instance, see Lindley and Miller, 1958) or of random permutations (for instance, see Winer, 1971). In this procedure, subjects or treatment units are assigned to treatment conditions according to how they coincide or correspond with a number on a table. For example, if the experimenter has two treatment conditions (experimental and control), he goes to a table of random permutation of some even number of digits (16 or 32, for instance), chooses a column, and then assigns the first subject or treatment unit on his list to the experimental condition if the first number is even, the second subject or treatment unit to the experimental condition if the second number is even, and the third subject or treatment unit to the control condition if the third number is odd. This procedure could be used to randomize not only subjects or treatment units but time of day, day of week, date of month, or any other factor that might vary in such a way as to confound the assignment of treatment units to conditions.

Readers should note that I have used the phrase *random assignment of subjects or treatment units* rather than the simple phrase *random assignment of subjects*. I have done so because one of the most frequent methodological errors made by those sophisticated in correlational techniques who attempt to do experimental research is to think they have randomized an entire subject population when they have randomized only certain units within the population. This error occurs repeatedly throughout the pages of *Experimental Study of Politics* (see Dawson, 1971; Dyson and Scioli, 1971; Lamare, 1971; Reback, 1971). The error usually occurs under one of two conditions. In the first, subjects are assigned at random as individuals to one of two experimental sessions. For example, in one session one hundred subjects see an antiwar film and in the other session one hundred subjects hear an antiwar lecture. A second condition under which this error is likely to occur is when groups, wards, or other units of subjects are assigned at random to experimental treatments. For example, certain wards may receive a great deal of party activity and others receive very little or none at all (Gertzog, 1970). Mere assignment of subjects to conditions in one of these fashions is not the error. The error occurs when subjects are assigned in these ways and then the data are analyzed by pooling the dependent variable scores for the individual subjects and doing statistical tests on the basis of an inflated number of degrees of freedom.

Let us examine these two error-prone assignment techniques in some detail. In doing so, we will examine hypothetical rather than real cases, so as not to single out any one of these new experiments in political psychology for special criticism.

Let us suppose that an experimenter wants to test the effects of a one-sided antiwar television program versus those of a two-sided program upon the attitudes of the general public. He discovers that the American Broadcasting System has made two pilot films—one film blatantly antiwar and antimilitary, the other film balancing much of this same antiwar material with a rebuttal by "General George I. (G.I.) Joseph." The experimenter draws a random sample of citizens living within a radius of fifty miles of his town (in order to cut down on the proportion of academics in his sample and study some "real people"). By offering his subjects fifty dollars for a two-hour session, he gets *all* of the potential subjects to agree to come down to the theater he has rented (so that they will not associate his study with the local college) on a night he has designated. Unfortunately, he has spent so much money on securing the film, drawing a true random sample of all adults, seducing them into coming to his special showing, and renting the theater that he can show the film only two times, once on Monday and once on Tuesday. He is not worried about this, however, because his subjects agree to come on exactly the night he tells them, and he assigns them to nights at random (using a random-number table).

E shows the one-sided film to one hundred subjects on Monday and the two-sided pilot to one hundred subjects on Tuesday. After each showing, he asks the subjects the same set of unobtrusive, cleverly disguised, highly valid, and highly reliable questions which tap their antiwar feelings, antimilitary attitudes, and pacifist inclinations. He also asks them a set of more direct policy-oriented questions about the ordering of American priorities. Finally, his graduate students call the subjects at home two months later and ask them some questions as part of a public opinion poll, which is not perceived by the subjects as in any way related to the experimenter's research.

He then analyzes his data. He computes the mean score for each of the two groups (one-sided and two-sided) and discovers that the differences between the two groups are not very big. Hence, he has to do statistical tests in order to convince journal editors and journal readers that he has discovered something more substantial than just a chance fluxation. Accordingly, he does a series of t tests on the differences between the means of the two groups, each having 198 degrees of freedom, and writes an article concluding that a one-sided communication is more effective than a two-sided communication in producing attitude change in this population. The journal editor rejects the article, noting that if the experimenter wanted to conclude that the different messages did make a difference, he should have used zero degrees of freedom in his t test (impossible, of course). If he wanted to conclude that "something which happened in the Monday session" produced more attitude change than "whatever it was that happened on Tuesday night," then he could still use 198 degrees of freedom.

This experimenter's problem was that in his procedure he confounded *intrasession history* with the independent variable (one-sided versus two-sided). If he had wanted to conclude that it was the difference between the messages (rather than an obnoxious drunk in his Army Reserve uniform at the Tuesday session or his own more confident and relaxed manner on Monday or the fire drill in the building next door on Monday or the breakdown of the boiler on Tuesday or some other more subtle, perhaps unspecifiable difference between what happened in the two sessions) that made a difference in the subjects' antiwar attitudes, he could have used one of two strategies. First, he could have arranged for each subject to see the one- or two-sided film alone. He could have used many television sets in a number of isolation booths or had subjects come to the theater at one- or two-hour intervals all week long. In this case he could have taken the average of each individual's score on the dependent variable and use a t test with 198 degrees of freedom. He could then conclude that it was the message alone and not the combination of message and session that produced the difference because each subject's individual session would have been unique. The irrelevant events—such as drunks in uniform, the fire drill, his own changes in mood (presumed to vary independently of the film he was showing), the changes in temperature in the building, and so on—would have been distributed across all sessions in a fashion which did not coincide exclusively with one of the communications. That is, the unique intrasession histories would have been randomly distributed across conditions.

As a second possible strategy, he could have had smaller numbers at each session and multiple replications of each session. For example, he could have assigned subjects to sessions on Monday, Tuesday, Wednesday, Thursday, and Friday evenings, held two sessions each night, and shown each film at one or the other of these sessions each night. The one-sided film could have been shown at the first session on three nights, and the two-sided film could have been shown at the first session on the other two nights. Which film would be shown first on which night could have been decided by a combination of counterbalancing and randomization. In this procedure, the one hundred subjects exposed to the one-sided film would have been distributed across five sessions of about twenty subjects each. The same would hold for the subjects exposed to the two-sided pilot. The data analysis should in this instance be based upon computing the average score for each session and then computing the average of the averages for the five one-sided sessions and the five two-sided sessions. The t test on the differences between these two final average of averages should be based upon eight degrees of freedom.

To repeat and summarize, this experimenter's difficulty grew out of his confounding of the nature of his communication (the properties of his independent variable) with intrasession history. Since the subjects on Monday night had in *common both* the one-sided communication *and* whatever happened in their session, they had to be treated as a single unit for the data analysis unless the experimenter wanted to conclude that it was this combination that was responsible for the observed difference. The problem, then, is not that the experiment was run in only two sessions. It could have been run in only one session and the data analyzed on the basis of individual scores if each subject had received his or her treatment as an individual. If, for example, subjects had *read* one- or two-sided newspaper editorials distributed at random throughout the *same* group, the data could have been analyzed at the individual level because *all* subjects would have had the same intrasession history. Hence, only the difference in reading material would account for the observed differences in attitudes, feelings, or opinions. The rule of thumb should be to analyze, as a unit, all subjects who have both a common intrasession history and a common experimental treatment. Since this analysis is usually accomplished by averaging an individual subject's scores within units (which increases the reliability of a unit score) and then averaging across units, the increase in reliability generally offsets the decrease in degrees of freedom.

The above error results from a confound within the experimental design. The second error, assigning units at random and analyzing on the basis of individuals, results from a violation of the assumptions underlying the mathematics of randomization. This error occurs in most studies of voting behavior where whole wards or precincts are assigned to some treatment condition—for example, when one set of precincts is flooded with emotional campaign materials and another with rational materials (Hartmann, 1935). It could also occur, however, in studies of political socialization, in which whole classrooms or schools are assigned the same curriculum. For experimental and quasi-experimental voting studies where this error did not occur, see Blydenburgh (1971); where the correct degrees of freedom were used; and Eldersveld and Dodge (1954) and Eldersveld (1956), where the randomization was on the basis of individuals rather than wards or precincts.

As another hypothetical example, let us suppose that an experimenter wants to test the effects of endorsement of a candidate by a well-regarded or a poorly regarded public figure upon voter preference. With the consent of the candidate, he picks thirty wards in which to distribute the literature and (using a table of random permutations) assigns the wards to one of three conditions: (1) Leaflets are distributed telling of the candidate's great qualities of leadership and probity; the leaflets are signed by the incumbent president of the United States, a person loved by everyone in this electoral district. (2) The same leaflets are distributed bearing the signatures of a famous local murderer, rapist, and child molester, a person uniformly hated by everyone in the district. (3) The same leaflets are distributed without a signature or other source identification. The experimenter then waits two weeks and sends legions of graduate students out to interview an equal-probability sample of voters drawn from the three districts. By means of Thematic Apperception Tests, Semantic Differentials, and some clever tests of his own creation, he is able to obtain a highly reliable and valid interval scale of preference for the candidate.

Because of his cleverness, his interviewers' resourcefulness, the huge amount of money he spent, and a tremendous amount of luck, this experimenter, then, obtained measures of candidate preference from 100 percent of his original sample, so that he had no sampling bias; and he secured data from one hundred subjects in each of his three wards. Since the leaflets were assigned at random and the sample was un-biased, he was certain that the three groups were equally likely to prefer the candidate before he bombarded them with his propaganda. Hence, he performed a three-level one-way analysis of variance upon his data, using F tests having 2 and 297 degrees of freedom. After examining the results, he concluded that it was better to be en-dorsed by a dearly loved incumbent president than by a hated murderer, rapist, and child molester but (interestingly enough) that it was better to have been endorsed by the latter than to distribute unsigned literature. The journal editor, unfortunately, concluded that the experimenter should have used F tests with 2 and 27 degrees of freedom in his various analyses, because unit of randomization and unit of analysis must be the same for tests of this sort. Since the experimenter had randomized on the basis of wards, his total N was 30, not 300, and his degrees of freedom had to be reduced accordingly. Unfortunately, when the new analyses were run, he found himself with no statistically significant results.

Rather than wade any further into the mathematics, let us attempt to get an intuitive grasp of the problem. The reason for randomization in this experiment was to equate the three treatment groups on the dependent variable and all other variables at the time of randomization. Since the unit of randomization was the ward rather than the individual, the wards composing the high-prestige treatment group were equal to the wards composing the other two treatment groups. In other words, the high-prestige treatment group—which equaled the other two treatment groups—was a group of wards, not a group of individuals.

The experimenter could have avoided this error if he had averaged scores within wards and then averaged the averages. He could also have recorded the percentage of the vote the candidate got in each ward and then averaged the per-centages across wards within treatment groups. The rule of thumb, then, is that the unit of randomization (persons, groups, wards, classrooms, legislative committees) and the unit of data analysis must be identical.

In the two examples illustrating these common errors in randomization, the hypothetical experimenter used parametric statistics (t and F tests) to assess the significance levels of his results. His errors could not have been avoided if he had used nonparametric tests (Chi squares, for example). The error was in violating the logic of randomization for equation of experimental treatment groups and would be reflected in the number of degrees of freedom chosen for any type of statistical test. The examples also involved only two- and three-level single-factor designs for simplicity of presentation. The logic, however, applies to multilevel and multifactor experimental designs as well.

One last point that should be raised before I leave this discussion of randomization is that matching and randomization can be combined to gain statistical precision in some circumstances, especially where the number of experimental units is small. Thus, in our last example the experimenter could have matched as nearly as possible on the vote for his candidate in the preceding election (or the nominee of his candidate's party) by creating ten groups of three wards, each ward having approximately the same voter-preference rates. Then one ward from each trio could be assigned at random to one of the experimental conditions. This procedure is called *blocking* in the statistical literature and is discussed intuitively in Campbell and Stanley (1963) and mathematically in Cox (1957), Feldt (1958), and Lindquist (1953).

Randomization in Field Settings. In the hypothetical examples above and in many actual experimental studies of political psychology, internal validity is frequently sacrificed to attain a certain measure of external validity. Films acquired from networks at considerable expense are used instead of less expensive television tapes or written materials created by the researcher. Random samples are drawn from a population of voters or all adults in a district. The research is conducted in field settings, where real elections or real committee decisions can be observed. Unfortunately, since all research is conducted within the limits of a finite (though occasionally large) budget, the resources devoted to increasing external validity will reduce the resources that an experimenter can devote to internal validity. This brings us to the researcher's dilemma: Increasing external validity may reduce internal validity to the point where the results are uninterpretable; but introducing more and more control to maximize internal validity may introduce more and more isolation, sterility, and artificiality—which reduces external validity to the point where the results are clear but ungeneralizable.

As with most real-life dilemmas, there is no ideal solution. Not only are we unable to conduct "crucial" studies in which two competing theories are pitted against each other and one of them destroyed by the empirical results (Campbell and Stanley, 1963), but we can rarely conduct perfect experiments in which both internal and external validity are maximized. What we will need, then, is programmatic rather than one-shot research. In programmatic research, a series of experiments (or studies) are conducted in which we compensate for flaws in one study by designing a second study which is free of those flaws but has a different set of weaknesses, which can be compensated for in a third study, and so on. Furthermore, in such a program the internal validity of each individual study should be maximized while the weaknesses in external validity should be compensated for by different studies. In fact, an experimental study (specifically excluding quasi-experimental studies) which does not have perfect internal validity is not worth doing. In experimental research, excuses for design flaws that jeopardize internal validity but are justified as necessary to increase external validity must be categorically rejected.

If the researcher is going to attempt an experiment, with all the effort and cost entailed in such research, he ought to emerge with a result that is clearly interpretable in a causal sense. However, once the internal validity has been achieved by proper randomization and the necessary control groups, then efforts should be made to increase external validity in a fashion that does not jeopardize internal validity.

A true experiment in a field setting, while very difficult to perform, does begin to approach an ideal solution to the dilemma. Frequently, researchers have overlooked the opportunities to do field experiments because the laboratory scientists were more comfortable with the ease and extreme control of the laboratory, and survey researchers simply did not think in experimental terms, finding it easier to measure differences in the variable of concern than to create them. Both types of researchers, however, should at least entertain the possibility that they might study a certain research question by means of a field experiment before settling for their most familiar method.

Field experiments may consist of simply transposing the laboratory into the field, taking the experiment and experimenters to the subjects rather than waiting for the subjects to come to the laboratory. Such studies have both internal validity, through randomization and control of experimental variations, and external validity insofar as they are in natural settings and the subjects are usually unaware of their participation in an experiment. For example, studies of bystander intervention (Bryan and Test, 1967; Piliavin, Rodin, and Piliavin, 1969) generally involve a team of researchers who fake an accident or an argument in a public place while another experimenter notes who intervened and in what manner under different experimental conditions. The above-cited studies of campaign techniques and of ethnicity and electoral choice are of this sort. In these field experiments, the randomization follows a procedure similar to that in laboratory experiments.

But still other possibilities for field experiments offer great opportunity for research and have not been exploited to any extent as yet. These take advantage of "naturally" occurring random assignments to gather meaningful data that are internally and externally valid. By "naturally" occurring random assignments we mean those set into motion independently of the experimenter.

The best example of this type of field experiment is the study by Siegel and Siegel (1957) of the effects of reference and membership groups upon attitude change. These researchers took advantage of the fact that Stanford University utilized a lottery to pick the women students who would get to live in highly desired "row housing." The women who wanted into row housing and those already living in row housing were higher on a modified F scale (Adorno and others, 1950) than other females on campus, but most Stanford women (regardless of housing) tended to score lower on the F scale the longer they were in school. The experimenters pre-tested the women who applied for row housing at the start of an academic year and then let the lottery create three experimental groups: (1) those who wanted in and did get into row housing; (2) those who wanted in and did not get in, but applied the next year; and (3) those who wanted in, did not get in, and did not apply again the next year. So far as F scale scores were concerned, this created (1) a group whose membership and reference groups were both high F; (2) a group whose membership group was low F but whose reference group was high F; (3) a group whose reference group and membership group were both low F. The result, consistent with reference-group and other social evaluation theories (Pettigrew,

1967), was that on a posttest a year later the first group showed the least decline in F scores while the third group showed the greatest decline.

Political psychologists may have other opportunities for field experiments which occur as a result of our roles as consultants or social reformers. Frequently, we are asked to advise a school board, legislative committee, or governmental administrative agency. The current emphasis upon evaluation and accountability by the United States Office of Education may provide excellent opportunities for research into political socialization and the political psychology of educational reform.

Along with Campbell (1969), we would stress the importance of pressing for random assignment under circumstances where not every unit (person, ward, school, classroom) can be subjected to the change at the same time. Random assignment is generally the fairest way to distribute experimental treatments in addition to having the properties of creating the conditions for a true experiment. For example, I was involved in planning and evaluating an alternative high school program in New Haven, Connecticut (Hawley and others, 1972). Many more students wanted into the program than could be admitted. Some school administrators and school board members initially favored establishing a screening committee to choose students by some set of criteria to be established by students, parents, teachers, administrators, and other interested persons. The social scientists, however, were able to convince all concerned that a lottery (stratified on certain racial groups to match the racial balance of the entire secondary school system) would be the fairest method of choosing students from the list of applicants. The acceptance of the lottery method satisfied a number of interests peculiar to various subgroups within the population involved in planning the new school and its program. It saved time, reduced or even eliminated political intrigues concerning who would be admitted, reduced the potential for a struggle over the admissions criteria, minimized the potential damage to the self-esteem of rejected students, and, incidentally, equated the admitted and nonadmitted groups of students on all independent and dependent variables (at the time of the lottery at any rate), and—especially important—it created a control group of nonadmitted students whose initial motivation to participate in the program was equal to that of the admitted students.

Naturally occurring experiments and those engineered by advisors as a means of equity have two great advantages over laboratory experiments. First, they have powerful variations in the independent variable; actually living in a row house does not compare in any way with role-playing such a relationship or being assigned to participate in a group for an hour. Second, they have high external validity. In addition, they are superior to survey studies because of their high internal validity. Field experiments of this sort may also have a disadvantage vis à vis laboratory experiments. Frequently the exact stimulus producing the change is hard if not impossible to specify. For example, the observed differences may result from exposure to an entire school curriculum or to only one course in that curriculum (Hawley and others, 1972). Similarly, differences observed after an experiment in racially integrated education might result from the intergration experience or from the fact that some students rode buses to school. These ambiguities may retard the development of middle-range theories in some cases; in others the theories are such blunt instruments that eliminating even gross alternatives can only help in sharpening them.

The rule of thumb, then, ought to be: Researchers should be on the lookout for field settings in which experiments can be performed, in which experiments are occurring "naturally," or in which the investigator can suggest randomization as the best and fairest means of deciding who gets what treatment. Whenever we hear or read of an instance where a chance mechanism is used to affect people's political lives or behavior, we should ask if this opportunity could be utilized for research purposes. Social psychologists, for example, have already started taking advantage of the selective service lottery to examine its effects upon social psychological attitudes (Apsler, 1972). Surely, political psychologists might be interested in whether the nineteen-year-old subjects in this experiment also have their political behavior affected.

Quasi-Experiments. When pretreatment equality of groups cannot be achieved through randomization, quasi-experimental or patchwork designs may still yield internally valid data with high external validity. The general principle involved is to introduce as much randomization as possible and to compensate for various threats to internal validity by finding comparison groups which enable an experimenter to infer that a specific threat to internal validity is highly implausible even if he is unable to rule it out entirely as a possible threat. A number of these quasi-experimental designs have been suggested in some detail (Campbell, 1968; Campbell and Stanley, 1963), and specific applications of them to concrete research questions have also been published (Campbell, 1969; Campbell and Ross, 1968).

Complicating Factors

We could stop our discussion at this point inasmuch as the basic principles of experimentation have been presented. However, political psychologists should be concerned with generalizing from specific studies to broader theoretical issues, and we usually (though not always) use human individuals or human institutions as the subjects and the experimenters in our studies. Because of this, the world of the experimenter is even more complex than the above presentation implied. In this section, we shall look quite briefly at these additional factors. Though our examination will be almost cursory (because of space limitations), these factors are important and the complete experimenter will have mastered them as well as other aspects of experimental design.

Multiple Measures and Methods. Frequently political psychologists wish to include individual-difference measures as part of their experimental designs. For example, Morrow (1972) included self-esteem and personal efficacy, two concepts measured by psychometric scales, along with an experimental manipulation of the status of the frustrator in his test of a social-psychological model of aggressive political behavior. In fact, probably because of our heavy reliance upon correlational methods in the past, most of our political-psychological concepts are operationalized by paper-and-pencil individual-difference measures (authoritarianism, liberalism-conservatism, dogmatism).

The variance associated with measures of this sort has at least three components: random-error variance, method variance, and variance contributed by differences in individual's standing on the trait or dimension. Error variance can be assessed and controlled by statistical tests of significance, but the other two are hopelessly confounded in a single study that uses only one method of measuring individual differences, and this confound is a possible threat to the external validity of the study. Good experimental procedures, therefore, should include both multiple methods of assessing the same individual-difference dimension of independent variables *and* multiple methods of measuring the dependent variables (see Campbell and Fiske, 1959).

Advocates of psychological control in experiments (variations in the experimental stimuli of the *same* treatment condition to increase "experimental realism" and create a uniform psychological state or perception) should be especially careful to use multiple "take" measures or checks upon their manipulations, since method and hypothesized psychological state are confounded in single-method procedures. On the other hand, advocates of a uniform stimulus presentation or stimulus control should be careful to replicate, using very different stimulus manipulations, since method and concept are confounded in a stimulus-control procedure. (For discussions of stimulus control versus psychological control, see Aronson and Carlsmith, 1968; Kiesler, Collins, and Miller, 1969.)

Experimenter Effects and Bias. In the 1960s, experimental researchers discovered the experimenter. As a result, new possible threats to both internal and external validity must be dealt with. The threat to internal validity was first called to our attention by R. Rosenthal's work (1966, 1969) on experimenter *bias*. This kind of bias is a threat to internal validity because the various persons who run the experiments for the researcher (influenced by the researcher's hypotheses or their own hypotheses regarding the outcome of the experiment) may act differently in different experimental conditions. This different, often quite subtle, behavior is thus confounded with differences in the experimental manipulations across treatment conditions. Discussion of procedures for controlling experimenter's bias (such as automation and "blind" experimenters) and criticisms of Rosenthal's original research may be found in Aronson and Carlsmith (1968) and Kiesler, Collins, and Miller (1969).

The threat to external validity results from the obvious fact that different experimenters are different. Different experimenters, quite independently of their expectations regarding the hypothesized outcome of the experiment, may produce different results; consequently, the results obtained by one experimenter may not generalize to those of other experimenters. Survey researchers have been aware of the different effects of various interviewers for some time (see Hyman and others, 1954), but experimental researchers began systematic examination of such effects much later (McGuigan, 1963; Kintz and others, 1965). As with experimenter bias, there are no across-the-board panaceas for the problem of experimenter effects. The best general approach is to consider the experimenter as a context variable (Kiesler, Collins, and Miller, 1969) and to employ more than one experimenter, each running all conditions of the experiment. This procedure permits assessment of the experimenter effect by including the experimenter as a random factor in the analysis of variance.

Demand Characteristics. Experimental arrangements and design may combine to pose a threat to internal validity (as well as to external validity, previously discussed). For example, Orne (1962) has proposed that subjects enter an experiment with a problem-solving orientation aimed at discovering what the experimenter wants them to do. Because the students who serve as subjects in most experiments value science, they will then do what they think the experimenter's theory calls for—

their notions being based upon the *demand characteristics* of the experimental situation (their analysis of the design, the cover story, and the like) and not upon cues given off by the experimenter. A similar formulation is Rosenberg's (1965b) concept of *evaluation apprehension,* which also assumes that subjects will do what they perceive as the normal or proper thing for them to do once they have figured out the experimenter's intention. Attempts to minimize the effects of this phenomenon have ranged from increasing the deception of the subjects in some way (through separated posttests, "preexperimental" experiments, elaborate cover stories) to careful analyses of the design for demand characteristics. These attempts are discussed in detail and different solutions proposed in Aronson and Carlsmith (1968) and Kiesler, Collins, and Miller (1969).

Ethics. Concern about the reactivity of experimental situations, demand characteristics, and the increasing experimental sophistication of their college student subjects led many psychological experimenters to move into field settings, where the subjects had no idea they were in an experiment, or to build ever more elaborate hoaxes into their experimental designs. As a result, pretesting of experimental manipulations and elaborate debriefings (or "de-hoaxings," as they are called in one laboratory-oriented psychology department) became increasingly necessary. (For the best description of careful pretesting and debriefing procedures, see Aronson and Carlsmith, 1968.) Eventually the manipulations began to rival the wildest and fondest dreams of the mad scientists who inhabit television's late, late shows. Understandably, a number of psychologists have become uneasy about the ethics involved in doing experiments in which there is a great deal of deception or stress created for human subjects, especially when it is the subjects who suffer and "science" or the scientists who benefit (Baumrind, 1964; Ring, 1967; Kelman, 1968c). The debate thus far has been mainly speculative and rhetorical, but the ethical issues involved in doing experimental or any sort of research should not be too readily dismissed simply because of the form in which they have been raised. Political psychology is an especially sensitive area, not only because of the manner in which our data might be gathered but also because of the use to which our findings might be put.

Final Note

It would be a gross exaggeration to claim that the discipline of political psychology will not advance until every scientist in the field is an expert in experimental technique. But it is also a serious mistake to dismiss out of hand experimental methodology as a tool for political-psychological research. To restate a theme that has run throughout this chapter, we need to develop testable middle-range theories and a stance toward research which allows us to use multiple methods: intensive interviews, projective tests, sample surveys, cross-cultural comparisons, content analyses, standardized tests, questionnaires, and other procedures still to be invented. Laboratory and field experiments should take a prominent place among these other methods and probably will as more and more and more political researchers sharpen their experimental skills by doing experiments.

14

SIMULATION:
ATTEMPTS AND
POSSIBILITIES

Rufus P. Browning

The scientist strives to see behavior more clearly, to tell us more about it, and to weave ever stronger links between what he sees and what he says. The chapters of this volume on surveys, experiments, and projective techniques all focus on distinctive ways of observing or seeing behavior. In the case of simulation, this chapter examines some special ways of saying—ways of describing behavior and of finding out what the descriptions signify.

Simulation methods may be used to describe and study the behavior of any system. The following social and individual processes have in fact all been studied with the help of simulation: referendum campaigns in local communities (Abelson and Bernstein, 1963); the decision making of a legislature faced with a series of bills (Cherryholmes and Shapiro, 1969); the responses of a politician to a flow of information and questions about his politically salient environment (Abelson and Carroll, 1965); and the decisions and interactions of nations (Guetzkow and others,

383

1963). In contrast to other descriptions, however, simulations are working models of the processes under study. All descriptions aim to communicate the main features of behavior. Simulations go beyond such descriptions in an effort to reproduce observed behavior, even of complex systems, with a high degree of precision. The ability to reproduce the behavior of a human system would imply a strong description of its processes; thus a working model of the system is desirable in itself. It is also a necessity because often the only way to understand a complex description fully is to carry out the cumulative implications of every statement in it.

Unfortunately, carrying out the implications of a complex descriptive model is frequently an impossibly burdensome task for a person to accomplish unaided. The solution is to rely on the technology of the computer (computer simulation) or on ways of involving human actors to play out the assumptions and conditions set forth in the model (games or mixed, man-machine simulation). To operate the computer model or the game with human players is to *simulate* the processes of the system represented in the model: "A hypothetical stream of behavior is generated that can be compared with the stream of behavior of the original system" (Clarkson and Simon, 1960, p. 920). In this manner, the implications of what is said about behavior can be compared precisely with what is observed, and better descriptions can be devised to fill the gaps uncovered by the comparison.

Capabilities for describing complex processes precisely and for reproducing the behavior of a human system are indeed desirable features of a method for scientific description. The reader should keep in mind that simulation, like other methods, has its costs as well as its benefits, and also the deeper warning that simple insights, even ambiguously stated, may fruitfully guide our thinking about behavior. The researcher must decide for himself whether a precise working model of a complex process is what is needed and whether it is worth the costs of development and use.

Conceptually, simulation models depart sharply from other ways of describing behavior. A large part of our knowledge about human behavior is stated in the form of static, correlational propositions: variable Y is said to be related to variable X. Considerations of the sequence and timing of events are frequently left implicit or ignored altogether. Not so in simulation: the aim of generating a stream of behavior over time requires constant attention to the sequences in which events can occur and the time periods involved. A high correlation between attitudes of political efficacy and, say, participation in politics is interesting, but a simulation requires a statement about what happens to participation when the attitude changes—whether participation changes as well, how soon, and in what way. Much more information is needed than is given by the correlation. Simulation requires strong statements about the relationships among a great many such events and conditions.

The need for precise description often entails the use of mathematical functions in simulation models. Sometimes it is possible to derive by logical methods the main consequences of such a model. Especially for complex models, however, derivation is not feasible, and computer simulation provides the only way to determine how the model behaves.

Sometimes mathematical descriptions are partly or entirely inappropriate for the phenomena under study. Before the advent of the computer, verbal models of complex behavior, models precise enough to reproduce behavior, were scarcely conceivable. The computer offers a general logical and symbol-processing capability that can be used to explore the implications of models that are precise but entirely non-mathematical in conception, a radical innovation in fields where behavior has appeared impossibly intricate to trace and not describable in mathematical form (for instance, thinking).

Computer simulation is sometimes too demanding a method. Suppose a researcher has a set of hypotheses about some processes of a system and about its basic structure but lacks confidence in his knowledge about other parts of the system. It may be possible to construct a simulation in which people, programmed in part by the structure and predetermined processes of the game, play out the roles of hypothetical actors in the system to which the simulation refers. Especially where it is genuinely difficult to observe closely the behavior and thinking of actors in the reference system, it may be fruitful to obtain observations about the behavior of people in a simulate. This is one of the motivations behind the sustained and fruitful (and continuing) development of the Inter-Nation Simulation (Guetzkow and others, 1963; Guetzkow, 1968, 1969; Smoker, 1968a, 1968b, 1970). The use of the term *reference system* rather than *real system* records the fact that we can compare a model only to some reference information about the real world, never to reality itself, which we know only through selected and interpreted statements (see Guetzkow, 1968).

Human or mixed man-machine simulation may suggest new explanations of behavior; may be used to replicate particular reference systems (for instance, particular time periods in international relations); may generate alternative futures or pasts that shed light on how such alternatives might occur; and may afford an unusually rich setting for laboratory experimentation (see Chapter Thirteen in this volume). Such simulations or games may be used also for teaching purposes. (For additional information, see Inbar and Stoll, 1971; Tansey and Unwin, 1969; Boocock and Schild, 1968.)

An experimental approach may be fruitful for computer simulations as well (Naylor, 1969, 1971). Experiments with a suitably valid simulation model may help the researcher understand the dynamics of the reference system; in policy applications, the effects of alternative policies can be evaluated.

In short, simulation is a set of methods for constructing hypothetical models of behavior and for generating their implications, in the search for better explanation and theory or for useful prediction. Simulations may be used to examine the consequences of alternative assumptions about behavior; for validation against particular real systems; or for the generation of data. The operations of a model may be carried out by hand, by computer, by human actors, or by combinations of these.

Simulation has had a brief but vigorous history. Raser (1969, ch. 3) traces the roots of modern simulations back to several centuries of military games, but more closely related developments in small-group experimentation, decision theory, and systems analysis occurred much more recently. Dutton and Starbuck (1971, ch. 1–2) note that work on machine and other physical models of behavior appeared as early as the last years of the nineteenth century, but almost all of the references in their bibliography on machine simulation of behavior have appeared since 1945— that is, since computers became available for research.

Herbert A. Simon's work stands at the origins of several strands of development of both computer and human simulations in behavioral science. With others, he developed and introduced to several fields the elements of a theory of decision making, by individuals and in groups and organizations (Simon, Smithburg, and Thompson, 1950; Simon, 1947; March and Simon, 1958). The theory created a strong impetus toward the systematic study of decision making. Simon's associates at Carnegie Institute of Technology included Richard Cyert and James March, who published in 1963 *A Behavioral Theory of the Firm*. Their theories of organizational decision making were made operational in the form of computer simulations that generated major decisions of various business organizations over time. Harold Guetzkow collaborated with March and Simon (1958) and went on to lead the mixed, man-machine Inter-Nation Simulation project at Northwestern University (Guetzkow and others, 1963). Simon's students have published many computer simulations. Simon himself, in association with Allen Newell especially, participated in a radical transformation of the study of thinking and problem solving through a series of computer simulation models and a theory of human information processing (Newell and Simon, 1956, 1972; Newell, Shaw, and Simon, 1958; and many other publications).

Several surveys of simulation in social science have been published. In my view, the best of those relevant to political psychology is a long article by Abelson (1968b), which should be required reading for anyone seriously interested in simulation. Four of the seven computer simulations that he describes in some detail are studies in political psychology. Abelson offers an extended and wise discussion of when and how to do computer simulation; Dutton and Starbuck (1971) have prepared somewhat different but also incisive suggestions in a book that includes an enormous bibliography and a good selection of articles on computer simulations, drawn from diverse sources. Guetzkow, Kotler, and Schultz (1972) bring together reviews of both human and computer simulations in many fields of social science, plus reports of particular simulations selected from the published literature. The text *Computer Simulation Techniques* (Naylor and others, 1966) offers useful advice and information, especially for simulation of mathematical models of a kind common in economics. (See also Coleman, 1964c, 1965b; Guetzkow, 1962; Cohen and Cyert, 1965.) Because so many authors have surveyed simulation methods and applications, I will emphasize suggestive uses rather than attempt an exhaustive coverage of simulations of individual, electoral, small-group, organizational, and organizational system behavior.

Individual Behavior

The theory of individual cognitive processes has been more sharply transformed and expanded by computer simulation than any other field in the behavioral sciences. That emerging success story has favorable implications for the study of individual political behavior because others can build on the concepts and methods developed there; borrowing may be fruitful even though the aims of research and the research settings of cognitive psychology are not on the face of it very close to the objectives and settings of research into political behavior.

What does it mean to the student of political psychology that researchers have developed the elements of a theory of human thinking and that they have been able to generate via computer simulation problem-solving behavior that closely approximates the behavior of human subjects? To motivate an answer to this query, we must have in mind some political actor whose thinking or choosing processes we would like to describe in detail, with a view to explaining the stream of behavior.

Official as Information-Processing System. To elucidate why and how we might go about studying the problem-solving process of a political officeholder, building on the theory and methods already developed in the context of formal problem solving, consider the problem facing the head of a large government department at budget time, when he receives requests from the chief officials of the bureaus in the department and must himself prepare from them a budget to submit to the legislature. It is of some interest to understand just how a department head handles this task. We know that some departments become veritable engines of innovation through their budget processes, while others wallow apathetically through the same formalities; the way that budget requests are treated, therefore, appears to be crucial (Browning, 1970). To guide our research into the department head's thinking, we refer to Newell and Simon's *Human Problem Solving* (1972). All of the italicized concepts in this section are defined and discussed in detail there.

Suppose that revisions of requests are developed and agreed to in meetings of the department head and his staff with each bureau chief and his staff. We sit in on these meetings, transcribe the discussions, and go over the head's behavior with him afterward, trying to tease out the thinking that generated his behavior, hoping eventually to formulate a working model of it. The budget meetings last four or five hours; our research strategy leads us to work first with this relatively short-term behavior. We are able to observe a series of meetings with different bureaus at about the same time. Thus, some features of the head's *task environment* are held constant, and we have an opportunity to observe his performance on a number of somewhat different problems within it (revising the budgets of the various bureaus). These tasks are genuinely problematic, not routine, for this department head. He will have objections to the requests before him, and he will know when a bureau's budget is finally acceptable; but its final shape, when he incorporates it into the department's budget, is built up only as the meeting proceeds. It depends on what he learns about the bureau's requests and operations and about the bureau officials themselves as he questions, cajoles, persuades, threatens, and reassures them during the meeting, and as they respond with information, objections (or acquiescence), and reconstructed justifications.

From study of the meetings and from conversation with the department head, we conclude that three goals define the immediate task for him: First of all, he seeks to convince the legislature that his department's budget requests should be granted, even though they involve large percentage increases and public funds are scarce. This goal entails both modification of bureau requests and improvement of the justifications for them. Second, he seeks to bring the bureaus into line with his goals for the agency. (In the longer run, his goals are shaped by his subordinates' best proposals and by experience.) Finally, he seeks to stimulate the bureau heads to allocate their full energies to the attainment of his goals, which involve substantial policy and organizational change and require continuing innovation by the bureaus. The second and third goals pose a most delicate problem of combining obedience and enthusiasm. All three goals could also be thought of as subsidiary to some higher goals for the department head, referring perhaps to the public purposes of his department and to his own career. While this may be the case, it is not necessary to specify these higher goals in order to generate his behavior in the meeting.

The department head's behavior is generated from a *problem space,* a representation of the task environment internal to him: facts of the request and of the bureau as he perceives them; of his own objectives and criteria of acceptability; of the methods he might use to find unacceptable requests, to determine the status of major problems and opportunities in the bureau, to improve faulty justifications, and to evaluate and shape the budget and the performance of the bureau; and of other aspects of the problem and possible solution procedures.

The department head has a rather rich repertoire of *methods.* Some of these are routine and trigger only small changes in the budget, like the addition of a sentence to a justification in order to tie a request more explicitly to the department's stated goals. One method, frequently applied, eliminates requests that the legislature is likely to criticize. Other methods of assessment and questioning open up whole areas of the budget for restructuring, and may lead to long sequences of questions and reformulations. Some of these searches for a better request will be abortive. Sometimes a second approach is taken to these items, and another way of organizing or justifying them developed; but some items that initially appeared salvageable turn out poorly and are dropped.

Particular *subgoals* evoked and applied in the course of the meeting include administrative considerations, such as matching a request for a new division to a rule of thumb for feasible rate of growth, taking into account the administrative burden of recruitment, training, and startup. Other subgoals refer not to the budget per se but to the interpersonal relationships at the meeting. Praise is mingled with criticism. Care is taken to avoid harsh criticism of a bureau chief in front of his staff. Both in the pattern of budget cuts and acceptances, and in the flow of verbal communication, the bureau chief is led to feel that the department head is helping him deal with the problems of his bureau; thus, an implicit exchange is established. A third set of subgoals refers to the bureau chief's understanding of the relationships between his bureau's structure, its budget, the major trends in its environment, and the goals of the department for the bureau. The department head probes the bureau chief to determine his perception of these relationships; if his perception is in any way deficient, time is taken to explain the relationships.

This particular department head is in some ways a difficult subject because his subgoal structure is so extensive and his repertoire of methods so rich. With less experienced, less highly motivated, and less intelligent officials, we would expect a less complex and extensive problem space. Nevertheless, we might be able with further study to describe not only his behavior but also some aspects of the structure of goals and methods that generates it. (We need not insist that our model of his behavior be capable of receiving and emitting natural language, however. A capacity for understanding and formulating sentences is an enormously difficult problem in itself; discretion dictates a symbolic representation of the task environment and of the methods applied by the department head. Newell and Simon do not demand of their computer models that they mutter and stutter like the human subjects, only that they make the same moves.)

Our reconstruction of his problem space is facilitated by the knowledge that the complexities are made of a relatively small number of *elementary information processes* and that the human information-processing system confronted with a task combines these processes in a finite number of *programs* that are triggered by particular kinds of subgoals. For example, our department head evokes a *discrimination net* to evaluate a bureau's request prior to the meeting. The net contains his major criteria for acceptance of requests. During the meeting unacceptable requests undergo a program of finer discriminations to specify precisely the difference between the request as it stands and an acceptable request; then goals are evoked and methods applied to reduce these differences, *difference reduction* being a common type of problem-solving goal and method.

The illustration can prove nothing, of course, but may suggest that interesting microprocesses of individual political behavior can be observed and modeled. To help us in this work, a substantial body of theory and method, developed in the study of formal problem solving (playing chess, proving logical theorems), is available.

Why Simulation? As we study the variety of department heads or other political figures, we will probably find large differences between them in the way they approach their tasks. Some department heads will not seek change, will not be interested in the problems of the bureaus, will not be sensitive to the needs of their subordinates, and will not apply criteria to their budgets sufficiently powerful to avoid legislative criticism. Either way, useful information is obtained. If a department head does well, studying his internal problem-solving processes gives us information about the task and about the psychology of successful performance. If he does poorly, we gain information about the nature of the internal mechanisms that limit his performance.

Newell and Simon suggest that a theory of individual performance must include both an analysis of the tasks involved and an analysis of rational adaptation to task requirements—and even, we might add, an analysis of irrational adaptations. In fact, these dual concerns are already clearly present in the existing correlational research on managerial styles and productivity (for example, Likert, 1967), phenomena rather similar in content and setting to the interactions between agency officials over their budgets, described above. Would it not be equally fruitful to apply a correlational approach to the budgetary process, over a set of agencies, measuring the relationship between administrative styles and the budgetary behavior of subordinate officials? This would also be fruitful, I believe, and I have no quarrel with it. The essential argument for choosing to describe precisely the microprocesses of behavior lies in the level of explanation desired. A simulation of individual behavior "posits a set of processes or mechanisms, that produce the behavior of the thinking human. . . . It does not simply provide a set of relations or laws about behavior from which one can often conclude what behavior must be" (Newell and Simon, 1972, p. 9). Rather than correlating a few selected features of the processes under study, Newell and Simon's simulation approach seeks to reconstruct the process itself, in model form. Obviously, this is a more detailed account of the events than is customary with a correlational approach. It is also a stronger account, setting forth less ambiguous statements about many more aspects of behavior and its generators.

Cognitive-Process Simulation. The concentration on process and on the explication of mechanisms sufficient to generate individual behavior is a radical shift of direction in psychology. In political psychology, too, such an approach takes a deeper slice of behavior and attempts a stronger description of it. As noted, cognitive-process simulation differs from a correlational approach to the relations between the attitudes and the actions of individuals, and the effects of actions. It differs also from a "whole-personality" approach, since it does not attempt to lay out all the important sources of action internal to the individual; rather, only those mechanisms sufficient to generate behavior in a particular task environment are posited. Third, Newell and Simon's information-processing descriptions of problem solving give much greater prominence to the intended rationality of the individual at a task than we are accustomed to in political psychology. Newell and Simon were able to assume that their subjects were properly motivated to perform the intellectual tasks set before them. The researchers could assume that the subjects really were trying to reach a well-defined goal, known to both subject and scientist.

In the context of formal problems, the end goal is common to all subjects; the intermediate methods and subgoals may differ from one person to another. But this is not necessarily the case in political or administrative problem solving. Different people bring different motivations to the same political position; the behavior of individual officials will be generated by partly different end goals. Because different goals create different subjective tasks in a given environment, political psychologists will want to extend the cognitive-process approach to include an explication of the motivational constructs, or goals, that various individuals bring to a task. Still, carrying the Newell-Simon theory of problem solving over into political psychology would probably induce a clearer recognition of the fact that political actors are commonly goal-directed and intendedly rational; a greater emphasis on an analysis of the task environment in which their goals and actions operate; and closer attention to the connections between goals and actions.

Newell and Simon's argument in favor of the analysis of rational behavior and of the task environment in which it occurs reflects in part simply their interest in formal problem solving. Nevertheless, political psychologists as well may profit from the suggestion that they understand thoroughly and clearly the rational content of the behavior they study. In some contexts, several kinds of rational behavior may be conceivable, corresponding to different subjective goals; or it may be useful to posit a goal and a variety of rational behavior on prior theoretical grounds—for example, ambition for higher office (Schlesinger, 1966) or for higher agency budgets (Niskanen, 1971).

Though rational behavior is the focus of Newell and Simon's simulation studies and may be a useful concept in political psychology as well, it is certainly not an inevitable focus of research using the simulation method. Any behavior occurring over time may be simulated, provided the subject's states and acts are truly strongly connected and adequate access to his behavior and thinking is feasible. For example, Kenneth Colby and his associates (Colby, 1965, 1968; Tesler, Enea, and Colby, 1968; Colby and Schank, 1973) have developed a body of theory and simulations of the client in a psychiatric setting, their aim being to construct mechanisms of personality sufficient to produce the observed verbal behavior of the client in response to the statements and questions of the therapist. The question of rationality does not arise in their work; but it is necessary, and possible in this case, that they have close access to the client's behavior and thinking and that his mental states and verbalizations be strongly connected to each other and to the stimuli emitted by the therapist.

The two requirements of intensive observational access and strongly connected behavior no doubt account for the tendency of simulation studies of individuals to focus on relatively short behavior sequences, in settings which permit unusually close observation and interviewing. Work on a formal problem is a matter of minutes; budget meetings last several hours; the psychiatric interview is one hour; the responses of the political ideologist modeled by Abelson (discussed below) might take a few seconds or a couple of minutes. To be sure, intensive work with these short sequences should prepare us for equally well-specified models of longer ones; but in the meantime, correlational and other approaches are still necessary if many instances of the longer sequences are to be studied at all, or if we are to reconstruct processes that have already taken place.

Though simulations are too demanding a method for modeling long or past sequences of behavior, or for portraying many different individuals, still we can find easy continuities of theory between familiar sorts of correlational and developmental studies, on the one hand, and simulations, on the other. For example, suppose we measure the motives for achievement, affiliation, and power of a set of politicians in policy-making positions, and then find that certain patterns of motivation are associated with distinctive patterns of behavior in office (Browning, 1968a, 1968b). In the parlance of problem-solving theory, we are tapping the particular goals (motives) that these individuals bring to a given task environment, and the methods (behavior) that they apply to reach their goals. If we regard our respondents as intendedly rational, we should not be surprised to find some correlation between the goals and the methods, between a concern for achievement and actions intended to produce it. In the correlational research mode, conceptualization and valid measurement of behavior and of the goals and expectations relevant in the task environment are crucial, and it is no small achievement for the researcher to obtain high and reliable correlations. In the simulation mode, conceptualization aims not at measurement of summarizing factors of personality but at construction, from the directly observed behavior and thinking of the subject, of mechanisms sufficient to reproduce behavior. We may still wish to call a particular program of criteria for evaluating situations and choosing actions "achievement motive," but we will have gone beyond detection of a mechanism linking situation and behavior to a precise specification of it.

Descriptions of political thinking as individuals try to adjust their actions to the demands of their goals and of the problematic environment are not yet available in sufficient detail to permit precise modeling, but it is clear that many fragments of such thinking can be obtained or constructed from interviews (Browning, 1969, ch. 4–5) and in some cases from analysis of the papers and public record and statements of well-known political figures (George and George, 1956). Barber's work on state legislators (1965) and especially his analysis of twentieth-century presidents of the United States (1972a) strives to bring out the structure of the personality mechanisms that generate performance in a given task environment. Barber interprets presidential psychology in terms of the demands that the task environment of the presidency places on the president—demands commonly recognized by the occupants of that difficult position even when they are not able to respond in an effective way to them. The president as problem solver comes through clearly in Barber's analysis, equipped in personality to cope rationally with some of the problems of the office, but unable in the face of other demands to find or apply methods of dealing with them that could lead to success in the light of his own goals.

Bardach's (1972) description and theoretical construction of highly rational political entrepreneurship is not explicitly psychological in orientation but still brings to light significant features of individual political thinking and behavior. What we see in Bardach's account of the repeal of mental commitment laws in California is the dynamic mobilization and manipulation of authorities and other interests in a complex, problematic political environment. The leaders of the repeal effort foresee opportunities and problems; map out strategies for building support and for adding to their capacity to obtain additional support; and neutralize, pacify, or outmaneuver the anticipated opposition. An opposing figure is placed in a situation constructed so as to damage his credibility and maximize the chances that his personality will lead him into irrational, counterproductive statements. Another prominent authority, known to oppose repeal and to fight tenaciously when cornered, is carefully soothed with personal praise and inclusion in repeal strategy meetings. The mechanisms that generate these strategies are not completely described, but some are well specified and others can be inferred from the detailed analysis of problem and behavior presented. No simulation is attempted, but the orientation of the study toward internal calculations and behavior process is akin to that of problem-solving simulations.

One might have conducted an explicitly psychological study of political effectiveness in the mental commitment repeal case, attempting perhaps to fit to the data a model of goal effectiveness as a function of position and of personal skill and style, and skill and style as a function of "personality characteristics." Measures of "political efficacy"; of authoritarianism; of achievement, power, and affiliative motivation; of manifest anxiety; of Machiavellianism—these or others might have been obtained, and surely some of them would be found closely related to one or more differences in measures of behavior among the political actors. It is difficult to believe that this approach, even skillfully executed, could yield an explanation as satisfactory as that provided by Bardach's less quantitative but better-grounded analysis. Instead of measures of "personality" detached from the task environment, Bardach is able to characterize, even if not completely, the state of mind and strategy of the principal actors at several stages in the unfolding campaign for repeal; the links between circumstance and mind, the mind and action, are reconstructed in a way that is most uncommon in correlational analysis.

The suggested analysis of the agency head's budget behavior, Bardach's account of political entrepreneurship, and the Newell-Shaw-Simon models of problem solving have in common a further characteristic that distinguishes them from correlational studies. All three concentrate not so much on individual differences and their effects—by definition the essence of the correlational method—as on explication of common forms of thinking and behavior. We know that there are many kinds of problem solvers, agency heads, and political entrepreneurs, but the main focus in these efforts is on the development of theory suitable to describe the range and basic characteristics of the behavior found. In effect, they seem to be saying, a better understanding of individual behavior is necessary before we throw our resources fully into exploration of the consequences of differences between individuals.

Are Simulation and Computer Essential? The studies discussed in the previous pages are like the simulations of individual problem solving in their focus on process, on close observation of behavior, and on reconstruction of internal mechanisms that generate behavior. Obviously, one does not have to use computer simulation to study the psychology of political behavior. Even given a concern for process, of what special use is simulation?

It is easier to recommend the intensive study of some interesting political and psychological process than it is to insist on the value of a computer simulation. No doubt many researchers would be content to rest with verbal accounts of the behavior they study, and there is much to study before verbal accounts become entirely inadequate. However, there are limits to what a verbal description of the mechanisms that generate performance can convey, because of the imprecision of words and because the structure of natural language does not force us to squeeze out ambiguity and to make all relationships explicit in the system we are describing. This essential ambiguity, and the lack of a sufficiently powerful method for generating the behavior described, must leave us with a large component of uncertainty that we have the right description, the right model of the actor's problem-solving system. Computer simulation does not allow ambiguity; it does force the user to make all relationships explicit; and the computer does offer a sufficiently powerful way of generating the implications of even a very complex description.

Although empirical work should usually be conducted in close support of a simulation effort, the researcher should expect a significant shift of time and energy toward questions of theoretical formulation and simulation technique. For this investment, researchers report heuristic benefits as well as advantages of precision and generating power. Colby (1965, p. 501) wrote of his simulations of neurotic processes that it was too early to plan extended empirical tests of the models: "At the moment their main contribution has been to clarify theory by forcing the theorist to be explicit about his system, its entities, and relations." In the same vein, Abelson (1968b, p. 292) suggests: "One virtue for the investigator in struggling with these flow-charting problems is that he may be forced into closer scrutiny of his own theory. . . . Once the investigator starts thinking about process timing, he must think more deeply about the psychology of the processes."

Indeed, it may be that the prime value of most social science simulations is heuristic (Freeman, 1971). Perhaps they should be appreciated for this even when a valid model is not attained. Depending on the stage of development of a particular field, an effort to pinpoint the gaps in knowledge may be precisely what is needed, and a valid model too much to hope for.

Newell and Simon (1972, p. 870) state that the computer was for them "an important tool, for it has permitted us to carry out, through simulation, detailed comparisons between theory and data, and to derive numerous empirical predictions from theory." These functions are so crucial for the specification and validation of a theory (though not for the initial statement of it) that it is difficult to see how Newell and Simon could have developed their theory without the use of the computer. Even so, they assert that "the computer as hardware" was not as important as "the new concepts of information-processing systems and the new formalisms and languages for describing such systems with precision" (p. 870). The conceptual innovations had roots in a growing interest in human thinking on the part of scholars in diverse fields, antedating the invention of the computer; no doubt the latter greatly stimulated the theoretical developments. In earlier publications of Newell and Simon and their associates, the computer models were prominent; by the time of the 1972 book they were able to describe the human information-processing system directly in terms more appropriate to the study of human behavior (and more comprehensible to human readers). The resulting theory was the goal, the simulations instrumental in its development and testing.

"Ideology Machine." Abelson's ideology machine, a model of a closed belief system, represents an approach with potentially great significance for political psychology. It is the only computer simulation extant that models political behavior of a politically interesting individual and is well grounded in psychology and (apparently) in data on the subject (Senator Barry Goldwater). The model portrays the performance of an individual confronted with statements or questions about events in international relations; for example, "Secretary Laird says the communists are planning to attack Thailand." One version of the model (Abelson and Carroll, 1965) has mechanisms to test statements for credibility; if a statement is found credible but upsetting—inconsistent with beliefs already in the system—the mechanism attempts denial and rationalization. Later reports (Abelson, 1968a, 1971, 1973) describe a capability for generating *scripts,* or potential event sequences, in response to questions about what will happen; these reports greatly strengthen and broaden the conceptualization of belief systems.

The structure of Abelson's model is already a contribution to the theory of attitude structure and of ideology in particular. The basic elements in the system are about five hundred nouns or noun phrases and one hundred verbs or verb phrases. A variety of relationships organizes these elements and provides the connections that permit inferences and answers. First and most simply, there is a horizontal relationship between elements: nouns are connected to verb-noun predicates, as in "Cambodia accepts U.S. aid," to establish the statements "believed" by the system. Second, elements are connected hierarchically: most nouns and verbs are classed within general categories; for instance, "Hungary" would belong to the class of "communist nations." It is an *instance* of "communist nation," and "communist nation" is a *quality* of "Hungary ." This relation permits the system to determine the credibility of a new statement by checking whether the statement is believed true of other instances in the category (induction) or whether it is believed true of the categories to which the instance belongs (deduction). A statement that includes a general verb category between two noun categories may define a *generic event;* for example, "(communist nation) (physically attack) (neutral nation)." The third relation within the belief system connects generic events to build up the scripts—sequences of generic events. Scripts permit the system to respond to a query about what will happen following a particular event. This event is located as an instance of a generic event; then the script that follows from that generic event is triggered, in effect as a model for what will happen in the particular case referred to by the original question. A script may include alternative possibilities, with different sequences flowing from each one.

Abelson (1971, p. 13) gives this illustration of a script-generated answer to the question "If communists attack Thailand, what will happen?" The model's answer: "If communists attack Thailand, communists take over unprepared nations unless Thailand ask-aid-from United States and United States give-aid-to Thailand." Obviously there are problems of style, but that is unimportant; the meaning of the answer is plausible.

Abelson's project is more difficult in several ways than the work on formal problem solving from which it springs. The goals and methods of formal problems are defined by the problems themselves in precise symbolic notation (for instance, logic) or in terms for which a notation can be readily invented. But the elements of a belief system are linguistic concepts and sentences; hence, the simplification that might be achieved via a symbolic notation for words would increase the distance between the model and the task environment of the subject, and would constrain the use of the model to pinpoint gaps in knowledge about the effects of language on belief. Construction of the model pinpointed certain gaps in the available knowledge about psycholinguistic processes. Subsequently, experiments were designed and carried out to fill the gaps (Gilson and Abelson, 1965; Kanouse and Abelson, 1967).

Abelson's effort to model one individual, and one with a well-developed and relatively closed belief system, is sensible. It would be desirable also to have a subject one could interview; most of the ideological content of the model was developed from public statements by Senator Goldwater. Interviews would bring the method of data collection closer to the Newell-Shaw-Simon method of observing subjects, obtaining their own verbal account of what they are thinking, and asking them questions about what they are doing and why.

In research on formal problem solving, researchers could simply take as given the goals of the subjects; they were assumed to be well motivated, and their goals and subgoals were defined by the problem. In Abelson's belief-system model, in contrast, all of the motivation and all of the particular goals and subgoals of the "problem" (of inconsistencies between beliefs) are part of the individual's belief structure and process, not part of an objective problem external to the system. Thus, knowing the person's problem space and getting it into the system are much more difficult. The gap between observation and model is especially painful for the "evaluations" that register affect in the model: "Every element, whether concept or predicate, carries a signed quantitative evaluation summarizing the resultant of all positive or negative affects attaching to the element" (Abelson and Carroll, 1965, p. 26). Where these quantities come from is not clear. Yet some method for obtaining them is essential, because important processes take the evaluations as input or operate upon them.

While the treatment of evaluations may involve an empirical gap in the model, apparently a good deal of interesting empirical work has been done in the construction of the belief system; unfortunately, this work has not to my knowledge been reported in published form. Abelson mentions that his method is to paraphrase the known beliefs of the subject and that "the paraphrasing procedure is extremely difficult" (Abelson and Carroll, 1965, p. 30), but the rules for paraphrasing are not given, nor, indeed, is the resulting belief-system model described except by illustration. Even if no simulation were involved, this work would be of interest, and its public availability is to be hoped for.

Simulation offers to students of ideology and of attitude structure and change an opportunity to describe their processes precisely and to generate tests of the validity of process models. (For discussion of these processes, see Chapters Three and Four in this volume.) Simulation is a demanding method, however, not routinely or easily applied to the description of individual political behavior and thinking. Clearly, a prior commitment to simulation in studies of political-psychological process carries a high-risk rating. But studies of process in political psychology, as we can see from recent work of this type, already make a strong contribution to knowledge and prepare the way for the more precise and reproducible statements that are the aim of simulation methods.

Computer Simulations of Electoral Behavior

The possibility of simulating the complexities of an election campaign on the computer has attracted several researchers. Because the earlier work in this subfield has been repeatedly reviewed by other authors, only truncated descriptions will be offered here.

Pool, Abelson, and Popkin (1965) attempted a simulation of the 1960 and 1964 presidential elections for prediction purposes (as contrasted with other simulations reviewed in this chapter, which aim for description of process). The model seeks to predict the vote of 480 groupings defined by socioeconomic characteristics; then knowledge of the extent to which each group is represented in the population of each state permits prediction of the vote by state. For a first effort, the model, based on data at least two years old but improved by some good guesses by the authors, did astonishingly well, achieving a correlation of .82 between the predicted and actual vote percentages for John F. Kennedy in thirty-two states outside the South (p. 57). A similar effort for the 1964 election managed a correlation of .90 with the state-by-state vote, including the South, with a median error of 3.4 percent (p. 174). The 1960 model is extensively reviewed by Rosenthal (1965).

Although the Pool-Abelson-Popkin model does not try to represent psychological dynamics explicitly, nevertheless some interesting findings of psychological relevance emerge from analysis of the model and of the huge data bank the authors assembled to support the model. For instance, they demonstrate that socioeconomic predispositions are only additively related to attitudes on a large number of issues. Multiplicative effects are rare except for "party-dominated" issues—those for which party identification is strongly related to attitude; on these issues, party identification interacts with other socioeconomic factors in their impact on attitude (Pool, Abelson, and Popkin, 1965, ch. 4).

Other voting simulations, by McPhee and associates and by Abelson and Bernstein, contain explicit representations of individuals and more or less elaborate arrangements for contact, communication, and influence among them. McPhee's model consists of processes for stimulation (for instance, from the media), for discussion among voters, and for learning (modification of dispositions) (McPhee and Smith, 1962; McPhee, Ferguson, and Smith, 1971). Although the McPhee model was used, with modifications, for limited predictive purposes (McPhee, 1963), it was designed to investigate via conceptual experiments macroprocesses of voter preferences extending over many elections. In one such application, McPhee and Ferguson (1962) used the model to test whether and under what conditions an electorate subjected to repeated strong disturbances from political crises and charismatic appeals will develop immunity to the effects of additional disturbances—an interesting question. But even though the model produces interesting results, and even though these results roughly parallel certain historical experiences, the model remains at the level of a tool for speculation because parts of it are not well grounded either in theory or in data. Rosenthal (1968, pp. 245–253) argues that some of the conclusions McPhee arrives at could have been obtained with simpler models and analyses, avoiding simulation altogether. (Rosenthal also explicates portions of McPhee's model that are not well defined in the original publications.) Both Rosenthal (p. 251) and Boudon (1965, p. 13) conclude that McPhee's model makes excessive demands for data on the microbehavior of voters—data that are in practice out of reach. Nevertheless, as a pioneering effort at a most difficult task, McPhee's work is still worth referring to and learning from.

Abelson and Bernstein's (1963) model of community referendum controversies similarly attempts to predict outcomes of a campaign from simulation of individual exposure, communication with others, and attitude change. (Francis, 1972, pp. 251–256, provides an explication of the model in flow-chart form.) The theoretical specification of the model is a tour de force in itself and suggests a worthwhile strategy for simulators: good theoretical work is interesting and important even if a simulation is not operationalized or not tested (but perhaps the simulation should not be promised until it has been tested); and careful development of the theory should precede the writing of the simulation model in any case. Abelson (1964) argued that available mathematical models of the distribution of attitudes subject to controversy tended to predict a movement of attitudes toward agreement, whereas the evidence from fluoridation referenda and some other controversies showed polarization: hence, the simulation, to obtain effects observed but not predicted. However, it is not clear that the very complex model set forth by Abelson and Bernstein was needed to account for polarization. Boudon (1965, p. 14) argues that "it would suffice to introduce the familiar hypothesis of selective exposure to generate bimodal distributions" of opinion. If and when confrontations of the model with data on fluoridation and school desegregation controversies appear in print, it should become possible to determine what degree of complexity is necessary to produce observed effects. The question raised about the need for complexity suggests a strategy of developing and testing simpler models against the data in the hope that the more complex model will not be necessary. Indeed, the model has so many parameters that it may be extremely difficult to test, as Boudon (1965) and Rosenthal (1968, pp. 253–254) argue.

Shaffer (1972) reviews the Pool-Abelson-Popkin and McPhee models and reports simulations of voting in the 1964 presidential election, using two different models, one based on a theory of the rational voter developed by Anthony Downs (1957), the other on a six-component multiple regression model developed at the Survey Research Center (Stokes, Campbell, and Miller, 1958; Stokes, 1966). Both of these models attempt prediction of individual votes with no mechanisms for interaction.

Shaffer shows ingenuity in obtaining measures for the concepts of Downs' model from the 1964 SRC survey data; however, students of voting behavior may still be less than satisfied with some of the measures used. For example, a key concept of Downs' model is "current party differential": the difference between the utility a voter has received from the party in power and the utility he could have expected from the opposition party (Downs, 1957, p. 40). For a measure of this variable, Shaffer (1972, p. 70) relies entirely on respondents' answers to the question "Do you think it will make any difference in how you and your family get along financially whether the Republicans or the Democrats win the election?" Also, the concept of "information costs" is represented in the model by a measure of total mass media use, a very different notion. In spite of these deficiencies in the data (which stem from the fact that the SRC survey was not designed to test the Downsian model), a modified version of the model, with the information-cost variable dropped altogether and a party-identification variable added to guide the votes of those respondents with zero "party differential," correctly predicted 66.6 percent of the reported votes and abstentions in the sample (p. 107).

The SRC six-component model attempts to explain an individual's voting choice as a function of his attitudes toward the Democratic and Republican candidates as persons; his attitudes toward the parties and candidates related to group benefits, domestic policy, and foreign policy; and his attitude toward the general performance of the parties in managing the government. It does this by regressing voting choice on measures of each of the six attitudes. By this method, multiple correlations of .72 to .75 are obtained for the four presidential elections studied, and a correlation of .98 between estimated and actual majorities over the same four contests (Stokes, 1966, p. 28).

The SRC model as it stands is not predictive: it takes the estimate of best-fitting regression parameters from the data on voting choice in each election, rather than predicting it. The weights so determined for the effects of the six attitudes on voting choice are different in each election. Because Shaffer wanted to predict votes, he adopted a different procedure. Values for each of the six attitude dimensions in the original SRC model were defined as "the arithmetic difference between a respondent's pro-Republican and pro-Democratic responses whose content relates to the dimension" (Stokes, 1966, p. 27). Shaffer apparently simply sums these differences across all six dimensions. (Shaffer refers to summation of "net Democratic preference valences" [p. 67], a term that is not defined.) This procedure produces a weighting of its own. Specifically, it would seem that Shaffer's procedure weights most heavily those attitude dimensions on which respondents are most widely polarized; that is, those dimensions on which the distribution of net partisan responses is most widely dispersed. Such a weighting has some intuitive appeal.

Shaffer predicts that all respondents with more responses favoring the Democratic party or candidate will vote Democratic; those with more responses favoring the Republicans will vote Republican; and those with equal numbers of responses favoring each party will abstain. This rule generates correct predictions for 69.5 percent of the sample's reported vote and abstention decisions (Shaffer, 1972, p. 121).

Neither the SRC nor the Downsian model qualifies as a simulation in the sense of generating the behavior of a system over time. These are one-shot predictions; nothing happens over time in the models. Furthermore, they are predictions from attitudinal data obtained at a time very close to the election itself. If one wishes to make best predictions from survey data obtained close to election day, there are better ways to do it. The SRC six-component model is probably best used as Stokes and his associates have used it; namely, to trace the net relation of each attitudinal component to voting choice over time. There is interest, of course, in the problem of defining "rational voting" and testing models of the rational voter against survey data (Shapiro, 1969). There is interest also in developing the theory of the campaign process, which several of the simulations mentioned above gloss over. Working at the Survey Research Center, Coombs, Fried, and Robinovitz (1968) reported the development of a computer simulation of the campaign as well as the vote in presidential elections. Schauland, Naylor, and Kornberg (1971) have built a man-machine simulation; one of its purposes is to give people practice at making simulated campaign decisions on such matters as allocation of resources, media mix, and issue stands.

Group and Organizational Processes

In the section of this chapter on individual behavior, an illustration of possible research on the problem-solving behavior of a department head was developed. Ordinarily, the group context of the proposed research would lead us to think of it as research in group interaction; but it would be much too difficult at this stage to develop models for all the participants and thus to generate their interactions; there-fore, it was proposed to take the responses of the other participants as given and attempt a model only of the thinking and statements of the head. Any research that tries to develop computer simulations of the thinking of more than one problem solver in a group is probably overambitious if the group task involves qualitative representations and moves or is otherwise complex, or if the members see the problem in different terms. Accordingly, researchers observe groups performing simple tasks under experimental control. Models are developed to describe behavior in the re-stricted problem space so created. Most computer simulations of small-group inter-action refer to such experimental settings. Simulations of more complex processes have left large parts of the model to be played by human actors, as in the Inter-Nation Simulation (but an all-computer model by Bremer, 1971, builds on the INS work); or they have yielded models of organizational decision rules without trying to trace the individual contributions and interactions. These efforts will be discussed in turn.

Small Groups. One laboratory situation that aims for a clear specification of conflict is the Prisoner's Dilemma game. The structure of rewards in this game is such that the two players gain if they cooperate with each other; if one cooperates and the other defects, the defector gains even more, but the cooperator loses; and if both defect, they both lose. Each player is constantly tempted to increase gains by defecting from mutual cooperation; but he also runs the risk that the other player will defect, too, thus turning gains to losses. The rational strategy is mutual coopera-tion, but this often does not occur for a large number of plays. The situation is genuinely problematic for the players.

Emshoff (1970) noted that one important model of the game (from Rapo-port and Chammah, 1965) reproduced only the mean behavior of a group of sub-jects and was not very useful for predicting an individual game; in addition, its predictions were not sensitive to different possible reward structures. He criticized other studies on the grounds that they failed to come up with a "unified" model that could reproduce the observed behavior. Emshoff proposed a computer simula-tion which would reproduce behavior in individual games, based on a general model of the behavior of the individual players. The model of the players is not an informa-tion-processing model of the Newell-Shaw-Simon type, but Emshoff did study the decision processes used by players; he then developed equations in which to express the effects of four key parameters on players' predicted moves. The parameters opera-tionalized were competitiveness, memory, foresight, and rigidity.

The competitiveness parameter enters into equations that determine a value to the player for the payoffs stated in the game—Emshoff had found that some subjects were responding not only to their own rewards but also to the possibility of getting more than the other player. The memory parameter determines how far back in the game a player's memory extends, and what weight is given to recent versus past moves. The foresight parameter measures the extent to which a player places a value on the expected future consequences of each move as well as on the reward expected directly from the move itself. These three parameters modify the value the player attaches to each possible move, given the conditions and previous moves of the game. The player then moves so as to maximize this subjective value. Rigidity has to do with a player's response to a cooperative move by the other player after a string of defecting moves by both players; the rigid player will continue to play so as to maximize the value of his next move (as altered by his competitiveness, memory, and foresight), whereas the nonrigid player will follow the other's coopera- tive move with cooperation. The rigidity parameter appears to be an ad hoc rule introduced to correct the failure of the model to predict cooperation in that particular situation.

Twenty games of thirty-five moves each were run in the laboratory and simulated with the model. The laboratory results were used to find the specific values for the eight parameters (four for each player) that gave the best fit for each of the twenty different games. Parameter values were assumed stable for the duration of a game. For each game, the model was simulated one thousand times, using one thousand randomly varied values for each of the eight parameters. The parameter values yielding the best fit to the laboratory result of the game were chosen to char- acterize it. "Best fit" means essentially the smallest number of errors in reproducing the individual players' moves; thiry-five moves for each player, where the first two moves of the model were simply assumed to be those of the human players.

When the best-fitting parameter values were used for each game, the model was able to reproduce moves with more than 80 percent accuracy, on the average, over all games. Large differences between games in accuracy of reproduction suggest that the model represents some games rather well but that variables not in the model affect play in other games. Trial runs showed also that it was able to generate a wide range of sequences of moves, corresponding to various patterns produced by human players.

Ability to reproduce play in laboratory games is an essential and difficult achievement. It is still less than prediction because the values of the parameters are taken from (chosen to give best fit to) the data reproduced. The next step in vali- dation would involve a determination of the stability of the parameters by first estimating their values from one set of moves and then trying to predict to a second set. A further extension might measure the parameters for players independently of plays of the game.

Computer simulations of laboratory groups are reported also by McWhinney (1962), Coe (1964), and Clarkson (1968); and of other aspects of social behavior by Loehlin (1968), Gullahorn and Gullahorn (1963, 1971), and Rainio (1965, 1966).

Emshoff's model is interesting because of the clarity with which conflict is defined in the Prisoner's Dilemma game, which has the advantage also of having been much studied. The model is interesting psychologically as well; the competitiveness parameter surely refers to a factor of general importance where goals conflict, and the memory and foresight parameters identify basic differences in cognitive reach among individuals. The simulation is at least promising.

Without going in great detail into studies of the PD game, we might find it instructive to compare Emshoff's approach with a mathematical approach to the game by Ofshe and Ofshe (1970a, 1970b). They explicate and test in several contexts a mathematical model that yields predictions both of coalition choices in a three-person coalition game and of cooperativeness in the PD game. In contrast to Emshoff, the Ofshes have made no effort to predict individual behavior; also, they predict behavior only after it has stabilized (usually after fifteen to thirty trials in their work), whereas Emshoff tried to reproduce behavior in the first thirty-five trials. Thus, the Ofshes' model is not so ambitious—but it is clearer, more general, better related to the theory of utility and choice, and better validated empirically than Emshoff's.

The Ofshes' model predicts the average performance of a group of subjects over many plays or trials of a game. In the coalition game, the measure of performance is the proportion of all the subject's choices in which he chooses a coalition with the player who is most likely to reciprocate (thus yielding the payoff for forming a coalition). In the PD game, the measure is the proportion of all moves that are cooperative, given the degree of cooperativeness shown by the other player. These are in both cases the choices that maximize individual payoffs in the long run.

In the Ofshes' work as in Emshoff's, a player's utility is based partly on his valuation of the rewards received by the other players, as well as on the payoffs he expects for himself. The inclusion of responses to the gains of others is an important addition to models of rational behavior in experimental games. In the coalition game, the Ofshes hypothesize that the players have some concern for an equitable distribution of payoffs among the three players, a concern which tempers the maximizing strategy of always choosing as coalition partner the other player who is most likely to reciprocate. To the extent that the observed behavior of the players turns out to be related to the equity function in the model, we might think of their behavior as corresponding to a situation in which political actors are guided by real concerns for the principle of equity, as they sometimes are. Another possibly analogous situation is the classic dual problem of forming coalitions sufficient to win both a party's nomination and the ensuing election. The coalition that wins the top prize in the nominating convention is constrained to offer the losing players sufficient side payments (lesser nominations, other offices, policy commitments) to retain their support in the election. This is not a concern for equity but might be conceptualized and measured in the same manner and produce the same effect on behavior.

In the Ofshes' model of the two-person PD game, players are thought to be concerned in part with gaining more than their opponents—a competitive orientation that modifies the simple maximizing strategy. Here again, we are familiar with the tendency of some political actors to seek not only gains for themselves but losses for others. In addition, sometimes the zero-sum structure of political situations seems to require competitive behavior if gains are not available except by imposing losses on other actors.

The models for both the coalition and the PD game define a player's utility for a move as the sum of (a) his utility for individual payoff from the move and (b) his utility for the effect of the move on the other players—the fairness or equity of the payoffs for them in the coalition game, and his relative gain over the opponent in the PD game. An equation is derived from this sum. Using the equation, one can estimate the parameters for the two sources of utility from data on play of the games.

The test of the model is its ability to generate predictions. The parameters are estimated from an experiment with a sample of subjects. Then, to test the model, another sample of subjects from the same population plays the game; their behavior is predicted by the model with the parameter values estimated from the behavior of the first sample. Thus, no information is taken from the data on the test condition to generate predictions for it. In addition, a change in the experimental treatment was made from the estimation experiment to the prediction experiment; this further strengthens the test of the model, because it is required to make accurate predictions under different conditions. The accuracy of the predictions obtained is astonishing. For example, under various conditions and for groups ranging in size from six to twenty-two, discrepancies between observed and predicted proportions of choices of the reciprocating player in the coalition game range from .0008 to .0328 (usually larger discrepancies for the smaller groups, as expected from sampling error), for proportions that fall in the range from .4 to .95 (Ofshe and Ofshe, 1970a, pp. 344–345).

Clearly, the model performs extraordinarily well at predicting the average performance of a group of players over a number of plays of the games. It estimates parameter values by a straightforward least-squares technique rather than through the awkward simulation-and-search method devised by Emshoff. The parameters have very clear and direct utility interpretations; although the model does not yet attempt predictions of individual behavior or of behavior on the early trials of the games, it appears to offer an excellent base for such efforts. Emshoff's model is also promising, but the approach taken by Ofshe and Ofshe may well prove to be more fruitful at the very tasks that Emshoff applied himself to.

The Ofshes are able to arrive at their model by further simplifying already simple game situations. Instead of setting three people to the coalition game, they began with one person facing two players whose moves were controlled by computer. In effect, they first studied individual behavior in a game setting; only later did they study freely interacting human players (Ofshe and Ofshe, 1970b). Instead of leaving the allocation of rewards between the members of a coalition as part of the game, they stipulated the reward for each member, thus removing another source of variability from play. Control is of course the obvious advantage of the experimental situation. With careful step-by-step introduction of complexities into the model and the experiment, it should be possible to elaborate upon both, obtaining in this way models that explain more intricate and varied behavior without sacrificing accuracy or theoretical clarity and simplicity.

Perhaps it will still be necessary eventually to adopt a simulation approach to individual behavior in these game situations. However, in contrast to the problems for which Newell, Shaw, and Simon built their models of problem solving, the coalition and Prisoner's Dilemma games are deliberately constructed to permit mathematical description. Hopefully, behavior in them will be more readily modeled in the simpler, more transparent mathematical form. (See Coleman, 1964c; Gregg and Simon, 1967; Dutton and Starbuck, 1971, Ch. 1, 3.)

Several promising developments in the study of real decision-making groups in government have not yet been adequately explored. They are introduced here not because they are immediately relevant to simulation but because they could be used to provide the data on which a clear conception of the group decision process might be built. The study of real groups should proceed along with the study of experimental ones.

An early contribution that has never been satisfactorily followed up was the work of the Conference Research Project at the University of Michigan in the late 1940s and 1950s. Researchers observed meetings in government departments and in firms, recording a large number of categories of behavior. Some of these categories referred to the interpersonal relationships and feelings in a group; others referred to the tasks that must be performed for the group to solve a problem and arrive at a decision. The research produced many interesting findings that qualify familiar assumptions; for example, the availability and use of facts was associated with high levels of consensus in groups that found themselves in disagreement over the substance of decisions but not in groups where conflict was intensely emotional and personal. Neither the urgency of an agenda item nor its importance to the welfare of the organization was related to the way conflict was handled or to the level of consensus reached (Guetzkow and Gyr, 1954). Numerous other findings raise questions about why and how the observed relationships occurred or why they occurred in many of the conferences but not in others.

One respect in which the observed conferences may have been underdescribed has to do with the content of the problems facing them. A review of studies of individual problem solving and of small experimental groups suggests that tight control over the task environment greatly facilitates the development and validation of models of behavior. What the field researcher lacks in control over his subjects must be obtained as much as possible via description. Knowledge about characteristics of the tasks facing real groups, and the goals and perceptions of the individual members, would facilitate our thinking about the process and outcomes of group decision.

A second promising idea for the study of group decision processes is realized in Barber's (1966) study of real governmental groups (town boards of finance) brought into the laboratory. Barber assigned all the boards the same tasks, thereby holding constant at least the objective task environment (though different boards and their individual members approached these tasks with varying goals, perceptions, and methods, some of which Barber describes). Many of Barber's findings depended directly on his ability to exercise control over aspects of each group's performance.

Gathering better information about the nature of the problems that groups face, and observing governmental groups in both natural and laboratory settings, should enhance our ability to develop more clearly defined explanations of the process of group decision. (See also Weick, 1965; Scott, 1965.)

Large Groups.   As we pass from the comparative simplicities of small groups, the researcher's problem is magnified many times. In practice, he has to write his description of behavior at a level that ignores most of the details of individual decision and interaction. He may decide to turn to a mixed man-machine simulation or to a game played entirely by human players, in order to generate data on which to build theory. The mixed and all-human simulations of organizations and systems have been used as rich experimental settings in which to trace the effects of personality characteristics on performance and outcomes. The all-computer simulations, in contrast, tend to squeeze out personality factors as these are commonly understood, or to avoid identifying observed behavior with particular individuals even though that is where it must originate. Nevertheless, some of these simulations are interesting to the student of political psychology because of the suggestive use they make of psychological theory to model organizational behavior.

Cherryholmes and Shapiro (1969) simulated on the computer roll-call voting in one session of the House of Representatives. A review of the literature suggested that much voting could be explained as a function of factors impinging on a legislator's self-interest—for instance, constituency characteristics—or predicted from his party membership. Most of the predictive work in the model is done by the predisposition phase of the model, using these sorts of predictors. Ideology was introduced as a conceptual variable but measured simply by the member's past voting record. Cherryholmes and Shapiro predicted that members whose self-interest and alliances created strong cross pressures on a particular bill would develop only weak predispositions for or against the bill. The simulation proposes that these members undertake additional communication about the bill. Via a probabilistic process, they are exposed to the stands of other members and of the president, and these may change the voting predispositions of the cross-pressured members. The communication phase improves slightly the already good predictions of members' votes. The cross-pressure mechanism and communication phase are consonant, in general terms, with the available knowledge about these phenomena as well as about the Congress. Cherryholmes and Shapiro's success at predicting 80–90 percent of individual votes testifies to the strong and clear self-interest of the legislators and to the public availability of information about the institutions and other factors to which that self-interest is tied. Congressmen's votes, at least, appear to be very largely determined by the interaction of widely shared goals of reelection and influence with identifiable characteristics of the member's environment.

One further aspect of Cherryholmes and Shapiro's method deserves mention. They might have estimated statistically the weights for the various attributes of a member vis-à-vis a bill in the predisposition phase of the model; instead, they chose to assign undoubtedly cruder weights on the basis only of the evidence already available in the research literature on the importance of the attributes. The model with the crude, preset weights was a stronger test of the existing level of knowledge about roll-call voting and represents a stronger theory than a statistical model, because the model as it stood took no information from the behavior (votes) it was intended to reproduce. A model that has to be given information about the behavior it is to replicate is less powerful in an important sense than one that makes predictions without any knowledge of the predicted behavior. (See Hanna, 1971, for a formal argument to this point and a measure of the information value of a model.) Following the test of the model, it is also appropriate now to estimate statistically the parameters for the hypothesized variables, to see whether a simpler model is just as efficient and to assess the stability of the parameters over several sessions of the Congress.

Computer simulations of organizational behavior have attempted with models of decision rules to generate the time paths of largely quantitative decision variables adjusted repeatedly by the organization under study, such as pricing and production decisions in firms (Cyert and March, 1963), budgetary allocations in governments (Crecine, 1967, 1969; Gerwin, 1969), and decisions of national leaders in an international system (Bremer, 1971). Particular decision rules specify what information about the organization and its performance is attended to, how this information impinges on goals, and what alternatives are considered. Commonly, it is not clear whether the decision rules stated for an organizational subunit inhere in one person or in a group. Nevertheless, some are certainly associated with individuals; in any case, decision rules of the kind described could be used to characterize individual decision making.

What kinds of decision processes are described in these models? What kinds of political behavior can be brought into focus with the concepts and methods put to use in them? Several of the simulations do describe behavior and to some extent the thinking of officeholders such as the urban school superintendent and his staff in Gerwin's study, and the municipal government departments, city council, and mayor in Crecine's work. Both studies describe largely routine decision rules for adjusting budgetary allocations among departments, functions, and accounts. The limitation to routine behavior and the emphasis on common adaptations to the organizational environment make the Crecine and Gerwin simulations more obviously relevant for the student of government budgeting than for political psychologists generally. One could describe and simulate a variety of modes of adaptation and decision in organizations, with an emphasis on individual differences. The Crecine and Gerwin studies establish base points for such an effort, with respect to budgeting.

Cyert and March's work on decision processes in firms and Bremer's simulation of national decision making (with many formulations patterned after Cyert and March's) operationalize concepts of attention, learning, level of aspiration, aspiration change, hostility, and reciprocity that are more familiar to psychologists. By way of illustration, one of the many models in Bremer's simulation provides that the rate of verbal or diplomatic hostility emitted by one nation toward another is a function of the rate of hostility anticipated from the other nation, multiplied by a reactivity parameter (a psychological characteristic?). Three characteristics of the dyadic relation may modify the expression of hostility predicted by that simple equation: power differences (weaker nations suppress hostility toward stronger ones) ; alliance relationships (nations suppress normal reactions to hostility when the other nation is an ally) ; and economic dependence (dependent nations suppress hostility). A particular nation might weight these constraints on its hostility differently than other nations (though no effort has been made yet to determine weights for actual nations).

Bremer posits that national officeholders seek to make their positions secure. The variable that operationalizes leaders' goals for security of office is an aspiration level for probability of continuing to hold office. The security-of-office aspiration enters into decisions such as the allocation of national resources to consumer goods rather than military forces or basic investment. Aspiration level is a function partly of aspiration level in the previous time period, partly of the level of security currently experienced, and partly of the security of officeholders in other, similar nations (a reference group). The possible different weightings for these three factors might represent cultural or psychological patterns. The parameter that transmits the effect of current experience is set so as to raise aspiration levels more rapidly when experience is favorable than they are lowered when experiencing is discouraging.

The organizational decision models all posit that the decision makers re-evaluate and possibly change their decisions each time period, which may be a week or a month for business units or a year or more for governmental budgeting and international relations. The models recycle each time period through the same structure of decisions, but under changing conditions as the decision environment is altered. The timing and regularity of recycling may be a feature of the process under study, as it is for governmental budgeting, or may be partly a construction in the model to impose some theoretical order on a less well-known or less well-structured process, like the cycle of national decisions in Bremer's simulation of an international system. The models assume some stability of decision rules over time, or simple mechanisms for altering decision rules from one period to the next.

The decision-rule formulations assume either a largely quantitative task environment (appropriations, force levels, prices; or, by extension, votes, organizational size) or a level of aggregation at which the researcher is willing to describe the relation between decisional situations and choices in mathematical terms, as in portions of Bremer's model. If the researcher is able to quantify features of the decision maker's environment as rates or probabilities (whether the decision maker thinks of them this way or not), and if detailed knowledge of his internal decision process is unimportant or too difficult to obtain, then the simulations of organizational decision offer many useful models. Extension to other phenomena depends on finding quantitative decision processes or on researchers' ingenuity at quantification and ability to develop the large data bases necessary to model the decision maker's task environment.

To the extent that the organizational decision models do not portray simply routine performances, they describe processes that are strongly goal-oriented and intendedly rational. Decision makers are seen as working at their tasks, motivated to achieve certain rather clearly defined goals by applying a limited number of familiar methods. Cognitive processes come to the fore. They may have their origins in the interaction of past experience and the personalities of individuals, but the origins are not examined or described in the models. Presumably it would be possible to study a number of decision makers at the same task, specify the differences in their decision processes, and proceed from there to investigate where the differences came from. It should be possible also to develop different models of the same decision task from study of human decision makers and to assess their performance under various hypothetical conditions. Thus, one could evaluate the rationality of the range of decision rules used. An example of this approach in economics is a study by Baumol and Quandt (1964) that investigates the consequences of a number of simple quantitative rules of thumb for pricing decisions; their performance was found surprisingly good under the limited conditions assumed. The context is distant from political psychology, but the method is of interest.

Man and Man-Machine Simulation of Systems

It is no coincidence that simulations dispensing with the computer in part or entirely are found associated with especially complex phenomena about which our ignorance is especially great. In spite of problems of complexity and of access for data collection, we still need to study the behavior of systems of organizations, in particular the international system. A simulation that includes human actors is one way of doing this. If we attempt a computer simulation or mathematical model of extremely complex behavior about which we know little, we will have to invent many processes to obtain the necessary closed model. It does not take very many inventions based neither on theory nor on data to render a model literally incredible. But if enough is known about the behavior of a system so that part of it can be defined at least tentatively, then people can be set to work carrying out the actions posited for the rest of it. This is the notion embodied in the Inter-Nation Simulation (INS) and its many versions and descendants.

In INS, people play the roles of major leaders of nations, deciding how to act toward other nations and how to allocate national resources, such as whether to spend more for consumer goods or for arms. The programmed portion of the simulation, whether calculated by hand or by computer, simulates basic economic and political structures and processes that shape the behavior of the human players in their decision-making roles. For instance, one function determines the level of consumer satisfaction that results from allocation of resources to consumer and other purposes; the level of consumer satisfaction subsequently affects the probability that the current set of leaders will continue to hold office. The functions of the programmed modules of the simulation and the actions of the human players feed into each other. The model builder is not faced with the impossible task of formulating mechanisms that could generate all the behavior of the simulated nations, but he can use various settings he creates as motivating structures to observe the behavior of the surrogate human actors.

A wide range of research efforts may be indicated by the term *simulation* applied to all-human or man-machine models. On the one hand, simulation means to some researchers an experiment in an enriched setting. This meaning is common in references to experimental studies of organizational phenomena, in which the experimenter creates a realistic task for a laboratory group and establishes levels of authority in it. Experienced actors as well as the usual student subjects may be brought into the laboratory (Barber, 1966), with special advantages and problems. Zelditch and Evan (1962) discuss the methodology of simulated bureaucracies. Typically, the tasks and structures invented by researchers have not been widely adopted; hence, there has been little continuity in development of theory from a succession of studies using essentially the same setting. Nevertheless, such enriched experiments may be efficient generators of information when control over variables is needed and not readily attainable in field research. Coleman's legislative game (1964a, 1966b) provides a setting whose characteristics deserve fuller exploration than they have received.

Both argument and evidence make a persuasive case for enrichment of experimental settings, if inferences beyond the boundaries of the laboratory are hoped for. In a neat demonstration of the effects of even minimal enrichment, Pilisuk and Rapoport (1964) gave two sets of subjects an identical Prisoner's Dilemma game, one in abstract form, the other with the same choices labeled as degrees of disarmament. Subjects were more cooperative in the disarmament version. Where a concern is to make inferences to a real system, an appropriately enriched setting has greater "proximal similarity" to the reference system (Raser, Campbell, and Chadwick, 1970; Abelson, 1968b, p. 279). This does not mean that all details of the setting need be "realistic," but it certainly argues for the inclusion of variables thought to interact with other variables in the reference system. The Inter-Nation Simulation and others in the same vein induce substantial information overload, uncertainty, complexity, and anxiety, all factors thought to affect behavior in the international system. A setting that lacked these features and was not labeled like real national decisions and international relations would be that much more distant in concept and behavior from real international systems. Inferences from laboratory to referent would be less well founded.

INS and its offspring are more than enriched experimental settings, however. They represent efforts to operationalize and connect "islands of theory" about diverse national and international processes. Human actors are used to generate decisions within the simulated nations not because the aim is to study individual behavior but because the difficulties in programming national decision functions are too great (Guetzkow, 1968, pp. 692–699). INS was created primarily to build the theory of international relations rather than to investigate the behavior of individuals in the simulated positions of national decision makers. There is some overlap between these uses, to be sure, since the behavior of the individual actors is a prime determinant of the behavior of the system.

Simulations of international processes are well reviewed and referenced by Smoker (1972). One important line of development has spawned a family of mixed man-machine simulations, devised for particular uses or to improve upon the theory embedded in INS, including Smoker's own International Processes Simulation. Another line seeks to develop explicit models of the behavior of the human actors and to test the models against the data from INS runs and against data from the real international system, as in Bremer's (1971) computer simulation of INS. For present purposes, attention focuses on the use of INS and related simulations either to study individual and small-group behavior or to study system behavior, with special sensitivity to the effects of individual differences. Two applications are discussed: (a) the study of individual cognitive processes and capabilities during decision making under conditions of stress, complexity, and information overload; and (b) the study of system behavior when actors are selected according to their personality characteristics. (For other studies of personality and cultural factors under simulated conditions, see M. G. Hermann, 1966; Druckman, 1968; Terhune and Firestone, 1967; C. F. Hermann, 1969; Powell, 1969. See also Chapter Ten in this volume; some of the assumptive frameworks discussed there could fruitfully be studied via simulations.)

Cognitive Phenomena. Research into the information-processing abilities and problems of the human actors in simulations is of special interest because it has been vigorously pursued and because it touches again upon the viewpoint expressed throughout this chapter about our need to understand cognitive processes in political behavior.

Using the Inter-Nation Simulation to study the behavior of individuals under the cognitively challenging decision conditions of that game, Driver (1962, 1965) divided players into nation-teams consisting of individuals with simple and with complex cognitive structure and process. Perhaps the clearest way to define these labels is to list the referents used in the classification procedure (Schroder, Driver, and Streufert, 1967). The responses of cognitively simple individuals are characterized by overgeneralization; hierarchical organization; absoluteness; inability to generate conflict or diversity; inability to view a situation from another person's point of view; inability to generate alternative perceptions and outcomes; and a tendency to seek structure, avoid delay, and close thinking quickly.

Driver's findings on the relation between cognitive structural complexity and aggression and irrationality in INS are intriguing. Groups made up of people with structurally simple cognition performed major aggressive acts (war and unprovoked arms buildup) three times more frequently than groups of cognitively complex persons (Driver, 1965, pp. 30–34). In the complex groups, aggressive behavior was instrumental to the achievement of other goals. In the "simple" groups, however, aggressive behavior tended to be related to attitudes toward violence rather than to goals prominent in the task environment of INS. If members of the group tended to be favorably disposed toward violence, then violence occurred irrationally and even at objectively low levels of stress. Violence as a response to frustration was much more likely for the simple-thinking groups than for those with more complex cognitive structures and processes (Driver, 1962; summarized by Schroder, Driver, and Streufert, 1967, p. 142). The line of research has been continued with a somewhat simpler simulation, the Tactical and Negotiations Game (Streufert and others, 1965; Streufert, Suedfeld, and Driver, 1965; Streufert and Streufert, 1969; Streufert, Streufert, and Castore, 1969). The findings constitute a strong argument for getting the house of cognitive processes in order and applying our knowledge of them to the study of political behavior.

Selecting Actors by Personality Characteristics. Hermann and Hermann (1967) conducted a pilot study, using INS, in which the assignment of players to roles in the simulation was based on the extent to which their personalities matched available knowledge about the personalities of particular historic actors—specifically, national leaders of European nations on the eve of World War I. One of the authors, a psychologist, studied materials on the leaders and developed a distinctive profile for each one. Categories of dominance, self-acceptance, and self-control appeared to differentiate among all ten of the leaders selected for matching. These characteristics and others identified in the analysis were measured in a group of people (high school students) by the California Psychological Inventory (Gough, 1956). Attitudes toward such concepts as suspicion, frankness, making decisions, peace, success, and war—also found to characterize one or another leader—were measured among the students by the Semantic Differential (Osgood, Suci, and Tannenbaum, 1957).

The players selected as matching most closely the personalities of the real leaders were placed in two runs of the INS, modified to simulate several days in July 1914—the few days just before war broke out. The history of developing conflict and events from the period preceding the simulated days were given to the players, in order to approximate in the simulation the conditions that shaped behavior in the reference system. Names of countries were fictitious, and particular events were altered in their details (but not in their meaning) in order to disguise the correspondence between simulate and reality. (The aim was to structure the players' behavior by the structure of the reference system, not by their memory of the actual outcome; nevertheless, some players did perceive a similarity between the simulation and the 1914 setting.)

One of the two runs carried out included players closely matched to the real leaders; the other, players less closely matched. Both in detail and in major outcomes, the run with matched players resembled the reference events much more closely than did the other run. The matched run was on the verge of war at the close of the simulation; the other run was preoccupied with plans for a conference called by one of the leaders. Numerous messages and conferences in the matched run resembled closely the events of the reference period.

One cannot draw firm conclusions from two INS runs with high school students. Still, the approach was bold, the method interesting, and the result suggestive. If replicable, the findings could validate, with respect to the pre-1914 reference system, both the scenario for the simulation and, most significantly, the selection and rating of personality traits and the matching of players to real leaders. The procedures for determining the personality characteristics of the leaders are of great interest in themselves and deserve a more complete and public account than they have received. We are learning to assess the personalities of leaders (George and George, 1956; Barber, 1972a), but the method applied by the Hermanns appears unique and worth further development. But then to have, in addition, a simulation method for validating the personality analysis opens up a range of new possibilities for students of political psychology.

Caveats

The reader will perceive the dominant tone of this chapter as optimistic— not for simulation generally or for all uses of it, but for some possible directions of research. It would be inappropriate to leave the matter at that, without pointing more clearly to major problems and requirements, and acknowledging the critics (Singer, 1965; Boudon, 1965; Zald and Schliewen, 1968; Rosenthal, 1965, 1968; Howrey and Kelejian, 1969; Powell, 1969; Shaw, 1971; Padioleau, 1969).

Validation. Most models and theories are intended to refer to some real phenomena, and sooner rather than later. If this is the case, the theorist should have in mind at the outset a procedure for validating his model, for comparing it with the reference system. Validation of simulations is still something of a new issue, but a number of good statements are available (Abelson, 1968b; Naylor and others, 1966; Naylor, 1969; C. F. Hermann, 1967; Dutton and Starbuck, 1971; MacRae and Smoker, 1967).

Not every model need refer directly to an existing real system. A simulation may involve a more limited examination of the implications of concepts and hypotheses: How do these ideas behave when put together? Day and Tinney (1968), for instance, examined through computer simulation the consequences of fragmented decision making, primitive learning, and satisficing (versus optimizing) decision rules in a hypothetical firm; their model is clearly not rich enough to represent a real firm, and the authors do not intend to validate the model. Nevertheless, a useful purpose is served by their demonstration. This does not mean we should avoid confrontation with data, but we need not undertake the confrontation every time we examine an idea.

A pointed use of simulation that does not fit readily into a conventional validation scheme is to suggest and evaluate alternatives to the real system. Smoker (1969, p. 11) argues: "It is possible to take the complementary position and to evaluate the 'real world' relative to the 'model world' incorporated in a simulation.

With this perspective the model world becomes an attempt to demonstrate or show or reveal the way parts of reality could or should be, and differences between the two worlds are rectified by changing aspects of reality through social and political action."

Perhaps the very term *validation* implies an inappropriate finality to the confrontation of data with model. A theoretical effort may stimulate our thinking or lead to the design of better research. It is reasonable to expect contributions of this sort rather than some kind of final validity (Raser, Campbell, and Chadwick, 1970). Furthermore, because many simulations are very complex, it is commonly more sensible to ascertain what parts of a simulation are invalid and to change them rather than to declare the whole model invalid.

Complexity, Sustained Development, and Cost. More than one simulation has been so complex as to exceed the capacity of its inventors to understand it, leading to "Bonini's paradox" (Dutton and Starbuck, 1971, p. 4; referring to Bonini, 1963): "Because the assumptions incorporated in the model are complex and their mutual interdependencies are obscure, the simulation program is no easier to understand than the real process was." Especially the computer modeler should ask: How complex must a model be to portray the behavior? It is a mistake to include in a model every detail one can observe in the real process.

Complex models of intrinsically interesting processes demand long, sustained development. The Inter-Nation Simulation and the Newell-Shaw-Simon work on problem solving fall into this category. Both have been developed by a large number of researchers over more than a decade; both will require more decades of revision and extension. Both projects have commanded significant resources and strong institutional support, and these were essential.

Simulation tends to be a slow and expensive way of doing research—in part, and justifiably, because of the complexity of the problems under study. In addition, however, the technology is very demanding and time-consuming, especially on the computer side of the method. Many a sad tale could be told about great aspirations that ended in stacks of useless computer output, obtained after anticipated weeks of work stretched into months, even years, of frustration with flighty student programmers, opaque computer systems, and frequent system changes.

Publication, Communication, and Parsimony. It is imprudent to promise a simulation before it has produced intelligible results, because it may never do so, in spite of good intentions and earnest effort. Many researchers, myself ruefully among them, have so strongly desired the final product that they came to expect it. Unfortunately, simulations have often turned out to be more problematic than they seemed to be at an earlier stage of development.

A different problem arises also from the overly strong wish for a running simulation. In several simulations reviewed in this chapter, interesting empirical and theoretical work has gone into the construction of a model but has not been fully described in print. Perhaps researchers should take their work and publications step by step, not concentrating so singlemindedly on the simulation that may eventually result. A gradual buildup of theory, data, and publications would also facilitate communication about the simulation, typically a difficult problem.

Frijda (1967) rightly criticizes computer simulators for failure to communicate their work adequately. Simulations are difficult to describe, and model builders have frequently neglected to present them unambiguously. If a complex simulation is worth doing, it must be worth describing in full detail and with careful attention to the requirements for adequate communication that Frijda sets forth. Moore (1968) suggests a standard format for the description of decision processes; Newell and Simon (1972) present a notation for information processes.

The detail incorporated in many simulations not only hinders communication but appears on the surface to place them at a severe disadvantage with respect to parsimony. A full exposition is not possible here (see Gregg and Simon, 1967, for a suggestive discussion), but some points may be set forth for consideration:

1. Simulations often make much stronger statements about the processes under study than do competing mathematical or verbal theories—more precise, more detailed, more extensive. The fact that two models are about the same process does not mean that they attempt equally ambitious explanations.

2. The hundreds or thousands of statements in a computer program (or in a scenario for an all-man or man-machine simulation) should not be equated with a small number of verbal or mathematical statements in a competing model. Much of the detail in a simulation program or scenario just copes with the technology. Gregg and Simon (1967) argue that mathematical models sometimes achieve an illusory parsimony by leaving implicit important features of a process that are made explicit in a simulation.

3. A theory is validated mainly by surviving tests of its predictions—efforts to disconfirm it and replace it with a competing explanation (Popper, 1959). If the theory is so ambiguous or general that no clear test of its predictions can possibly be developed, then its validity cannot be determined by scientific investigation—a state of affairs that typically generates more heat than light. A theory whose statements are precise, detailed, unambiguous, and explicit is therefore much to be preferred. While simulation models do not necessarily represent good theory, they are likely to be strong in the important ways noted. Some loss of parsimony may be a price well worth paying. Nevertheless, as suggested earlier in this chapter, mathematical methods are sometimes more suitable, especially where the environment of the modeled behavior is quantified and simple, as it may be in an appropriately controlled experiment.

Clearly, we stand at an early point in the use of simulation to develop knowledge about behavior generally and political-psychological behavior in particular. We see some achievements and more possibilities, and a falling away of naïve exuberance for the method. Abelson's (1968b, p. 346) closing statement is still apt: "The potentialities of the technique are indeed exciting, but it will take much more time to realize them than had been anticipated. Miracles are not to be expected; progress is."

15

THE NEW FRONTIER
OF PROJECTIVE
TECHNIQUES

Jeanne N. Knutson

The area known today as political psychology has been shaped by the research instruments used and by the research interests to which these instruments have been directed. To date, the political psychologist's principal tools have been scales employed in survey research, the focused interview, the psychobiography, and—to a much lesser extent—content analysis. But many other techniques developed for the study of human behavior—participant observation, the laboratory and natural experiment, computer and human simulation, and a variety of projective techniques—offer possibilities for increasing our understanding of the intrapsychic basis of politics. Since research instruments shape the content as well as the form of the data gathered (Knutson, 1972b), it has become increasingly

For their thoughtful critiques of the draft version of this chapter, I would like to express public appreciation to Leopold Bellak, Fred I. Greenstein, William E. Henry, and Paul H. Mussen.

important to widen the armamentarium of political psychology in order to check both our favorite hypotheses and our "established facts" against different types of data. The intellectual security which such multimethod research provides has been clearly recognized (Campbell and Fiske, 1959).

Additionally, total reliance on personality scales for our knowledge of the intrapsychic dimensions of political behavior is analogous to being limited to the stated preferences of a sample of voters in Bend, Oregon, in predicting the outcome of a national election. The employment of a variety of research methods increases both the range of human subjects on which inquiry can be feasibly focused and the type of information which may be gathered. Further, methods vary in their "discovery power," with this power differential being a function of both the properties of the method and the use to which it is put. An experienced interviewer, for instance, can uncover sensitive areas unavailable to questionnaire research. At the same time, the breadth of data provided by easily administered forced-choice survey questions cannot be approached by the more personalized depth methods.

This chapter explores the utility of employing projective techniques in political research as an adjunct to the limited methods now in use. Since such use has been rare, this subject is in many ways a new frontier. Like other frontiers, the explorer's investment is likely to be considerable and the rewards exciting but uncertain. Yet the rich and varied literature on projective techniques can help us to assess the utility of expending energy in this direction by elucidating some basic issues involving the meaning of "projective" in this sense, the import of the subject's response, and the possible advantages which would outweigh the considerable investment of investigator time.

Historical Perspective

Undoubtedly, the precursor of the projective techniques available today is the technique of free association developed by Sigmund Freud. Through this method, it was early recognized that each individual has a "subjective or experiential side" (Bolgar, 1956), which is causally related to his overt behavior; furthermore, the best way to become privy to this inner world is to provide an unstructured situation which the person is free to structure in his idiosyncratic way. Although the free-association method remains the paradigm of such understanding, it requires considerable expertise and time; consequently, researchers have tried to develop other methods for tapping inner predispositions. Concurrently, the assumptions about personality on which interpretations of responses are based have undergone considerable revision.

Since the late nineteenth century, psychologists have frequently employed unstructured stimuli to test individual differences and to measure mental content. Word-association tests developed by Carl Jung, James Cattell, and Francis Galton were soon followed by picture-association studies reported by H. L. Brittain, L. A. Schwartz, D. J. Van Lennep, and A. Binet (Harrison, 1965; Lindzey, 1961). It was not, however, until the advent of Hermann Rorschach's famous inkblot test in the 1920s that, through the medium of psychoanalytic concepts, association to unstructured stimuli became connected to personality theory (Rabin, 1968). Shortly afterward, L. K. Frank (1939) and Henry Murray (1938) independently discovered the commonality behind the various tests of association and separately coined the terms *projective techniques* and *projective methods* to cover this form of research (with the historical priority belonging to Murray). As Frank's seminal monograph stated, "The dynamic conception of personality as a process of organizing experience and structuralizing life space in a field leads to the problem of how we can reveal the way an individual personality organizes experience, in order to disclose or at least gain insight into that individual's private world of meanings, significances, patterns, and feelings" (p. 402).

Various other early studies uncovered, in perception and memory, systematic biases that could be related to personality factors. For example, the selective-perception phenomenon was clearly illustrated in an early study of the development of social attitudes in a southern community (Horowitz and Horowitz, 1938). Another study of that period (Seeleman, 1940–1941) found correlations ranging from .64 to .71 between a direct test of social attitudes and a recall of Negro and white photographs. In addition, Edwards (1941) published evidence supporting the hypothesis that individuals tend to forget information which conflicts with existing frames of reference and to remember information which harmonizes. Thus, not only through psychoanalysis but through the fields of perception and memory, psychologists were led to study the phenomenon of the selective ways in which an individual structures stimuli.

The term *projection* has been able to cover this phenomenon because of changes in the connotations of that word. According to Freudian theory, what occurs in the mechanism of projection is that "internal perception is suppressed, and, instead, its content, after undergoing a certain degree of distortion, enters consciousness in the form of an external perception" (Lindzey, 1961, p. 30).

> The essence of this conservative view is captured very well by Murray, who suggests that an orthodox definition of projection implies (a) an actual misperception in which the individual believes something that is manifestly false concerning another; (b) this misperception involves attributing to the other person a tendency directed toward either the perceiver or toward a third person; (c) the tendency is an important part of the perceiver's own personality; (d) the tendency is unacceptable to the perceiver and he is unaware of its existence in his own makeup; (e) the function of the process is to maintain self-esteem, or to escape from anxiety.

However, projective techniques owe their name not to this psychoanalytic mechanism of projection but rather to what Lindzey has called "generalized projection"— namely, "a normal process whereby the individual's inner states or qualities influence his perception and interpretation of the outer world." Thus, the term *projection,* outside of psychoanalytic discussions, is today assumed to include such intrapsychic mechanisms as (1) broad processes of ascribing one's feelings and views to others, (2) ways in which personality needs distort perception, and (3) the mechanism of classical projection rationalized by intellectual justification for the projection—a phenomenon frequently employed in ethnocentrism (Murstein and Pryer, 1959; also see Chapter Six above).

Efforts to explore and measure the workings of this widened process termed *projection* led to the development of countless varieties of techniques. In addition to the Rorschach inkblots and such picture-association methods as Murray's Thematic Apperception Test, projective techniques include various devices involving minimal cueing, such as auditory stimuli to which individuals give their interpretation, incompleted sentences for which subjects supply the ending, story-completion procedures, word-association tests, and drawing and drawing-completion tests. Shneidman (1965, p. 500) summarizes the commonality of these techniques as "psychological measurement devices which are characterized (1) on the *stimulus* side by *ambiguity* in the stimulus, (2) on the *response* side by the *multiplicity* of responses permitted the subject in an open situation where the responses do not have a right or wrong character, and (3) in the *interpretation* aspect by the interest of the interpreter in the *unconscious* or latent aspects of personality and in their amenability to holistic personality analysis."

One might ask why, in sum, if projection is a basic and inescapable feature of each person's dynamics, it is necessary to bother developing pictures, auditory stimuli, elaborate stages with figures, word lists, and other devices. Why, in other words, does the researcher not simply ask each subject to tell five stories or give ten random statements? Murray (1943, p. 2) suggests that devices such as his TAT cards have three advantages over collecting segments of subjects' thoughts which are not produced in response to specific stimuli: "It has been found (1) that pictures are effective in stirring the imagination; (2) that they serve to force the subject to deal, in his own way, with certain classical human situations; and finally (3) that the advantages of using standard stimuli are here, as in other tests, considerable."

Projective Responses

As stated previously, the intellectual tradition by which projective techniques were wedded to personality theory was psychoanalytic. Thus, when the intrapsychic needs interpreted from Rorschach and TAT responses did not correspond to the respondent's observed behavior, a variety of psychoanalytic concepts—including reaction formation, denial, repression, sublimation, and displacement—were employed to account for the discrepancy. Concurrent with the psychoanalytically influenced interpretation of responses to projective techniques went (and with researchers in this tradition still goes) an emphasis on content (story themes and outcomes) rather than on the formal or stylistic features of the responses (Murstein, 1963, p. 62).

With the growing influence of ego psychology in the 1950s, however, the view of what projective responses mean began to change. Psychologists began to believe that intrapsychic needs may provide the basic stimuli for a person's responses but that the type and direction of response are mediated by the functional capacity of the person's ego structure (such as ability to rationalize, degree of awareness of social press, capacity to organize). In spite of Murray's emphasis on the similarities between TAT stories and other types of fantasy (specifically daydreaming), present projective theory has come to emphasize the differences rather than the similarities between these verbal products.

While the element of fantasy (unguided free association without manifest continuity) is undoubtedly present in projective responses, it is recognized to be fantasy mediated by ego processes. In Freudian terms, this fantasy is secondary-rather than primary-process material. The growing understanding that the projective response is "mediated fantasy" is instructive because it epitomizes an important shift in meaning. From its earlier association with dreams, drug states, and other hypnogogic phenomena, *fantasy* has now come to refer to structured as well as unstructured imaginative processes. This broader usage reflects a differing view of the meaning of the projective response; hence, the continued application of "fantasy" to projective techniques represents another case of new wine in old bottles.

The usefulness of projective responses is not seen as being reduced because they are now understood to represent an individual's inner life seen in terms of his personalized coping activities and his own view of likely behavioral outcomes. On the contrary, students of behavior have increasingly recognized such mediated psychic needs as essential to understanding and predicting overt behavior. Indeed, "the manner in which a person copes with his problems is the most revealing thing about him. . . . Insofar as one can single out a particular flaw in current views of ego defense, it is that writers on the subject have failed to mention the tremendous importance of constructive strategies as a means of avoiding the vicissitudes that make crippling defenses necessary" (Smith, Bruner, and White, 1956, pp. 282–283).

Thus, it is today generally recognized that what has been labeled "cognitive control" (Gardner and others, 1959) intervenes between and mediates the impact of need on response. "The duty of cognitive control is to relate the functioning of (a) the gratification of drives, (b) the modulation and delay of drive consummation, and (c) the appraisal of reality and reconciliation of environmental forces and internal tension to each other within the person" (Murstein, 1963, p. 68). The earlier view of a direct relationship between inner needs and projective responses (Adorno and others, 1950) has generally been replaced by the understanding that the relationship between need and response is influenced by a number of other intrapsychic factors. Hence, whereas early work (Sanford, 1936) demonstrated that intrapsychic needs influence a person's way of structuring a situation (both what he perceives and what he ignores), other research began to illustrate that projective response is influenced by such factors as the degree of drive arousal and of anxiety arousal. Further, as the concept of perceptual defense was clearly demonstrated, experimental evidence also indicated "that it is the acceptable, although perhaps deprived, needs that are most frequently expressed in projective material" (Eriksen, 1954, p. 139).

The traditional position that motives are directly expressed in projective (particularly TAT) responses—perhaps most ably defended by Atkinson (1961) and McClelland and his associates (1953)—has been both challenged and illuminated by Lazarus (1966) in his "substitutive" theory, which states that "motives appear in fantasy when they are not expressed behaviorally." Lazarus's theory actually supports the thesis that motives are directly expressed in projective responses since he provides theoretical rationale for cases where direct expression of motives does not occur. Thus, his theory is consistent with Atkinson's (1961) statement that it is necessary to specify the conditions when motives are expressed and, further, when they are related to overt behavior.

Lazarus (1966, p. 485) further suggests that TAT stories can vary on a continuum from playful fantasy to problem-solving behavior necessary to gratify an aroused motive—and, indeed, usually reflect both factors. "Depending on the mix, the contents will either directly or substitutively reflect motivations, positive correlations with relevant behavior occurring in the case of the former, negative in the latter." He suggests that this mix is influenced by both personality and situational factors (and is true in *any* situation in which psychologists use behavior to infer motives): "The instrumental (goal-oriented) forms undoubtedly will increase relatively under conditions that emphasize logical, coherent, socially meaningful stories that are consistent with a minimally ambiguous stimulus." Thus, needs may be expressed or not and may be expressed through fantasy or goal-oriented responses, depending on the degree of need arousal, opportunities for its satisfaction, and the situational parameters relating to fantasy production.

With the increasing realization that there are various determinants of how intrapsychic needs influence projective responses and that the respondent may exercise a good deal of conscious control over his responses, there has come a corresponding realignment of scoring techniques: "To get away from these easily censorable responses, clinicians seem to be turning in increasing numbers to the use of formalistic variables which reflect *how* the story is told more than *what* the subject tells" (Murstein, 1963, p. 364). In this vein, Riessman and Miller (1958) note that it is important to know how story length (as well as story theme) is affected by the subject's social class.

This distinction between content and structural variables has played an increasingly important role in determining the meaning of projective responses. As noted above, content variables refer to "the semantic meaning of the fantasy response, and, in practice, there is strong emphasis on attitudinal and motivational meaning" (Kagan, 1961, p. 196). Structural variables, however, deal with how the response is made rather than the meaning of the response and can refer to a variety of processes.

> First, a structural variable can include the syntax of the subject's verbal behavior and the ordering of language units in the verbal response . . . the preferred use of specific language forms over others . . . the preferred perceptual organization of the stimulus . . . the coherence and logic of the fantasy production . . . the tendency to "go beyond" what is given in the external stimulus. . . . One might also include the nonthematic behavior of the subject (e.g., his resistance or his subjective reaction to the examiner) [Kagan, 1961, pp. 196–198].

As a result of this emphasis on structural variables, a high degree of quantification now often replaces the earlier, predominantly qualitative, assessment methods. This realignment has troubled a number of projective theorists. Atkinson (1961, pp. 227–228), for example, suggests that examining isolated variables may obviate the purpose for which projective measures were designed—namely, to study the whole person. And Shneidman (1965, pp. 504–507) has incisively noted:

> The worst indictment of projective techniques in America is not their lack of rigor or validity—which . . . can be viewed as an irrelevant demand from the 'other point of view'—but rather that they themselves have not consistently pursued a global understanding of their human subjects but

have been content rigidly to use one or two techniques to which they have oftentimes become cultishly cathected. . . . The normative aspirations of projective techniques can also be seen as a clear case of trying to placate the other tribe's totem.

Concurrent with the interest in (and debate over) the utility of quantifying projective responses is the realization that situational or extrapsychic factors must be considered when one assesses the responses of subjects. In addition to interviewer cues (as mentioned by Lazarus, above), various studies of stimulus cards show that the card itself "is by far the most important determinant of the content of a TAT response" (Murstein, 1963, p. 195). Based on this understanding, a number of researchers (Harrison, 1965; Sigel and Hoffman, 1956; Feshbach, 1961) suggest that projective devices which are custom-made to elicit the response area of interest are of value. As Feshbach (1961, p. 137) notes, however, the use of focused stimuli still leaves the problems of inference to be solved: "It is by now evident that we should not expect to find a simple, uniform relationship between 'covert' fantasy expression of a motive and 'overt' behavioral expressions. The proper question is not 'What is the relationship?' but rather 'Under what conditions would we expect to find a positive, inverse, or negligible correlation?' "

Indeed, problems of inference have been the focus of the most concerned attention from projective theorists. Henry (1960, pp. 18–19) summarizes the issue:

> We do assume that behavior bears some discoverable, if not direct, relation to underlying dynamics. And conversely, we do suppose that a particular pattern of inner dynamic relations has some greater tendency to be related to one pattern of overt behavior than to another. . . . The success of predictions of overt behavior is, however, greatly limited by our very scanty knowledge of what psychological issues will manifest themselves in which kind of behavior under what circumstances of correlative internal dynamics and of external pressures and sanctions.

For example, a study of lower- and middle-class boys (Mussen and Naylor, 1954) demonstrated that expression of aggression varies with both the degree of negative sanctions on aggression in the class group and the degree to which the person anticipates punishment for the expression of such aggression. Another study (Kagan, 1956) further illustrated that the expression of overt aggression varies in relation to (1) the strength of the need, (2) the amount of anxiety accompanying the need, and (3) the kind of aggressive behavior; in general, the relationship between fantasy productions and overt aggression was closer when the fantasized aggressive behavior was closely related to the overt criterion.

The levels of inference required and the resulting demands on the user of projective techniques are well stated by Korner (1965, pp. 24–25): "It is important that we are aware that our tests merely record behavior and that we can arrive at clinical insights only through inference, which in turn requires a thorough familiarity with the principles of psychodynamics on the part of the interpreter." Korner goes on to observe that projective techniques are as yet of limited relevance because they are slices of behavior and thus their utility rests on the inferences made about these behavior segments. It is here, however, that psychology, and particularly personality theory, is presently lacking in knowledge (see Chapter Two above), and thus this deficit is felt equally by all other forms of behavioral measurement. As Korner notes, successful prediction depends on the solution of two complex and perhaps unsolvable problems:

> The first one is the detection of all the innumerable variables that are at work in the process of an individual's reality adaptation to a need. It is probably not only the existence of these variables but also their interaction which determines what form his adaptation will take. The other problem is to find the secret of ego synthesis, which probably consists of an organismic process involving more than the sum of the variables at work and which possibly is at the root of all the clinical discrepancies mentioned before [p. 31].

Thus, both projective behavior and reality behavior are valid indications of internal predispositions, but between a person's needs and his behavior lie many intervening variables which need to be delimited.

In sum, the meaning of projective responses has changed with the changing emphases in personality theory and in psychometrics. Projective responses are now seen as *mediated* and *situationally influenced* expressions of intrapsychic needs. Although much research effort has been directed toward specifying what the mediating and situational variables are, the problems of levels of inference and of multi-determined causality have generally been unexplored. These serious issues, however, in many ways reflect the state of the art in psychology—or at least in personality measurement; thus, their existence does not provide an adequate reason to disallow the utility of projective techniques in the study of political behavior.

Projective Techniques and Other Methodologies

An area of particular interest to those using projective techniques in research is the relation between data gathered on projective measures and that acquired from more direct means. Of the number of studies focused on this area, the following are illustrative.

Propper (1970), replicating an earlier study by Davids and Pildner (1958), measured alienation by using a series of TAT cards and a sentence-completion test (the projective measures), as well as a self-rating scale and an affection questionnaire (the direct measures). Both studies found all intercorrelations to be significant at the .01 level, "suggesting that Davids' objective and projective instruments are indexing the same dimensions of the alienation syndrome" (Propper, 1970, p. 43).

In another study (Proshansky, 1943), ambiguous pictures of labor situations were intermingled with more typical TAT scenes as the projective measures. The ratings from the subjects' descriptions correlated .77 and (in a second sample) .67 with a direct verbal scale of attitudes toward labor. Such correlations appear unusually high. As Eriksen (1954, p. 440) notes in his summary of the literature: "In some experiments correlations of about .6 have been reported, [but] more typically the correlations have run about .4 or .5."

The area of the relationship between direct and projective scores has been carefully analyzed by Zimbardo (1964, p. 197), who criticizes direct measures of motivation employed after an experiment "because the subjects might not have been consciously aware of nor able to verbalize their true feelings, and the measure might evoke resistance in subjects for whom admitting to a state such as anxiety (or fear) calls into question their masculinity." This viewpoint is supported by Campbell (1957a) and McClelland (1958) and, of course, is very meaningful in view of the sensitive nature of much research in political psychology. Several interesting studies illustrate the value of employing projective measures of affect and motivation as a means of tapping areas in which anxiety is a factor. For example, Sarnoff and Zimbardo (1961) used a projective postexperimental measure (subjects were shown a photograph of a poker-faced person, who was supposedly about to participate in the same experiment, and asked to judge this person's reaction). They found a significant correlation between subjects' projections of anxiety and the anxiety arousal of experimental conditions to which they had been subjected, while a direct scale measure did not discriminate between conditions. In another well-known study, Clark (1952) presented TAT cards to sexually stimulated subjects (1) in a classroom setting and (2) in a fraternity (where subjects were under the influence of alcohol). He found that the subjects used significantly more symbolic sexual imagery but less manifest primary sexual imagery in their stories in the classroom, whereas in the fraternity their use of these categories was reversed.

In another interesting analysis of the relationship between projective and direct measures, Zimbardo and Formica (1963) found a correlation of .75 between direct and projective measures but discovered that subjects who had admitted auto-biographically (prior to the study) to reserved natures in expressing emotions were significantly more likely to express anxiety in projective measures than in the direct measure. The authors suggest that the method of data gathering should be tailored to the expressive nature of the subjects, but they unfortunately provide no evidence illustrating which measure was a better indicator of the actual anxiety felt by the subjects. It would be useful to replicate this study and to employ additionally a physiological measure of anxiety.

Other data suggest not only that different subjects may utilize projective devices in different ways but also that projective and direct responses may have different meanings. One study (De Charms and others, 1955) measured the need for achievement in the standard way (through specially designed TAT cards) and in a direct way (through answers to questions). The investigators found that two different dimensions were being measured (which correlated +.23). Subjects who were consciously achieving on the direct measure tended to be conformists, with a high valuation of authority, a low valuation of unsuccessful people, and high scores on the F scale. Indirect achievers, on the other hand, tended to have internalized standards of excellence and to perform in a superior way on various tasks. It is not clear why the investigators were surprised that two different dimensions appeared, since there is a predictable psychodynamic difference between assertion and action in this area. That is, it is one thing to state categorically that one conforms well to a major social value; it is quite a different thing to use one's abilities creatively in goal-oriented behavior. I believe that this is an important point, because the often-found disparity between different measures purportedly assessing the same dimensions could frequently be predicted from a careful analysis of the constraints inherent in the measures themselves (thus dispelling some unnecessary gloom surrounding the area of psychometrics).

In a careful summary of indirect measures, Campbell (1950, pp. 30–31) notes that none of the many studies he reviewed illustrated that the indirect tests have higher validity than the direct tests. However, the case for face validity of these indirect measures is usually better than for direct measures. "In a number of the disguised, structured tests, the distribution of scores and measures of internal consistency demonstrates unequivocally that nonrandom, systematic errors, differences in perceptions, etc. exist, of which the respondents are presumably unaware. These systematic unconscious 'biases' are well worth study in their own right, and seem to lie close to the functional meaning of attitude."

In another thoughtful article, Campbell (1957b, pp. 207–208) discusses the relation of projective techniques to other methods. He finds three main differences. The first distinction is between voluntary and objective tests. "In the *voluntary* test the respondent is given to understand that any answer is acceptable, and that there is no external criterion of correctness against which his answers will be evaluated." The second distinction is between indirect and direct tests. "In the *direct* test, the respondent's understanding of the purpose of the test and the psychologist's understanding are in agreement." The third difference distinguishes free-response from structured tests. "The *free-response* format has the advantage of not suggesting answers or alternatives to the respondent, of not limiting the range of alternatives available, nor of artificially expanding it through the suggestions provided in the prepared alternatives." The classical projective measures are voluntary, indirect, and free-response; projective techniques exist, however, for all permutations of these dimensions except voluntary-direct-structured and two types that are inappropriate for personality measurement (objective–direct–free-response and objective-direct-structured).

One final distinction should be made between projective techniques and other methods. Two sets of investigators (Hanfmann and Getzels, 1955; Greenstein and Tarrow, 1970) have raised a distinction between projective and what they call "semiprojective" measures. These investigators use the term *semiprojective* to refer to data-gathering techniques such as story-completion tests, "which are like fully projective tests in that they involve fantasy elaboration on a stimulus, but which are unlike them in two respects:

(1) The stimulus content is more structured and culturally patterned. It is ordinarily *aspects* of the stimulus, rather than the entire stimulus, that are left ambiguous, and the ambiguities are carefully adjusted in order to expose the respondent to specific issues with which the investigator is concerned. Alternatively, the stimulus may be unambiguous but *problematic*, as in story completions that pose a dilemma in which a choice must be made between two equally desirable—or undesirable—options. In this case, the ambiguity is in how to resolve the dilemma. (2) The resulting data are interpreted at a surface (sociocultural) rather than a deep (psychodiagnostic) level. That is, the interpretive interest is in what orthodox projective testers ordinarily treat as chaff: values, cognitions, perceptual sets, characteristic ways of perceiving typical social situations, expecta-

tions about actions that will take place under specified circumstances, and so forth [Greenstein and Tarrow, 1970, pp. 501–502].

It appears to me that the above discussion raises an inconsequential, if not invalid, distinction. Projective techniques, as Campbell (1957b) has noted, vary in their degree of focus; what these investigators are describing are voluntary, free-response, and either direct or indirect tests—and thus in the tradition of classical projective techniques. Furthermore, projective techniques (like the so-called semiprojective techniques) are also based on carefully adjusted ambiguity; that is, although the stimulus rests on a large degree of psychological ambiguity, successful projective techniques must present a fairly well-structured situation—or at least, as with TAT cards, the physical ambiguity must be minimal (Harrison, 1965). Finally, as we noted earlier, there are many different scoring interests, focusing on various levels and a wide range of psychic functioning and situationally determined behavior; the above-described scoring options fit well within traditional, nonclinical interests.

Projective techniques, then, can measure significant aspects of what direct measures seek to capture, but most of the variance between these types of measures is presently unaccounted for. (For a more detailed analysis of problems of validity, see Buros, 1965.) Perhaps the degree of missing variance can be significantly reduced by a clearer understanding of the use which different personality types make of different techniques of assessment. It also appears necessary to define the target dimension more sharply, so that both the direct and indirect measures are similarly focused and there is some intellectual confidence that they both measure the same phenomenon. Finally, it should be underscored that projective techniques refer to a wide variety of data-gathering devices which bear commonality because they are voluntary and usually indirect measures. Both a wide range of scoring focuses and methodologies and an equally vast array of structured ambiguity are at home within this commonality.

Politically Relevant Uses

Projective techniques probably have proved most useful so far in the area of ethnocentrism. Guggenheim (1969), for example, used projective techniques to focus on two previously separately documented relationships: (1) between being black and expressing lowered self-esteem and/or self-hatred, and (2) between cumulative, chronic failure and an inability to realistically appraise task requirements, with chronic failure presumably associated with being black in America. Connecting these two issues is the view that level of aspiration is a function of self-esteem and that self-esteem is a facet of self-concept. Guggenheim's study thus analyzed the interrelationships of ethnic background, expectations for achievement, actual achievement, and self-esteem. His subjects (162 sixth-grade children from a Manhattan elementary school) were asked to "Draw a person like yourself" as a special version of Machover's Draw-a-Person Test and were given a set of ten Semantic Differential Scales (Osgood, Suci, and Tannenbaum, 1957) related to the picture in order to assess self-esteem. This procedure was followed because "problems of social desirability and defensive responses which loom large when measuring self-esteem do not seem to be adequately controlled in the phenomenological [self-rating] framework [usually employed]" (p. 69). On the basis of the semantic differential scales, 56 black and white children were selected, differentiated on the basis of high or low self-esteem. This sample was then given a specially designed achievement test which was administered three times under different degrees of information regarding actual achievement.

Guggenheim found that black children, as predicted, had significantly greater discrepancies between actual achievement and expectation of achievement, but this phenomenon was unrelated to degree of self-esteem. Information regarding actual achievement reduced the discrepancy scores for the subjects as a whole. The amount of discrepancy, however, was less important than the direction of the discrepancy between actual and expected achievement: "Eighty-six percent of the Negro pupils, as compared to 58 percent of the white pupils, overestimated the number of problems they thought they would get right." There was a similarly significant difference in overestimation between high- and low-esteem children. with high self-esteem children also tending to predict higher scores than they achieved. Finally, while white children had significantly higher achievement scores than did black children, low-esteem white children had significantly higher expectation scores than did low-esteem black children (and there was no significant difference between the high-esteem groups). This use of projective techniques thus suggests the surprising conclusion that while black children do exhibit generally lower school performance (a phenomenon being attacked by federally funded programs to raise their self-esteem), black children do not differ from white children in self-esteem. The performance-relevant personality difference may rather be defensive, overambitious, and unrealistic goal-setting behavior.

Several other studies fall in this area. Johnson (1949) successfully illustrated the development of Anglo-Spanish attitudes in the Southwest through specially designed TAT pictures. Seeleman (1940–1941), as mentioned previously, found high correlations in two studies between a direct test of social attitudes and a recall of Negro and white photographs. Morgan (1945) investigated attitudes toward the Japanese at the end of World War II. By employing an unusual projective technique he attempted to counter the reduction in predictive value of public opinion polls caused by "self-deceit" on issues which are highly emotion-laden. Using as subjects 170 students from psychology classes at Northwestern University, Morgan first assessed their attitudes toward the Japanese by four items embedded in a fifty-item direct-attitude questionnaire. He then attempted to measure the veridical degree of the questionnaire answers by giving respondents "two similar syllogisms, one containing terms which have no personal value and the other involving personal convictions or controversial issues; the differences in the patterns of response to the two syllogisms can be used as an index of the direction of the personal bias of the respondents" (p. 27). (For evidence of the degree to which paired syllogisms can measure personal bias, see his two earlier studies: Morgan and Morton, 1944, 1945.)

Morgan then employed the issues in the four direct-attitude questions in four different syllogisms which were paired with four control syllogisms which used emotionally indifferent terms. (These pairs were not given in juxtaposition.) For example, one direct question stated: "The Japanese are not assimilable in American society." The corresponding syllogism stated: "If it is true that some Japanese people are not assimilable in American society, it is logical to conclude: (1) All Japanese people are assimilable in American society. (2) Some Japanese people are assimilable in American society. (3) No Japanese people are assimilable in American society. (4) Some Japanese people are not assimilable in American society. (5) No logical conclusion can be drawn from the given statement." The control syllogism which logically corresponded to the above stated: "If it is true that some pills are not poison and if it is true that some poisons are not green, it is logical to conclude: (1) All pills are green. (2) Some pills are green. (3) No pills are green. (4) Some pills are not green. (5) No logical conclusion can be drawn from the given statement."

While the direct measure did not offer this understanding, data from the syllogisms clearly indicated a pull toward tolerance (over the logical choice pattern evidenced on the control syllogism). For example, whereas 85 percent of the sample (on the direct question) did not feel that "Japanese are inherently more cruel than white men" (and thus did not agree with popular propaganda statements of the times), the control syllogism choice was logically equivalent to the paired syllogism choice that "80 percent of the Japanese people are cruel"; on the emotion-laden paired syllogism, however, the subjects tended to reject this ethnocentric statement in favor of "No logical conclusion can be drawn from the given statement." Thus this use of projective techniques helped to separate the factors of socially desirability, popular responses, and intrapsychic proclivities.

To political psychologists, the best-known use of projective techniques in studying ethnocentrism is undoubtedly found in *The Authoritarian Personality* (Adorno and others, 1950). (For a detailed discussion of this study and of the development of its most visible contribution, the F scale, see Chapter Six in this volume. See Christie and Jahoda, 1954, for an analysis of validity problems in this study.) Two further studies of this subject illustrate the utility of projective techniques in providing a clearer understanding of the psychodynamics of the prejudiced personality. In one study (Goldberg and Stern, 1952), a group of five hundred college freshmen were given the E and F scales, with the highs and lows being selected for further study. These subjects were given several projective techniques, including the Rorschach, the TAT, and a sentence-completion test. As in the original Berkeley study, it was found that ethnocentrics tended to repress or reject impulses, to hold contradictory and distant parental images, and to show an absence of nurturant capacities. In a second study (Sarnoff, 1951), one hundred Jewish male students were differentiated into highs and lows on an anti-Semitism scale from the Berkeley study and then given TAT cards and the Michigan Sentence Completion Test. Subjects high in ethnocentrism tended to have more negative and fewer positive attitudes toward parents and toward themselves, to be more frequently passive in the face of interpersonal hostility, and to be less prone to retaliate against aggressors (that is, as noted in the previous study, to deny or repress impulses). Thus, data from these studies support the biographical and projective data gathered during the Berkeley research.

The relationship between ethnocentrism and intolerance of ambiguity, a major focus of the Berkeley authoritarianism work, received additional confirmation in a study by Block and Block (1951). These authors hypothesized that both ethnocentrism and intolerance of ambiguity are "subordinate manifestations" of a more central personality dimension, which they labeled "ego control." (For a discussion of levels of intrapsychic analysis, see Chapter Two in this volume.) Using sixty-five males (homogeneous in social status and intelligence) from an elementary psychology course, Block and Block first separated their subjects into overcontrollers, who "bind their tensions excessively"; undercontrollers, who "do not bind their tensions sufficiently"; and appropriate controllers. This separation was made by judgments of stories told by the subjects to three Murray TAT cards.

Next, the experimenters made use of a different type of projective test: the well-known autokinetic phenomenon of the apparent movement of a pinpoint of light focused on a wall of a darkened room. The subjects (in a hundred trials over a forty-five-minute period) were asked to turn off their light by button the instant they perceived it to move, and to write down the distance that it moved. Raters divided the subjects' scores on the basis of whether, over the series of trials, the subject had established a norm or frame of reference for the degree of light movement. A statistically significant relationship (at the .02 level) was found between the establishment of a norm in the autokinetic experiment and a high score on the Berkeley ethnocentrism scale. Further (at significance levels ranging between .05 and .01), overcontrollers were found to be highest in ethnocentrism, undercontrollers were lowest, and appropriate controllers fell in between. Here the employment of a quite different method of measurement and a different point of view made an important contribution by confirming the thesis of the Berkeley study, which had employed another technique to measure intolerance of ambiguity.

Also in this area is an ongoing study of the effects on moral development (in Kohlberg's terms) of the stress and violence which children in Northern Ireland are today experiencing (Fields, 1972). In a preliminary study in December 1971, the author interviewed twelve Catholic and twelve Protestant children from slum-dwelling families in Belfast and an equal number (minus four Protestant children) in Dublin, employing a ten-card TAT and the Tapp questions on rules and laws (Tapp and Kohlberg, 1971). The TAT responses were analyzed in terms of Arnold's (1962) method of story sequence analysis. Preliminary analysis indicates that the children in Belfast

> are pessimistic and fatalistic. The people in their stories have little or no control over their fate. They may choose to run away from "troubles" but the trouble pursues them. People have incomprehensible motives for destruction and children are quite helpless to contravert them. You may work hard to accomplish a task but more often your efforts end up in failure. Death and destruction are inevitable. When you try to correct an injustice, you are hurt in the end. Ordinarily you try to tell others and get them to help you, but they neither listen nor help. War is an everyday fact of life and military action inevitably leads to grief and death. The prognosis, on the basis of motivation index scores, is quite dim. . . . The children of Dublin, who share a similar cultural context but have not personally experienced war in their streets, demonstrate a more optimistic outlook. They have more concern with interpersonal relations and with the necessity for being good and "making amends." Their prognosis by motivation index scores would appear to be more optimistic. The range of motivation index scores is parallel with those of children in the United States and, in fact, somewhat higher than those of correspondingly lower class [Fields, 1972, p. 13].

In general, this TAT response analysis gives an understanding of the psychodynamics underlying the finding that—unlike the Dublin sample and the United States sample reported by Tapp and Kohlberg—the war-stressed Belfast sample does not evidence the age-related trend of moral development but generally remains at the lowest level, suggesting that "the present conflict will effect a truncation in the development of moral judgment for the next generation of the Northern Irish."

Turning from the dimensions of ethnocentrism, Dies (1968) reports a study dealing with the subject of efficacy, an area of continuing interest to political psychologists. Specifically, Dies was concerned with Rotter's (1966) dimension of internality-externality and employed the method—developed by Witkin and his associates (1954)—of scoring TAT stories for story figures' ability to cope with environmental and intrapersonal conflicts. The subjects (forty female psychiatric nursing students) were given Rotter's internality-externality scale and two weeks later were asked to write stories to seven TAT cards. Their TAT scores allowed correct classification of 80 percent of the subjects as to which end of the internality-externality scale their score fell. (This correlation was unrelated to grades or to mental health, as these factors were judged by experienced clinicians.) As noted in the previous section, there is a pressing need to understand why a direct measure picks up different scores for some respondents than does a projective measure; and thus deviant case analysis of the 20 percent whose scores did not agree would have been most helpful. This criticism is particularly important here since a secondary analysis of the TAT stories of the deviant scorers in terms of the subjects' scale responses might provide data leading to a refinement of our understanding of the dimension of efficacy.

A second study which generally falls into this area of efficacy is reported by Mussen and Wyszynski (1952). The focus of this study is personality differences between politically active and apathetic; for this purpose, the subjects selected were 156 University of Wisconsin undergraduates between the ages of seventeen and twenty-seven. In this study, the authors used a version of the projective question delimited by Levinson (1950, pp. 545–548) as "an application of the general principles of projective techniques to the questionnaire method and to the study of the dynamics of ideology. A projective question is an open-ended question which is answered in a few words or lines and which deals with unusual events or experiences likely to have emotional significance for the individual. Care is taken to give the question a 'homey,' even humorous, wording; also, an emphasis on the universal nature of certain emotional experiences (e.g., moods, embarrassment) may make the subject feel freer in giving an answer." Although this method is similar to other projective techniques, Levinson noted a number of advantages to its use in sociopsychological research: the items are readily comprehended; they can be answered quickly ("eight items require only ten to fifteen minutes"); they need no detailed instructions; and, since they are admirably suited to questionnaire use, they provide a useful multimethod validation of dimensions measured in scale items.

In the Mussen-Wyszynski (1952) study (at significance levels varying between .05 and .10), a number of meaningful differences appeared in the intrapsychic orientation of the active and the apathetic. Political apathy was seen as a fundamental part of a basic passive orientation, identified by characteristics including "inability to recognize personal responsibility or to examine—or even accept—[one's] own emotions and feelings; vague, incomprehensible feelings of worry, insecurity, and threat; complete, unchallenging acceptance of constituted authority (social codes, parents, religion) and conventional values" (p. 78). The politically active, on the other hand, do not have feelings of insecurity and threat, and show "an emphasis on strivings for ego satisfactions, independence, maturity, and personal happiness. . . . The sensitivity to others' feelings, emotions, and conflicts which is revealed by the politically active may also be interpreted as part of a generally active orientation, since it may represent an outgoing response: an attempt to understand, and empathize with, others" (pp. 78–79). The investigators also note, however, that the positive desire to make social contributions must be accompanied by a lack of sense of threat for activity to be actualized and point out that authoritarianism (as measured by the F scale) does not differentiate between the active and the apathetic student.

Another research focus is the area of power, achievement, and affiliation motivation. First of all, Veroff and his associates (Veroff, 1961; Veroff and others, 1960) used these dimensions in what, to my knowledge, is the only study in which projective techniques were employed with a national sample (other than perhaps some possibly projective questions). Although the interests of this nationwide study of three basic motivations are generally unrelated to politics, a number of relationships (for example, between the target dimensions and socioeconomic status) could be fruitfully reviewed by the political psychologist for heuristic purposes.

In a directly political analysis of this dimension, Browning and Jacob (1964) gave the McClelland TAT series to a sample of fifty elected officials in two Louisiana parishes (67 percent of the elected officials) and, in an eastern city, to a random sample of twenty-three businessmen-politicians. They found that neither affiliation, power, nor achievement differentiated the politicians from the nonpoliticians. However, "politicians in high-potential positions scored much higher in both achievement and power motivation than their matched sample (N = nine pairs)" (p. 85). Thus, this controlled analysis suggests the existence of a relationship between role requirements and personality type which their initial aggregate-level analysis missed.

Several other political studies report imaginative uses of projective methods. Green and Stacey (1966) investigated the relationship between voting choice and self-image. The investigators showed their subjects eight photographs of males and asked the subjects to order the pictures along eight dimensions of personality (for instance, "Which of these men would you say was the most/least determined and confident? Now arrange the others in between"—p. 13). Each subject was then asked which of the men he most/least would like to be, "thus providing an index of preferred and rejected identification." Finally, the subjects were told that four of the men in the photographs were members of the Conservative Party and that four were staunch Labour Party supporters, and they were asked to guess which was which. The random sample—consisting of eighty male voters who lived in London—was composed of twenty middle-class Conservatives, twenty middle-class Labourites, twenty working-class Conservatives, and twenty working-class Labourites.

Green and Stacey's data revealed that each of the four subject groups (at a significance level of .05) had markedly different self-images, except for the two working-class groups. The data also indicated a high relation between a subject's

party affiliation and the affiliation attributed to the photograph identified most positively by the subject, suggesting that a shared self-image may be an imporant factor in
a person's voting preferences. Interestingly, the working-class Conservatives usually
identified positively with the photographs of the presumed Conservatives, but they
also tended to reject the presumed Conservatives as strongly as the two Labour
groups did (selecting a presumed Conservative from photographs chosen for rejected
identification). This finding suggests that working-class Conservatives have considerable ambivalence about their political orientation. Thus this study may have uncovered a fissure—in the form of a lack of personal identification with the
Conservative image—in the bedrock of lower-class Conservatism, as well as evidence
for the existence of a shared working-class identification which transcends party lines.

Two other studies used a political cartoon to study attitudes. Fromme (1941)
analyzed attitudes toward war, using as subjects thirty-five nonrandomly selected men.
Each subject was interviewed for four to seven hours and given (as a basis for the
interview probes) the SPSSI "Survey of Opinion on Methods of Preventing War."
After the interview, in order to judge the stability of a subject's answers, the interviewer presented conflicting answers from an imaginary poll of experts. Additionally,
Fromme used five political cartoons, with the original captions removed; the subjects
were asked to choose the most appropriate caption from among four. The subjects
were also given five TAT pictures, especially designed for the study. In spite of this
wealth of data, the investigator offered no definitive analysis of his materials but
did present suggestive evidence that "yes-no" responses (to the SPSSI Survey) about
half the time did *not* indicate the subject's true meaning.

Fillmore Sanford (1950b) reported a more carefully designed study which
also used the cartoon as a projective technique. Sanford's study, which focused on
leadership and authority, employed a random sample (N = 963) of Philadelphians.
The immediate concern of the study was what people worry about. Fairly early in
the hour-long interview, the subjects were asked, "Do you think you worry more or
less than most people?" and then "What sort of thing do you worry about most?"
Later in the interview, the subjects were shown a cartoon which depicted a person
with a problem which the subject was asked to specify. The subjects were also asked
when they sought advice and what kind of advice they needed.

> While 159 (16.5 percent) give no answers [to the cartoon queries], this
> does not compare too unfavorably with the 13.2 percent who do not
> answer the direct question on worries or with the 13.8 percent who fail
> to answer the question on the sort of advice needed. (For four of the six
> pictures used in the complete study, the percentage of "no answers" runs
> around 4 percent.) In terms of the technical feasibility of the pictures,
> there is the additional factor that most people interviewed appear to
> enjoy responding to the pictures. . . . They represent, apparently, a
> pleasant change of pace in a long interview [pp. 699–701].

Sanford also felt that the pictures elicited more specific and personal answers and
thus "gets past the psychological censor which often operates in the standard face-to-
face interview" (p. 701).

In the Sanford study, 201 people were retested one month later. The cartoon
was as or more reliable than other measures; and, according to Sanford, the reliability

would have been higher "had the coding been based on categories of a more psychological or more genotypical nature" rather than "relatively superficial ones, based on the clearly manifest content of the answers" (pp. 701–703). Sanford's retest analysis indicated that the pictures elicited basic attitudes rather than simply indicating socially desirable responses. (The politically relevant findings of this study are reported in Sanford, 1950a.) These findings raise the important issue in the use of projective techniques of the ways in which reliability is affected when coding moves from a simple response description (low reliability) to broader categories in terms of themes or story imports (generally high reliability) to coding based on inferences about intrapsychic processes (reliability issue unclear).

Another study employing a somewhat different technique in politically relevant research is reported by Hanfmann and Getzels (1955), who gave a specially constructed "Episodes Test" to a sample of Soviet refugees (forty-one men and ten women) living in Munich plus a control sample of Americans. The episodes (described above) consisted of a series of brief verbal descriptions of interpersonal situations (five familial and five extrafamilial). The subject was asked to describe the probable development and outcome of the episode. The technique was labeled "semiprojective" because "it addresses itself to the level of realistic, social-directed action, rather than to that of fantasy, and elicits material that is not too far removed from the subject's conscious attitudes and from his manifest behavior" (p. 1).

Hanfmann and Getzels (1955) found that Americans were more likely to see difficulties as internal; the Russians, as social and/or political. Additionally, the Russians expressed significantly more positive feelings toward the social group and did not feel as weak, helpless, or unconfident vis-à-vis the group as did the American subjects. In short, "the Russians do not feel compelled, as the Americans are, to defend their individual integrity against the group" (pp. 34–35). Correlated with this, the Russians were less hero-oriented, but rather tended to express more spontaneous empathy for all the actors. Of equal value are some distinctions that did not occur: "The data of the episodes do not yield any material that would indicate a greater incidence of authoritarian character traits in one or in the other national group," nor were there any great differences in other "essential personality variables" such as aggression and affection—thus negating national-character arguments (pp. 36–37). In many ways, this study illustrates the importance of employing projective techniques, for the responses give evidence not only of *what* attitude is held but also of *why* it is held (its meaning and importance to the person in terms of his own needs and values).

Another study in which the psychic-social nexus receives focus is the lengthy psychoanalytically oriented study of a Mexican village reported by Fromm and Maccoby (1970). Over a period of many years, a variety of research techniques (participant observation, Rorschach tests, the TAT, in-depth questionnaires) probed the character types of the villagers (in terms of Fromm's typology) and the relationship between social character and behavior in a number of areas. The authors (p. 7) stated their thesis as follows: "We believe that just as psychoanalysis studies the character of an individual in terms of analyzing the underlying forces which in a structuralized form make up his character and motivate him to feel and think in certain ways, the character common to a whole group, *social character,* has the same dynamic function and can be studied empirically." While their research design obviated the causal evidence they sought, the investigators present impressive correlations between social character (such as exploitative or productive hoarding) and such behavioral indices as assumption of and functioning in family roles, degree of alcoholism, type of crops planted, and degree of economic success. Important here is the sensitive nature of the data derived from projective techniques and the value of employing such a technique in studying intrapsychic dynamics of a generally nonliterate population.

Finally, three studies in political socialization have employed projective techniques as a necessary antidote to the almost total reliance here on data shaped by survey methods. First is a study by Greenstein and Tarrow (1970) of children in America, France, and Great Britain. The preliminary report focuses on the methodology used (an episodes technique similar to the one employed by Hanfmann and Getzels) and presents as data only a few illustrative case studies, so that the value of their techniques of measurement remains to be assessed. Some of the episodes deal indirectly with political themes (and are thus termed "parapolitical") ; others are directly political. An example of the former is as follows: "A group of children of your own age are playing. Some of them want to play one game. Others want another. There are not enough children to play both. Finish the story." An example of a political episode: "One day the President (substitute Queen in England, President of the Republic in France) was driving his car to a meeting. Because he was late he was driving very fast. The police stop the car. Finish the story."

Greenstein and Tarrow (p. 505) suggest that their measures help to fill the "imperfect fit between inner perceptual experience and its representation in survey data" and make this cogent comment: "No doubt many survey respondents express, in Converse's (1970) term, 'nonattitudes' rather than actual attitudes when queried by the pollster. But it would seem likely that in addition there are people who do hold opinions, or at least reasonably stable 'outlooks,' and who are simply unable to make the connection between their own thought patterns and the formalized mold provided for them by the authors of survey questionnaires." The results of this study will certainly be of major interest to political psychologists.

A second use of projective techniques in political socialization research is found in reports of work by Adelson and O'Neil (1966), using 120 children taken equally from the fifth, seventh, ninth, and twelfth grades. Their interview schedule was based on the following premise: "Imagine that a thousand men and women, dissatisfied with the way things are going in their country, decide to purchase and move to an island in the Pacific; once there, they must devise laws and modes of government." After this imaginary format was offered to and accepted by the subjects, the children were asked to discuss a number of hypothetical issues:

> For example, the subject was asked to choose among several forms of government and to argue the merits and difficulties of each. Proposed laws were suggested to him; he was asked to weigh their advantages and liabilities and answer arguments from opposing positions. The interview leaned heavily on dilemma items, wherein traditional issues in political theory are actualized in specific instances of political conflict, with the subject asked to choose and justify a solution. The content of our inquiry ranged widely to include, among others, the following topics: the scope

and limits of political authority, the reciprocal obligations of citizens and state, utopian views of man and society, conceptions of law and justice, the nature of the political process.

The investigators suggested a sound rationale for choosing this projective method of exploring the development of a sense of community: "Our pretesting had taught us that direct questions on such large and solemn issues, though at times very useful, tended to evoke simple incoherence from the cognitively unready, and schoolboy stock responses from the facile." Employment of this technique yielded a rich data base from which it was possible to comprehend not only what the children understood of the target concept at each developmental level but also both their misconceptions and the dynamics which served to unite these misconceptions. The nuances of shifts from an egocentric to a sociocentric perspective are particularly well reflected in these data.

In addition to these two socialization studies, I am currently engaged in a research project with a similar focus. (See Knutson, 1974, for a preliminary report.) This work employs a specially developed political version of the TAT, designed to correspond to empirical evidence (discussed earlier) that (1) focused cards tend to be most predictive of target behavior; (2) cards that are psychologically ambiguous but physically structured have been most successful; and (3) cards need not depict figures similar to the subject's sex, culture, or class—indeed, the most useful cards are often set in other times or cultures in order to relax the subject's defenses so as to elicit psychically meaningful, veridical responses, although such responses would be unacceptable to the subject if conscious and/or verbalized.

The ten cards of what is called the Political Thematic Apperception Measure (PTAM) were developed to correspond to ten basic themes in politics and to elicit (when present) five basic intrapsychic need-areas, as delimited by Maslow (physiological, safety or security, affection and belongingness, esteem and self-actualization). The theme cards are:

1. Legalized Force (aggression): the beneficial vs. deleterious effects, the identification of the subject with protagonist as "victim" or society as "victimized," etc.: *the necessity and role of legalized force*

2. Human Nature: seen as basically cooperative, antagonistic in a Hobbesian sense, etc.: *the ability which humans possess to solve human problems*

3. Authority: useful and beneficent, threatening and alien, etc.: *the relation which it is necessary to make with authority*

4. Leader-Follower: the necessary relation between leader and group; leader as object or subject of authority: *the basis of the decision-making process*

5. Security in Society: the safety or danger of communal life, etc.: *the ability of men to live communally and handle antisocial acts*

6. Youth: seen as an alienated or integrated group, object of hostility, curiosity, affection, etc.: *the function and role of generational differences*

7. Locus of Authority: internal or external, with man as actor or puppet: *the ability of man to rationally shape his destiny*

8. Group-Individual: the ability of a group to satisfy an individual's needs (especially affection and esteem): *the group as deprivational or nurturing of an individual's relational needs*

9. Poverty: as due to human failure, social conditions, fate, etc.: *social vs. individual responsibility for those falling below norms and the causality of social dependence*

10. Systemic Loyalty: country as ego alien, deserving of higher regard than self, etc.: *the power of the system to claim allegiance*

A preliminary study used these cards[1] to explore the politicization of young children (fourteen subjects in each of the third and sixth grades). Analysis indicates that children at this age have well-defined views of themselves and others; on a pre-political level, they have a full range of ideological stances similar to the more politicized viewpoints held by their elders. In this study, the children were also asked to tell "what you are thinking about and feeling" when shown ten politically relevant magazine pictures (for instance, of President Nixon, of a policeman, and of a prisoner in jail) and to define, if possible, eighteen political concepts (such as democracy, laws, Republican). The combined projective responses suggest—contrary to the predominant assumptions in socialization literature—that many children are at best neutral and at times quite hostile to political objects; the data further indicate that children have clearly defined and personally meaningful beliefs about basic (as opposed to time-bound) political issues—such as how criminals should be viewed and what role war should have. In sum, this assessment method allowed young children to discuss comprehensively subjects which (1) would be far too difficult for their verbal ability if asked in questionnaire form, (2) would often lead to "schoolboy" responses, parroting little-understood definitions and ideological segments, and (3) would elicit a "positivity" effect if cues were given so that any socially "right" answer was available.

Research Advantages

To the typical—that is, skeptical—political psychologist, far from at ease with clinical methods and clinical analysis, the above literature review may be interesting but may also raise a number of serious reservations. He may wonder, for instance, about the considerable time necessary for data gathering and evaluation, the development of the requisite skills, the necessity of validating new instruments (such as the PTAM) or new uses of old instruments (explicating the political relevance of standard Rorschach responses), and he may experience as well the conservative force of inertia (both professional and personal). Therefore, the present section deals with enumeration of the special advantages offered by the assessment techniques that have come to light in the literature review. These advantages are in part overlapping;

[1] Copies of these cards are available from the author to interested political psychologists who wish to use them for research purposes. Requests should be sent to the author at The Wright Institute, 10837 Via Verona, Los Angeles, California 90024.

their number, however, is suggestive of the potential of projective techniques for political psychologists.

Two of these advantages have been already discussed. First, as Greenstein and Tarrow (1970) note, projective techniques help to narrow the distance between the researcher's determined view of the respondent's inner reality and that inner reality as perceived and employed by the respondent. Thus, both the investigator and his subject are assured that responses are rich in meaning *and* are the choice of the subject. Additionally, however, responses can later be classified and ordered along more generally meaningful dimensions in an aggregate analysis. Second, as discussed by Campbell (1950), the systematic biases which appear in projective responses provide a more adequate case for face validity than do the typical casually employed, unvalidated personality scales.

Next—and intimately related to the above—projective techniques reduce and standardize the external constraints which inevitably shape the expression of intra-psychic predispositions, so that predispositions stand out with greater clarity (Fromme, 1941). As Greenstein and Tarrow (1970, pp. 498–499) note, "Clinicians have argued that the open-endedness of projective procedures contributes to their diagnostic utility by ensuring that the categories a respondent uses are his own rather than those built into the test." It is well understood today that behavior is the result of personality interacting with social and cultural norms and values and with situational constraints. By the use of projective techniques, it is possible to determine and con-trol the influence of situational constraints; intercultural research may then make it possible to isolate the influence of cultural and social factors. Projective techniques thus may facilitate our understanding of the determining influence of predispositions on behavior.

In addition, projective techniques are of great heuristic value because they provide rich opportunity to learn about what we continually attempt to measure gropingly. This advantage was brilliantly illustrated in research on the authoritarian personality (for instance, Frenkel-Brunswik and Sanford, 1945), where hypotheses concerning psychogenesis and psychodynamics were developed and refined from projective data and then employed as a theoretical basis for scale development (see Chapter Six above). Thus, projective techniques allow exploration of the dimensions underlying the target behavior. In the Hanfmann-Getzels (1955) study, for example, the data not only illustrated that Russians and Americans differ along fairly obvious dimensions of social and individual values, but also made it possible to ascertain the intrapsychic toll which such differences exact and the unitary nature of personality from which such diversity stemmed. Thus, projective techniques allow us to under-stand motivations which the respondent is unaware of or only barely so (Klopfer, 1968), and also those which the investigator, in all his wisdom, cannot previously know of or intuit.

In addition, projective techniques can be scored in ways which focus on how the respondent organizes intrapsychic imperatives while simultaneously organizing and integrating focused situational variables. In other words, projective techniques provide a unique way of assessing the manner in which a person responds. Indeed, a basic rationale behind the use of this assessment method has been that "personality reveals some of its organization and ways of organizing experience when the person is given more or less ambiguous stimuli to interpret and in the process projects his own idiosyncratic feelings, meanings, and ideas" (Harrison, 1965, p. 563). Instead of merely giving evidence of "how much" of a trait a respondent possesses, the projective technique makes palpable the *modus vivendi* of the person in which any target trait operates (Murstein, 1961, p. 3). Thus, to employ projective responses only to assess a single personality dimension obviates the valuable contribution which configurational analysis makes possible.

Also inherent in a study of the manner in which a person typically responds is the advantage—as suggested above—of a holistic approach to personality. As Atkinson (1961, p. 227) has commented, "When you go at projectives the way some of us have, looking only at isolated motives (achievement, power, affiliation), you lose contact with the whole person." Projective data, however, allow interpretation on *both levels*. Not only can assessments be made similar to the trait measurements of personality scales, but personality can also be seen as an open-ended process.

An additional advantage of employing projective techniques in political-psychological research is clearly the opportunity to delimit the conditions under which a need or trait may be expressed, as well as the manner (the intensity and direction) in which expression is likely to occur. Once a separate area of intrapsychic functioning has been delimited, it is imperative that the political psychologist determine under what conditions and in what manner that predisposition is likely to become operative. As the requirement for political relevance circumscribes the employment of laboratory experimentation (Knutson, 1972b; see also Chapter Thirteen in this volume), specially constructed projective measures provide an additional way to assess the situational imperatives which are likely to engage intrapsychic predispositions. Thus, in the area of projective theory predictive validity may be a more important and valid goal than concurrent validity (Klopfer, 1968). As previously discussed, prediction is a problem that has plagued personality research as a whole (Korner, 1965; see also Chapter Two above). Projective techniques suggest a fruitful avenue of increasing our predictive powers in this area.

Further, projective techniques provide a wealth of data. Responses can be scored to illustrate a variety of theoretical perspectives; they are not limited to the immediate focus of the investigator but may be reanalyzed by others in terms of different or unthought-of perspectives (Block and Haan, 1971). If drawn from a meaningful sample, such data thus provide a "bank" of information and an avenue of access which has been too seldom traveled into the wealth of material accumulated for psychiatric purposes (see, for instance, Almond, 1954; Lasswell, 1930). The richness of the data provided by projective techniques is of course related to its heuristic importance. As Greenstein and Tarrow (1970, p. 531) noted: "We have been constantly impressed by the number of serendipitous, theoretically interesting themes that emerge in our sample." (This idea is well illustrated in Veroff, 1961.)

Another major advantage in using projective techniques is that they provide an opportunity to study motivations that may be clearly delimited but are socially undesirable and/or ego-alien to the respondent. Thus, investigators are better equipped to surmount the barrier of social desirability which is now understood to shape the meaning of scale responses (as well as other types of human behavior). As noted by Morgan (1945, p. 219): "The fact of the matter is that a survey is likely to be most accurate when the data assembled are based on drab or settled issues and is most untrustworthy when the question is one on which opinion is divided, when violent emotions are involved, or when mutual distrust prevails." On the other hand, in giving projective responses, the subject "often allows himself a greater degree of freedom of expression because he is not openly telling about himself and giving his own ideas about real people and how they act" (Aron, 1950, p. 489). The opportunity to have a veridical view of inner predispositions is intimately tied to the fact that projective techniques are "less susceptible to faking. Even if an individual has some psychological sophistication and is familiar with the general nature of a particular instrument, such as the Rorschach or TAT, it is still unlikely that he can predict the intricate ways in which his responses will be scored and interpreted. Moreover, the examinee soon becomes absorbed in the task and hence is less likely to resort to the customary disguises and restraints of interpersonal communication" (Anastasi, in Greenstein and Tarrow, 1970, p. 488).

Of further value in employing projective techniques is their facility of administration, particularly as a way of engaging the interest of those with little skill and/or ease in accomplishing verbal tasks or achieving in testing situations. Riessman and Miller (1958), for example, have found that projective techniques are particularly effective tools in research with lower socioeconomic groups. A number of other investigators (for example, Green and Stacey, 1966; Greenstein and Tarrow, 1970) have spontaneously noted that their subjects enjoyed this research task. Related to this advantage is another opportunity—namely, that projective techniques "will make possible the use of large and representative samples in testing personality hypotheses heretofore based on and tested by the study of small numbers of people drawn from the 'captive' undergraduate population" (F. Sanford, 1950b, p. 709).

Another reason for employing projective techniques in political research touches on an area of particular concern to investigators in this area. Projective techniques make possible comparisons across cultural and age groups (Greenstein and Tarrow, 1970) because it is possible to employ the same research stimuli with subjects who vary widely in verbal fluency, mother tongue, social class, and age. Thus, projective techniques provide a valuable asset to those interested in developmental and cross-cultural research.

Finally, projective techniques offer a way in which the more methodologically conscious investigator of today can validate his conclusions. As noted above, projective questions fit well within the constraints of survey research. A further step removed but still offering the same advantage are the numerous other methods of projective measurement. When it is possible to achieve a high degree of accuracy in predicting the response of a subject on a direct measure from his response on a projective measure (or vice versa), the investigator can be a good deal more comfortable that he is tapping a psychically meaningful, stable response pattern and that he adequately understands the meaning of that pattern. (For a further discussion of this point, see Chapter Two in this volume.)

Projective techniques, then, offer a number of advantages which urge their inclusion in the research tools employed by political psychologists. While the advantages touch on a wide variety of areas, most compelling to me is the opportunity to widen our data base. Projective responses can be coded and designed to elicit predispositions in sensitive areas where—apart from captive college samples—it is not usually feasible to probe. Cross-cultural comparison and developmental studies are aided as a similar stimulus can be used with samples which vary widely in demographic characteristics. Finally, projective techniques make it possible for a deeper understanding of the manner in which an individual organizes his inner and outer reality, as well as the probable direction and intensity of such organization.

Overview

Projective techniques are no panacea, free of methodological problems and research limitations. Like every other method of assessment, they offer certain unique advantages as well as clear drawbacks. The above review suggests that they may complement in valuable ways more traditional measures which are currently employed and allow access into arenas generally closed to political research. In addition, I believe that their use will promote the development of political psychology by their imperious demands for explication of what we set out to measure. A projective response is an open-ended resource; what we choose to see its content and form as revealing about its author is nonobvious. Thus, the use of projective techniques requires especially rigorous attention to the validity of those levels of inference— from the intrapsychic to political behavior—which we select to employ (Knutson, 1972b).

Taken as a whole, the advantages discussed above should lead to greater specification of process assumptions, as we study intrapsychic dynamics under different sets of constraints. Thus, the processes of bargaining and decision making, of attitude formation, and of the development of political ideology are likely areas for the focus of future research. In addition, projective techniques can serve as a necessary antidote to past heavy reliance on survey research questionnaires and can help us assess standard results gained thereby. Projective responses thus make it possible to enrich aggregate analysis by individual-level data and—as the above discussion of socialization studies suggests—to vitalize some simplistic assumptions (by, for example, exploring the dynamics of extremism and conformity). Past use has also suggested that projective techniques present an interviewee with an enjoyable and welcome change from a stock set of questions and answers, as well as providing access to the meaning of his written records; hence, they may also be of value to those concerned with the study of leadership. (For a valuable example of the use of these techniques to analyze personal records, see Bellak, 1966.)

The view that projective techniques provide an unclouded window to the unconscious has departed and has been replaced by some sobering caveats. With these caveats, however, the projective response has become more useful to the political psychologist. Gaining recognition is a view of projective responses as focused segments of behavior, which are expressions of intrapsychic needs mediated by ego processes, by (experimentally isolable) social and role conventions, and by cultural values. Within this wider meaning, projective techniques hold forth the promise of enriching our scientific understanding by making us more deeply aware of the ways in which inner and outer reality are individually shaped into political behavior.

16

POLITICAL PSYCHOLOGY: A PLURALISTIC UNIVERSE

Fred I. Greenstein

"Political psychology" has two referents: the psychological components of human political behavior and the academic endeavor of applying psychological knowledge to the explanation of politics. Political psychology in the first sense is a permanent part of the human condition, fundamentally implicated in the extraordinary achievements of the species, but also in the chronic difficulties mankind faces in living in peace and managing material and human resources. The profound human need to come to grips with political psychology in the first sense accounts for the need for systematic development of political psychology in the second sense.

For reasons I shall attempt to suggest (in the first two sections of this chapter), students of politics have been slow to construct bridges between political science and psychology. That there now should be a *Handbook of Political Psychology* seems to signal a major—and highly promising—change in intellectual climate. Each of the preceding chapters in this handbook is an impressive accomplishment, not only for the substantial amount of literature, much of it quite recent, that is summarized, but also for the originality of the contributor's own synthesis. And just as the individual chapters each go beyond their bibliographical building blocks, the collective impression left by the full array of chapters considerably exceeds the sum of the parts. In short, political psychology as an interdisciplinary endeavor seems finally to be alive, well, and sufficiently developed not to recede with the next shift in academic fashions.

There appears to be no way to "do justice" to each of the richly diverse contributions to a volume of this sort, particularly if the concluding chapter is also to make its own statement. My tack, therefore, has been to compose an essay (in the last three sections of this chapter) building on my own program over the years of seeking to clarify investigative strategies for the study of political psychology (Greenstein, 1969; Greenstein and Lerner, 1971). In that essay I seek simultaneously to argue a series of propositions about the peculiar properties of political psychology and to make at least some reference to each of the fifteen chapters that precede mine, pointing to connections among them and among other elements in the pluralistic universe of political psychology not reviewed in this volume. Although I draw extensively on the formulations of several of the contributors, I have merely alluded to other chapters of equal importance which did not lend themselves to my argument, and have discussed the topic of several of the chapters rather than the specific points made by the authors. What follows, therefore, is neither a summary nor an evaluation of the other chapters, each of which needs to be approached on its own terms.

Institutional Connections Between Psychology and Political Science

The disciplines of political science and psychology have some common roots. Both can be traced to Plato and the pre-Socratics. Both represent enduring preoccupations of mankind. Both have antecedents in philosophy, theology, and ethics and are more and more difficult to distinguish from those endeavors the further one looks back into intellectual history. Neither was present in universities as an officially titled discipline before the nineteenth century.

But in spite of the elements of common heritage, there are significant divergences as well. Political science departments evolved from law schools and departments of history as well as drawing on philosophy and kindred fields. Some of the most sizable tributaries leading into the endeavors summarized by the term *psychology* have their origins in the natural, and especially the life, sciences. Furthermore, psychology became well grounded and entrenched in its institutional settings and traditions in the nineteenth century; political science has been a slowly developing phenomenon of the twentieth century.

There are far more psychologists than political scientists in the United States, probably because psychology—especially in the post–World War II years—has become intricately and complexly intertwined in the society as an applied pursuit, as well as being lodged in the academy, whereas political science is largely an academic endeavor. In 1947 the American Psychological and American Political Science Associations had approximately the same number of members; by 1957 the former was more than twice the size of the latter, although both had grown markedly (Behavioral and Social Sciences Survey, 1969, p. 23). I am informed by the APA and APSA national offices that in 1972 the former had 2927 Fellows (members judged to have made distinguished contributions) and 23,870 Regular Members (members with Ph.D.s); the latter had only 12,402 members in the nearest equivalent category to APA Regular Members and Fellows combined—individual (non-student) members.

The growth of interest within political science in what is now called the behavioral sciences was presaged in the great University of Chicago political science department of the 1920s led by Charles E. Merriam, who in his *New Aspects of Politics* (1925) explicitly called for a scientific political science that would draw on other disciplines, including psychology. At that time Merriam's student and colleague, Harold D. Lasswell, became the Founding Father of political psychology as an academic subdiscipline. It was many years, however, until work informed by disciplines other than law and the humanities began to appear with frequency in periodicals like *The American Political Science Review,* first in the late 1940s and then increasingly in the 1950s.

The behavioral science emphasis in political science, popularly labeled "behaviorism" or "behavioralism," with no intended allusion to the behaviorism of Pavlov and Watson, was pronounced a success (and hence ready to be assimilated and transcended) by one of the movement's key figures, Robert A. Dahl, in his 1961 essay "The Behavioral Approach in Political Science: Epitaph for a Monument to a Successful Protest." Yet it is interesting to look at the *Biographical Directory of the American Political Science Association* published in the same year (American Political Science Association, 1961). The 1961 APSA directory gave members of the association the opportunity to list the full range of cognate fields that interested them. Of the numerous "other disciplines" in which political scientists evinced an interest, there were more references to history (471) and economics (279) than to either of the two disciplines which, from the standpoint of a logic-of-the-behavioral-sciences rationale set forth below, "ought" to be the twin pillars of political science: sociology and psychology. Dahl's epitaph evidently was a bit premature. *Between* sociology and psychology, moreover, the preference was clearly for the former, with 188 references to sociology and only 69 to psychology.[1]

Much of the interest in psychology that *was* expressed by APSA members in 1961 seems to have reflected not preoccupation with psychological aspects of the political process but rather quite narrow and technical interest in the traditional

[1] The 1968 APSA directory (APSA, 1968) *did* list "political psychology" as one of the categories among which members could choose in expressing their interests, but strangely enough did not include the more recognized category "political sociology." Reference to "political psychology" was made by 462 APSA members, a roughly sixfold increase during a period when overall APSA membership doubled, but only about 3 percent of the association's membership. The most recent directory (APSA, 1973) uses still another set of sub-disciplinary categories, one which makes it impossible to estimate the total number of members disposed to profess an interest in psychology. (There *is* a listing for a subset of political psychology, "personality and motivation," which was chosen by 238 members of the association.)

applied specialty of personnel management and assessment on the part of civil servants and students of public administration. Thus, at that time, those political scientists with a behavioral science bent were drawn toward sociology. (The 1961 interest in economics seems to have had a traditional nexus in the economic institutions that impinge on government rather than representing an intellectual commitment to the analytic tools and perspectives of modern economics. By the end of that decade, economics was still another strand in "behavioral" and "post-behavioral" political science—for example, via the public choice literature.)

Another more fundamental sign of the greater tropism of political scientists toward sociology than toward psychology is that political scientists and sociologists have in fact worked together on similar problems in similar ways, whereas there are far fewer evidences of such connections between political scientists and psychologists. Thus political scientists and sociologists often publish in each other's journals; political scientists and psychologists rarely do. Within sociology a recognized subfield— political sociology—explicitly takes note of sociology's connections with political science. The American Psychological Association has divisions of industrial psychology, military psychology, esthetics, and even philosophical psychology, but none of political psychology.

Logical and Empirical Connections Between Psychology and Political Science

Modern political science has reached out more to sociology than to psychology partly because of the stimulus properties of the academic discipline of psychology as it is commonly practiced, if not as it inevitably *must* be practiced. For many psychologists it is a central if unarticulated major premise *not* to conceive of their science as one which attempts to explain concrete instances of behavior in particular sociopolitical contexts. Rather, in the phrase of one psychologist, Richard Littman (1961), psychology is often seen as a "socially indifferent" discipline.

Littman's observations were made before the increasing preoccupation throughout the 1960s and early 1970s in all the behavioral sciences with "relevance." He used "indifference" in a technical sense to refer not to a callousness about practical utility but rather to a basic strategy of inquiry. In seeking universal principles of behavior, Littman suggested, the psychologist has traditionally *stripped away* elements that are specific—for example, to the behavior of a congressional committee or at a political convention. "Psychologists do study and must study things and activities possessing social content. . . . It is only that psychology has been a science that abstracts out of all these content-characterized behaviors the concepts which form the jargons of its subdisciplines." This may thereby contribute to the development of universal laws, but there is a negative consequence: "When colleagues in other disciplines (mainly sociology, anthropology, political science, and economics) turn to psychology for help, they are disappointed and, indeed, often aggrieved. What they begin to read with enthusiasm they put down with depression. What seemed promising turns out to be sterile, palpably trivial, or false and, in any case, a waste of time" (p. 235). When psychologists *do* pronounce on problems of politics and society,[2] Littman argues, their observations often are "naïve" and "conventional"

[2] Those willing to comment on psychological aspects of politics usually have been

because they "are ignorant of the historical dimensions of most social activity" and "do not see the complex interweaving of institutions and arrangements." Psychologists, he suggests, "tend to be like laymen when they confront social phenomena," particularly those that involve large-scale patterns because "the main areas of social activity are only the *place* where psychologists study interesting sorts of things, rather than being the *focus of inquiry*."

But, Littman continues, the reciprocal of psychologists' insensitivity to sociopolitical realities is the proclivity of nonpsychologists in their analyses of politics and society to "posit incorrect or weak laws about individual humans." Both sides of Littman's thesis are profoundly germane to the diverse literatures of political psychology and will be illustrated at various points in this chapter.

Even though the links between political science and sociology seem to have been stronger to date than those between political science and psychology, the study of politics needs to be firmly grounded in *both* disciplines. We can demonstrate this statement on two levels: (1) by considering what appears to be the broad general purposes and preoccupations of the three disciplines and (2) by looking closely at the problem of explaining political or, for that matter, any other kind of patterned human behavior.

As disciplines, psychology and sociology have directly complementary and equally far-reaching concerns. The territorial imperatives of these two disciplines appear to be dual: first, in Inkeles' (1963, p. 319) phrase, psychology deals with "the personal system," sociology with "the social system." Second, psychology is concerned with those determinants of behavior that arise from within individuals, whereas sociology focuses on the effects of the environment, especially the human environment, on individuals' behavior. In each case the discipline is conceived of as a basic science, unbounded in the specific modes and contexts of human activity with which it may be concerned.

It follows from the universal ambitions of sociology and psychology that all institution-specific disciplines, the two most notable being political science and economics, are derivatives in a logical sense from the two basic disciplines. As Herbert Simon (1959, p. 253) puts it with reference to economics, any "verified generalizations about human economic behavior must have a place in the more general theories of human behavior to which psychology and sociology aspire." The reasons (from the standpoint of the present abstract reconstruction) for according the institution-specific fields independent disciplinary status is the amount of specialized knowledge necessary to deal with their subject matter and the importance of that subject matter for the conduct of human affairs.

We have already made it clear that the real-world denizens of academic departments do not fit neatly into analytic ideal types, in that actual political scientists have drawn more on sociology than on psychology. It is also the case that the disciplinarians of sociology and psychology overlap enormously in what they actually do. Sociologists often study individuals and intrapsychic variables, even though they frequently profess to draw the line at attitudes and to be not interested in something called "personality." Indeed, some of the most important contributors to the political

---

not academic psychologists but psychoanalysts like Erich Fromm or culture-and-personality anthropologists like Margaret Mead.

psychology literature (including two contributors to this volume, Hyman and Yinger) are sociologists. Psychologists, in fact, are frequently interested in groups and are sufficiently interested in the environment, the source of "stimuli," that for some psychologists, like B. F. Skinner, it is hard to see just where the psyche fits in at all. As M. Brewster Smith remarks in his chapter in this volume, a Skinnerian emphasis would incapacitate students of political behavior, since *actors* and *actions* are central to their concerns. Most political actions of any analytic interest call for psychological as well as environmental explanations, for reasons suggested in Noam Chomsky's (1959) well-known critique of Skinner's *Verbal Behavior*. Chomsky defends what Smith calls "a psychology that bets on the strategy of accounting for the flux of observed social behavior by abstracting analytically two classes of inferred, reconstructed determinants: features of the situation of action and inferred *dispositions* or properties of the behaving person." Referring to Skinner's reluctance to accept inferences about human dispositions as evidence for explaining behavior, Chomsky (p. 27) points out:

> Insofar as independent neurophysiological evidence is not available, it is obvious that inferences concerning the structure of the organism are based on observation of behavior and outside events. Nevertheless, one's estimate of the relative importance of external factors and internal structures in the determination of behavior will have an important effect on the direction of research. . . . Putting it differently, anyone who sets himself the problem of analyzing the causation of behavior will (in the absence of independent neurophysiological evidence) concern himself with the only data available, namely the record of inputs to the organism and the organism's present response, and will try to describe the function specifying the response in terms of the history of inputs. . . . There are no possible grounds for argument here. . . . The differences that arise between those who affirm and those who deny the importance of the specific "contribution of the organism" to learning and performance concern the particular character and complexity of this function, and the kinds of observations and research necessary for arriving at a precise specification of it.

Chomsky then goes on to comment: *"If the contribution of the organism is complex,* the only hope of predicting behavior even in a gross way will be through a very indirect program of research that begins by studying the detailed character of the behavior itself and the particular capacities of the organism involved" (emphasis supplied). Since in politics "the organism" (actor) *is* manifestly complex in its contributions to political behavior, at least in some circumstances, Chomsky's account of what is involved in explaining behavior leads to the same conclusion as our discussion of the logic of academic disciplines: Political studies must be jointly social and psychological.

Often, as Betty Glad points out in this volume, the complex contributions of the personal properties of political actors to their behavior are remarked upon by political analysts only when that behavior deviates from what might "normally" be expected of an actor in similar circumstances. And such is the reliance of political scientists on sociological premises that psychological explanatory notions are left implicit or deliberately not introduced if a situational explanation can be found.

Commonly, psychological explanation seems to find its way into political analysis as a self-conscious activity via the back door. When situational explanation does not seem satisfying, there is an impulse to turn to psychological explanations. The sequence is picturesquely illustrated by B. A. Farrell (1963, p. 11): "When we are ordinarily puzzled by someone, for example, our new neighbor next door, what puzzles us are the apparent inconsistencies in his life and general conduct. Thus, our new neighbor might say he is very interested in gardening, but he lets his large garden go to ruin; when his luggage came, it was seen to contain various pieces of sporting equipment, but he appears to play no sport and hardly goes out at all." In effect, we generate a prediction of how a person in this situation "should" behave. Because our neighbor's behavior seems inconsistent with our prediction, we begin to seek further information about his inner dispositions. Our puzzlement is likely to cease and our investigation is likely to come to a rest if we learn a bit more about the individual's situation. Farrell's illustration concludes: "But when we discover that his wife has just died, that gardening and sport were joint activities of theirs, and that he is still too distressed by her death to take up the normal round again, we then feel we have solved the puzzle—that we now understand him."

This "situational" explanation, of course, contains many—we might even say mainly—psychological elements. However, the explanatory impulse is to treat our neighbor's perceptions and feelings as epiphenomena of his circumstances and to focus only on his circumstances in our explanatory account of him. And if psychological explanatory factors tend to be admitted through the back door, attention to underlying personality structures and psychodynamics tends, as it were, to be admitted only through the window, late at night. Where the actor's behavior seems explicable neither as a reflexive action to his environment nor in terms of his conscious orientations—for example, if it could be shown that the neighbor in Farrell's example had never *had* a wife—then the tendency would be to turn to the tool kit of clinical psychology for an explanation.

Ordinarily this rationale is implicit, but occasionally, as in Theodore Abel's (1945, p. 459) critique of psychological explanations of Nazism, the assumption is explicitly stated: "In dealing with social problems, we should always bear in mind the dictum of . . . Durkheim, namely, 'social facts must be interpreted by social facts.' This rule teaches focusing our attention first of all on historical processes, on aspects of social structure, on group mores, and on sentiments for clues to causal factors. The logical rider to this rule is that only if we fail to obtain a satisfactory explanation in terms of social processes should we go beyond the realm of social facts and invoke the aid of psychology."

For another formulation which seems—by the very act of definition—explicitly to equate psychological analysis with the analysis of deviance, we may note Linton's (1945, p. 26) use of the term *personality:* "In general, all the individuals who occupy a given position in the structure of a particular society will respond to many situations in very much the same way. That any one individual of such a group manifests this response proves nothing about his personality except that he has normal learning ability. His personal predispositions will be revealed not by his culturally patterned responses but by his deviations from the culture pattern." By this reasoning there would be little interest in an account of the personal orientations toward their political leaders of the vast majority of politically quiescent or "cooperative" American citizens. There *would* be interest, however, if like the President's Commission on the Assassination of President John F. Kennedy (1964, pp. 669-740) we were attempting to explain the behavior of Lee Harvey Oswald. Similarly, psychological analyses would be not necessary in explanations of the great bulk of political leaders, but they would be in the cases of dramatically successful or unsuccessful leaders whose achievements or failings could not readily be attributed to external circumstances. Yet, as Glad points out in Chapter Eleven in this volume, it is scarcely satisfactory to reserve psychological explanations for the extraordinary and to imply that normal and typical behavior is not psychologically interesting.

According to Glad, my own inventory of conditions requiring political analysts to take account of psychological factors (Greenstein, 1967; 1969, ch. 2) is open to precisely the criticism that it treats political psychology as a means of explaining deviance, rather than as an enterprise applicable to the full range of political behavior.[3] The discussion in question is a distillation of two assertions made over the years: assertions by *critics* of the use of psychological data to explain political behavior—critics who nevertheless acknowledged that under some circumstances it is important to look at psychological variables; assertions by *defenders* of political-psychological analysis, who went on to indicate circumstances under which it would *not* be profitable to seek psychological determinants of behavior. The qualifying statements by both the critics and the defenders of political psychological analysis converge in a single set of contingent statements, the following pair of propositions being examples: Variations in the personal qualities of actors are more likely to account for variations in their behavior to the degree that the actors are placed in *ambiguous* (new, complex, or contradictory) *situations*. Variations in personal qualities are more likely to account for behavioral variations to the degree that actors are in situations where *sanctions are not attached to alternative courses of action*.

Propositions of the foregoing sort should, however, merely be thought of as indications of the *necessary* conditions for analyzing psychological antecedents of behavior, rather than as indications of the *sufficient* conditions. Furthermore, the entire emphasis on such contingencies (whether the situation is ambiguous, whether there are sanctions) results from the reliance of the behavioral sciences on a particular intellectual convention for the explanation of behavior—namely, the examination of concomitant variation. Within the logic of variable analysis, the analyst's energies are expended in seeking antecedent factors which covary with the phenomena being explained. But whenever the phenomenon of concern to the analyst does not vary— for example, in unambiguous or sanctioned situations where political actors with differing psychological properties behave in the same way—the impulse is to seek no further antecedents of the behavior in question.

Analysis of concomitant variation is an attractive intellectual mode because of the leverage it provides for testing hypotheses about causality. To be reminded of the difficulties of explaining invariant behavior, one need only consider the

[3] Changes in the ordering of the propositions and in a number of other parts of the discussion between my earlier version (Greenstein, 1967) and my revised version (Greenstein, 1969, ch. 2) were introduced in an only partly successful effort to deal with precisely the point raised by Glad—a point that was pressed on me by Michael Lerner, who not coincidentally shares Glad's interest in intensive single-case analysis.

tortured history of attempts to account for that virtual cultural universal, the incest taboo. Yet this example also cuts in the other direction. The incest taboo evidently reflects fundamental ingredients in the human condition, and there appears to be no justification for failing to study fundamental phenomena because one's analytic modes are better adapted to studying that which is less fundamental.

It is instructive to shift from the logic of variable analysis to the logic of behavior, returning to the familiar formula just reviewed (and discussed in this volume by Davies and Knutson as well as Smith) that behavior is a function of the situation impinging on the person and the person's dispositions. We immediately recognize that *all* situational stimuli are mediated by actors with psychological properties. Much human behavior—including the great bulk of "conforming" and especially habitual behavior—is not even evoked by immediate situational stimuli. And even within the logic of variable analysis, what is treated as a variable depends upon the interests of the investigator, so that behavior viewed as invariant from one standpoint may vary in interesting ways from another. Further, for some purposes the entire logic of variable analysis becomes strained, and it becomes more comfortable to take a case-by-case approach. Political analysts need to be interested in single (especially well-placed) individuals and in case studies in general (Eckstein, forthcoming); and such interests tend to reduce the sway of variable analysis and to increase the desirability of studying conformity as well as deviance.

The notion that we need accounts of conforming as well as of nonconforming behavior is congenial to a school of sociological and anthropological thought which concerns itself with the psychological prerequisites of social systems. Writers on this topic have been concerned with personality and role requirements. One way we can think of any social or political system, they point out, is in terms of the sets of actions that must be performed in order to maintain it in existence. What roles must be filled in the system, and what are their requirements? People must be motivated to fill these roles, whether by the satisfaction they receive from the role performance, by other gratifications they are accorded, or because of sanctions inflicted for performance or nonperformance. Even where role performance depends upon sanctions, psychological understanding of why people respond to particular rewards and punishments is important. For, as Spiro (1961, p. 102) notes, "Unless the members of a society have certain personality drives which can be reduced by acquiring positive, and avoiding negative, sanctions, it is unlikely that these sanctions would serve as techniques of social control. . . . Social sanctions serve as techniques of social control because they function as motivational variables."

According to this way of thinking, the task of the political psychologist would be to understand the psychological underpinnings of the commonplace and normal in political behavior, no less than the obscure and unexpected. This would be a comprehensive undertaking and presumably would involve "the psychological 'mapping' or 'census' of major subgroups and total societal populations" (Inkeles, 1963, p. 383). Included would be analyses of the various roles and personnel in the political system, asking questions such as: What kinds of people are selected to fill each role? How do the personal characteristics of the role incumbents affect their role performance? How does filling a role affect the role incumbent? Moreover, such analysis need not assume that role requirements are static, or even that they cannot be substantially altered by the role incumbents themselves. (On role and personality, see Levinson,

1959; for a discussion of the importance of studying "common forms of thinking and behavior" rather than simply focusing on "individual differences and their effects," see the conclusion to Browning's discussion, in this volume, of Bardach's work on political entrepreneurship and the Newell-Shaw-Simon models of problem solving.)

Problems in the Study of Political Psychology

The following remarks, stimulated by the fifteen previous chapters, are designed to illustrate four general propositions about the nature of "real-world" political psychology and therefore about the intellectual requirements of the academic subdiscipline of the same name. These are propositions which can be simply stated, but which have implications that run deep and that are very often unappreciated. Taken together they help to explain the slowness to take root of academic political psychology and the many resistances political scientists have shown to accepting and drawing on the existing political psychology literature. The propositions:

1. The connections between psychological phenomena and political behavior and processes are complex and often indirect.

2. The complexity and indirectness of connection are such that political psychologists need to invest considerable effort in conceptualizing their investigations and framing their research in terms of explicit theories that take account of the diverse types of predispositional and environmental antecedents of individual and collective behavior.

3. The previous points art not meant as a counsel of vagueness ("It's all so complicated! So what can we say?"), but instead lead to a highly specific admonition: "Search for contingent relationships—for interactive rather than direct effects." A successful search may entail finding structural effects in which, for example, a particular psychological factor has different properties and consequences in different sociopolitical settings. It also may be dependent on identifying psychological typologies which differentiate among political actors in terms of the way they will respond to similar environmental stimuli. (Knutson quotes Allport's [1937, p. 325] delightful analogy: "The same heat that melts the butter hardens the egg.")

4. Finally, I repeatedly revert to an issue not discussed in any detail in my own earlier writings on this topic, but very commonly raised by those political scientists whose experiences have provided them with detailed inside exposure to the intricacies of government and politics and to the specialized norms of the political process. Most efforts at the formal application of the diverse theories and methodologies of psychology (and psychiatry) to politics seem to the close political observer (and the political actor) to be insensitive to "political realities," including their psychological components. By the same token, the common-sense psychological political explanations by nonpsychologists tend to lack rigor and theoretical grounding. In short, there is a gap in the extant literature between political *psychology* and *political* psychology.

Davies' introductory chapter, "Origins and Dimensions of Political Psychology," very substantially amplifies the points made above about the slowness with which political psychology has emerged from the broad matrix of psychological inquiry, the nature of that matrix, and the buzzing, blooming diversity of the political-psychological inquiry to date. The three chapters that then follow under the heading "Basic Psychological Constructs"—Knutson on personality, Smith on attitude, and Lane on belief—each parallel Davies' introduction in seeking to connect political psychology with certain general problems of psychological inquiry.

In the latter part of his chapter, Smith presents an up-to-date summary exposition of his exceptionally useful "map" for the analysis of personality and politics. This map, which is valuably complemented by Knutson's similar formulation in her chapter on personality, serves as a convenient way to visualize the connections among the diverse antecedents of human behavior: situational stimuli; opinions and attitudes; the patterns of personality predispositions that underlie attitudes and opinions; personal socializing experiences that determine psychological predispositions; and overarching societal and political institutions, past and present, that provide the wider context of individual political and social development of behavior.

The panel numbered III in Smith's Figure 1 provides a key to the "functional approach" to the study of attitudes—the approach that Smith and another contributor to this volume, Katz (1960), have been instrumental in developing. This approach, which stresses that political and other social orientations may serve different functions in the psychic economies of different individuals, encourages flexible multivariate conceptualization of political thought and behavior, in that it recognizes the complexity and diversity of human motivation. Assumptions of the sort that underlie the Smith and Katz formulations sensitize one to recognize a particularly politically important pair of complementary complexities: (1) Similar patterns of political orientation and behavior can perform different psychological functions for different individuals (for instance, one politician may, in Smith's terminology, be basing his political behavior on object-appraisal needs, another on ego-defensive needs). (2) Essentially the same pattern of motivational needs may exhibit itself in different behavior patterns (as in left- and right-wing authoritarianism).

Smith notes that his map and the functional approach more generally have had greater influence in political science than in his own discipline. This may be appropriate. Psychologists are able to practice a division of labor that leads some investigators to focus on affect and the emotions, some on social conformity and nonconformity, and some on cognitive patterns (the three general functions that opinions may serve for the personality); but political scientists, precisely *because* theirs is an applied specialty and they are interested in concrete behavior, need to consider the whole panoply of psychic possibilities.

Since political scientists are inevitably forced to grapple with the complexity of real-world political behavior and its many bewildering complications, they are likely to find it difficult to inform their inquiries in a fruitful way with psychologies that see humanity in terms of a restricted range of traits. Hall and Lindzey (1957) in their summary of diverse personality theories remark that psychoanalytic psychology enables one to see the social actor as "a full-bodied individual living partly in a world of reality and partly in a world of make-believe, beset by conflicts and inner contradictions, yet capable of rational thought and action, moved by forces of which he has little knowledge and by aspirations which are beyond his reach, by turn confused and clear-headed, frustrated and satisfied, hopeful and despairing, selfish and altruistic; in short, a complex human being" (p. 72).

Both Smith and Katz, in their chapters in this volume, cogently point out the shortcomings of personality theories that focus *only* on Freud's earlier concerns, the unconscious and the ego defenses. As Smith puts it, "a less restrictive conception of personality is also possible, and . . . has much to recommend it." Nevertheless, because frameworks like Smith's and Katz's for examining the motivational basis of political orientations make it possible to consider *both* the inner depth *and* the outer periphery of psychic dispositions, they are peculiarly useful for those who are less interested in the intradisciplinary issues within psychology than in being alert to all of the facets of individual character that may affect political behavior.

The main part of Smith's chapter consists of a detailed account and evaluation of the several proliferating psychological literatures on attitudes and the conditions under which they arise, persist, and change. Smith draws on an impressive inventory (derived by Zimbardo and Ebbeson from Karlins and Abelson) of forty propositions and subpropositions about the conditions under which attitudes are subject to influence. Yet, as Smith points out, in spite of the vast effort and ingenuity that have gone into the study of attitudes, the number of nonobvious findings in the literature is not astounding, and the less obvious findings are subject to interesting controversies and failures of replication. Moreover, Smith reminds us, there are substantial discrepancies, which Hovland noted a number of years ago, between experimental findings about opinion change and observations about the effects of influence efforts in actual field contexts. These discrepancies, which probably help account for the continuing failure of psychologists studying attitudes and students of politics studying voting and public opinion to draw in detail on each other's work, provide a first illustration of the final two propositions enunciated at the start of the section—that connections between psychology and politics are likely to be complexly interactive (and therefore not easily replicated from one context to the next) and that "pure" psychological theories may often be inapplicable to "applied" political realities.

Knutson's treatment of the study of personality and politics contrasts usefully with the extended chain of commentary that I presented on this topic (Greenstein, 1969). She delves in considerable detail into the substance of diverse personality theories and the concrete findings of personality research, whereas I attempted to ask in a general way how questions about personality and politics can be clearly phrased, what kinds of questions typically arise in personality-and-politics inquiry, and what might be necessary in establishing a systematic program of inquiry around the diverse types of questions or analytic tasks.

Knutson's discussion of the differences between trait personality theories and holistic theories does not describe an unbridgeable gulf, since examination of the *pattern* of presenting traits of an individual or type in the light of some appropriate personality theory will ordinarily lead to more holistic formulations about overall personality dynamics and about the antecedents of these dynamics. (Compare Greenstein, 1969, ch. 3.) Nevertheless, Knutson does point to a genuine distinction to which students of political psychology need to be sensitive. In what, if any, kind of formal personality theory should political analysts seek to ground their work? As Hall and Lindzey (1957, p. 557) wisely suggest, there is more to be said for immersing oneself in a theory one finds congenial and then using it skeptically and eclectically to inform one's work than in seeking to synthesize a master theory. My own predilection, following from the observation made above about the merits of Smith's rather comprehensive vision of the dimensions of psychic phenomena, is for a holistic rather than a trait approach. Trait psychologies are of use for certain things that students of political psychology do, notably correlational analyses. But if one seeks to examine the actual political behavior of actors *in context,* it becomes necessary to think of personal qualities as more than disaggregated bundles of traits. The political scientist resembles the clinician in that each needs to make a prediction about *this* patient, or this political actor, in *this* concrete reality context. (Deliberately simplified diagnoses can sometimes be analytically suggestive, however.) See Payne (1972) and Payne and Woshinsky (1972) for an interesting effort to apply a single-trait motivational typology to political analysis.

Lane's chapter on political belief in this volume goes over many of the same issues as Smith's psychology-grounded chapter on political attitudes; but for Lane, the political scientist, the adjective *political* is at least as important as the noun. The mosaic of propositions listed by Smith was derived from the innumerable studies by psychologists who (precisely as Littman indicates) are indifferent whether their subject matter is explicitly political. Psychologists have studied opinions in manifestly political contexts, but they seem as eager to look at attitudes toward tooth brushing (Janis and Feshbach, 1953) or even toward the eating of grasshoppers (Smith, 1961). What emerges from Lane's analysis is an account of belief in which both content of belief and the sociopolitical context in which belief arises are important. Lane's contention that belief systems are necessary to enable political and other social actors to thread their ways through life reaches back to the still impressive discussion by Walter Lippmann (1922) of how "pictures inside our heads of the world beyond . . . reach" mediate human encounters with reality.

Lane also draws extensively on the sociology-of-knowledge literature, again illustrating the way in which the requirements of political analysis seem often to lead political scientists, even psychologically oriented political scientists like Lane (see Lane, 1959b, 1962, 1972), to rely more on sociology than on psychology. In a sense, Mannheim's (1949) classic work on ideology and utopia is directly cognate for sociology to the once-thriving industry of attitude research within psychology.

Niemi, in his succinct summary of the political socialization literature that has burgeoned forth so extraordinarily since the introduction of that term by Hyman (1959), reports on the notable expansion of knowledge about the events occurring in panel II of Smith's map—namely, the social environment as a context for the development of personality and the acquisition of attitudes. Not least in this accomplishment has been the major national survey of American high school seniors with which Niemi has been associated (see, for example, Jennings and Niemi, 1968b).

For the most part, political socialization research has dealt with the antecedents of what Almond and Verba (1963) call "subject" and "citizen" orientations: nonleaders' dispositions vis-à-vis the political order and their own participation therein. There are unfortunately still few bridges between the socialization and the political recruitment literatures; although there is much fragmentary information about the in-role socialization experiences of political leaders, that information is not yet systematically summarized. In addition, the issues about the fundamental properties of belief and personality dealt with in the Smith, Knutson, and Lane chapters obviously have important preadult antecedents, and these have not been dealt with in the political socialization literature. Nor have most students of political socialization drawn explicitly on developmental psychology (but see Merelman,

1969)—apparently because most of the shapers of the political socialization literature have been interested in learning about the advent of political orientations with an ultimate view to contributing to the understanding of how political systems function rather than with an intrinsic interest in human development. Consequently, they have tended to pay attention to psychological structures such as party identification—which have great political consequences but do not play a sufficient part in human development to interest students of development in general—and to ignore more "fundamental" aspects of development. (For an expansion of this point, see Greenstein, 1970a.)

Following Niemi's chapter, the two remaining chapters in the section on "Forming and Maintaining Stable Orientations" deal with two of the most extensive of the several literatures in which a psychological or social-psychological typology is applied to political behavior—the authoritarian and the anomie-alienation literatures. Of the two, and of typologies in general, the authoritarian construct is by far the most widespread psychological classification scheme to have been applied to political psychology. Christie and Cook (1958) were able to list 260 bibliographical references relating to the authoritarian personality through 1956, only six years after publication of *The Authoritarian Personality*. This inventory preceded the point at which the analysis of response sets in F scale questionnaires became a booming source of articles in psychology journals. A 1967 literature review required a short monograph (Kirscht and Dillehay). In spite of the many critiques of the authoritarian construct (perhaps the most easily accessible and well rounded of them being the chapter on authoritarianism in Roger Brown's [1965] social psychology textbook) interest in authoritarian character and personality endures. In 1972 numerous articles (for example, Gabennesch, Simpson, Herzon, Kohn, Wright, Thompson and Michel, and Roghmann and Sodeur) using the term *authoritarian* and addressing themselves directly to issues involved in this literature continued to appear. Furthermore, the issue of authoritarianism is one which from the beginning extended itself well beyond the domain of formal government politics into studies of authoritarian child-rearing practices, religious habits, approaches to the perception and treatment of mental illness, and so forth.

Sanford, whose chapter is informed by his research with Adorno, Frenkel-Brunswik, and Levinson in the team that produced *The Authoritarian Personality* (1950), notes that the phenomenon of psychological authoritarianism was sufficiently evident in the daily life of the Germany of the 1920s and 1930s to lead the group of scholars in the Institute for Social Research to emigrate in advance of active Nazi persecution. It seems to me that at base the interest in authoritarianism, despite the critiques, may persist because once sensitized to the notion that some individuals have reciprocal needs to dominate "inferiors" and to kowtow to "superiors," we all recognize instances of this type of individual in our everyday environments.

In *Personality and Politics* I quote Fielding's assertion (in 1747) that "slaves and flatterers . . . exact the same taxes on all below them which they themselves pay to all above them." Another striking example of the long-standing recognition in the conventional wisdom of the culture of phenomena described in *The Authoritarian Personality* is Samuel Butler's description of the Victorian clergyman Theobald Pontifex in *The Way of All Flesh* (published in 1903). Sanford in this volume describes one of the defining traits of the authoritarian syndrome, "authoritarian aggression," as the ego-defensive strategy of one who "has identified himself with the ingroup authorities of his childhood and found in the tendency to punish wrongdoing in others a safe and fairly well-sanctioned outlet for his aggression." Butler presents an episode in which Theobald, already in "a bad temper," is offended at his young son's pronunciation of "come" as "tum." Butler describes Theobald's effort to instruct his young son to give up the baby-talk pronunciation of the word.

> "Ernest," said Theobald, from the armchair in front of the fire, where he was sitting with his hands folded before him, "don't you think it would be very nice if you were to say 'come' like other people, instead of 'tum'?"
>
> "I do say tum," replied Ernest, meaning that he had said "come"
> . . .
> Theobald noticed that he was being contradicted in a moment . . .
> "No, Ernest, you don't," he said, "you say nothing of the kind, you say 'tum,' not 'come.' Now say 'come' after me, as I do."
> "Tum," said Ernest, at once, "is that better?" I have no doubt he thought it was, but it was not.
> "Now, Ernest, you are not taking pains, you are not trying as you ought to do . . .
> The boy remained silent for a few seconds and then said "tum" again.
> I laughed, but Theobald turned to me impatiently and said, "Please do not laugh, Overton, it will make the boy think it does not matter, and it matters a great deal;" then turning to Ernest he said, "Now, Ernest, I will give you one more chance, and if you don't say 'come,' I shall know that you are self-willed and naughty."
> He looked very angry, and a shade came over Ernest's face, like that which comes upon the face of a puppy when it is being scolded without understanding why. The child saw well what was coming now, was frightened, and, of course, said "tum" once more.
> "Very well, Ernest," said his father, catching him angrily by the shoulder. "I have done my best to save you, but if you will have it so, you will," and he lugged the little wretch, crying by anticipation, out of the room. A few minutes more and we could hear screams coming from the dining-room, and knew that poor Ernest was being beaten.

Butler is worth quoting at this length both to illustrate the social reality of the constellation of traits described in the authoritarian construct and for the period-piece tone of its specific details. The latter helps illustrate Sanford's interesting observation that, since the pioneering study he and his Berkeley associates conducted in the early post–World War II years, there does appear to have been genuine characterological change in society. At the same time, it would be premature to compose an obituary for the original typology, as can be seen from Rupert Wilkinson's recent (1972) use of the typology for a broad-gauged survey of a remarkably diverse array of political trends.

Sanford's references to such features of the classical authoritarian syndrome as "rigid adherence" to "middle-class values" and "moral indignation with respect to the behavior of other people" seem remarkably *un*dated in the context of the

1972 presidential campaign, which included such ingredients of sociomoral polarization as a defense of "Gay Liberation" by a homosexual delegate to the Democratic National Convention and the defection of many middle-class ethnic and working-class voters from the traditional Democratic coalition, at least partly in reaction to life-style issues. Hyman and Sheatsley convincingly showed in their influential 1954 critique of *The Authoritarian Personality* that many of the values and attitudes associated with the authoritarian "symptomatology" were not necessarily the outward manifestations of the psychodynamics posited by the Berkeley investigators (that is, reaction formations to repressed antiauthority impulses), but instead were conventionally learned working-class cognitions. But, as Christie (1954) argued, it still seemed likely that some individuals who exhibit authoritarian presenting patterns, perhaps especially those of middle-class backgrounds, did so because of ego-defensive psychodynamic antecedents. An interesting possibility, in view of the evidence of a migration of rigid child-rearing practices "downward" in the social structure (Bronfenbrenner, 1958) and in view of the affluent backgrounds of the first wave of radical student activists in the 1960s (Flacks, 1967), is that new-style working-class authoritarianism may have a stronger ego-defensive component than old-style working-class authoritarianism.

Smith's map, with its built-in assumption that outward behavioral patterns may perform different inner functions for different individuals, is tailor-made for clarifying the requirements of establishing whether and to what degree authoritarian patterns have a basis in learned cognitions (Smith's "object appraisal" category) or in ego-defensive needs. Only a handful of the countless studies of authoritarianism—a notable example being the ingenious experimental study of authoritarianism and repression by Kogan (1956)—provided solid evidence of the original explanation that authoritarianism is in essence an outward manifestation of the play of mechanisms of ego defense. But the cognitivists—for example, Selznick and Steinberg (1969), on whose work Sanford comments so generously—seem to me often to err in the opposite direction from the original Berkeley group; that is, they fail to conceive of the possibility that both kinds of authoritarianism—ego-defensive as well as cognitive—may exist and that the initial conceptualization of research and development of instrumentation should take this into account. Furthermore, it is not just in the authoritarianism literature that mechanical application of a psychodiagnostic instrument to members of diverse social groups appears to have misclassified the conventional cognitive patterns of particular social groups as psychodynamic symptomatology. Gynther (1972) argues that this is precisely what occurs when the MMPI scores of American blacks are interpreted in terms of white norms.

Yinger's chapter on anomie and alienation deals with the array of typologies within sociology that may well earn the-most-tangled-empirical-literature award, which would no doubt be earned by the authoritarianism literature within psychology. There have been a very large number of empirical ventures, psychometric scales, and statistical data-reduction procedures, in which responses to questionnaire items designed to measure the Durkheim- and Marx-derived concepts of anomie and alienation were intercorrelated and sometimes also used in conjunction with items from scales designed to measure authoritarianism. Yet this literature remains far from having reached a "final" empirical closure.

Both the anomie-alienation literature and the authoritarianism literature have been complexly extended, controversial, and plagued by the formula "failure to replicate" because of a pair of complementary problems. The first of these problems is insufficient awareness that relationships between psychological dispositions and political behavior ought *in principle* to be highly variable, depending upon further aspects of the social and psychological context. Yinger has been a continuing spokes-man for the sort of contextual social-psychological analysis, which is also called for by Smith's mapping formulation and in Knutson's personality chapter. While Yinger does not systematically summarize his own general conceptualization of the overall strategies appropriate for studying psychology and sociopolitical structure in the present volume (for his earlier statements, see Yinger, 1963, 1965), his view about the need for systematic simultaneous attention of psychological and sociological factors informs his treatment of the checkered bodies of literature he reviews and helps to clarify. As he comments, "There is not a single empirical investigation of anomie and deviant behavior . . . that has systematically included simultaneous aspects of collectivity, subgroup, and individual attributes in relation to deviant behavior." Eliminate the word *deviant* and substitute *political* behavior and we have a somewhat, but fortunately not completely, accurate characterization of the general state of systematic attention to the interaction of the social and the psychological in political behavior research.

The second problem is that the anomie-alienation literature and the authori-tarianism literature have suffered from shortcomings in instrumentation. As Sanford suggests, there has been an inordinate reliance on standard, fixed-choice attitude and personality scale measures (whether or not corrected for response set) to the exclusion of other measurement devices, such as controlled clinical procedures, projective devices of the sort discussed by Knutson in this volume, and unobtrusive field observation procedures. Too often, investigators have "operationalized" phe-nomena of the greatest complexity via crude measures of the independent variables; they have failed to recognize that a multitude of dispositional and environmental factors may contribute to a single item of behavior, that different types of actors will respond differently to similar environmental influences, and that even slightly differ-ent environmental contexts may yield quite different patterns of behavior.

For a good example of a study that breaks out of the standard psychometric mode, the reader should examine Smith's (1965) use of Q-sort techniques to code psychiatric interviews in a study of authoritarianism. Of the many studies over the years in which personality inventories and attitude scales are intercorrelated, perhaps the most carefully designed and sensitively analyzed is the body of data on American citizens and their leaders collected by Herbert McClosky in the late 1950s and subsequently reported by McClosky and his associates (McClosky, 1958; McClosky and Schaar, 1965; McClosky, 1967a; DiPalma and McClosky, 1970; Sniderman and Citrin, 1971).

Katz's chapter on patterns of leadership is the first of three chapters that appear under the heading "The Nexus of Individual and Polity." Literally, of course, there is no "nexus" between individuals and polities in that the latter are composed of the former. For this reason, my own predilection is to borrow the language used to connect microeconomic and macroeconomic phenomena and to speak of "aggrega-tion" (Greenstein, 1969). Nevertheless, in the case of leaders—especially pivotally placed, role-defining leaders—it seems appropriate to think of the individual as a separate entity acting on the polity.

In dealing with the motivational underpinnings of leadership styles and behavior, one can usefully return for still another application of the left side of the personality and personal dispositions panel (III) in Smith's map, which, like Katz's own seminal work, suggests that attitudes and other political behavior may to varying degrees serve diverse motives. A number of motivational classifications are possible. Smith's, which resembles Freud's tripartite conception of psychic structure, distinguishes the rational-cognitive ("object appraisal"), the social ("mediation of self-other relationships"), and the emotions-management ("ego defense and externalization") needs of individuals.

Each of Smith's functions can be linked with a leadership type. His category "mediation of self-other relationships" (response to social influences) provides a useful lever for understanding the political behavior of many—perhaps the great bulk of all—democratic leaders. Many politicians are likely to be preselected and then further socialized by their roles into a psychological stance in which sensitivity to others and their demands provides a principal motivational engine for the leader's continuing activities. This sort of leader, who resembles Riesman's (1950) other-directed type, is likely to come forth with such formulas as the following assertion, quoted by V. O. Key (1958, p. 497n) : "I have outlined my views without equivocation and those views will be my continued views unless the people at meetings and through cards and letters give evidence of the voters' opposition." To the degree that a political or other actor's behavior is motivated by conformity needs, that behavior, as Goldhamer (1950, p. 353) has pointed out, is likely to "have a somewhat fortuitous character in relation to [other aspects of] the personality and be dependent largely on attendant situational factors."

Such an other-directed leadership style resembles one of the leadership types in Barber's interesting schema of leadership styles developed in his study of Connecticut state legislators (Barber, 1965) and expanded on in his typological analysis of twentieth-century American presidents (Barber, 1972a). The style in question is called "the spectator" in Barber's first book and the "passive-positive" in his 1972 book. Among American presidents, William Howard Taft and Warren G. Harding appear to fit this category. Barber's classification schema is based on a dichotomous cross-classification of politicians in terms of two variables—their level of political activity (active-passive) and the general emotional tone of their stance toward life (positive-negative).

But leaders are not all chameleonlike passive-positives. Indeed, as Lewis Dexter (1969, pp. 159–160) has noted in a masterful treatment of the social psychology of the relationships among representatives and their constituents, even when a politician seeks to mirror his constituency, the shapelessness of public demands may make it impossible for him *not* to lead. Independence on the part of leaders also is often *imposed* by features of the interpersonal networks that surround them, as when a congressman who consciously *seeks* to subordinate himself to constituency opinion encounters in the course of attempting to do so the very constituency activists who take their own cues from the congressman himself. Thus, even the political leader with conformist social needs in fact finds politics a kind of Rorschach.

Smith's two other functional categories also can serve as psychological modalities around which distinctive leadership styles cluster, meshing suggestively with two other of the Barber categories. Smith's "ego defense and externalization" category seems to converge with Barber's "advertiser" or "active-negative" type (Wilson, Hoover, Lyndon Johnson, Nixon), presidents who Barber feels were prone to "act out" inner tensions in their behavior in office. And Smith's "object appraisal" category parallels Barber's "active-positive" type (Franklin Roosevelt, Truman, Kennedy), who takes a generally rational approach to appraising and coping with the objects he encounters in the political arena. Barber's fourth type, "the reluctant" or "passive-negative," is perhaps less likely than the others to reflect distinctive personality needs in that this type of individual (for instance, Coolidge or Eisenhower) is typically someone who dislikes politics but is drafted to political office because of his esteem in the community.[4]

Barber's *The Lawmakers* (1965) concludes (pp. 219–227) with an important theoretical attack on the general problem of whether political leaders as a class have distinctive personality constellations and, if so, what kind. Barber's formulation is an exemplary instance of contextual treatment of social and psychological variables. The political career, he points out, is negatively valued by most Americans. Politics is a "late-entry" occupation, as well. Thus, the individual who shifts from political activism in the general population to more or less full-time political activity needs both to justify to himself a career change and to explain to others his entry into a somewhat disreputable activity. These external social pressures increase the motivational threshold for political participation, Barber argues. Only individuals with exceptionally powerful needs to do so will take the necessary step. This motivation may come from compensatory needs to propitiate the psychic deficiencies which, in Barber's opinion, commonly motivate his advertisers, spectators, and in some cases his reluctants; or it may come from the need for self-fulfillment on the part of individuals with special emotional and cognitive strengths. (Compare the application of Maslow's "self-actualization" formulation to politics by Davies, 1963, and Knutson, 1972a.)

Thus, Barber's analysis explicitly assumes the diversity of motivation of different types of political actors and strongly suggests that efforts such as DiRenzo's (1967) application of a Rokeach dogmatism scale to Italian legislators, with a view to "distinguishing a general personality type that constitutes the professional politician" (p. 6), are doomed to failure. (For an expansion of this point, see Greenstein, 1970b.) The same criticism applies to other efforts (for example, Hennessy, 1959; Schwartz, 1969) to establish a unimodal political-leadership personality type.

---

[4] Barber's work on presidential character is discussed in this volume by both Knutson and Katz. I agree with them about the desirability of further conceptional clarification and operationalization of the variables that define his typology. For example, the two dichotomized variables of affect and activity might be treated as continuous variables, and the affect variable might be so conceived as to take account of ambivalence and mood swings. Knutson and Katz seem to me to underestimate the degree to which Barber's formulations have already received some quantitative grounding in the correlational data he presents in *The Lawmakers* and the carefully ordered case-material presentations in both *The Lawmakers* and *The Presidential Character*. It should be noted that Barber redefined his affect variable from "affect toward role" to "general outlook on life" in his presidential study, presumably because all individuals who make their way through the recruitment process to the presidency are at least somewhat positive toward that role.

This criticism of efforts to find *the* personality of *the* political leader is in no way incons:stent with Lasswell's (1930) famous formula asserting that "Political Man" displaces private motives on public objects, rationalizing them in the public interest. Lasswell's "Political Man" refers both to more and to less than all actors in what society conventionally labels the political arena; he has in mind *power seekers,* excluding politicians not oriented to power and including power seekers in the church, business, and other areas. From his earliest work on personality and politics to the present, it has been a central Lasswellian tenet that the tatterdemalion array of individuals who happen to become inducted into the diverse array of roles constituting the formal political process are unlikely to have common psychological properties. Therefore, Lasswell has argued, the political psychologist needs to identify functionally distinctive political roles (regardless of their formal institutional nexus) and then to seek distinctive psychological concomitants (Lasswell, 1930, ch. 4; Lasswell, 1948, ch. 1). One of the few studies to take this admonition seriously is the fascinating analysis of politicians in diverse functional roles and political settings by Browning and Jacob (1964). (For the empirical delineation of a political personality type reminiscent of Lasswell's Political Man, see Browning, 1968b.)

Barber's treatment of presidential personalities and political styles provides a valuable extension of Richard Neustadt's penetrating analysis of the role requirements of the modern American presidency, discussed by Katz in his survey of "patterns of leadership." Katz is a psychologist who hews more closely to analysis of how psychological processes exhibit themselves in specific institutional contexts than the archetypically "socially indifferent" psychologist referred to by Richard Littman. (See his editorial in Volume 1, Number 1, of the *Journal of Social and Personality Psychology* [1965], urging more psychological research that takes realistic account of social contexts.) Katz's sensitivity to specific institutional configurations and their implications for political roles leads him to summarize sympathetically Neustadt's analysis of how Franklin Roosevelt deliberately snarled the lines of authority among his subordinates in order to maintain presidential control of policy making. A less politically astute psychologist might well merely attribute such a presidential leadership practice to "poor administration."

In spite of Katz's political perspicacity, a comparison of Katz's references to the American presidency and Neustadt's discussion (which, while not stated in a formalized manner, is susceptible to more or less formal summary) provides a further illustration of proposition 4 at the beginning of this section, dealing with the differences between psychologists' and political scientists' perspectives on politics. Neustadt discusses many more aspects of the political psychology of presidents that are presidency-specific than does Katz; and Katz is far more likely than Neustadt to deal with the psychology of leadership as a general phenomenon.

Apart from practicing political science as a vocation, through his service with Truman and Kennedy, Neustadt has had extensive participant-observer experience with the tribal mores along the Potomac. This experience informs his delineation of a presidential role (or rather a range of role possibilities) which is in many respects *sui generis* and therefore only partially susceptible to analysis in terms of generalized organization and leadership theories. The modern president has enormous formal powers of the sort that Neustadt metaphorically describes as "clerical." But formal powers do not automatically entail *leadership* in the sense of a distinctive presidential impact on *his* administration. Furthermore, while the president can *in principle* act unilaterally to *tell* his "subordinates" what to do, in most instances peremptory command (as practiced, for example, when Truman dismissed MacArthur) is so politically costly as to be only a last resort.

The president's command power within the government is limited, not only because of the constitutional separation of powers but also because the fragmentation of the American political system is inconsistent with organizing even the administrative branch (much less the entire government) on a classically pyramidal basis. The model of hierarchy applies better to some aspects of the president's jurisdiction than to others, but in general it is useful to think of the president as being surrounded by a series of semiautonomous individuals and entities, among whom there are many reciprocal interdependencies, rather than as the head of any "subordinates" other than those on his official staff. Both the norms of national politics and the realities of the reciprocities make the president a bargainer and a persuader, to the degree that his own self-definition of his role leads him to want to accomplish ends for which the cooperation of others is necessary—that is, to the degree that he has any goals other than that of being inactive.

An ideal-typical Neustadt president—one who is seeking to leave a mark on public policy and has the professionalism to know what a president can and cannot do in the American political context—behaves in ways which, if duplicated in the daily behavior of an individual not responding to similar situational imperatives, would seem to reflect excessive, perhaps even pathological, vanity and opportunism. First, he exhibits a hypertrophy of a certain kind of rather coolly aloof empathy, leading him constantly to ask of other political actors, "What does he want?" "How can I arrange matters so it is in *his* interest to want to do what *I* want him to do?" Second, such a president cultivates a kind of controlled narcissism, recognizing the great instrumental importance of having a formidable "professional reputation"— that is, a reputation among his significant others in the Washington policy-making community as someone who systematically and consistently is prepared to reward his allies and punish his adversaries to advance his policy goals. Finally, the president who practices Neustadt's how-to-succeed-in-the-White-House precepts will, as Katz notes, often deliberately set his associates at counterpurposes (even if he does not actually play them off against one another in Franklin Roosevelt fashion) and will in general comport himself in ways that maximize his own decision-controlling options. (On the social psychology of presidents' relationships with their advisers, see George, 1971, and Janis, 1972.)

From the standpoint of Barber's political-leadership characterology, a Neustadtian president cannot by definition be one of Barber's two passive types. One wants, of course, to assume that an effective president "ought" to fall into Barber's rational, problem-solving-oriented, "active-positive" category. But, as Barber (1972b) pointed out in his pre-1972 election attempt to assess Nixon and McGovern in terms of his typology, the active-positive individual—probably as a result of his own relative lack of anxiety—tends to lack an empathic "resonance" with the fears and hopes of others. And, in fact, two of the three twentieth-century presidents who presided over the most substantial policy innovations—Wilson and Johnson (but not the third, Roosevelt)—fall into Barber's category of the active-negative leader for whom leadership plays ego-defensive functions. The enigmatic Abraham Lincoln would also have at least intermittently fit into this category.

Katz's concern with leadership, especially as amplified here to take account of leaders' styles and personalities, is closely paralleled by Glad's chapter on psycho-biography, which I shall therefore refer to here rather than in connection with the other four essays in the methodological section. There is a well-worn debate within psychology about the problem, in Gordon Allport's (1962) phrase, of "the general and the unique in psychological science." For some psychologists—more so for clini-cians than for the seekers of general laws referred to by Littman—personality analysis is not satisfactory unless it is capable of application to specific individuals in all of their personal distinctiveness. For others, the individual is useful at best as a source of illustrative material in presentations of data designed to support universal generali-zations. Whatever may be appropriate for psychology, the political analysis cannot content itself with the strategy of ignoring the concrete particularity of the individual actor. The analyst of the modern, institutionalized American presidency, for example, has only six cases at his disposal—Franklin Roosevelt, Truman, Eisenhower, Kennedy, Johnson, and Nixon.

Even though some political analysts may seek to transcend individual cases, the society's needs for understanding are such that other political analysts (whatever their training and formal connections) are bound to look at the interaction of role and personality in these five individuals. This need, of course, goes well beyond the American presidency, as can be seen by the intense critical interest with which new psychological interpretations of historically pivotal figures are received—for example, Lacy Baldwin Smith (1971) on Henry VIII and Langer's belatedly published (1972) psychodiagnosis of Hitler (conducted for the American government during World War II), as well as many other of the psychobiographies referred to in Glad's chapter.

Stating it generally, analyses of the psychological properties of individual political actors are necessary to the degree that two conditions obtain. First, *the actor is lodged in a role which leaves some room for the role incumbent's personal qualities to contribute to variance in role performance.* Some roles are sufficiently open-ended and encumbered as to resemble the Rorschach inkblot. Such roles in-evitably exhibit the personal qualities of role incumbents. Other roles are so hedged by external pressures—a limiting case might be the galley slave—that individual role incumbents are largely substitutable for one another. (See the discussion of "actor dispensability" in Greenstein, 1969, ch. 2, as well as the remarks in this chapter on necessary versus sufficient conditions for using psychological data.)

Among contemporary leadership roles, the official positions of leaders in totalitarian nations and in developing nations in which the political forces impinging upon government are loosely institutionalized probably leave more room for personal idiosyncrasy to come into play than do the roles of leaders of industrialized democ-racies with well-institutionalized interest groups. Leadership roles in the new nations appear to have some of the same malleability that was evident in the premodern West. Norman Cantor (1967, p. 136) says of the kingship in Angevin England: "Royal government was always heavily dependent on the king's personality, and without an intelligent and energetic monarch on the throne the effectiveness of royal administration and law was bound to be diminished. On the other hand, a king of great qualities could have a profound impact on the expansion of royal authority." Similarly, in contemporary preindustrial settings, the personality of a Sukarno, an Nkruma, or a Nasser appears to leave a vivid imprint on role performance. A striking recent illustration of the lability of political roles in the new nations is provided by the behavior of General Idi Amin of Uganda, who expelled his nation's 50,000 Asian residents after reporting that God had instructed him to do so in a dream and whom one journalist (Munnion, 1972) described as a "heavyweight boxer, flyweight philosopher, and seemingly punch-drunk president [who has] transformed life in his . . . state into a nightmare of terror for inhabitants of all hues."

Tucker (1965) comments on the profound effect the personality of a totalitarian leader can have on both the leadership style in a political system and on the overall performance of the system, not as in the Third World case because of the vacuum of forces surrounding the leader, but rather because the bureaucratic structure of the totalitarian state serves "as a conduit of the dictatorial psychology." If, on the other hand, we look at the institutionalization of leadership in industrialized democracies, it may seem at first glance as if the "role requirements" virtually totally mold the behavior of leaders. We note, for example, that various American presidents —for instance, Truman (Rogow and Lasswell, 1963) and Nixon—have behaved in the White House in ways not generally expected on the basis of their previous careers, and that politicians of different ideological persuasions tend to converge in their political programs in a two-party system (Downs, 1957, ch. 8). Nevertheless, even leaders of developed democracies, whose roles force somewhat similar behavior upon them, may vary rather strikingly in the conduct of their duties. One need only compare the styles in office of American presidents to recognize the many aspects of personal variation possible even within well-institutionalized roles (Hargrove, 1966; Barber, 1972a).

Reference to the American president, who used to be described in a multiply ambiguous locution as "the most powerful democratic leader in the world," brings us to the second factor which makes it incumbent upon political analysts to attend to an individual actor's psychological properties. *The greater the consequences of the actor's behavior, the more necessary it is to study that leader intensively.* Even if only nuances of personal variation are evident from role incumbent to role incumbent, the choices faced by political leaders are often balanced so delicately that the added personal feather—and it may be more than a feather—can be decisive. The modern American president is in some respects (especially where congressional approval is necessary) extraordinarily encumbered. But he also is a human lynch pin in a thermonuclear-weapons equilibrium—which, if disturbed, could wipe out much of the earth's population in a matter of hours. Short of the thermonuclear-weapons-launching powers of the president—which seem fortunately to be unusable—are his capacities for exercising only imperfectly restrained powers for prosecuting undeclared limited wars. For a somewhat loosely argued version of a thesis that can be defended more rigorously on Lyndon Johnson's personal responsibilities for the Vietnam escalation, see Wicker (1968).

This reminder of the impact of American presidential behavior on the stability of the international political arena provides an appropriate transition to Kelman and Bloom's valuable discussion of "Assumptive Frameworks in International Politics." By "assumptive frameworks" they mean the complex of underlying assumptions in terms of which "national decision makers, opinion leaders, or involved citizens . . . formulate specific opinions and arrive at decisions on issues of international politics." Thus, their discussion is in part about the kind of basic psychological issue discussed by Smith and Lane in their chapters on attitudes and beliefs, rather than about the mixture of psychological and structural concerns that would be involved in linking data on individuals aggregatively into full-fledged accounts of institutional functioning. The Kelman-Bloom discussion does differ from those of Smith and Lane, however, in its emphasis on decision makers and the influential minority outside of government rather than on the full population (mass orientations toward foreign policy are notoriously weakly grounded and labile) and in a further respect: Kelman and Bloom place a particular emphasis on assumptive frameworks which they feel are inadequate in that they "impose unnecessary limits on the range of alternatives considered in the formulation and execution of policy."

While the treatment of assumptive frameworks that makes up the major part of Kelman and Bloom's chapter is not addressed to locating assumptive frameworks in their sociopolitical contexts, Kelman and Bloom make clear, in the literature summary with which their chapter begins, that they reject the emphasis of those writers on international conflict, from William James (1910) on, who assume that the causes of war are exclusively psychological. Echoing the other critics of the war-is-in-the-minds-of-men school of thought, such as Waltz (1959), Kelman and Bloom comment that they hope to see developed "not a complete and self-contained social-psychological theory of international relations, but a general theory of political behavior at the system level in which social-psychological factors play a part, once the points in the process at which they are applicable have been properly identified."

> To focus attention on the individual actor does not imply that such an analysis can provide a total picture of international political processes. Certainly, every participant in both the national and international systems, at whatever level he makes his contribution, is heavily influenced by the political, economic, and social realities that surround him, and acts within the constraints and procedures of institutional structures. Moreover, once an individual actor has developed a point of view, made a decision, or taken a politically relevant action, he has contributed only one of a large number and variety of inputs out of which a political outcome is shaped. There is no substitute for analysis of the structural mechanisms and systemic processes that select among the myriad of individual inputs and mold them into final policy decisions.

Both the foregoing passage by Kelman and Bloom and Kelman's other writings (for instance, Kelman, 1965, pp. 565–607; Kelman, 1970) underline the point that psychological data are necessary (as the sociologizers fail to appreciate) but not sufficient (as the psychologizers fail to appreciate) to understand international politics. Yet, in a way that parallels the differences between Katz's and Neustadt's treatments of the presidency, the Kelman-Bloom discussion does not exhibit the same sense of the specific norms, style of behavior, and perceived contingencies of international political actors that is to be found in some of the writings in what Kelman and Bloom refer to as "the traditional discipline of international relations."

Kelman and Bloom make no claims about the distribution, of their several presumptive frameworks in populations of leaders, but instead focus on why the frameworks appear to be inaccurate or dysfunctional and what alternative frameworks might replace them. Nevertheless, by specifying possible cognitive and affective sets that govern political behavior, their formulation naturally connects with empirical efforts to observe, delineate, and classify frames of reference in actual populations; for example, the "folk taxonomy" studies of cognitive anthropologists such as Tyler (1969) and the attempts to characterize political leaders' operational codes and conceptions of the rules of the game by political scientists such as Leites (1959) and George (1969).

Furthermore, given the importance of well-placed individual actors in political behavior, one inevitably is led to compare categorizations of types of assumptive frameworks, like those presented by Kelman and Bloom, with the actual frameworks of individual decision makers, so far as these can be ascertained, recognizing that abstract types of framework will inevitably seem "thin" when compared with the variegated thought and behavior of a complex, sophisticated individual. If one, for example, compares Landau's (1972) detailed reconstruction of Henry Kissinger's thought and behavior with the Kelman-Bloom frameworks, at least one consistency and one inconsistency are evident. Kissinger's balance-of-power frame of reference is consistent with the Kelman-Bloom assumptive framework that treats the nation-state as supreme (it would be hard to see how a national *representative* could escape this framework), but Kissinger does *not* appear to have viewed the Vietnam conflict in aggressor-defender terms, whatever the rhetoric of the president he served.

Therefore, as Kelman and Bloom further develop their interesting analysis of assumptive frameworks, it is to be hoped that they will establish links with the literature on actual leaders' frameworks, whether collective or individual. Correct *description* of existing assumptive frameworks has some bearing on the task of *prescribing* alternative frameworks and persuading decision makers to adopt them. One of the points in the inventory of propositions about attitude change presented by Smith is that "a communicator's effectiveness is increased if he initially expresses some views that are also held by his audience."

Those political scientists who, like Neustadt, specialize in analyzing politics in roughly the same terms that politicians experience politics have been among the critics of efforts to apply notions derived from psychology to the resolution and elimination of international conflict. One such writer is the sometime State Department consultant–political scientist Robert Osgood (not to be confused with the psychologist Charles Osgood). The very title of Osgood's book, *Ideals and Self-Interest in America's Foreign Relations* (1953), in itself suggests a set of ubiquitous concerns of the politician that some psychologists describing and prescribing for international politics (especially those of the minds-of-men school) have been wont to ignore, or to treat in a wholly pejorative manner. These are concerns with national power in a world at least partly composed of adversary relationships, genuine conflicts of interest, and the absence of an international social order which even remotely resembles the sociopolitical conditions that minimize the use of violence within the so-called stable nations.

Such concerns led Osgood some years ago (1955) to point to what he considered three fundamentally incorrect premises behind much of the psychological literature on conflict resolution—that the "normal" state of relations among nations is harmonious rather than competitive (on this point Osgood's argument can be assimilated to the broader school of thought that emphasizes the functions of social conflict), that it is possible usefully to discuss international tensions *qua* tensions "abstracted from the actual political circumstances in which they occur," and that "conflicts of national interest and power" are "merely the superficial symptoms of some sociopsychological malady and not . . . anything fundamentally inherent in the existing conditions of international society." Kelman's own writings (1965, 1970, and the passage with Bloom quoted above) constitute an important source of reorientation of international political psychology in the direction of political realism. Yet there do continue to be persistent differences in emphasis in the way that psychological aspects of international politics are treated by writers who come to these issues with different disciplinary backgrounds—differences that are at once a source of creative intellectual tension and an evidence of a still imperfect scholarly synthesis.

Political scientists such as Key and Munger (1959) sometimes phrase the desideratum of attending to the distinctive norms and situational demands of the political arena in terms of the desirability of studying "politics" *rather* than "psychology" or "sociology." This is an unfortunate usage: the psychology (sociology) of politics is just as psychological (sociological) as any aspect of the parent discipline, but behind the shaky semantics is a point of fundamental importance about the need to take account of what is distinctive about political contexts and dispositions. In this connection, Burton's experimental efforts to encourage conflict resolution by Greek and Turkish Cypriots and Doob's similar experiments with Africans of different nationalities, as fascinating as they are, are likely to arouse less enthusiasm among political scientists than among psychologists for precisely the reasons Kelman and Bloom recognize as accounting for their efficacy in the experimental context: these procedures bring "together representatives of nations or national (ethnic) communities involved in active conflict, for face-to-face communication in a relatively isolated setting, free from governmental and diplomatic protocol."

From the standpoint of the concerns of political scientists, it may be more to the point to develop experimental settings with demand characteristics like those in the interesting experimental attempt by Herman and Herman (1967) to simulate the outbreak of World War I. The Hermans explicitly encouraged their experimental subjects to assume a psychological mode that is ubiquitous in political life and certain other aspects of social life, but rarely studied by psychologists—that of the *agent* or *representative*. A number of years ago Kelman (1965, p. 597) pointed to the desirability of incorporating "into the laboratory situation the significant *conditions* of the international situation," and more recently Michel and Dillehay (1969) have sought to study reference behavior of representatives. The Herman and Herman simulation also is interesting in its imaginative effort to "match" the personalities of the simulation subjects with those of the principal great-power leaders and their agents in 1914. Here again the problem of realism arises, however. As commendable as this matching effort was, there is a breathtaking inferential leap between 1960's

American high school students who have been classified on the basis of California Psychological Inventory and Semantic Differential personality tests and induced to play a hypothetical simulation game and the actual behavior in 1914 of Nicholas II, Wilhelm II, Berthelot, Grey, and their compatriots.

If Kelman and Bloom, in focusing on the psychological phenomenon of assumptive frameworks, are not explicitly concerned in their chapter with aggregating micro-level data to account for macro-level patterns, Davies surely *does* have this interest in the second of his chapters in this handbook. The topics referred to in his title—aggression, violence, revolution, and war—run the gamut from the individual to the intersocietal levels. Furthermore, Davies is alone among the contributors in emphasizing that the individual psyche is rooted in nontrivial ways in its somatic base, drawing on some of the work (especially with infrahuman subjects) that takes account of the physiochemical antecedents of behavior.

One source of difficulty with the challenging literatures discussed by Davies is the diversity of the phenomena subsumed by the terms *aggression* and *violence*. Even ruling out what Davies excludes in his initial definitional discussion, an extraordinarily varied range of somatic and motivational antecedents ought in principle to be responsible for such diverse phenomena as crimes of passion, premeditated murder, violence ensuing from racial conflict, so-called official violence such as capital punishment and the use of physical force by police, wartime violence by coolly professional soldiers, the violence of passionate zealots, and so forth. It is only a semantic accident that singular terms apply to such varied phenomena. In this area, as in that of establishing the psychological qualities of politicians, it would seem necessary to identify functionally discrete types of violence and aggression in order to identify reasonably stable and distinctive antecedents.

There is a second difficulty with the challenging bodies of literature discussed by Davies, especially when they are viewed in relation to one another. This is the problem of "reductionism," which Davies frequently alludes to, and its obverse, the task of systematically aggregating individual-level data to account for system-level phenomena. Expanding on my own summary of a chain of linkage (Greenstein, 1969, ch. 5) to take account of issues discussed by Davies, we need to recognize that the relationships are not necessarily simple and direct along the following causal chain: (1) genetic and acquired physiochemical dispositions, (2) childhood environmental influences, (3) adult personality, (4) adult sociopolitical orientations, (5) individual behavior, and (6) collective sociopolitical outcomes. Thus: "Similar somatic resources (1) and similar childhood environmental experiences (2) can produce different personalities, if only because of the many complex ways in which (1) and (2) can interact.

We have already noted that similar personalities (3) can accommodate different (if not the full possible range of) sociopolitical orientations (4).

Sociopolitical orientations (4) such as those discussed by Smith and Lane do not in themselves lead to predictable behavior patterns because behavior also is a function of situational influences (Panel IV of Smith's map).

Finally, individual actions (5) are far from simply additive in accounting for collective phenomena (6): millions of actions by peasants may count for less than the behavior of a Lenin."

The point of enumerating all these junctures and potential disjunctions is not to deny that, say, the nature of endocrine functioning or cortical structures in humankind may be consequential for conflict within and between nations, but rather to insist on explicit, self-conscious examination of the way different "levels" of phenomena are interconnected.

A quite striking and suggestive research report by Peter Bourne (1971), former chief of the Neuropsychiatry Section of the U.S. Army Medical Team in Vietnam, uses both physiochemical and psychological data in an analysis that is consistent with the monitory themes of this chapter. Using medical and logistical technology which was not available as recently as the Korean war, Bourne measured adrenal function via levels of 17-hydro-oxycorticosteroid in urine, thus obtaining a physical measure of chronic inner stress. He studied members of a helicopter medical aid team and a Special Forces group on hazardous duty in Vietnam. There were regular psychiatric interviews and physiochemical measurements during episodes of relative quiet and during periods of intense combat or imminent threat of combat. Previous research had established normal 17-hydro-oxycorticosteroid levels and normal alterations of level in individuals subjected to stress (race drivers, runners, patients prior to open-heart surgery).

Bourne's findings exhibit exactly the sort of complexly interactive pattern I have been suggesting "ought" to be found in careful, theoretically informed analyses of the connections between psychological and physiological variables with behavior. Contrary to the assumption that military activity is likely to have its motivating basis in states of emotional excitation, the helicopter medical crew members (all of whom were enlisted men) showed abnormally *low* levels of adrenal secretion. These levels did not vary as the intensity of combat exposure increased, although they *did* vary under situations of *personal* stress, such as severe accidental injury. The helicopter crewmen appeared able to ward off severe anxiety by concentrating on the mechanical tasks at hand and by a series of psychological defenses of a magical-fatalistic sort.

The Special Forces combat team exhibited a somewhat different pattern and certainly one that justifies still another use on my part of the overworked term "complex." Members of this team, which was in enemy territory and "under constant threat of attack by an overwhelmingly superior force," also showed lower mean secretion levels than normal populations. But the secretion levels of officers were significantly higher than those of the enlisted men, and this difference was wholly consistent with the psychiatric evidence that the officers underwent severe stress as a result of the uncertainty and responsibility of leadership, whereas the enlisted men "bound" anxiety via bravado, magical thinking, and a concentration of the routine mechanical aspects of their tasks. Furthermore, at the point of imminent enemy attack on the camp, officers' secretion levels *rose* dramatically and those of enlisted men *declined*. Bourne (1971, p. 287) advances the following speculation at the conclusion of his paper:

> At first glance, it might appear that these findings in humans contradict the extensive data on the physiological aspects of aggressive behavior in animals. However, closer examination indicates that, for many reasons, warfare among nations cannot be equated either psychologically or physiologically with aggressive behavior in animals. First, it is highly institutionalized, with the individual soldier having virtually no control over and

little emotional investment in the decisions made by his leaders. He finds himself compelled to follow their wishes, and his concern becomes one of surviving in a socially acceptable way rather than being in a state of personal aggressive arousal. Second, warfare, particularly for the pilot dropping bombs or even the foot soldier using a gun, has become a mechanistic act which in most instances is quite depersonalized. Much of the time the soldier feels he is merely doing a job and experiences little sense of animosity or aggressivity. Third, human psychic processes enable man to divorce himself emotionally from events that are threatening or aggressive in a way which presumably animals are incapable of doing.

Bourne's conclusion fits remarkably well with the carefully reasoned recent discussion and data presentation by Ray (1972), who argues against the widespread assumption among some political psychologists that "psychopathological" or at least aggressive attitudes are the necessary antecedents of "militarism"; both commentators deny that a single dispositional state can account for military behavior. In this respect, it is also interesting to note Dicks' (1972) conclusion, on the basis of his psychiatric interviews with Nazi S.S. killers, that conformity needs rather than psychiatric disorders of the sort that produce aggressive symptomatology motivated their behavior.

I now turn to an overly brief set of remarks on four of the five chapters in the "Methods of Inquiry" section. (Glad's chapter has already been discussed.) In reprinting his methodological papers, Samuel Stouffer (1962) commented that the one most sought after by students requesting reprints was "Some Observations on Study Design" (pp. 290–299). This essay of Stouffer's might usefully be read as a bridge to the methodological chapter in this volume by McConahay on experiments and by Hyman on surveys, in that it elegantly shows how the full experimental design of experimental group, control group, and before-after measurement is both a research design ideal and the basis of the explanatory logic in the many investigations that for one reason or another fall short of experimental design, notably surveys.

Hyman's ingenious invocation of the "most ingenious paradox" from *The Pirates of Penzance* is by way of recognition that, in spite of the supremacy in theory of experimental design, it is nonexperimental survey research with all of its causal ambiguities that has rendered the bulk of important, nonobvious, statistically grounded contributions to political psychology. My own resolution of this paradox will by now be painfully predictable. Surveys take account of how orientations and behavior exhibit themselves in the actual settings of the "real world." If, as I have been arguing, the concrete contexts of politics are highly consequential and cannot be "stripped away" or abstracted without grievous loss, then it will not be surprising if we find political analysts turning to the survey in most instances—or occasionally to the field experiment for such specialized problems as the study of how to enhance voter turnout. It also will not be surprising to find that "conflicting results [are] derived from experimental and field studies" (Hovland, 1959).

McConahay's chapter on experimentation, which because of the paucity of bona fide political experiments focuses perforce on methodological and design issues, begins with an extraordinarily interesting illustration, from the literature on male and female sexuality, of one way in which experiments *can* be more interesting than surveys. As McConahay's example makes clear, the experimenter automatically includes in his design situational as well as dispositional variables, thus correcting for one major shortcoming in the survey literature. Surveys have produced mountains of psychological data, but much less in the way of a capacity to predict behavior, because of the absence in most surveys of evidence about the environmental antecedents of behavior.

Both McConahay's discussion of experiments and Browning's balanced, lucid treatment of simulation point to the advantages of the methodologies of deliberate and radical simplification for the clarification of key theoretical issues about causal relationships. The seeming paradox in the three complementary methodologies of surveying, experimentation, and simulation is that as capacity for precise, controlled treatment of data increases, capacity to deal realistically and convincingly with "recognizably important issues" often seems to decrease. And when the techniques for precise simplification are tinkered with to accommodate to the nonsimplified nature of reality, we are in danger of winding up with the worst of all worlds, a model so complex that it does not allow clear interpretation and is not even an empirical slice of "the real world," an outcome discussed in Browning's interesting comments about "Bonini's paradox." In spite of the problems of realism inherent in simulation and experimentation, the gain in clarity about causal relationships and control over data makes it highly desirable that they continue to be employed and perfected.

Hyman, McConahay, Browning, and Knutson (in her valuable review of projective testing procedures in terms of their application to political analysis) are all commendably innocent of methodological imperialism. They recognize the importance of multiple, complementary techniques of inquiry, even within an investigative mode. The general notion that no finding is adequately documented without "a triangulation of measurement processes" (Webb and others, 1966, p. 3) is well recognized, if not always acted on, within psychology (Campbell and Fiske, 1959). It needs to be better recognized by political scientists. Thus, we may hope to see more studies with mixed instrumentation and research design. An issue of sufficient importance and complexity might well call for surveys using projective as well as conventional nonprojective instruments, which are paralleled by coordinate experiments, simulations, life histories, and field and archival observations. More often, of course, it is the more or less free marketplace of individual scholarly enrepreneurship that produces such diversity, rather than a single master research design.

Literatures Not Covered in This Volume

The publishing dates of the successive handbooks of social psychology were 1935, 1954, and 1965, and the magnitude of the project increased dramatically with each edition (Murchison, 1935, 1 volume; Lindzey, 1954, 2 volumes; Lindzey and Aronson, 1968–1969, 5 volumes). Clearly each earlier handbook failed to cover some of the topics in the following handbook, either because the topic was not ripe for review or because the appropriate reviewer was unavailable.

This volume lacks literature summaries on some important topics for the unassailable reason that the relevant literatures have not yet been produced. Inventories of potential but presently nonexistent literatures, like censuses of unborn populations, probably serve largely as projective tests of the compiler of the inventory. My only suggestion about future needs is a broad one, following from much of what I have said: there is a great deal of important but unsystematic psychological content in the many, many writings within political science (and overlapping the work of journalists). Integration of the political and the psychological in political psychology is undoubtedly one of the major tasks ahead.

Of those political psychology literatures that presently exist, but which it was not convenient to review in this volume, several are worth noting, following the main headings of the table of contents:

1. Smith notes that for purposes of expository clarity he has omitted from his map reference to a critically important class of phenomena that intervene between stable personal predispositions and situational stimuli: *perceptions*. Perhaps the single most interesting (but difficult to achieve at the present stage of knowledge) addition to the section of this handbook on basic psychological constructs would have been a review of what is presently known about political perception and the related issues of attention and selective exposure to political stimuli (see, for example, Freedman and Sears, 1965). The importance of systematically understanding the interaction between the goals of political actors and their perceptions of their environments is a theme running through Browning's chapter in this volume.

2. Under the heading "Forming and Maintaining Stable Orientations," this handbook contains Niemi's excellent review of the literature on the childhood antecedents of adult citizen and subject behavior, but there are no reviews of the better-developed literature on the adult aspects of these phenomena. Fortunately, there is an excellent and highly comprehensive recent review article by Sears (1969) and literature reviews on voting by Converse and political participation by Verba and Nie appear in still another handbook: *The Handbook of Political Science* (1974). Reviews are also available elsewhere of what might be called the old and new comparative political psychology literature, the former being the traditional culture-and-personality writings (Inkeles and Levinson, 1954, 1969); the latter, the political-culture literature (Pye and Verba, 1965). In addition, the time may be ripe for reviews of typological literatures other than those discussed by Sanford and Yinger—for example, dogmatism (Rokeach, 1960) and Machiavellianism (Christie and Geis, 1970), or for a reexamination of the numerous other studies correlating personality traits with political orientations and behavior, or for a summary of the numerous scattered studies of the objective and subjective characteristics of different populations of political leaders and activists (for example, Salisbury, 1966; Conway and Feigert, 1968).

3. The section in this volume on "The Nexus of Individual and Polity" could at some point (the present time is probably premature) be expanded to review the range of particular types of political contexts (such as legislatures and courts) and the more or less distinctive psychological demands they may make on political actors. In addition, there are the many challenging, if not invariably clear, broad psycho-philosophical characterizations of polity and society by writers such as Brown (1959), Fromm (1941), and Marcuse (1959), which could usefully be reviewed in terms of their empirical and normative implications.

4. Of the present methodological chapters, only Knutson's, on the under-utilized but promising approach of projective techniques, deals with instrumentation. For a discussion of the more conventional approach to eliciting political-psychological observations from populations of individuals—namely, the questionnaire and

attitude scale—see Oppenheim (1966). Parallel to the chapters in this volume on surveys, experimentation, and simulation, there are available sources that can introduce the student of political psychology to two other fundamental resources used by political scientists to gather data, particularly data on how institutions operate: field studies (McCall and Simmons, 1969) and archival and library studies (Vose, forthcoming).

The Literatures of Political Psychology: Let Many Flowers Bloom

Having taken the unconventional tack of summarizing my conclusions earlier in this chapter, there remains only one final point to make—that it is misleading to speak of political psychology in the singular. It is chimerical to imagine that a "truly comprehensive" handbook will ever be possible, or even desirable. As Donald Campbell (1969b) has pointed out in his proposal for a "fish-scale" approach to the unity of knowledge, it is impossible for any single work to encompass all of the diverse data, methodologies, and perspectives that might be applied to the issues it seeks to cover. But some integration will occur if inquiries are so organized that one investigation or specialty partially overlaps another, after the fashion of the successive overlappings of the scales of a fish. As reassuring as Campbell's image is in an intellectual universe in which one can never "adequately cover the literature," the fish-scale metaphor does not go quite far enough. Even if "knowledge" *did* have bounded contours and we did know the shape of the fish and therefore could supply it with all of its scales, we would still have to take account of the inevitability and desirability that diverse viewpoints be expressed about each set of issues. In short, we need not only the overlapping scales but also alternative renderings of each of the scales.

As a result of the widespread intellectual ferment within political psychology that this volume exhibits we can expect substantial expansion of the universe of political psychology. The cumulating logic of inquiry points to this. So does the need of our species to come to grips with its own condition—before we are too late. But it is neither inevitable nor necessarily desirable that the future handbooks of political psychology will reveal a universe that is less pluralistic than the stimulating array of theory, conceptualization, and evidence to be found in the present volume.

REFERENCES

ABCARIAN, G., AND STANAGE, S. "Alienation and the Radical Right." *Journal of Politics,* 1965, *27,* 776–796.

ABEL, T. "Is a Psychiatric Interpretation of the German Enigma Necessary?" *American Sociological Review,* 1945, *10,* 457–464.

ABELSON, H., COHEN, R., HEATON, E., AND SLIDER, C. "Public Attitudes Toward an Experience with Erotic Materials." *Technical Reports of the Commission on Obscenity and Pornography.* Vol. 6. Washington, D.C.: U.S. Government Printing Office, 1970.

ABELSON, R. P. "Mathematical Models of the Distribution of Attitudes Under Controversy." In N. Frederiksen and H. Gulliksen (Eds.), *Contributions to Mathematical Psychology.* New York: Holt, 1964.

ABELSON, R. P. "Psychological Implication." In R. P. Abelson, E. Aronson, W. J. McGuire, T. M. Newcomb, M. J. Rosenberg, and P. H. Tannenbaum (Eds.), *Theories of Cognitive Consistency: A Sourcebook.* Chicago: Rand McNally, 1968a.

ABELSON, R. P. "Simulation of Social Behavior." In G. Lindzey and E. Aronson (Eds.), *The Handbook of Social Psychology.* (Rev. Ed.) Vol. 2. Reading, Mass.: Addison-Wesley, 1968b.

ABELSON, R. P. "The Ideology Machine." Paper prepared for annual meeting of American Political Science Association, Chicago, 1971.

ABELSON, R. P. "The Structure of Belief Systems." In K. Colby and R. Schank (Eds.), *Computer Simulation of Thought and Language.* San Francisco: Freeman, 1973.

ABELSON, R. P., ARONSON, E., MC GUIRE, W. J., NEWCOMB, T. M., ROSENBERG, M. J., AND TANNENBAUM, P. H. (Eds.) *Theories of Cognitive Consistency: A Sourcebook.* Chicago: Rand McNally, 1968.

471

ABELSON, R. P., AND BERNSTEIN, A. "A Computer Simulation Model of Community Referendum Controversies." *Public Opinion Quarterly*, 1963, *27*, 93–122.

ABELSON, R. P., AND CARROLL, J. D. "Computer Simulation of Individual Belief Systems." *American Behavioral Scientist*, 1965, *8*, 24–30.

ABERBACH, J. D. "Alienation and Political Behavior." *American Political Science Review*, 1969, *63*, 86–99.

ABERBACH, J. D., AND WALKER, J. L. "Political Trust and Racial Ideology." *American Political Science Review*, 1970, *64*, 1199–1219.

ABERLE, D. F. "The Psychosocial Analysis of a Hopi Life History." In Y. A. Cohen (Ed.), *Social Structure and Personality: A Casebook*. New York: Holt, 1961.

ABRAHAM, K. "Amenhotep (Ikhnaton): A Psychoanalytic Contribution to the Understanding of His Personality and the Monotheistic Cult of Anton." *Imago*, 1912, *1*, 334–360. Translated in *Psychoanalytic Quarterly*, 1935, *4*, 537–569.

ABRAMSON, P. "Political Efficacy and Political Trust Among Black School-Children: Two Explanations." *Journal of Politics*, 1972, *34*, 1243–1275.

ABRAMSON, P., AND INGLEHART, R. "The Development of Systematic Support in Four Western Democracies." *Comparative Political Studies*, 1970, *2*, 419–442.

ADELSON, J. "A Study of Minority Group Authoritarianism." *Journal of Abnormal and Social Psychology*, 1953, *48*, 477–485.

ADELSON, J. "The Political Imagination of the Young Adolescent." *Daedalus*, 1971, *100*, 1013–1050.

ADELSON, J., AND O'NEIL, R. "Growth of Political Ideas in Adolescence: The Sense of Community." *Journal of Personality and Social Psychology*, 1966, *4*, 295–306.

ADELSON, J., AND O'NEIL, R. "Growth of the Idea of Law in Adolescence." *Developmental Psychology*, 1969, *1*, 327–332.

ADELSON, J., AND SULLIVAN, P. "Ethnocentrism and Misanthropy." *American Psychologist*, 1952, *7*, 330.

ADLER, A. *Understanding Human Nature*. New York: Fawcett World Library, 1969. Originally published 1927.

ADLER, N., AND HARRINGTON, C. *The Learning of Political Behavior*. Glenview, Ill.: Scott, Foresman, 1970.

ADORNO, T. "Anti-Semitism and Fascist Propaganda." In E. Simmel (Ed.), *Anti-Semitism: A Social Disease*. New York: International Universities Press, 1946.

ADORNO, T., FRENKEL-BRUNSWIK, E., LEVINSON, D., AND SANFORD, N. *The Authoritarian Personality*. New York: Harper, 1950. With a preface by Max Horkheimer.

AGGER, R. E., GOLDSTEIN, M., AND PEARL, S. "Political Cynicism: Measurement and Meaning." *Journal of Politics*, 1961, *23*, 477–506.

AGGER, R., AND OSTROM, V. "The Political Structure of a Small Community." *Public Opinion Quarterly*, 1956, *20*, 89–102.

ALGER, C. F. "Comparison of Intranational and International Politics." *American Political Science Review*, 1963, *57*, 406–419.

ALKER, H. A. "Is Personality Situationally Specific or Intrapsychically Consistent?" *Journal of Personality*, 1972, *40*, 1–16.

ALLAND, A., JR. *The Human Imperative*. New York: Columbia University Press, 1972.

ALLINSMITH, W., AND ALLINSMITH, B. "Religious Affiliation and Politico-Economic Attitude." *Public Opinion Quarterly*, 1948, *12*, 377–389.

ALLISON, G. T. *Essence of Decision*. Boston: Little, Brown, 1971.

ALLPORT, F. *Social Psychology*. Boston: Houghton Mifflin, 1924.

ALLPORT, G. W. "The Composition of Political Attitudes." *American Journal of Sociology*, 1930, *35*, 220–228.

ALLPORT, G. W. "Attitudes." In C. Murchison (Ed.), *A Handbook of Social Psychology.* Worcester, Mass.: Clark University Press, 1935. Pp. 798–844. Reprinted in G. W. Allport, *The Nature of Personality.* Reading, Mass.: Addison-Wesley, 1950.

ALLPORT, G. W. *Personality: A Psychological Interpretation.* New York: Holt, 1937.

ALLPORT, G. W. "Personality: A Problem for Science or a Problem for Art?" *Review of Psychology,* 1938, *1,* 488–502.

ALLPORT, G. W. *The Use of Personal Documents in Psychological Science,* Bulletin 49. New York: Social Science Research Council, 1942.

ALLPORT, G. W. "The General and the Unique in Psychological Science." *Journal of Personality,* 1962, *30,* 405–422.

ALLPORT, G. W., BRUNER, J. S., AND JANDORF, E. M. "Personality Under Social Catastrophe: Ninety Life Histories of the Nazi Revolution." *Character and Personality,* 1941, *10,* 1–22.

ALLPORT, G. W., AND ODBERT, H. "Trait-Names: A Psycho-Lexical Study." *Psychological Monographs,* 1936, *47,* whole No. 211.

ALMOND, G. A. *The Appeals of Communism.* Princeton: Princeton University Press, 1954.

ALMOND, G. A. *The American People and Foreign Policy.* New York: Harcourt, 1950. New York: Praeger, 1960a.

ALMOND, G. A. "Introduction: A Functional Approach to Comparative Politics." In G. Almond and J. Coleman (Eds.), *The Politics of the Developing Areas.* Princeton: Princeton University Press, 1960b.

ALMOND, G. A. "A Comparative Study of Interest Groups and the Political Process." In H. Eckstein and D. E. Apter (Eds.), *Comparative Politics.* New York: Free Press, 1963.

ALMOND, G. A., AND VERBA, S. *The Civic Culture: Political Attitudes and Democracy in Five Nations.* Princeton, N.J.: Princeton University Press, 1963. Boston: Little, Brown, 1965.

American Political Science Association. *Biographical Directory.* (4th Ed.) Washington, D.C., 1961, 1968.

American Political Science Association. *Biographical Directory.* (6th Ed.) Washington, D.C., 1973.

ANDERSON, B., ZELDITCH, M., JR., TAKAGI, P., AND WHITESIDE, D. "On Conservative Attitudes." *Acta Sociologica,* 1965, *8,* 189–204.

ANGELL, R. C. "Preferences for Moral Norms in Three Problem Areas." *American Journal of Sociology,* 1962, *67,* 650–660.

APSLER, R. "Effects of the Draft Lottery and a Laboratory Analogue on Attitudes." *Journal of Personality and Social Psychology,* 1973.

ARDREY, R. *African Genesis.* New York: Dell, 1961.

ARDREY, R. *The Territorial Imperative.* New York: Atheneum, 1966.

ARENDT, H. *The Origins of Totalitarianism.* New York: Harcourt, 1951.

ARNOLD, M. *Story Sequence Analysis.* New York: Columbia University Press, 1962.

ARON, B. "The Thematic Apperception Test in the Study of Prejudiced and Unprejudiced Individuals." In T. Adorno, E. Frenkel-Brunswik, D. Levinson, and R. N. Sanford (Eds.), *The Authoritarian Personality.* New York: Harper, 1950.

ARONOFF, J. *Psychological Needs and Cultural Systems.* Princeton, N.J.: Van Nostrand, 1967.

ARONOFF, J. "Psychological Needs as a Determinant in the Formation of Economic Systems: A Confirmation." *Human Relations,* 1970, *23,* 123–138.

ARONSON, E., AND CARLSMITH, J. M. "Experimentation in Social Psychology." In G. Lindzey and E. Aronson (Eds.), *The Handbook of Social Psychology.* (Rev. Ed.) Vol. 2. Reading, Mass.: Addison-Wesley, 1968.

ASCH, S. E. *Social Psychology.* Englewood Cliffs, N.J.: Prentice-Hall, 1952.

ATKINSON, J. "Discussion of Paper by R. Lazarus." In J. Kagan and C. Lesser (Eds.), *Contemporary Issues in Thematic Apperceptive Methods.* Springfield, Ill.: Thomas, 1961.

AXELROD, J., FREEDMAN, M., HATCH, W., KATZ, J., AND SANFORD, N. *Search for Relevance.* San Francisco: Jossey-Bass, 1969.

AZRAEL, J. "Soviet Union." In J. Coleman (Ed.), *Education and Political Development.* Princeton: Princeton University Press, 1965.

BAIN, R. "Spencer's Love for George Eliot." *Psychoanalytic Review,* 1927, *14,* 37–55.

BALDWIN, A. L. "Personal Structure Analysis: A Statistical Method for Investigating the Single Personality." *Journal of Abnormal and Social Psychology,* 1942, *37,* 163–183.

BALES, R. F. "Task Roles and Social Roles in Problem-Solving Groups." In E. Maccoby, T. M. Newcomb, and E. L. Hartley (Eds.), *Readings in Social Psychology.* New York: Holt, 1958.

BANFIELD, E. *The Moral Basis of a Backward Society.* New York: Free Press, 1958.

BARAKAT, H. "Alienation: A Process of Encounter Between Utopia and Reality." *British Journal of Sociology,* 1969, *20,* 1–10.

BARBER, J. D. *The Lawmakers: Recruitment and Adaptation to Legislative Life.* New Haven, Conn.: Yale University Press, 1965.

BARBER, J. D. *Power in Committees: An Experiment in the Governmental Process.* Chicago: Rand McNally, 1966.

BARBER, J. D. *The Presidential Character: Predicting Performance in the White House.* Englewood Cliffs, N.J.: Prentice-Hall, 1972a.

BARBER, J. D. "The Question of Presidential Character." *Saturday Review,* 23 September, 1972b, pp. 62–66.

BARDACH, E. *The Skill Factor in Politics: Repealing the Mental Commitment Laws in California.* Berkeley: University of California Press, 1972.

BARKER, E. "Authoritarianism of the Political Right, Center and Left." *Journal of Social Issues,* 1963, *19,* 63–74.

BARNARD, C. I. *The Functions of the Executive.* Cambridge, Mass.: Harvard University Press, 1938.

BASS, B. "Authoritarianism or Acquiescence." *Journal of Abnormal and Social Psychology,* 1955, *51,* 616–623.

BAUMOL, W. J., AND QUANDT, R. E. "Rules of Thumb and Optimally Imperfect Decisions." *American Economic Review,* 1964, *54,* 23–46.

BAUMRIND, D. "Some Thoughts on Ethics of Research: After Reading Milgram's 'Behavioral Study of Obedience.'" *American Psychologist,* 1964, *19,* 421–423.

BAUMRIND, D. "Child Care Practices Anteceding Three Patterns of Preschool Behavior." *Genetic Psychology Monographs,* 1967, *75,* 43–88.

BAY, C. *The Structure of Freedom.* Stanford, Calif.: Stanford University Press, 1958.

BECK, P. "Youth and the Politics of Realignment." In R. Niemi (Ed.), *New Views of Children and Politics.* San Francisco: Jossey-Bass, forthcoming, 1974.

BECK, S. J. "The Science of Personality: Nomothetic or Idiographic?" *Psychological Review,* 1953, *60,* 353–359.

BECKER, H. P. "Normative Reactions to Normlessness." *American Sociological Review,* 1960, *25,* 803–810.

BECKER, H. S. "Social Observation and Social Class Studies." In D. Sills (Ed.), *International Encyclopedia of the Social Sciences.* New York: Macmillan, 1968.

Behavioral and Social Sciences Survey Committee. *The Behavioral and Social Sciences: Outlook and Needs.* Englewood Cliffs, N.J.: Prentice-Hall, 1969.

BELL, D. *The End of Ideology: On the Exhaustion of Political Ideas in the Fifties.* New York: Free Press, 1960.

BELL, D. (Ed.) *The Radical Right.* Garden City, N.Y.: Doubleday, 1963.

BELL, W. "Anomie, Social Isolation, and Class Structure." *Sociometry,* 1957, *20,* 105–116.

BELL, W., HILL, R., AND WRIGHT, C. *Public Leadership.* San Francisco: Chandler, 1961.

BELLAK, L. "Somerset Maugham: A Thematic Analysis of Ten Short Stories." In R. White (Ed.), *The Study of Lives.* Chicago: Aldine-Atherton, 1966.

BEM, D. "Self-Perception: An Alternative Interpretation of Cognitive Dissonance Phenomena." *Psychological Review,* 1967, *74,* 183–200.

BENEDICT, R. *Patterns of Culture.* Boston: Houghton Mifflin, 1934.

BERADT, C. *The Third Reich of Dreams.* Chicago: University of Chicago Press, 1968.

BERELSON, B., LAZARSFELD, P., AND MC PHEE, W. *Voting: A Study of Opinion Formation in a Presidential Election.* Chicago: University of Chicago Press, 1954.

BERGER, A. S., GAGNON, J. H., AND SIMON, W. "Pornography: High School and College Years." *Technical Reports of the Commission on Obscenity and Pornography.* Vol. 9. Washington, D.C.: U.S. Government Printing Office, 1970.

BERKOWITZ, L. *Aggression: A Social Psychological Analysis.* New York: McGraw-Hill, 1962.

BERKOWITZ, L. (Ed.) *The Roots of Aggression: A Re-examination of the Frustration-Aggression Hypothesis.* New York: Atherton, 1969.

BERKOWITZ, L. "The Study of Urban Violence: Some Implications of Laboratory Studies of Frustration and Aggression." *American Behavioral Scientist,* March-April 1971, pp. 14–17.

BETTELHEIM, B. *The Informed Heart.* New York: Free Press, 1960.

BETTELHEIM, B. *The Children of the Dream.* New York: Avon, 1969.

BILLY, J.-S. "Le Probleme de la Finalité des Societés Politiques et les Explications Ideologiques." *International Social Science Bulletin,* 1953, *5,* 51–74.

BLACK, M. *Critical Thinking.* Englewood Cliffs, N.J.: Prentice-Hall, 1946.

BLALOCK, H. M. *Social Statistics.* New York: McGraw-Hill, 1960.

BLAU, P. *Exchange and Power in Social Life.* New York: Wiley, 1964.

BLAU, P. M., AND SCOTT, W. R. *Formal Organizations.* San Francisco: Chandler, 1962.

BLAUNER, R. *Alienation and Freedom: The Factory Worker and His Industry.* Chicago: University of Chicago Press, 1964.

BLITZER, C. *An Immortal Commonwealth: The Political Thought of James Harrington.* New Haven: Yale University Press, 1960.

BLOCK, JACK. "Personality Measurement: Overview." In D. Sills (Ed.), *International Encyclopedia of the Social Sciences.* New York: Macmillan, 1968.

BLOCK, JEANNE. "Generational Continuity and Discontinuity in the Understanding of Societal Rejection." *Journal of Personality and Social Psychology,* 1972, *22,* 333–345.

BLOCK, J. AND BLOCK, J. "An Investigation of the Relationship Between Intolerance of Ambiguity and Ethnocentrism." *Journal of Personality,* 1951, *19,* 303–311.

BLOCK, J., AND HAAN, N. *Lives Through Time.* Berkeley: Bancroft Books, 1971.

BLOCK, J. HAAN, N., AND SMITH, M. B. "Socialization Correlates of Student Activism." *Journal of Social Issues,* 1969, *25,* 143–177.

BLONDEL, J. *Voters, Parties, and Leaders.* Hammondsworth, England: Penguin Books, 1963.

BLOOM, B. *Stability and Change in Human Characteristics.* New York: Wiley, 1965.

BLUMENTHAL, M. D., AND OTHERS. *Justifying Violence: Attitudes of American Men.* Ann Arbor: University of Michigan Institute for Social Research, 1972.

BLYDENBURGH, J. C. "A Controlled Experiment to Measure the Effects of Personal Contact Campaigning." *Midwest Journal of Political Science,* 1971, *15,* 365–381.

BODER, D. P. "The Adjective-Verb Quotient: A Contribution to the Psychology of Language." *Psychological Record,* 1940, *3,* 310–343.

BOLGAR, H. "A Re-evaluation of Projective Theory." In B. Klopfer (Ed.), *Advances in Rorschach Technique.* Vol. 2. New York: World Book Co., 1956.

BONINI, C. P. *Simulation of Information and Decision Systems in the Firm.* Englewood Cliffs, N.J.: Prentice-Hall, 1963.

BOOCOCK, S. S., AND SCHILD, E. O. (Eds.) *Simulation Games in Learning.* Beverly Hills, Calif.: Sage Publications, 1968.

BOUDON, R. "Reflexions sur la Logique des Modèles Simulés." *European Journal of Sociology,* 1965, *6,* 3–20.

BOURNE, P. G. "Altered Adrenal Function in Two Combat Situations in Viet Nam." In B. E. Eleftheriou and J. P. Scott (Eds.), *The Physiology of Aggression and Defeat.* New York: Plenum, 1971.

BOWLBY, J. *Attachment.* New York: Basic Books, 1969.

BOYD, E. "Sex in Biography." *Harper's,* 1932, *165,* 752–759.

BRECHT, A. *Political Theory: The Foundations of Twentieth Century Political Thought.* Princeton: Princeton University Press, 1959.

BREED, W., AND KTSANES, T. "Pluralistic Ignorance in the Process of Opinion Formation." *Public Opinion Quarterly,* 1961, *25,* 382–392.

BREMER, S. A. *National and International Systems: A Computer Simulation.* (Doctoral dissertation, Michigan State University) Ann Arbor, Mich.: University Microfilms, 1971. No. 71-18, 175.

BRICKMAN, P., SHAVER, P., AND ARCHIBALD, P. "American Tactics and American Goals in Vietnam as Perceived by Social Scientists." In W. Isard (Ed.), *Vietnam: Issues and Alternatives.* Cambridge, Mass.: Schenkman, 1969.

BRIDGMAN, P. W. *The Logic of Modern Physics.* New York: Macmillan, 1928.

BRIM, JR., O., AND WHEELER, S. *Socialization After Childhood: Two Essays.* New York: Wiley, 1966.

BRINTON, C. *The Anatomy of Revolution.* Englewood Cliffs, N.J.: Prentice-Hall, 1938. New York: Vintage, 1965.

BRODIE, B. A. "A Psychoanalytic Interpretation of Woodrow Wilson." *World Politics,* 1957, *9,* 413–422.

BRODIE, F. M. *Thaddeus Stevens.* New York: Norton, 1966.

BRONFENBRENNER, U. "Socialization and Social Class Through Time and Space." In E. E. Maccoby, T. M. Newcomb, and E. L. Hartley (Eds.), *Readings in Social Psychology.* (3rd Ed.) New York: Holt, 1958.

BRONFENBRENNER, U. *Two Worlds of Childhood.* New York: Russell Sage, 1970.

BROWN, D. M. *The White Umbrella: Indian Political Thought from Manu to Gandhi.* Berkeley: University of California Press, 1959.

BROWN, D., AND BRSTRYN, D. "College Environment, Personality and Social Ideology of Three Ethnic Groups." *Journal of Social Psychology,* 1956, *44,* 279–288.

BROWN, D., FREEDMAN, M., SANFORD, N., AND WEBSTER, H. "Personality Development During the College Years." *Journal of Social Issues,* 1956, *12*(41).

BROWN, J. F. *Psychology and the Social Order.* New York: McGraw-Hill, 1936.

BROWN, N. O. *Life Against Death.* Middletown: Wesleyan University Press, 1959.

BROWN, R. *Social Psychology.* New York: Free Press, 1965.

BROWN, S. R. "Consistency and the Persistence of Ideology: Some Experimental Results." *Public Opinion Quarterly,* 1970, *34,* 60–68.

BROWN, S. R. "Experimental Design and the Structuring of Theory." *Experimental Study of Politics,* 1971, *1,* 1–41.

BROWNING, R. P. "Hypotheses About Political Recruitment: A Partially Data-Based Computer Simulation." In W. D. Coplin (Ed.), *Simulation in the Study of Politics.* Chicago: Markham, 1968a.

BROWNING, R. P. "The Interaction of Personality and Political System in Decisions to Run for Office: Some Data and a Simulation Technique." *Journal of Social Issues,* 1968b, *24,* 93–109.

BROWNING, R. P. *Businessmen in Politics: Motivation and Circumstances in the Rise to Power.* (Doctoral dissertation, Yale University) Ann Arbor, Mich.: University Microfilms, 1969. No. 69-12, 908.

BROWNING, R. P. "Innovative and Non-innovative Decision Processes in Government Budgeting." In I. Sharkansky (Ed.), *Policy Analysis in Political Science.* Chicago: Markham, 1970.

BROWNING, R., AND JACOB, H. "Power Motivation and the Political Personality." *Public Opinion Quarterly,* 1964, *28,* 75–90.

BROWNLEE, K. A. *Statistical Theory and Methodology in Science and Engineering.* New York: Wiley, 1960.

BRUNER, J. S., GOODNOW, J. J., AND AUSTIN, G. A. *A Study of Thinking.* New York: Wiley, 1956.

BRYAN, J., AND TEST, M. "Models and Helping: Naturalistic Studies of Aiding Behavior." *Journal of Personality and Social Psychology,* 1967, *6,* 400–407.

BUDNER, S. "Intolerance of Ambiguity as a Personality Variable." *Journal of Personality,* 1962, *30,* 29–50.

BULLOUGH, B. "Alienation in the Ghetto." *American Journal of Sociology,* 1967, *72,* 469–478.

BURKE, E. *Reflections on the Revolution in France.* Chicago: Regnery, 1955. Originally published 1790.

BUROS, O. K. (Ed.) *The Sixth Mental Measurements Yearbook.* Highland Park, N.J.: Gryphon Press, 1965.

BURTON, J. W. *Conflict and Communication: The Use of Controlled Communication in International Relations.* London: Macmillan, 1969.

BURTON, J. W. *World Society.* Cambridge: Cambridge University Press, 1972.

BURTON, R., AND WHITING, J. "The Absent Father and Cross Sex Identity." *Merrill-Palmer Quarterly,* 1961, *7,* 85–95.

BUSHMAN, R. L. "On the Uses of Psychology: Conflict and Conciliation in Benjamin Franklin." *History and Theory,* 1966, *5,* 225–240.

BUTLER, D., AND STOKES, D. *Political Change in Britain.* New York: St. Martin's, 1969.

BWY, D. "Dimensions of Social Conflict in Latin America." In L. H. Masotti and D. R. Bowen (Eds.), *Riots and Rebellion: Civil Violence in the Urban Community.* Beverly Hills, Calif.: Sage, 1968.

CAHALAN, D. "Correlates of Respondent Accuracy in the Denver Validity Survey." *Public Opinion Quarterly,* 1968, *32,* 607–621.

CAMPBELL, A., CONVERSE, P., MILLER, W., AND STOKES, D. *The American Voter.* New York: Wiley, 1960.

CAMPBELL, A., CONVERSE, P., MILLER, W., AND STOKES, D. *Elections and the Political Order.* New York: Wiley, 1966.

CAMPBELL, A., GURIN, G., AND MILLER, W. *The Voter Decides.* New York: Harper, 1954.

CAMPBELL, A., AND SCHUMAN, H. "Racial Attitudes in Fifteen American Cities." In *Supplemental Studies for the National Advisory Committee on Civil Disorders.* Washington, D.C.: U.S. Government Printing Office, July 1968, pp. 11–67.

CAMPBELL, D. T. "The Indirect Assessment of Social Attitudes." *Psychological Bulletin,* 1950, *47,* 15–38.

CAMPBELL, D. T. "Factors Relevant to the Validity of Experiments in Social Settings." *Psychological Bulletin,* 1957a, *54,* 297–312.

CAMPBELL, D. T. "A Typology of Tests, Projective and Otherwise." *Journal of Consulting Psychology,* 1957b, *21,* 207–210.

CAMPBELL, D. T. "Recommendations for APA Test Standards Regarding Construct, Trait, or Discriminant Validity." *American Psychologist,* 1960, *15,* 546–553.

CAMPBELL, D. T. "Social Attitudes and Other Acquired Behavioral Dispositions." In S. Koch (Ed.), *Psychology: A Study of a Science.* Vol. 6. New York: McGraw-Hill, 1963. Pp. 94–172.

CAMPBELL, D. T. "Quasi-Experimental Design." In D. L. Sills (Ed.), *International Encyclopedia of the Social Sciences.* Vol. 5. New York: Macmillan, 1968.

CAMPBELL, D. T. "Reforms as Experiments." *American Psychologist,* 1969a, *24,* 409–429.

CAMPBELL, D. T. "Ethnocentrism of Disciplines and the Fish-Scale Model of Omniscience." In M. Sherif and C. W. Sherif (Eds.), *Interdisciplinary Relationships in the Social Sciences.* Chicago: Aldine, 1969b.

CAMPBELL, D. T., AND FISKE, D. W. "Convergent and Discriminant Validation by the Multitrait-Multimethod Matrix." *Psychological Bulletin,* 1959, *56,* 81–105.

CAMPBELL, D. T., AND MC CANDLESS, B. "Ethnocentrism, Xenophobia and Personality." *Human Relations,* 1951, *4,* 186–192.

CAMPBELL, D. T., AND ROSS, H. L. "The Connecticut Crackdown on Speeding: Time-Series Data in Quasi-Experimental Analysis." *Law and Society Review,* 1968, *3*(1), 33–53.

CAMPBELL, D. T., AND STANLEY, J. C. "Experimental and Quasi-Experimental Designs for Research on Teaching." In N. L. Gage (Ed.), *Handbook of Research on Teaching.* Chicago: Rand McNally, 1963.

CANNING, R. R., AND BAKER, J. M. "Effect of the Group on Authoritarian and Non-Authoritarian Persons." *American Journal of Sociology,* 1959, *64,* 579–581.

CANTOR, N. F. *The English: A History of Politics and Society to 1760.* New York: Simon and Schuster, 1967.

CANTRIL, H. *The Politics of Despair.* New York: Basic Books, 1958.

CANTRIL, H. *The Pattern of Human Concerns.* New Brunswick, N.J.: Rutgers University Press, 1965.

CARLSMITH, J. M., COLLINS, B. E., AND HELMREICH, R. L. "Studies on Forced Compliance. I: The Effect of Pressure for Compliance on Attitude Change Produced by Face-to-Face Role-Playing and Anonymous Essay Writing." *Journal of Personality and Social Psychology,* 1966, *4,* 1–13.

CARR, L. G. "The Srole Items and Acquiescence." *American Sociological Review,* 1971, *36,* 287–293.

CASH, W. J. *The Mind of the South.* New York: Knopf, 1941.

CASPARY, W. "The 'Mood Theory': A Study of Public Opinion and Foreign Policy." *American Political Science Review,* 1970, *64,* 536–547.

CATTELL, R. "New Concepts for Measuring Leadership in Terms of Group Syntality." *Human Relations,* 1951, *4,* 161–184.

CATTELL, R. *Personality and Motivation: Structure and Measurement.* Yonkers-on-Hudson, N.Y.: World Book, 1957.

CENTERS, R. *The Psychology of Social Classes.* Princeton: Princeton University Press, 1949.

CHEIN, I. *The Science of Behavior and the Image of Man.* New York: Basic Books, 1972.

CHERRYHOLMES, C. H., AND SHAPIRO, M. J. *Representatives and Roll Calls: A Computer Simulation of Voting in the Eighty-Eighth Congress.* Indianapolis: Bobbs-Merrill, 1969.

CHICKERING, A. *Education and Identity.* San Francisco: Jossey-Bass, 1969.

CHILD, I. L., STORM, T., AND VEROFF, J. "Achievement Themes in Folk Tales Related to Socialization Practice." In J. W. Atkinson (Ed.), *Motives in Fantasy, Action and Society.* Princeton: Van Nostrand, 1958.

CHOMSKY, N. "Review of *Verbal Behavior* by B. F. Skinner." *Language,* 1959, *35,* 26–58.

CHRISTIANSEN, B. "The Scientific Status of Psychoanalytic Clinical Evidence." *Inquiry,* 1964, *7,* 47–49.

CHRISTIE, R. "Authoritarianism Re-examined." In R. Christie and M. Jahoda (Eds.), *Studies in the Scope and Method of "The Authoritarian Personality."* New York: Free Press, 1954.

CHRISTIE, R. "Eysenck's Treatment of the Personality of Communists." *Psychological Bulletin,* 1956, *53,* 411–430.

CHRISTIE, R., AND COOK, P. "A Guide to Published Literature Relating to the Authoritarian Personality Through 1956." *Journal of Psychology,* 1958, *45,* 171–199.

CHRISTIE, R., AND GEIS, F. L. (Eds.) *Studies in Machiavellianism.* New York: Academic Press, 1970.

CHRISTIE, R., HAVEL, J., AND SEIDENBERG, B. "Is the F Scale Irreversible?" *Journal of Abnormal and Social Psychology,* 1958, *56,* 143–159.

CHRISTIE, R., AND JAHODA, M. (Eds.) *Studies in the Scope and Method of "The Authoritarian Personality".* New York: Free Press, 1954.

CLARK, L. P. *Lincoln: A Psycho-biography.* New York: Scribner's, 1933.

CLARK, R. "The Projective Measurement of Experimentally Induced Levels of Sexual Motivation." *Journal of Experimental Psychology,* 1952, *44,* 391–399.

CLARKE, J. "Family Structure and Political Socialization Among Urban Black Children: Some Observations on Father Absence." *Midwest Journal of Political Science,* 1973.

CLARKSON, G. P. E. "Decision Making in Small Groups: A Simulation Study." *Behavioral Science,* 1968, *13,* 288–305.

CLARKSON, G. P. E., AND SIMON, H. A. "Simulation of Individual and Group Behavior." *American Economic Review,* 1960, *50,* 920–932.

CLAUSEN, A. R. "Response Validity: Vote Report." *Public Opinion Quarterly,* 1968, *32,* 588–606.

CLINARD, M. B. (Ed.) *Anomie and Deviant Behavior: A Discussion and Critique.* New York: Free Press, 1964.

CLOWARD, R. A., AND OHLIN, L. E. *Delinquency and Opportunity.* New York: Free Press, 1960.

CNUDDE, C., AND NEUBAUER, D. *Empirical Democratic Theory.* Chicago: Markham, 1969.

COE, R. M. "Conflict, Interference and Aggression: Computer Simulation of a Social Process." *Behavioral Science,* 1964, *9,* 186–196.

COHEN, A. K. "The Sociology of the Deviant Act: Anomie Theory and Beyond." *American Sociological Review,* 1965, *30,* 5–14.

COHEN, K. J., AND CYERT, R. M. "Simulation of Organizational Behavior." In J. G. March (Ed.), *Handbook of Organizations.* Chicago: Rand McNally, 1965.

COHN, T. S. "The Relation of the F Scale to a Response to Answer Positively." *American Psychiatrist,* 1953, *8,* 335. (Abstract)

COHN, T., AND CARSCH, H. "Administration of the F Scale to a Sample of Germans." *Journal of Abnormal and Social Psychology,* 1954, *49,* 471.

COKER, F. W. *Recent Political Thought.* New York: Appleton-Century, 1934.

COLBY, K. M. "Computer Simulation of Neurotic Processes." In R. W. Stacy and B. D. Waxman (Eds.), *Computers in Biomedical Research.* Vol. 1. New York: Academic Press, 1965.

COLBY, K. M. "A Programmable Theory of Cognition and Affect in Individual Personal Belief Systems." In R. P. Abelson, E. Aronson, W. J. McGuire, T. M. Newcomb, M. J. Rosenberg, and P. H. Tannenbaum (Eds.), *Theories of Cognitive Consistency: A Source Book.* Chicago: Rand McNally, 1968.

COLBY, K. M., AND SCHANK, R. (Eds.) *Computer Simulation of Thought and Language*. San Francisco: Freeman, 1973.

COLEMAN, J. S. "Relational Analysis: The Study of Social Organization with Survey Methods." *Human Organization*, 1958, *17*, 28–36.

COLEMAN, J. S. *The Adolescent Society*. New York: Free Press, 1961.

COLEMAN, J. S. "Collective Decisions." *Sociological Inquiry*, 1964a, *34*, 166–181.

COLEMAN, J. S. "Implications of the Findings on Alienation." *American Journal of Sociology*, 1964b, *70*, 76–78.

COLEMAN, J. S. "Mathematical Models and Computer Simulation." In R. E. L. Faris (Ed.), *Handbook of Modern Sociology*. Chicago: Rand McNally, 1964c.

COLEMAN, J. S. (Ed.) *Education and Political Development*. Princeton: Princeton University Press, 1965a.

COLEMAN, J. S. "The Use of Electronic Computers in the Study of Social Organizations." *European Journal of Sociology*, 1965b, *6*, 89–107.

COLEMAN, J. S. *Equality of Educational Opportunity*. Washington: United States Office of Education, 1966a.

COLEMAN, J. S. *The Game of Democracy*. Washington, D.C.: National 4-H Club Foundation, 1966b.

COLES, R. "The Limits of Psychiatry." *Progressive,* May 1967, pp. 32–34.

Commission on Obscenity and Pornography. *Report of the Commission on Obscenity and Pornography*. New York: Bantam, 1970.

COMSTOCK, C. "Swing Voters: A Comparison of Attitudes on Leadership Style and on the War in Viet Nam, Expressed by Undecided Voters and by Supporters of McGovern and Nixon." Berkeley, Calif.: Wright Institute, 1972.

COMSTOCK, C., AND DUCKLES, R. "The Assessment of Destructiveness in Personality: Working Papers." Berkeley, Calif.: Wright Institute, 1972.

CONNELL, R. "Research and Thought on the Development of Political Beliefs in Children: A Critical Survey." Paper presented at meeting of Australasian Political Studies Association, Sydney, August 1969.

CONVERSE, P. E. "The Nature of Belief Systems in Mass Publics." In D. E. Apter (Ed.), *Ideology and Discontent*. New York: Free Press, 1964.

CONVERSE, P. E. "Of Time and Partisan Stability." *Comparative Political Studies,* 1969, *2*, 139–171.

CONVERSE, P. E. "Attitudes and Non-Attitudes: Continuation of a Dialogue." In E. Tufte (Ed.), *The Quantitative Analysis of Social Problems*. Reading, Mass.: Addison-Wesley, 1970.

CONVERSE, P. E. "Non-voting Among Young Adults in the United States." In W. Crotty, D. Freeman, and D. Gatlin (Eds.), *Political Parties and Political Behavior*. Boston: Allyn and Bacon, 1971.

CONVERSE, P. E. "Public Opinion and Voting Behavior." In F. I. Greenstein and N. W. Polsby (Eds.), *The Handbook of Political Science*. Vol. 6. Reading, Mass.: Addison-Wesley, forthcoming.

CONVERSE, P. E., AND DUPEUX, G. "Politicization of the Electorate in France and the United States." *Public Opinion Quarterly,* 1962, *26*, 1–23.

CONVERSE, P. E., AND SCHUMANN, H. "Silent Majorities and the Vietnam War." *Scientific American,* 1970, *222*, 17–25.

CONWAY, M. M., AND FEIGERT, F. B. "Motivation, Incentive Systems, and the Political Party Organization." *American Political Science Review,* 1968, *62*, 1159–1173.

COOMBS, S. L., FRIED, M., AND ROBINOVITZ, S. H. "An Approach to Election Simulation Through Modular Systems." In W. D. Coplin (Ed.), *Simulation in the Study of Politics*. Chicago: Markham, 1968.

COOPERSMITH, S. *The Antecedents of Self-Esteem.* San Francisco: Freeman, 1967.

CORNBLETH, C. "Political Socialization and the Social Studies: Political Beliefs of Mexican-American Youth." Paper presented at meeting of American Educational Research Association, New York, February 1971.

CORNFIELD, J., AND TUKEY, J. W. "Average Values of Mean Squares in Factorials." *Annals of Mathematical Statistics,* 1956, *27,* 907–949.

COSER, L. *The Functions of Social Conflict.* New York: Free Press, 1956.

COUCH, A., AND KENISTON, K. "Yeasayers and Naysayers: Agreeing Response Set as a Personality Variable." *Journal of Abnormal and Social Psychology,* 1960, *60,* 151–174.

COX, D. R. "The Use of a Concomitant Variable in Selecting an Experimental Design. *Biometrika,* 1957, *44,* 150–158.

COX, D. R. *Planning of Experiments.* New York: Wiley, 1958.

CRAWFORD, T. J., AND NADITCH, M. "Relative Deprivation, Powerlessness, and Militancy: The Psychology of Social Protest." *Psychiatry,* 1970, *33,* 208–223.

CRECINE, J. P. "A Computer Simulation Model of Municipal Budgeting." *Management Science,* 1967, *13,* 786–815.

CRECINE, J. P. *Governmental Problem-Solving, A Computer Simulation of Municipal Budgeting.* Chicago: Rand McNally, 1969.

CRITTENDEN, J. "Aging and Party Affiliation." *Public Opinion Quarterly,* 1962, *26,* 648–657.

CRONBACH, L. *Educational Psychology.* New York: Harcourt, 1963.

CRONBACH, L., AND MEEHL, P. "Construct Validity in Psychological Tests." *Psychological Bulletin,* 1955, *52,* 281–302.

CROSSMAN, R. (Ed.) *The God That Failed.* New York: Harper, 1949.

CROTTY, W. J. "Party Effort and Its Impact on the Vote." *American Political Science Review,* 1971, *65,* 439–450.

CROW, W. J. "A Study of Strategic Doctrines Using the Inter-Nation Simulation." *Journal of Conflict Resolution,* 1963, *7,* 580–589.

CRUTCHFIELD, R. "Character and Conformity." *American Psychologist,* 1955, *10,* 191–198.

CUMMINGS, E., AND HENRY, W. *Growing Old: The Process of Disengagement.* New York: Basic Books, 1961.

CUTLER, N. "Generation, Maturation and Party Affiliation: A Cohort Analysis." *Public Opinion Quarterly,* 1970, *33,* 583–588.

CUTLER, S. J. "Membership in Voluntary Associations and the Theory of Mass Society." Unpublished Doctoral dissertation, University of Michigan, 1969.

CUTRIGHT, P. "Measuring the Impact of Local Party Activity on the General Election Vote." *Public Opinion Quarterly,* 1963, *27,* 372–386.

CUTRIGHT, P., AND ROSSI, P. H. "Grass Roots Politicians and the Vote." *American Sociological Review,* 1958, *23,* 171–179.

CYERT, R. M., AND MARCH, J. G. *A Behavioral Theory of the Firm.* Englewood Cliffs, N.J.: Prentice-Hall, 1963.

DAHL, R. A. "The Behavioral Approach in Political Science: Epitaph for a Monument to a Successful Protest." *American Political Science Review,* 1961, *55,* 763–772.

DAVIDS, A. "Comparison of Three Methods of Personality Assessment: Direct, Indirect and Projective." *Journal of Personality,* 1955, *23,* 432–440.

DAVIDS, A., AND PILDNER, H. "Comparison of Direct and Projective Methods of Personality Assessment Under Different Conditions of Motivation." *Psychological Monographs,* 1958, *72,* whole No. 464.

DAVIES, A. F. *Private Politics: A Study of Five Political Outlooks.* Melbourne: Melbourne University Press, 1966.

DAVIES, A. F. "Criteria for the Political Life History." *Historical Studies of Australia and New Zealand,* 1967, *13*(49), 76–85.

DAVIES, A. "The Child's Discovery of Nationality." *Australian and New Zealand Journal of Sociology*, 1968, *4*, 107–125.

DAVIES, J. C. "The Political Implications of Psychoanalytic and Academic Psychology." Unpublished doctoral dissertation, University of California, Berkeley, 1952.

DAVIES, J. C. "Toward a Theory of Revolution." *American Sociological Review*, 1962, *27*, 5–19.

DAVIES, J. C. *Human Nature in Politics*. New York: Wiley, 1963.

DAVIES, J. C. "The Family's Role in Political Socialization." *Annals of the American Academy of Political and Social Science*, 1965, *361*, 10–19 (September).

DAVIES, J. C. "The J-Curve of Rising and Declining Satisfactions as a Cause of Some Great Revolutions and a Contained Rebellion." In H. D. Graham and T. R. Gurr (Eds.), *The History of Violence in America*. New York: Bantam, 1969.

DAVIES, J. C. "Violence and Aggression: Innate or Not?" *Western Political Quarterly*, 1970, *23*, 611–623.

DAVIES, J. C. (Ed.) *When Men Revolt and Why*. New York: Free Press, 1971.

DAVIES, J. C. "The Need Hierarchy and Political Theory." Unpublished manuscript, 1972.

DAVOL, S. H., AND REIMANS, G. "The Role of Anomie as a Psychological Concept." *Journal of Individual Psychology*, 1959, *15*, 215–225.

DAWSON, P. A. "The Structural Nature of Attitudes: An Experimental Investigation of Attitudes Toward the War in Viet Nam." *Experimental Study of Politics*, 1971, *1*, 61–86.

DAWSON, R. E., AND PREWITT, K. *Political Socialization*. Boston: Little, Brown, 1969.

DAY, R. H., AND TINNEY, E. H. "How to Co-operate in Business Without Really Trying: A Learning Model of Decentralized Decision Making." *Journal of Political Economy*, 1968, *76*, 583–600.

DEAN, D. G. "Alienation: Its Meaning and Measurements." *American Sociological Review*, 1961, *26*, 753–758.

DE CHARMS, R. *Personal Causation: The Internal Affective Determinants of Behavior*. New York: Academic Press, 1968.

DE CHARMS, R., MORRISON, H., REITMAN, W., AND MC CLELLAND, D. "Behavioral Correlates of Directly and Indirectly Measured Achievement Motivation." In D. McClelland (Ed.), *Studies in Motivation*. New York: Appleton-Century, 1955.

DE FLEUR, M., AND DE FLEUR, L. "The Relative Contribution of Television as a Learning Source for Children's Occupational Knowledge." *American Sociological Review*, 1967, *32*, 777–789.

DE GRAZIA, S. "Mahatma Gandhi: The Son of His Mother." *Political Quarterly*, 1948a, *19*, 336–348.

DE GRAZIA, S. *The Political Community: A Study of Anomie*. Chicago: University of Chicago Press, 1948b.

DE LAMATER, J., KATZ, D., AND KELMAN, H. C. "On the Nature of National Involvement: A Preliminary Study." *Journal of Conflict Resolution*, 1969, *13*, 320–357.

DELGADO, J. M. R. *Physical Control of the Mind*. New York: Harper, 1969.

DENNIS, J. *Political Learning in Childhood and Adolescence: A Study of Fifth, Eighth, and Eleventh Grades in Milwaukee, Wisconsin*. Technical Report No. 98. Madison: University of Wisconsin Research and Development Center for Cognitive Learning, 1969.

DENNIS, J. *A Survey and Bibliography of Contemporary Research on Political Learning and Socialization*. Occasional Paper No. 8. Madison: University of Wisconsin Research and Development Center for Cognitive Learning, 1967; updated version, 1971.

DENNIS, J. *Socialization to Politics: A Reader*. New York: Wiley, 1973.

DENNIS, J., BILLINGSLEY, K., AND THORSON, S. *A Pilot Experiment in Early Childhood*

Political Learning. Technical Report No. 63. Madison: Wisconsin Research and Development Center for Cognitive Learning, 1968.

DENNIS, J., AND MC CRONE, D. "Preadult Development of Political Party Identification in Western Democracies." *Comparative Political Studies,* 1970, *3,* 243–263.

DE RIVERA, J. *The Psychological Dimension of Foreign Policy.* Columbus, Ohio: Merrill, 1968.

DEUTSCH, K. W. *The Nerves of Government.* New York: Free Press, 1963.

DEUTSCH, M. "A Theory of Cooperation and Competition." *Human Relations,* 1949, *2,* 129–152.

DEUTSCH, M. "Trust, Trustworthiness, and the F Scale." *Journal of Abnormal and Social Psychology,* 1960, *61,* 138–141.

DEUTSCH, M., AND KRAUSS, R. M. "The Effect of Threat on Interpersonal Bargaining." *Journal of Abnormal and Social Psychology,* 1960, *61,* 181–189.

DEUTSCHER, I. *Stalin: A Political Biography.* New York: Oxford University Press, 1949.

DEVEREAUX, G. "Charismatic Leadership and Crisis." *Psychoanalysis and the Social Sciences,* 1955, *4,* 145–157.

DE VOTO, B. "The Skeptical Biographer." *Harper's,* 1933, *166,* 181–192.

DEXTER, L. A. *The Sociology and Politics of Congress.* Chicago: Rand McNally, 1969.

DEXTER, L. A. *Elite and Specialized Interviewing.* Evanston, Ill.: Northwestern University Press, 1970.

DICKS, H. V. "The Authoritarian Personality: A Critical Appreciation." *Human Relations,* 1951, *4,* 203–211.

DICKS, H. V. *Licensed Mass Murder: A Socio-Psychological Study of Some S.S. Killers.* New York: Basic Books, 1972.

DIES, R. "Development of a Projective Measure of Perceived Locus of Control." *Journal of Projective Techniques and Personality Assessment,* 1968, *32,* 487–490.

DIETZEL, C., AND ABELES, N. "Thematic Drive Expression and Self-Esteem." *Journal of Personality Assessment,* 1971, *35,* 442–447.

DI PALMA, G., AND MC CLOSKY, H. "Personality and Conformity: The Learning of Political Attitudes." *American Political Science Review,* 1970, *64,* 1054–1073.

DI RENZO, G. J. *Personality, Power and Politics: A Social Psychological Analysis of the Italian Deputy and His Parliamentary System.* Notre Dame, Ind.: University of Notre Dame Press, 1967.

DOLLARD, J. *Criteria for the Life History.* New Haven: Yale University Press, 1935.

DOLLARD, J., DOOB, L. W., MILLER, N. E., MOWRER, O. H., AND SEARS, R. R. *Frustration and Aggression.* New Haven: Yale University Press, 1939.

DOLLARD, J., AND MOWRER, O. H. "A Method of Measuring Tension in Written Documents." *Journal of Abnormal and Social Psychology,* 1947, *42,* 3–32.

DONALD, D. H. "Between History and Psychology: Reflections on Psychobiography." Paper presented at meeting of American Psychiatric Association, Dallas, May 1972.

DOOB, L. W. "The Behavior of Attitudes." *Psychological Review,* 1947, *54,* 135–156.

DOOB, L. W. (Ed.) *Resolving Conflict in Africa: The Fermeda Workshop.* New Haven: Yale University Press, 1970.

DOOB, L. W. "The Impact of the Fermeda Workshop on the Conflicts in the Horn of Africa." *International Journal of Group Tensions,* 1971, *1,* 91–101.

DOOLEY, L. "Psychoanalytic Studies of Genius." *American Journal of Psychology,* 1916, *27,* 363–416.

DOUVAN, E., AND WALKER, A. M. "The Sense of Effectiveness in Public Affairs." *Psychological Monographs,* 1956, *70* (no. 22), 1–19.

DOWNS, A. *An Economic Theory of Democracy.* New York: Harper, 1957.

DRIVER, M. J. "Conceptual Structure and Group Processes in an Inter-Nation Simulation.

Part One: The Perception of Simulated Nations." *Educational Testing Service Research Bulletin,* 1962, RB 62-15.

DRIVER, M. J. *A Structural Analysis of Aggression, Stress and Personality in an Inter-Nation Simulation.* Institute Paper No. 97. Lafayette, Ind.: Institute for Research in the Behavioral, Economic and Management Sciences, Purdue University, 1965.

DRUCKMAN, D. "Ethnocentrism in the Inter-Nation Simulation." *Journal of Conflict Resolution,* 1968, *12,* 45–68.

DUBERMAN, M. "Politics and the Man," *New York Times,* December 10, 1967.

DULLES, A. W. "A Foreign-Affairs Scholar Views the Real Woodrow Wilson." *Look,* 13 December 1966.

DURBIN, E. F. M., AND BOWLBY, J. *Personal Aggressiveness and War.* London: Kegan Paul, 1939.

DURKHEIM, E. *The Division of Labor in Society.* New York: Free Press, 1933. Originally published 1893.

DURKHEIM, E. *Suicide.* New York: Free Press, 1951. Originally published 1897.

DUTTON, J. M., AND STARBUCK, W. H. *Computer Simulation of Human Behavior.* New York: Wiley, 1971.

DYE, T. R., AND ZEIGLER, L. H. *The Irony of Democracy.* Belmont, Calif.: Wadsworth, 1970.

DYMOND, R. "Can Clinicians Predict Individual Behavior?" *Journal of Personality,* 1954, *61,* 339–342.

DYSON, J. W., AND SCIOLI, F. P. "An Experimental Test of Consistency Theory." *Experimental Study of Politics,* 1971, *1,* 118–138.

EASTON, D. *A Systems Analysis of Political Life.* New York: Wiley, 1965.

EASTON, D., AND DENNIS, J. "The Child's Acquisition of Regime Norms." *American Political Science Review,* 1967, *61,* 25–38.

EASTON, D., AND DENNIS, J. *Children in the Political System.* New York: McGraw-Hill, 1969.

EASTON, D., AND HESS, R. D. "The Child's Political World." *Midwest Journal of Political Science,* 1962, *6,* 229–246.

ECKHARDT, W., AND LENTZ, T. F. "Factors of War/Peace Attitudes." *Peace Research Reviews,* 1967, *1*(5).

ECKSTEIN, H. "Case-Study and Theory in Political Science." In F. I. Greenstein and N. W. Polsby (Eds.), *The Handbook of Political Science.* Reading, Mass.: Addison-Wesley, forthcoming.

EDEL, L. "The Biographer and Psycho-Analysis." *International Journal of Psycho-Analysis,* 1961, *42,* 458–466.

EDINGER, L. J. "Political Science and Political Biography: Reflections on the Study of Leadership." *Journal of Politics,* 1964, *26,* 423–439, 648–676.

EDINGER, L. J. *Kurt Schumacher: A Study in Personality and Political Behavior.* Stanford, Calif.: Stanford University Press, 1965.

EDWARDS, A. L. "Political Frames of Reference as a Factor Influencing Recognition." *Journal of Abnormal and Social Psychology,* 1941, *36,* 34–50.

EDWARDS, A. L. *Experimental Design in Psychological Research.* (Rev. Ed.) New York: Holt, 1960.

EDWARDS, L. P. *The Natural History of Revolution.* Chicago: University of Chicago Press, 1927.

EINSTEIN, A., AND FREUD, S. *Why War?* Paris: International Institute of Intellectual Cooperation, 1932.

ELDERSVELD, S. J. "Experimental Propaganda Techniques and Voting Behavior." *American Political Science Review,* 1956, *50,* 154–165.

ELDERSVELD, S. J. *Political Parties.* Chicago: Rand McNally, 1964.

ELDERSVELD, S. J., AND DODGE, R. W. "Personal Contact or Mail Propaganda? An Experiment in Voting Turnout and Attitude Change." In D. Katz, D. Cartwright, S. Eldersveld, and A. M. Lee (Eds.), *Public Opinion and Propaganda*. New York: Dryden, 1954.

ELMS, A., AND MILGRAM, S. "Personality Characteristics Associated with Obedience and Defiance Toward Authoritative Command." *Journal of Experimental Research in Personality*, 1966, *1*, 282–289.

EMSHOFF, J. R. "A Computer Simulation Model of the Prisoner's Dilemma." *Behavioral Science*, 1970, *15*, 304–317.

ENDLEMAN, R. "Review of *The University Crisis Reader.*" *Contemporary Sociology*, 1972, *1*, 3–9.

ENGLE, B., AND FRENCH, T. M. "Some Psychodynamic Reflections upon the Life of Solon." *Psychoanalytic Quarterly*, 1951, *20*, 253–273.

ERBE, W. "Social Involvement and Political Activity: A Replication and Elaboration." *American Sociological Review*, 1964, *29*, 198–215.

ERIKSEN, C. "Needs in Perception and Projective Techniques." *Journal of Projective Techniques*, 1954, *18*, 435–440.

ERIKSON, E. H. "Hitler's Imagery and German Youth." *Psychiatry*, 1942, *5*, 475–493.

ERIKSON, E. H. *Childhood and Society*. (2nd ed.) New York: Norton, 1963. Originally published 1950.

ERIKSON, E. H. "The Problem of Ego Identity." *Journal of the American Psychoanalytic Association*, 1956, *4*, 58–121.

ERIKSON, E. H. *Young Man Luther: A Study in Psychoanalysis and History*. New York: Norton, 1958.

ERIKSON, E. H. "The Strange Case of Freud, Bullitt, and Woodrow Wilson: I (A Dubious Collaboration)." *New York Review of Books*, 9 February 1967.

ERIKSON, E. H. "On the Nature of Psycho-Historical Evidence: In Search of Gandhi." *Daedalus*, 1968, *97*, 695–730.

ERIKSON, E. H. *Gandhi's Truth*. New York: Norton, 1969.

ERNST, M. L., AND LOTH, D. *Report on the American Communist*. New York: Holt, 1952.

ETZIONI, A. *The Active Society*. New York: Free Press, 1968.

ETZIONI, A. "Social-Psychological Aspects of International Relations." In G. Lindzey and E. Aronson (Eds.), *The Handbook of Social Psychology*. (2nd Ed.) Vol. 5. Reading, Mass.: Addison-Wesley, 1969.

EULAU, H., BUCHANAN, W., FERGUSON, L. C., AND WAHLKE, J. C. "Career Perspectives of American State Legislators." In D. Marvick (Ed.), *Political Decision Makers*. New York: Free Press, 1961.

EULAU, H., AND SCHNEIDER, P. "Dimensions of Political Involvement." *Public Opinion Quarterly*, 1956, *20*, 128–142.

EVAN, W. "Cohort Analysis of Survey Data: A Procedure for Studying Long Term Opinion Change." *Public Opinion Quarterly*, 1959, *23*, 63–72.

EYSENCK, H. J. *The Psychology of Politics*. London: Routledge and Keagan Paul, 1954a.

EYSENCK, H. J. "The Science of Personality: Nomothetic!" *Psychological Review*, 1954b, *61*, 339–342.

FAGEN, R. "Cuba: The Political Content of Adult Education." In R. Sigel (Ed.), *Learning About Politics*. New York: Random House, 1970.

FALK, J. L. "Issues Distinguishing Idiographic from Nomothetic Approaches to Personality Theory." *Psychological Review*, 1956, *63*, 53–62.

FANON, F. *The Wretched of the Earth*. New York: Grove Press, 1968.

FARBER, M. L. "The Problem of National Character: A Methodological Analysis." *Journal of Psychology*, 1950, *30*, 307–316.

FARRELL, B. A. Introduction. Sigmund Freud, *Leonardo Da Vinci and a Memory of His Childhood.* Harmondsworth, Middlesex, England: Penguin Books, 1963.

FEARING, F. "Psychological Studies of Historical Personalities." *Psychological Bulletin,* 1927, *24,* 521–539.

FEIERABEND, I. K., AND FEIERABEND, R. L. "Aggressive Behaviors Within Polities, 1948–1962. A Cross-National Study." *Journal of Conflict Resolution,* 1966, *10,* 249–271.

FEIERABEND, I. K., AND FEIERABEND, R. L. "Systematic Conditions of Political Aggression: An Application of Frustration-Aggression Theory." In I. K. Feierabend, R. L. Feierabend, and T. R. Gurr (Eds.), *Anger, Violence, and Politics.* Englewood Cliffs, N.J.: Prentice-Hall, 1972.

FEIERABEND, I. K., FEIERABEND, R. L., AND GURR, T. R. (Eds.) *Anger, Violence, and Politics.* Englewood Cliffs, N.J.: Prentice-Hall, 1972.

FEIERABEND, I. K., FEIERABEND, R. L., AND NESVOLD, B. A. "Social Change and Political Violence: Cross-National Patterns." In H. D. Graham and T. R. Gurr (Eds.), *The History of Violence in America.* New York: Bantam Books, 1969.

FELDMAN, K., AND NEWCOMB, T. *The Impact of College on Students.* San Francisco: Jossey-Bass, 1969.

FELDT, L. S. "A Comparison of the Precision of Three Experimental Designs Employing a Concomitant Variable." *Psychometrika,* 1958, *23,* 335–353.

FENDRICH, J. M., AND AXELSON, L. J. "Marital Status and Political Alienation Among Black Veterans." *American Journal of Sociology,* 1971, *77,* 245–261.

FERGUSON, G. A. *Statistical Analysis in Psychology and Education.* New York: McGraw-Hill, 1959.

FESHBACH, S. "The Influence of Drive Arousal and Conflict upon Fantasy Behavior." In J. Kagan and G. Lesser (Eds.), *Contemporary Issues in Thematic Apperceptive Methods.* Springfield, Ill.: Thomas, 1961.

FESTINGER, L. *A Theory of Cognitive Dissonance.* Stanford, Calif.: Stanford University Press, 1957.

FESTINGER, L., AND CARLSMITH, J. M. "Cognitive Consequences of Forced Compliance." *Journal of Abnormal and Social Psychology,* 1959, *58,* 203–210.

FIEDLER, F. E. "The Contingency Model: A Theory of Leadership Effectiveness." In H. Proshansky and B. Seidenberg (Eds.), *Basic Studies in Social Psychology.* New York: Holt, 1965.

FIEDLER, F. E. *A Theory of Leadership Effectiveness.* New York: McGraw-Hill, 1967.

FIELD, J., AND ANDERSON, R. "Ideology in the Public's Conceptualization of the 1964 Election." *Public Opinion Quarterly,* 1969, *33,* 380–398.

FIELDS, R. "Conversations with Children Under Siege." Unpublished manuscript, 1972.

FINIFTER, A. W. "Dimensions of Political Alienation." *American Political Science Review,* 1970, *64,* 389–410.

FISHBEIN, M. "An Investigation of the Relationship Between Beliefs About an Object and the Attitude Toward That Object." *Human Relations,* 1963, *16,* 233–240.

FISHBEIN, M. "Attitude and the Prediction of Behavior." In M. Fishbein (Ed.), *Readings in Attitude Theory and Measurement.* New York: Wiley, 1967.

FISHER, R. A. *Statistical Methods for Research Workers.* London: Oliver and Boyd, 1925.

FISHER, R. A. *The Design of Experiments.* London: Oliver and Boyd, 1935.

FISHER, R. J. "Third Party Consultation: A Method for the Study and Resolution of Conflict." *Journal of Conflict Resolution,* 1972, *16,* 67–94.

FISHMAN, J. A. *Language and Nationalism.* Rowley, Mass.: Newbury, 1972.

FLACKS, R. "The Liberated Generation: An Exploration of the Roots of Student Protest." *Journal of Social Issues,* 1967, *23,* 52–75.

FRANCIS, W. L. "Political Process Simulations." In H. Guetzkow, P. Kotler, and R. L. Schultz (Eds.), *Simulation in Social and Administrative Science.* Englewood Cliffs, N.J.: Prentice-Hall, 1972.

FRANK, J. D. *Persuasion and Healing: A Comparative Study of Psychotherapy.* Baltimore: Johns Hopkins Press, 1961.

FRANK, L. K. "Projective Methods for the Study of Personality." *Journal of Psychology,* 1939, *8,* 389–413.

FREE, L. "Gauging Thresholds of Frustration." In J. C. Davies (Ed.), *When Men Revolt and Why.* New York: Free Press, 1971.

FREEDMAN, J. L., AND SEARS, D. O. "Selective Exposure." In L. Berkowitz (Ed.), *Advances in Experimental Social Psychology.* Vol. 2. New York: Academic Press, 1965.

FREEDMAN, R., HAWLEY, A. H., LANDECKER, W. S., LENSKI, G. E., AND MINER, H. M. *Principles of Sociology.* (Rev. Ed.) New York: Holt, 1956.

FREEMAN, L. "Two Problems in Computer Simulation in the Social and Behavioral Sciences." *Social Science Information,* 1971, *10,* 103–112.

FRENCH, J. R. P., AND RAVEN, B. H. "The Bases of Social Power." In D. Cartwright (Ed.), *Studies in Social Power.* Ann Arbor: University of Michigan Press, 1959.

FRENKEL-BRUNSWIK, E. "Further Explorations by a Contributor." In R. Christie and M. Jahoda (Eds.), *Studies in the Scope and Method of "The Authoritarian Personality."*. New York: Free Press, 1954.

FRENKEL-BRUNSWIK, E., AND SANFORD, R. N. "Some Personality Factors in Anti-Semitism." *Journal of Psychology,* 1945, *20,* 271–291.

FREUD, S. *Leonardo da Vinci: A Psycho-Sexual Study of an Infantile Reminiscence.* New York: Dodd, Mead, 1932. Originally published 1910.

FREUD, S. *Group Psychology and the Analysis of the Ego.* London: Hogarth, 1922.

FREUD, S. *Civilization and Its Discontents.* London: Hogarth, 1930.

FREUD, S. *New Introductory Lectures in Psycho-Analysis.* London: Hogarth, 1933.

FREUD, S., AND BULLITT, W. C. *Thomas Woodrow Wilson: A Psychological Study.* Boston: Houghton Mifflin, 1967.

FREY, F. "Surveying Peasant Attitudes in Turkey." *Public Opinion Quarterly,* 1963, *27,* 335–355.

FRIEDRICH, C. J., AND CHAPMAN, J. (Eds.) *Nomos VI: Justice.* New York: Atherton, 1963.

FRIJDA, N. H. "Problems of Computer Simulation." *Behavioral Science,* 1967, *12,* 59–67.

FROMM, E. *Escape from Freedom.* New York: Holt, 1941.

FROMM, E. *Man for Himself.* New York: Holt, 1947.

FROMM, E. *The Sane Society.* Greenwich: Fawcett Publications, 1955.

FROMM, E., AND MACCOBY, M. *Social Character in a Mexican Village: A Sociopsychoanalytic Study.* Englewood Cliffs, N.J.: Prentice-Hall, 1970.

FROMME, A. "On the Use of Certain Qualitative Methods of Attitude Research: A Study of Opinions on the Methods of Preventing War." *Journal of Social Psychology,* 1941, *13,* 429–459.

FUESS, C. M. "Debunkery and Biography." *Atlantic,* 1933, *151,* 347–356.

GABENNESCH, H. "Authoritarianism as World View." *American Journal of Sociology,* 1972, *77,* 857–875.

GAGE, N., AND CHATTERGEE, B. "The Psychological Meaning of Acquiescence Set: Further Evidence." *Journal of Abnormal and Social Psychology,* 1960, *60,* 280–283.

GALTUNG, J. "Social Position, Party Identification and Foreign Policy Orientation: A Norwegian Case Study." In J. N. Rosenau (Ed.), *Domestic Sources of Foreign Policy.* New York: Free Press, 1967.

GALTUNG, J. "Foreign Policy Opinion as a Function of Social Position." In J. N. Rosenau

(Ed.), *International Politics and Foreign Policy*. (2nd Ed.) New York: Free Press, 1969.

GAMSON, W. A. *Power and Discontent*. Homewood, Ill.: Dorsey Press, 1968.

GAMSON, W. A., AND MODIGLIANI, A. *Untangling the Cold War: A Strategy for Testing Rival Theories*. Boston: Little, Brown, 1971.

GARCIA, C. "An Inquiry into the Development of Political System Values Among Mexican-American Children." Unpublished manuscript, University of New Mexico, 1972.

GARDNER, R., HOLZMAN, P., KLEIN, G., LINTON, H., AND SPENCE, D. "Cognitive Control, A Study of Individual Consistencies in Cognitive Behavior." *Psychological Issues*, 1959, *1*, No. 4.

GARRATY, J. A. "The Interrelations of Psychology and Biography." *Psychological Bulletin*, 1954, *51*, 569–582.

GARRATY, J. A. *The Nature of Biography*. New York: Knopf, 1957.

GEORGE, A. L. "Power as a Compensatory Value for Political Leaders." *Journal of Social Issues*, 1968, *24*, 29–49.

GEORGE, A. L. "The 'Operational Code': A Neglected Approach to the Study of Political Leaders and Decision-Making." *International Studies Quarterly*, 1969, *13*, 190–222.

GEORGE, A. L. "Some Uses of Dynamic Psychology in Political Biography: Case Materials on Woodrow Wilson." In F. I. Greenstein and M. Lerner (Eds.), *A Source Book for the Study of Personality and Politics*. Chicago: Markham, 1971.

GEORGE, A. L. "The Case for Multiple Advocacy in Making Foreign Policy." *American Political Science Review*, 1972, *66*, 751–785.

GEORGE, A. L., AND GEORGE, J. L. *Woodrow Wilson and Colonel House: A Personality Study*. New York: Dover, 1956.

GERTZOG, I. N. "The Electoral Consequences of a Local Party Organization's Registration Campaign: The San Diego Experiment." *Polity*, 1970, *3*, 247–264.

GERWIN, D. *Budgeting Public Funds*. Madison: University of Wisconsin Press, 1969.

GIERKE, O. *Political Theories of the Middle Age*. Trans. F. W. Maitland. Boston: Beacon, 1958.

GILBERT, D., AND LEVINSON, D. "Role Performance, Ideology and Personality in Mental Hospital Aides." In M. Greenblatt and others (Eds.), *The Patient and the Mental Hospital*. New York: Free Press, 1957.

GILBERT, G. M. *The Psychology of Dictatorship*. New York: Ronald Press, 1950.

GILSON, C., AND ABELSON, R. P. "The Subjective Use of Inductive Evidence." *Journal of Personality and Social Psychology*, 1965, *2*, 301–310.

GLAD, B. *Charles Evans Hughes and the Illusions of Innocence*. Urbana: University of Illinois Press, 1966.

GLAD, B. "Review of C. Beradt, *The Third Reich of Dreams*." *American Political Science Review*, 1968, *62*, 545.

GLAD, B. "The Significance of Personality for Role Performance as Chairman of the Senate Foreign Relations Committee: A Comparison of Borah and Fulbright." Paper presented at annual meeting of American Political Science Association, New York, 1969.

GLENN, N. "Aging, Disengagement and Opinionation." *Public Opinion Quarterly*, 1969, *33*, 17–33.

GLENN, N. "Problems of Comparability and Trend Studies with Opinion Poll Data." *Public Opinion Quarterly*, 1970, *34*, 82–91.

GLENN, N., AND GRIMES, M. "Aging, Voting and Political Interest." *American Sociology Review*, 1968, *33*, 563–575.

GLOCK, C. (Ed.) *Survey Research in the Social Sciences*. New York: Russell Sage, 1967.

GOLDBERG, S., AND STERN, G. "The Authoritarian Personality and Education." *American Psychologist*, 1952, *7*, 372–375.

GOLDHAMER, H. "Public Opinion and Personality." *American Journal of Sociology*, 1950, *55*, 346–354.

GORDEN, R. L. *Interviewing: Strategy, Techniques, and Tactics*. Homewood, Ill.: Dorsey Press, 1969.

GORDON, L. "A Comment on Political Orientation and Riot Participation." *American Sociological Review*, 1972, *37*, 379.

GOSNELL, H. F. *Getting Out the Vote*. Chicago: University of Chicago Press, 1927.

GOTTERSFELD, H., AND DOZIER, G. "Changes in Feelings of Powerlessness in a Community Action Program." *Psychological Reports*, 1966, *10*, 978.

GOTTFRIED, A. *Boss Cermak of Chicago*. Seattle: University of Washington Press, 1962.

GOTTSCHALK, L., KLUCKHOHN, C., AND ANGELL, R. *The Use of Personal Documents in History, Anthropology and Sociology*. New York: Social Science Research Council, n.d.

GOUGH, H. G. *California Psychological Inventory*. Palo Alto, Calif.: Consulting Psychologists Press, 1956.

GOUGH, H., AND SANFORD, N. "Rigidity as a Psychological Variable." Mimeographed. Institute of Personality Assessment and Research, University of California, Berkeley, 1952.

GRAHAM, H. D., AND GURR, T. R. (Eds.) *The History of Violence in America*. Report to the National Violence Commission. New York: Bantam, 1969.

GRANBERG, D. "War Expectancy and the Evaluation of a Specific War." *Journal of Conflict Resolution*, 1969, *13*, 546–549.

GREEN, R., AND STACEY, B. "A Flexible Projective Technique Applied to the Measurement of the Self-Image of Voters." *Journal of Projective Techniques and Personality Assessment*, 1966, *30*, 12–15.

GREENACRE, P. *Swift and Carroll*. New York: International Universities Press, 1955.

GREENBERG, E. "Children and the Political Community: A Comparison Across Racial Lines." *Canadian Journal of Political Science*, 1969, *2*, 471–492.

GREENBERG, E. "Black Children and the Political System." *Public Opinion Quarterly*, 1970a, *34*, 333–345.

GREENBERG, E. "Children and Government: A Comparison Across Racial Lines." *Midwest Journal of Political Science*, 1970b, *14*, 249–275.

GREENBERG, E. (Ed.) *Political Socialization*. New York: Atherton, 1970c.

GREENBLATT, M., LEVINSON, D. J., AND WILLIAMS, R. H. (Eds.) *The Patient and the Mental Hospital*. New York: Free Press, 1957.

GREENSTEIN, F. I. "The Benevolent Leader: Children's Images of Political Authority." *American Political Science Review*, 1960, *54*, 934–943.

GREENSTEIN, F. I. *Children and Politics*. New Haven: Yale University Press, 1965.

GREENSTEIN, F. I. "The Impact of Personality on Politics: An Attempt to Clear Away the Underbrush." *American Political Science Review*, 1967, *61*, 629–641.

GREENSTEIN, F. I. "Harold D. Lasswell's Concept of Democratic Character." *Journal of Politics*, 1968a, *30*, 696–709.

GREENSTEIN, F. I. "Socialization: Political Socialization." In D. Sills (Ed.), *International Encyclopedia of the Social Sciences*. New York: Macmillan, 1968b.

GREENSTEIN, F. I. *Personality and Politics*. Chicago: Markham, 1969.

GREENSTEIN, F. I. "A Note on the Ambiguity of 'Political Socialization': Definitions, Criticisms and Strategies of Inquiry." *Journal of Politics*, 1970a, *32*, 969–977.

GREENSTEIN, F. I. "Review of *Personality, Power and Politics*." *Political Science Quarterly*, 1970b, *85*, 365–368.

GREENSTEIN, F. I. "The Study of Personality and Politics: Overall Considerations." In F. I. Greenstein and M. Lerner (Eds.), *A Source Book for the Study of Personality and Politics.* Chicago: Markham, 1971.

GREENSTEIN, F. I., AND LERNER, M. *A Source Book for the Study of Personality and Politics.* Chicago: Markham, 1971.

GREENSTEIN, F. I., AND TARROW, S. "The Study of French Political Socialization." *World Politics,* 1969, *22,* 95–137.

GREENSTEIN, F. I., AND TARROW, S. "Political Orientations of Children: The Use of a Semi-Projective Technique in Three Nations." Sage Professional Papers in Comparative Politics 01-0009, *1,* 479–558. Beverly Hills: Sage, 1970.

GREGG, L. W., AND SIMON, H. A. "Process Models and Stochastic Theories of Simple Concept Formation." *Journal of Mathematical Psychology,* 1967, *4,* 246–276.

GRONSETH, E. "The Impact of Father Absence in Sailor Families on the Personality Structure and Social Adjustment of Adult Sailor Sons." In N. Anderson (Ed.), *Studies of the Family.* Vol. 2, Part 1. Göttingen: Vanderhoeck and Ruprecht, 1957.

GUEDALLA, P. "The Method of Biography." *Journal of the Royal Society of Arts,* July 1939, pp. 925–936.

GUETZKOW, H. *Multiple Loyalties.* Princeton: Princeton University Press, 1955.

GUETZKOW, H. (Ed.) *Simulation in Social Science: Readings.* Englewood Cliffs, N.J.: Prentice-Hall, 1962.

GUETZKOW, H. "Some Correspondences Between Simulations and 'Realities' in International Relations." In M. Kaplan (Ed.), *New Approaches to International Relations.* New York: St. Martin's, 1968.

GUETZKOW, H. "Simulations in the Consolidation and Utilization of Knowledge About International Relations." In D. G. Pruitt and R. C. Snyder (Eds.), *Theory and Research on the Causes of War.* Englewood Cliffs, N.J.: Prentice-Hall, 1969.

GUETZKOW, H., ALGER, C. F., BRODY, R. A., NOEL, R. C., AND SNYDER, R. C. *Simulation in International Relations: Developments for Research and Teaching.* Englewood Cliffs, N.J.: Prentice-Hall, 1963.

GUETZKOW, H., AND GYR, J. "An Analysis of Conflict in Decision-Making Groups." *Human Relations,* 1954, *7,* 367–381.

GUETZKOW, H., KOTLER, P., AND SCHULTZ, R. L. (Eds.) *Simulation in Social and Administrative Science.* Englewood Cliffs, N.J.: Prentice-Hall, 1972.

GUGGENHEIM, F. "Self-Esteem and Achievement Expectations for White and Negro Children." *Journal of Projective Techniques and Personal Assessment,* 1969, *33,* 63–71.

GUILFORD, J. *Personality.* New York: McGraw-Hill, 1959.

GULLAHORN, J., AND GULLAHORN, J. E. "A Computer Model of Elementary Social Behavior." *Behavioral Science,* 1963, *8,* 354–362.

GULLAHORN, J., AND GULLAHORN, J. E. "Computer Simulation of Role Conflict Resolution." In J. M. Dutton and W. H. Starbuck (Eds.), *Computer Simulation of Human Behavior.* New York: Wiley, 1971.

GURIN, G., VEROFF, J., AND FELD, S. *Americans View Their Mental Health: A Nationwide Interview Study.* New York: Basic Books, 1959.

GURIN, P. "Motivation and Aspirations of Southern Negro College Youth." *American Journal of Sociology,* 1970, *75,* 607–631.

GURIN, P., GURIN, G., LAO, R. C., AND BEATTIE, M. "Internal-External Control in the Motivational Dynamics of Negro Youth." *Journal of Social Issues,* 1969, *25,* 29–53.

GURR, T. R. *Why Men Rebel.* Princeton: Princeton University Press, 1970.

GUSFIELD, J. R. "Mass Society and Extremist Politics." *American Sociological Review,* 1962, *27,* 19–30.

GUYTON, A. C. *Textbook of Medical Physiology.* (3rd Ed.) Philadelphia: Saunders, 1966.

GYNTHER, M. D. "White Norms and Black MMPIs: A Prescription for Discrimination." *Psychology Bulletin,* 1972, *78,* 386–402.

HAAS, E. B. *Beyond the Nation-State: Functionalism and International Organization.* Stanford, Calif.: Stanford University Press, 1964.

HAIRE, M. "Projective Techniques in Marketing Research." *Journal of Marketing,* 1950, 649–656.

HALL, C. S., AND LINDZEY, G. *Theories of Personality.* New York: Wiley, 1957.

HALL, E. "Will Success Spoil B. F. Skinner?" An Extensive Interview. *Psychology Today,* 1972, *6,* 65ff.

HAMBLIN, R. L. "The Dynamics of Racial Discrimination." *Social Problems,* 1962, *10,* 103–121.

HAMILTON, R. "A Research Note on the Mass Support for 'Tough' Military Initiatives." *American Sociological Review,* 1968, *33,* 439–445.

HANFMANN, E., AND GETZELS, J. "Interpersonal Attitudes of Former Soviet Citizens, as Studied by a Semi-Projective Method." *Psychological Monographs,* 1955, *389,* whole issue.

HANNA, J. F. "Information-Theoretic Techniques for Evaluating Simulation Models." In J. M. Dutton and W. H. Starbuck (Eds.), *Computer Simulation of Human Behavior.* New York: Wiley, 1971.

HARGROVE, E. C. *Presidential Leadership: Personality and Political Style.* New York: Macmillan, 1966.

HARLOW, H. F. "Mice, Monkeys, Men and Motives." *Psychological Review,* 1953, *60,* 23–32.

HARLOW, H. F., AND HARLOW, M. K. "Social Deprivation in Monkeys." *Scientific American,* 1962, *207,* 136–146.

HARLOW, H. F., AND SUOMI, S. J. "Induced Psychopathology in Monkeys." *Engineering and Science* (Pasadena: California Institute of Technology), 1970, *33,* 8–14.

HARLOW, H. F., AND ZIMMERMAN, R. R. "The Development of Affectional Response in Infant Monkeys." *Proceedings of the American Philosophical Society,* 1958, *102,* 501–509.

HARNED, L. "Authoritarian Attitudes and Party Activity." *Public Opinion Quarterly,* 1961, *25,* 393–399.

HARRIS, D., GOUGH, H., AND MARTIN, W. E. "Children's Ethnic Attitudes: II. Relationship to Parental Beliefs Concerning Child Training." *Child Development,* 1950, *21,* 169–181.

HARRISON, R. "Thematic Apperceptive Methods." In B. Wolman (Ed.), *Handbook of Clinical Psychology.* New York: McGraw-Hill, 1965.

HARTMAN, D. A. "The Psychological Point of View in History: Some Phases of the Slavery Struggle." *Journal of Abnormal Psychology,* 1922–1923, *17,* 261–273.

HARTMANN, G. W. "A Field Experiment on the Comparative Effectiveness of 'Emotional' and 'Rational' Political Leaflets in Determining Election Results." *Journal of Abnormal and Social Psychology,* 1935, *31,* 99–114.

HARVEY, O. J., HUNT, D. E., AND SCHRODER, H. M. *Conceptual Systems and Personality Organization.* New York: Wiley, 1961.

HATHAWAY, S., AND MC KINLEY, J. C. *Manual for the Minnesota Multiphasic Personality Inventory.* (Rev. Ed.) New York: Psychological Corporation, 1951.

HAWLEY, W. D., MC CONAHAY, J. B., MC CONAHAY, S. F., NELSON, K., AND GRUBER, J. E. *An Evaluation of High School in the Community.* New Haven: Educational Research Services, 1972.

HAY, J., AND NICOLAY, J. G. *Abraham Lincoln.* Chicago: University of Chicago Press, 1966. Originally published 1886.

HAYS, W. L. *Statistics for Psychologists.* New York: Holt, 1963.

HAYTHORN, W., COUCH, A., HAEFNER, D., LANGHAM, P., AND CARTER, L. "The Behavior of

Authoritarian and Equalitarian Personalities in Groups." *Human Relations,* 1956a, *9,* 57–74.

HAYTHORN, W., COUCH, A., HAEFNER, D., LANGHAM, P., AND CARTER, L. "The Effects of Varying Combinations of Authoritarianism and Equalitarianism in Leaders and Followers." *Journal of Abnormal and Social Psychology,* 1956b, *53,* 210–219.

HEIDER, F. *The Psychology of Interpersonal Relations.* New York: Wiley, 1958.

HEIST, P. "Diversity in College Students' Characteristics." *Journal of Educational Psychology,* 1960, *33,* 279–291.

HEMPEL, C. G. *Aspects of Scientific Explanations.* New York: Free Press, 1965.

HENNESSY, B. "Politicals and Apoliticals: Some Measurements of Personality Traits." *Midwest Journal of Political Science,* 1959, *3,* 336–355.

HENRY, W. "The Thematic Apperception Test." In A. Carr and others (Eds.), *The Prediction of Overt Behavior Through the Use of Projective Techniques.* Springfield, Ill.: Thomas, 1960.

HERMAN, S. N. *Israelis and Jews: The Continuity of an Identity.* New York: Random House, 1970.

HERMANN, C. F. "Validation Problems in Games and Simulations with Special Reference to Models of International Politics." *Behavioral Science,* 1967, *12,* 216–231.

HERMANN, C. F. *Crises in Foreign Policy: A Simulation Analysis.* Indianapolis: Bobbs-Merrill, 1969.

HERMANN, C. F., AND HERMANN, M. G. "An Attempt to Simulate the Outbreak of World War I." *American Political Science Review,* 1967, *61,* 400–416.

HERMANN, M. G. "Testing a Model of Psychological Stress." *Journal of Personality,* 1966, *34,* 381–396.

HERO, A., JR. "Liberalism-Conservatism Revisited: Foreign vs. Domestic Federal Policies, 1937–1967." *Public Opinion Quarterly,* 1969, *33,* 399–408.

HERRING, E. P. *The Politics of Democracy.* New York: Holt, 1940.

HERSEY, J. *The Algiers Motel Incident.* New York: Bantam, 1968.

HERZON, F. D. "A Review of Acquiescence Response Set in the California F Scale." *Social Science Quarterly,* June 1972, pp. 66–78.

HESS, R. "The Socialization of Attitudes Toward Political Authority: Some Cross National Comparisons." *International Social Science Journal,* 1963, *15,* 542–559.

HESS, R., AND EASTON, D. "The Child's Image of the President." *Public Opinion Quarterly,* 1960, *24,* 632–644.

HESS, R., AND TORNEY, J. *The Development of Political Attitudes in Children.* Chicago: Aldine, 1967.

HIMELHOCH, J. "Tolerance and Personality Needs: A Study of the Liberalization of Ethnic Attitudes Among Minority Group College Students." *American Sociological Review,* 1950, *15,* 79–88.

HIRSCH, H. *Poverty and Politicization.* New York: Free Press, 1971.

HITSCHMANN, E. "Some Psycho-Analytic Aspects of Biography." *International Journal of Psycho-Analysis,* 1956, *37,* 265–269.

HOBBES, T. *Leviathan.* Oxford: Clarendon, 1946. Originally published–1651.

HOFSTADTER, R. *The Paranoid Style in American Politics and Other Essays.* New York: Knopf, 1965.

HOFSTADTER, R. "The Strange Case of Freud, Bullitt, and Woodrow Wilson: II." *New York Review of Books,* 9 February 1967, pp. 3–8.

HOLLANDER, E. "Authoritarianism and Leadership Choice in a Military Setting." *American Psychologist,* 1953, *8,* 368–369.

HOLLANDER, E. P. "Conformity, Status and Idiosyncrasy Credit." *Psychological Review,* 1958, *65*(2), 117–127.

HOLLANDER, E. P., AND JULIAN, J. P. "Studies in Leader Legitimacy, Influence and Innovation." In L. Berkowitz (Ed.), *Advances in Experimental Social Psychology*. Vol. 5. New York: Academic Press, 1970.

HOLLINGSHEAD, A. *Elmtown's Youth*. New York: Wiley, 1949.

HOLST, E. VON, AND ST. PAUL, U. VON. "Electrically Controlled Behavior." *Scientific American*, March 1962, *206*, 50–59.

HOLSTI, O. R. "Comparative 'Operational Codes' of Recent U.S. Secretaries of State: John Foster Dulles." Paper presented at meeting of American Political Science Association, New York, September 1969.

HOLSTI, O. R., BRODY, R. A., AND NORTH, R. C. "The Management of International Crisis: Affect and Action in American-Soviet Relations." In D. G. Pruitt and R. C. Snyder (Eds.), *Theory and Research on the Causes of War*. Englewood Cliffs, N.J.: Prentice-Hall, 1969. Pp. 62–79.

HOLT, R. R. "The Nature of TAT Stories as Cognitive Products: A Psychoanalytic Approach." In J. Kagan and G. Lesser (Eds.), *Contemporary Issues in Thematic Apperceptive Methods*. Springfield, Ill.: Thomas, 1961.

HOLT, R. R. Unpublished working paper. Research Center for Mental Health, New York. University, 1972.

HOLTZMAN, W. "Personality Measurement: Personality Inventories." In D. Sills (Ed.), *International Encyclopedia of the Social Sciences*. New York: Macmillan, 1968.

HOLZBERG, J. D. "The Clinical and Scientific Methods: Synthesis or Antithesis?" *Journal of Projective Techniques*, 1957, *21*, 227–242.

HOLZBERG, J. D. "The Clinical and Scientific Methods: Synthesis or Antithesis?" *Journal of Personality*, 1962, *30*, 377–403.

HOMANS, G. *The Human Group*. New York: Harcourt, 1950.

HOOK, S. *The Hero in History*. Boston: Beacon, 1943.

HORKHEIMER, M. (Ed.) *Studien über Autorität und Familie*. Paris: Alcan, 1966.

HORNEY, K. *The Neurotic Personality of Our Time*. New York: Norton, 1937.

HORNEY, K. *Neurosis and Human Growth*. New York: Norton, 1950.

HOROWITZ, E., AND HOROWITZ, R. "Development of Social Attitudes in Children." *Sociometry*, 1938, *1*, 301–338.

HOROWITZ, I. L., AND LIEBOWITZ, M. "Social Deviance and Political Marginality: Toward a Redefinition of the Relation Between Sociology and Politics." *Social Problems*, 1968, *15*, 280–296.

HORST, P. "The Prediction of Personal Adjustment and Individual Cases." In P. F. Lazarsfeld and M. Rosenberg (Eds.), *The Language of Social Research: A Reader in the Methodology of Social Research*. New York: Free Press, 1955.

HORTON, J. "The Dehumanization of Anomie and Alienation: A Problem in the Ideology of Sociology." *British Journal of Sociology*, 1964, *15*, 283–300.

HORTON, J. E., AND THOMPSON, W. E. "Powerlessness and Political Negativism: A Study of Defeated Local Referendums." *American Journal of Sociology*, 1962, *67*, 485–493.

HOVLAND, C. I. "Reconciling Conflicting Results Derived from Experimental and Survey Studies of Attitude Change." *American Psychologist*, 1959, *14*, 8–17.

HOVLAND, C. I., AND JANIS, I. L. *Personality and Persuasibility*. New Haven: Yale University Press, 1959.

HOVLAND, C. I., JANIS, I. L., AND KELLEY, H. H. *Communication and Persuasion*. New Haven: Yale University Press, 1953.

HOVLAND, C. I., LUMSDAINE, A. A., AND SHEFFIELD, F. D. *Experiments in Mass Communication: Studies in Social Psychology in World War II*. Vol. 3. Princeton, N.J.: Princeton University Press, 1949.

HOWARD, J. W., JR. "Judicial Biography and the Behavioral Persuasion." Paper Presented at meeting of American Political Science Association, New York, September 1969.

HOWARD, J., AND SOMERS, R. "Resisting Institutional Evil from Within." In N. Sanford and C. Comstock (Eds.), *Sanctions for Evil*. San Francisco: Jossey-Bass, 1971.

HOWREY, P., AND KELEJIAN, H. H. "Simulation Versus Analytical Solutions." In T. H. Naylor (Ed.), *The Design of Computer Simulation Experiments*. Durham, N.C.: Duke University Press, 1969.

HUGHES, H. S. *History as an Art and as a Science*. New York: Harper, 1964.

HUNT, J. "Traditional Personality Theory in the Light of Recent Evidence." *American Scientist*, 1965, *53*, 80–96.

HUNT, W., CRANE, W., AND WAHLKE, J. "Interviewing Political Elites in Cross-Cultural Comparative Research." *American Journal of Sociology*, 1964, *70*, 59–68.

HUNTINGTON, S. P. "Conservatism as an Ideology." *American Political Science Review*, 1957, *51*, 454–473.

HYMAN, H. H. "Community Background in Public Opinion Research." *Journal of Abnormal and Social Psychology*, 1945, *40*, 411–413.

HYMAN, H. H. *Survey Design and Analysis*. New York: Free Press, 1955.

HYMAN, H. H. *Political Socialization*. New York: Free Press, 1959.

HYMAN, H. H. *Secondary Analysis of Sample Surveys: Principles, Procedures, and Potentialities*. New York: Wiley, 1972a.

HYMAN, H. H. "Strategies in Comparative Survey Research." In R. Smith (Ed.), *Social Science Methods*. New York: Free Press, 1972b.

HYMAN, H. H., COBB, W. J., FELDMAN, J. J., HART, C. W., AND STEMBER, C. H. *Interviewing in Social Research*. Chicago: University of Chicago Press, 1954.

HYMAN, H. H., LEVINE, G., AND WRIGHT, C. "Studying Expert Informants by Survey Methods: A Cross-National Inquiry." *Public Opinion Quarterly*, 1967, *31*, 9–26.

HYMAN, H. H., AND SHEATSLEY, P. B. "Some Reasons Why Information Campaigns Fail." *Public Opinion Quarterly*, 1947, *11*, 412–423.

HYMAN, H. H., AND SHEATSLEY, P. B. "Trends in Public Opinion on Civil Liberties." *Journal of Social Issues*, 1953, *9*, 6–16.

HYMAN, H. H., AND SHEATSLEY, P. B. *"The Authoritarian Personality*—A Methodological Critique." In R. Christie and M. Jahoda (Eds.), *Studies in the Scope and Method of "The Authoritarian Personality."* New York: Free Press, 1954.

HYMAN, H. H., AND SHEATSLEY, P. B. "Attitudes Toward Desegregation." *Scientific American*, 1956, *195*, 35–39.

HYMAN, H. H., AND SINGER, E. (Eds.) *Readings in Reference Group Theory and Research*. New York: Macmillan, 1968.

INBAR, M., AND STOLL, C. *Simulation and Gaming in Social Science*. New York: Free Press, 1971.

INGLEHART, R. "Changing Value Priorities and European Integration." *Journal of Common Market Studies*, 1971a, *10*, 1–36.

INGLEHART, R. "The Silent Revolution in Europe: Intergenerational Change in Post-Industrial Societies." *American Political Science Review*, 1971b, *65*, 991–1017.

INKELES, A. "Sociology and Psychology." In S. Koch (Ed.), *Psychology: A Study of a Science*. New York: McGraw-Hill, 1963, Pp. 317–387.

INKELES, A., AND LEVINSON, D. J. "National Character: The Study of Modal Personality and Sociocultural Systems." In G. Lindzey and E. Aronson (Eds.), *The Handbook of Social Psychology*. (2nd Ed.) Reading, Mass.: Addison-Wesley, 1969. Originally published 1954.

INSKO, C. A. *Theories of Attitude Change*. New York: Appleton-Century, 1967.

ISRAEL, F. L. *Nevada's Key Pittman*. Lincoln: University of Nebraska Press, 1963.

JAHODA, G. "The Development of Children's Ideas About Country and Nationality. Part I: The Conceptual Framework." *British Journal of Educational Psychology,* 1963a, *33,* 47–60.

JAHODA, G. "The Development of Children's Ideas About Country and Nationality. Part II: National Symbols and Themes." *British Journal of Educational Psychology,* 1963b, *33,* 143–153.

JAHODA, G. "Children's Concepts of Nationality: A Critical Study of Piaget's Stages." *Child Development,* 1964, *35,* 1081–1092.

JAKOBOVITS, L. A. "Evaluational Reactions to Erotic Literature." *Psychological Reports,* 1965, *16,* 985–994.

JAMES, W. *The Principles of Psychology.* New York: Dover, 1950. Originally published–1890.

JAMES, W. "The Moral Equivalent of War." *International Conciliation,* 1910 (27), 3–20.

JANIS, I. L. "Decisional Conflicts: A Theoretical Analysis." *Journal of Conflict Resolution,* 1959, *3,* 6–27.

JANIS, I. L. "Groupthink Among Policy Makers." In N. Sanford and C. Comstock (Eds.), *Sanctions for Evil.* San Francisco: Jossey-Bass, 1971.

JANIS, I. L. *Victims of Groupthink.* Boston: Houghton Mifflin, 1972.

JANIS, I. L., AND FESHBACH, S. "Effects of Fear-Arousing Communications." *Journal of Abnormal and Social Psychology,* 1953, *48,* 78–92.

JANIS, I. L., AND SMITH, M. B. "Effects of Education and Persuasion on National and International Images." In H. C. Kelman (Ed.), *International Behavior: A Social Psychological Analysis.* New York: Holt, 1965.

JANOWITZ, M., AND MARVICK, D. "Authoritarianism and Political Behavior." *Public Opinion Quarterly,* 1953, *17,* 185–201.

JAROS, D. "Children's Orientations Toward the President: Some Additional Theoretical Considerations and Data." *Journal of Politics,* 1967, *29,* 368–387.

JAROS, D. *Socialization to Politics.* New York: Praeger, 1972.

JAROS, D., HIRSCH, H., AND FLERON, F., JR. "The Malevolent Leader: Political Socialization in an American Subculture." *American Political Science Review,* 1968, *62,* 564–575.

JENNINGS, H. H. *Leadership and Isolation: A Study of Personality in Interpersonal Relations.* New York: Longmans, 1943.

JENNINGS, M., AND NIEMI, R. "Patterns of Political Learning." *Harvard Educational Review,* 1968a, *38,* 443–467.

JENNINGS, M., AND NIEMI, R. "The Transmission of Political Values from Parent to Child." *American Political Science Review,* 1968b, *62,* 169–184.

JENNINGS, M., AND NIEMI, R. *Families, Schools and Political Learning.* Princeton, N.J.: Princeton University Press, forthcoming, 1974.

JESSOR, R., GRAVES, T., HANSON, R. C., AND JESSOR, S. L. *Society, Personality and Deviant Behavior.* New York: Holt, 1968.

JOHNSON, A. "Tendencies of Recent American Biography." *Yale Review,* 1912, *1,* 390–403.

JOHNSON, C. "An Experimental Analysis of the Origin and Development of Racial Attitudes with Special Emphasis on the Role of Bilingualism." Unpublished doctoral dissertation, University of Colorado, 1949.

JOHNSON, G. W. *Randolph of Roanoke.* New York: Minton, Beach, 1929.

JONES, E. "The Case of Louis Bonaparte, King of Holland." *Journal of Abnormal Psychology,* 1913, p. 289.

JONES, E. *The Life and Work of Sigmund Freud.* New York: Basic Books, 1953, 1955, 1957. 3 Vols.

JONES, H. M. "Methods in Contemporary Biography." *English Journal,* 1932, *21,* 113–122.

JONES, M., BAYLEY, N., MAC FARLANE, J., AND HONZIK, M. *The Course of Human Development.* Waltham, Mass.: Xerox College Publishing, 1971.

JOSEPHSON, E., AND JOSEPHSON, M. (Eds.) *Man Alone: Alienation in Modern Society.* New York: Dell, 1962.

JOSEPHSON, M. "Historians and Mythmakers." *Virginia Quarterly Review,* 1940, *16,* 92–109.

KAGAN, J. "The Measurement of Overt Aggression from Fantasy." *Journal of Abnormal and Social Psychology,* 1956, *52,* 390–393.

KAGAN, J. "Stylistic Variables in Fantasy Behavior." In J. Kagan and G. Lesser (Eds.), *Contemporary Issues in Thematic Apperceptive Methods.* Springfield, Ill. Thomas, 1961.

KAGAN, J. "Motives and Development." *Journal of Personality and Social Psychology,* 1972, *22,* 51–66.

KAGAN, J., AND MOSS, H. *Birth to Maturity.* New York: Wiley, 1962.

KAMIN, L. J. "Ethnic and Party Affiliations of Candidates as Determinants of Voting." *Canadian Journal of Psychology,* 1958, *12,* 205–212.

KANOUSE, D. E., AND ABELSON, R. P. "Language Variables Affecting the Persuasiveness of Simple Communications." *Journal of Personality and Social Psychology,* 1967, *7,* 158–163.

KAPLAN, M. A. "Review of Klineberg's *The Human Dimension in International Relations.*" *American Political Science Review,* 1964, *58,* 682–683.

KARDINER, A., AND OTHERS. *The Psychological Frontiers of Society.* New York: Columbia University Press, 1945.

KARIEL, H. S. "The Political Relevance of Behavioral and Existential Psychology." *American Political Science Review,* 1967, *61,* 334–342.

KARLINS, M., AND ABELSON, H. I. *Persuasion: How Opinions and Attitudes Are Changed.* (2nd Ed.) New York: Springer, 1970.

KATZ, D. "The Functional Approach to the Study of Attitudes." *Public Opinion Quarterly,* 1960, *24,* 163–204.

KATZ, D. "Editorial." *Journal of Personality and Social Psychology,* 1965, *1,* 1–2.

KATZ, D. "The Practice and Potential of Survey Methods in Psychological Research." In C. Glock (Ed.), *Survey Research in the Social Sciences.* New York: Russell Sage, 1967.

KATZ, D., AND ELDERSVELD, S. "The Impact of Local Party Activity upon the Electorate." *Public Opinion Quarterly,* 1961, *25,* 1–24.

KATZ, D., AND KAHN, R. L. *The Social Psychology of Organizations.* New York: Wiley, 1966.

KATZ, D., MC CLINTOCK, C., AND SARNOFF, I. "Ego-Defense and Attitude Change." *Human Relations,* 1956, *9,* 27–45.

KATZ, D., MC CLINTOCK, C., AND SARNOFF, I. "The Measurement of Ego Defense as Related to Attitude Change." *Journal of Personality,* 1957, *25,* 465–474.

KATZ, D., AND SCHANCK, R. *Social Psychology.* New York: Wiley, 1938.

KATZ, D., AND STOTLAND, E. "A Preliminary Statement to a Theory of Attitude Structure and Change." In S. Koch (Ed.), *Psychology: A Study of a Science.* Vol. 3. New York: McGraw-Hill, 1959.

KATZ, E., AND LAZARSFELD, P. F. *Personal Influence: The Part Played by People in the Flow of Mass Communication.* New York: Free Press, 1955.

KATZ, J. (Ed.) *No Time for Youth.* San Francisco: Jossey-Bass, 1968.

KELLEY, H. H. "Two Functions of Reference Groups." In G. E. Swanson, T. M. Newcomb, and E. L. Hartley (Eds.), *Readings in Social Psychology.* 2nd Ed. New York: Holt, 1952.

KELLEY, H. H. "Attribution Theory in Social Psychology." In D. Levine (Ed.), *Nebraska Symposium on Motivation.* Lincoln: University of Nebraska Press, 1967.

KELLY, E. "Consistency of the Adult Personality." *American Psychologist,* 1955, *10,* 659–681.

KELMAN, H. C. "Compliance, Identification and Internalization: Three Processes of Attitude Change." *Journal of Conflict Resolution,* 1958, *2,* 51–60.

KELMAN, H. C. (Ed.) *International Behavior: A Social-Psychological Analysis.* New York: Holt, 1965.

KELMAN, H. C. "Education for the Concept of a Global Society." *Social Education,* 1968a, *32,* 661–666.

KELMAN, H. C. "International Relations: Psychological Aspects." In D. L. Sills (Ed.), *International Encyclopedia of the Social Sciences.* Vol. 8. New York: Macmillan, 1968b.

KELMAN, H. C. *A Time to Speak: On Human Values and Social Research.* San Francisco: Jossey-Bass, 1968c.

KELMAN, H. C. "Patterns of Personal Involvement in the National System: A Social-Psychological Analysis of Political Legitimacy." In J. N. Rosenau (Ed.), *International Politics and Foreign Policy.* (2nd Ed.) New York: Free Press, 1969.

KELMAN, H. C. "The Role of the Individual in International Relations: Some Conceptual and Methodological Considerations." *Journal of International Affairs,* 1970, *24,* 1–17.

KELMAN, H. C. "Language as an Aid and Barrier to Involvement in the National System." In J. Rubin and B. H. Jernudd (Eds.), *Can Language Be Planned? Sociolinguistic Theory and Practice for Developing Nations.* Honolulu: University Press of Hawaii, 1971.

KELMAN, H. C. "The Problem-Solving Workshop in Conflict Resolution." In R. L. Merritt (Ed.), *Communication in International Politics.* Urbana: University of Illinois Press, 1972.

KELMAN, H., AND BARCLAY, J. "The F Scale as a Measure of Breadth of Perspective." *Journal of Abnormal and Social Psychology,* 1963, *67,* 608–615.

KELMAN, H. C., AND EZEKIEL, R. S., with the collaboration of R. B. Kelman. *Cross-National Encounters: The Personal Impact of an Exchange Program for Broadcasters.* San Francisco: Jossey-Bass, 1970.

KELMAN, H. C., AND LAWRENCE, L. H. "Assignment of Responsibility in the Case of Lt. Calley: Preliminary Report on a National Survey." *Journal of Social Issues,* 1972, *28*(1), 177–212.

KENISTON, K. *The Uncommitted: Alienated Youth in American Society.* New York: Harcourt, Brace and World, 1965.

KENNAN, G. F. "It's History, But Is It Literature?" *New York Times Book Review,* April 26, 1959.

KENYON, S. "The Development of Political Cynicism Among Negro and White Adolescents." Paper presented at meeting of American Political Science Association. New York, September 1969.

KERR, H. H. "Changing Attitudes Through International Participation: European Parliamentarians and Integration." *International Organization,* 1973, *27,* 45–83.

KEY, V. O., JR. *Politics, Parties and Pressure Groups.* 4th ed. New York: Crowell, 1958.

KEY, V. O., JR. *Public Opinion and American Democracy.* New York: Knopf, 1961.

KEY, V. O., JR. *The Responsible Electorate: Rationality in Presidential Voting.* Cambridge: Harvard University Press, 1966.

KEY, V. O., JR. AND MUNGER, F. "Social Determinism and Electoral Decision: The Case of Indiana." In E. Burdick and A. J. Brodbeck (Eds.), *American Voting Behavior.* New York: Free Press, 1959.

KIELL, N. *Psychological Studies of Famous Americans.* New York: Twayne, 1964.

KIESLER, C. A., COLLINS, B. E., AND MILLER, N. *Attitude Change: A Critical Analysis of Theoretical Approaches.* New York: Wiley, 1969.

KILLIAN, L. M. "Leadership in the Desegregation Crisis: An Institutional Analysis." In M. Sherif (Ed.), *Intergroup Relations and Leadership*. New York: Wiley, 1962.

KILLIAN, L. M., AND SMITH, C. U. "Negro Protest Leaders in a Southern Community." *Social Forces,* 1960, *38,* 253–257.

KINSEY, A. C., POMEROY, W. B., AND MARTIN, C. E. *Sexual Behavior in the Human Male.* Philadelphia: Saunders, 1948.

KINSEY, A. C., POMEROY, W. B., MARTIN, C. E., AND GEBHARD, P. H. *Sexual Behavior in the Human Female.* Philadelphia: Saunders, 1953.

KINTZ, B., DELPRATO, D., METTE, D., PERSONS, C., AND SCHAPPE, R. "The Experimenter Effect." *Psychological Bulletin,* 1965, *63,* 223–232.

KIRBY, D. "A Counter-Culture Explanation of Student Activism." *Social Problems,* 1971, *19,* 203–216.

KIRSCHT, J. P., AND DILLEHAY, R. C. *Dimensions of Authoritarianism: A Review of Research and Theory.* Lexington: University of Kentucky Press, 1967.

KISH, L. *Survey Sampling.* New York: Wiley, 1965.

KLECKA, W. "Applying Political Generations to the Study of Political Behavior: A Cohort Analysis." *Public Opinion Quarterly,* 1971, *35,* 358–373.

KLINEBERG, O. *Tensions Affecting International Understanding.* New York: Social Science Research Council, 1950.

KLINEBERG, O. *The Human Dimension in International Relations.* New York: Holt, 1964.

KLINEBERG, O. "Prejudice: The Concept." In D. Sills (Ed.), *International Encyclopedia of the Social Sciences.* New York: Macmillan, 1968.

KLINEBERG, O., AND ZAVALLONI, M. *Nationalism and Tribalism Among African Students.* Paris: Mouton, 1969.

KLOPFER, W. "The Metamorphosis of Projective Methods." *Journal of Projective Techniques and Personality Assessment,* 1968, *32,* 402–404.

KLUCKHOHN, C., AND MURRAY, H. A. "Personality Formation: The Determinants." In C. Kluckhohn, and H. A. Murray (Eds.), *Personality in Nature, Society and Culture.* (2nd Ed.) New York: Knopf, 1953.

KLUCKHOHN, F. R., AND STRODTBECK, F. L. *Variations in Value Orientation.* New York: Harper, 1961.

KNUTSON, J. "Personality Correlates of Political Belief: Left, Right and Center." Chicago: American Political Science Association, 1971.

KNUTSON, J. *The Human Basis of the Polity: A Psychological Study of Political Men.* Chicago: Aldine-Atherton, 1972a.

KNUTSON, J. "Some Problems of Assessment in Political Psychology." Washington, D.C.: American Political Science Association, 1972b.

KNUTSON, J. "The Political Relevance of Self-Actualization." In A. Wilcox (Ed.), *Public Opinion and Political Attitudes.* New York: Wiley, 1973.

KNUTSON, J. "Individual Differences in Pre-political Ideology: The Basis of Political Learning." In R. Niemi (Ed.), *New Views of Children and Politics.* San Francisco: Jossey-Bass, forthcoming, 1974.

KOCH, S. "Epilogue." In S. Koch (Ed.), *Psychology: A Study of Science.* Vol. 3. New York: McGraw-Hill, 1959.

KOESTLER, A. *The Ghost in the Machine.* New York: Macmillan, 1967.

KOESTLER, A. "Man—One of Evolution's Mistakes?" *New York Times Magazine,* 19 October 1969, pp. 28ff.

KOGAN, N. "Authoritarianism and Repression." *Journal of Abnormal and Social Psychology,* 1956, *53,* 34–37.

KOGAN, N., AND WALLACH, M. *Risk Taking: A Study in Cognition and Personality.* New York: Holt, 1964.

KOHLBERG, L. "Development of Moral Character and Moral Ideology." In M. L. Hoffman and L. W. Hoffman (Eds.), *Review of Childhood Development.* Vol. 1. New York: Russell Sage, 1964.

KOHLBERG, L. "Moral Development." In D. Sills (Ed.), *International Encyclopedia of the Social Sciences.* Vol. 10. New York: Macmillan, 1968.

KOHLBERG, L. *Stages in the Development of Moral Thought and Action.* New York: Holt, 1971.

KOHN, P. M. "The Authoritarianism-Rebellion Scale: A Balanced F Scale with Left-Wing Reversals." *Sociometry,* 1972, *35,* 176–189.

KOMORITA, S. S. "Cooperative Choice in a Prisoner's Dilemma Game." *Journal of Personality and Social Psychology,* 1965, *2,* 741–745.

KORNER, A. "Theoretical Considerations Concerning the Scope and Limitations of Projective Techniques." In B. Murstein (Ed.), *Handbook of Projective Techniques.* New York: Basic Books, 1965.

KORNHAUSER, W. *The Politics of Mass Society.* New York: Free Press, 1959.

KRAMER, G. H. "The Effects of Precinct-Level Canvassing on Voting Behavior." *Public Opinion Quarterly,* 1970, *34,* 560–572.

KRAUT, R. E., AND MC CONAHAY, J. B. "An Experimental Study of the Effects of 'Public Opinion Polling' and Alienation Reduction upon Turnout in Primary Elections." Paper presented at annual meeting of American Political Science Association, Chicago, 1971.

KRAUT, R. E., AND MC CONAHAY, J. B. "An Experimental Study of the Effects of Being Interviewed upon Voting in Subsequent Primary Elections." Unpublished paper, Yale University, 1972.

KRECH, D. "The Chemistry of Learning." *Saturday Review,* 20 January 1968, pp. 48–68.

KROEBER, A. L. *Configurations of Culture Growth.* Berkeley: University of California Press, 1944.

KROEBER, A. L., AND PARSONS, T. "The Concepts of Culture and of Social System." *American Sociological Review,* 1958, *23,* 582–583.

KROEBER, T. "The Coping Functions of the Ego Mechanisms." In R. White (Ed.), *The Study of Lives.* New York: Atherton, 1966.

KUBIE, L. S. *Neurotic Distortion of the Creative Process.* New York: Noonday Press, 1961.

LAMARE, J. W. "University Education in American Government: An Experimental Approach to a Growing Problem." *Experimental Study of Politics,* 1971, *1,* 122–148.

LAMBERT, W. E., AND KLINEBERG, O. *Children's Views of Foreign Peoples: A Cross-National Study.* New York: Appleton-Century, 1967.

LAMPRECHT, F., EICHELMAN, B., THOA, N. B., WILLIAMS, R. B., AND KOPIN, I. J. "Rat Fighting Behavior: Serum Dopamine-B-Hydroxylase and Hypothalamic Tyrosine Hydroxylase." *Science,* 1972, *177,* 1214–1215.

LANDAU, D. *Kissinger: The Uses of Power.* Boston: Houghton Mifflin, 1972.

LANE, R. E. "Political Character and Political Analysis." *Psychiatry,* 1953, *16,* 387–398.

LANE, R. E. "Political Personality and Electoral Choice." *American Political Science Review,* 1955, *49,* 173–190.

LANE, R. E. "Fathers and Sons: Foundations of Political Belief." *American Sociological Review,* 1959a, *24,* 502–511.

LANE, R. E. *Political Life: Why People Get Involved in Politics.* New York: Free Press, 1959b.

LANE, R. E. *The Liberties of Wit: Humanism, Criticism and the Civic Mind.* New Haven: Yale University Press, 1961.

LANE, R. E. *Political Ideology: Why the American Common Man Believes What He Does.* New York: Free Press, 1962.

LANE, R. E. "The Decline of Politics and Ideology in a Knowledgeable Society." *American Sociological Review*, 1966, *31*, 649–662.

LANE, R. E. "Personality, Political: The Study of Political Personality." In D. Sills (Ed.), *International Encyclopedia of the Social Sciences*. New York: Macmillan, 1968.

LANE, R. E. *Political Thinking and Consciousness*. Chicago: Markham, 1969.

LANE, R. E. *Political Man*. New York: Free Press, 1972.

LANE, R. E., AND SEARS, D. O. *Public Opinion*. Englewood Cliffs, N.J.: Prentice-Hall, 1964.

LANGER, W. C. *The Mind of Adolf Hitler: The Secret Wartime Report*. New York: Basic Books, 1972.

LANGER, W. L. "The Next Assignment." *American Historical Review*, 1958, *63*, 283–304.

LANGTON, K. "Peer Group and School and the Political Socialization Process." *American Political Science Review*, 1967, *61*, 751–758.

LANGTON, K. *Political Socialization*. New York: Oxford University Press, 1969.

LANGTON, K., AND JENNINGS, M. "Political Socialization and the High School Civics Curriculum in the United States." *American Political Science Review*, 1968, *62*, 852–867.

LAPONCE, J. A., AND SMOKER, P. (Eds.) *Experimentation and Simulation in Political Science*. Toronto: University of Toronto Press, 1972.

LASKI, H. *Communism*. New York: Holt, 1927.

LASSWELL, H. D. *Psychopathology and Politics*. Chicago: University of Chicago Press, 1930.

LASSWELL, H. D. *World Politics and Personal Insecurity*. New York: McGraw-Hill, 1935. New York: Free Press, 1965.

LASSWELL, H. D. "Agitation." In *Encyclopedia of the Social Sciences*. Vol. 1. New York: Macmillan, 1936a.

LASSWELL, H. D. *Politics: Who Gets What, When, How*. New York: Whittlesey House, 1936b.

LASSWELL, H. D. *Power and Personality*. New York: Viking, 1948.

LASSWELL, H. D. *The Political Writings of Harold D. Lasswell*. New York: Free Press, 1951.

LASSWELL, H. D. "The Selective Effect of Personality on Political Participation." In R. Christie and M. Jahoda (Eds.), *Studies in the Scope and Method of "The Authoritarian Personality."* New York: Free Press, 1954.

LASSWELL, H. D. "The Political Science of Science." *American Political Science Review*, 1956, *50*, 961–979.

LASSWELL, H. D. *Psychopathology and Politics: A New Edition with Afterthoughts by the Author*. New York: Viking, 1960.

LASSWELL, H. D. "A Note on 'Types' of Political Personality: Nuclear, Correlational, Developmental." *Journal of Social Issues*, 1968, *24*, 81–91.

LASSWELL, H. D., AND KAPLAN, A. *Power and Society: A Framework for Political Inquiry*. New Haven: Yale University Press, 1950.

LASSWELL, H. D., AND LERNER, D. (Eds.) *World Revolutionary Elites*. Cambridge: MIT Press, 1965.

LATANE, B., AND DARLEY, J. M. *The Unresponsive Bystander: Why Doesn't He Help?* New York: Appleton-Century, 1970.

LAZARSFELD, P. F., BERELSON, B., AND GAUDET, H. *The People's Choice*. New York: Duell, 1944. New York: Columbia University Press, 1948.

LAZARUS, R. "A Substitutive-Defensive Conception of Apperceptive Fantasy." In J. Kagan and G. Lesser (Eds.), *Contemporary Issues in Thematic Apperceptive Methods*. Springfield, Ill.: Thomas, 1961.

LAZARUS, R. *Personality and Adjustment*. Englewood Cliffs, N.J.: Prentice-Hall, 1963.

LAZARUS, R. "Story Telling and the Measurement of Motivation." *Journal of Consulting Psychology*, 1966, *30*, 483–487.

LEGGETT, J. C. *Class, Race and Labor: Working-Class Consciousness in Detroit.* New York: Oxford University Press, 1968.

LEIGHTON, A. H. *The Governing of Men.* Princeton: Princeton University Press, 1945.

LEITES, N. *On the Game of Politics in France.* Stanford, Calif.: Stanford University Press, 1959.

LERNER, D. *The Passing of Traditional Society.* New York: Free Press, 1958.

LEVENS, H. "Organizational Affiliation and Powerlessness: A Case Study of the Welfare Poor." *Social Problems,* 1968, *16,* 18–32.

LEVENTHAL, H., JACOBS, R., AND KUDIRKA, N. "Authoritarianism, Ideology and Political Candidate Choice." *Journal of Abnormal and Social Psychology,* 1964, *69,* 539–549.

LEVIN, M. "Social Climates and Political Socialization." *Public Opinion Quarterly,* 1961, *25,* 596–606.

LE VINE, R. "Political Socialization and Culture Change." In C. Geertz (Ed.), *Old Societies and New States.* New York: Free Press, 1963.

LEVINSON, D. J. "Projective Questions in the Study of Personality and Ideology." In T. Adorno, E. Frenkel-Brunswik, D. Levinson, and R. N. Sanford (Eds.), *The Authoritarian Personality.* New York: Wiley, 1950.

LEVINSON, D. J. "Authoritarian Personality and Foreign Policy." *Journal of Conflict Resolution,* 1957, *1,* 37–47.

LEVINSON, D. J. "The Relevance of Personality for Political Participation." *Public Opinion Quarterly,* 1958, *22,* 3–10.

LEVINSON, D. J. "Role, Personality, and Social Structure in the Organizational Setting." *Journal of Abnormal and Social Psychology,* 1959, *58,* 170–180.

LEVINSON, D. J. "Conservatism and Radicalism." In D. Sills (Ed.), *International Encyclopedia of the Social Sciences.* New York: Macmillan, 1968.

LEVINSON, D. J., AND HUFFMAN, P. "Traditional Family Ideology and Its Relation to Personality." *Journal of Personality,* 1955, *23,* 251–273.

LEVINSON, D. J., AND SANFORD, N. "A Scale for the Measurement of Anti-Semitism." *The Journal of Psychology,* 1944, *17,* 339–370.

LEVY, D. M. "Anti-Nazis: Criteria of Differentiation." *Psychiatry,* 1948, *11,* 125–167.

LEVY, L. H. *Conceptions of Personality.* New York: Random House, 1970.

LEWIN, K. *Field Theory in Social Science.* New York: Harper, 1951.

LEWIS, F. "What is Alienation? The Career of a Concept." *New Politics,* 1962, *1,* 116–134.

LEWIS, O. *Tepoztlan, Village in Mexico.* New York: Holt, 1960.

LIEBSCHUTZ, S., AND NIEMI, R. "Political Socialization Among Black Children: The Development of Attitudes and the Impact of Curriculum and Teachers." In R. Niemi (Ed.), *New Views of Children and Politics.* San Francisco: Jossey-Bass, forthcoming, 1974.

LIFTON, R. J. *Thought Reform and the Psychology of Totalism: A Study of "Brainwashing" in China.* New York: Norton, 1961.

LIFTON, R. J. *Death in Life. Survivors of Hiroshima.* New York: Random House, 1968.

LIKERT, R. *The Human Organization: Its Management and Value.* New York: McGraw-Hill, 1967.

LINDLEY, D. V., AND MILLER, J. C. P. *Cambridge Elementary Statistical Tables.* Cambridge University Press, 1958.

LINDQUIST, E. F. *Design and Analysis of Experiments in Psychology and Education.* Boston: Houghton Mifflin, 1953.

LINDZEY, G. (Ed.) *Handbook of Social Psychology.* Reading, Mass.: Addison-Wesley, 1954. 2 Vols.

LINDZEY, G. *The Assessment of Human Motives.* New York: Holt, 1958.

LINDZEY, G. *Projective Techniques and Cross-Cultural Research.* New York: Appleton-Century, 1961.

LINDZEY, G., AND ARONSON, E. (Eds.) *The Handbook of Social Psychology*. Reading, Mass.: Addison-Wesley, 1968–1969. 5 Vols. (2nd Ed.).

LINTON, R. *The Cultural Background of Personality*. New York: Appleton-Century, 1945.

LIPPMANN, W. *Public Opinion*. New York: Harcourt, 1922.

LIPSET, S. M. "Some Social Requisites of Democracy." *American Political Science Review*, 1959, *53*, 69–105.

LIPSET, S. M. *Political Man, The Social Bases of Politics*. New York: Doubleday, 1960.

LIPSET, S. M. *The First New Nation: The United States in Historical and Comparative Perspective*. New York: Basic Books, 1963.

LIPSET, S. M. "Three Decades of the Radical Right: Coughlinites, McCarthyites, and Birchers." In D. Bell (Ed.), *The Radical Right*. Garden City, N.Y.: Doubleday, 1964.

LIPSET, S. M., AND RAAB, E. *The Politics of Unreason*. New York: Harper, 1970.

LIPSET, S. M., TROW, M., AND COLEMAN, J. *Union Democracy*. New York: Free Press, 1956.

LIPSITZ, L. "Work Life and Political Attitudes: A Study of Manual Workers." *American Political Science Review*, 1964, *58*, 951–962.

LIPSITZ, L. "Working-Class Authoritarianism: A Reevaluation." *American Sociological Review*, 1965, *30*, 103–109.

LIPSKY, M. "Protest as a Political Resource." *American Political Science Review*, 1968, *62*, 1144–1158.

LITT, E. "Civic Education, Community Norms and Political Indoctrination." *American Sociological Review*, 1963, *28*, 69–75.

LITTMAN, R. A. "Psychology: The Socially Indifferent Science." *American Psychologist*, 1961, *16*, 232–236.

LOEHLIN, J. C. *Computer Models of Personality*. New York: Random House, 1968.

LOEVINGER, J. "The Meaning and Measurement of Ego Development." *American Psychologist*, 1966, *21*, 195–206.

LOEVINGER, J., AND WESSLER, R. *Measuring Ego Development*. Vol. 1. *Construction and Use of a Sentence Completion Test*. San Francisco: Jossey-Bass, 1970.

LORENZ, K. *On Aggression*. New York: Bantam, 1967. Originally published 1963 as Der Sogenannte Bose: Zur Naturgeschichte der Aggression.

LORINSKAS, R. A., HAWKINS, B. W., AND EDWARDS, S. "The Persistence of Ethnic Voting in Rural and Urban Areas: Results from the Controlled Election Method." *Social Science Quarterly*, 1969, *49*, 871–899.

LOVEJOY, A. *The Great Chain of Being*. Cambridge, Mass.: Harvard University Press, 1936.

LOWE, C. M., AND DAMANKOS, F. J. "Psychological and Sociological Dimensions of Anomie in a Psychiatric Population." *Journal of Social Psychology*, 1968, *74*, 65–74.

LOWE, F., AND MC CORMACK, T. "A Study of the Influence of Formal and Informal Leaders in an Election Campaign." *Public Opinion Quarterly*, 1956, *20*, 651–662.

LOWENSTEIN, K. "Ideologies and Their Institutions: The Problem of Their Circulation." *Western Political Quarterly*, 1953a, *6*, 689–706.

LOWENSTEIN, K. (Rapporteur) "Report of the Second International Congress of Political Science, 1952." *International Social Science Bulletin*, 1953b, *5*.

LOWENTHAL, L., AND GUTERMAN, N. *Prophets of Deceit*. New York: Harper, 1949.

LUTTERMAN, K. G., AND MIDDLETON, R. "Authoritarianism, Anomia, and Prejudice." *Social Forces*, 1970, *48*, 485–492.

LYLE, W. H., AND LEVITT, E. E. "Permissiveness, Authoritarianism, and Parental Discipline of Grade School Children." *Journal of Abnormal and Social Psychology*, 1955, *51*, 42–46.

LYND, H. M. "Must Psychology Aid Reaction?" In *Toward Discovery*. New York: Sarah Lawrence College, 1965.

LYND, R. S., AND LYND, H. M. *Middletown: A Study in Contemporary American Culture.* New York: Harcourt, 1929.

LYND, R. S., AND LYND, H. M. *Middletown in Transition.* New York: Harcourt, 1937.

LYNN, D., AND SAWREY, W. "Effects of Father Absence on Norwegian Boys and Girls." *Journal of Abnormal and Social Psychology,* 1959, *19,* 258–262.

LYONS, S. "The Political Socialization of Ghetto Children. *Journal of Politics,* 1970, *32,* 288–304.

MC CALL, G. J., AND SIMMONS, J. L. (Eds.) *Issues in Participant Observation: A Text and Reader.* Reading, Mass.: Addison-Wesley, 1969.

MC CLELLAND, D. "Methods of Measuring Human Motivation." In J. Atkinson (Ed.), *Motives in Fantasy, Action and Society.* Princeton: Van Nostrand, 1958.

MC CLELLAND, D., ATKINSON, J., CLARK, R., AND LOWELL, E. *The Achievement Motive.* New York: Appleton-Century, 1953.

MC CLELLAND, D. *The Achieving Society.* New York: Free Press, 1967.

MC CLOSKY, H. "Conservatism and Personality." *American Political Science Review,* 1958, *52,* 27–45.

MC CLOSKY, H. "Personality and Attitude Correlates of Foreign Policy Orientation." In J. N. Rosenau (Ed.), *Domestic Sources of Foreign Policy.* New York: Free Press, 1967a. Pp. 51–109.

MC CLOSKY, H. "Survey Research in Political Science." In C. Glock (Ed.), *Survey Research in the Social Sciences.* New York: Russell Sage, 1967b. Pp. 63–143.

MC CLOSKY, H., AND DAHLGREN, H. "Primary Group Influence on Party Loyalty." *American Political Science Review,* 1959, *53,* 757–776.

MC CLOSKY, H., AND SCHAAR, J. H. "Psychological Dimensions of Anomy." *American Sociological Review,* 1965, *30,* 14–40.

MACCOBY, E., MATTHEWS, R., AND MORTON, A. "Youth and Political Change." *Public Opinion Quarterly,* 1954, *18,* 23–29.

MACCOBY, M. "Emotional Attitudes and Political Choices." *Politics and Society,* 1972, *2,* 211.

MC CONAUGHY, J. B. "Certain Personality Factors of State Legislators in South Carolina." *American Political Science Review,* 1950, *44,* 897–903.

MC DILL, E. L., AND RIDLEY, J. C. "Status, Anomia, Political Alienation, and Political Participation." *American Journal of Sociology,* 1962, *68,* 205–213.

MC DOUGALL, W. *Introduction to Social Psychology.* (14th Ed.) Boston: Luce, 1921. Originally published 1908.

MC FARLAND, A. S. *Power and Leadership in Pluralist Systems.* Stanford, Calif.: Stanford University Press, 1969.

MC GEE, H. "Measurement of Authoritarianism and Its Relation to Teachers' Classroom Behavior." Unpublished doctoral dissertation. University of California, Berkeley, 1954.

MC GUIGAN, F. J. "The Experimenter: A Neglected Stimulus Object." *Psychological Bulletin,* 1963, *60,* 421–428.

MC GUIRE, W. J. "A Syllogistic Analysis of Cognitive Relationships." In M. J. Rosenberg, C. I. Hovland, W. J. McGuire, R. P. Abelson, and J. W. Brehm (Eds.), *Attitude Organization and Change.* New Haven: Yale University Press, 1960.

MC GUIRE, W. J. "Inducing Resistance to Persuasion." In L. Berkowitz (Ed.), *Advances in Experimental Social Psychology.* Vol. 1. New York: Academic Press, 1964.

MC GUIRE, W. J. "The Nature of Attitudes and Attitude Change." In G. Lindzey and E. Aronson (Eds.), *The Handbook of Social Psychology.* (Rev. Ed.) Vol. 3. Reading, Mass.: Addison-Wesley, 1968.

MC ILLWAIN, C. H. *The High Court of Parliament and Its Supremacy.* New Haven: Yale University Press, 1910.

MAC IVER, R. *Society, A Textbook of Sociology.* New York: Holt, 1937.

MAC IVER, R. *The Web of Government.* New York: Macmillan, 1948.

MAC KINNON, W. J., AND CENTERS, R. "Authoritarianism and Internationalism." *Public Opinion Quarterly,* 1956, *20,* 621–630.

MC PHAIL, C. "Civil Disorder Participation: A Critical Examination of Recent Research." *American Sociological Review,* 1971, *36,* 1058–1073.

MC PHEE, W. N. "Note on a Campaign Simulator." In W. N. McPhee (Ed.), *Formal Theories of Mass Behavior.* New York: Free Press, 1963.

MC PHEE, W. N., AND FERGUSON, J. "Political Immunization." In W. N. McPhee and W. A. Glaser (Eds.), *Public Opinion and Congressional Elections.* New York: Free Press, 1962.

MC PHEE, W. N., FERGUSON, J., AND SMITH, R. B. "A Model for Simulating Voting Systems." In J. M. Dutton and W. H. Starbuck (Eds.), *Computer Simulation of Human Behavior.* New York: Wiley, 1971.

MC PHEE, W. N., AND SMITH, R. B. "A Model for Analyzing Voting Systems." In W. N. McPhee and W. A. Glaser (Eds.), *Public Opinion and Congressional Elections.* New York: Free Press, 1962.

MAC RAE, J., AND SMOKER, P. "A Vietnam Simulation." *Journal of Peace Research,* 1967, *4,* 1–24.

MC WHINNEY, W. H. "Simulating the Communication Network Experiments." *Behavioral Science,* 1962, *9,* 80–84.

MAIER, N. R. F. *Frustration: The Study of Behavior Without a Goal.* New York: McGraw-Hill, 1949.

MALONE, D. "Biography and History." In J. R. Strayer (Ed.), *The Interpretation of History.* Princeton: Princeton University Press, 1943.

MANN, F. C. "Toward an Understanding of the Leadership Role in Formal Organizations." In R. Dubin, G. Homans, and D. Miller (Eds.), *Leadership and Productivity.* San Francisco: Chandler, 1964.

MANN, M. "The Social Cohesion of Liberal Democracy." *American Sociological Review,* 1970, *35,* 423–439.

MANNHEIM, K. *Ideology and Utopia.* Trans. L. Wirth and E. Shils. New York: Harcourt, 1949.

MARCH, J. G., AND SIMON, H. A., with H. Guetzkow. *Organizations.* New York: Wiley, 1958.

MARCUSE, H. *Eros and Civilization.* Boston: Beacon Press 1959. Rev. Ed., 1966.

MARK, V. H., AND ERVIN, F. R. *Violence and the Brain.* New York: Harper, 1970.

MARTIN, W. C., AND BENGTON, V. L. "Alienation and Age: A Context Specific Approach." Unpublished manuscript, 1971.

MARTIN, J. G., AND WESTIE, F. R. "The Tolerant Personality." *American Sociological Review,* 1959, *24,* 521–528.

MARVICK, D., AND BAYES, J. "Domains and Universes: Problems in Concerted Use of Multiple Data Files for Social Science Inquiries." In M. Dogan and S. Rokkan (Eds.), *Quantitative Ecological Analysis in the Social Sciences.* Cambridge: MIT Press, 1969.

MARX, K. *Early Writings.* Trans. T. B. Bottomore. New York: McGraw-Hill, 1964. Originally published 1844.

MARX, K. "Wage Labor and Capital." In K. Marx and F. Engels, *Selected Works in Two Volumes.* Vol. 1. Moscow, Foreign Languages Publishing House, 1849. See also R. C. Tucker (Ed.), *The Marx-Engels Reader.* New York: Norton, 1972.

MARX, K., AND ENGELS, F. *The Manifesto of the Communist Party.* New York: International Publishers, 1968. Originally published 1848.

MASLOW, A. H. "The Dynamics of Psychological Security-Insecurity." *Character and Personality,* 1941–1942, *10,* 331–344.

MASLOW, A. H. "Authoritarian Character Structure." *Journal of Social Psychology,* 1943a, *18,* 401–411.

MASLOW, A. H. "Dynamics of Personality Organization: II." *Psychological Review,* November 1943b, *50,* 370–396.

MASLOW, A. H. "A Theory of Human Motivation." *Psychological Review,* 1943c, *50,* 370–396.

MASLOW, A. H. *Motivation and Personality.* New York: Harper, 1954.

MASLOW, A. H. "Power Relationships and Patterns of Personal Development." In A. Kornhauser (Ed.), *Problems of Power in American Democracy.* Detroit: Wayne State University Press, 1957.

MATTHEWS, D., AND PROTHRO, J. *Negroes and the New Southern Politics.* New York: Harcourt, 1966.

MATZA, D. "Subterranean Traditions of Youth." *Annals of the American Academy of Political and Social Science,* 1961, *338,* 102–118.

MAY, H. F. *Protestant Churches and Industrial America.* New York: Harper, 1949.

MAY, M. A. *A Social Psychology of War and Peace.* New Haven: Yale University Press, 1943.

MAY, R. *Power and Innocence: A Search for the Sources of Violence.* New York: Norton, 1972.

MAZLISH, B. (Ed.) *Psychoanalysis and History.* Englewood Cliffs, N.J.: Prentice-Hall, 1963.

MAZLISH, B. *In Search of Nixon: A Psychohistorical Inquiry.* New York: Basic Books, 1972.

MEAD, M. *Soviet Attitudes Toward Authority.* New York: McGraw-Hill, 1951.

MEIER, D. L., AND BELL, W. "Anomia and Differential Access to the Achievement of Life Goals." *American Sociological Review,* 1959, *24,* 189–202.

MERELMAN, R. "The Development of Political Ideology: A Framework for the Analysis of Political Socialization." *American Political Science Review,* 1969, *63,* 750–767.

MERELMAN, R. "The Development of Policy Thinking in Adolescence." *American Political Science Review,* 1971a, *65,* 1033–1047.

MERELMAN, R. *Political Socialization and Educational Climates.* New York: Holt, 1971b.

MERRIAM, C. E. *New Aspects of Politics.* Chicago: University of Chicago Press, 1925. (Revised 1931; reprinted revision, with a foreword by Barry D. Karl, published 1970.)

MERRIAM, C. E. *American Political Ideas, 1865–1917.* New York: Macmillan, 1929.

MERRIAM, C. E. *The Making of Citizens: A Comparative Study of Methods of Civic Training.* Chicago: University of Chicago Press, 1931.

MERRIAM, C. E. *Political Power.* New York: Collier, 1964. Originally published 1934.

MERTON, R. K. *Social Theory and Social Structure.* (Rev. Ed.) New York: Free Press, 1957. (Enlarged edition 1968.)

MICHEL, J. B., AND DILLEHAY, R. C. "Reference Behavior Theory and the Elected Representative." *Western Political Quarterly,* 1969, *22,* 759–773.

MICHELS, R. *Political Parties.* New York: Free Press, 1915. Reprinting, 1949.

MIDDLETON, R. "Alienation, Race and Education." *American Sociological Review,* 1963, *28,* 973–977.

MIDDLETON, R., AND PUTNEY, S. "Political Expression of Adolescent Rebellion." *American Journal of Sociology,* 1963, *68,* 527–535.

MIDLARSKY, M., AND TANTER, R. "Toward a Theory of Political Instability in Latin America." *Journal of Peace Research,* 1967, *3,* 209–227.

MILBRATH, L. W. *Political Participation: How and Why Do People Get Involved in Politics?* Chicago: Rand McNally, 1965.

MILBRATH, L. W., AND KLEIN, W. W. "Personality Correlates of Political Participation." *Acta Sociologica,* 1962, *6,* 53–66.

MILGRAM, S. "Behavioral Study of Obedience." *Journal of Abnormal and Social Psychology,* 1963, *67,* 371–378. Reprinted in W. G. Bennis and others (Eds.), *Interpersonal Dynamics: Essays and Readings in Human Interaction.* Homewood, Ill.: Dorsey Press, 1964.

MILGRAM, S. "Some Conditions of Obedience and Disobedience to Authority." *Human Relations,* 1965, *18,* 57–76.

MILLER, C. R., AND BUTLER, E. W. "Anomia and Eunomia: A Methodological Evaluation of Srole's Anomia Scale." *American Sociological Review,* 1966, *31,* 400–406.

MILLER, D. R., AND SWANSON, G. E. *The Changing American Parent.* New York: Wiley, 1958.

MILLER, D. R., AND SWANSON, G. E. *Inner Conflict and Defense.* New York: Holt, 1960.

MILLER, J. G. "Living Systems: The Organization." *Behavioral Science,* 1972, *17,* 1–182.

MILLER, S. M., AND RIESSMAN, F. "Working Class Authoritarianism: A Critique of Lipset." *British Journal of Sociology,* 1961, *12,* 263–276.

MILLER, W. "One Party Politics and the Voter." *American Political Science Review,* 1956, *50,* 707–725.

MILLETT, K. *Sexual Politics.* Garden City, N.Y.: Doubleday, 1970.

MISCHEL, W. *Personality and Assessment.* New York: Wiley, 1968.

MISIAK, H., AND SEXTON, V. *History of Psychology.* New York: Grune and Stratton, 1966.

MITRANY, D. *A Working Peace System.* Chicago: Quadrangle Books, 1966.

MIZRUCHI, E. H. "Social Structure and Anomia in a Small City." *American Sociological Review,* 1960, *25,* 645–654.

MIZRUCHI, E. H. *Success and Opportunity: A Study of Anomie.* New York: Free Press, 1964.

MODIGLIANI, A. "Hawks and Doves, Isolationism and Political Distrust: An Analysis of Public Opinion on Military Policy." *American Political Science Review,* 1972, *66,* 960–978.

MONYPENNY, W. F., AND BUCKLE, G. E. *The Life of Benjamin Disraeli.* New York: Macmillan, 1913–1920. 6 Vols.

MOORE, C. G. "Simulation of Organizational Decision Making: A Survey." In W. D. Coplin (Ed.), *Simulation in the Study of Politics.* Chicago: Markham, 1968.

MORGAN, J. "Attitudes of Students Toward the Japanese." *Journal of Social Psychology,* 1945, *21,* 219–222.

MORGAN, J., AND MORTON, J. "The Distortion of Syllogistic Reasoning Produced by Personal Conviction." *Journal of Social Psychology,* 1944, *20,* 39–59.

MORGAN, J., AND MORTON, J. "Distorted Reasoning as an Index of Public Opinion." *School and Society,* 1945, *57,* 333–335.

MORLEY, J. *The Life of William Ewart Gladstone.* New York: Macmillan, 1903. 3 Vols.

MORROW, C. "Aggression Against Whom?" Unpublished doctoral dissertation, Yale University, 1972.

MOYER, K. E. *The Physiology of Hostility.* Chicago: Markham, 1971.

MUELLER, J. "Presidential Popularity from Truman to Johnson." *American Political Science Review,* 1970, *64,* 18–34.

MUELLER, J. "Trends in Popular Support for the Wars in Korea and Vietnam." *American Political Science Review,* 1971, *65,* 358–375.

MUMFORD, L. "The Task of Modern Biography." *English Journal,* 1934, *23,* 1–9.

MUNNION, C. "If Idi Amin of Uganda Is a Madman, He's a Ruthless and Cunning One." *New York Times Magazine,* 12 November 1972.

MURCHISON, C. (Ed.) *A Handbook of Social Psychology.* Worcester, Mass.: Clark University Press, 1935.

MURPHY, G., AND LIKERT, R. *Public Opinion and the Individual.* New York: Harper, 1938.

MURPHY, G., MURPHY, L. B., AND NEWCOMB, T. M. *Experimental Social Psychology.* (Rev. Ed.) New York: Harper, 1937.

MURRAY, H. A. *Explorations in Personality.* New York: Oxford University Press, 1938.

MURRAY, H. A. "In Nomine Diaboli." *New England Quarterly,* 1941, *24,* 435–452.

MURRAY, H. A. *Thematic Apperception Test Manual.* Cambridge: Harvard University Press, 1943.

MURRAY, H. A. "Personality: Components of an Evolving Personological System." In D. Sills (Ed.), *International Encyclopedia of the Social Sciences.* New York: Macmillan, 1968.

MURRAY, H. A., AND KLUCKHOHN, C. "Outline of a Conception of Personality." In C. Kluckhohn and H. A. Murray (Eds.), *Personality in Nature, Society and Culture.* New York: Knopf, 1949.

MURSTEIN, B. "The Role of the Stimulus in the Manifestation of Fantasy." In J. Kagan and G. Lesser (Eds.), *Contemporary Issues in Thematic Apperceptive Methods.* Springfield, Ill.: Thomas, 1961.

MURSTEIN, B. *Theory and Research in Projective Techniques.* New York: Wiley, 1963.

MURSTEIN, B. *Handbook of Projective Techniques.* New York: Basic Books, 1965.

MURSTEIN, B., AND PRYER, R. "The Concept of Projection: Review." *Psychological Bulletin,* 1959, *56,* 353–374.

MUSSEN, P., AND NAYLOR, H. "The Relationship Between Overt and Fantasy Aggression." *Journal of Abnormal and Social Psychology,* 1954, *49,* 235–240.

MUSSEN, P., AND WYSZYNSKI, A. "Personality and Political Participation." *Human Relations,* 1952, *5,* 65–82.

National Opinion Research Center. *Opinion News,* August 1948.

NAYLOR, T. H. (Ed.) *The Design of Computer Simulation Experiments.* Durham, N.C.: Duke University Press, 1969.

NAYLOR, T. H. (Ed.) *Computer Simulation Experiments with Models of Economic Systems.* New York: Wiley, 1971.

NAYLOR, T. H., BALINTFY, J. L., BURDICK, D. S., AND CHU, K. *Computer Simulation Techniques.* New York: Wiley, 1966.

NEAL, A. G., AND RETTIG, S. "Dimensions of Alienation Among Manual and Non-manual Workers." *American Sociological Review,* 1963, *28,* 599–608.

NEAL, A. G., AND RETTIG, S. "On the Multidimensionality of Alienation." *American Sociological Review,* 1967, *32,* 54–64.

NEAL, A. G., AND SEEMAN, M. "Organizations and Powerlessness: A Test of the Mediation Hypothesis." *American Sociological Review,* 1964, *29,* 216–226.

NELSON, J. I. "Anomie: Comparisons Between the Old and New Middle Class." *American Journal of Sociology,* 1968, *74,* 184–192.

NETTLER, G. "A Measure of Alienation." *American Sociological Review,* 1957, *22,* 670–677.

NETTLER, G. "A Further Comment on 'Anomy.'" *American Sociological Review,* 1965, *30,* 762–763.

NETTLER, G., AND HUFFMAN, J. "Political Opinion and Personal Security." *Sociometry,* 1957, *20,* 51–66.

NEURINGER, C. "The Relationship Between Authoritarianism, Rigidity and Anxiety." *Journal of General Psychology,* 1964, *71,* 169–175.

NEUSTADT, R. E. *Presidential Power: The Politics of Leadership.* New York: Wiley, 1960.

NEWCOMB, T. *Personality and Social Change.* New York: Holt, 1943.

NEWCOMB, T. M. "Some Patterned Consequences of Membership in a College Community." In T. M. Newcomb and E. L. Hartley (Eds.), *Readings in Social Psychology*. New York: Holt, 1947.

NEWCOMB, T., KOENIG, K., FLACKS, R., AND WARWICK, D. *Persistence and Change*. New York: Wiley, 1967.

NEWELL, A. *Human Problem Solving*. Englewood Cliffs, N.J.: Prentice-Hall, 1972.

NEWELL, A., SHAW, J. C., AND SIMON, H. A. "Elements of a Theory of Human Problem Solving." *Psychological Review*, 1958, *65*, 151–166.

NEWELL, A., AND SIMON, H. A. "The Logic Theory Machine: A Complex Information Processing System." *IRE Transactions on Information Theory*, 1956, It-2, 61–79.

NEWELL, A., AND SIMON, H. A. *Human Problem Solving: A New Approach to the Psychology of Human Problem Solving Based on Detailed Analyses of Human Behavior and Basic Studies of the Information Processing Systems*. Englewood Cliffs, N.J.: Prentice-Hall, 1972.

NEWELL, A., TONGE, F. M., FEIGENBAUM, E. A., GREEN, B. F., KELLY, H. A., AND MEALY, G. *Information Processing Language V Manual*. (2nd Ed.) Englewood Cliffs N.J.: Prentice-Hall, 1964.

NICOLSON, H. *The Development of English Biography*. London: Hogarth, 1927.

NIE, N., POWELL, G., JR., AND PREWITT, K. "Social Structure and Political Participation: Developmental Relationships, I." *American Political Science Review*, 1969a, *63*, 361–378.

NIE, N., POWELL, G., JR., AND PREWITT, K. "Social Structure and Political Participation: Developmental Relationships, II." *American Political Science Review*, 1969b, *63*, 808–832.

NIEMI, R. "Review of R. Hess and J. Torney, *The Development of Political Attitudes in Children*." *Contemporary Psychology*, 1969, *14*, 497–498.

NIEMI, R. "Collecting Information About the Family: A Problem in Survey Methodology." In J. Dennis (Ed.), *Socialization to Politics: A Reader*. New York: Wiley, 1973.

NISKANEN, W. *Bureaucracy and Representative Government*. Chicago: Aldine-Atherton, 1971.

NIYEKAWA, A. M. "Factors Associated with Authoritarianism in Japan." Unpublished doctoral dissertation, New York University, 1960.

NOELLE, E., AND NEUMANN, E. *The Germans: Public Opinion Polls 1947–1966*. Allensbach and Bonn: Verlag für Demoskopie, 1967.

NOELLE-NEUMANN, E. "Wanted: Rules for Wording Structured Questionnaires." *Public Opinion Quarterly*, 1970, *34*, 191–201.

NOGEE, P., AND LEVIN, M. "Some Determinants of Political Attitudes Among College Voters." *Public Opinion Quarterly*, 1958, *22*, 449–463.

NORMAN, W. "Toward an Adequate Taxonomy of Personality Attributes: Replicated Factor Structures in Peer Nomination Personality Ratings." *Journal of Abnormal and Social Psychology*, 1963, *66*, 574–583.

NORTH, R. C., BRODY, R. A., AND HOLSTI, O. R. "Some Empirical Data on the Conflict Spiral." *Peace Research Society (International) Papers*, 1964, *1*, 1–14.

NOVE, A. *Economic Rationality and Soviet Politics, or Was Stalin Really Necessary?* New York: Praeger, 1964.

OCHS, S. *Elements of Neurophysiology*. New York: Wiley, 1965.

OFSHE, R., AND OFSHE, S. L. "Choice Behavior in Coalition Games." *Behavioral Science*, 1970a, *15*, 337–349.

OFSHE, R., AND OFSHE, S. L. *Utility and Choice in Social Interaction*. Englewood Cliffs, N.J.: Prentice-Hall, 1970b.

OGBURN, W. F. *Social Change with Respect to Culture and Original Nature.* New York: Huebsch, 1922.

OLDS, J. "Pleasure Centers of the Brain." *Scientific American,* October 1956, *195,* 106–116.

OLDS, J. "Self-Stimulation of the Brain." *Science,* 1958, *127,* 315–324.

OLDS, M. E., AND OLDS, J. "Approach-Escape Interactions in Rat Brain." *American Journal of Physiology,* 1962, *203,* 803–810.

OLSEN, M. E. "Alienation and Political Opinions." *Public Opinion Quarterly,* 1965, *29,* 200–212.

OLSEN, M. E. "Perceived Legitimacy of Social Protest Actions." *Social Problems,* 1968, *15,* 297–310.

OLSEN, M. E. "Two Categories of Political Alienation." *Social Forces,* 1969, *47,* 288–299.

O'NEIL, W. M., AND LEVINSON, D. "A Factorial Exploration of Authoritarianism and Some of Its Ideological Concomitants." *Journal of Personality,* 1954, *22,* 449–463.

OPPENHEIM, A. N. *Questionnaire Design and Attitude Measurement.* New York: Basic Books, 1966.

OPPENHEIMER, F. *The State.* Indianapolis: Bobbs-Merrill, 1914.

ORBELL, J. M., DAWES, R. M., AND COLLINS, N. J. "Grass Roots Enthusiasm and the Primary Vote." *Western Political Quarterly,* 1972, *25,* 249–259.

ORNE, M. T. "On the Social Psychology of the Psychological Experiment with Particular Reference to Demand Characteristics and Their Implications." *American Psychologist,* 1962, *17,* 776–783.

ORUM, A. (Ed.) *The Seeds of Politics: Youth and Politics in America.* Englewood Cliffs, N.J.: Prentice-Hall, 1972.

OSGOOD, C. E. *An Alternative to War or Surrender.* Urbana: University of Illinois Press, 1962.

OSGOOD, C. E. "Calculated De-escalation as a Strategy." In D. G. Pruitt and R. C. Snyder (Eds.), *Theory and Research on the Causes of War.* Englewood Cliffs, N.J.: Prentice-Hall, 1969.

OSGOOD, C. E., SUCI, G. J., AND TANNENBAUM, P. H. *The Measurement of Meaning.* Urbana: University of Illinois Press, 1957.

OSGOOD, R. E. *Ideals and Self-Interest in America's Foreign Relations.* Chicago: University of Chicago Press, 1953.

OSGOOD, R. E. "A Critique of Clinical Psychological Approaches to the Explanation of International Conflict." *Social Problems,* 1955, *2,* 176–180.

OSTROGORSKI, M. *Democracy and the Organization of Political Parties.* New York: Macmillan, 1902.

PADIOLEAU, J.-G. "Note sur les simulations en Sociologie Politique." *Revue Française de Sociologie,* 1969, *10,* 201–210.

PAIGE, G. D. *The Korean Decision.* New York: Free Press, 1968.

PAMMETT, J. "The Development of Political Orientations in Canadian School Children." *Canadian Journal of Political Science,* 1971, *4,* 132–141.

PARROTT, G., AND BROWN, L. "Political Bias in the Rokeach Dogmatism Scale." *Psychological Reports,* 1972, *30,* 805–806.

PARRY, H., AND CROSSLEY, H. "Validity of Responses to Survey Questions." *Public Opinion Quarterly,* 1950, *14,* 61–80.

PARSONS, T. *The Social System.* New York: Free Press, 1950.

PARSONS, T. *Structure and Process in Modern Societies.* New York: Free Press, 1960.

PARSONS, T., AND SHILS, E. A. (Eds.) *Toward a General Theory of Action.* New York: Harper, 1951.

PASSINI, F., AND NORMAN, W. "A Universal Conception of Personality Structure?" *Journal of Personality and Social Psychology,* 1966, *4,* 44–49.

PATCHEN, M. *The American Public's View of U.S. Policy Toward China.* New York: Council on Foreign Relations, 1964.

PATRICK, J. "The Impact of an Experimental Course 'American Political Behavior' on the Knowledge, Skills and Attitudes of Secondary School Students." *Social Education,* 1972, *36,* 168–179.

PAVLOV, I. P. *Conditioned Reflexes.* New York: Dover, 1960. Originally published 1927.

PAYNE, J. C. *Incentive Theory and Political Process: Motivation and Leadership in the Dominican Republic.* Lexington, Mass.: Heath, 1972.

PAYNE, J. L., AND WOSHINSKY, O. H. "Incentives for Political Participation." *World Politics,* 1972, *24,* 518–546.

PAYNE, R. "The Effect of Preshock on Pain-Elicited Aggression." Paper presented at meeting of Western Psychological Association, San Diego, March 1968.

PEABODY, D. "Attitude Content and Agreement Set in Scales of Authoritarianism, Dogmatism, Anti-Semitism, and Economic Conservatism." *Journal of Abnormal and Social Psychology,* 1961, *63,* 1–12.

PEAK, H. *Observations on the Characteristics and Distribution of German Nazis.* Washington, D.C.: American Psychological Association, 1945.

PEAK, H. "Problems of Objective Observation." In L. Festinger and D. Katz (Eds.), *Research Methods in the Behavioral Sciences.* New York: Dryden, 1953.

PEAR, T. H. (Ed.) *Psychological Factors of Peace and War.* London: Hutchinson, 1950.

PEARLIN, L. I. "Alienation from Work: A Study of Nursing Personnel." *American Sociological Review,* 1962, *27,* 314–326.

PELZ, D. C. "Leadership Within a Hierarchical Organization." *Journal of Social Issues,* 1951. *7,* 49–55.

PERRY, S. E. "Notes on the Role of the National: A Social-Psychological Concept for the Study of International Relations." *Journal of Conflict Resolution,* 1957, *1,* 346–363.

PETTEE, G. S. *The Process of Revolution.* New York: Harper, 1938.

PETTIGREW, T. "Personality and Sociocultural Factors in Intergroup Attitudes: A Cross-National Comparison." *Journal of Conflict Resolution,* 1958, *2,* 29–42.

PETTIGREW, T. F. "Social Evaluation Theory: Convergences and Applications." In D. Levine (Ed.), *Nebraska Symposium on Motivation.* Lincoln: University of Nebraska Press, 1967.

PIAGET, J. *The Moral Judgment of the Child.* New York: Free Press, 1965. Originally published 1932.

PIAGET, J., AND WEIL, A. "The Development in Children of the Idea of the Homeland and of a Relation with Other Countries." *International Social Science Bulletin,* 1951, *3,* 561–578.

PIERCE, E. L. *Memoir and Letters of Charles Sumner.* London: Sampson Low, 1878–1893. 4 Vols.

PILIAVIN, I., RODIN, J., AND PILIAVIN, J. A. "Good Samaritanism: An Underground Phenomenon?" *Journal of Personality and Social Psychology,* 1969, *13,* 289–299.

PILISUK, M., AND RAPOPORT, A. "A Non-Zero Sum Game Model of Some Disarmament Problems." *Peace Research Society (International) Papers,* 1964, *1,* 57–58.

PILISUK, M., AND SKOLNICK, P. "Inducing Trust: A Test of the Osgood Proposal." *Journal of Personality and Social Psychology,* 1968, *8,* 121–133.

PIN, E. "Hypotheses Relative à la Desaffection Religieuse dans les Classes Inferieures." *Social Compass,* 1962, *9,* 515–537.

PINE, F., AND LEVINSON, D. J. "Two Patterns of Ideology, Role Concepion, and Personality Among Mental Hospital Aides." In M. Greenblatt, D. J. Levinson, and R. H. Williams (Eds.), *The Patient and the Mental Hospital.* New York: Free Press, 1957.

PINNER, F. "Parental Overprotection and Political Distrust." *Annals of the American Academy of Political and Social Science,* 1965, *361,* 58–70.

POOL, I. DE S., ABELSON, R. P., AND POPKIN, S. *Candidates, Issues and Strategies: A Computer Simulation of the 1960 and 1964 Presidential Elections.* (2nd Ed.) Cambridge: MIT Press, 1965.

POPPER, K. R. *The Logic of Scientific Discovery.* New York: Basic Books, 1959.

POWELL, C. A. "Simulation: The Anatomy of a Fad. A Critique and a Suggestion with Respect to Its Use in the Study of International Conflict." *Acta Politica,* 1969, *4,* 299–330.

POWELL, E. H. *The Design of Discord: Studies of Anomie.* New York: Oxford University Press, 1970.

President's Commission on the Assassination of President John F. Kennedy. *Report.* Washington, D.C.: U.S. Government Printing Office, 1964.

PREWITT, K., EULAU, H., AND ZISK, B. "Political Socialization and Political Roles." *Public Opinion Quarterly,* 1966–1967, *30,* 569–582.

PREWITT, K., AND OKELLO-OCULI, J. "Political Socialization and Political Education in the New Nations." In R. Sigel (Ed.), *Learning About Politics.* New York: Random House, 1970.

PRICE, D. E., AND LUPFER, M. "Volunteers for Gore: The Impact of a Precinct-Level Canvass in Three Tennessee Cities." *Journal of Politics,* 1973.

PROCTOR, C. H. "Comment on Carr's Srole Items." *American Sociological Review,* 1971, *36,* 1107–1108.

PROPPER, M. "Direct and Projective Assessment of Alienation Among Affluent Adolescent Males." *Journal of Projective Techniques and Personality Assessment,* 1970, *34,* 41–44.

PROSHANSKY, H. "A Projective Method for the Study of Attitudes." *Journal of Abnormal and Social Psychology,* 1943, *38,* 383–395.

PROTHRO, E. T., AND MELIKIAN, L. "The California Public Opinion Scale in an Authoritarian Culture." *Public Opinion Quarterly,* 1953, *17,* 353–362.

PRUITT, D. G. "Definition of the Situation as a Determinant of International Action." In H. C. Kelman (Ed.), *International Behavior: A Social-Psychological Analysis.* New York: Holt, 1965.

PRUITT, D. G., AND GAHAGAN, J. P. "Campus Crisis: The Search for Power." Unpublished manuscript, State University of New York at Buffalo, 1972.

PRUITT, D. G., AND SNYDER, R. C. (Eds.) *Theory and Research on the Causes of War.* Englewood Cliffs, N.J.: Prentice-Hall, 1969.

PUTNAM, R. "Studying Elite Culture: The Case of 'Ideology.'" *American Political Science Review,* 1971, *65,* 651–681.

PYE, L. W. "Personal Identity and Political Ideology." In D. Marvick (Ed.), *Political Decision Makers.* New York: Free Press, 1961.

PYE, L. W. *Politics, Personality and Nation Building.* New Haven: Yale University Press, 1962.

PYE, L. W., AND VERBA, S. (Eds.) *Political Culture and Political Development.* Princeton: Princeton University Press, 1965.

QUAY, W. B., BENNETT, E. L., ROSENZWEIG, M. R., AND KRECH, D. "Effects of Isolation and Environmental Complexity on Brain and Pineal Organ." *Physiology and Behavior,* 1969, *4,* 489–494.

RABIN, A. *Projective Techniques in Personality Assessment.* New York: Springer, 1968.

RAINIO, K. "Social Interaction as a Stochastic Learning Process." *European Journal of Sociology,* 1965, *6,* 68–88.

RAINIO, K. "A Study on Socio-metric Group Structure: An Application of a Stochastic

Theory of Social Interaction." In J. Berger, M. Zelditch, Jr., and B. Anderson (Eds.), *Sociological Theories in Progress*. Boston: Houghton Mifflin, 1966.

RANSFORD, H. E. "Isolation, Powerlessness and Violence: A Study of Attitudes and Participation in the Watts Riot." *American Journal of Sociology,* 1968, *73,* 581–591.

RAPOPORT, A. "Conflict Resolution in the Light of Game Theory and Beyond." In P. Swingle (Ed.), *The Structure of Conflict.* New York: Academic Press, 1970.

RAPOPORT, A., AND CHAMMAH, A. M. *Prisoner's Dilemma: A Study in Conflict and Cooperation.* Ann Arbor: University of Michigan Press, 1965.

RAPOPORT, D. "Principles Underlying Projective Techniques." *Character and Personality,* 1942, *10,* 213–219.

RASER, J. R. "Personal Characteristics of Political Decision-Makers: A Literature Review." *Peace Research Society (International) Papers,* 1966, *5,* 161–181.

RASER, J. R. *Simulation and Society: An Exploration of Scientific Gaming.* Boston: Allyn and Bacon, 1969.

RASER, J. R., CAMPBELL, D. T., AND CHADWICK, R. W. "Gaming and Simulation for Developing Theory Relevant to International Relations." *General Systems,* 1970, *15,* 183–204.

RASER, J. R., AND CROW, W. J. "A Simulation Study of Deterrence Strategies." In D. G. Pruitt and R. C. Snyder (Eds.), *Theory and Research on the Causes of War.* Englewood Cliffs, N.J.: Prentice-Hall, 1969.

RAY, J. J. "Militarism, Authoritarianism, Neuroticism and Antisocial Behavior." *Journal of Conflict Resolution,* 1972, *16,* 319–340.

REBACK, G. L. "The Effects of Precinct-Level Voter Contact Activities on Voting Behavior." *Experimental Study of Politics,* 1971, *1,* 65–98.

REED, J., JR. *The Enduring South.* Lexington, Mass.: Heath, 1972.

REICH, C. *The Greening of America.* New York: Random House, 1970.

REICH, W. *The Mass Psychology of Fascism.* (3rd Ed.) New York: Orgone Press, 1946. Originally published 1933.

RENSHON, S. *The Psychological Origins of Political Efficacy: The Need for Personal Control.* Washington, D.C.: American Political Science Association, 1972.

RICHARDS, I. A. *Practical Criticism.* New York: Harcourt, 1954.

RICHARDSON, L. F. *Arms and Insecurity.* Chicago: Quadrangle Books, 1960.

RIESMAN, D. *The Lonely Crowd.* New Haven: Yale University Press, 1950.

RIESMAN, D., AND GLAZER, N. *Faces in the Crowd: Individual Studies in Character and Politics.* New Haven: Yale University Press, 1952.

RIESSMAN, F., AND MILLER, S. "Social Class and Projective Tests." *Journal of Projective Techniques,* 1958, *22,* 432–439.

RING, K. "Experimental Social Psychology: Some Sober Questions About Some Frivolous Values." *Journal of Experimental Social Psychology,* 1967, *3,* 113–123.

ROAZEN, P. *Freud: Political and Social Thought.* New York: Knopf, 1968.

ROBERTS, A. H., AND JESSOR, R. "Authoritarianism, Punitiveness and Perceived Social Status." *Journal of Abnormal and Social Psychology,* 1958, *56,* 311–314.

ROBERTS, A. H., AND ROKEACH, M. "Anomie, Authoritarianism and Prejudice: A Replication." *American Journal of Sociology,* 1956, *61,* 355–358.

ROBINSON, C. J. "Malcolm Little as a Charismatic Leader." Paper presented at meeting of American Political Science Association, Los Angeles, September 1970.

ROBINSON, J. A., ANDERSON, L., HERMANN, M., AND SNYDER, R. "Teaching with Internation Simulation and Case Studies." *American Political Science Review,* 1966, *60,* 53–65.

ROBINSON, J. A., HERMANN, C. F., AND HERMANN, M. G. "Search Under Crisis in Political

Gaming and Simulation." In D. G. Pruitt and R. C. Snyder (Eds.), *Theory and Research on the Causes of War.* Englewood Cliffs, N.J.: Prentice-Hall, 1969.

ROBINSON, J. P., AND HEFNER, R. "Multidimensional Differences in Public and Academic Perceptions of Nations." *Journal of Personality and Social Psychology,* 1967, 7, 251–259.

ROBINSON, J. P. AND HEFNER, R. "Perceptual Maps of the World." *Public Opinion Quarterly,* 1968, 32, 273–280.

ROBINSON, J. P., RUSK, J., AND HEAD, K. *Measures of Political Attitudes,* Ann Arbor, Mich.: Survey Research Center, 1968.

ROBINSON, J. P., AND SHAVER, P. *Measures of Social Psychological Attitudes.* Ann Arbor, Mich.: Survey Research Center, 1969.

ROBINSON, W. "The Motivational Structure of Political Participation." *American Sociological Review,* 1952, 17, 151–156.

ROETHLISBERGER, F. J., AND DICKSON, W. J. *Management and the Worker.* Cambridge: Harvard University Press, 1939.

ROGERS, E. *Diffusion of Innovations.* New York: Free Press, 1962.

ROGERS, H., JR., AND TAYLOR, G. "The Policeman as an Agent of Regime Legitimation." *Midwest Journal of Political Science,* 1971, 15, 72–86.

ROGHMANN, K., AND SODEUR, W. "The Impact of Military Service on Authoritarian Attitudes: Evidence from West Germany." *American Journal of Sociology,* 1972, 78, 418–433.

ROGOW, A. A. *James Forrestal: A Study of Personality, Politics and Policy.* New York: Macmillan, 1963.

ROGOW, A. A. "Review of V. Wolfenstein, *The Revolutionary Personality.*" *American Political Science Review,* 1968, 62, 604–666.

ROGOW, A. A., AND LASSWELL, H. D. *Power, Corruption and Rectitude.* Englewood Cliffs, N.J.: Prentice-Hall, 1963.

ROHTER, I. S. "The Genesis of Political Radicalism: The Case of the Radical Right." In S. Sigel (Ed.), *Learning About Politics: A Reader in Political Socialization.* New York: Random House, 1970.

ROIG, C., AND BILLON-GRAND, F. *La Socialisation Politique des Enfants: Contribution à l'étude de la Formation des Attitudes Politiques en France.* Paris: Librairie Armand Colin, 1968.

ROKEACH, M. "The Nature and Meaning of Dogmatism." *Psychological Review,* 1954, 61, 194–204.

ROKEACH, M. "Political and Religious Dogmatism: An Alternative to the Authoritarian Personality." *Psychological Monographs,* 1956, 70, 1–43.

ROKEACH, M. *The Open and Closed Mind: Investigations into the Nature of Belief Systems and Personality Systems.* New York: Basic Books, 1960.

ROKEACH, M. *Beliefs, Attitudes, and Values: A Theory of Organization and Change.* San Francisco: Jossey-Bass, 1968.

ROPER, E. *You and Your Leaders: Their Actions and Your Reactions, 1936–1956.* New York: Morrow, 1957.

RORER, L. C. "The Great Response-Style Myth." *Psychological Bulletin,* 1965, 63, 129–156.

ROSENAU, J. N. *National Leadership and Foreign Policy: A Case Study in the Mobilization of Public Support.* Princeton: Princeton University Press, 1963.

ROSENAU, J. N. "Pre-Theories and Theories of Foreign Policy." In R. B. Farrell (Ed.), *Approaches to Comparative and International Politics.* Evanston, Ill:. Northwestern University Press, 1966.

ROSENAU, J. N. (Ed.) *Domestic Sources of Foreign Policy.* New York: Free Press, 1967.

ROSENBERG, M. "Some Determinants of Political Apathy." *Public Opinion Quarterly,* 1954, 18, 349–366.

ROSENBERG, M. "Misanthropy and Political Ideology." *American Sociological Review,* 1956, *21,* 690–695.

ROSENBERG, M. "Misanthropy and Attitudes Toward International Affairs." *Journal of Conflict Resolution,* 1957, *1,* 340–345.

ROSENBERG, M. *The Logic of Survey Analysis.* New York: Basic Books, 1968.

ROSENBERG, M. J. "An Analysis of Affective-Cognitive Consistency." In M. J. Rosenberg, C. I. Hovland, W. J. McGuire, R. P. Abelson, and J. W. Brehm (Eds.), *Attitude Organization and Change: An Analysis of Consistency Among Attitude Components.* New Haven: Yale University Press, 1960.

ROSENBERG, M. J. "Images in Relation to the Policy Process: American Public Opinion on Cold-War Issues." In H. C. Kelman (Ed.), *International Behavior: A Social-Psychological Analysis.* New York: Holt, 1965a.

ROSENBERG, M. J. "When Dissonance Fails: On Eliminating Evaluation Apprehension from Attitude Measurement." *Journal of Personality and Social Psychology,* 1965b, *1,* 28–42.

ROSENBERG, M. J. "Attitude Change and Foreign Policy in the Cold War Era." In J. N. Rosenau (Ed.), *Domestic Sources of Foreign Policy.* New York: Free Press, 1967. Pp. 111–159.

ROSENBERG, M. J., AND ABELSON, R. P. "An Analysis of Cognitive Balancing." In M. J. Rosenberg, C. I. Hovland, W. J. McGuire, R. P. Abelson, and J. W. Brehm (Eds.), *Attitude Organization and Change: An Analysis of Consistency Among Attitude Components.* New Haven: Yale University Press, 1960.

ROSENBERG, M. J., VERBA, S., AND CONVERSE, P. E. *Vietnam and the Silent Majority. The Dove's Guide.* New York: Harper, 1970.

ROSENTHAL, H. "Election Simulation." *European Journal of Sociology,* 1965, *6,* 21–42.

ROSENTHAL, H. "Voting and Coalition Models in Election Simulations." In W. D. Coplin (Ed.), *Simulation in the Study of Politics.* Chicago: Markham, 1968.

ROSENTHAL, R. *Experimenter Effects in Behavioral Research.* New York: Appleton-Century, 1966.

ROSENTHAL, R. "Interpersonal Expectations: Effects of the Experimenter's Hypothesis." In R. Rosenthal and R. L. Rosnow (Eds.), *Artifact in Behavioral Research.* New York: Academic Press, 1969.

ROSENTHAL, R., AND ROSNOW, R. L. (Eds.) *Artifact in Behavioral Research.* New York: Academic Press, 1969.

ROSSITER, C. *The Political Thought of the American Revolution.* New York: Harcourt, 1953.

ROSTOW, W. W. *The Process of Economic Growth.* New York: Norton, 1952.

ROSZAK, T. *The Making of a Counter Culture.* Garden City, N.Y.: Doubleday, 1969.

ROTTER, J. B. "Generalized Expectancies for Internal Versus External Control of Reinforcement." *Psychological Monographs,* 1966, *80* (no. 1), 1–28.

RUGGIERO, G. DE. *The History of European Liberalism.* Trans. R. G. Collingwood, London: Oxford University Press, 1927.

RUSHING, W. A. "Class, Culture and Social Structure and Anomie." *American Journal of Sociology,* 1971, *76,* 857–872.

RUSSET, B. M. "Inequality and Instability: The Relation of Land Tenure to Politics." *World Politics,* 1964, *16,* 442–454.

RUSTOW, D. A. "The Study of Leadership." *Daedalus,* 1968, *97.*

RUTHERFORD, B. "Psychopathology, Decision-Making and Political Involvement." *Journal of Conflict Resolution,* 1966, *10,* 387–407.

SALISBURY, H. *The 900 Days.* New York: Harper, 1969.

SALISBURY, R. H. "The Urban Party Organization Member." *Public Opinion Quarterly,* 1966, *29,* 550–564.

SANFORD, F. *Authoritarianism and Leadership.* Philadelphia: Stephenson Brothers, 1950a.

SANFORD, F. "The Use of a Projective Device in Attitude Surveying." *Public Opinion Quarterly,* 1950b, *14,* 697–709.

SANFORD, N. "The Effect of Abstinence from Food upon Imaginal Processes: A Preliminary Experiment." *Journal of Psychology,* 1936, *2,* 129–136.

SANFORD, N. "Individual and Social Change in a Community Under Pressure: The Oath Controversy." *Journal of Social Issues,* 1953, *9,* 25–42.

SANFORD, N. "Recent Developments in Connection with the Investigation of the Authoritarian Personality." *Sociological Review* (New Series, British), 1954, *2,* 11–33.

SANFORD, N. "The Approach of the Authoritarian Personality." In J. L. McCary (Ed.), *Psychology of Personality.* New York: Logos Press, 1956.

SANFORD, N. "Impact of a Women's College upon Its Students." In A. Traxler (Ed.), *Long-Range Planning for Education.* Washington, D.C.: American Council on Education, 1957.

SANFORD, N. "The Professor Looks at the Student." In R. Cooper (Ed.), *The Two Ends of the Log.* Minneapolis: University of Minnesota Press, 1958.

SANFORD, N. "Knowledge of Students Through the Social Studies." In N. Brown (Ed.), *Spotlight on the College Student.* Washington, D.C.: American Council on Education, 1959a.

SANFORD, N. "Motivation of High Achievers." In O. D. David (Ed.), *The Education of Women: Signs for the Future.* Washington, D.C.: American Council on Education, 1959b.

SANFORD, N. "The Development of Maturity of Personality in College." In T. R. McConnell (Ed.), *Selection and Educational Differentiation.* Berkeley, Calif.: Field Service Center and Center for the Study of Higher Education, University of California, 1960a.

SANFORD, N. "Theories of Higher Education and the Experimental College." In S. Harris (Ed.), *Higher Education in the United States.* Cambridge: Harvard University Press, 1960b.

SANFORD, N. "Recent Research on the American College Student." In N. Brown (Ed.), *Orientation to College Learning.* Washington, D.C.: American Council on Education, 1961.

SANFORD, N. "Ends and Means in Higher Education." In K. Smith (Ed.), *Current Issues in Higher Education.* Washington, D.C.: National Education Association, 1962a.

SANFORD, N. *The American College: A Psychological and Social Interpretation of the Higher Learning.* New York: Wiley, 1962b.

SANFORD, N. "The Freeing and Acting Out of Impulse in Late Adolescence: Evidence from Two Cases." In R. White (Ed.), *The Study of Lives: Essays on Personality in Honor of Henry A. Murray.* New York: Atherton, 1963.

SANFORD, N. (Ed.) *College and Character: A Briefer Version of "The American College."* New York: Wiley, 1964a.

SANFORD, N. "Ego Processes in Learning." In N. M. Lambert and others (Eds.), *The Protection and Promotion of Mental Health in Schools.* Public Health Service Publication 1226, Mental Health Monograph 5. Washington, D.C.: U.S. Department of Health, Education and Welfare, 1964b.

SANFORD, N. "Psychological and Developmental Aspects of the Adolescent Years as They Apply to the Use of Alcohol." In H. B. Bruyn (Ed.), *Alcohol and College Youth.* Berkeley, Calif.: American College Health Association, 1966a.

SANFORD, N. *Self and Society: Social Change and Individual Development.* New York: Atherton, 1966b.

SANFORD, N. *Where Colleges Fail: A Study of the Student as a Person.* San Francisco: Jossey-Bass, 1967.

SANFORD, N. "Education for Individual Development." *American Journal of Orthopsychiatry,* 1968a, *30,* 858–868.

SANFORD, N. "Personality: The Field." In D. Sills (Ed.), *International Encyclopedia of the Social Sciences.* New York: Macmillan, 1968b.

SANFORD, N. "The University and the Life of the Student: The Next 100 Years." In J. Walsh (Ed.), *The University in a Developing World Society.* South Bend, Ind.: University of Notre Dame Press, 1968c.

SANFORD, N. "Research with Students as Action and Education." *American Psychologist,* 1969, *24,* 544–546.

SANFORD, N. "The Campus Crisis in Authority." *Educational Record,* 1970a, pp. 112–115.

SANFORD, N. *Issues in Personality Theory.* San Francisco: Jossey-Bass, 1970b.

SANFORD, N. "Whatever Happened to Action Research?" *Journal of Social Issues,* 1970c, *26,* 3–23.

SANFORD, N. "Academic Culture and the Teacher's Development." *Soundings,* 1971–1972, 357–371.

SANFORD, N. "The New Values and Faculty Response." In E. McGrath (Ed.), *Prospects for Renewal.* San Francisco: Jossey-Bass, 1972.

SANFORD, N., ADKINS, M., MILLER, R. B., AND COBB, E. "Physique, Personality, and Scholarship." *Monographs of the Society for Research in Child Development,* 1943, *8.*

SANFORD, N., AND COMSTOCK, C. (Eds.) *Sanctions for Evil.* San Francisco: Jossey-Bass, 1971.

SANFORD, N., WEBSTER, H., AND FREEDMAN, M. "Impulse Expression as a Variable of Personality." *Psychological Monographs,* 1957, *71.*

SARBIN, T. R., AND ADLER, N. "Self-Reconstitution Processes: A Preliminary Report." *Psychoanalytic Review,* 1970–1971, *57,* 599–616.

SARNOFF, I. "Identification with the Aggressor: Some Personality Correlates of Anti-Semitism Among Jews." *American Psychologist,* 1951, *6,* 319–320.

SARNOFF, I. "Psychoanalytic Theory and Social Attitudes." *Public Opinion Quarterly,* 1960, *24,* 251–279.

SARNOFF, I. *Personality Dynamics and Development.* New York: Wiley, 1962.

SARNOFF, I., AND KATZ, D. "The Motivational Bases of Attitude Change." *Journal of Abnormal and Social Psychology,* 1954, *49,* 115–124.

SARNOFF, I., AND ZIMBARDO, P. "Anxiety, Fear and Social Affiliation." *Journal of Abnormal and Social Psychology,* 1961, *62,* 356–363.

SAWYER, J., AND GUETZKOW, H. "Bargaining and Negotiation in International Relations." In H. C. Kelman (Ed.), *International Behavior: A Social-Psychological Analysis.* New York: Holt, 1965.

SCHACHT, R. *Alienation.* Garden City, N.Y.: Doubleday, 1971. With an introductory essay by Walter Kaufman.

SCHAULAND, H., NAYLOR, T. H., AND KORNBERG, A. "ELECTION: A Campaign Simulator." Paper prepared for annual meeting of American Political Science Association, Chicago, 1971.

SCHEIN, E. H., SCHNEIER, I., AND BARKER, C. H. *Coercive Persuasion: A Socio-Psychological Analysis of "Brainwashing" of American Civilian Prisoners by the Chinese Communists.* New York: Norton, 1961.

SCHELLING, T. C., AND HALPERIN, M. H. "Pre-emptive, Premeditated and Accidental War." In D. G. Pruitt and R. C. Snyder (Eds.), *Theory and Research on the Causes of War.* Englewood Cliffs, N.J.: Prentice-Hall, 1969.

SCHILDER, P. "The Analysis of Ideologies as a Psycho-Therapeutic Method Especially in Group Treatment." *American Journal of Psychiatry,* 1936, *93,* 601–617.

SCHLESINGER, A. M. JR., *The Age of Roosevelt*. Vol. 2. *The Coming of the New Deal*. Boston: Houghton Mifflin, 1959.

SCHLESINGER, J. A. *Ambition in Politics: Political Careers in the United States*. Chicago: Rand McNally, 1966.

SCHMIDL, F. "Psychoanalysis and History." *Psychoanalytic Quarterly*, 1962, *31*, 532–548.

SCHNEIDER, J. "The Cultural Situation as a Condition for the Achievement of Fame." *American Sociological Review*, 1937, *2*, 480–491.

SCHOENBERGER, R. A. "Conservatism, Personality and Political Extremism." *American Political Science Review*, 1968, *62*, 868–877.

SCHRODER, H. M., DRIVER, M. J., AND STREUFERT, S. *Human Information Processing*. New York: Holt, 1967.

SCHUMAN, H. "The Random Probe." *American Sociological Review*, 1966, *31*, 218–222.

SCHWARTZ, D. C. "Toward a Theory of Political Recruitment." *Western Political Quarterly*, 1969, *22*, 552–571.

SCHWARTZ, D. C. "A Theory of Revolutionary Behavior." In J. C. Davies (Ed.), *When Men Revolt and Why*. New York: Free Press, 1971.

SCHWARTZ, M. *Public Opinion and Canadian Identity*. Berkeley: University of California Press, 1967.

SCOTT, W. A. "Attitude Measurement." In G. Lindzey and E. Aronson (Eds.), *The Handbook of Social Psychology*. (Rev. Ed.) Vol. 2. Reading, Mass.: Addison-Wesley, 1968.

SCOTT, W. R. "Field Methods in the Study of Organizations." In J. G. March (Ed.), *Handbook of Organizations*. Chicago: Rand McNally, 1965.

SEARS, D. O. "Review of R. Hess and J. Torney, *The Development of Political Attitudes in Children*." *Harvard Educational Review*, 1968, *38*, 571–578.

SEARS, D. O. "Political Behavior." In G. Lindzey and E. Aronson (Eds.), *The Handbook of Social Psychology*. (2nd Ed.) Vol. 5. Reading, Mass.: Addison-Wesley, 1969.

SEARS, D. O., AND MC CONAHAY, J. B. *The Politics of Violence*. Boston: Houghton Mifflin, 1973.

SEELEMAN, V. "The Influence of Attitude upon the Remembering of Pictorial Material." *Archives of Psychology of N.Y.*, 1940–1941, *36*, 258.

SEEMAN, M. "On the Meaning of Alienation." *American Sociological Review*, 1959, *24*, 783–791.

SEEMAN, M. "Alienation and Social Learning in a Reformatory." *American Journal of Sociology*, 1963, *69*, 270–283.

SEEMAN, M. "Alienation, Membership and Political Knowledge: A Comparative Study." *Public Opinion Quarterly*, 1966, *30*, 353–367.

SEEMAN, M. "Alienation and Knowledge: A Comparative Study of Powerlessness and Learning." *Sociometry*, 1967a, *30*, 105–123.

SEEMAN, M. "On the Personal Consequences of Alienation in Work." *American Sociological Review*, 1967b, *32*, 273–285.

SEEMAN, M. "The Urban Alienations: Some Dubious Theses from Marx to Marcuse." *Journal of Personality and Social Psychology*, 1971, *19*, 135–143.

SEEMAN, M. "The Signals of '68: Alienation in Pre-Crisis France." *American Sociological Review*, 1972, *37*, 385–402.

SELZNICK, G. J., AND STEINBERG, S. *The Tenacity of Prejudice: Anti-Semitism in Contemporary America*. New York: Harper, 1969.

SERENO, R. *The Rulers*. New York: Praeger, 1962.

SHAFFER, W. R. *Computer Simulations of Voting Behavior*. New York: Oxford University Press, 1972.

SHAND, A. F. *The Foundations of Character*. London: Macmillan, 1914.

SHAPIRO, M. J. "Rational Political Man: A Synthesis of Economic and Social-Psychological Perspectives." *American Political Science Review,* 1969, *63,* 1106–1119.

SHAW, R. E. "Cognition, Simulation and the Problem of Complexity." *Journal of Structural Learning,* 1971, *2,* 31–44.

SHERIF, C. W., SHERIF, M., AND NEBERGALL, R. E. *Attitude and Attitude Change: The Social Judgment Approach.* Philadelphia: Saunders, 1965.

SHERIF, M. *The Psychology of Social Norms.* New York: Harper, 1936.

SHERIF, M. "Group Influences upon the Formation of Norms and Attitudes." In T. M. Newcomb and E. L. Hartley (Eds.), *Readings in Social Psychology.* New York: Holt, 1947.

SHERIF, M., AND CANTRIL, H. *The Psychology of Ego-Involvements.* New York: Wiley, 1947.

SHERIF, M., AND HOVLAND, C. I. *Social Judgment: Assimilation and Contrast Effects in Communication and Attitude Change.* New Haven: Yale University Press, 1961.

SHNEIDMAN, E. *Thematic Test Analysis.* New York: Grune and Stratton, 1951.

SHNEIDMAN, E. "Projective Techniques." In B. Wolman (Ed.), *Handbook of Clinical Psychology.* New York: McGraw-Hill, 1965.

SHURE, G. H., MEEKER, R. J., AND HANSFORD, E. A. "The Effectiveness of Pacifist Strategies in Bargaining Games." *Journal of Conflict Resolution,* 1965, *9,* 106–117.

SIEGEL, A. E., AND SIEGEL, S. "Reference Groups, Membership Groups and Attitude Change." *Journal of Abnormal and Social Psychology,* 1957, *55,* 360–364.

SIGEL, I., AND HOFFMAN, M. "The Predictive Potential of Projective Tests for Nonclinical Populations." *Journal of Projective Techniques,* 1956, *20,* 261–264.

SIGEL, R. "Assumptions About the Learning of Political Values." *Annals of the American Academy of Political and Social Science,* 1965, *361,* 1–9.

SIGEL, R. *Learning About Politics.* New York: Random House, 1970.

SIGUSCH, V., SCHMIDT, G., REINFELD, R., AND WEIDERMANN-SUTOR, I. Psychosexual Stimulation: Sex Differences." *Journal of Sex Research,* 1970, *6,* 10–24.

SILBERSTEIN, F. B., AND SEEMAN, M. "Social Mobility and Prejudice." *American Journal of Sociology,* 1959, *65,* 258–264.

SIMMONS, J. "Liberalism, Alienation and Personal Disturbance." *Sociology and Social Research,* 1965, *49,* 456–464.

SIMMONS, J. L. "Some Intercorrelations Among Alienation Measures." *Social Forces,* 1966, *44,* 370–372.

SIMON, H. A. *Administrative Behavior: A Study of Decision-Making Processes in Administrative Organization.* New York: Macmillan, 1947.

SIMON, H. A. "Theories of Decision-Making in Economics and Behavorial Science." *American Economic Review,* 1959, *40,* 253–283.

SIMON, H. A., SMITHBURG, D. W., AND THOMPSON, V. A. *Public Administration.* New York: Knopf, 1950.

SIMON, J., AND RESCHER, P. "Cause and Counterfactual." *Philosophy of Science,* 1963, *33,* 323–340.

SIMPSON, E. L. *Democracy's Stepchildren.* San Francisco: Jossey-Bass, 1971.

SIMPSON, G. E., AND YINGER, J. M. *Racial and Cultural Minorities.* (4th Ed.) New York: Harper, 1972.

SIMPSON, M. "Authoritarianism and Education: A Comparative Approach." *Sociometry,* 1972, *35,* 223–234.

SIMPSON, R. L., AND MILLER, H. M. "Social Status and Anomia." *Social Problems,* 1963, *10,* 256–264.

SINGER, J. D. "The Level-of-Analysis Problem in International Relations." In K. Knorr and S. Verba (Eds.), *The International System.* Princeton: Princeton University Press, 1961.

SINGER, J. D. "Inter-Nation Influence: A Formal Model." *American Political Science Review*, 1963, *57*, 420–430.

SINGER, J. D. "Data-Making in International Relations." *Behavioral Science*, 1965, *10*, 68–80.

SINGER, J. D. "Man and World Politics: The Psycho-Cultural Interface." *Journal of Social Issues*, 1968, *24*, 127–156.

SINGER, J. D. "The Correlates of War Project: Interim Report and Rationale." *World Politics*, 1972, *24*, 243–270.

SKINNER, B. F. *Walden Two*. New York. Macmillan, 1948.

SKINNER, B. F. *Verbal Behavior*. New York: Appleton-Century, 1957.

SKINNER, B. F. *Beyond Freedom and Dignity*. New York: Knopf, 1971.

SMELSER, N. J., AND W. T. (Eds.) *Personality and Social Systems*. New York: Wiley, 1965.

SMITH, B. F. *Adolf Hitler*. Stanford, Calif.: Hoover Institution on War, Revolution and Peace, 1967.

SMITH, E. E. "The Power of Dissonance Techniques to Change Attitudes." *Public Opinion Quarterly*, 1961, *25*, 626–639.

SMITH, G. H. "Liberalism and Level of Information." *Journal of Education and Psychology*, 1948a, *39*, 65–81.

SMITH, G. H. "The Relation of 'Enlightenment' to Liberal-Conservative Opinions." *Journal of Social Psychology*, 1948b, *28*, 3–17.

SMITH, L. B. *Henry VIII: The Mask of Royalty*. London: Jonathan Cape, 1971.

SMITH, M. B. "Review of *The Authoritarian Personality*." *Journal of Abnormal and Social Psychology*, 1950, *45*, 775–779.

SMITH, M. B. "Opinions, Personality and Political Behavior." *American Political Science Review*, 1958, *52*, 1–17.

SMITH, M. B. "An Analysis of Two Measures of 'Authoritarianism' Among Peace Corps Teachers." *Journal of Personality*, 1965, *33*, 513–535.

SMITH, M. B. "Attitude Change." In D. Sills (Ed.), *International Encyclopedia of the Social Sciences*. Vol. 1. New York: Macmillan, 1968a.

SMITH, M. B. "Competence and Socialization." In J. Clausen (Ed.), *Socialization and Society*. Boston: Little Brown, 1968b.

SMITH, M. B. "A Map for the Analysis of Personality and Politics." *Journal of Social Issues*, 1968c, *24*, 15–28.

SMITH, M. B. "Personality in Politics. A Conceptual Map, with Application to the Problem of Political Rationality." In O. Garceau (Ed.), *Political Research and Political Theory: Essays in Honor of V. O. Key, Jr.* Cambridge: Harvard University Press, 1968d.

SMITH, M. B. "Allport, Murray, and Lewin on Personality Theory: Notes on a Confrontation." *Journal of the History of the Behavioral Sciences*, 1971a, *7*, 353–362.

SMITH, M. B. "Review of Fromm and Maccoby's *Social Character in a Mexican Village*." *Contemporary Psychology*, 1971b, *16*, 635.

SMITH, M. B. "Is Experimental Social Psychology Advancing?" Review of L. Berkowitz (Ed.), *Advances in Experimental Social Psychology*, Vols. 1–5. *Journal of Experimental Social Psychology*, 1972, *8*, 86–96.

SMITH, M. B. "Is Psychology Relevant to New Priorities?" *American Psychologist*, 1973.

SMITH, M. B., BRUNER, J., AND WHITE, R. *Opinions and Personality*. New York: Wiley, 1956.

SMOKER, P. *Analyses of Conflict Behaviours in an International Processes Simulation and an International System 1955–60*. Evanston, Ill.: International Processes Simulation Project, Northwestern University, 1968a.

SMOKER, P. *International Processes Simulation: A Man-Computer Model*. Evanston, Ill.: International Processes Simulation Project, Northwestern University, 1968b.

SMOKER, P. "Social Research for Social Anticipation." *American Behavioral Scientist*, 1969, *12*, 7–13.

SMOKER, P. "International Processes Simulation: An Evaluation." *Peace Research Reviews*, 1970, *4*.

SMOKER, P. "International Relations Simulations." In H. Guetzkow, P. Kotler, and R. L. Schultz (Eds.), *Simulation in Social and Administrative Science*. Englewood Cliffs, N.J.: Prentice-Hall, 1972.

SNIDERMAN, P. M., AND CITRIN, J. "Psychological Sources of Political Belief: Self-Esteem and Isolationist Attitudes." *American Political Science Review*, 1971, *65*, 401–417.

SNOW, EDGAR, *Red Star over China*. New York: Grove Press, 1968. Originally published 1938.

SNYDER, R. C., BRUCK, H. W., AND SAPIN, B. (Eds.) *Foreign Policy Decision-Making*. New York: Free Press, 1962.

SOKOL, R. "Power Orientation and McCarthyism." *American Journal of Sociology*, 1968, *73*, 443–452.

SOMIT, A., TANENHAUS, J., WILKE, W., AND COOLEY, R. "The Effect of the Introductory Political Science Course on Student Attitudes Toward Personal Political Participation." *American Political Science Review*, 1958, *52*, 1129–1132.

SOREL, G. *Reflections on Violence*. New York: Collier, 1961. Originally published 1908.

SOROKIN, P. *The Sociology of Revolution*. Philadelphia: Lippincott, 1925.

SPIRO, M. "Social Systems, Personality, and Functional Analysis." In B. Kaplan (Ed.), *Studying Personality Cross-Culturally*. New York: Harper, 1961.

SPITZ, R. A. "The Role of Ecological Factors in Emotional Development in Infancy." *Child Development*, 1949, *20*, 145–155.

SPITZ, R. A. *A Genetic Field Theory of Ego Formation: Its Implications for Pathology*. New York: International Universities Press, 1959.

SROLE, L. "Social Integration and Certain Corollaries: An Exploratory Study." *American Sociological Review*, 1956, *21*, 709–716.

SROLE, L. "A Comment on 'Anomy.'" *American Sociological Review*, 1965, *30*, 757–762.

STAGNER, R. "Fascist Attitudes: Their Determining Conditions." *Journal of Social Psychology*, 1936, *7*, 438–454.

STANLEY, J. C. "Fixed, Random and Mixed Models in the Analysis of Variance as Special Cases of Finite Model III." *Psychological Reports*, 1956, *2*, 369.

STANTON, A. H., AND PERRY, S. E. (Eds.) *Personality and Political Crisis*. New York: Free Press, 1951.

STAPEL, J. "The Convivial Respondent." *Public Opinion Quarterly*, 1947–1948, *11*, 524–529.

STARK, S. "Toward a Psychology of Charisma: I. The Innovation Viewpoint of Robert Tucker." *Psychological Reports*, 1968, *23*, 1163–1166.

STARK, S. "Toward a Psychology of Charisma: II. The Pathology Viewpoint of James C. Davies." *Psychological Reports*, 1969, *24*, 88–90.

STARK, W. *The Sociology of Religion*. New York: Fordham University Press, 1967. 3 Vols.

STEVENSON, H., AND STUART, E. "A Developmental Study of Racial Awareness in Young Children." *Child Development*, 1958, *29*, 399–409.

STOKES, D. E. "Some Dynamic Elements of Contests for the Presidency." *American Political Science Review*, 1966, *60*, 19–28.

STOKES, D. E., CAMPBELL, A., AND MILLER, W. E. "Components of Electoral Decision." *American Political Science Review*, 1958, *52*, 367–387.

STOKES, D. E., AND MILLER, W. E. "Party Government and the Saliency of Congress." *Public Opinion Quarterly*, 1962, *26*, 531–546.

STOUFFER, S. A. *Communism, Conformity and Civil Liberties*. New York: Doubleday, 1955.

STOUFFER, S. A. *Social Research to Test Ideas: Selected Writings of Samuel A. Stouffer.* New York: Free Press, 1962.

STOUFFER, S. A., AND OTHERS. *The American Soldier. Studies in Social Psychology in World War II.* Vol. 1: *Adjustment in Army Life.* Vol. 2: *Combat and Its Aftermath.* Princeton: Princeton University Press, 1949.

STRACHEY, L. *Eminent Victorians.* New York: Capricorn Ed., 1963. Originally published 1918.

STRAUSS, H. J. "Revolutionary Types: Russia, 1905." *Journal of Conflict Resolution,* 1973, *17.*

STRAUSS, L. *The Political Philosophy of Hobbes.* Trans. E. M. Sinclair. Chicago: University of Chicago Press, 1952.

STREUFERT, S., CLARDY, M., DRIVER, M., KARLINS, M., SCHRODER, H. M., AND SUEDFELD, P. "A Tactical Game for the Analysis of Complex Decision Making in Individuals and Groups." *Psychological Reports,* 1965, *17,* 723–729.

STREUFERT, S., AND STREUFERT, S. "Effects of Conceptual Structure, Failure and Success on Attribution of Causality and Interpersonal Attitudes." *Journal of Personality and Social Psychology,* 1969, *2,* 138–147.

STREUFERT, S., STREUFERT, S., AND CASTORE, C. "Complexity, Increasing Failure and Decision Making." *Journal of Experimental Research in Personality,* 1969, *3,* 293–300.

STREUFERT, S., SUEDFELD, P., AND DRIVER, M. "Conceptual Structure, Information Search and Information Utilization." *Journal of Personality and Social Psychology,* 1965, *2,* 736–740.

STREUNING, E. L., AND RICHARDSON, A. H. "A Factor Analytic Exploration of the Alienation, Anomia and Authoritarianism Domain." *American Sociological Review,* 1965, *30,* 768–776.

SULLIVAN, H. S. "Conceptions of Modern Psychiatry." *Psychiatry,* 1940, *3,* 1–117.

SUTTON, F. X., HARRIS, S. E., KAYSEN, C., AND TOBIN, J. *The American Business Creed.* Cambridge: Harvard University Press, 1956.

SWINGLE, P. "Dangerous Games." In P. Swingle (Ed.), *The Structure of Conflict.* New York: Academic Press, 1970a.

SWINGLE, P. (Ed.) *The Structure of Conflict.* New York: Academic Press, 1970b.

SYKES, G. (Ed.) *Alienation: The Cultural Climate of Modern Man.* New York: Braziller, 1964. 2 Vols.

TAJFEL, H. "The Formation of National Attitudes: A Social-Psychological Perspective." In M. Sherif and C. W. Sherif (Eds.), *Interdisciplinary Relationships in the Social Sciences.* Chicago: Aldine, 1969.

TANNENBAUM, A. J. (Issue Ed.) "Alienated Youth." *Journal of Social Issues,* 1969, *25.*

TANSEY, P. J., AND UNWIN, D. *Simulation and Gaming in Education.* London: Methuen, 1969.

TANTER, R. "International War and Domestic Turmoil: Some Contemporary Evidence." In H. D. Graham and T. R. Gurr (Eds.), *The History of Violence in America.* New York: Bantam, 1969.

TANTER, R., AND MIDLARSKY, M. "A Theory of Revolution." *Journal of Conflict Resolution,* 1967, *11,* 264–280.

TAPP, J., AND KOHLBERG, L. "Developing Senses of Law and Legal Justice." *Journal of Social Issues,* 1971, *27,* 65–92.

TAPPER, E., AND BUTLER, R. "Continuity and Change in Adolescent Political Party Preferences." *Political Studies,* 1970, *18,* 390–394.

TAVISS, I. "Changes in the Form of Alienation: The 1900's Versus 1950's." *American Sociological Review,* 1969, *34,* 46–57.

TAWNEY, R. H. *Religion and the Rise of Capitalism.* Gloucester, Mass.: Smith, 1963. Originally published 1926.

TAWNEY, R. H. *Equality.* New York: Harcourt, 1929.

TAYLOR, J. "A Personality Scale of Manifest Anxiety." *Journal of Abnormal and Social Psychology,* 1953, *48,* 285–290.

TEMPLETON, F. "Alienation and Political Participation: Some Research Findings." *Public Opinion Quarterly,* 1966, *30,* 249–261.

TERHUNE, K. W. "The Effects of Personality in Cooperation and Conflict." In P. Swingle (Ed.), *The Structure of Conflict.* New York: Academic Press, 1970.

TERHUNE, K. W., AND FIRESTONE, J. M. *Psychological Studies in Social Interaction and Motives* (SIAM). Phase 2: Group Motives in an International Relations Game. CAL Report No. VX-2018-G-2. Buffalo, N.Y.: Cornell Aeronautical Laboratory, 1967.

TESLER, L., ENEA, H., AND COLBY, K. M. "A Directed Graph Representation for Computer Simulation of Belief Systems." *Mathematical Biosciences,* 1968, *2,* 19–40.

THIBAUT, J. W., AND RIECKEN, H. W. "Authoritarianism, Status and the Communication of Aggression." *Human Relations,* 1955, *8,* 95–120.

THOMAS, L. "Political Attitude Congruence Between Politically Active Parents and College-Age Children: An Inquiry into Family Political Socialization." *Journal of Marriage and the Family.* 1971, *33,* 375–386.

THOMAS, W. I. "The Unadjusted Girl." Excerpted in M. Janowitz (Ed.), *W. I. Thomas on Social Organization and Social Personality.* Chicago: University of Chicago Press, 1966. Pp. 117–139. Originally published 1923.

THOMAS, W. I., AND ZNANIECKI, F. *The Polish Peasant in Europe and America.* Vol. 1. Boston: Badger, 1918.

THOMPSON, R. C., AND MICHEL, J. B. "Measuring Authoritarianism: A Comparison of the F and D Scales." *Journal of Personality,* 1972, *40,* 180–190.

THOMPSON, W. E., AND HORTON, J. E. "Political Alienation as a Force in Political Action." *Social Forces,* 1960, *38,* 190–195.

THORNDIKE, R., AND GALLUP, G. "Verbal Intelligence of the American Adult." *Journal of Genetic Psychology,* 1944, *30,* 75–85.

THURSTONE, L. L. "Attitudes Can Be Measured." *American Journal of Sociology,* 1928, *33,* 529–554.

TILLER, P. "Father Absence and Personality Development of Children in Singular Families." Vol. 2, Part 2. In N. Anderson (Ed.), *Studies of the Family.* Göttingen: Vanderhoeck and Ruprecht, 1957.

TOCQUEVILLE, A. DE. *The Old Regime and the French Revolution.* New York: Harper, 1856.

TOLLEY, H., JR. "Socialization to War: A Questionnaire Study of Children's Attitudes and Knowledge." Paper presented at meeting of American Political Science Association, Washington, D.C., September 1972.

TOLMAN, E. C. *Drives Toward War.* New York: Appleton-Century, 1942.

TOZZER, A. M. "Biography and Biology." *American Anthropologist,* 1933, *35,* 418–432.

TROTSKY, L. *The History of the Russian Revolution.* New York: Simon and Schuster, 1932.

TRUEBLOOD, C. K. "Sainte-Beuve and the Psychology of Personality." *Character and Personality,* 1939, *8,* 120–143.

TUCKER, R. C. "The Dictator and Totalitarianism." *World Politics,* 1965, *17,* 555–583.

TURK, H. "Comparative Urban Studies in Interorganizational Relations." *Sociological Inquiry,* 1969, *39,* 108–110.

TURK, H. "Interorganizational Networks in Urban Society: Initial Perspectives and Comparative Research." *American Sociological Review,* 1970, *35,* 1–19.

TURNER, R. H. "The Public Perception of Protest." *American Sociological Review,* 1969, *34,* 815–830.

TURNER, R. H., AND KILLIAN, L. M. *Collective Behavior.* Englewood Cliffs, N.J.: Prentice-Hall, 1957.

TYLER, S. A. (Ed.) *Cognitive Anthropology.* New York: Holt, 1969.

UNDERWOOD, B. J. *Psychological Research,* New York: Appleton-Century, 1957.

VAILLANCOURT, P. "The Stability of Children's Political Orientations: A Panel Study." Paper presented at meeting of American Political Science Association, Los Angeles, September 1970.

VALEN, H., AND KATZ, D. *Political Parties in Norway.* Oslo: University of Oslo Press, 1964.

VAUGHN, G., AND WHITE, K. "Conformity and Authoritarianism Re-examined." *Journal of Personality and Social Psychology,* 1966, *3,* 363–366.

VERBA, S. *Small Groups and Political Behavior.* Princeton: Princeton University Press, 1961.

VERBA, S., BRODY, R. A., PARKER, E. B., NIE, N. H., POLSBY, N. W., EKMAN, P., AND BLACK, G. S. "Public Opinion and the War in Vietnam." *American Political Science Review,* 1967, *61,* 317–333.

VERBA, S., AND NIE, N. *Participation in America.* New York: Harper, 1972.

VERBA, S., AND NIE, N. "Citizenship and Civil Milieu." In F. I. Greenstein and N. W. Polsby (Eds.), *The Handbook of Political Science.* Reading, Massachusetts: Addison-Wesley, 1974.

VEROFF, J. "The Use of Thematic Apperception to Assess Motivation in a Nationwide Interview Study." *Psychological Monographs,* 1960, *74*(12).

VEROFF, J. "Thematic Apperception in a Nationwide Sample Survey." In J. Kagan and G. Lesser (Eds.), *Contemporary Issues in Thematic Apperceptive Methods.* Springfield, Ill.: Thomas, 1961.

VICARY, J. "Word Association and Opinion Research." *Public Opinion Quarterly,* 1948, *12,* 81–98.

VOSE, C. E. "Manuscript Collections and Reference Books as Data for Political Science." In F. I. Greenstein and N. W. Polsby (Eds.), *The Handbook of Political Science.* Vol. 2. Reading, Mass.: Addison-Wesley, forthcoming.

WALLACH, M. "Commentary: Active-Analytical vs. Passive-Global Cognitive Functioning." In S. Messick and J. Ross (Eds.), *Measurement in Personality and Cognition.* New York: McGraw-Hill, 1962.

WALLAS, G. *Human Nature in Politics.* New York: Knopf, 1921. Originally published 1908.

WALTER, J., AND STINNETT, N. "Parent-Child Relationships: A Decade Review of Research." *Journal of Marriage and the Family.* 1971, *33,* 70–111.

WALTZ, K. N. *Man, the State, and War.* New York: Columbia University Press, 1959.

WARNER, L. G., AND DEFLEUR, M. L. "Attitude as an Interactional Concept: Social Constraint and Social Distance as Intervening Variables Between Attitudes and Actions." *American Sociological Review,* 1969, *34,* 153–169.

WARNER, W. L. *Democracy in Jonesville.* New York: Harper, 1949.

WATSON, J. B. *Behaviorism.* Chicago: University of Chicago Press, 1961. Originally published 1924.

WEBB, E. J., CAMPBELL, D. T., SCHWARTZ, R. D., AND SECHREST, L. B. *Unobtrusive Measures: Nonreactive Research in the Social Sciences.* Chicago: Rand McNally, 1966.

WEBER, M. *The Protestant Ethic and the Spirit of Capitalism.* New York: Scribner's 1958. Originally published 1904–1905.

WEBER, M. *The Theory of Social and Economic Organization.* Trans. M. Henderson and T. Parsons. New York: Oxford University Press, 1947. Originally published 1922.

WEBSTER, H., FREEDMAN, M., AND HEIST, P. "Personality Changes in College Students." In N. Sanford (Ed.), *The American College.* New York: Wiley, 1962.

WEBSTER, H., SANFORD, N., AND FREEDMAN, M. "A New Instrument for Studying Authoritarianism in Personality." *Journal of Psychology,* 1955, *40,* 73–84.

WEDGE, B. "Khrushchev at a Distance—A Study of Public Personality." *Transaction,* October 1968.

WEICK, K. E. "Laboratory Experimentation with Organizations." In J. G. March (Ed.), *Handbook of Organizations*. Chicago: Rand McNally, 1965.

WEINSTEIN, E. A. "Denial of Presidential Disability: A Case Study of Woodrow Wilson." *Psychiatry*, 1967, *30*, 376–390.

WELDON, T. D. *The Vocabulary of Politics*. London: Penguin, 1953.

WESTBY, D. L., AND BRAUNGART, R. G. "The Alienation of Generations and Status Politics: Alternative Explanations of Student Political Activism." In R. Sigel (Ed.), *Learning About Politics: A Reader in Political Socialization*. New York: Random House, 1970.

WHITE, R. K. *Nobody Wanted War: Misperception in Vietnam and Other Wars*. Garden City, N.Y.: Doubleday, 1968.

WICKER, T. *JFK and LBJ: The Influence of Personality upon Politics*. New York: William Morrow, 1968.

WILKINSON, R. *The Broken Rebel: A Study in Culture, Politics and Authoritarian Character*. New York: Harper, 1972.

WILLCOX, W. B. *Portrait of a General*. New York: Knopf, 1964.

WILLIAMS, R., AND WRIGHT, C. "Opinion Organization in a Heterogeneous Adult Population." *Journal of Abnormal and Social Psychology*, 1955, *51*, 559–564.

WILLNER, A. R. *Charismatic Political Leadership: A Theory*. Research Monograph 32. Princeton: Center of International Studies, Princeton University, 1968.

WILLNER, A. R. "Quasi-Revolutionary Charismatic Political Leaders and Periods of Crisis." Paper presented at meeting of American Political Science Association, New York, September 1969.

WILSON, J. Q. "The Strategy of Protest: Problems of Negro Civic Action." *Journal of Conflict Resolution*, 1961, *3*, 291–303.

WILSON, J. Q. "Review of Gottfried's *Boss Cermak of Chicago*." *American Journal of Sociology*, 1962, *68*, 375.

WILSON, J. Q. "Violence, Pornography and Social Science." *Public Interest*, 1971, *22*, 45–61.

WILSON, R. A. "Anomie in the Ghetto: A Study of Neighborhood Type, Race and Anomie." *American Journal of Sociology*, 1971, *77*, 68–88.

WILSON, W. *Constitutional Government in the United States*. New York: Columbia University Press, 1908.

WINER, B. J. *Statistical Principles in Experimental Design*. (2nd Ed.) New York: McGraw-Hill, 1971.

WIRTH, L. "Consensus and Mass Communication." *American Sociological Review*, 1948, *13*, 1–15.

WISH, M., DEUTSCH, M., AND BIENER, L. "Differences in Conceptual Structures of Nations: An Exploratory Study." *Journal of Personality and Social Psychology*, 1970, *16*, 361–373.

WITKIN, H. A., DYK, R. B., FATERSON, H. F., GOODENOUGH, D. R., AND KARP, S. A. *Psychological Differentiation: Studies of Development*. New York: Wiley, 1962.

WITKIN, H., LEWIS, H., HERTZMAN, M., MACHOVER, K., MEISSNER, P., AND WAPNER, S. *Personality Through Perception*. New York: Harper, 1954.

WOLFENSTEIN, E. V. *The Revolutionary Personality: Lenin, Trotsky and Gandhi*. Princeton: Princeton University Press, 1967.

WOLFENSTEIN, E. V. *Personality and Politics*. Belmont, Calif.: Dickenson, 1969.

WOLFERS, A. "The Actors in International Politics." In W. T. R. Fox (Ed.), *Theoretical Aspects of International Relations*. Notre Dame, Ind.: University of Notre Dame Press, 1959.

WOLFINGER, R. E. "The Influence of Precinct Work on Voting Behavior." *Public Opinion Quarterly*, 1963, *27*, 387–398.

WOODWARD, J., AND ROPER, E. "Political Activity of American Citizens." *American Political Science Review*, 1950, *44*, 872–885.

WOODWARD, W. E. *George Washington: The Image and the Man*. New York: Boni and Liverwright, 1926.

WRIGHT, C., AND CANTOR, M. "The Opinion Seeker and Avoider: Steps Beyond the Opinion Leader Concept." *Pacific Sociological Review*, 1967, *10*, 33–43.

WRIGHT, J. D. "The Working Class, Authoritarianism, and the War in Vietnam." *Social Problems*, 1972, *20*, 134–150.

WRIGHT, Q. *A Study of War*. (Abridged Ed.) Chicago: University of Chicago Press, 1964.

WRIGHT, Q. "The Study of War." In D. Sills (Ed.), *International Encyclopedia of the Social Sciences*. Vol. 16. New York: Macmillan, 1968.

WYATT, F. "Review of P. Greenacre, *Swift and Carroll: A Psychoanalytic Study of Two Lives.*" *Contemporary Psychology*, 1956, *1*, 105–107.

WYLIE, L. *Village in the Vaucluse*. New York: Harper, 1964.

YINGER, J. M. "Research Implications of a Field View of Personality." *American Journal of Sociology*, 1963, *68*, 580–592.

YINGER, J. M. *Toward a Field Theory of Behavior: Personality and Social Structure*. New York: McGraw-Hill, 1965.

YINGER, J. M. *The Scientific Study of Religion*. New York: Macmillan, 1970.

YOUNG, O. R. *The Intermediaries: Third Parties in International Crises*. Princeton: Princeton University Press, 1967.

YOUNG, P. V. *Scientific Social Surveys and Research*. (4th. Ed.) Englewood Cliffs, N.J.: Prentice-Hall, 1966.

ZALD, M. N., AND SCHLIEWEN, R. "Ethno-Methodology and Simulation of Organizational Decision Making." In W. D. Coplin (Ed.), *Simulation in the Study of Politics*. Chicago: Markham, 1968.

ZELDITCH, M., JR., AND EVAN, W. M. "Simulated Bureaucracies: A Methodological Analysis." In H. Guetzkow (Ed.), *Simulation in Social Science: Readings*. Englewood Cliffs, N.J.: Prentice-Hall, 1962.

ZELIGS, M. *Friendship and Fratricide, An Analysis of Whittaker Chambers and Alger Hiss*. New York: Viking, 1966.

ZELLMAN, G., AND SEARS, D. "Childhood Origins of Tolerance for Dissent." *Journal of Social Issues*, 1971, *27*, 109–136.

ZIBLATT, D. "High School Extracurricular Activities and Political Socialization." *Annals of the American Academy of Political and Social Science*, 1965, *361*, 20–31.

ZIMBARDO, P. "Relationship Between Projective and Direct Measures of Fear Arousal." *Journal of Abnormal and Social Psychology*, 1964, *68*, 196–199.

ZIMBARDO, P. "The Human Choice: Individuation, Reason and Order Versus Deindividuation, Impulse and Chaos." In D. Levine (Ed.), *Nebraska Symposium on Motivation*. Lincoln: University of Nebraska Press, 1969.

ZIMBARDO, P., AND EBBESEN, E. B. *Influencing Attitudes and Changing Behavior*. Reading, Mass.: Addison-Wesley, 1969.

ZIMBARDO, P., AND FORMICA, R. "Emotional Comparison and Self-Esteem as Determinants of Affiliation." *Journal of Personality*, 1963, *31*, 141–162.

INDEX

Author

526

Subject